SCENE 1 /// The Girl Who Slips Through Floors

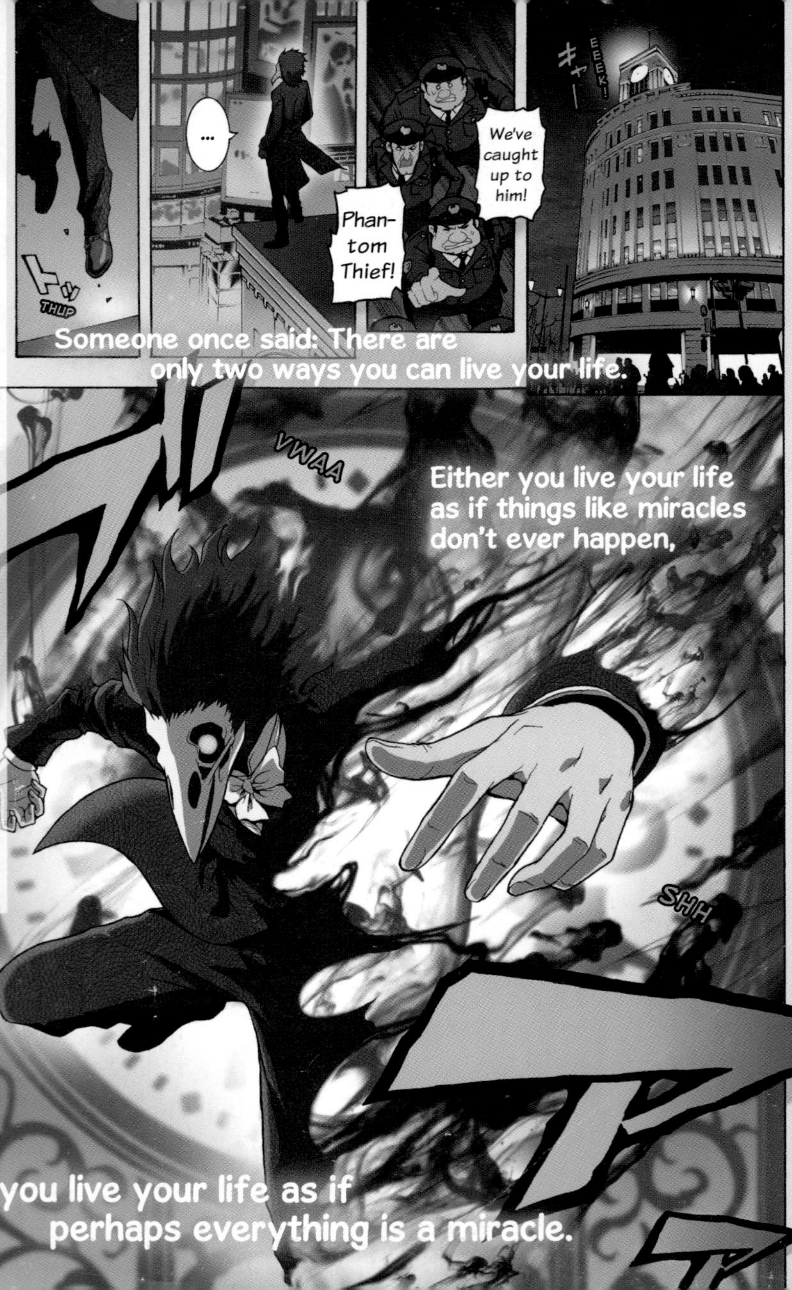
キャー
EEEK!
We've caught up to him!
Phantom Thief!
...
トッ
THUP
Someone once said: There are only two ways you can live your life.
Either you live your life as if things like miracles don't ever happen,
VWAA
SHH
or you live your life as if perhaps everything is a miracle.

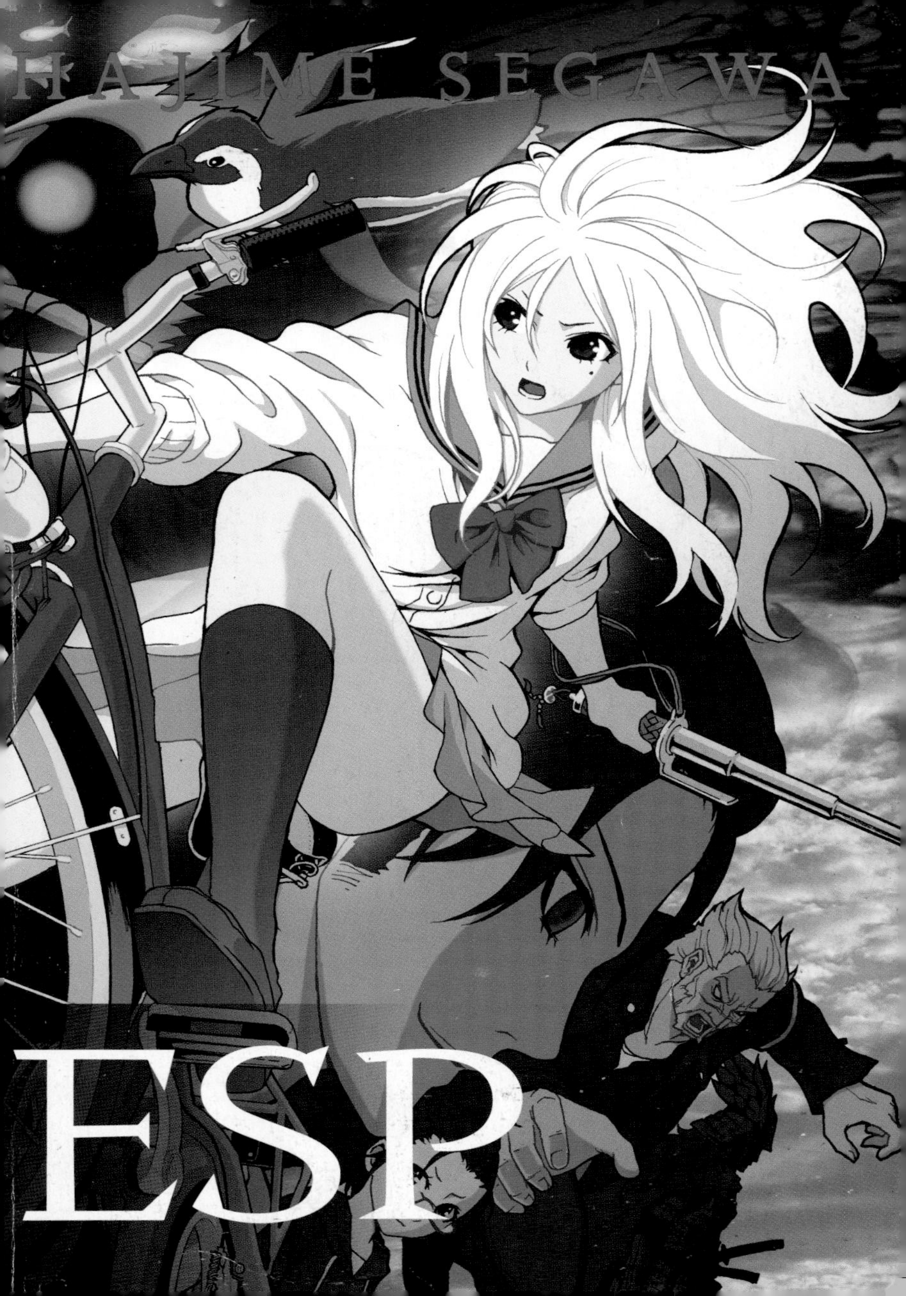
HAJIME SEGAWA
ESP

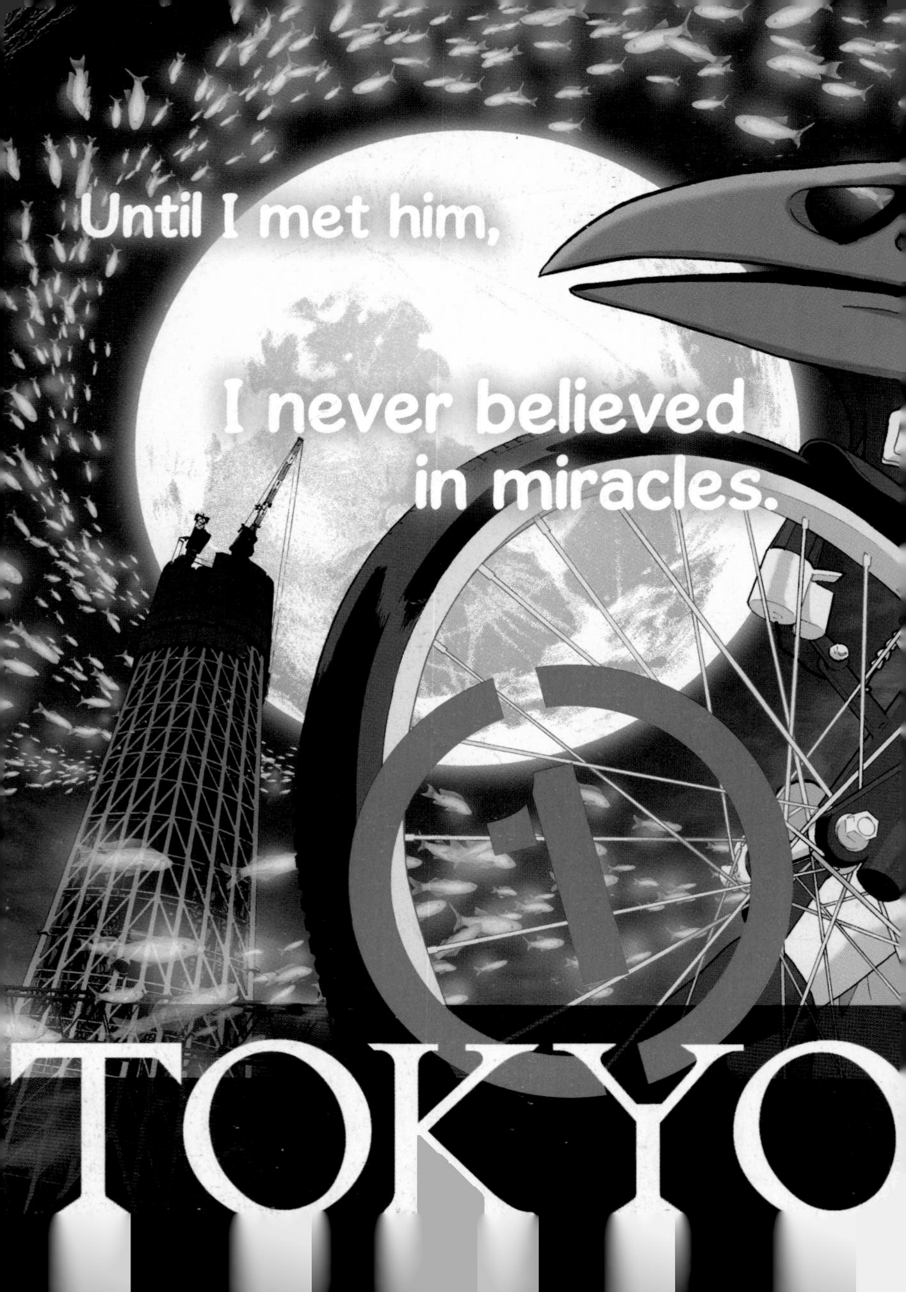
Until I met him,
I never believed
in miracles.
TOKYO

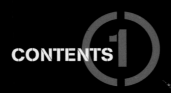

CONTENTS

Hajime Segawa Presents

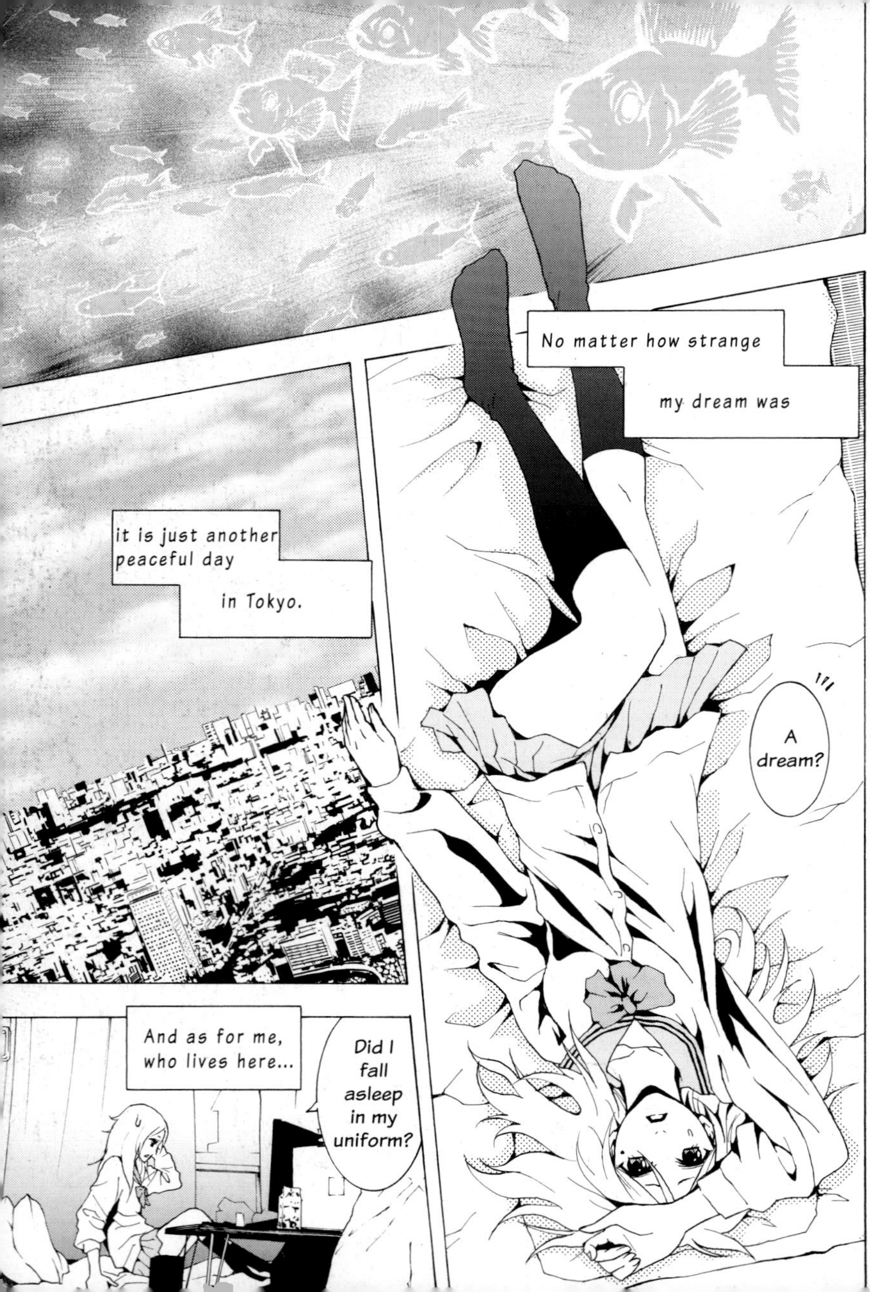
No matter how strange
my dream was
A dream?
it is just another peaceful day
in Tokyo.
And as for me, who lives here...
Did I fall asleep in my uniform?

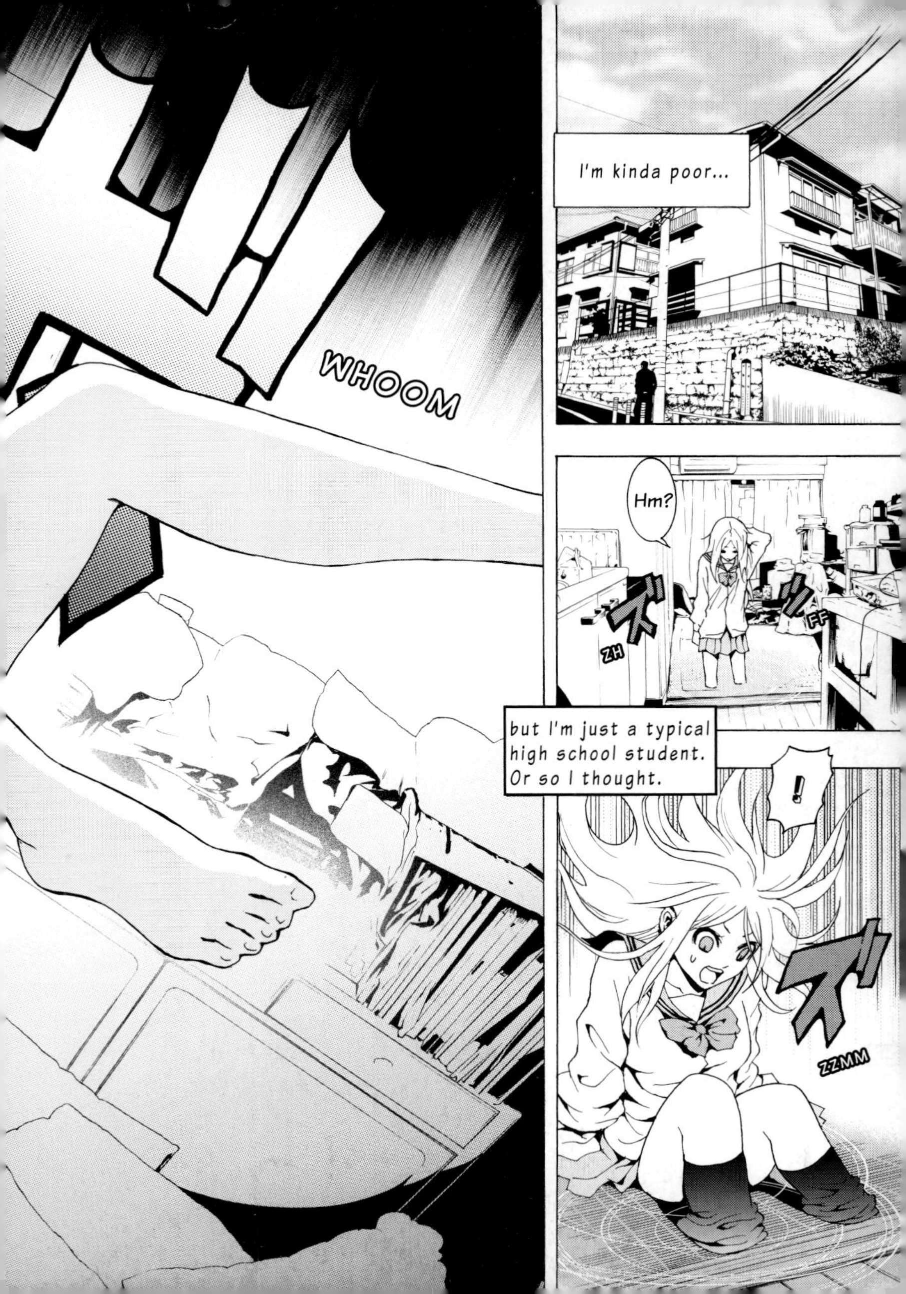
I'm kinda poor...
Hm?
FF
ZH
but I'm just a typical high school student. Or so I thought.
!
ZZMM
WHOOM

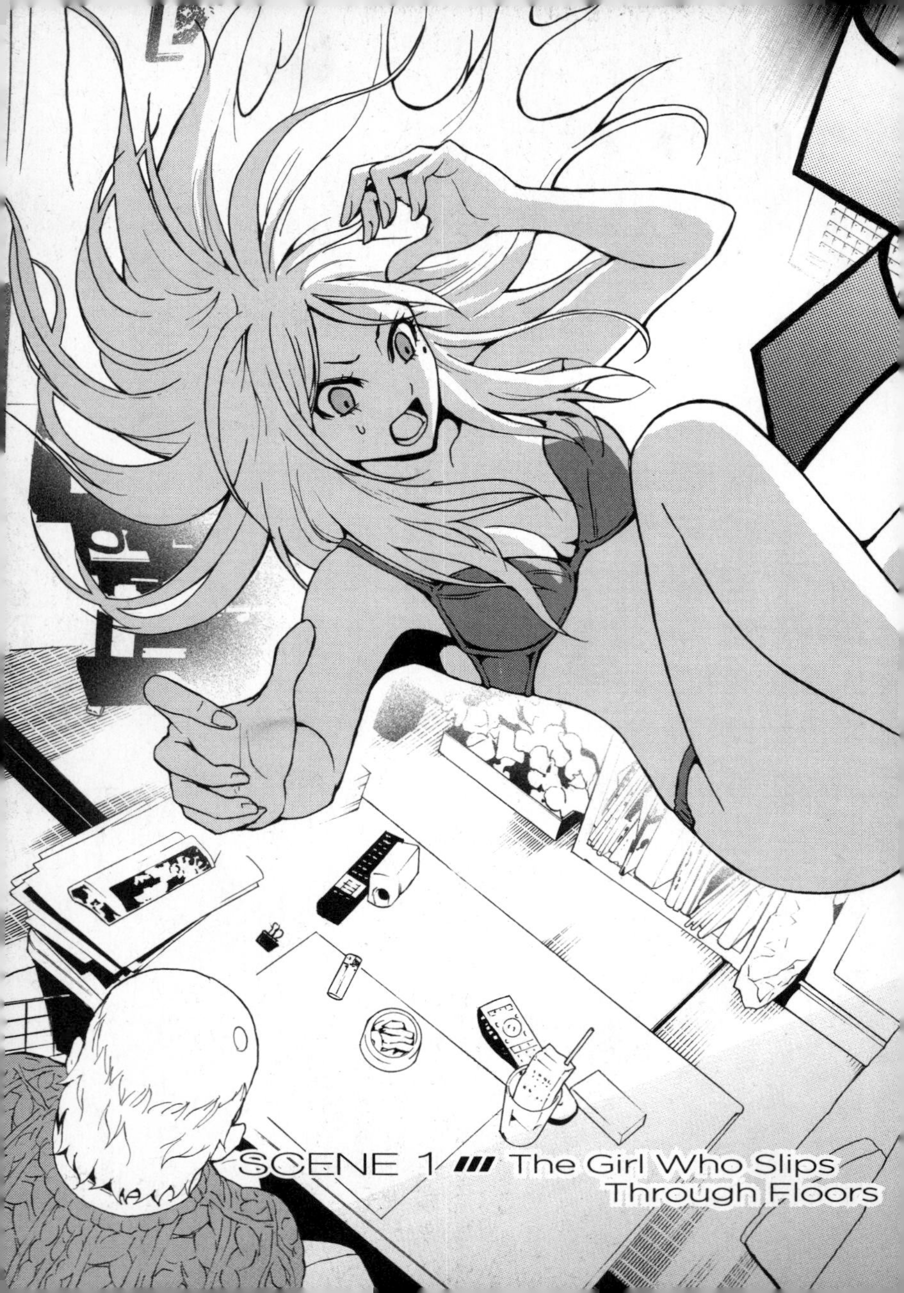
SCENE 1 /// The Girl Who Slips Through Floors

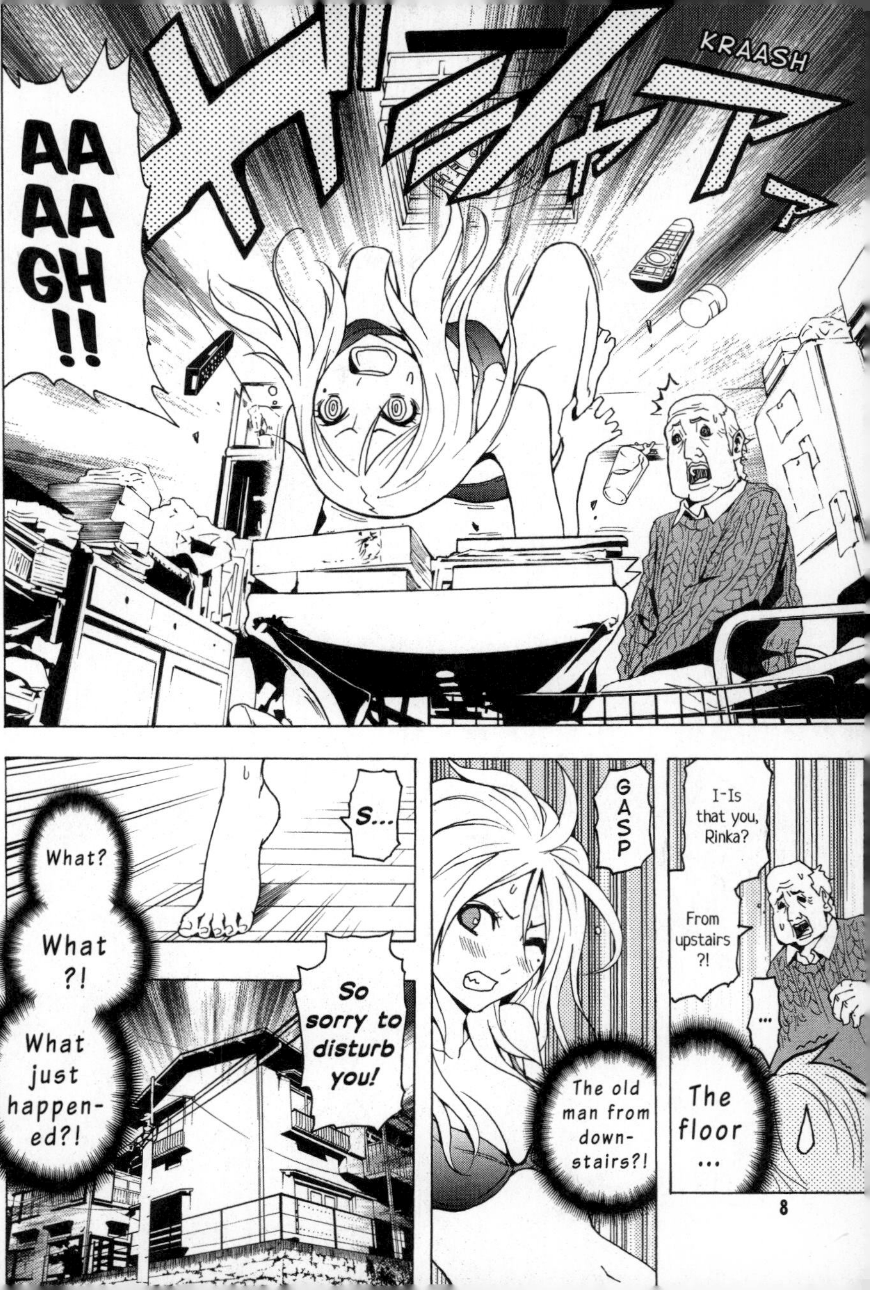
KRAASH
AAAAGH!!
I-Is that you, Rinka?
From upstairs?!
...
The floor ...
GASP
The old man from down-stairs?!
S...
So sorry to disturb you!
What?
What?!
What just happen-ed?!

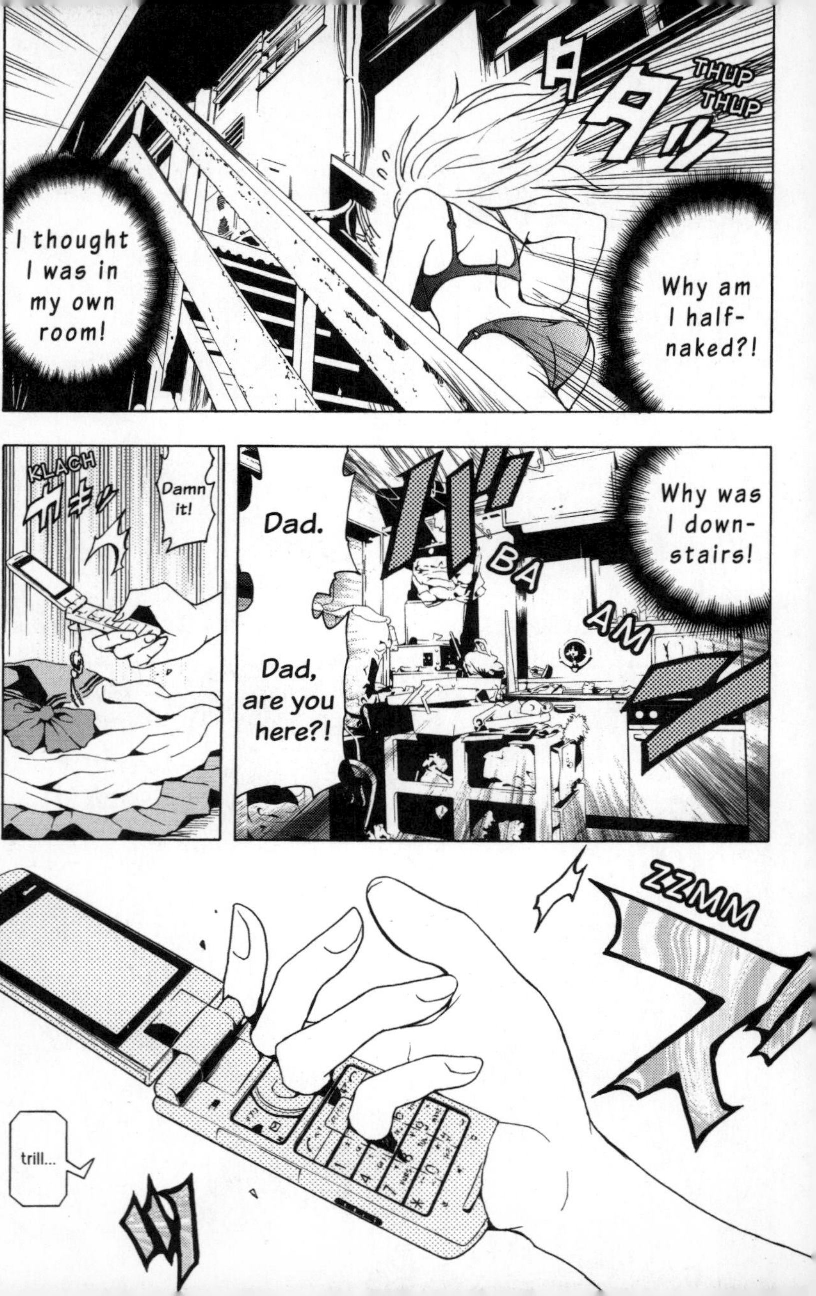
THUP THUP
Why am I half-naked?!
I thought I was in my own room!
Why was I downstairs!
Dad.
BA AM
Dad, are you here?!
KLACH
Damn it!
ZZMM
trill...

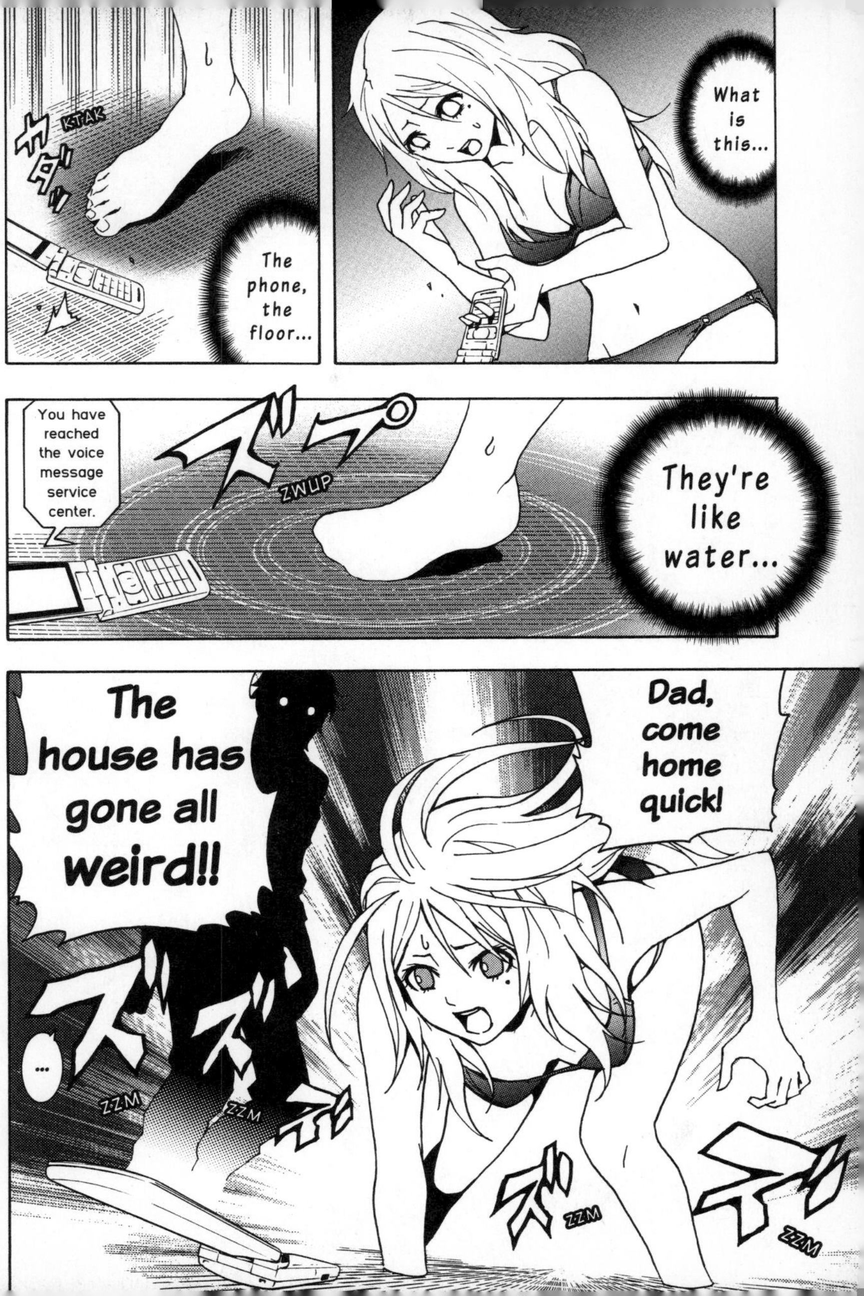
What is this...
KTAK
The phone, the floor...
They're like water...
ZWUP
You have reached the voice message service center.
Dad, come home quick!
The house has gone all weird!!
ZZM
ZZM
ZZM
ZZM
...

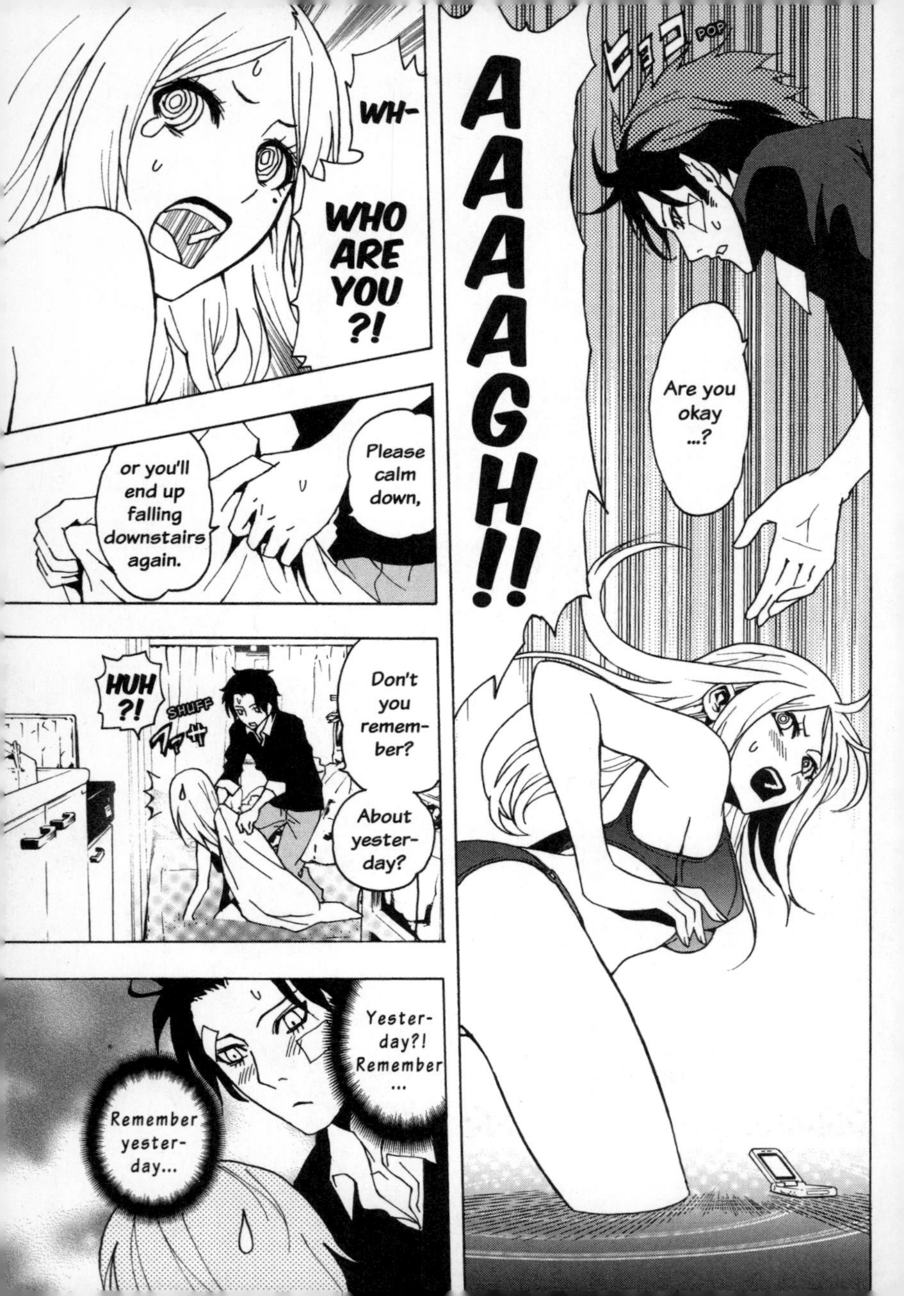

POP
Are you okay ...?
AAAAAGH!!
WH-
WHO ARE YOU ?!
Please calm down,
or you'll end up falling downstairs again.
Don't you remem-ber?
About yester-day?
HUH ?!
SHUFF
Yester-day?! Remember ...
Remember yester-day...

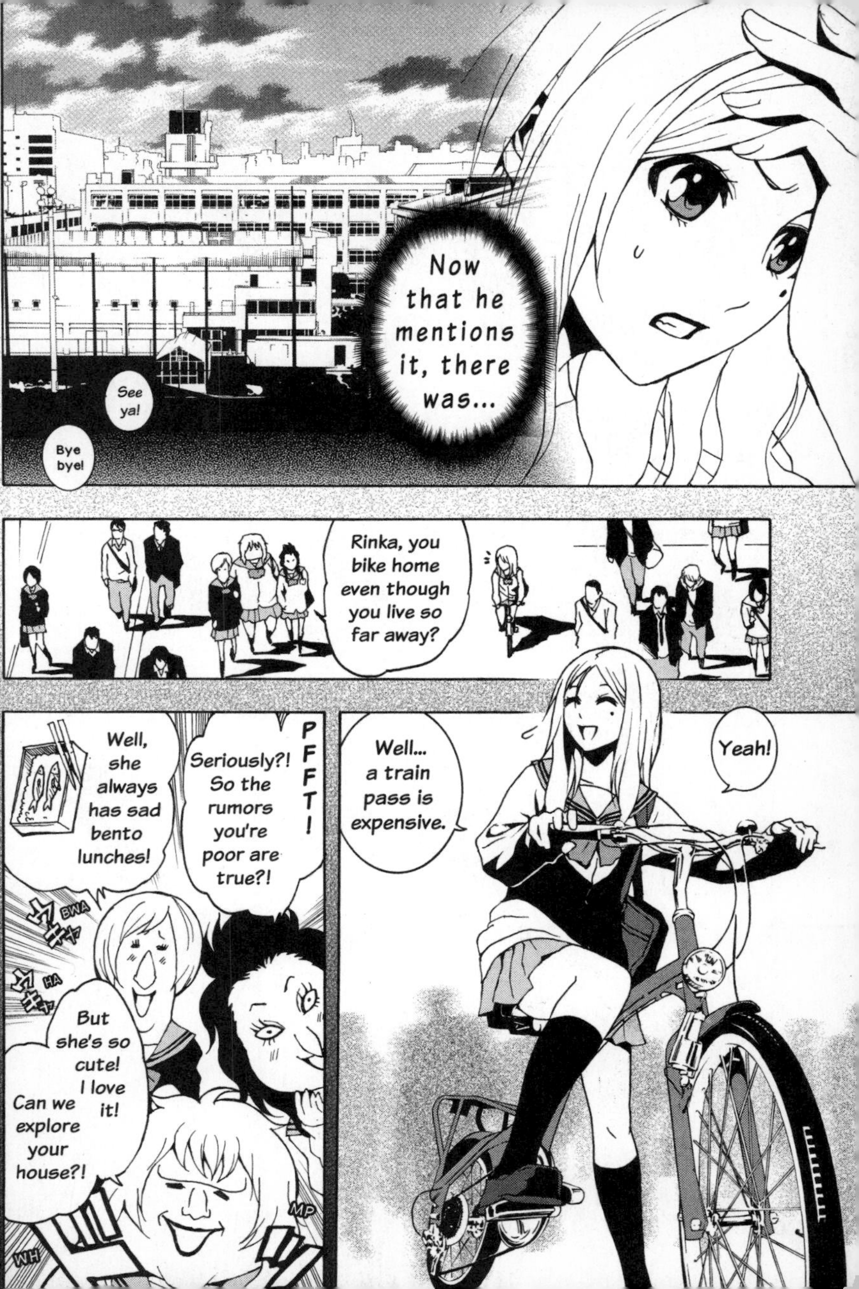
Now that he mentions it, there was...
See ya!
Bye bye!
Rinka, you bike home even though you live so far away?
Yeah!
Well... a train pass is expensive.
PFFT!
Seriously?! So the rumors you're poor are true?!
Well, she always has sad bento lunches!
BWA
HA
But she's so cute! I love it!
Can we explore your house?!
MP
WH

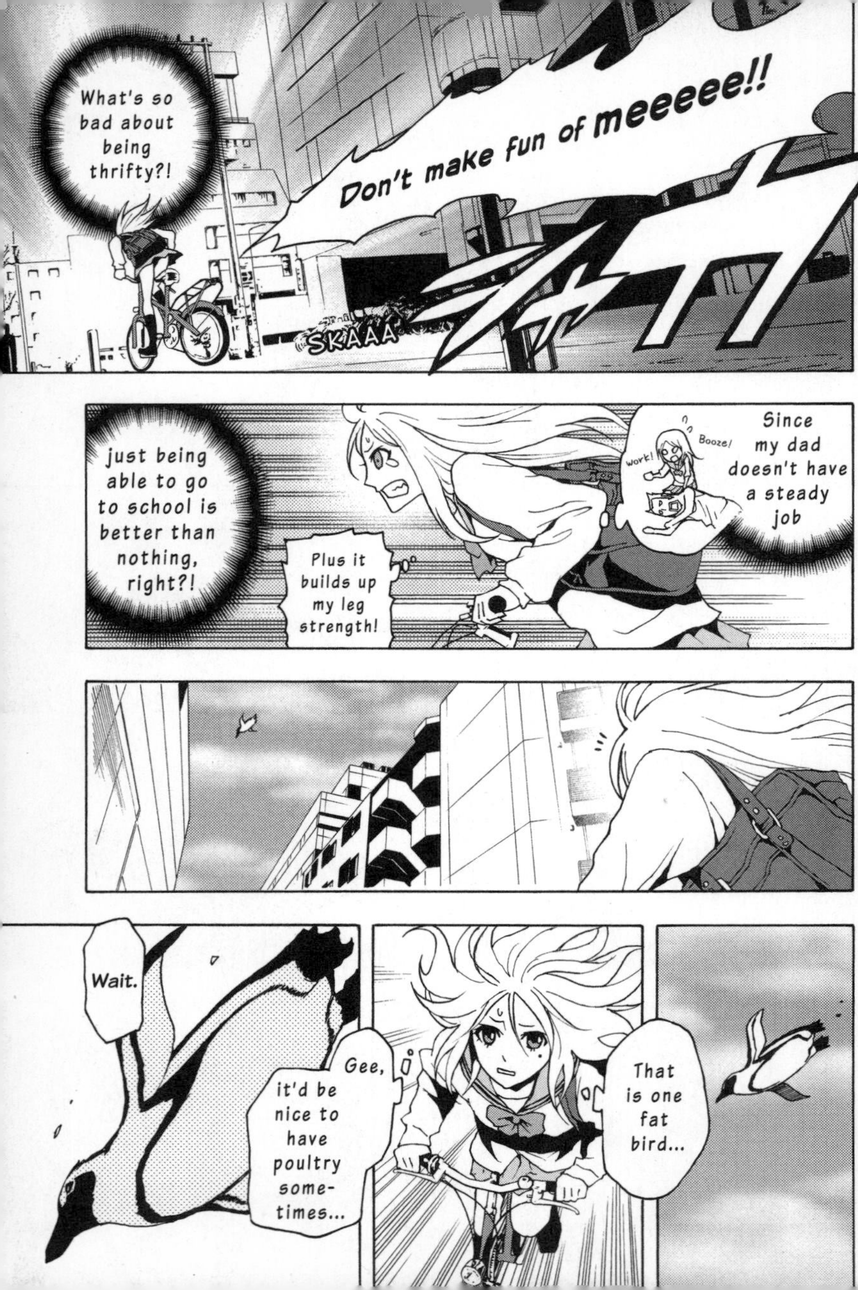
Don't make fun of meeeeee!!
What's so bad about being thrifty?!
SKAAA
Since my dad doesn't have a steady job
Booze!
Work!
just being able to go to school is better than nothing, right?!
Plus it builds up my leg strength!
That is one fat bird...
Gee, it'd be nice to have poultry some-times...
Wait.

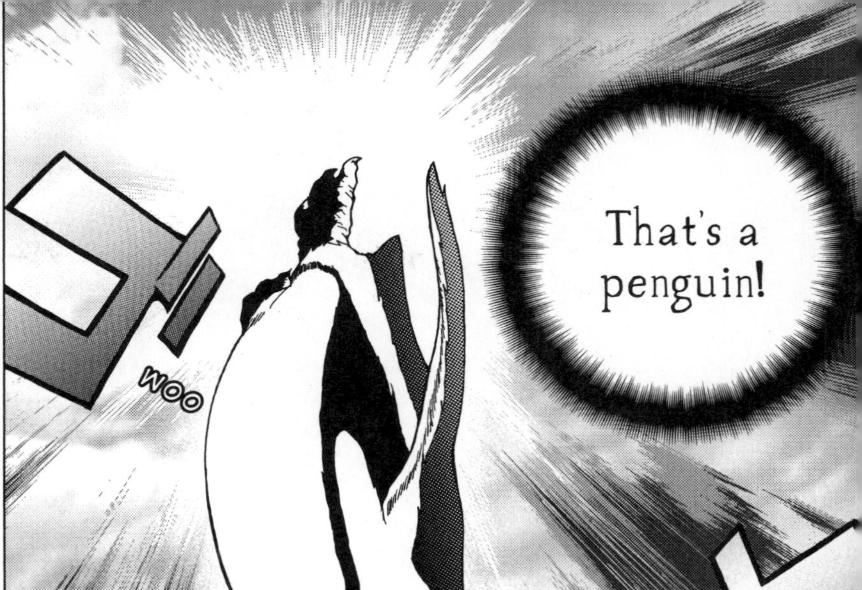
That's a penguin!
WOO
SH
A flying penguin!
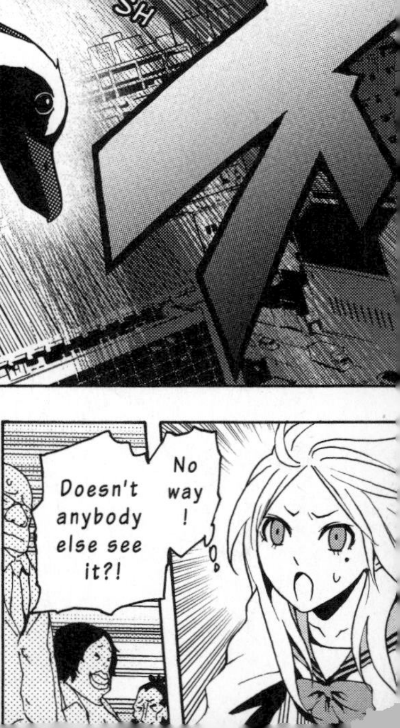
No way!
Doesn't anybody else see it?!
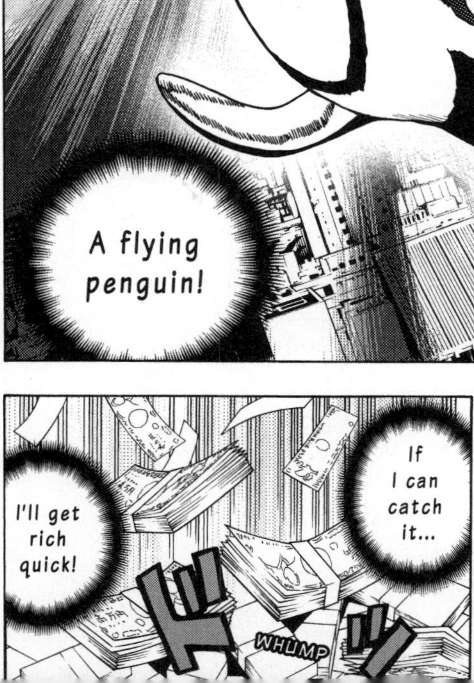
If I can catch it...
I'll get rich quick!
WHUMP

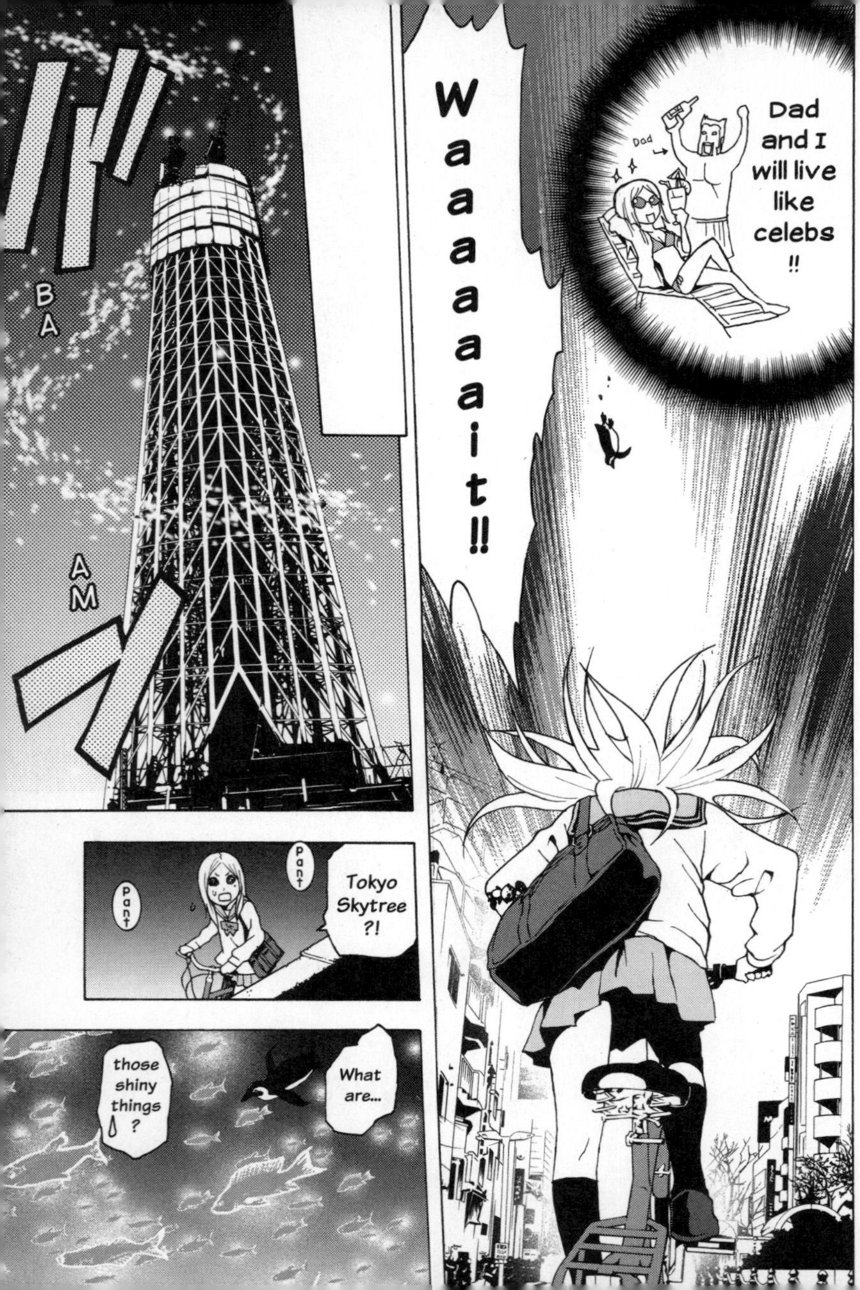
Dad and I will live like celebs !!
Dad
Waaaaaaait!!
BAAM
pant
pant
Tokyo Skytree ?!
What are...
those shiny things ?

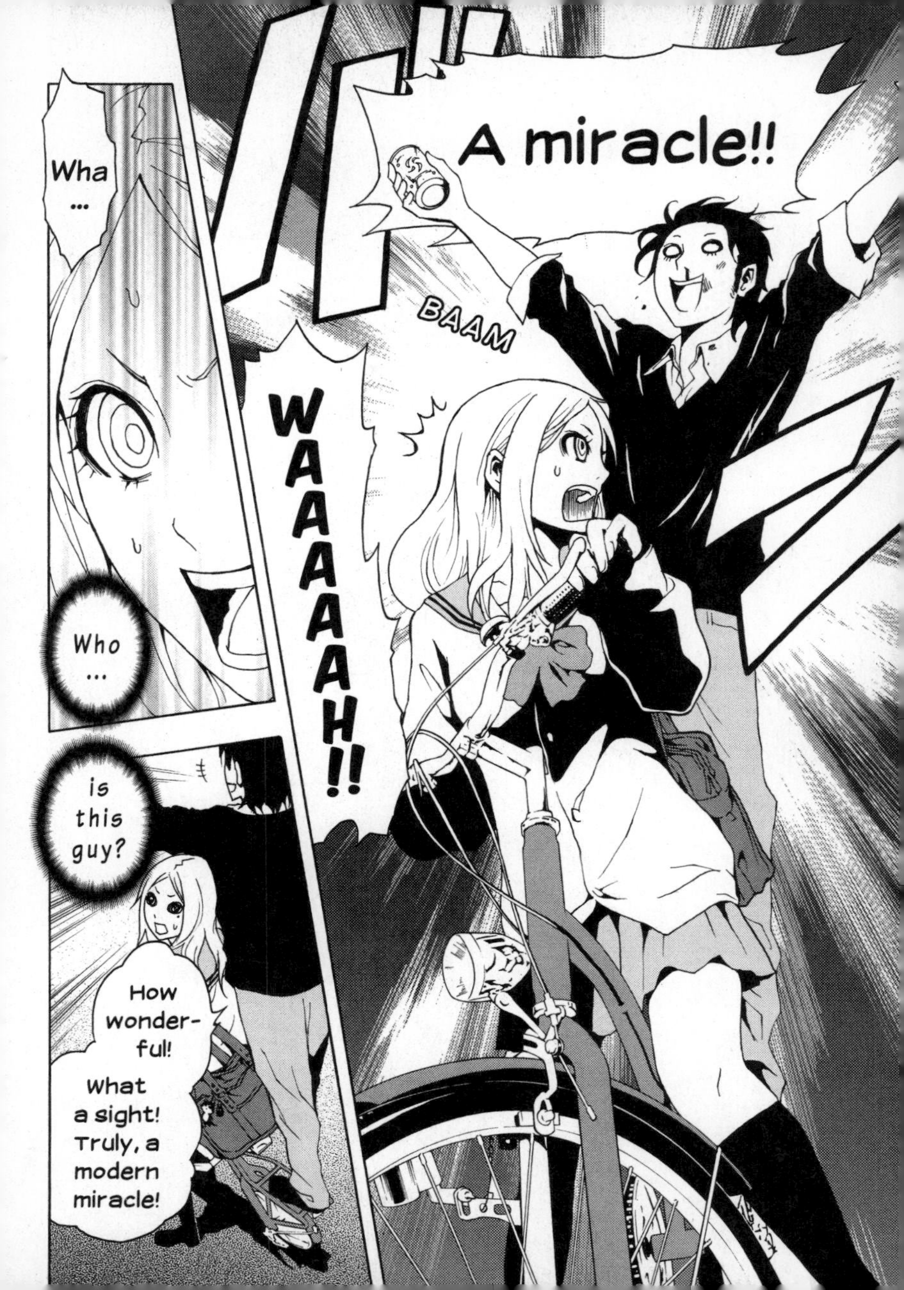
A miracle!!
BAAM
WAAAAAAH!!
Wha...
Who...
is this guy?
How wonderful!
What a sight! Truly, a modern miracle!

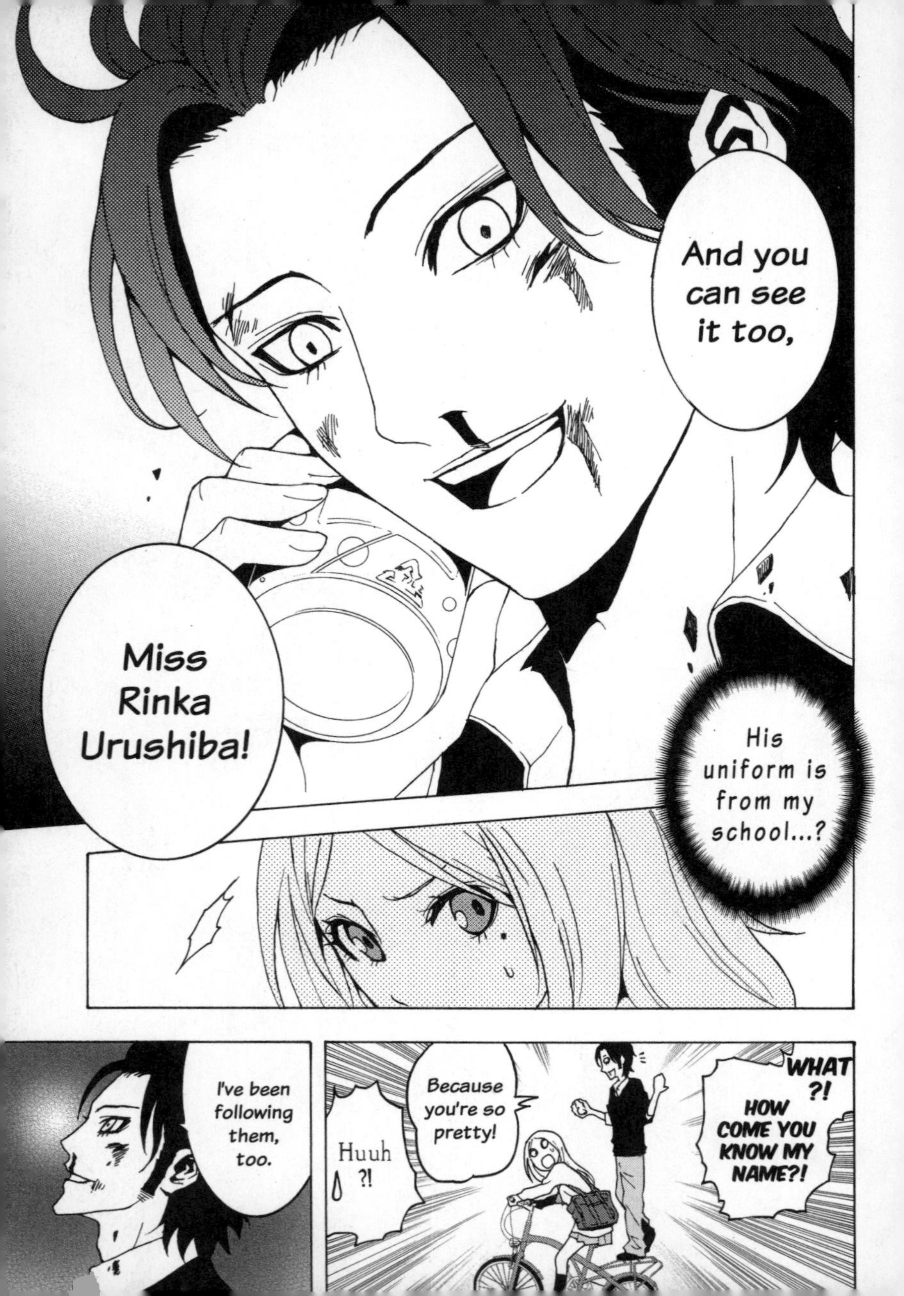
And you can see it too,
Miss Rinka Urushiba!
His uniform is from my school...?
WHAT?! HOW COME YOU KNOW MY NAME?!
Because you're so pretty!
Huuh ?!
I've been following them, too.

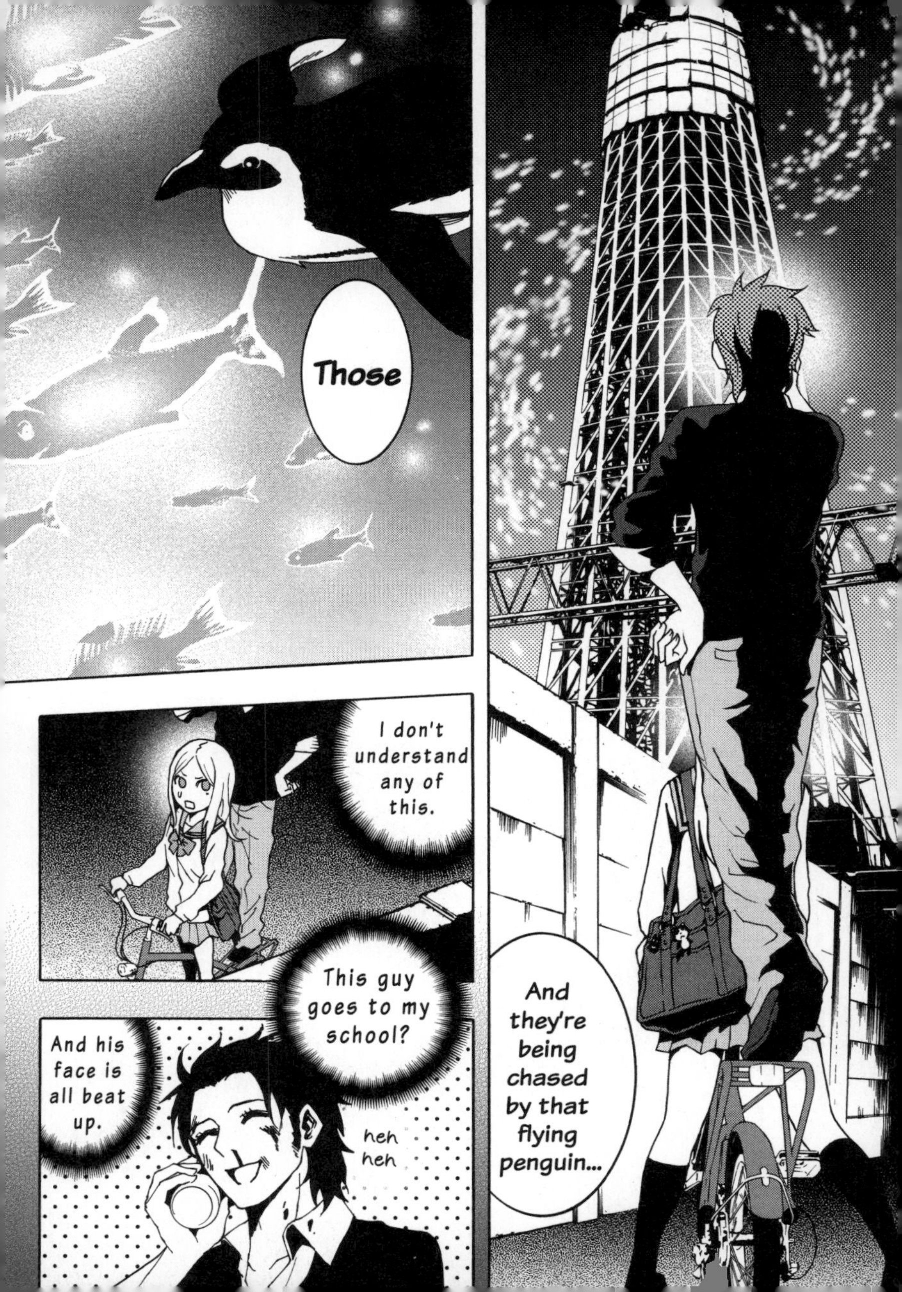
And they're being chased by that flying penguin...
Those
I don't understand any of this.
This guy goes to my school?
And his face is all beat up.
heh heh

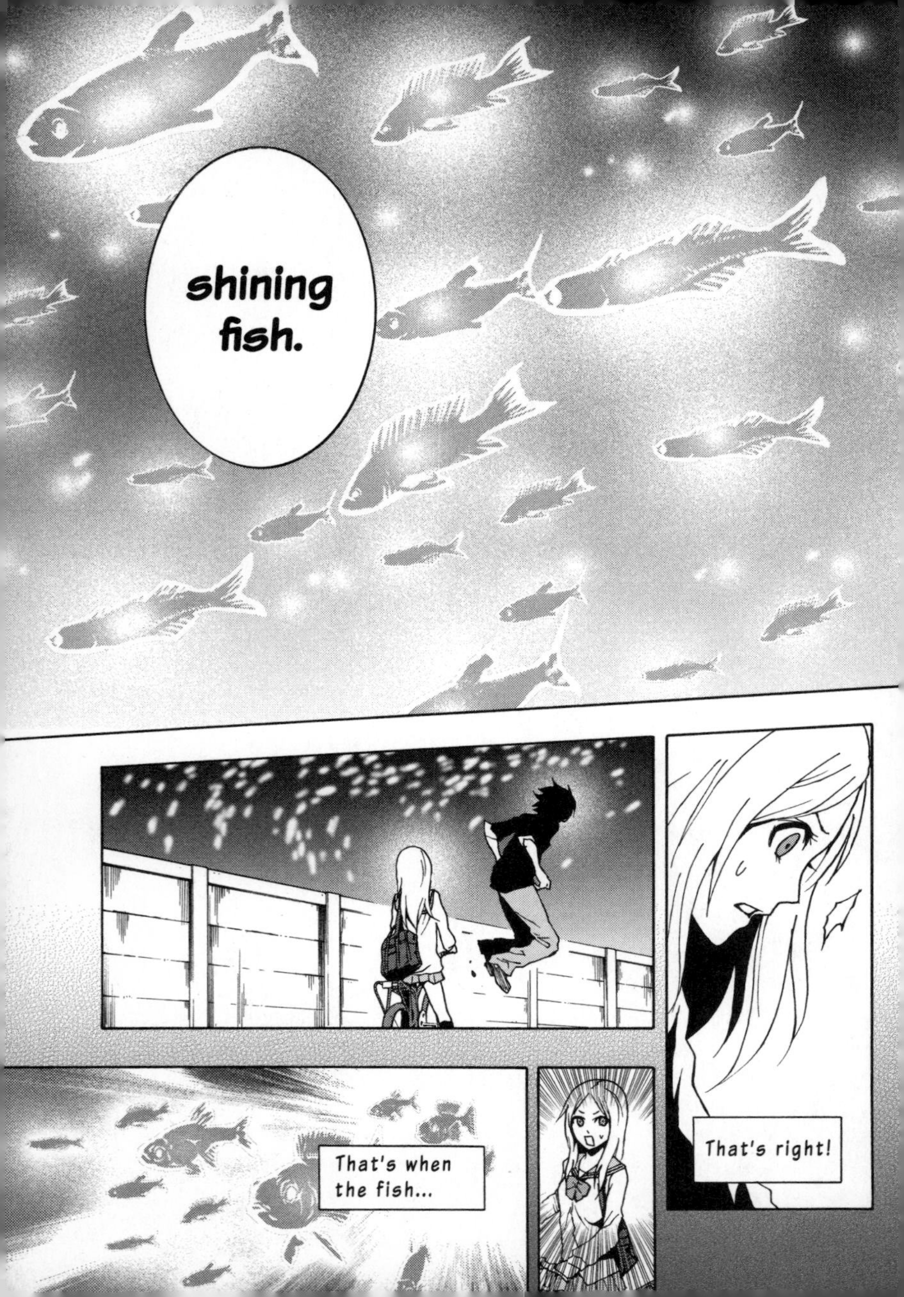
shining fish.
That's right!
That's when the fish...

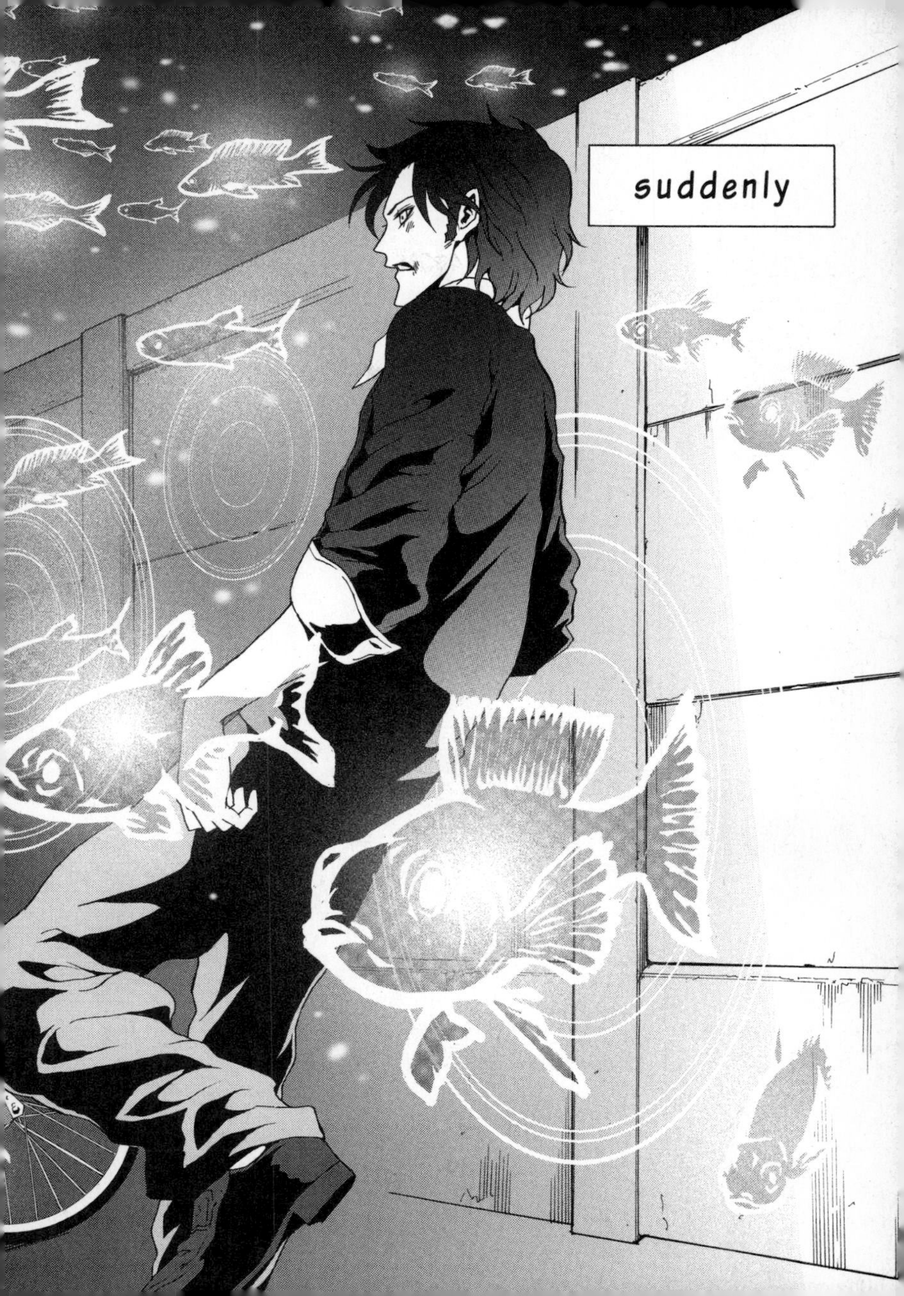
suddenly

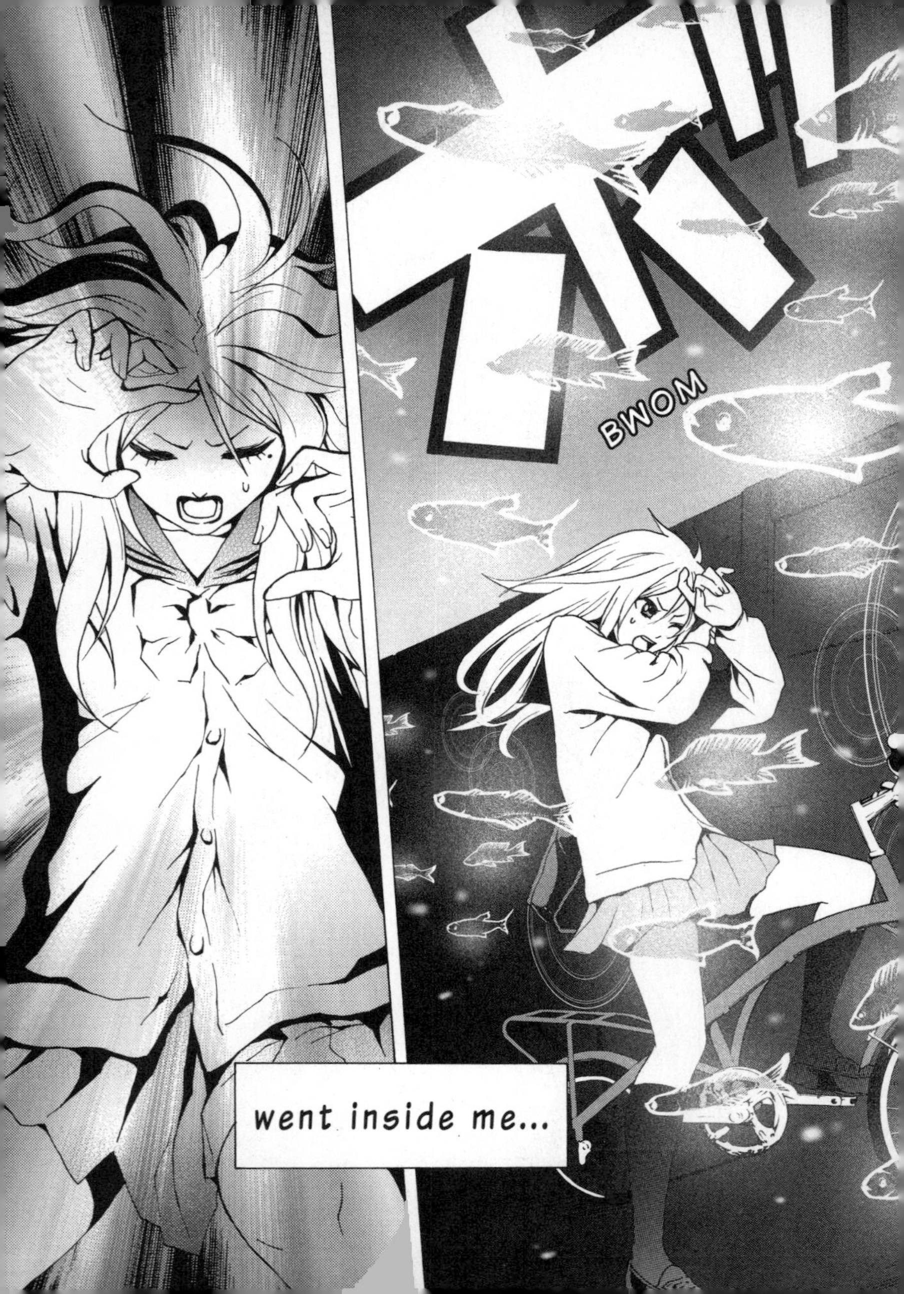
BWOM
went inside me...

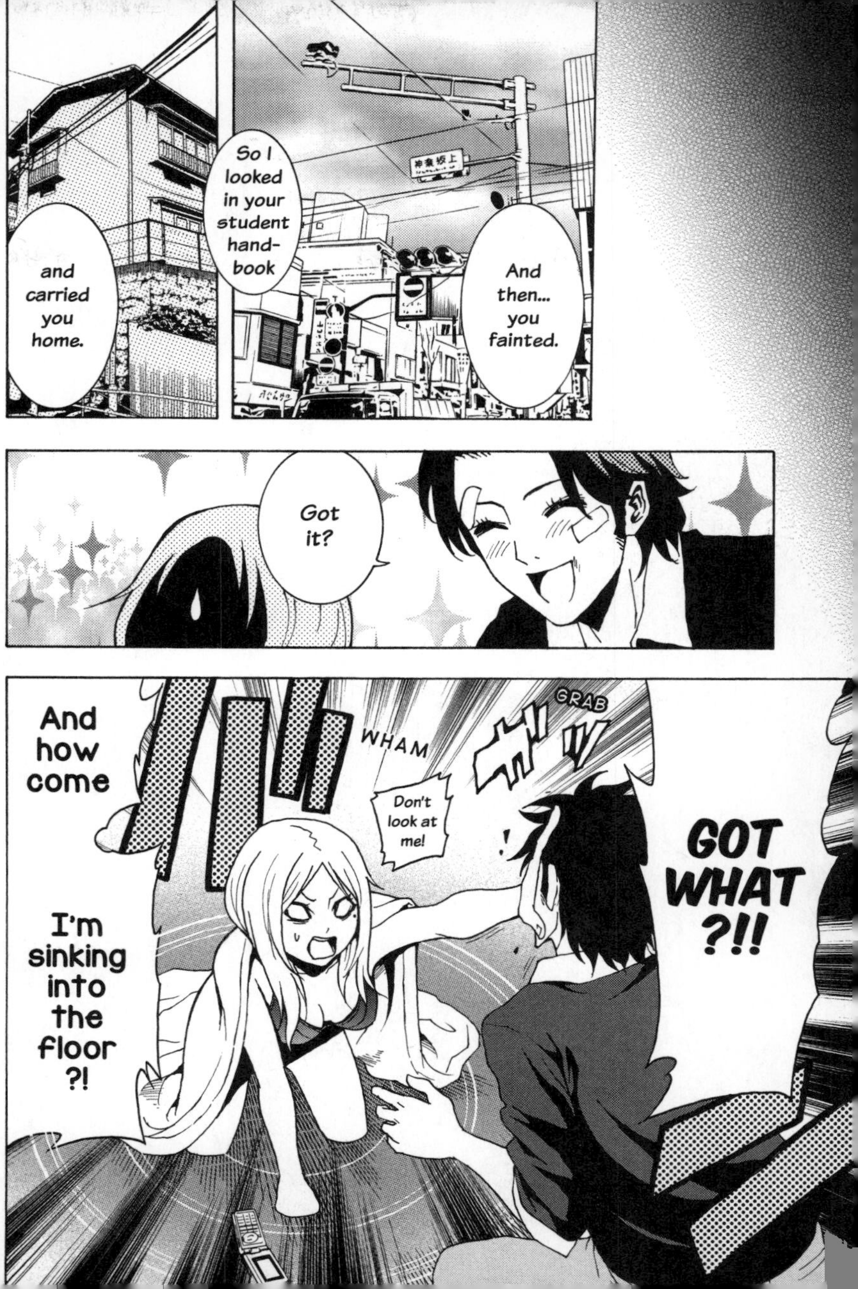

And then... you fainted.
So I looked in your student hand-book
and carried you home.
Got it?
GOT WHAT ?!!
GRAB
Don't look at me!
WHAM
And how come I'm sinking into the floor ?!

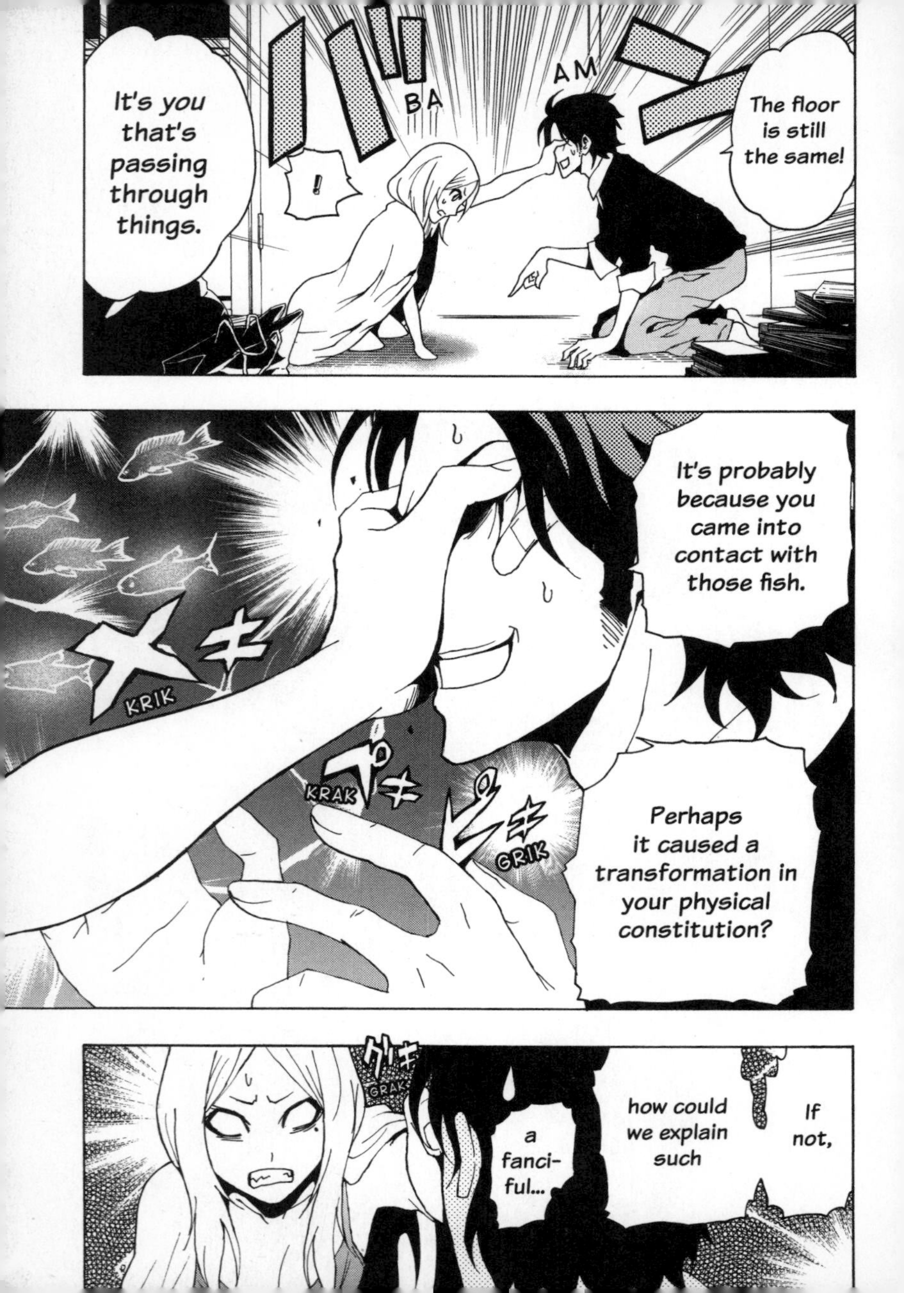
The floor is still the same!
BA
AM
!
It's you that's passing through things.
It's probably because you came into contact with those fish.
Perhaps it caused a transformation in your physical constitution?
KRIK
KRAK
GRIK
If not,
how could we explain such
a fanci-ful...
GRAK

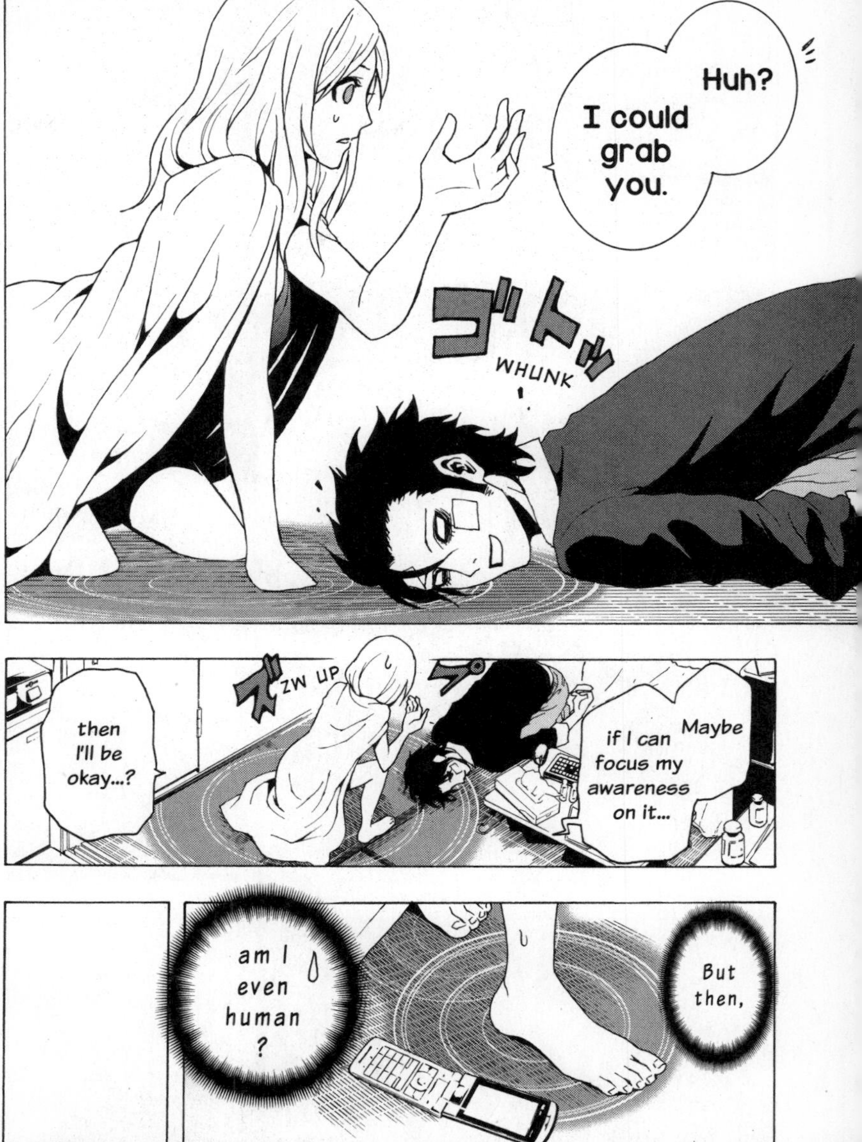

Huh? I could grab you.
ゴトッ
WHUNK
Maybe if I can focus my awareness on it...
ZW UP
then I'll be okay...?
But then,
am I even human?

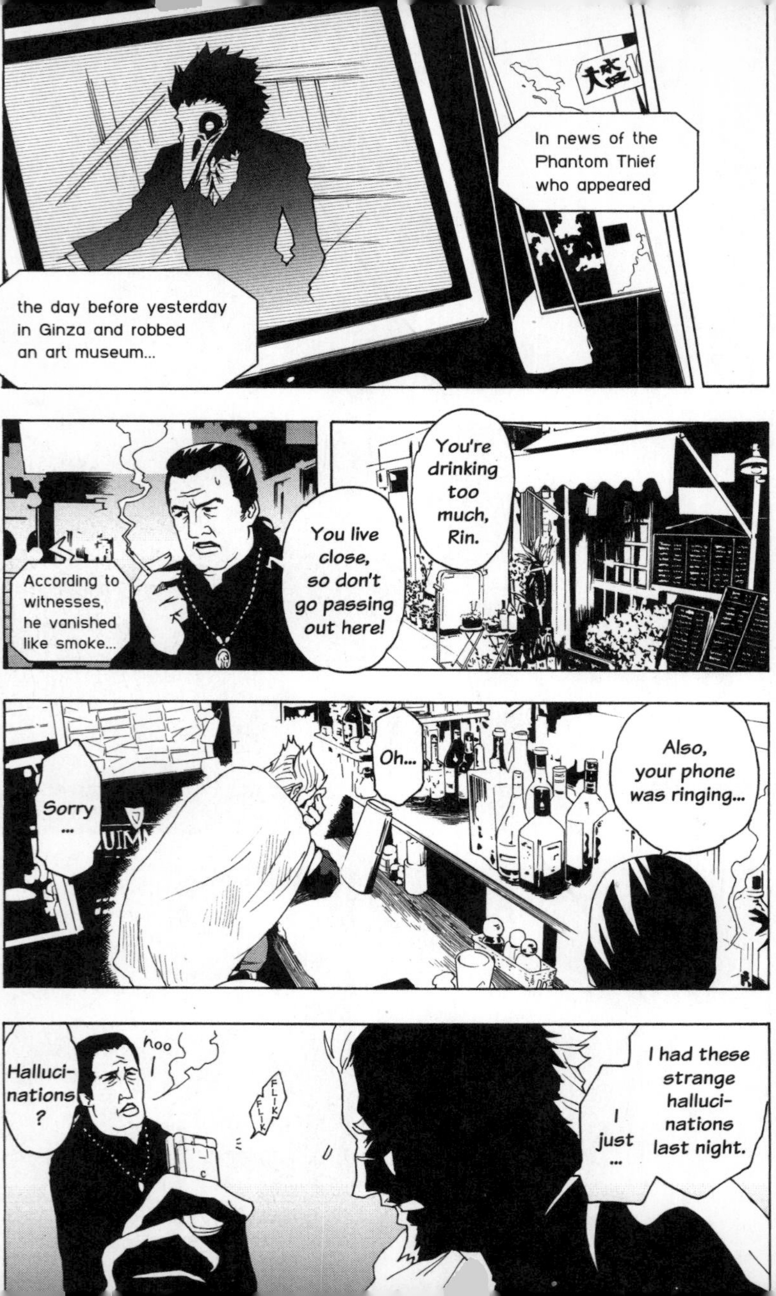
In news of the Phantom Thief who appeared
the day before yesterday in Ginza and robbed an art museum...
You're drinking too much, Rin.
You live close, so don't go passing out here!
According to witnesses, he vanished like smoke...
Also, your phone was ringing...
Oh...
Sorry ...
I had these strange halluci-nations last night.
I just ...
FLIK FLIK
hoo
Halluci-nations ?

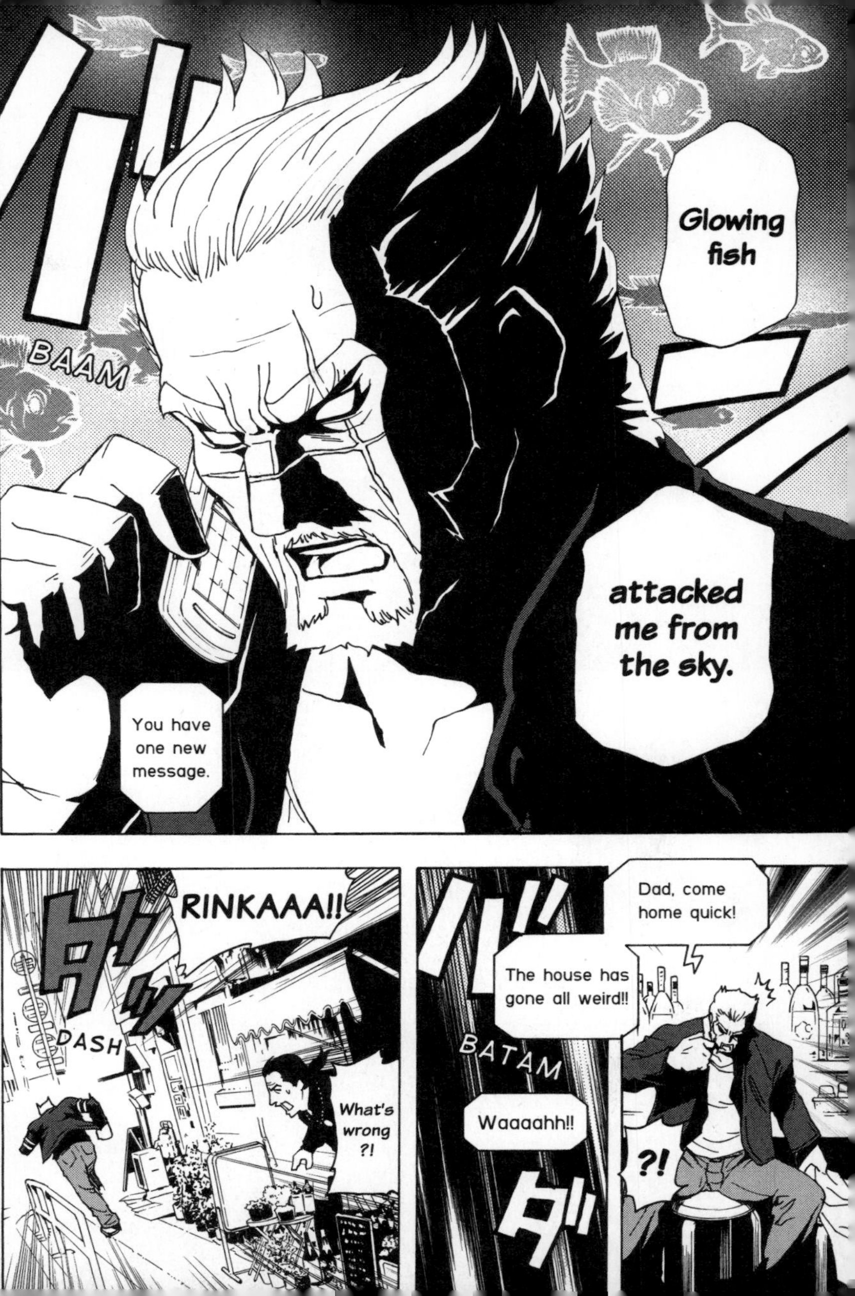
Glowing fish
attacked me from the sky.
BAAM
You have one new message.
Dad, come home quick!
The house has gone all weird!!
BATAM
?!
Waaaahh!!
RINKAAA!!
DASH
What's wrong ?!

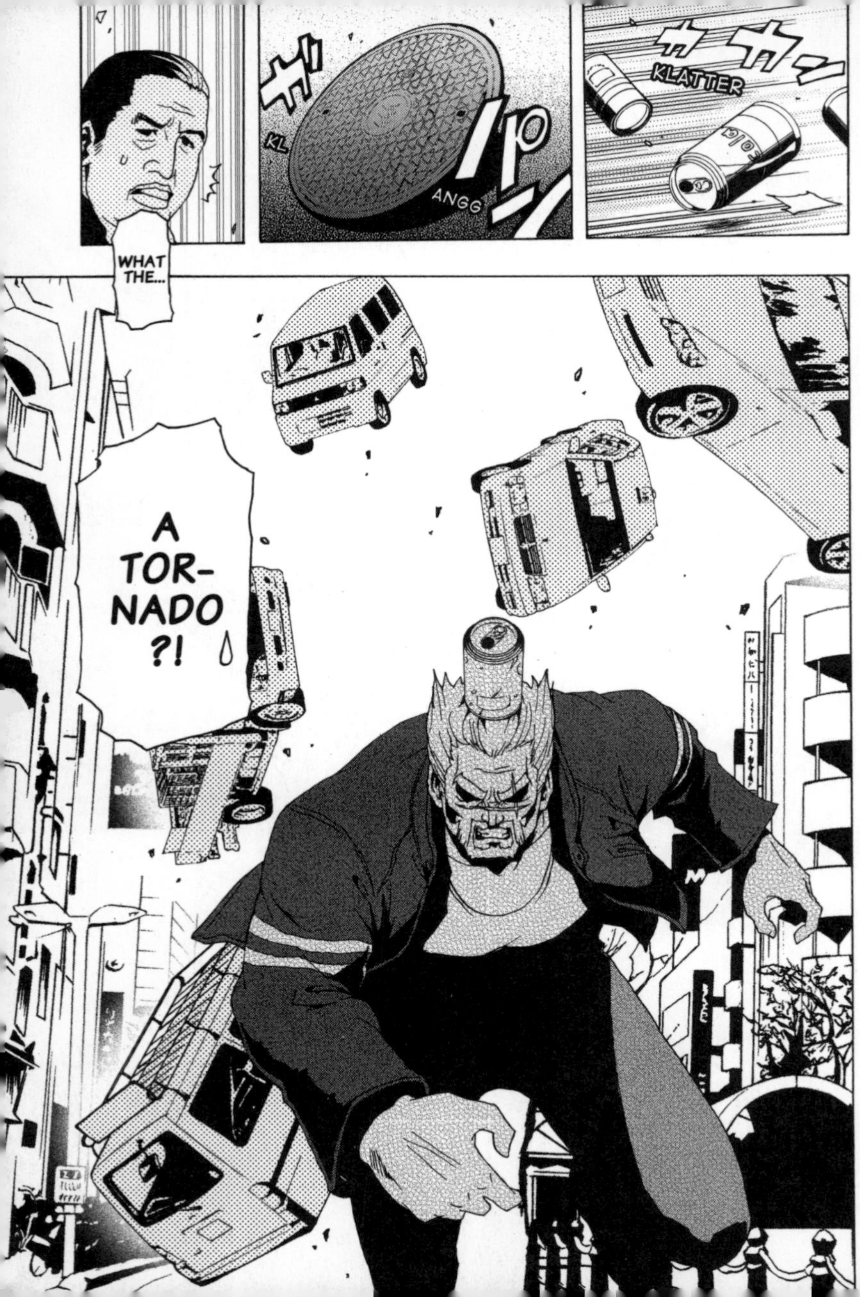
KLATTER
KL
ANGG
WHAT THE...
A TOR-
NADO
?!

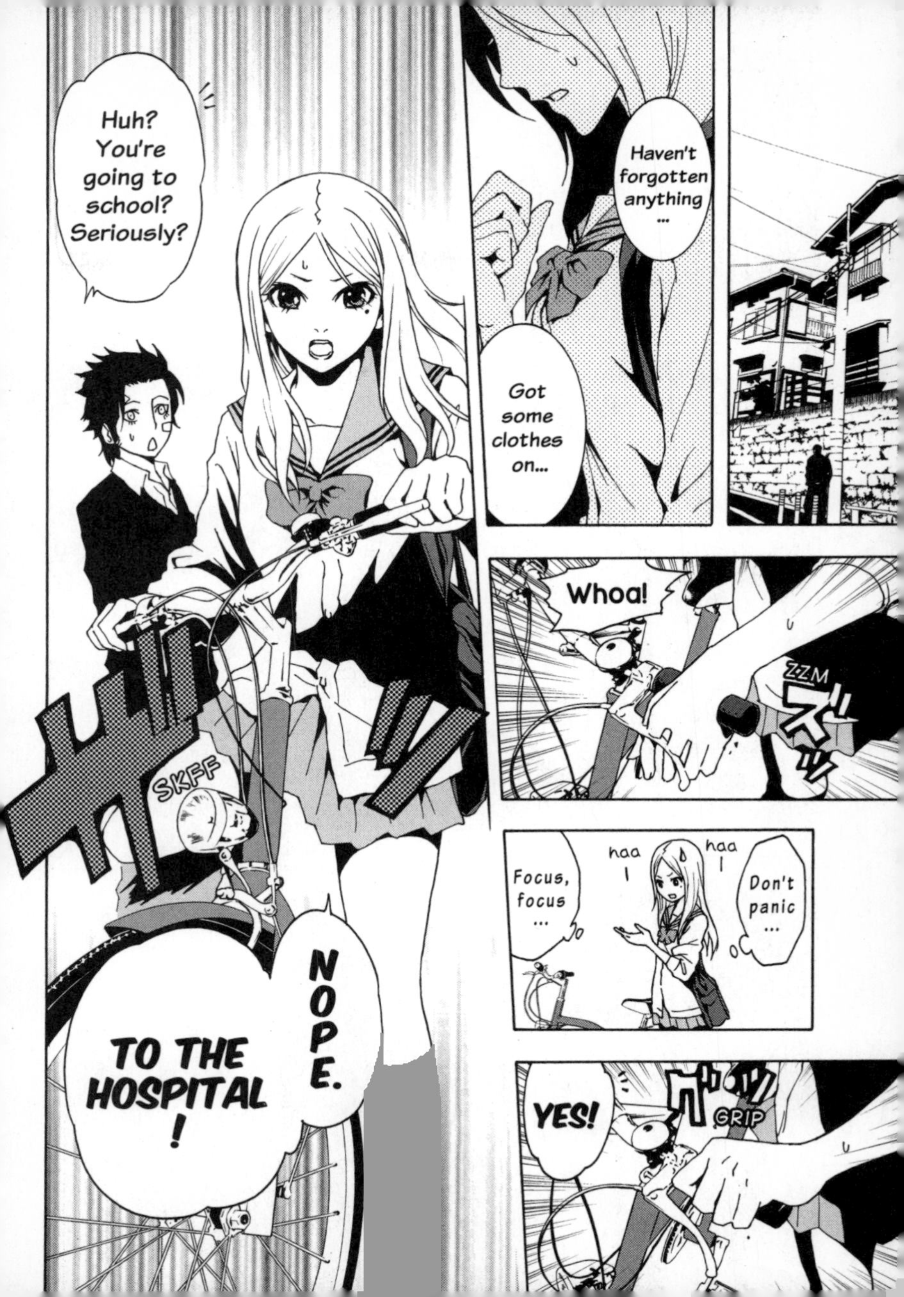

Haven't forgotten anything ...
Got some clothes on...
Whoa!
ZZM
Don't panic ...
haa
haa
Focus, focus ...
YES!
GRIP
Huh? You're going to school? Seriously?
NOPE.
TO THE HOSPITAL!
SKFF

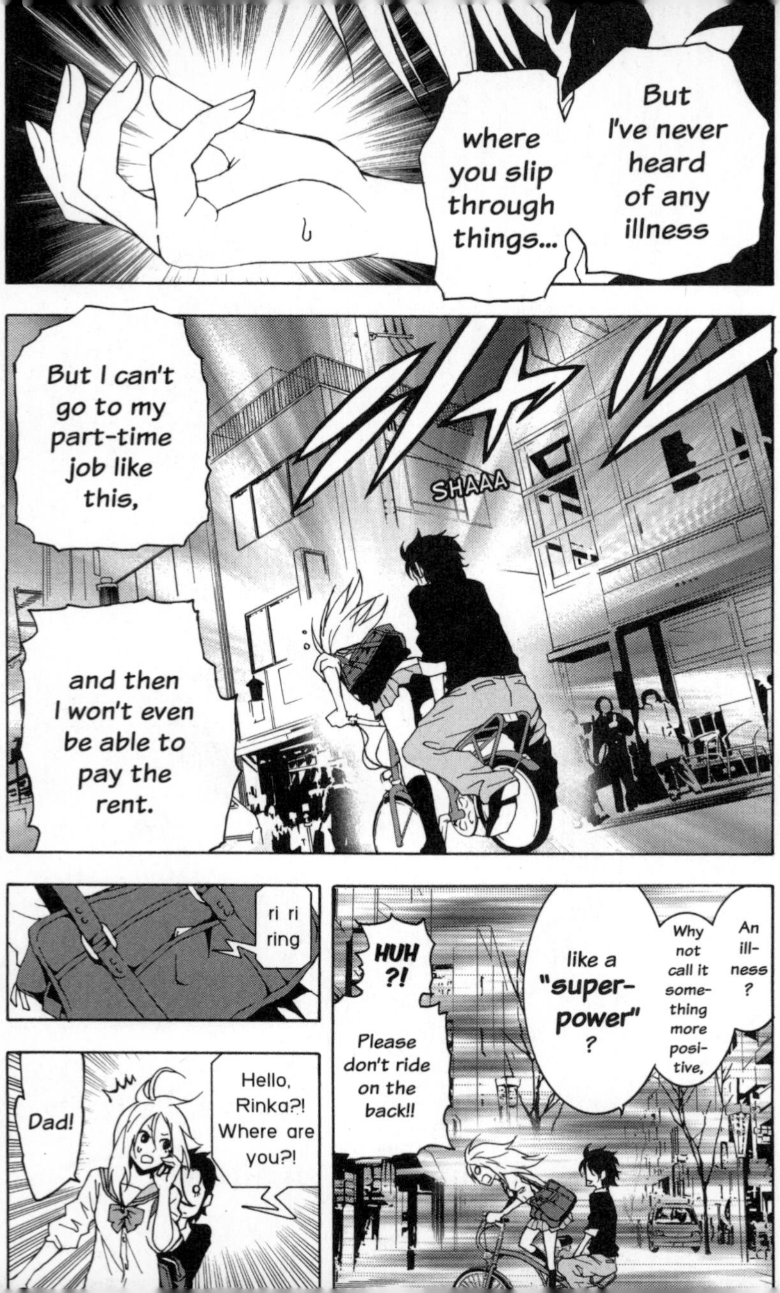
But I've never heard of any illness
where you slip through things...
But I can't go to my part-time job like this,
SHAAA
and then I won't even be able to pay the rent.
An illness?
Why not call it something more positive,
like a "super-power"?
HUH?!
Please don't ride on the back!!
ri ri ring
Hello, Rinka?! Where are you?!
Dad!

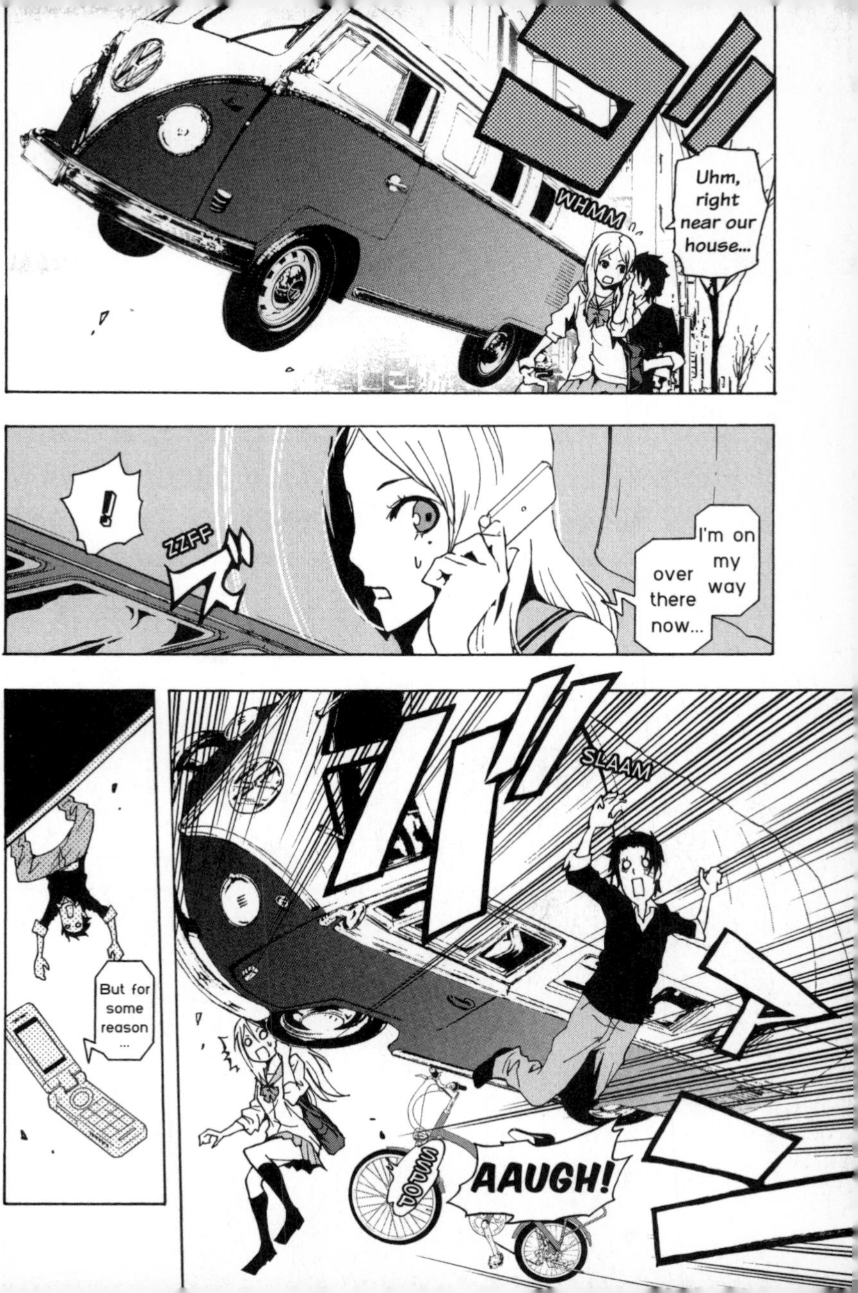
WHMM
Uhm, right near our house...
!
ZZFF
I'm on my way over there now...
SLAAM
AAUGH!
But for some reason ...

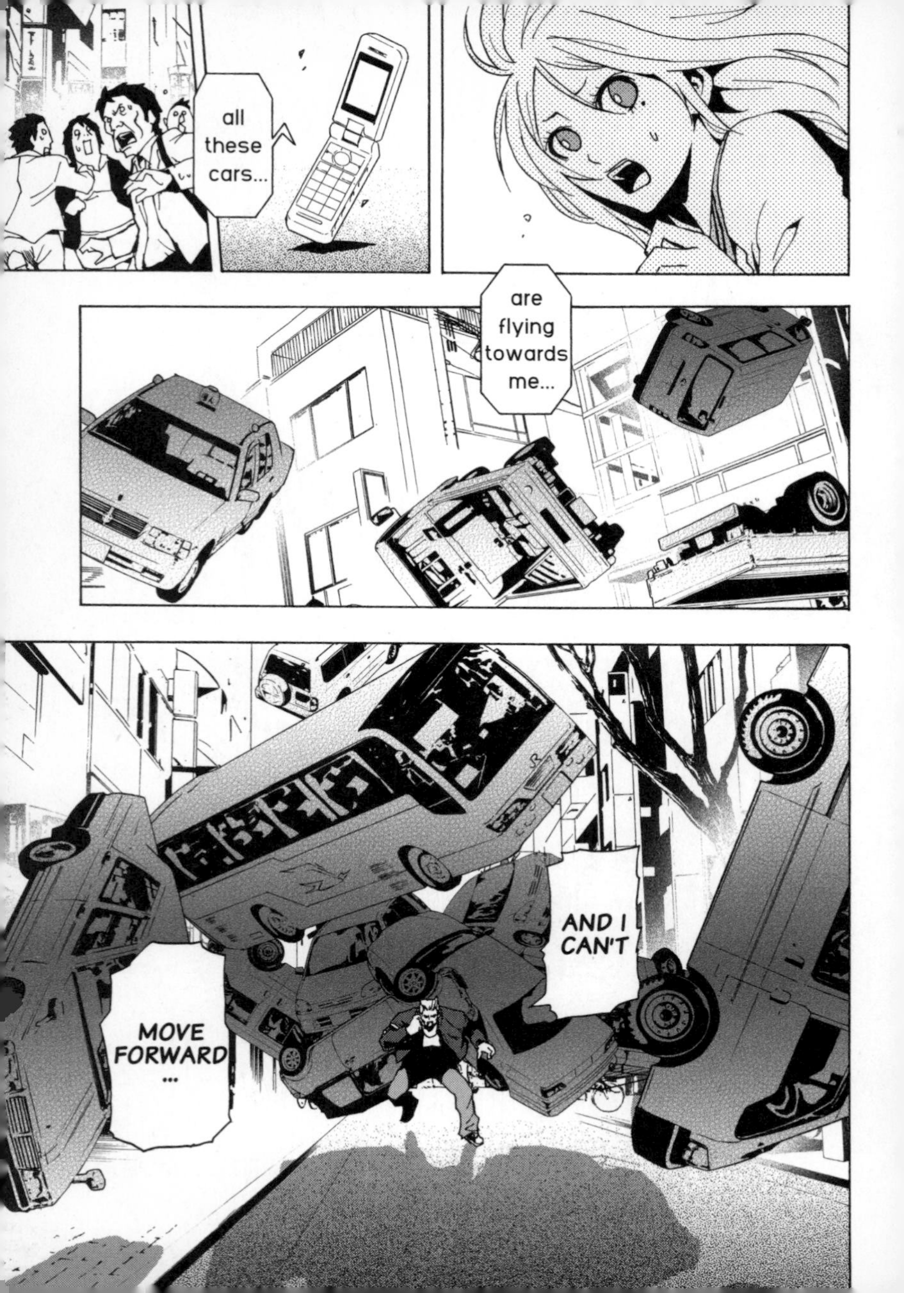
all these cars...
are flying towards me...
AND I CAN'T
MOVE FORWARD ...

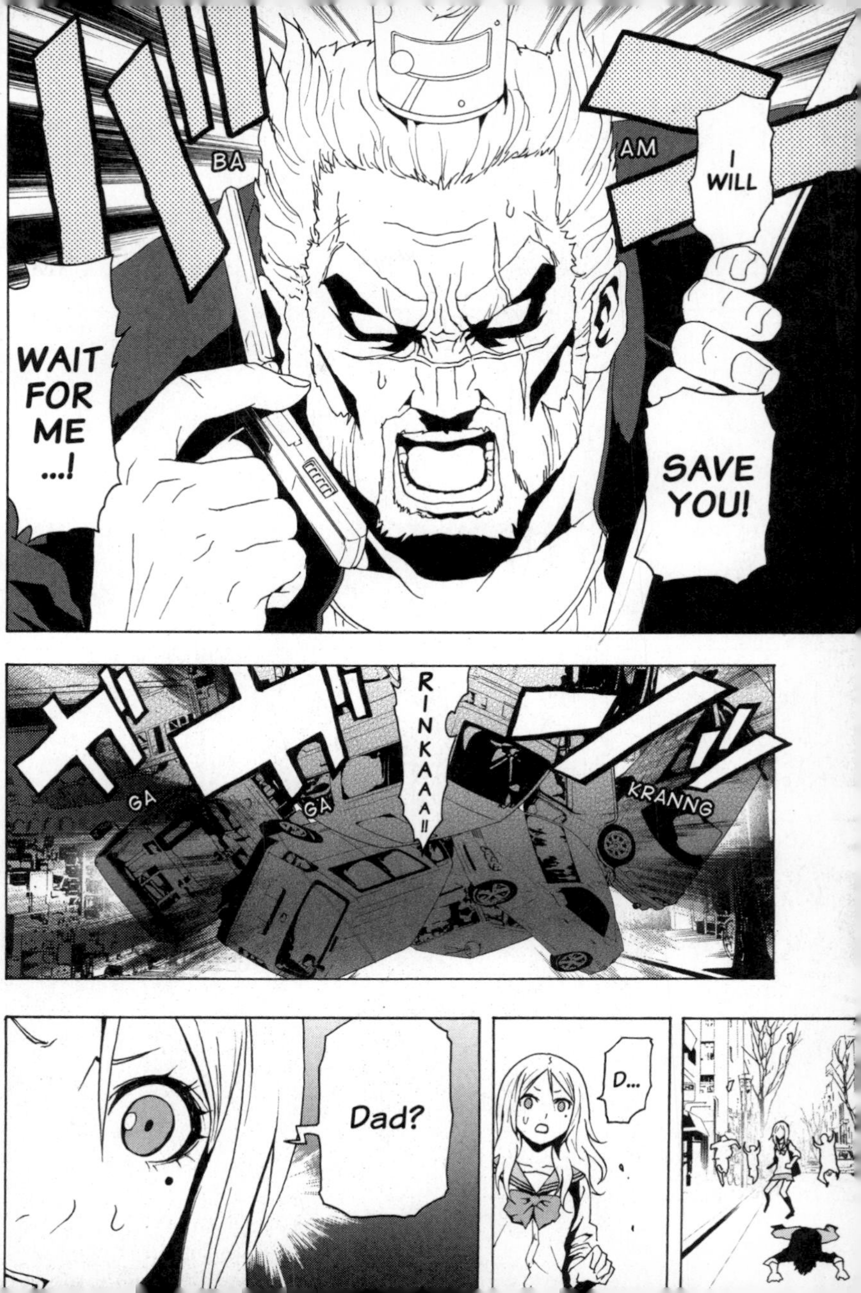
AM
I WILL
SAVE YOU!
BA
WAIT FOR ME ...!
KRANNG
RINKAAA!!
GA
GA
D...
Dad?

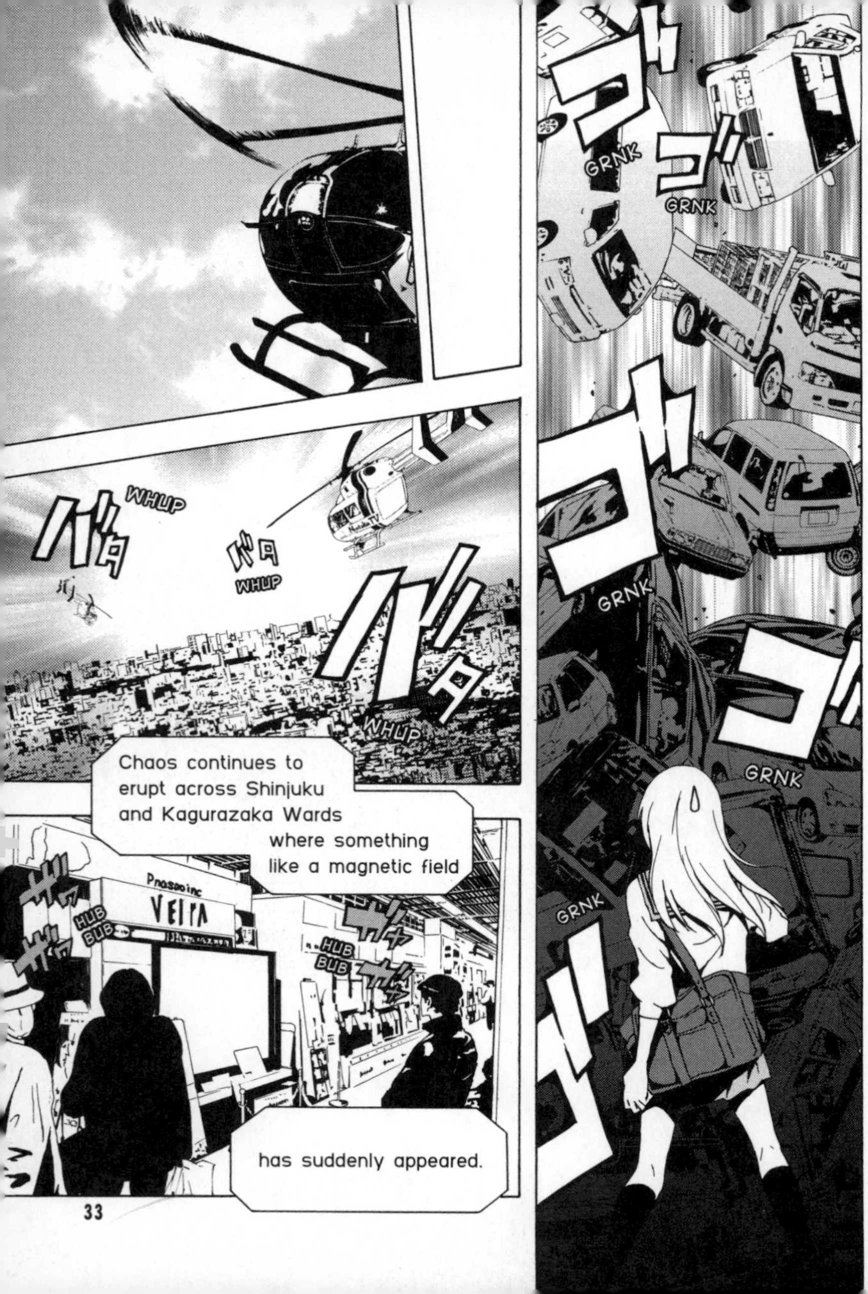
GRNK
GRNK
GRNK
GRNK
GRNK
WHUP
WHUP
WHUP
Chaos continues to erupt across Shinjuku and Kagurazaka Wards
where something like a magnetic field
HUB BUB
HUB BUB
has suddenly appeared.

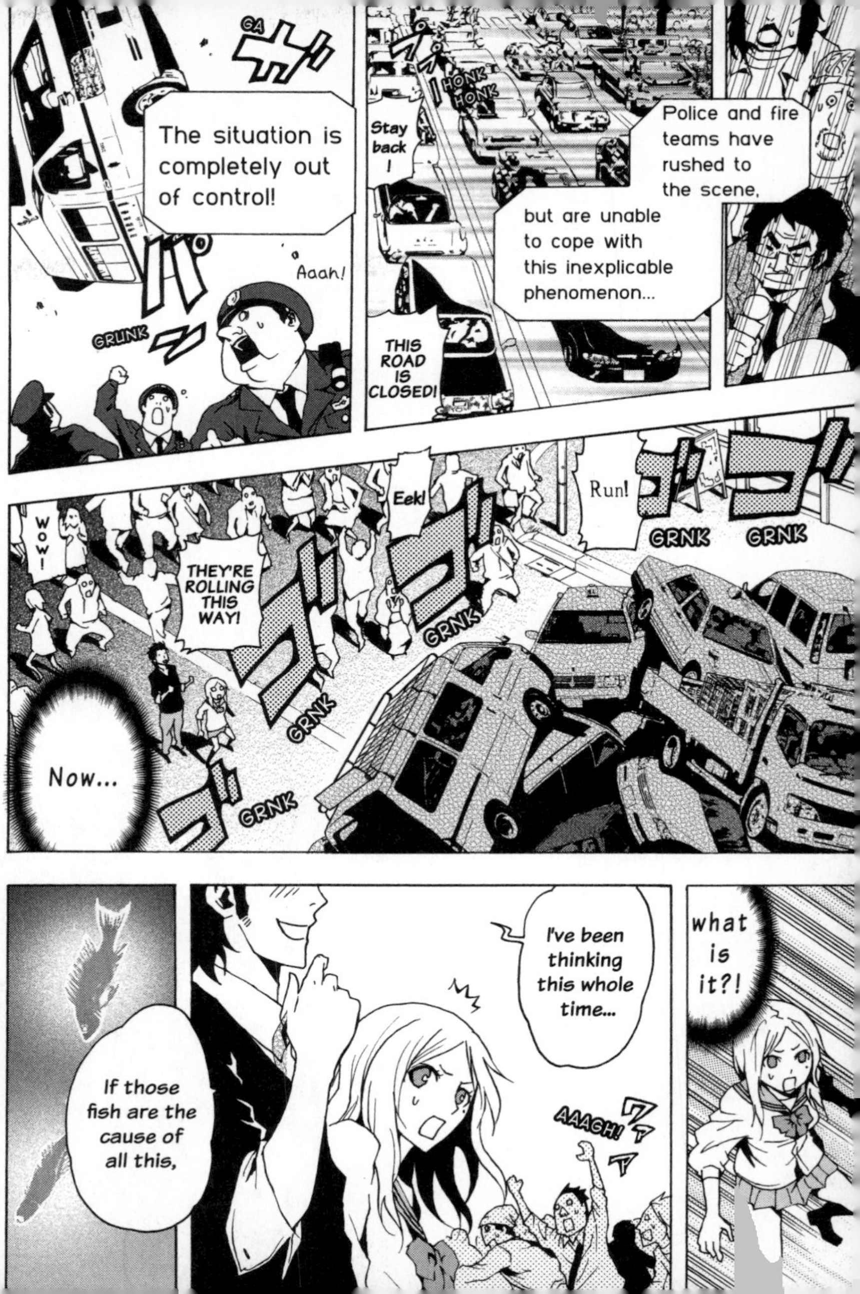
Police and fire teams have rushed to the scene,
but are unable to cope with this inexplicable phenomenon...
HONK HONK
Stay back!
THIS ROAD IS CLOSED!
GA
The situation is completely out of control!
Aaah!
GRUNK
Run!
GRNK
GRNK
Eek!
GRNK
THEY'RE ROLLING THIS WAY!
WOW!
GRNK
Now...
GRNK
what is it?!
I've been thinking this whole time...
AAAGH!
If those fish are the cause of all this,

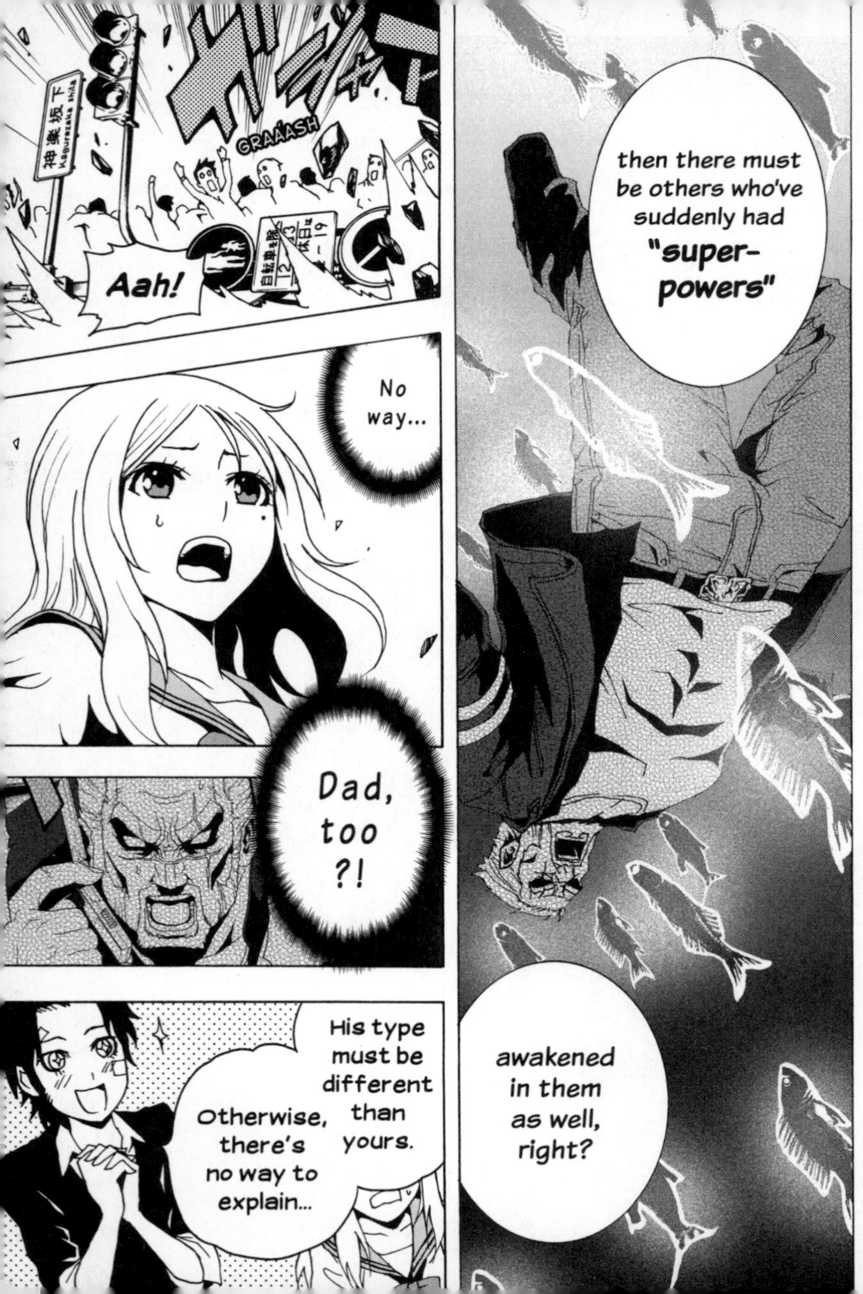

then there must be others who've suddenly had "super-powers"
awakened in them as well, right?
GRAAASH
神楽坂下
Kagurazaka shita
Aah!
No way...
Dad, too ?!
His type must be different than yours.
Otherwise, there's no way to explain...

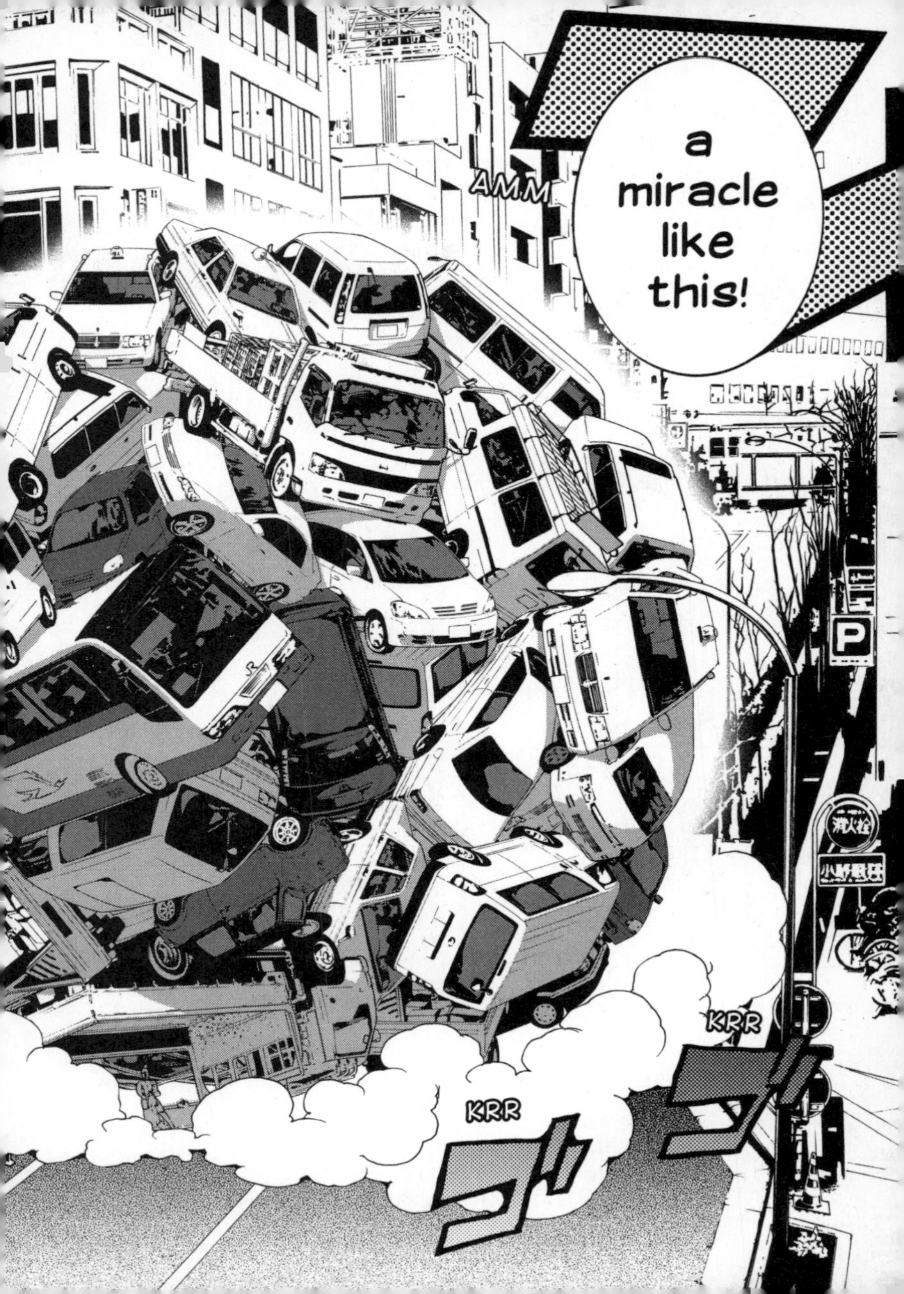
a miracle like this!
AMM
KRR
KRR

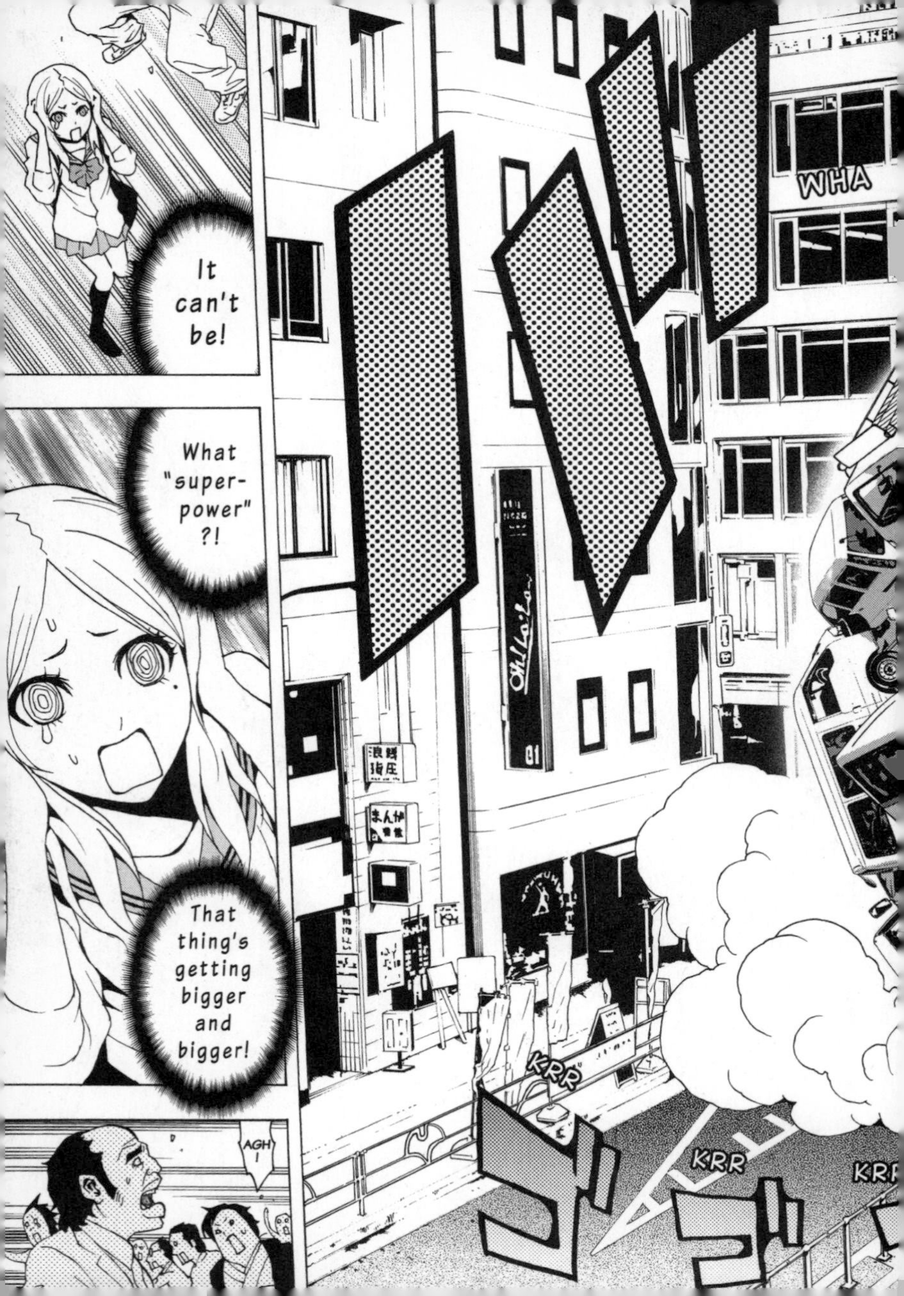
WHA
KRR
KRR
KRR
It can't be!
What "super-power"?!
That thing's getting bigger and bigger!
AGH!

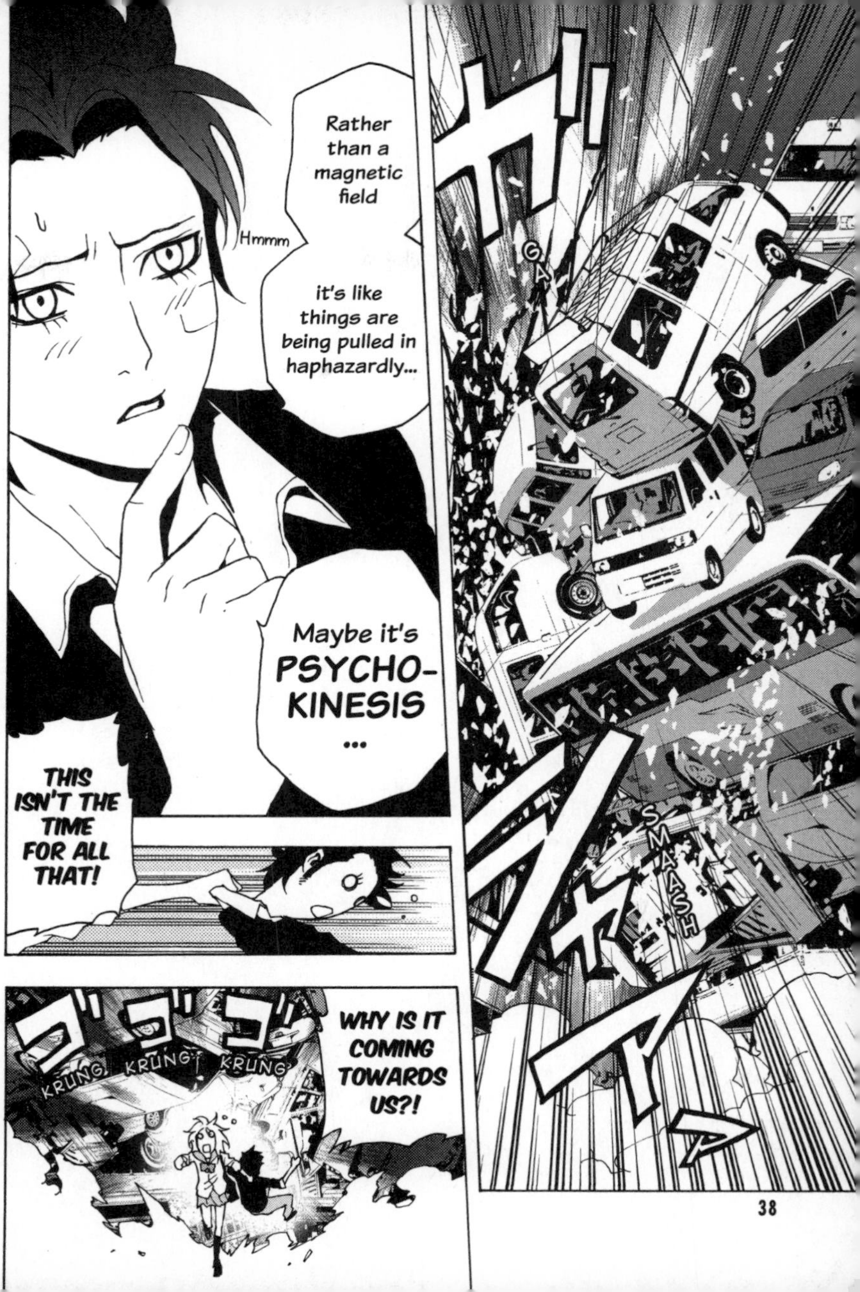
GA
SMASH
Rather than a magnetic field
Hmmm
it's like things are being pulled in haphazardly...
Maybe it's PSYCHO-KINESIS ...
THIS ISN'T THE TIME FOR ALL THAT!
WHY IS IT COMING TOWARDS US?!
KRUNG
KRUNG
KRUNG

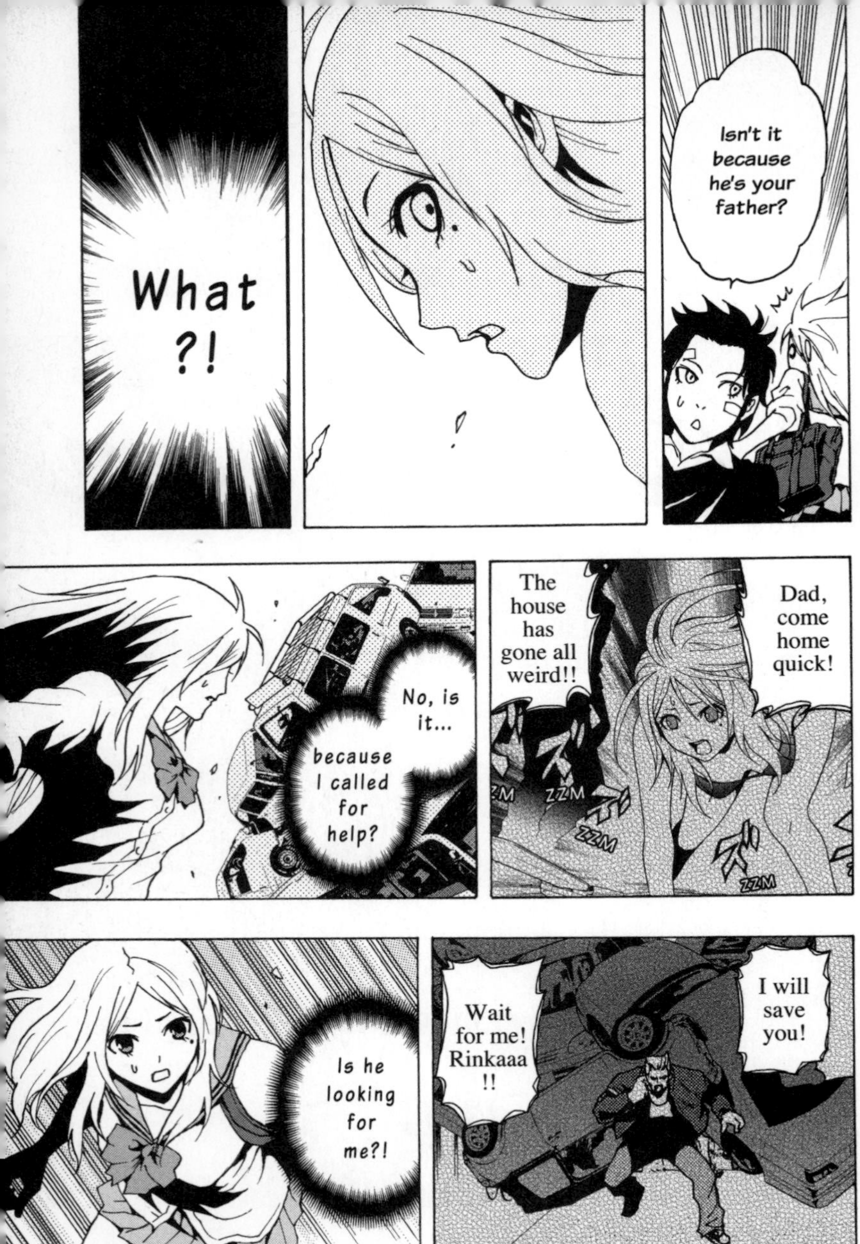
Isn't it because he's your father?
What ?!
Dad, come home quick!
The house has gone all weird!!
ZZM
ZZM
ZZM
ZZM
No, is it...
because I called for help?
I will save you!
Wait for me! Rinkaaa !!
Is he looking for me?!

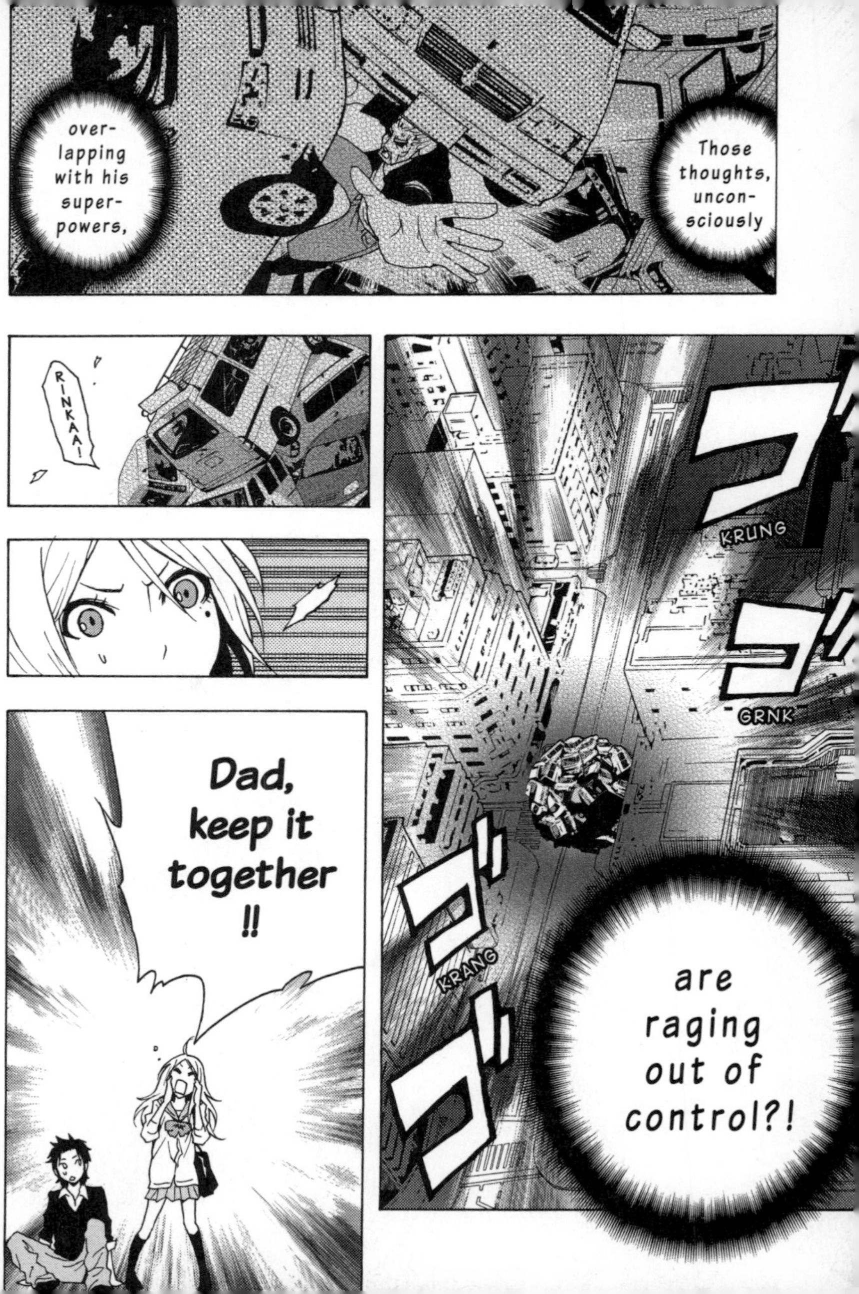
Those thoughts, unconsciously
overlapping with his superpowers,
KRUNG
GRNK
KRANG
are raging out of control?!
RINKAA!
Dad, keep it together!!

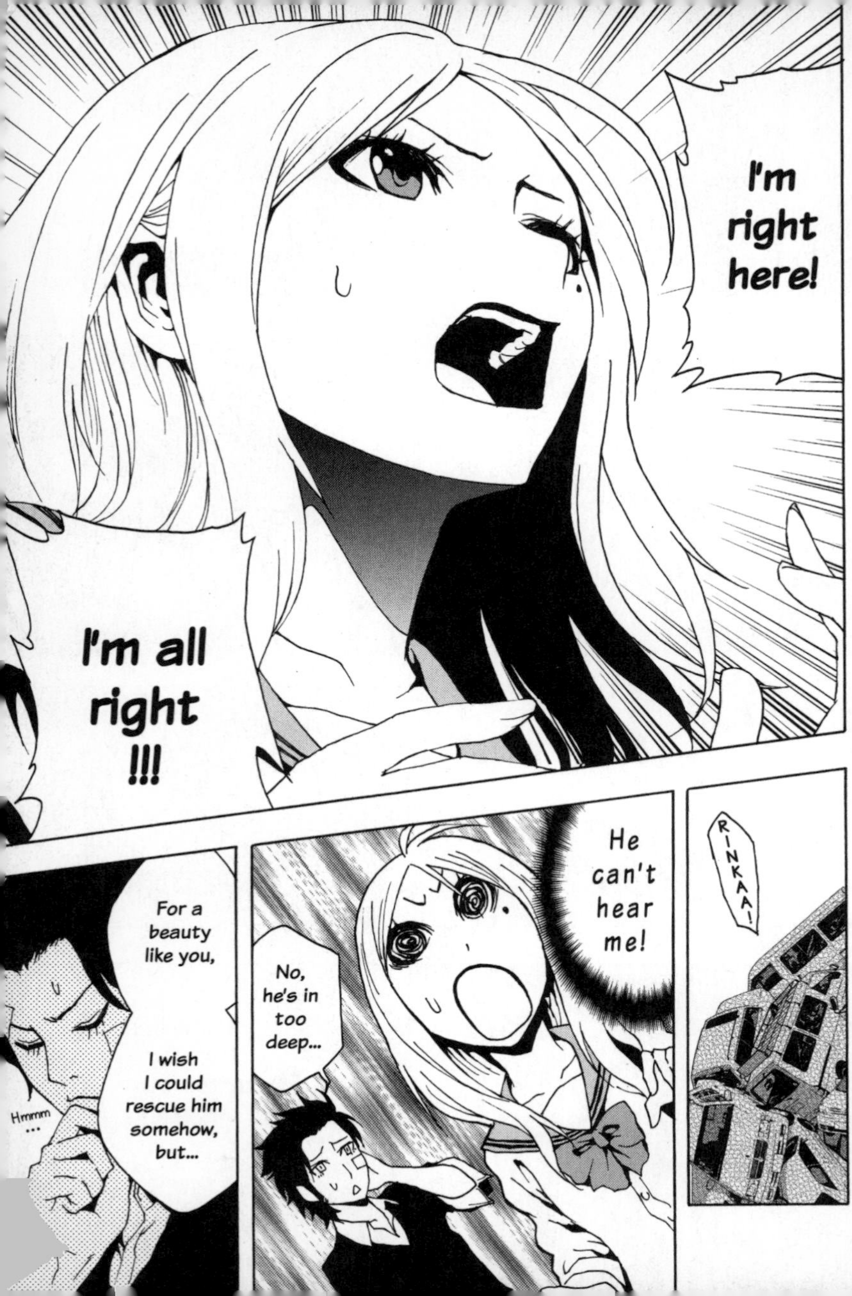
I'm right here!
I'm all right !!!
RINKAA!
He can't hear me!
No, he's in too deep...
For a beauty like you,
I wish I could rescue him somehow, but...
Hmmm ...

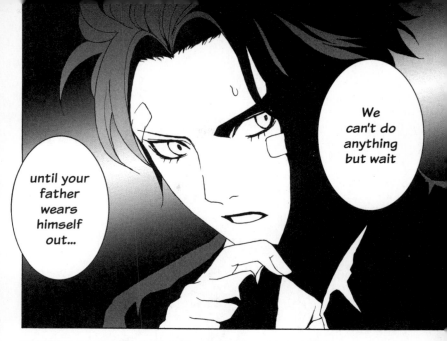

We can't do anything but wait

until your father wears himself out...

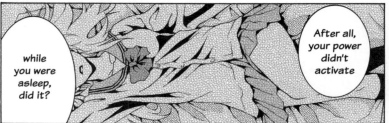

After all, your power didn't activate

while you were asleep, did it?

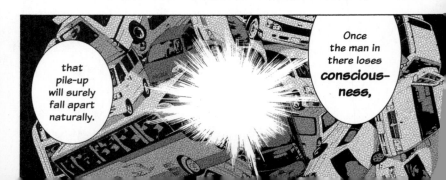

Once the man in there loses **conscious-ness,**

that pile-up will surely fall apart naturally.

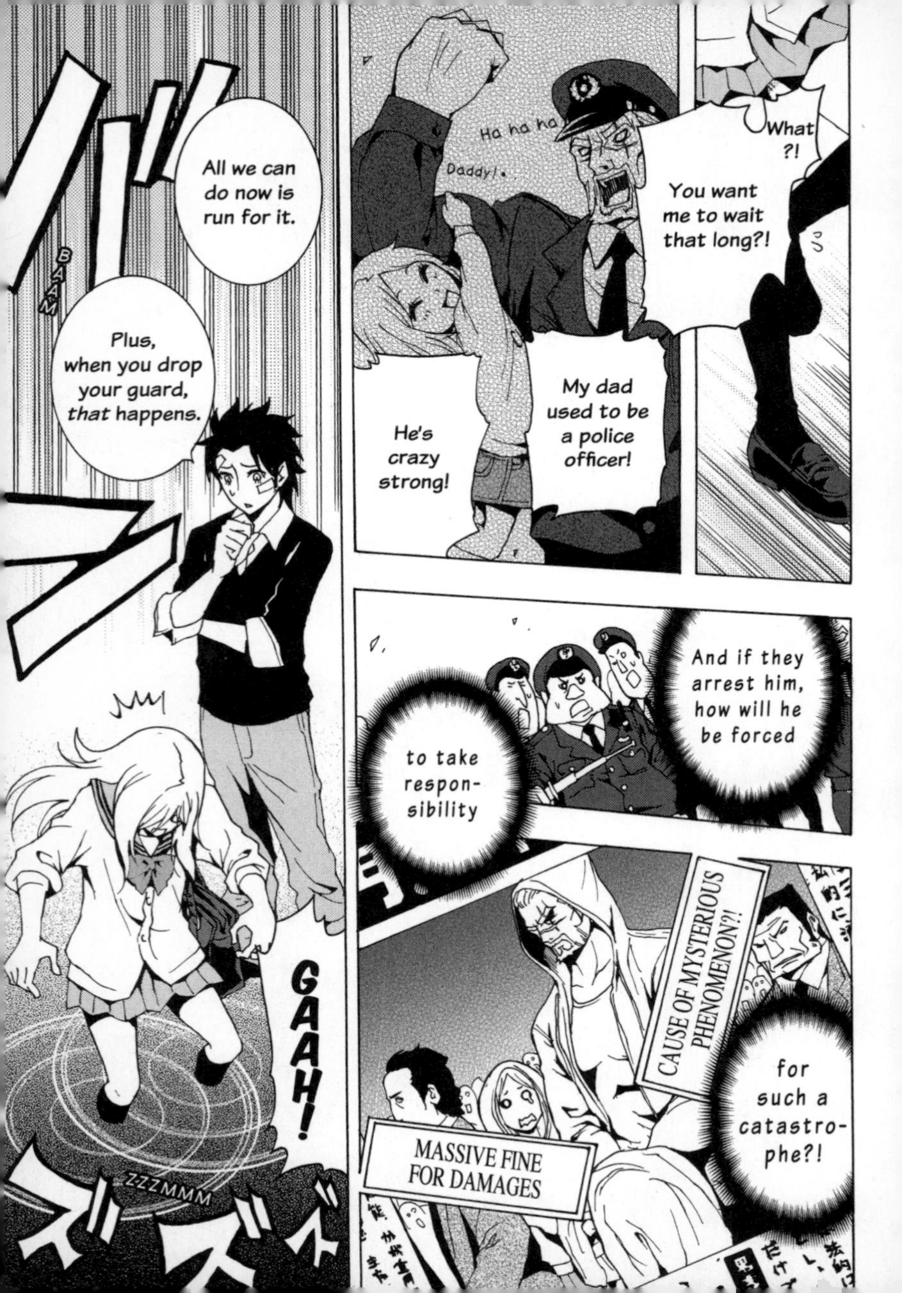
What?!
You want me to wait that long?!
Ha ha ha
Daddy!
My dad used to be a police officer!
He's crazy strong!
And if they arrest him, how will he be forced
to take respon-sibility
CAUSE OF MYSTERIOUS PHENOMENON?!
for such a catastro-phe?!
MASSIVE FINE FOR DAMAGES
All we can do now is run for it.
BAAAM
Plus, when you drop your guard, *that* happens.
GAAAH!
Z-Z-ZMMM

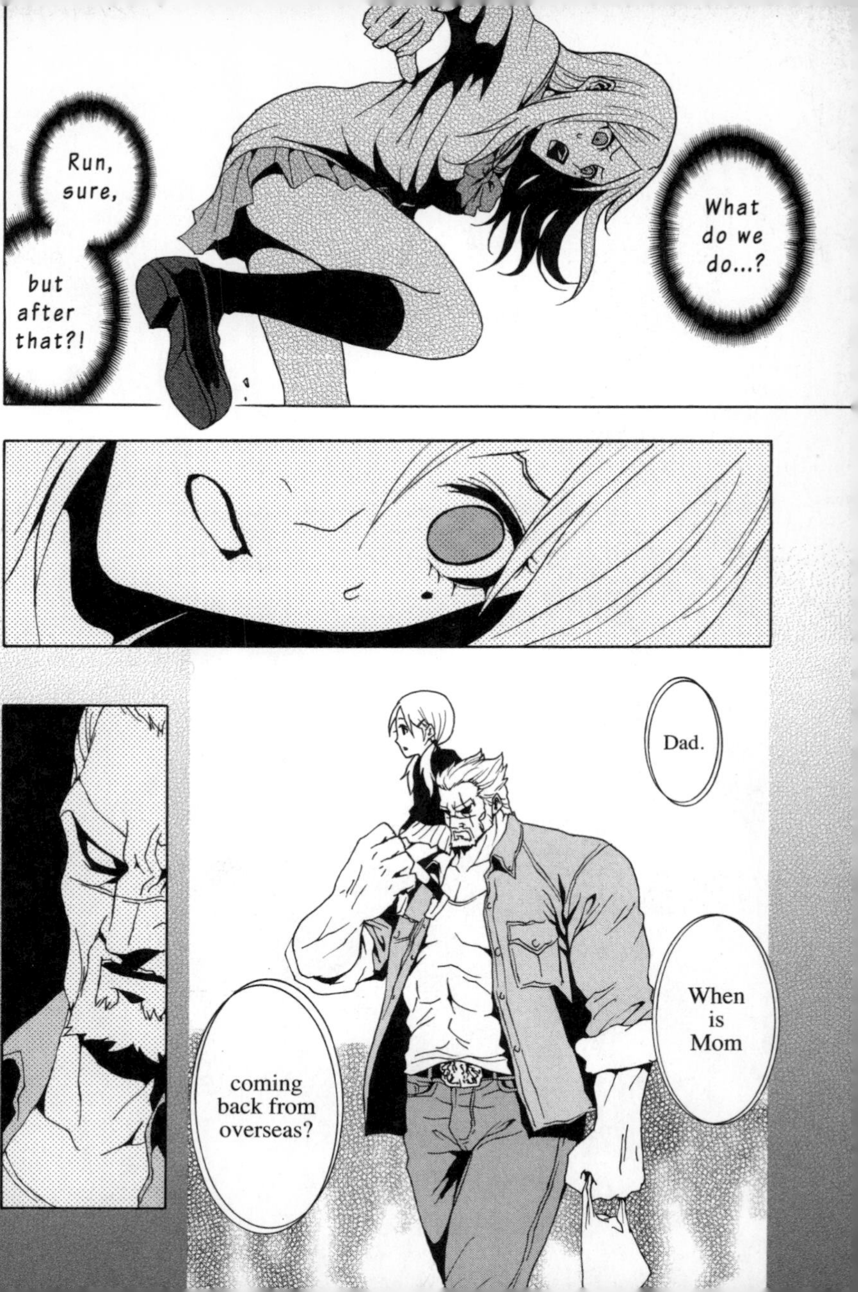
What do we do...?
Run, sure,
but after that?!
Dad.
When is Mom
coming back from overseas?

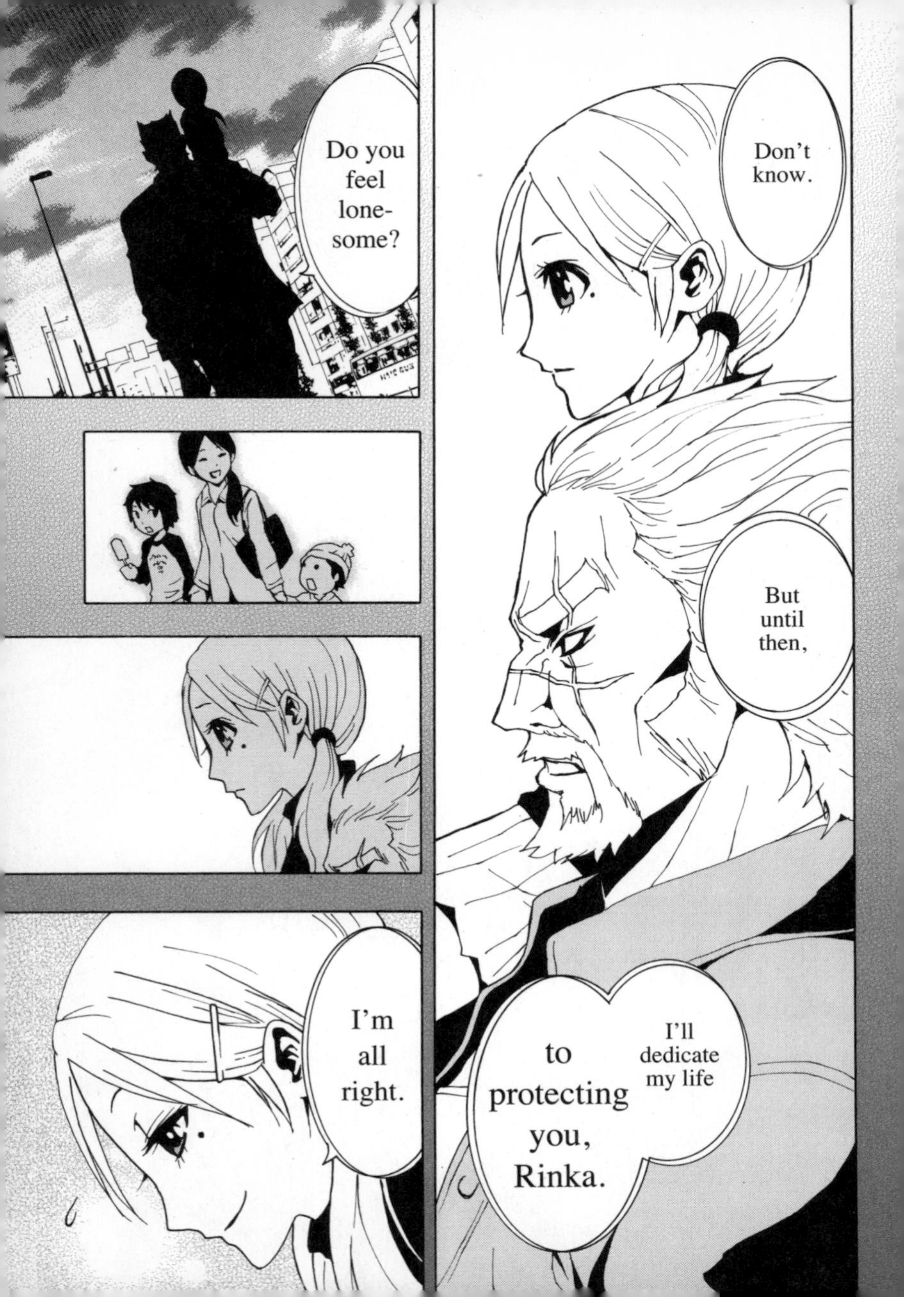

Don't know.
But until then,
I'll dedicate my life
to protecting you, Rinka.
Do you feel lone-some?
I'm all right.

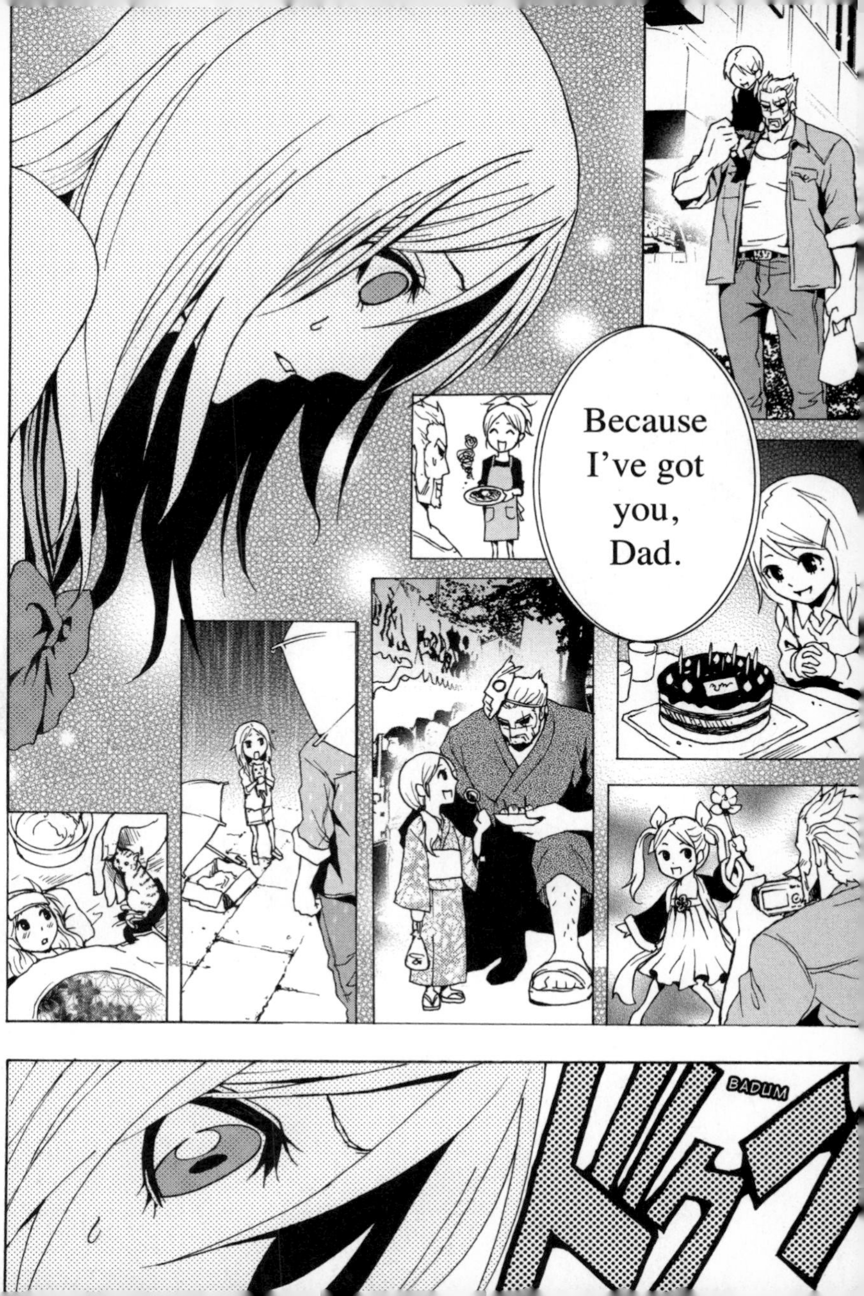
Because I've got you, Dad.
BADUM

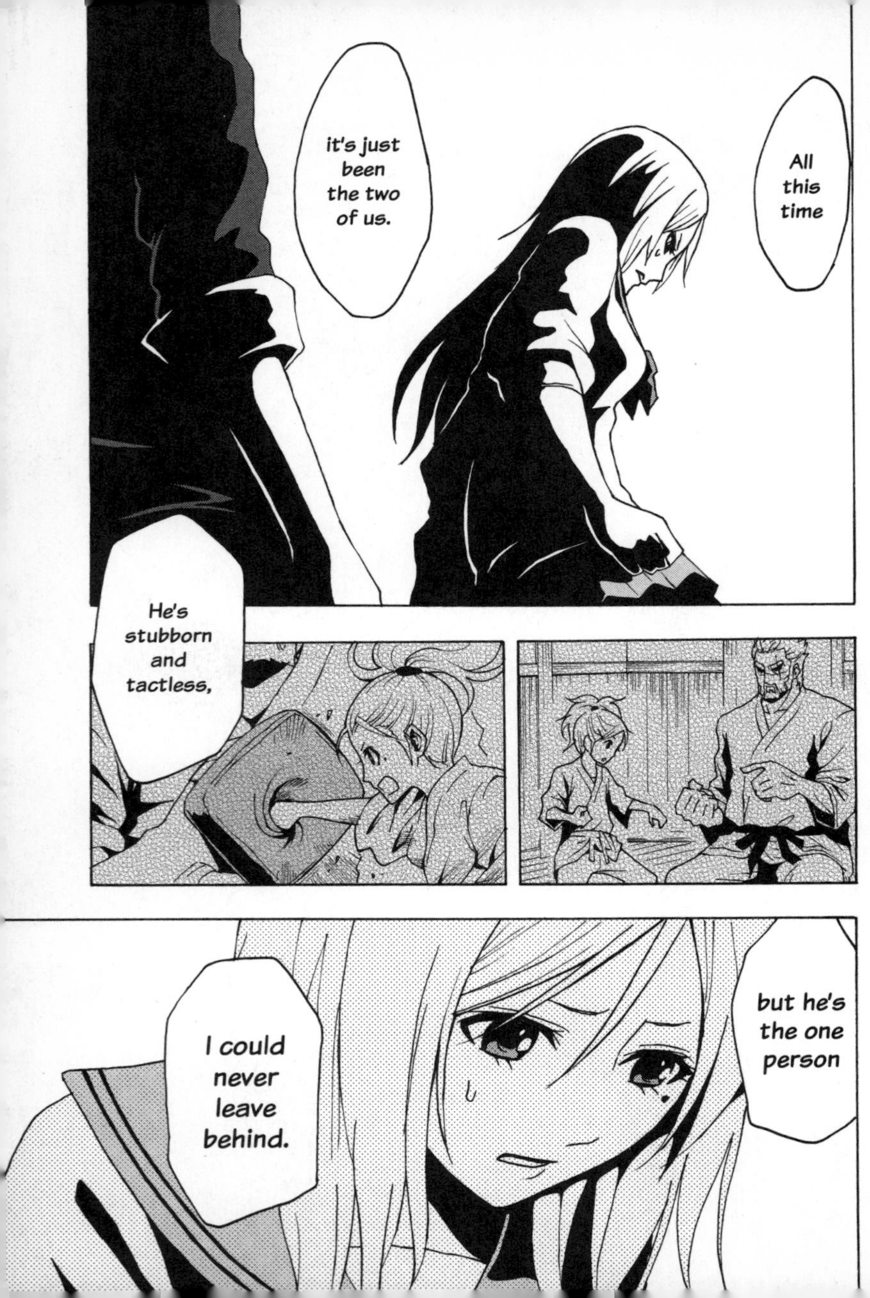
All this time
it's just been the two of us.
He's stubborn and tactless,
but he's the one person
I could never leave behind.

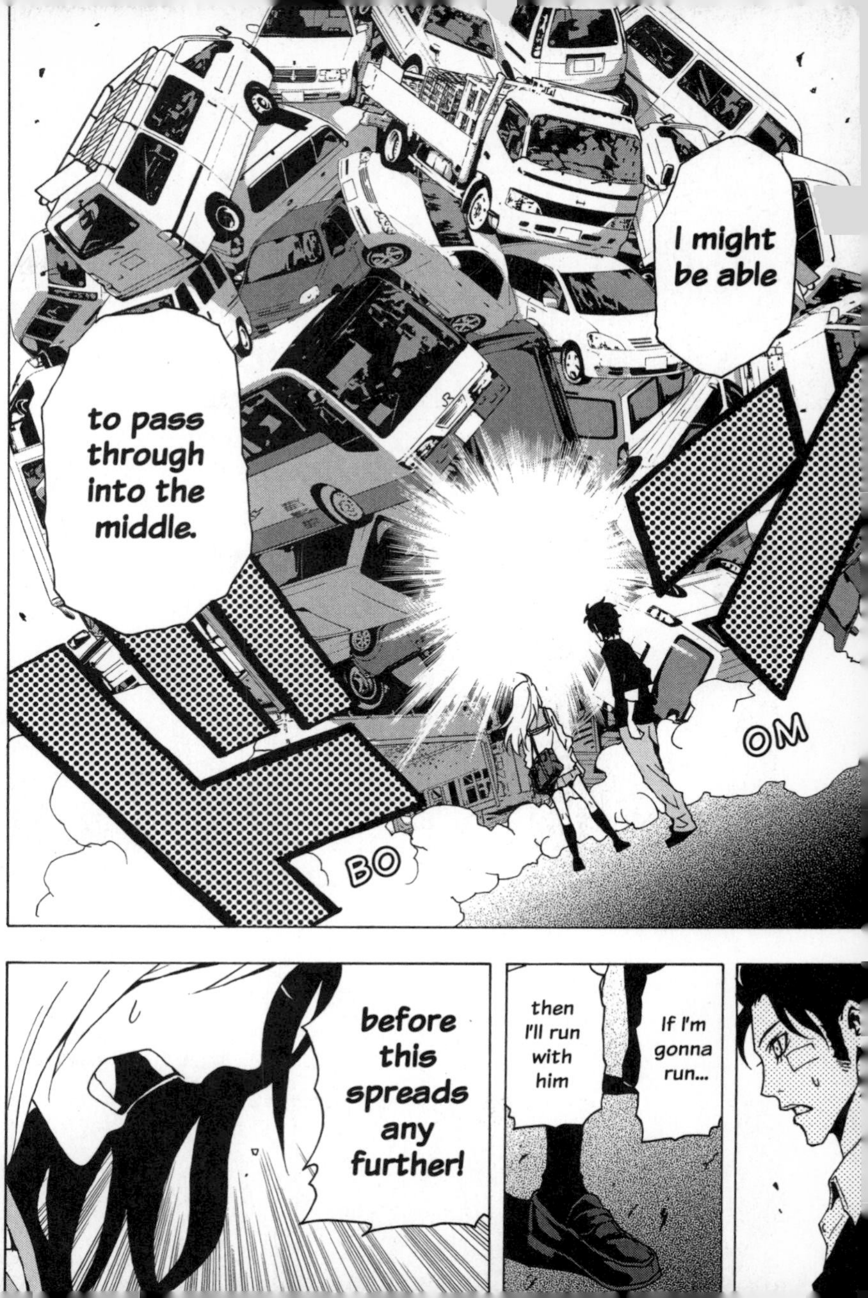
I might be able
to pass through into the middle.
BO
OM
If I'm gonna run...
then I'll run with him
before this spreads any further!

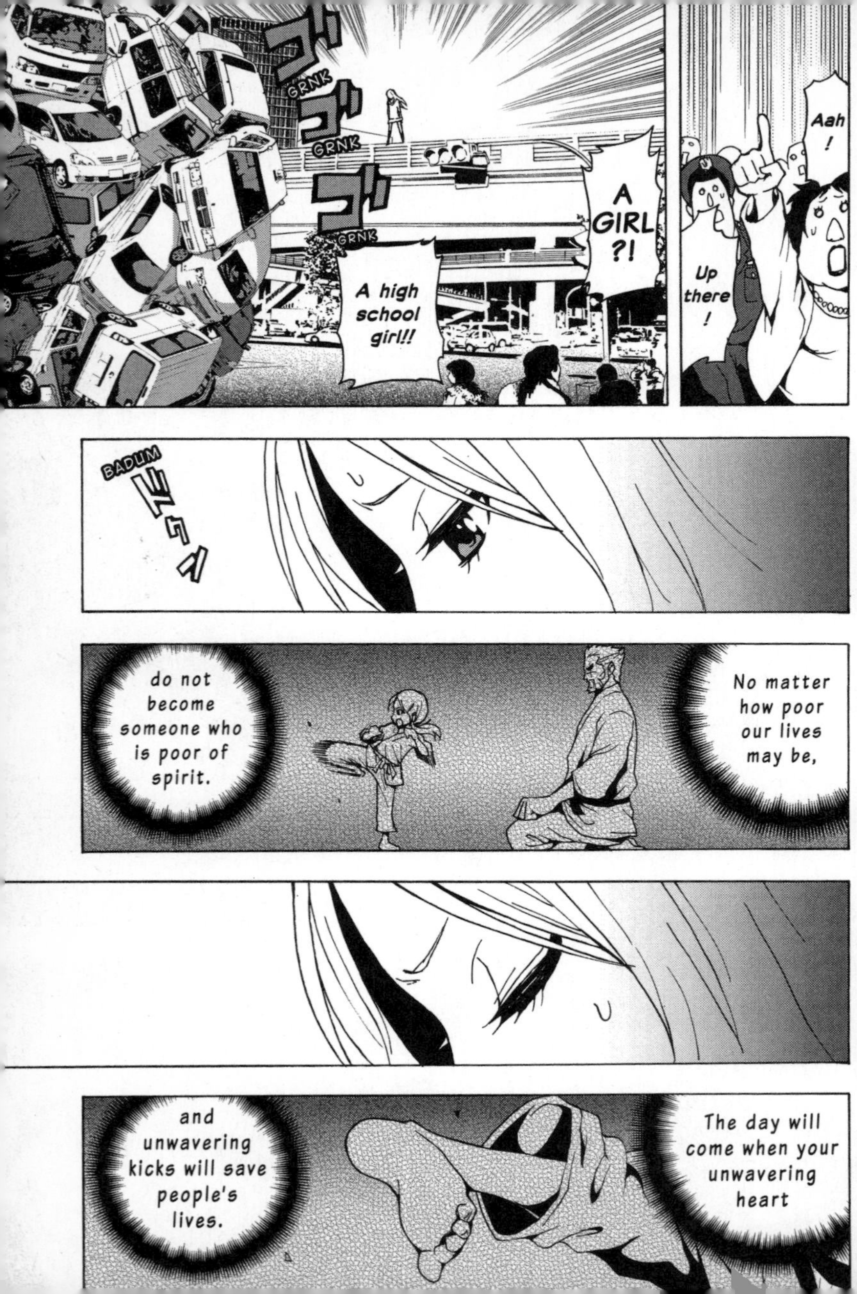
Aah!
Up there!
A GIRL?!
GRNK
GRNK
GRNK
A high school girl!!
BADUM
No matter how poor our lives may be,
do not become someone who is poor of spirit.
The day will come when your unwavering heart
and unwavering kicks will save people's lives.

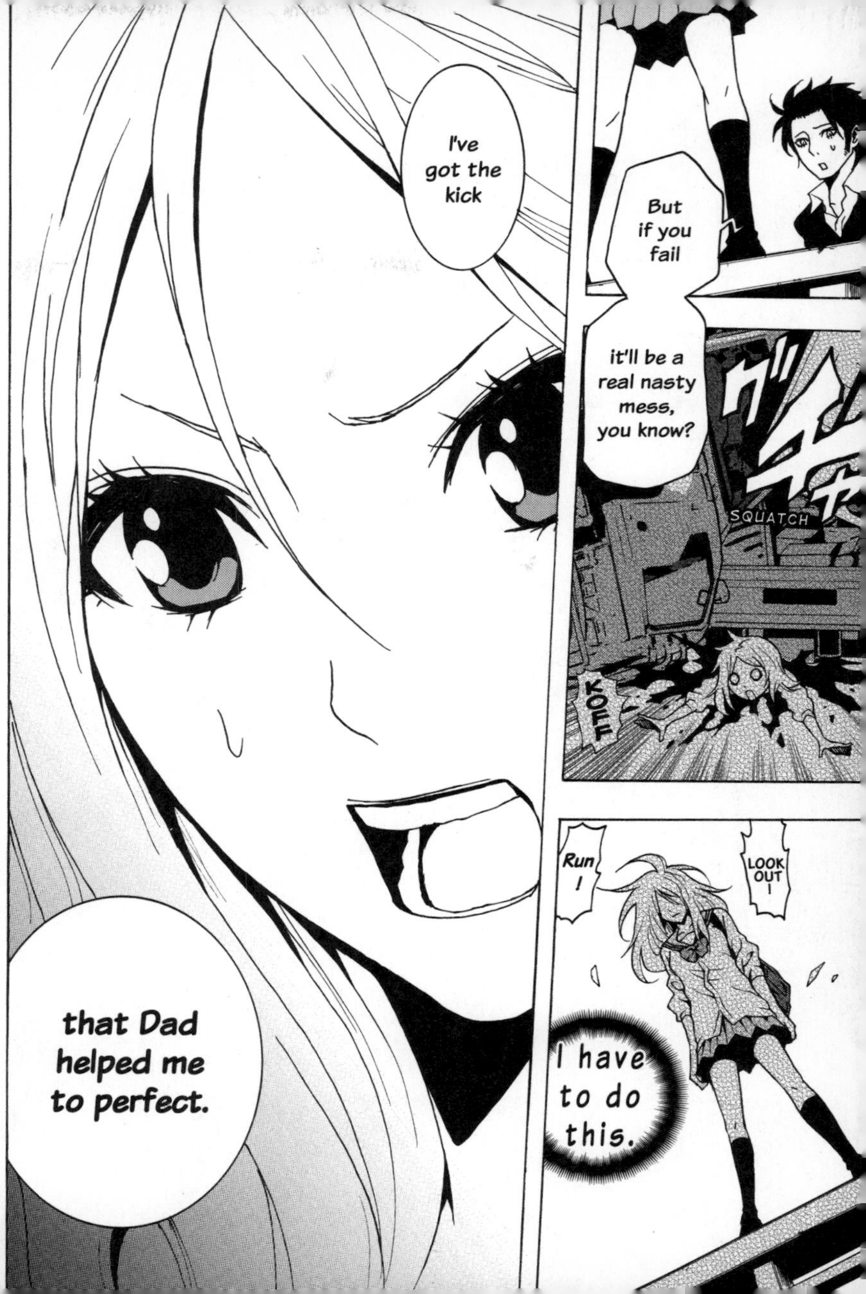
But if you fail
it'll be a real nasty mess, you know?
SQUATCH
KOFF
LOOK OUT!
Run!
I have to do this.
I've got the kick
that Dad helped me to perfect.

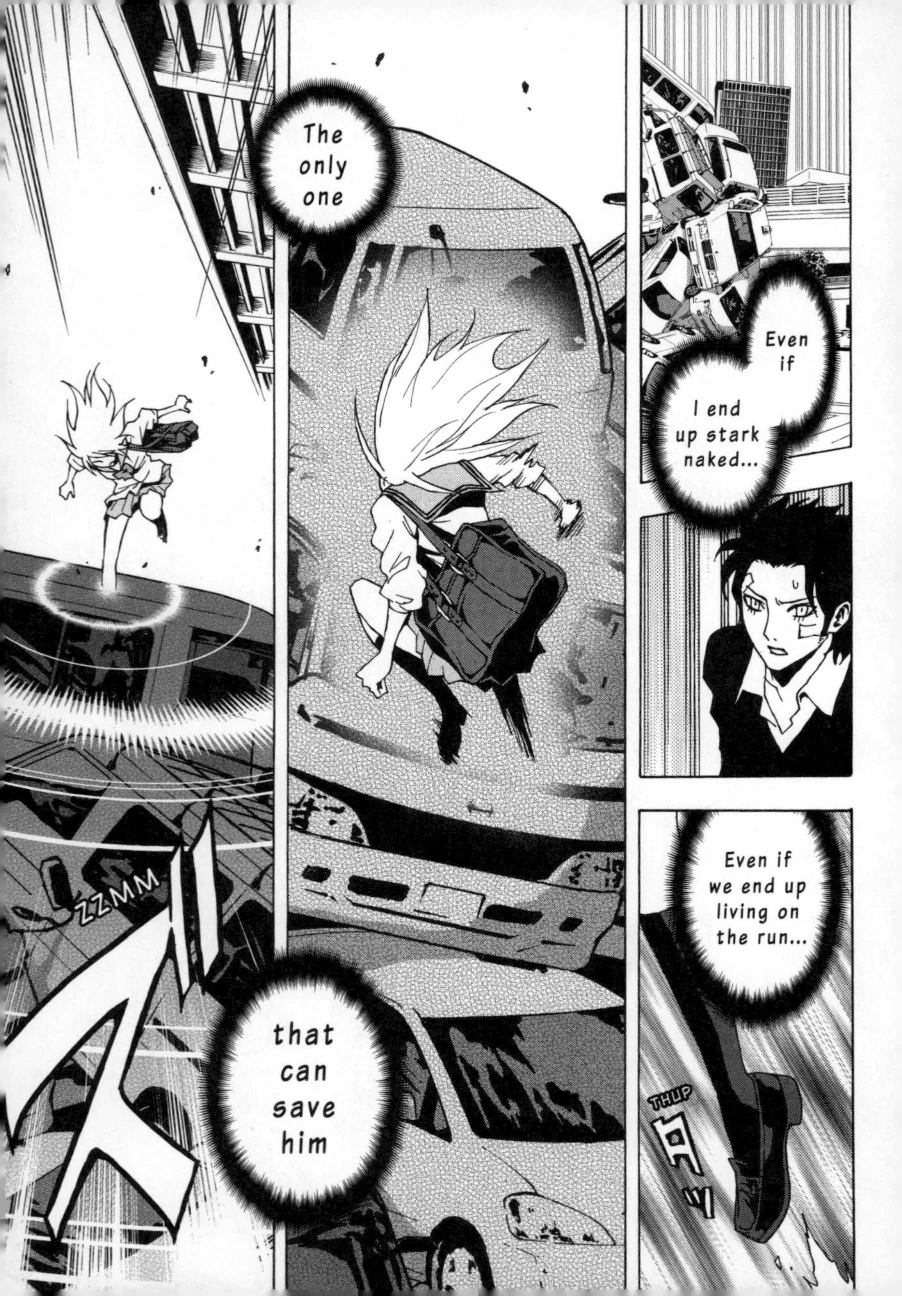
Even if I end up stark naked...
Even if we end up living on the run...
THUP
The only one
that can save him
ZZMM

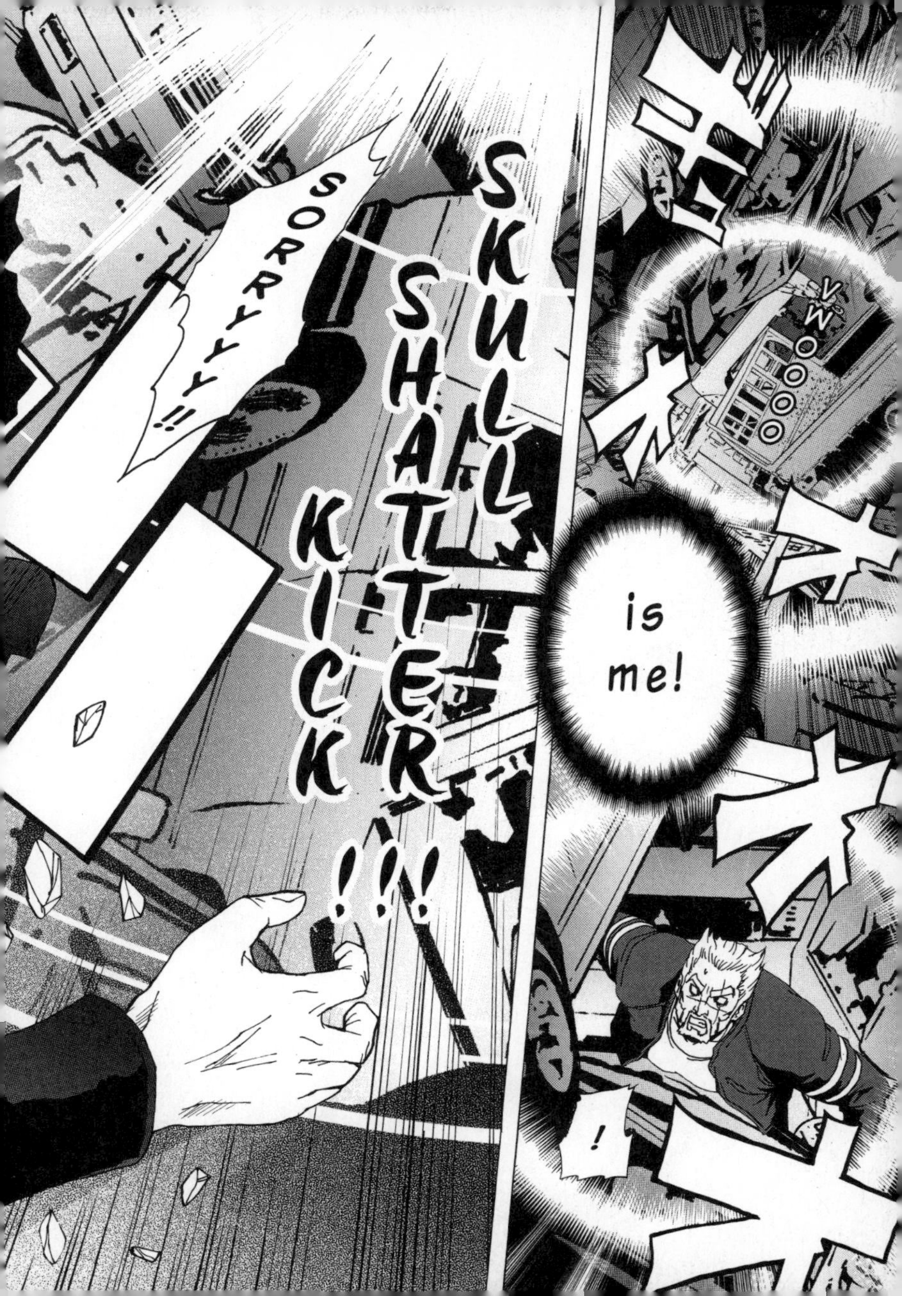
VWOOOO
is me!
!
SKULL SHATTER KICK!!!
SORRYYYY!!

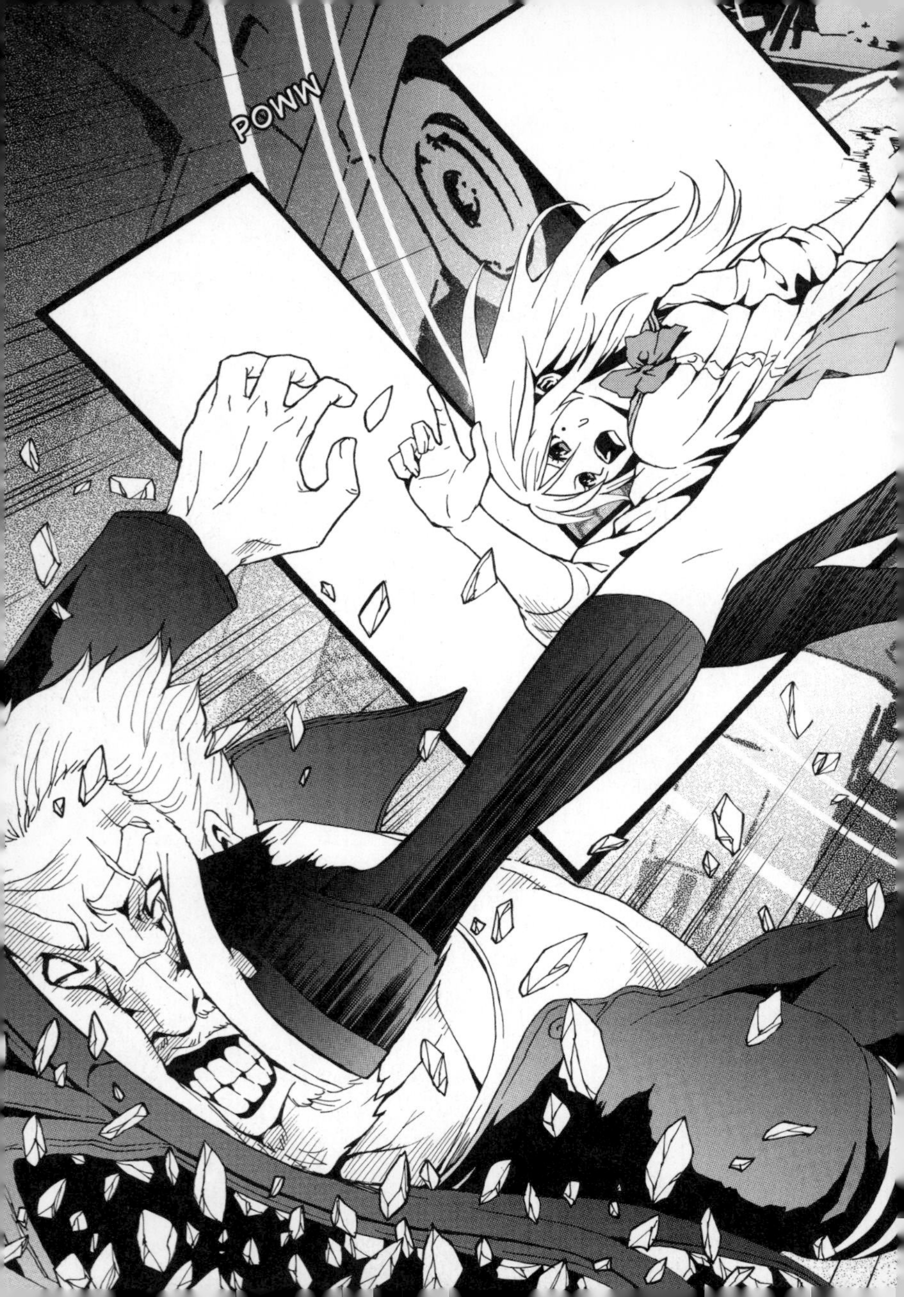
POWW

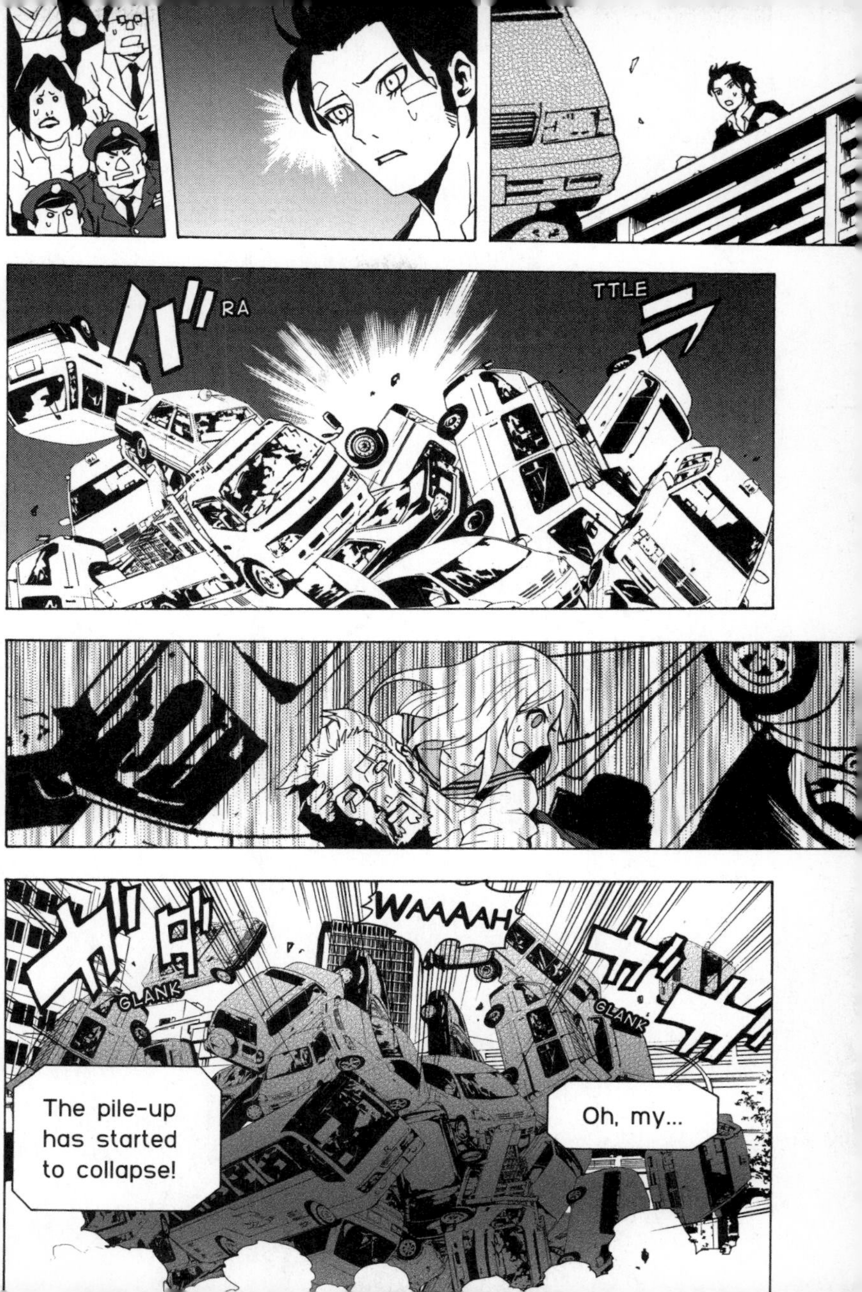
TTLE
RA
WAAAAH
GLANK
GLANK
Oh, my...
The pile-up has started to collapse!

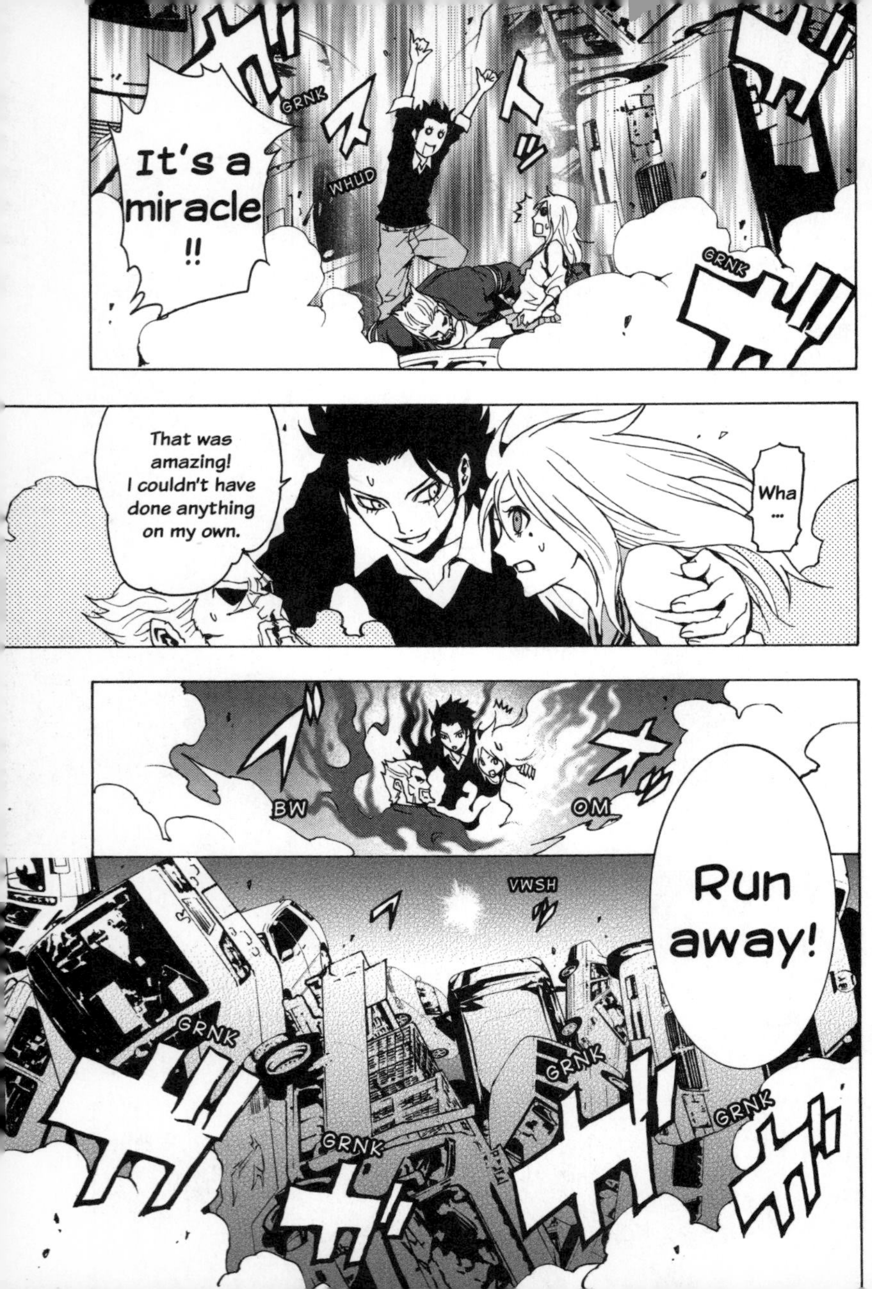
GRNK
WHUD
It's a miracle !!
GRNK
Wha ...
That was amazing! I couldn't have done anything on my own.
OM
BW
Run away!
VWSH
GRNK
GRNK
GRNK
GRNK

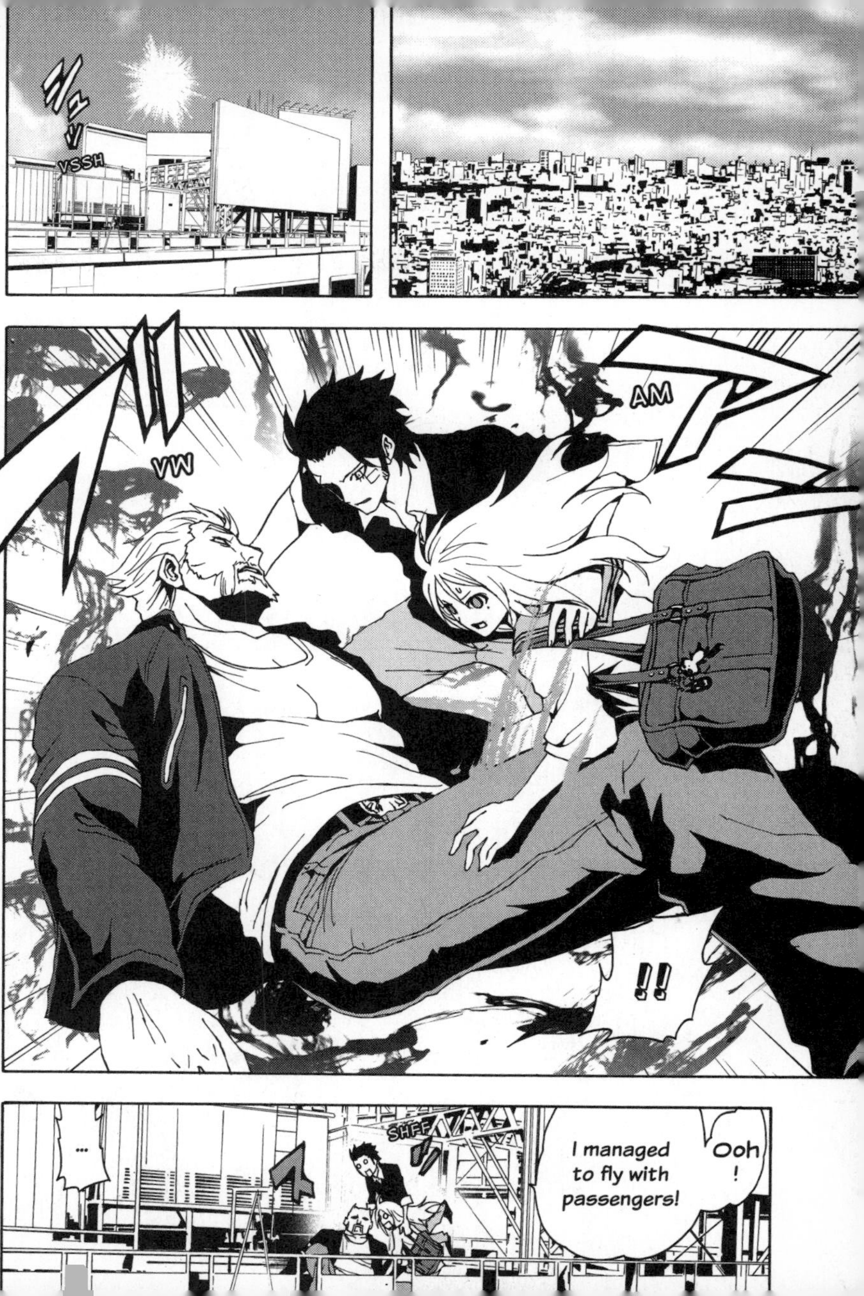
VSSH
AM
VW
!!
Ooh!
I managed to fly with passengers!
SHFF
...

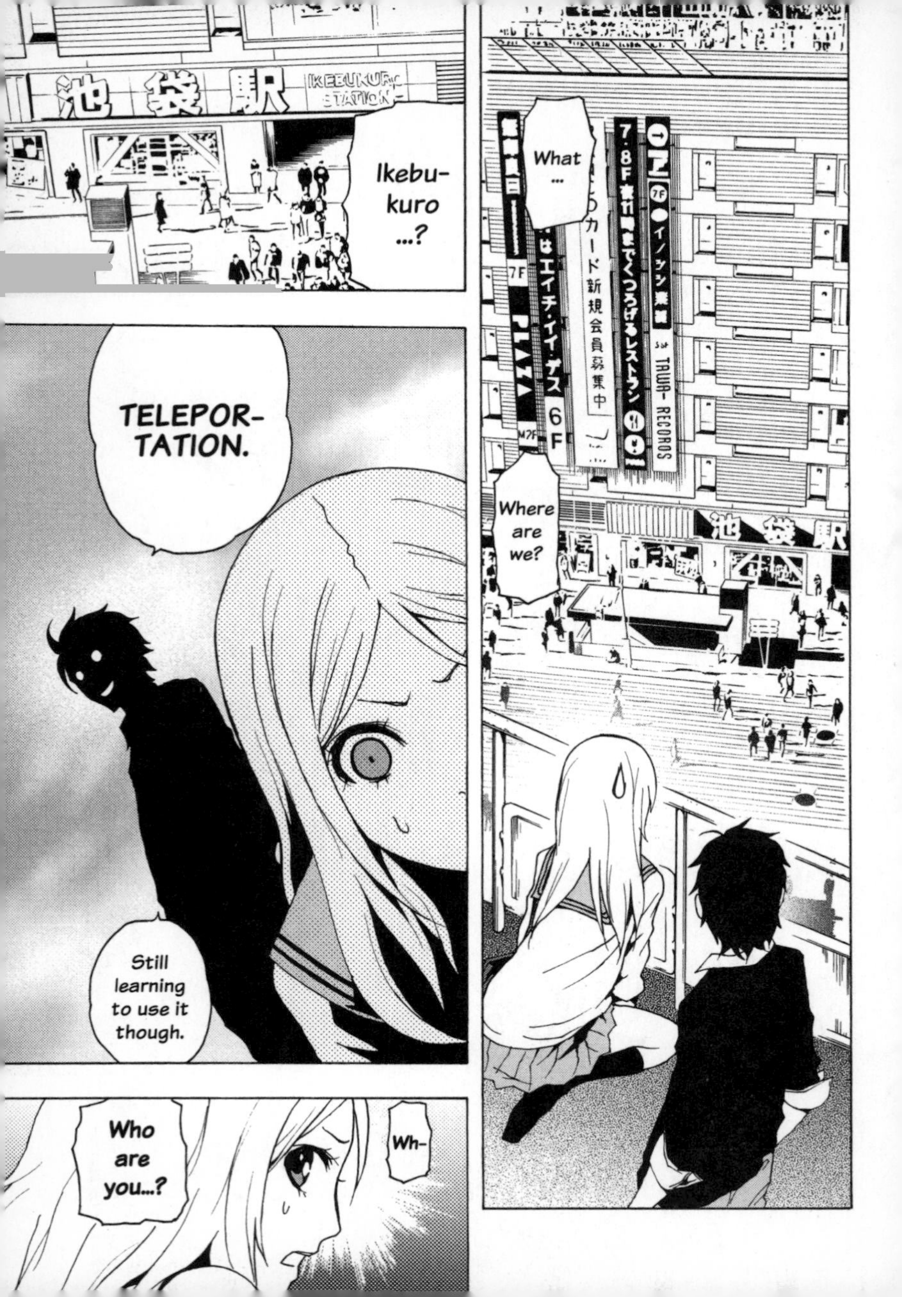
What ...
Where are we?
池袋駅
7.8F夜11時までくつろげるレストラン
カード新規会員募集中
池袋駅
Ikebu-kuro ...?
TELEPOR-TATION.
Still learning to use it though.
Wh-
Who are you...?

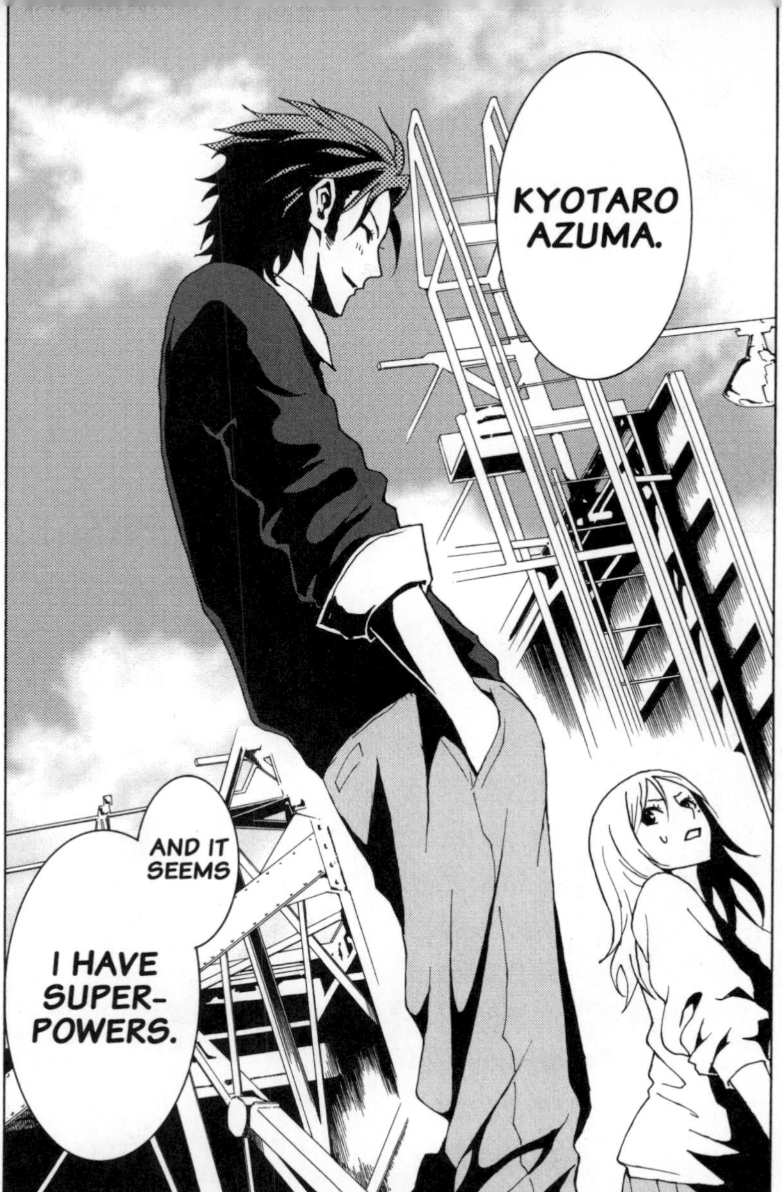
KYOTARO AZUMA.
AND IT SEEMS
I HAVE SUPER-POWERS.

SCENE 1 /// END

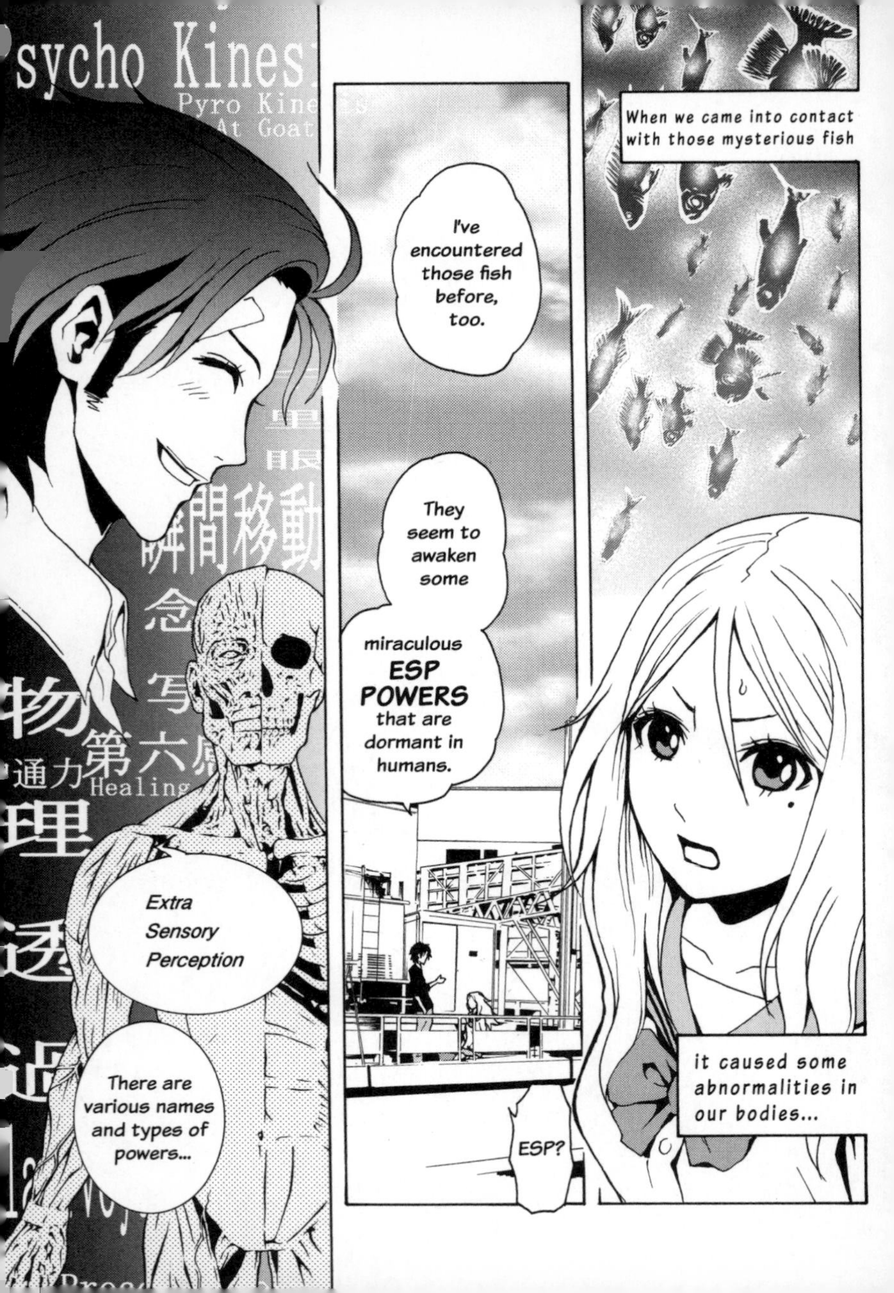
When we came into contact with those mysterious fish
it caused some abnormalities in our bodies...
I've encountered those fish before, too.
They seem to awaken some
miraculous ESP POWERS that are dormant in humans.
ESP?
sycho Kinesi
Pyro Kine
At Goat
間移動
第六
通力
Healing
Extra Sensory Perception
There are various names and types of powers...

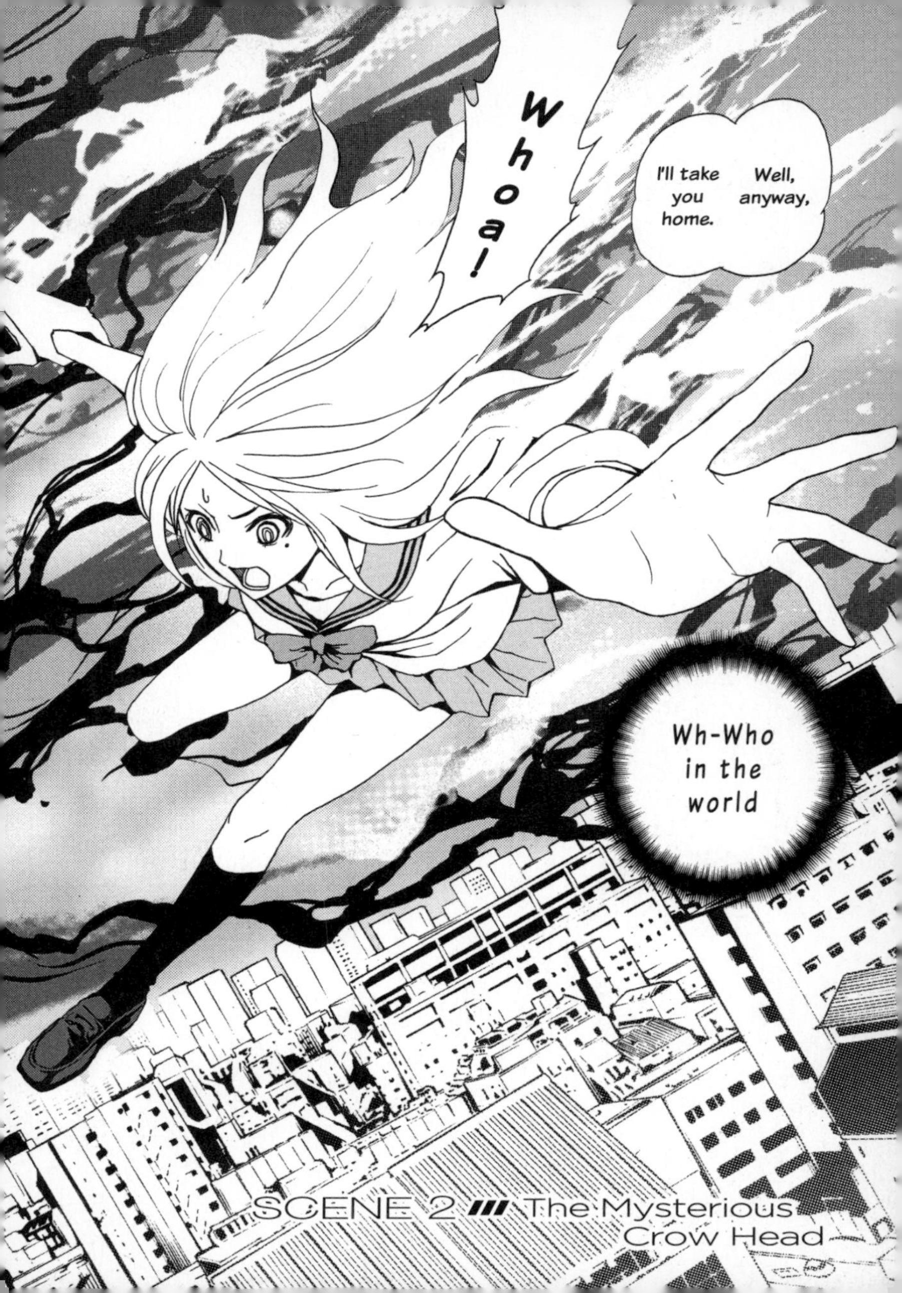
Well, anyway, I'll take you home.
Whoa!
Wh-Who in the world
SCENE 2 /// The Mysterious Crow Head

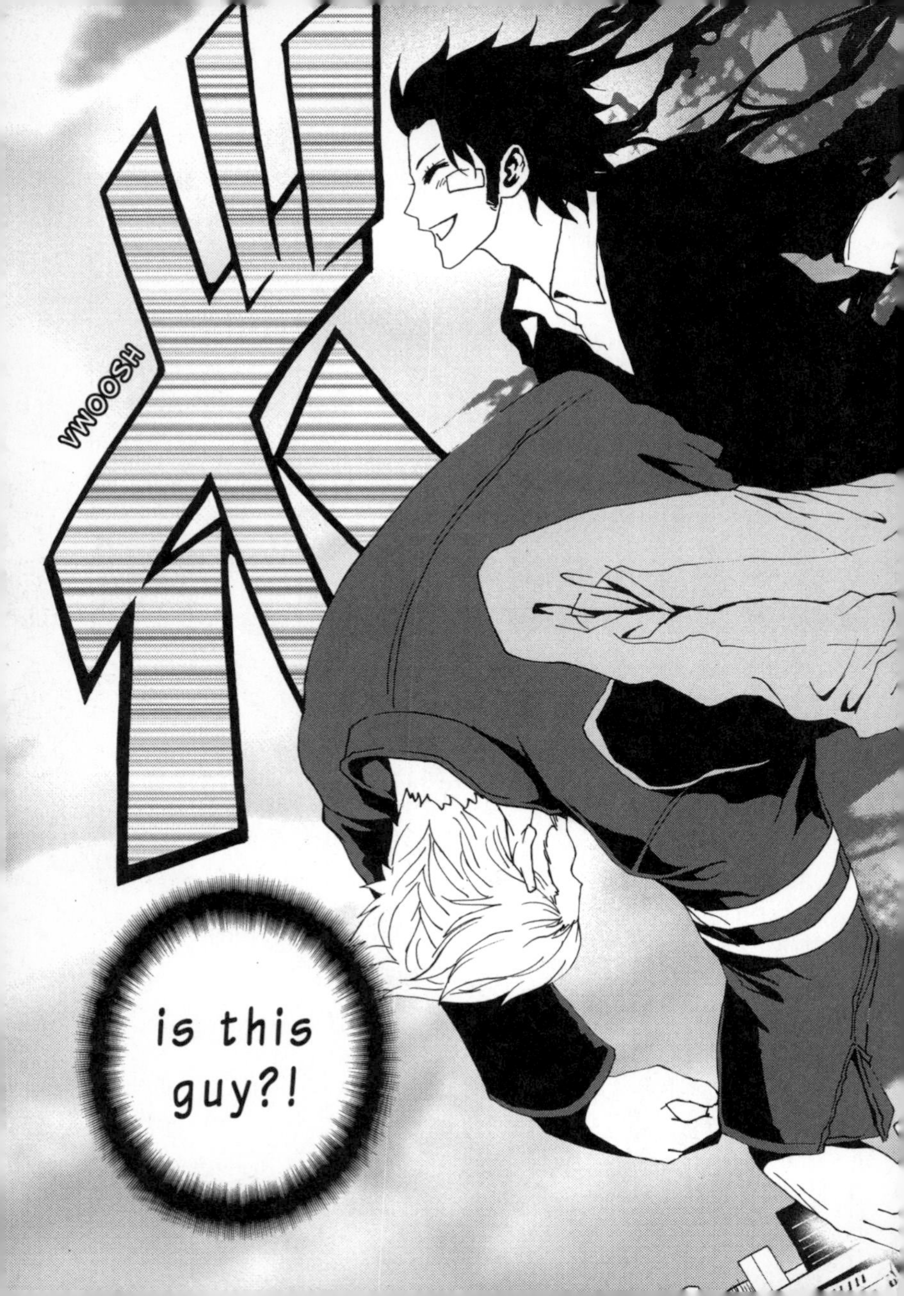
VWOOSH
is this guy?!

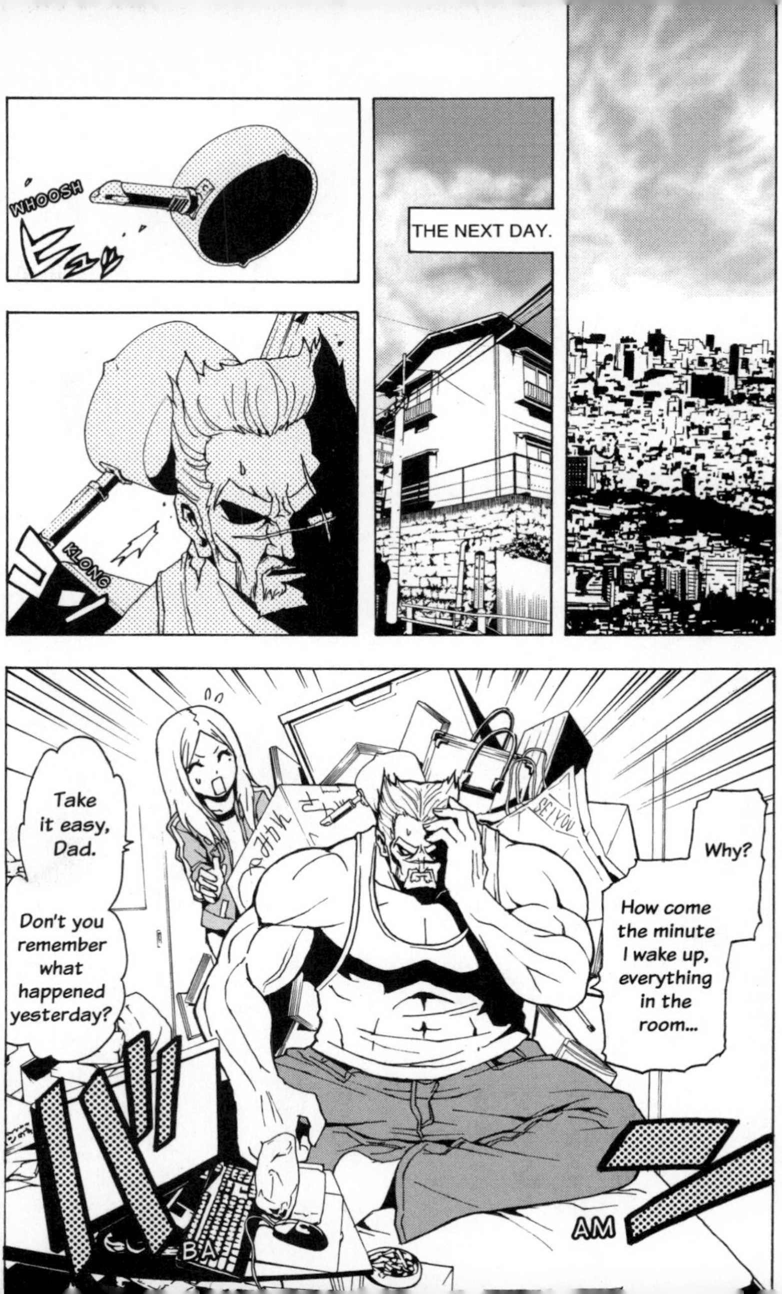
THE NEXT DAY.
WHOOSH
KLONG
Why?
How come the minute I wake up, everything in the room...
Take it easy, Dad.
Don't you remember what happened yesterday?
SEIYOU
AM
BA

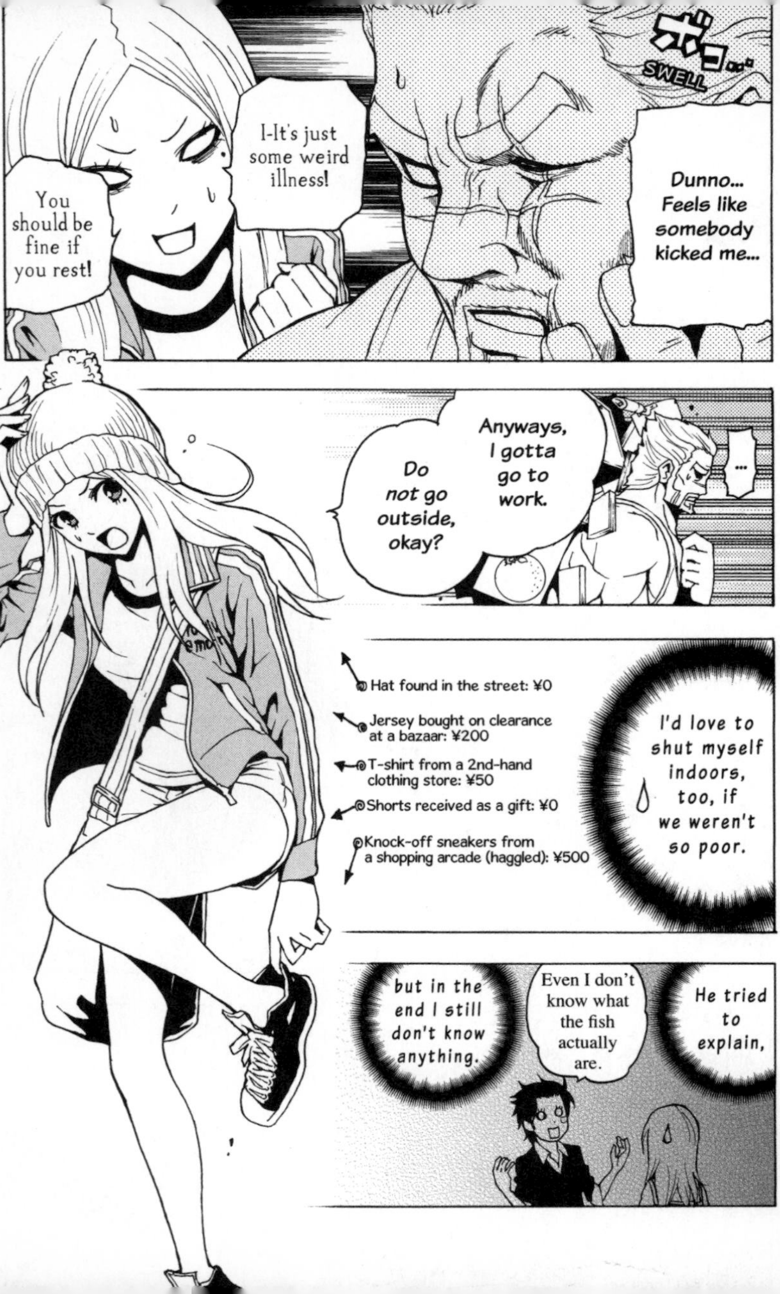
ボコ
SWELL
Dunno... Feels like somebody kicked me...
I-It's just some weird illness!
You should be fine if you rest!
...
Anyways, I gotta go to work.
Do not go outside, okay?
I'd love to shut myself indoors, too, if we weren't so poor.
He tried to explain,
Even I don't know what the fish actually are.
but in the end I still don't know anything.
Hat found in the street: ¥0
Jersey bought on clearance at a bazaar: ¥200
T-shirt from a 2nd-hand clothing store: ¥50
Shorts received as a gift: ¥0
Knock-off sneakers from a shopping arcade (haggled): ¥500

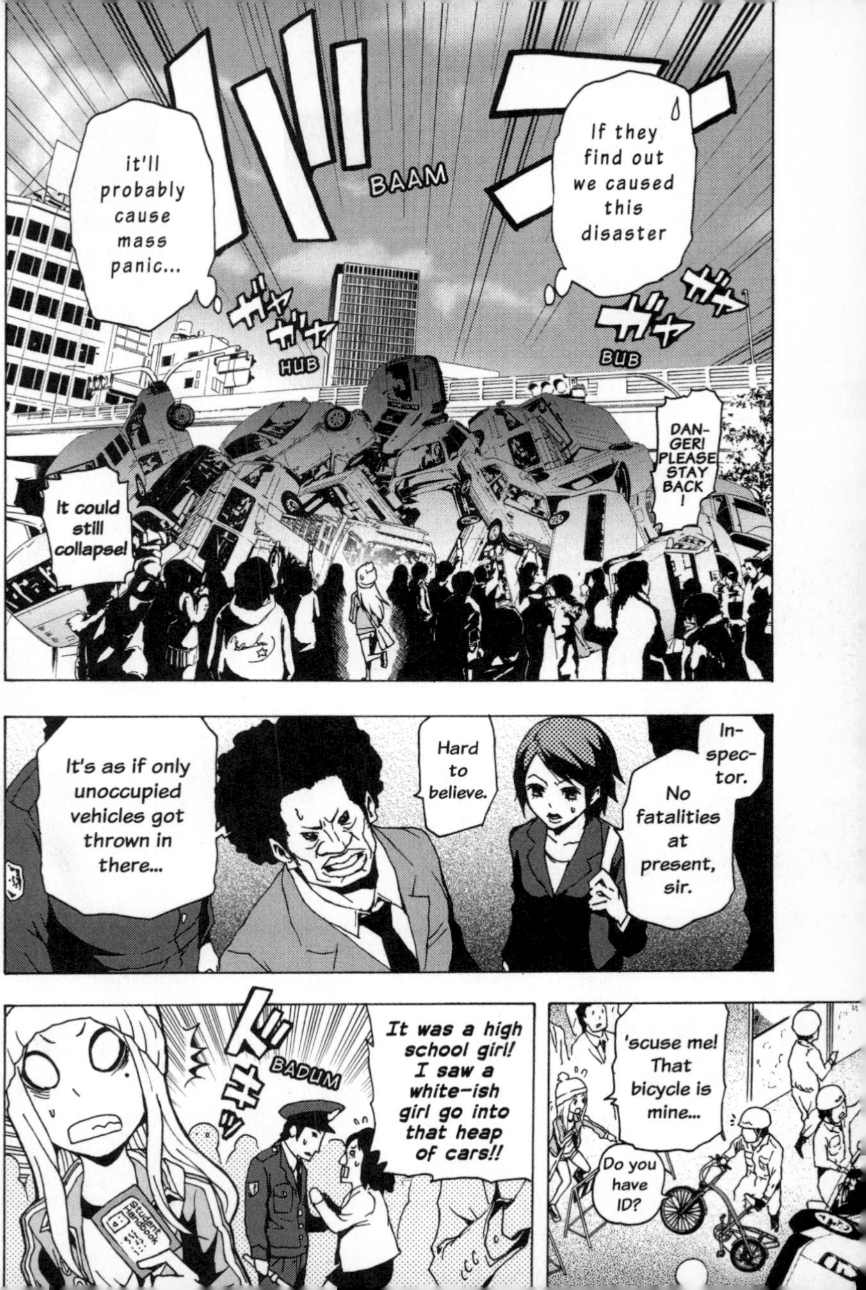
If they find out we caused this disaster
BAAM
it'll probably cause mass panic...
ガヤ
ガヤ
BUB
ガヤ
ガヤ
HUB
DAN-GER! PLEASE STAY BACK!
It could still collapse!
In-spec-tor. No fatalities at present, sir.
Hard to believe.
It's as if only unoccupied vehicles got thrown in there...
'scuse me! That bicycle is mine...
Do you have ID?
It was a high school girl! I saw a white-ish girl go into that heap of cars!!
ドキッ
BADUM
Student Handbook

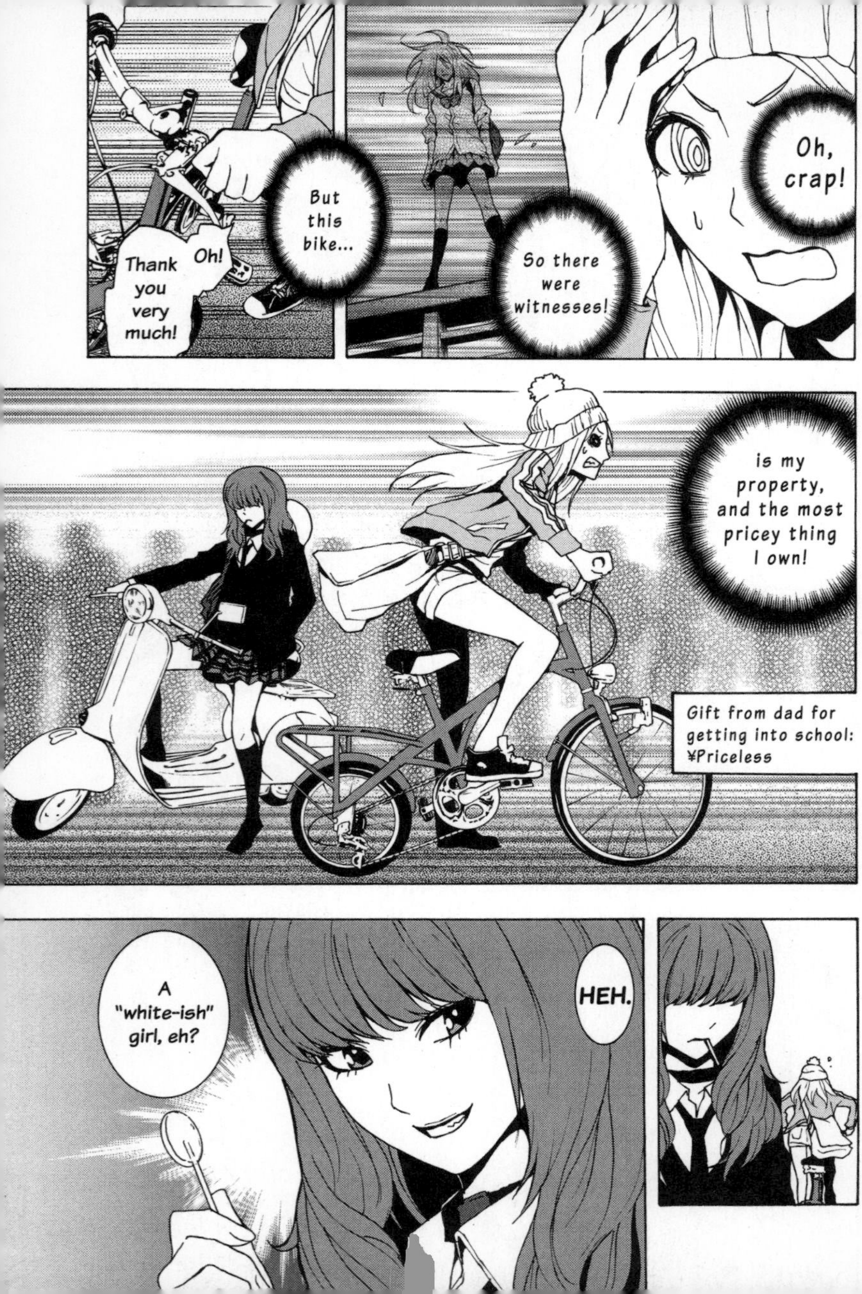
Oh, crap!
So there were witnesses!
But this bike...
Oh!
Thank you very much!
is my property, and the most pricey thing I own!
Gift from dad for getting into school: ¥Priceless
HEH.
A "white-ish" girl, eh?

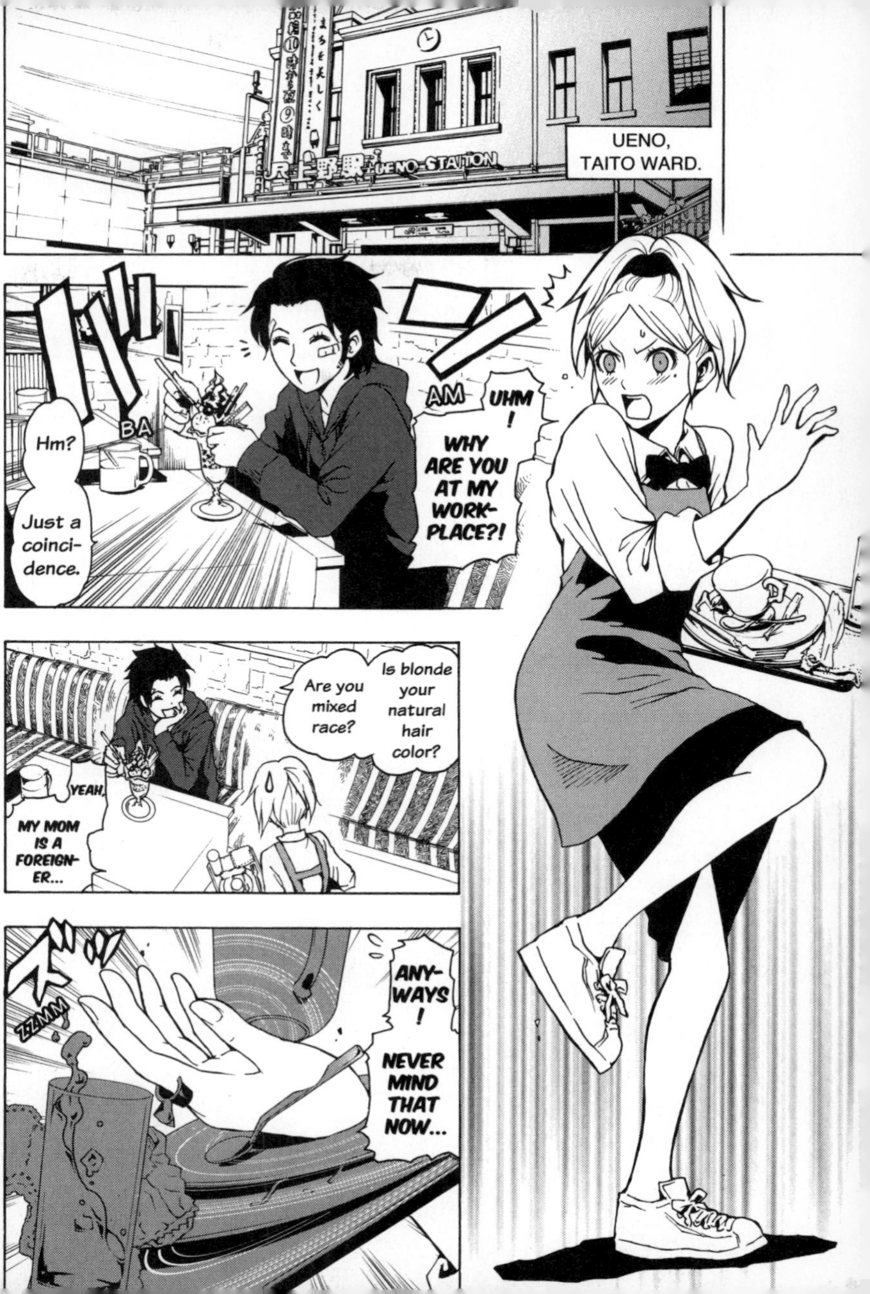
UENO, TAITO WARD.
UHM!
WHY ARE YOU AT MY WORKPLACE?!
AM
BA
Hm?
Just a coincidence.
Is blonde your natural hair color?
Are you mixed race?
YEAH,
MY MOM IS A FOREIGNER...
ANYWAYS!
NEVER MIND THAT NOW...
ZZMM

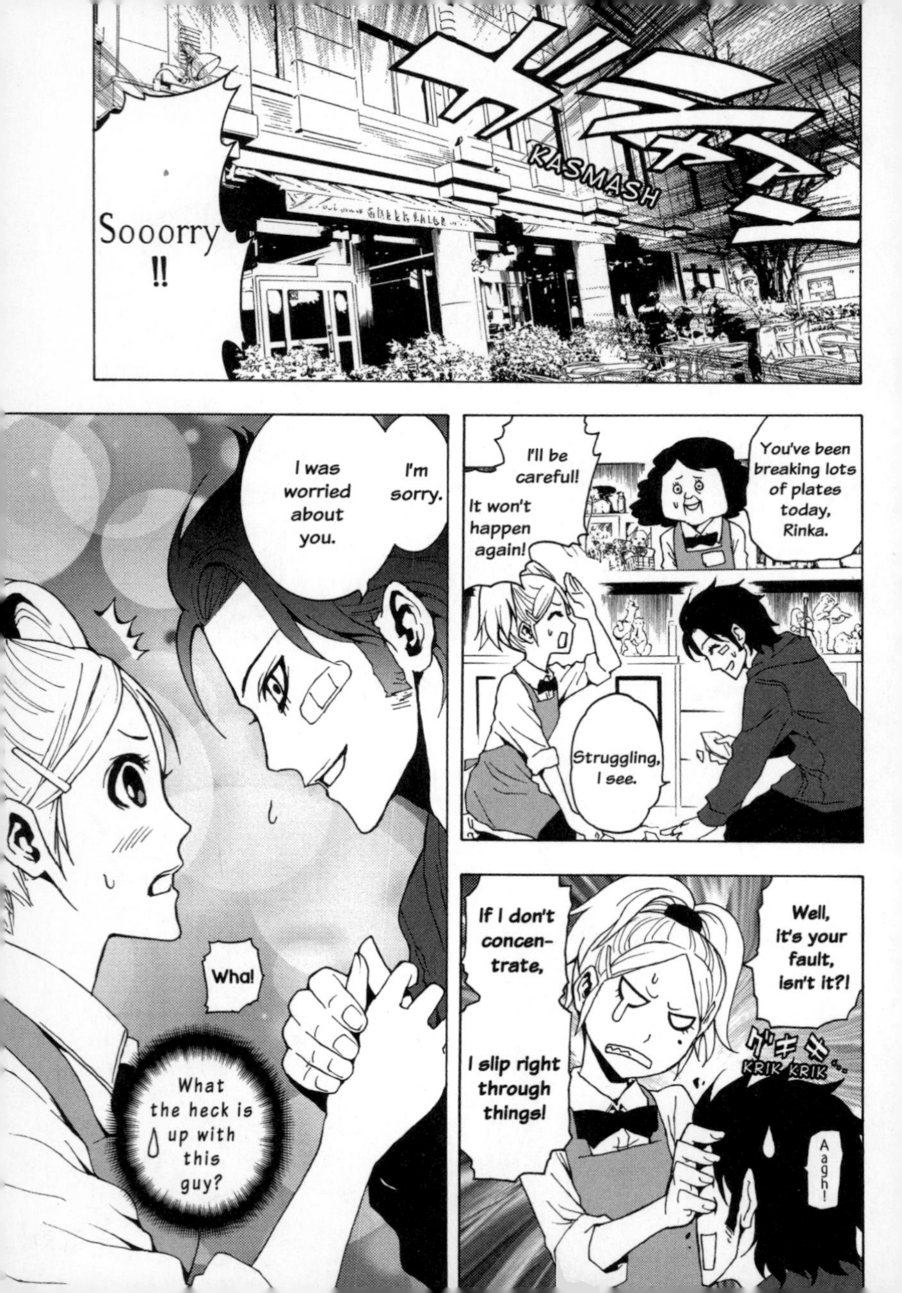
KASMASH
Sooorry !!
You've been breaking lots of plates today, Rinka.
I'll be careful!
It won't happen again!
Struggling, I see.
Well, it's your fault, isn't it?!
KRIK KRIK
If I don't concen-trate,
I slip right through things!
Aagh!
I'm sorry.
I was worried about you.
Wha!
What the heck is up with this guy?

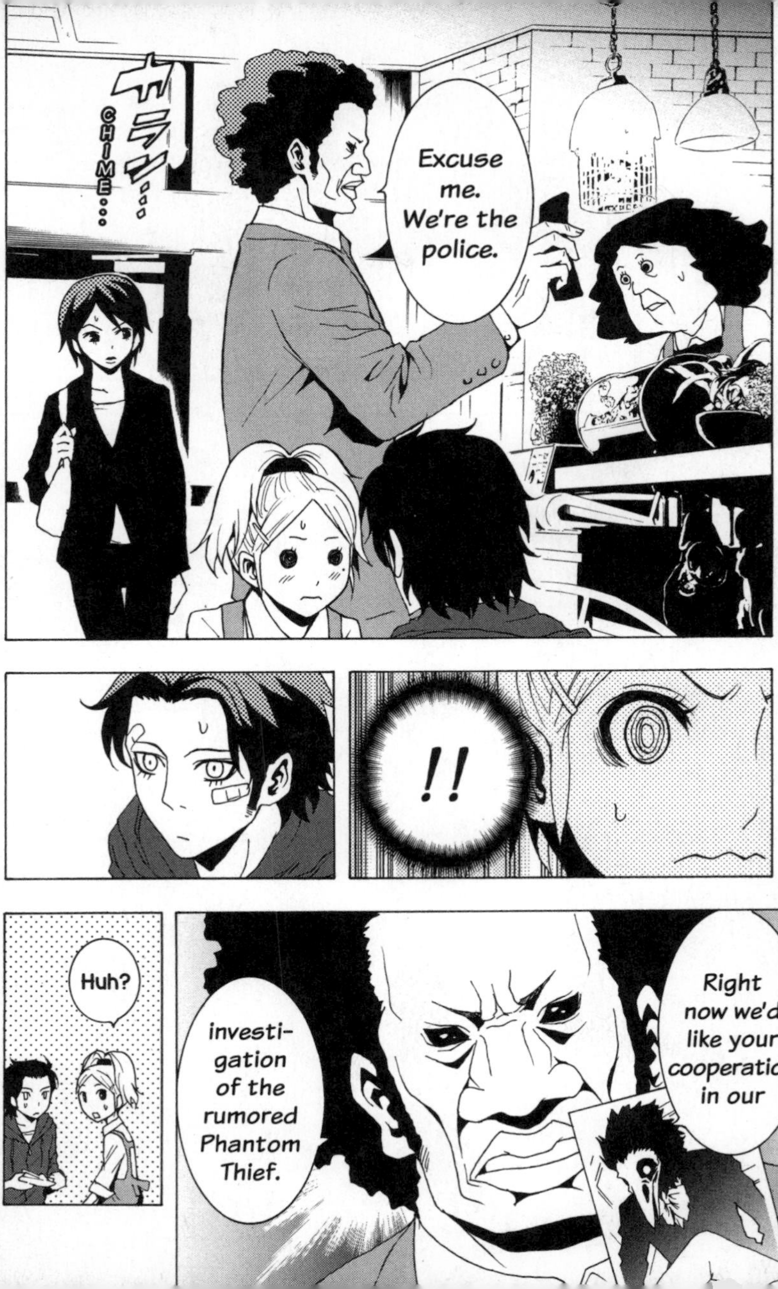
カラン…
CHIME…
Excuse me. We're the police.
!!
Right now we'd like your cooperation in our
investigation of the rumored Phantom Thief.
Huh?

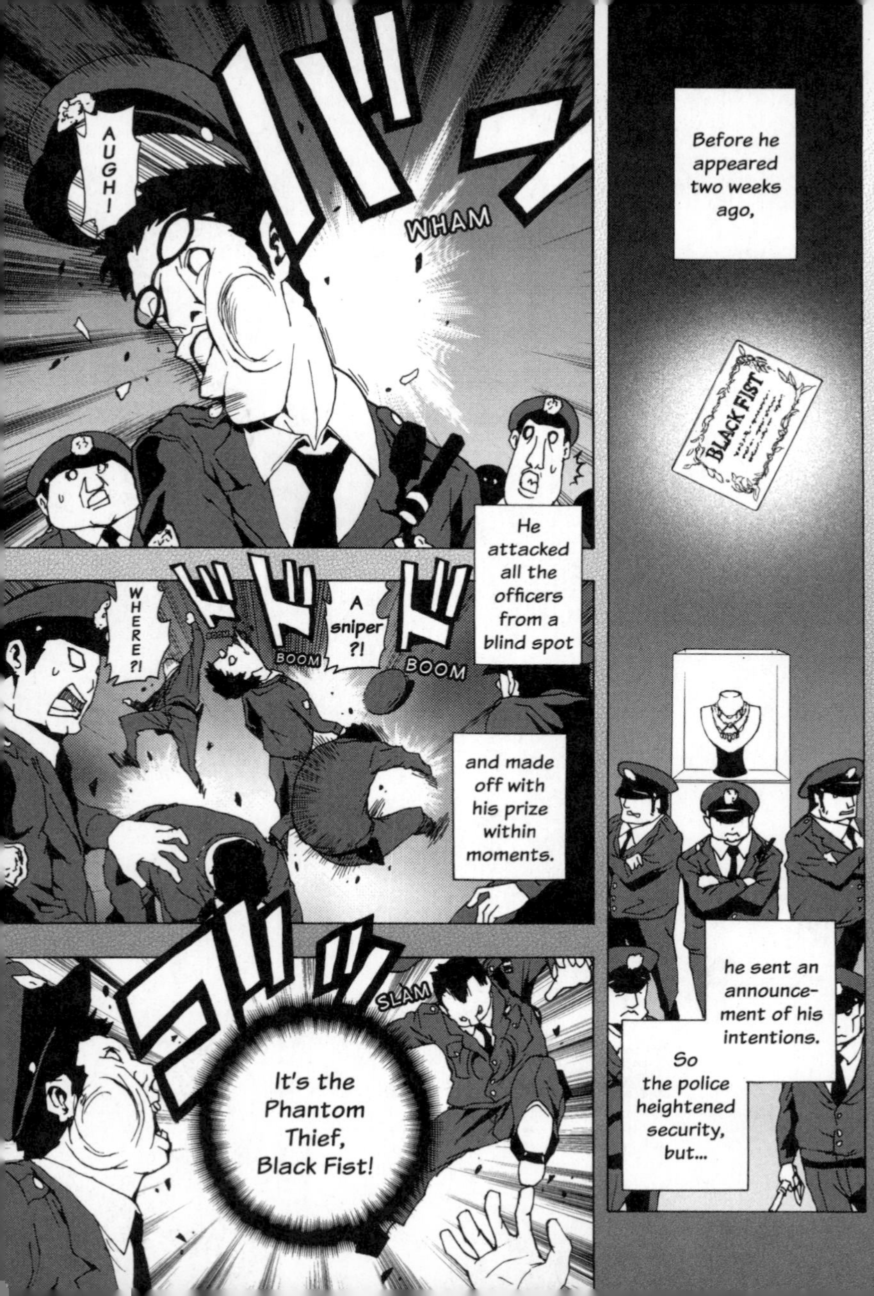
Before he appeared two weeks ago,
BLACK FIST
he sent an announcement of his intentions.
So the police heightened security, but...
AUGH!
WHAM
He attacked all the officers from a blind spot
WHERE?!
A sniper?!
BOOM
BOOM
and made off with his prize within moments.
SLAM
It's the Phantom Thief, Black Fist!

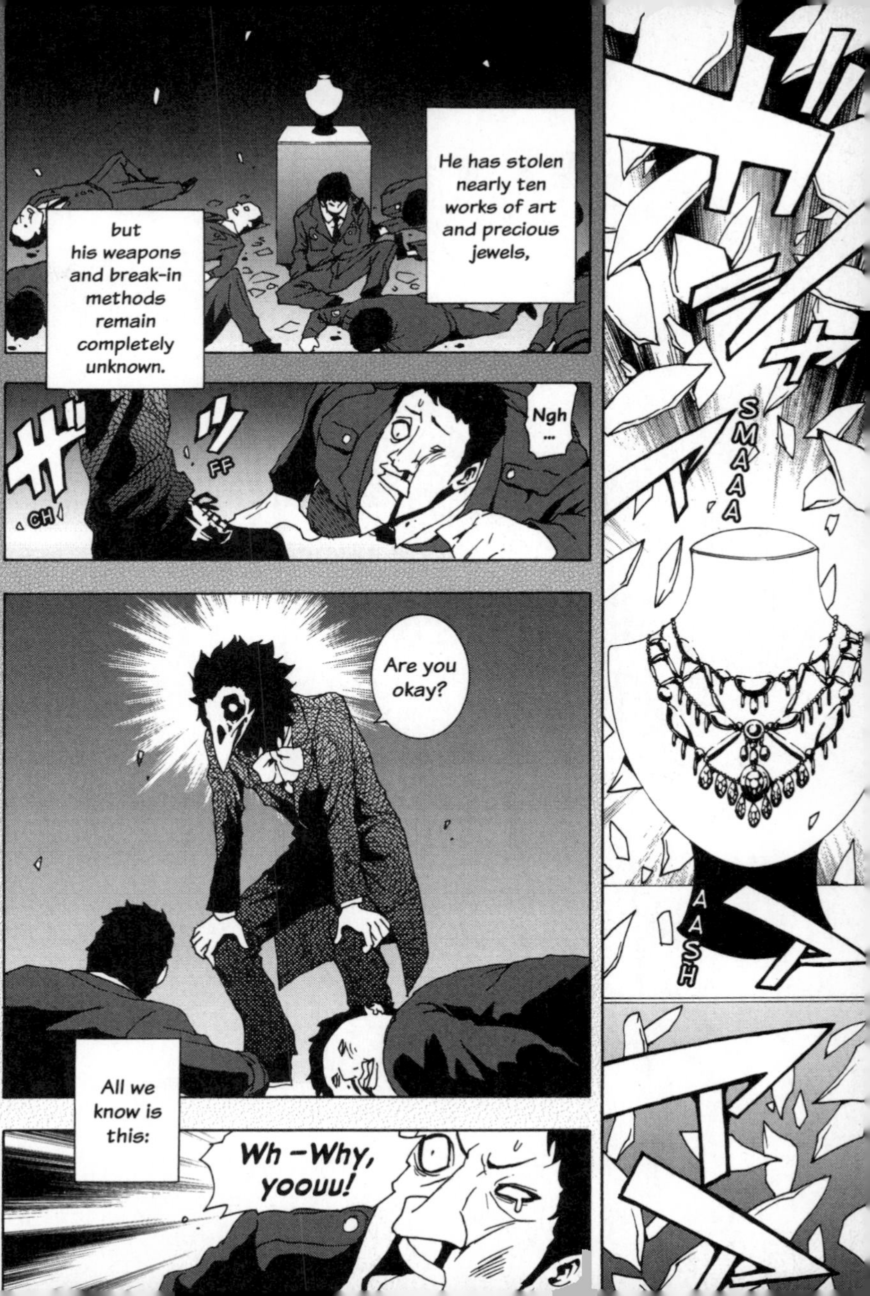
SMAAAAA
AASH
He has stolen nearly ten works of art and precious jewels,
but his weapons and break-in methods remain completely unknown.
Ngh...
FF
CH
Are you okay?
All we know is this:
Wh-Why, yoouu!

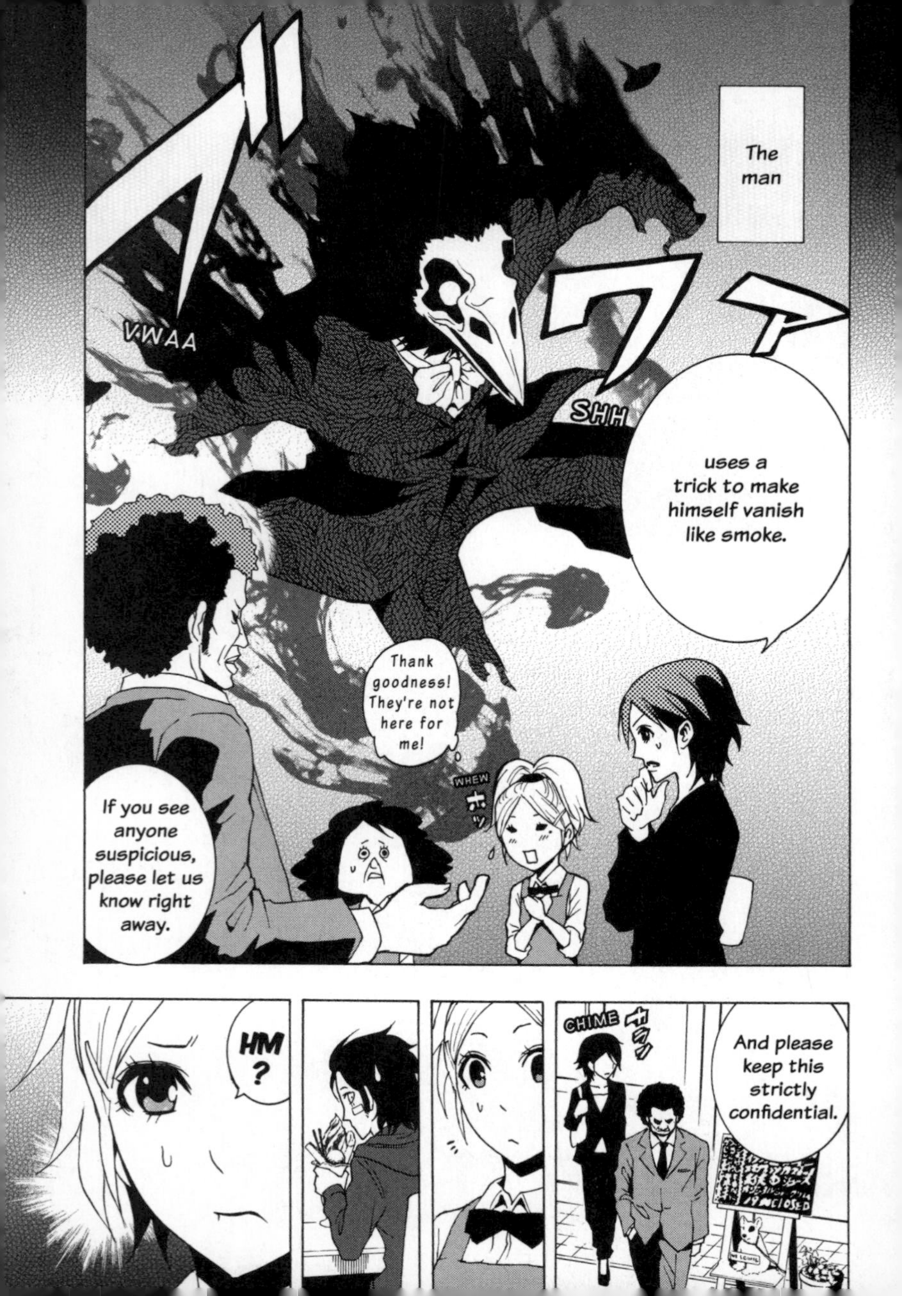
The man
VWAA
SHH
uses a trick to make himself vanish like smoke.
Thank goodness! They're not here for me!
WHEW
If you see anyone suspicious, please let us know right away.
And please keep this strictly confidential.
CHIME
HM?

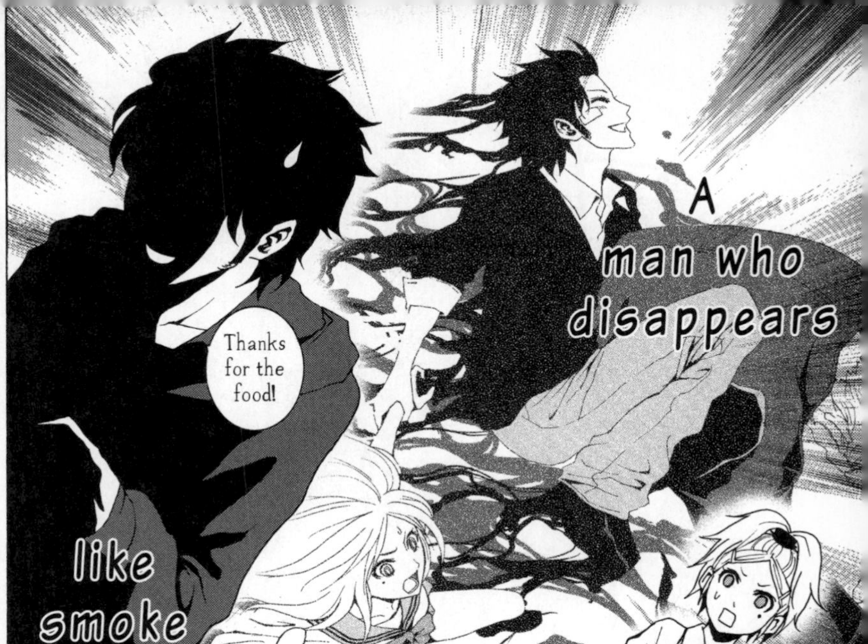
A man who disappears
Thanks for the food!
like smoke ?!
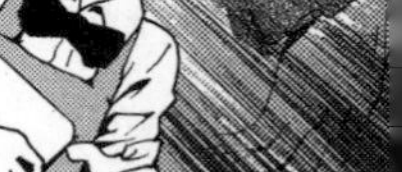
But, wait...
If they came here to request our help...
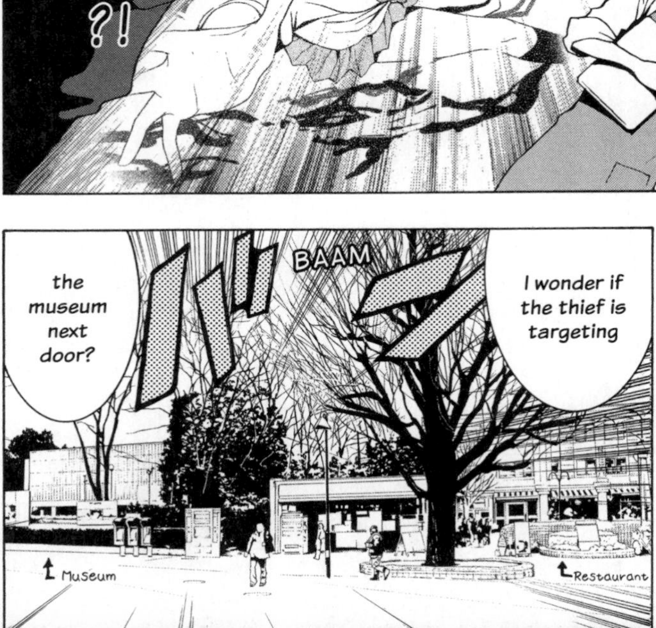
BAAM
I wonder if the thief is targeting
the museum next door?
Museum
Restaurant

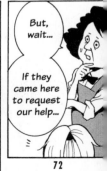

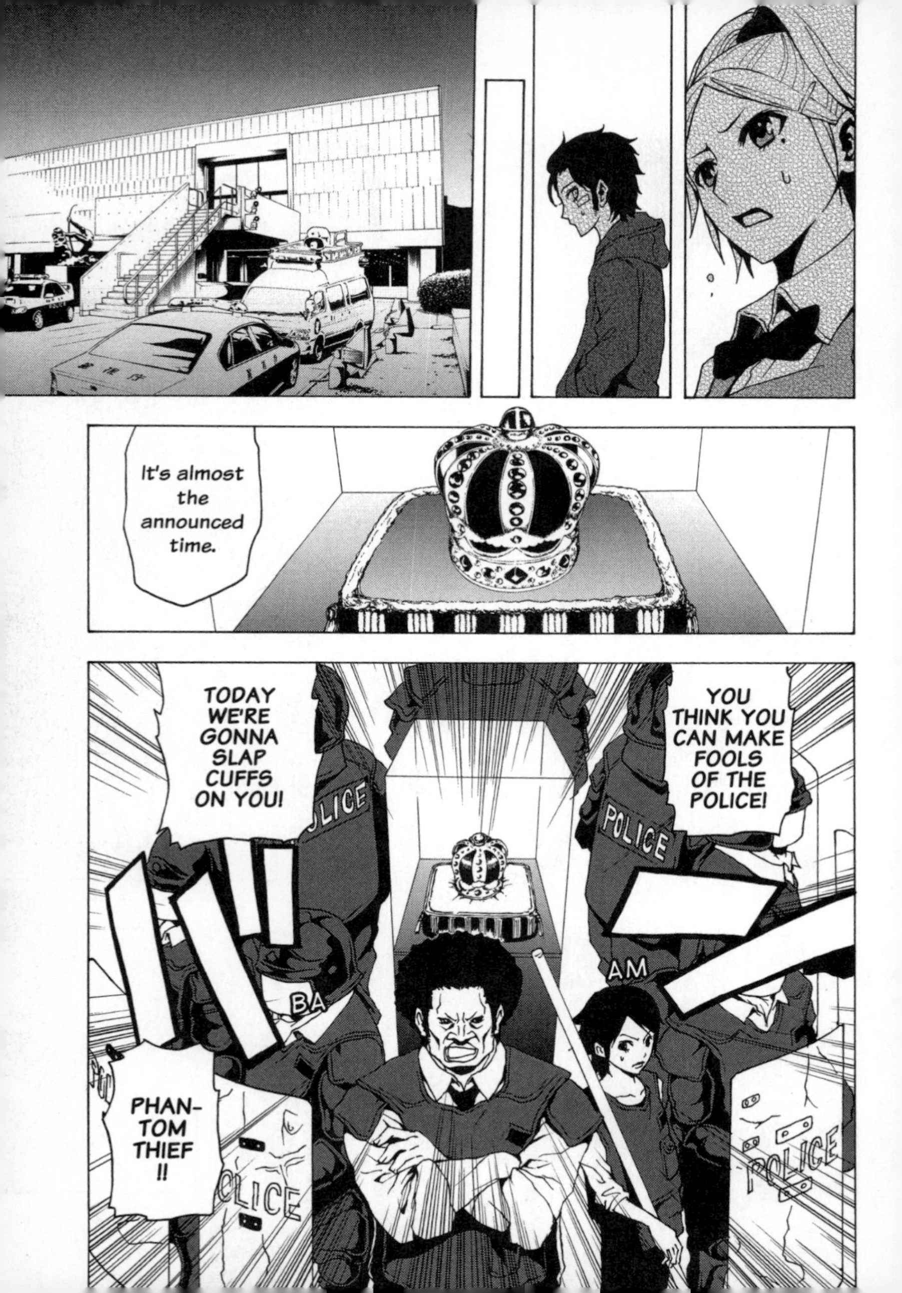
It's almost the announced time.
YOU THINK YOU CAN MAKE FOOLS OF THE POLICE!
TODAY WE'RE GONNA SLAP CUFFS ON YOU!
AM
BA
PHAN-TOM THIEF !!

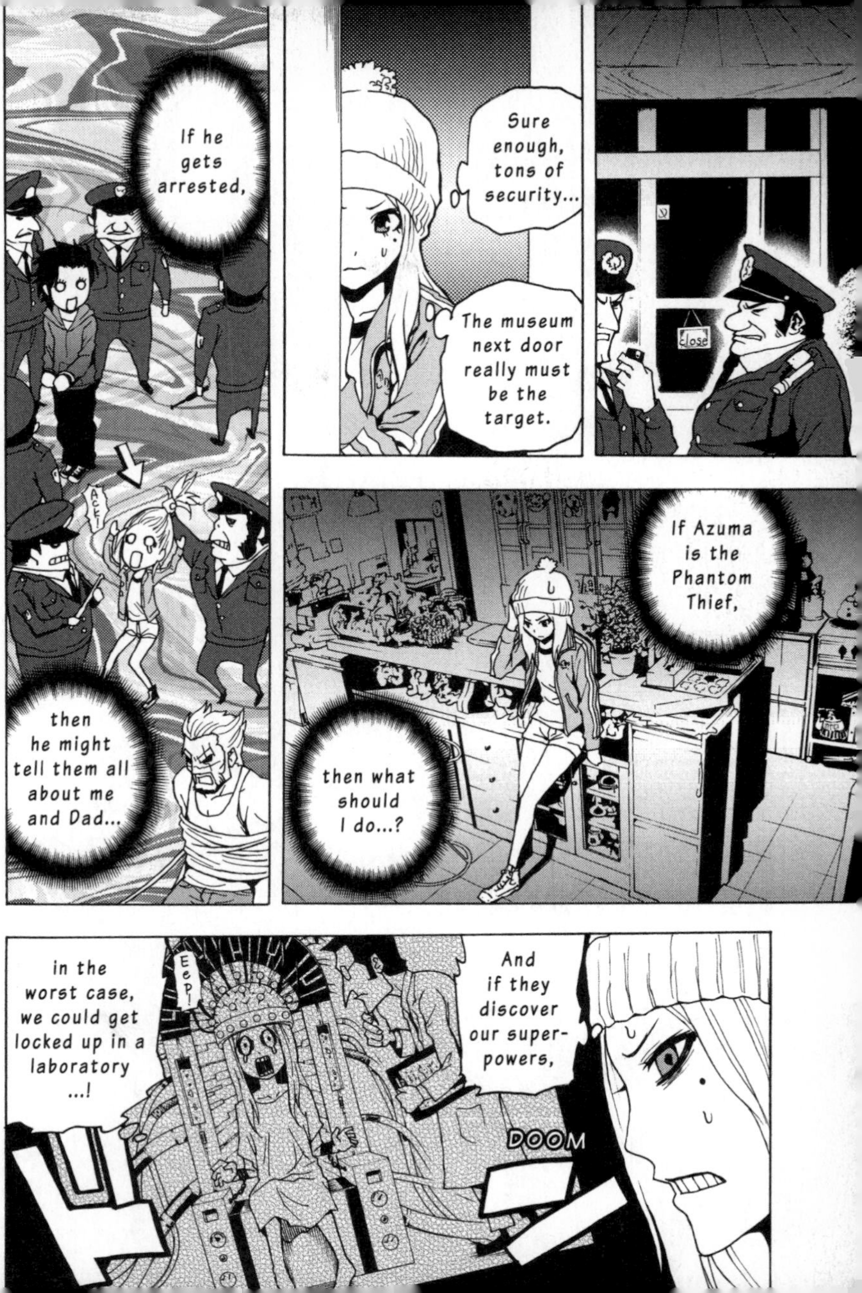
close
Sure enough, tons of security...
The museum next door really must be the target.
If Azuma is the Phantom Thief,
then what should I do...?
If he gets arrested,
ACK!
then he might tell them all about me and Dad...
And if they discover our super-powers,
in the worst case, we could get locked up in a laboratory ...!
EeP!
DOOM

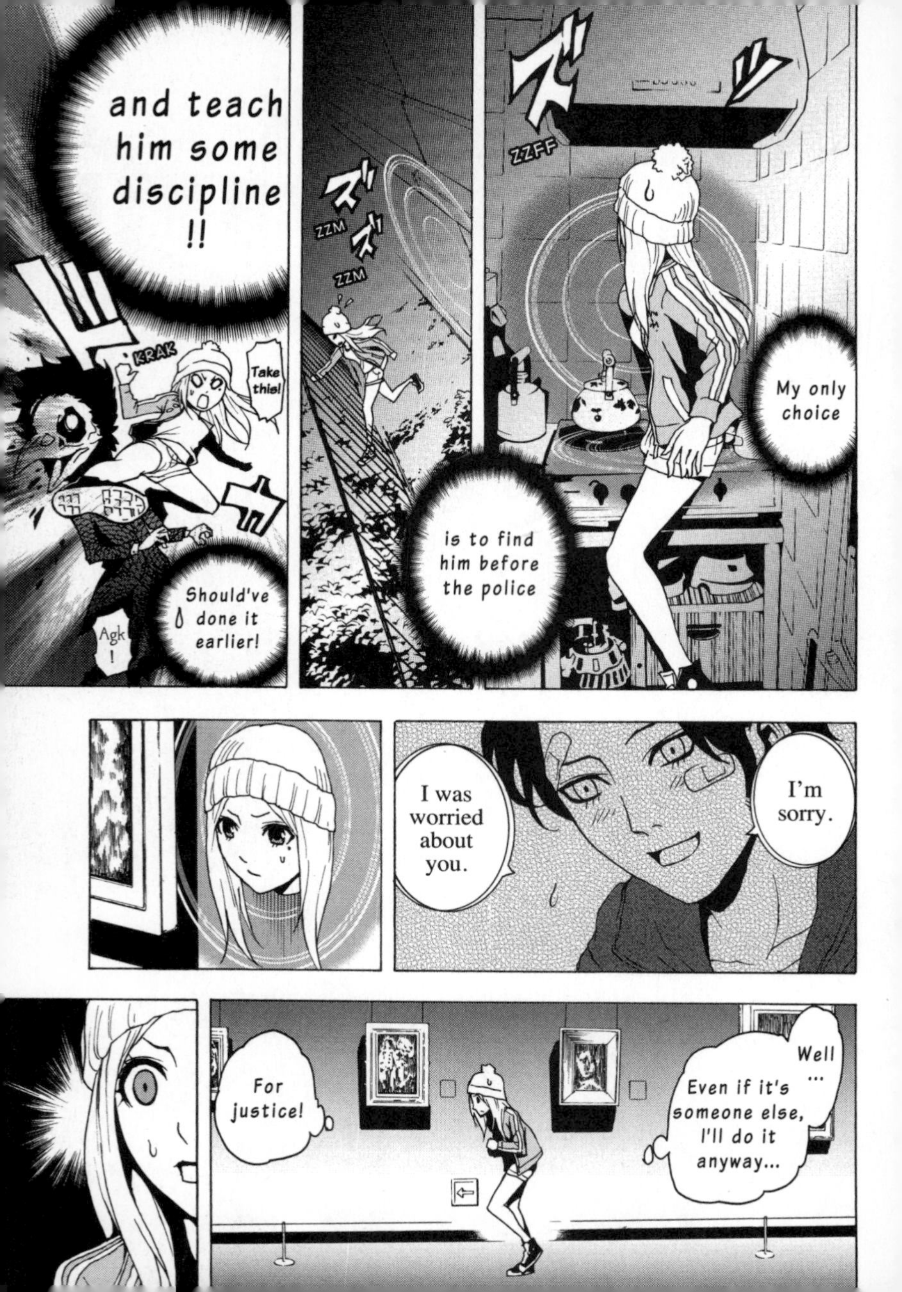
ZZFF
My only choice
is to find him before the police
ZZM
ZZM
and teach him some discipline !!
KRAK
Take this!
Should've done it earlier!
Agk !
I'm sorry.
I was worried about you.
Well ...
Even if it's someone else, I'll do it anyway...
For justice!

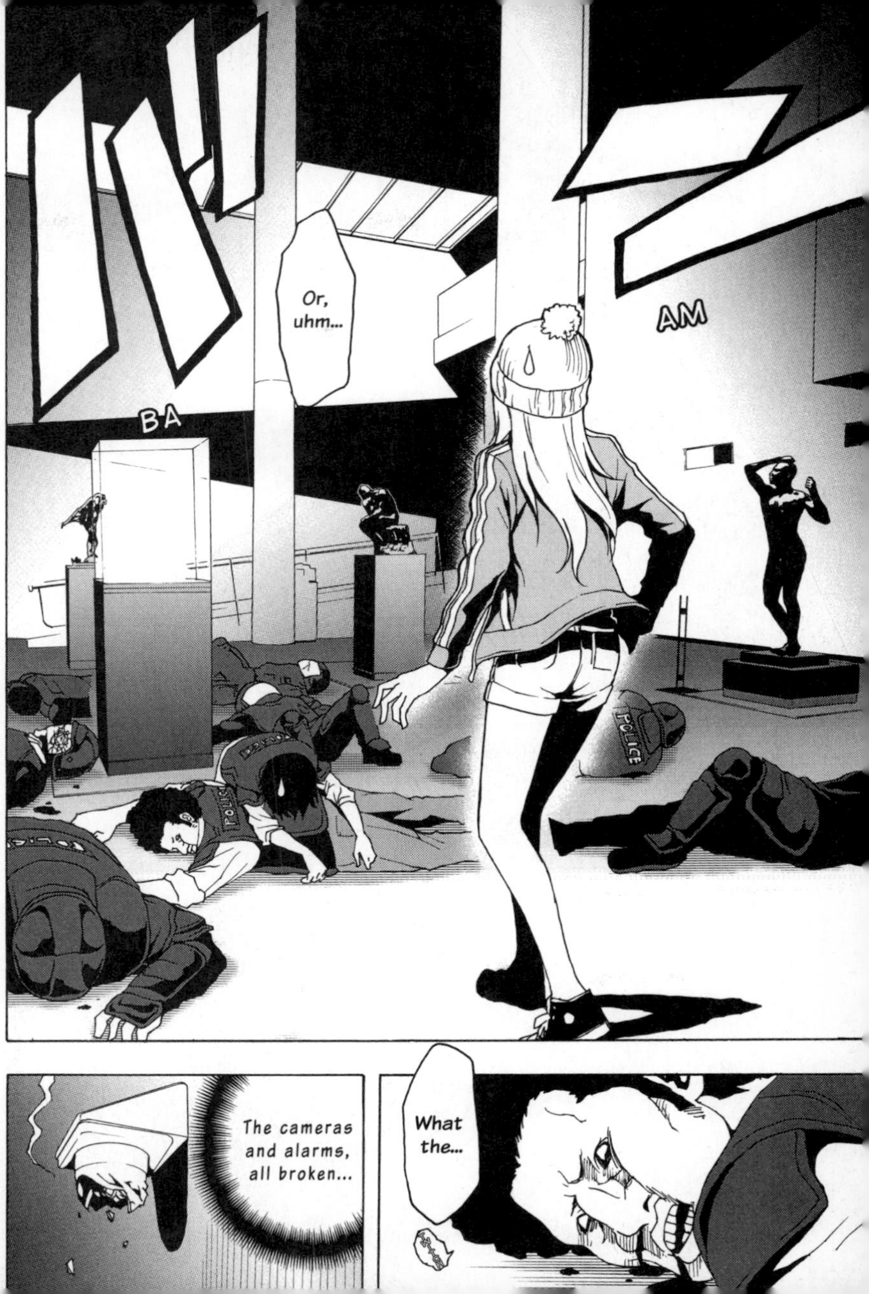
BA
AM
Or, uhm...
POLICE
What the...
The cameras and alarms, all broken...

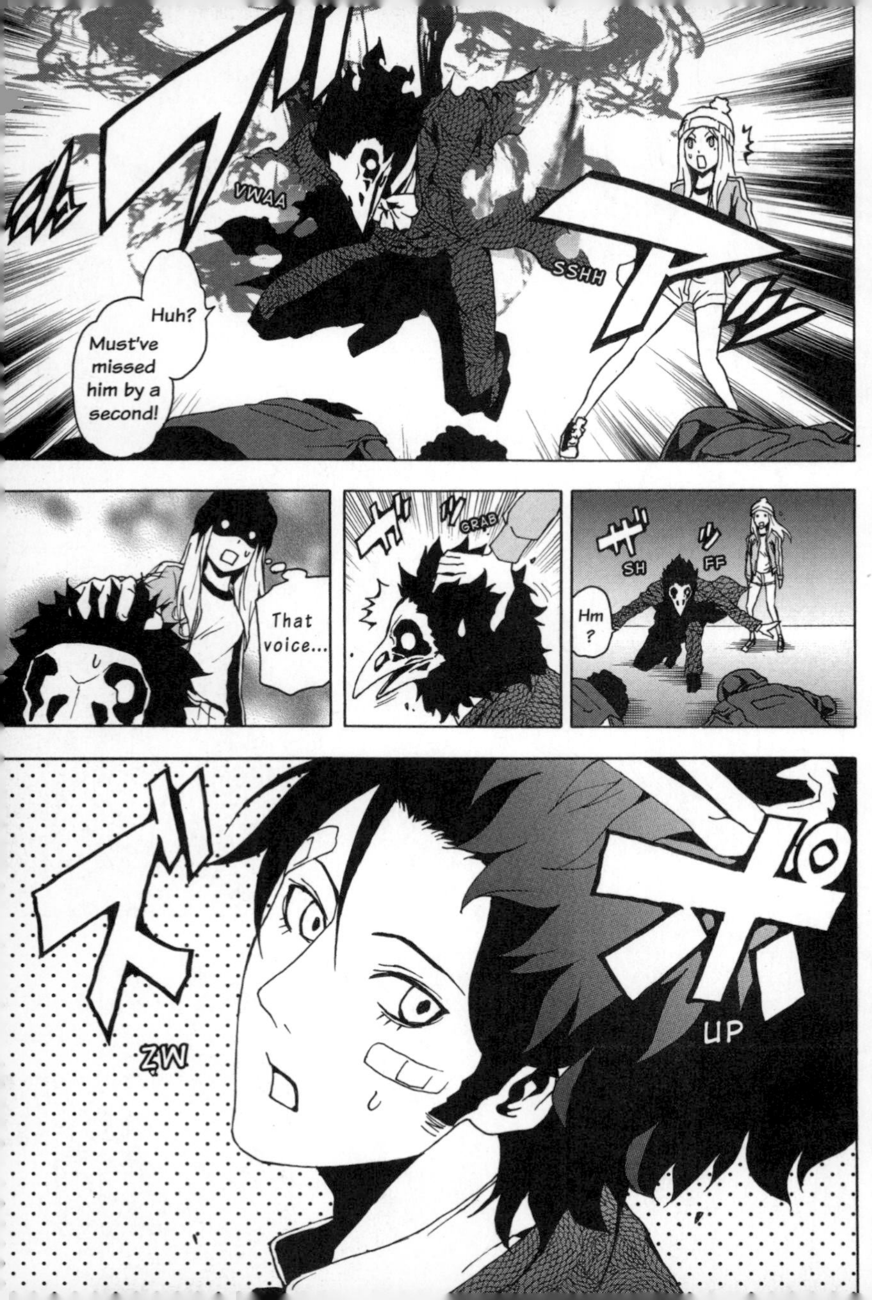
VWAA
SSHH
Huh? Must've missed him by a second!
SH
FF
Hm?
GRAB
That voice...
UP
ZW

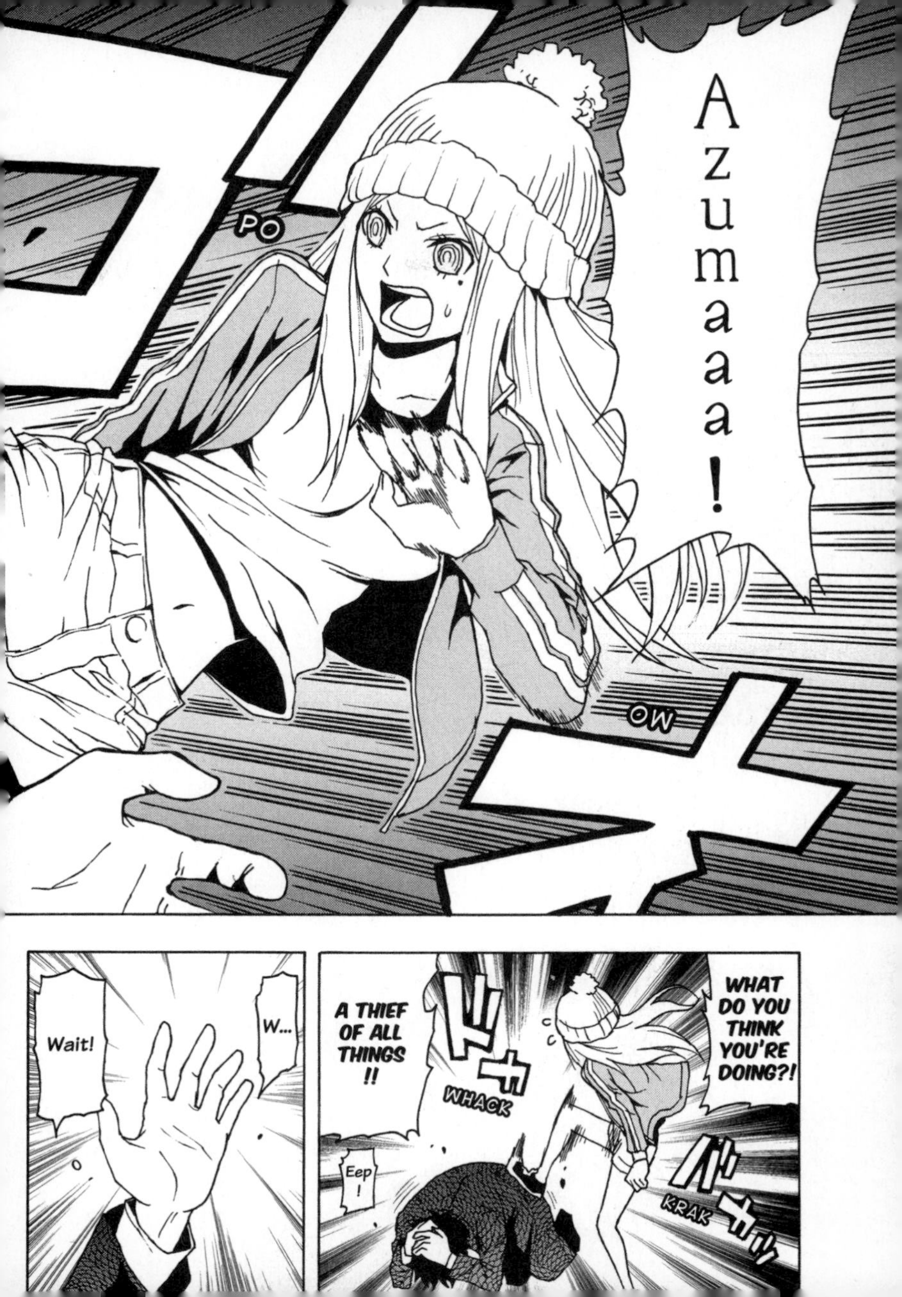
Azumaaa!
PO
OW
WHAT DO YOU THINK YOU'RE DOING?!
A THIEF OF ALL THINGS !!
WHACK
KRAK
Eep!
W...
Wait!

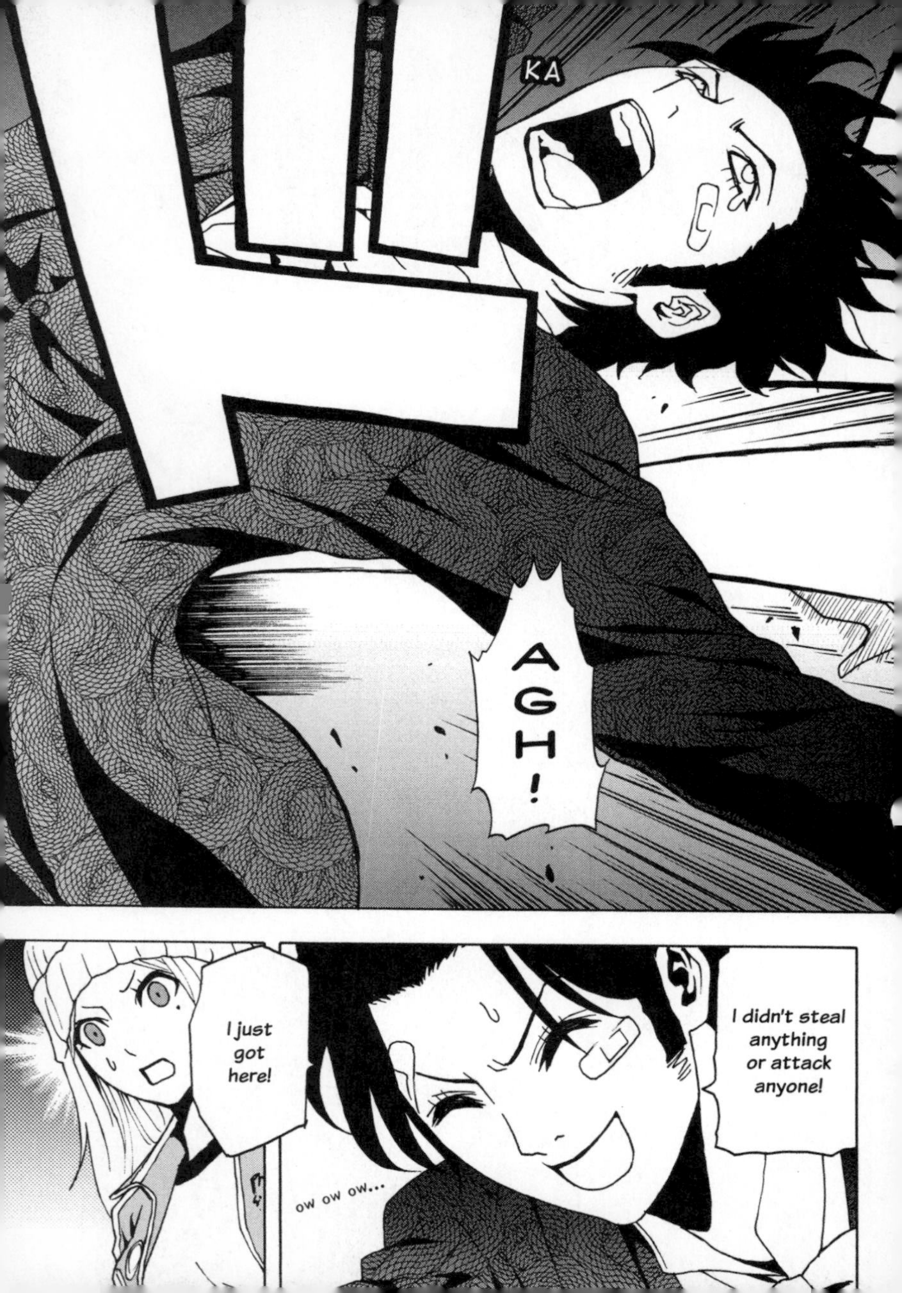
KA
AGH!
I didn't steal anything or attack anyone!
ow ow ow...
I just got here!

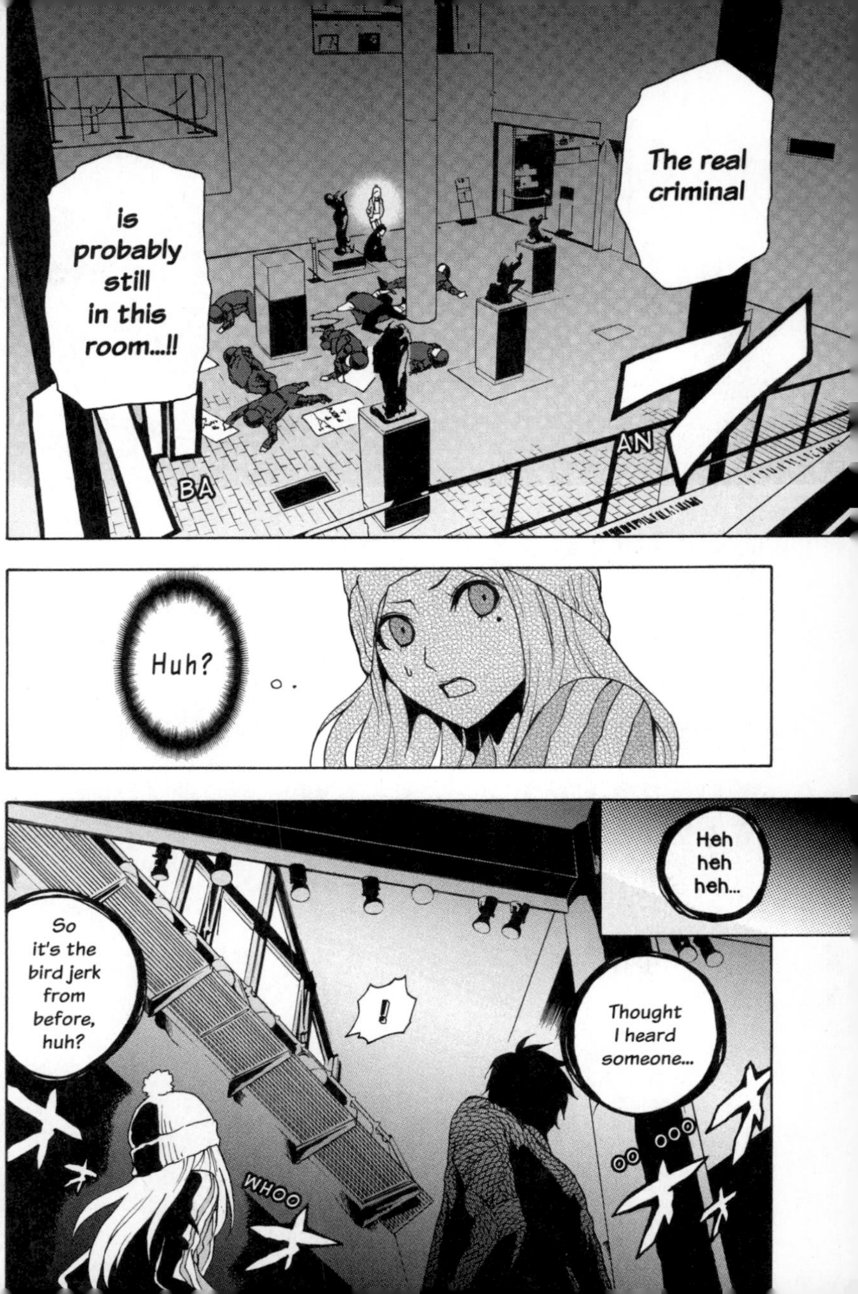

The real criminal
is probably still in this room...!!
AN
BA
Huh?
Heh heh heh...
Thought I heard someone...
!
So it's the bird jerk from before, huh?
OOO
OO
WHOO

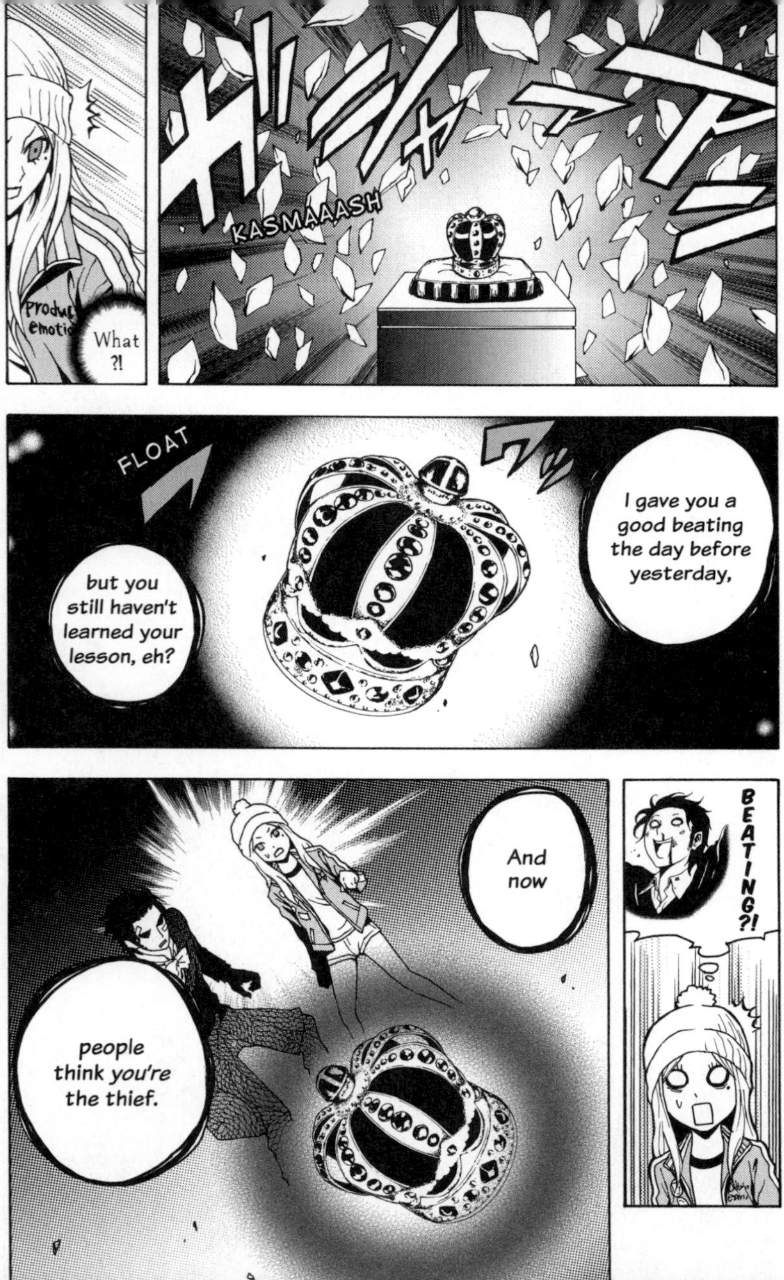
KASMAAASH
What ?!
FLOAT
I gave you a good beating the day before yesterday,
but you still haven't learned your lesson, eh?
BEATING?!
And now
people think *you're* the thief.

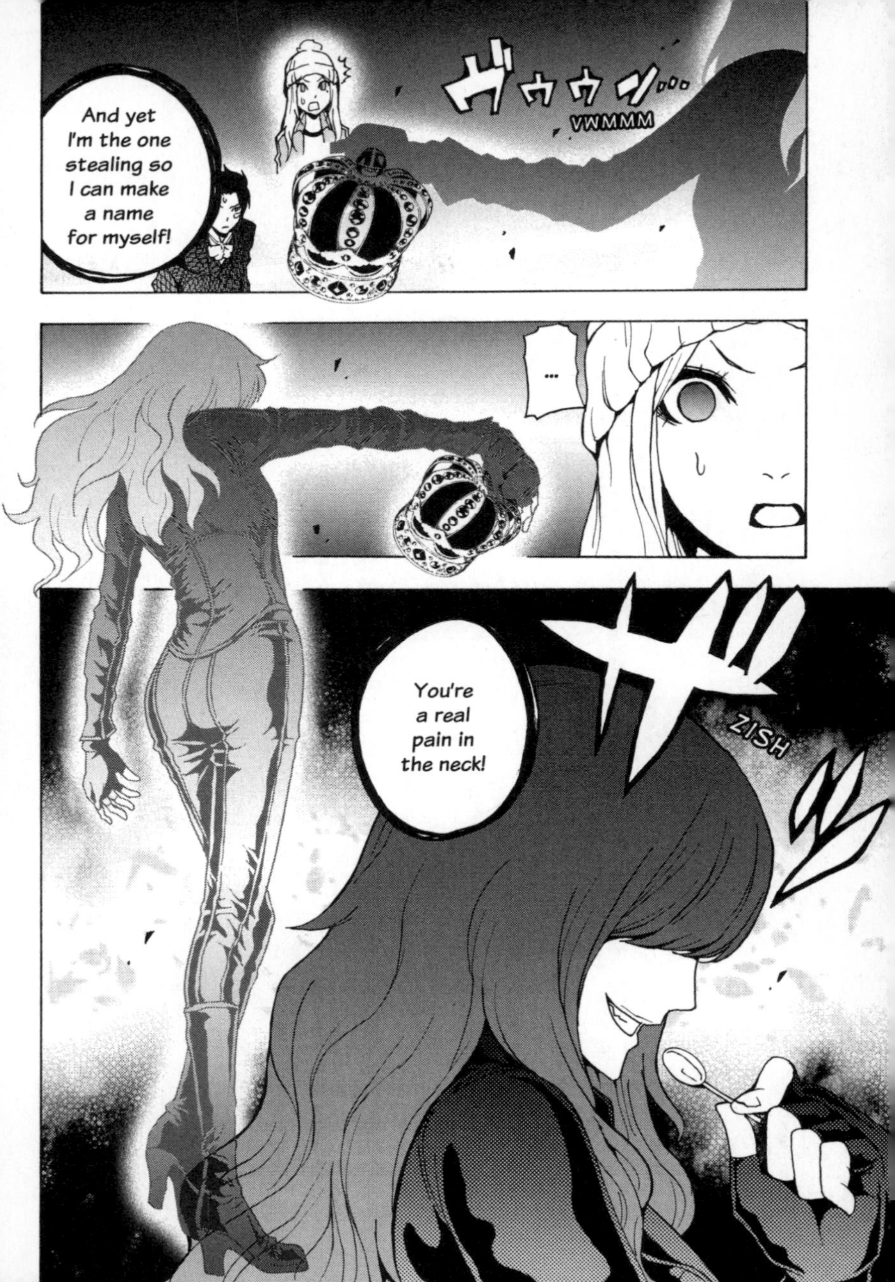
ヴゥゥン…
VWMMM
And yet I'm the one stealing so I can make a name for myself!
...
ザッ
ZISH
You're a real pain in the neck!

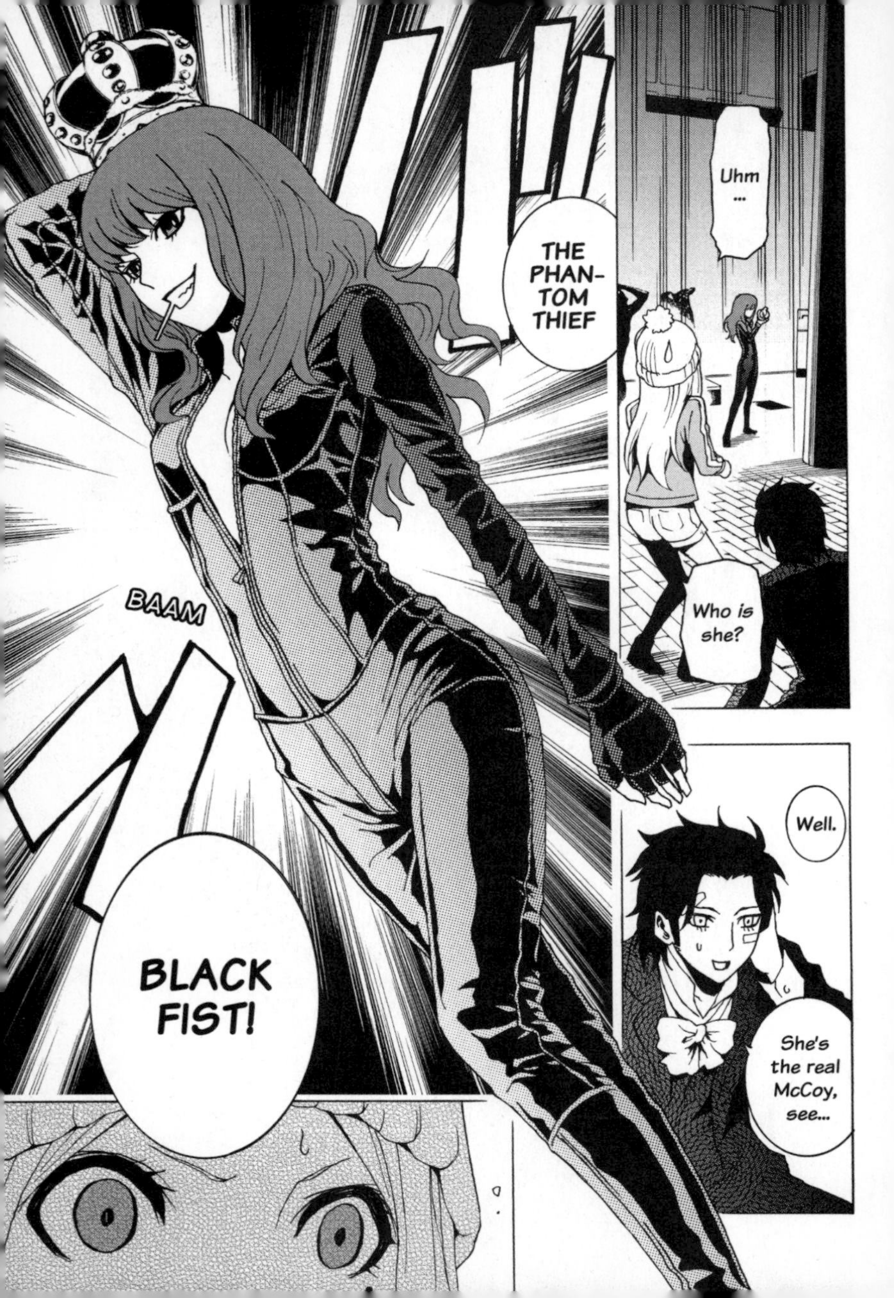
Uhm ...
Who is she?
Well.
She's the real McCoy, see...
THE PHAN-TOM THIEF
BAAM
BLACK FIST!

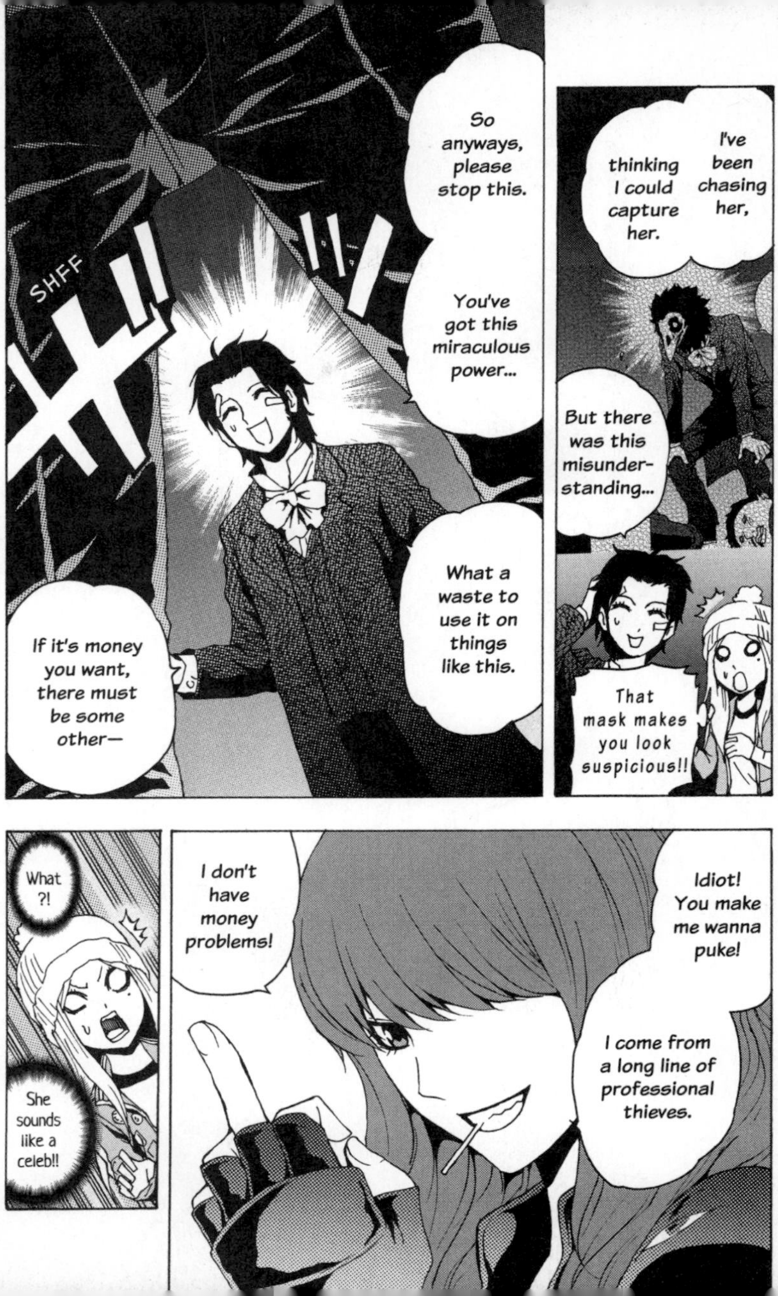
I've been chasing her,
thinking I could capture her.
But there was this misunder-standing...
That mask makes you look suspicious!!
So anyways, please stop this.
SHFF
You've got this miraculous power...
What a waste to use it on things like this.
If it's money you want, there must be some other—
Idiot! You make me wanna puke!
I don't have money problems!
I come from a long line of professional thieves.
What ?!
She sounds like a celeb!!

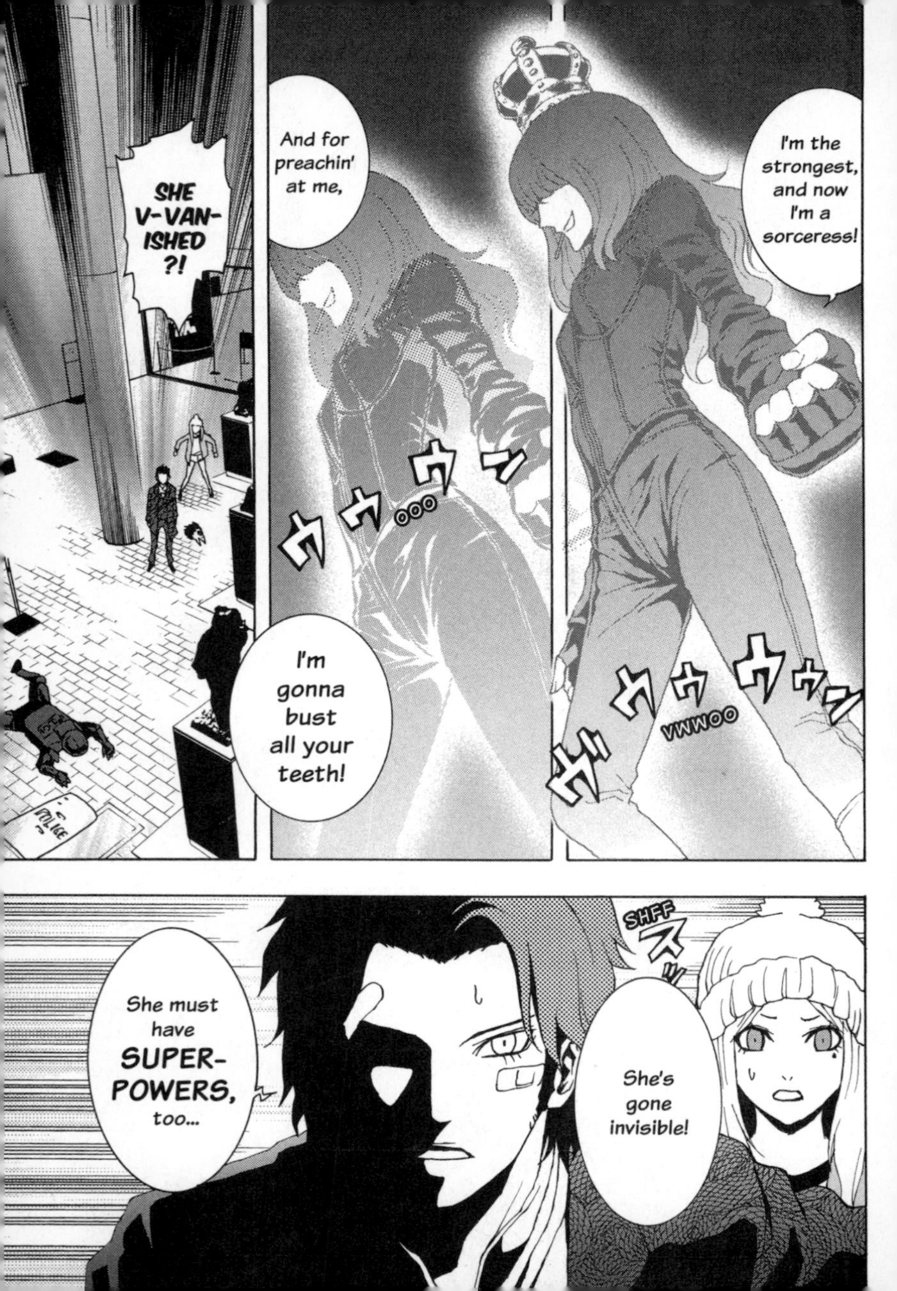
I'm the strongest, and now I'm a sorceress!
VWWOO
And for preachin' at me,
OOO
I'm gonna bust all your teeth!
SHE V-VANISHED ?!
SHFF
She's gone invisible!
She must have SUPER-POWERS, too...

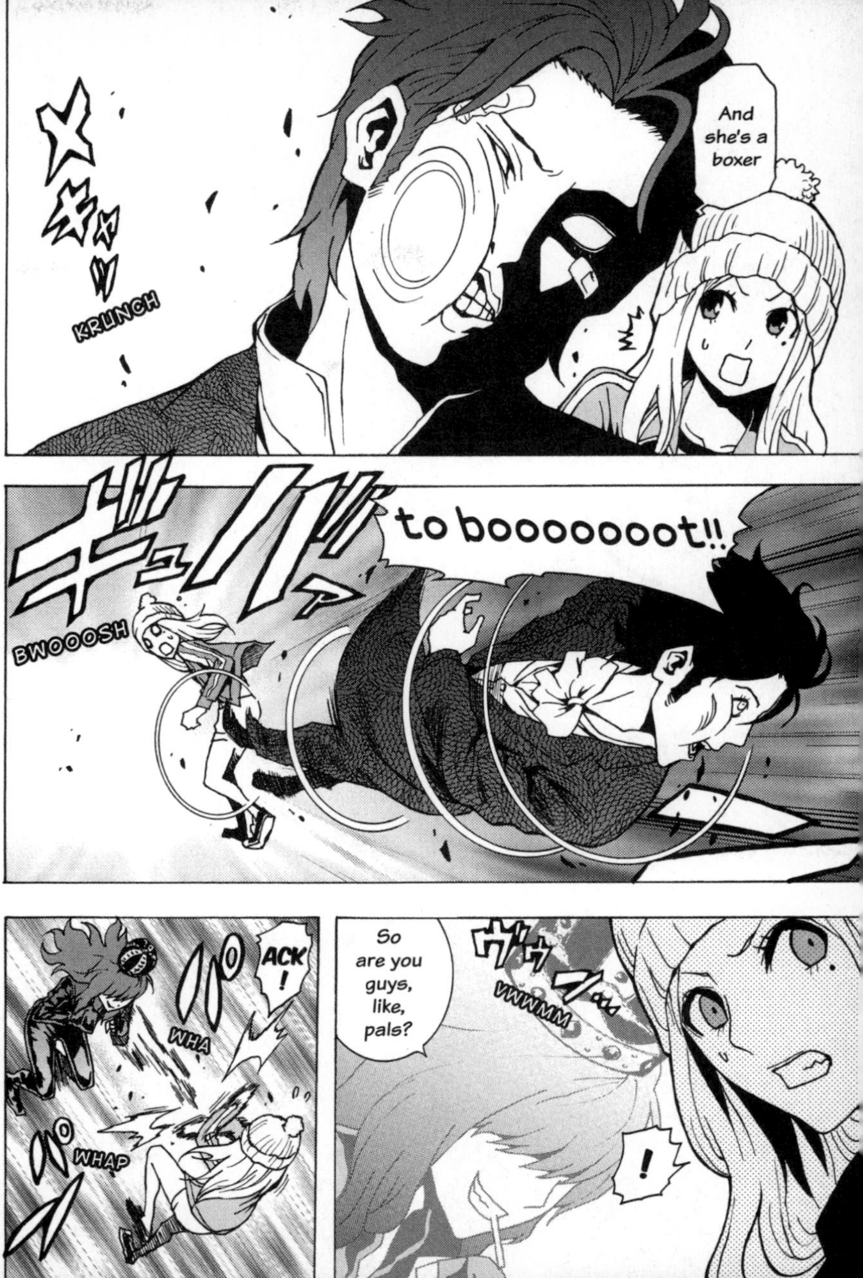
And she's a boxer
KRUNCH
!
to booooooot!!
BWOOOSH
So are you guys, like, pals?
VWWMM
!
ACK!
WHA
WHAP

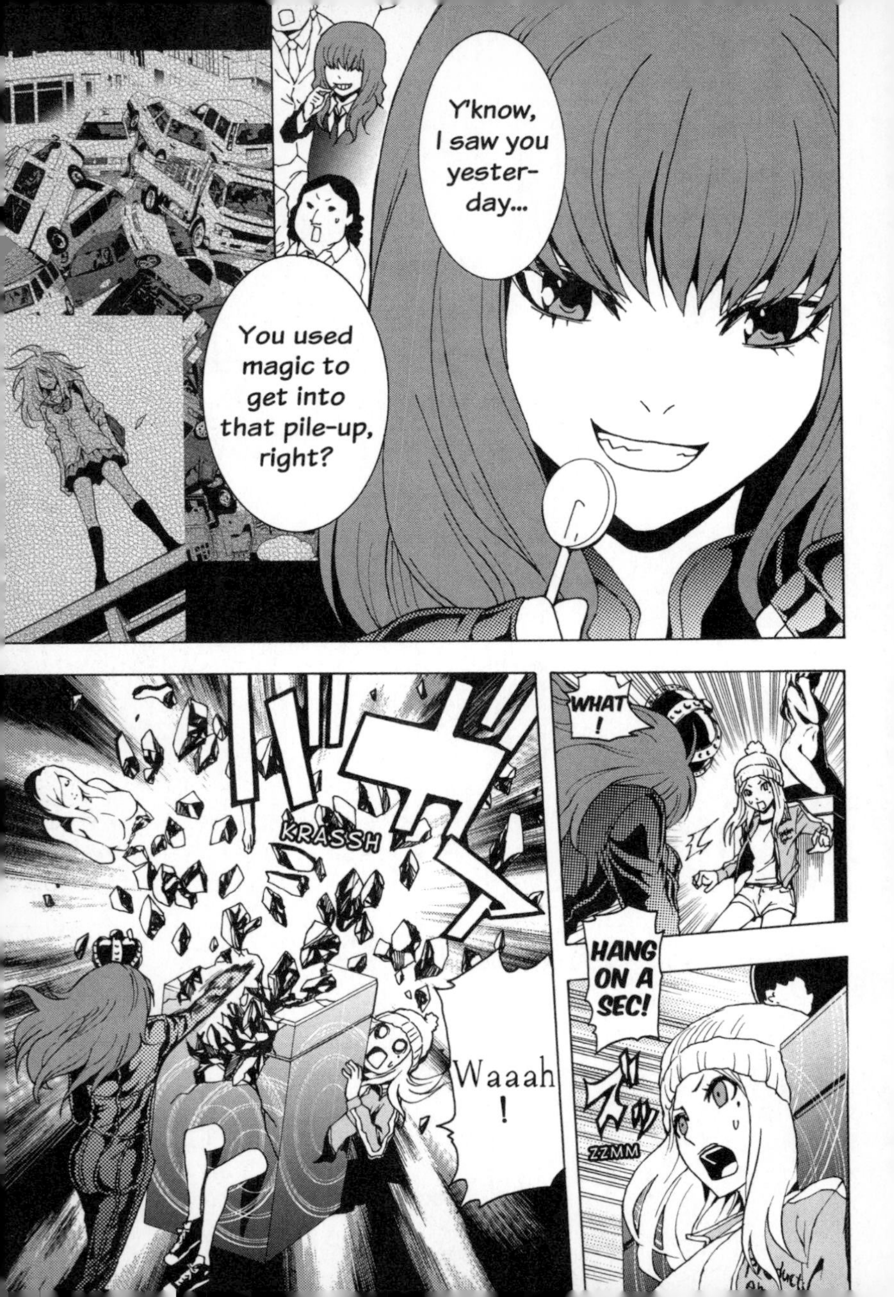
Y'know, I saw you yester-day...
You used magic to get into that pile-up, right?
WHAT!
HANG ON A SEC!
ZZMM
KRASSH
Waaah!

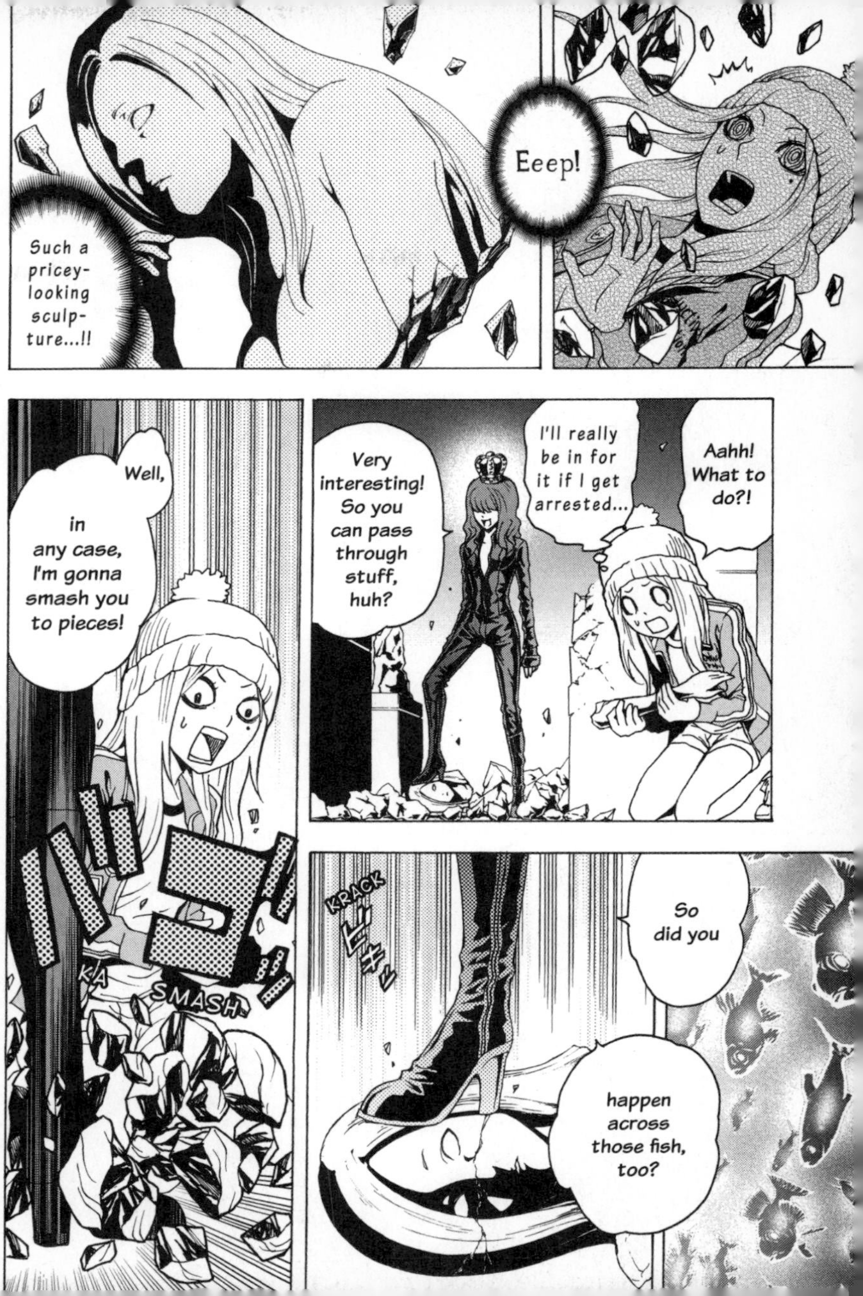
Eeep!
Such a pricey-looking sculpture...!!
Aahh! What to do?!
I'll really be in for it if I get arrested...
Very interesting! So you can pass through stuff, huh?
KRACK
So did you
happen across those fish, too?
Well,
in any case, I'm gonna smash you to pieces!
KA SMASH

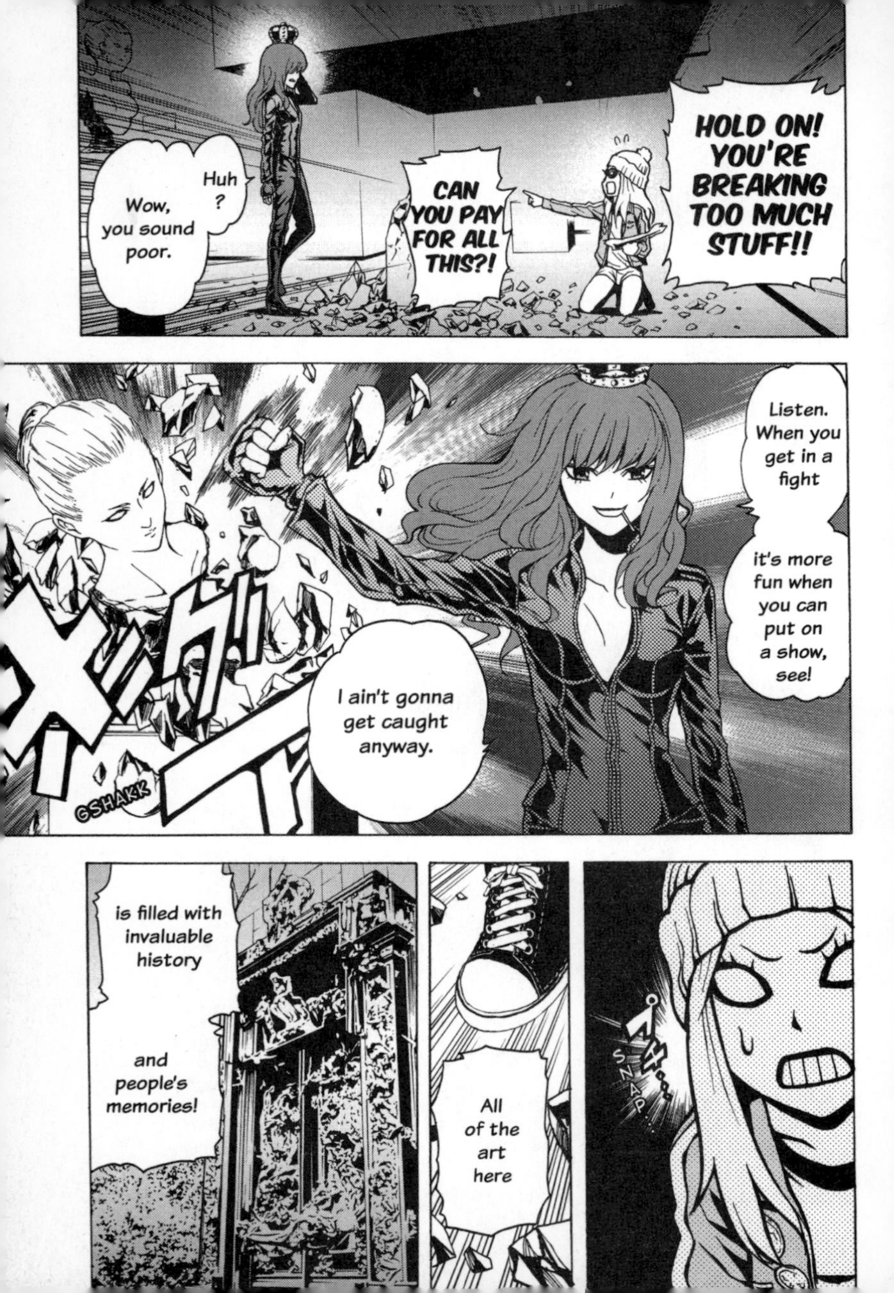
HOLD ON! YOU'RE BREAKING TOO MUCH STUFF!!
CAN YOU PAY FOR ALL THIS?!
Huh?
Wow, you sound poor.
Listen. When you get in a fight
it's more fun when you can put on a show, see!
I ain't gonna get caught anyway.
GSHAKK
SNAP...
All of the art here
is filled with invaluable history
and people's memories!

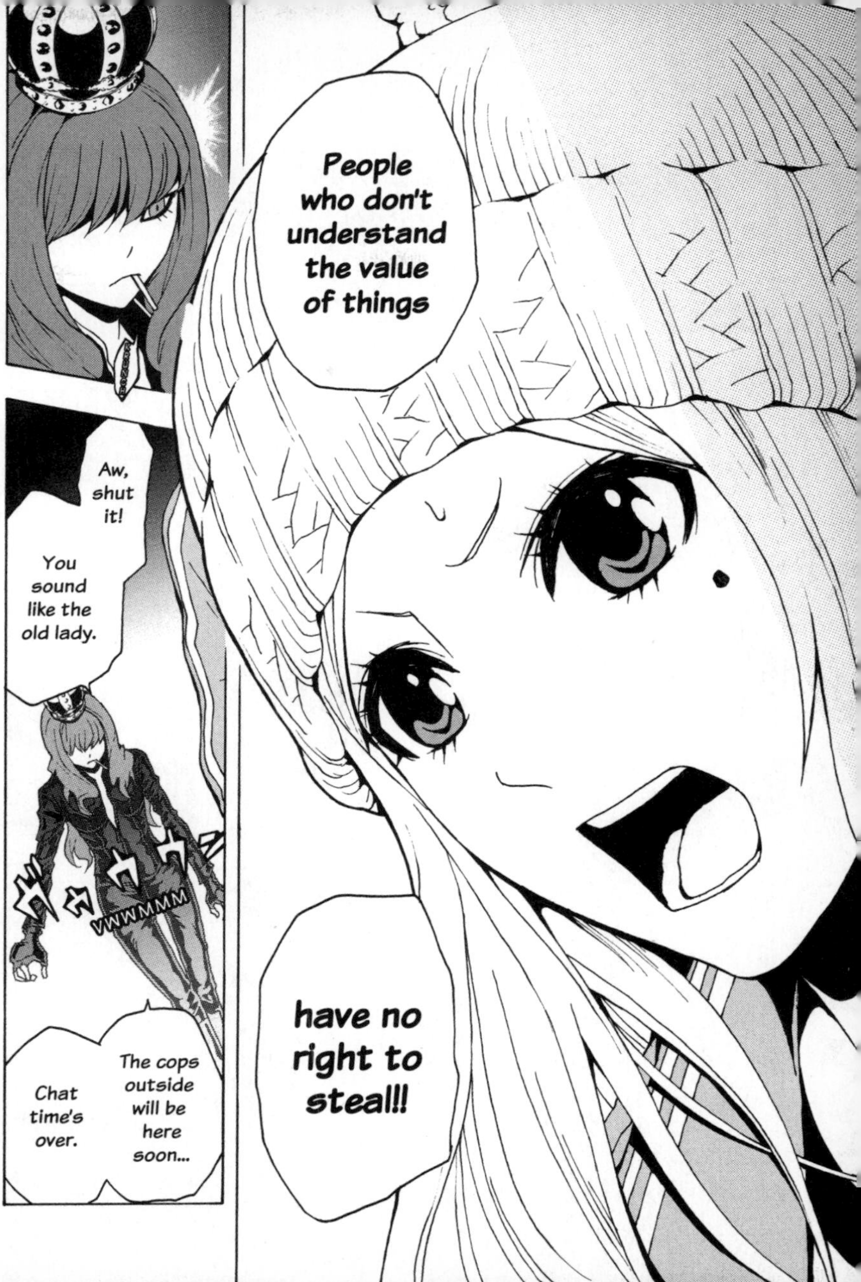
People who don't understand the value of things
have no right to steal!!
Aw, shut it!
You sound like the old lady.
VWWMMM
The cops outside will be here soon...
Chat time's over.

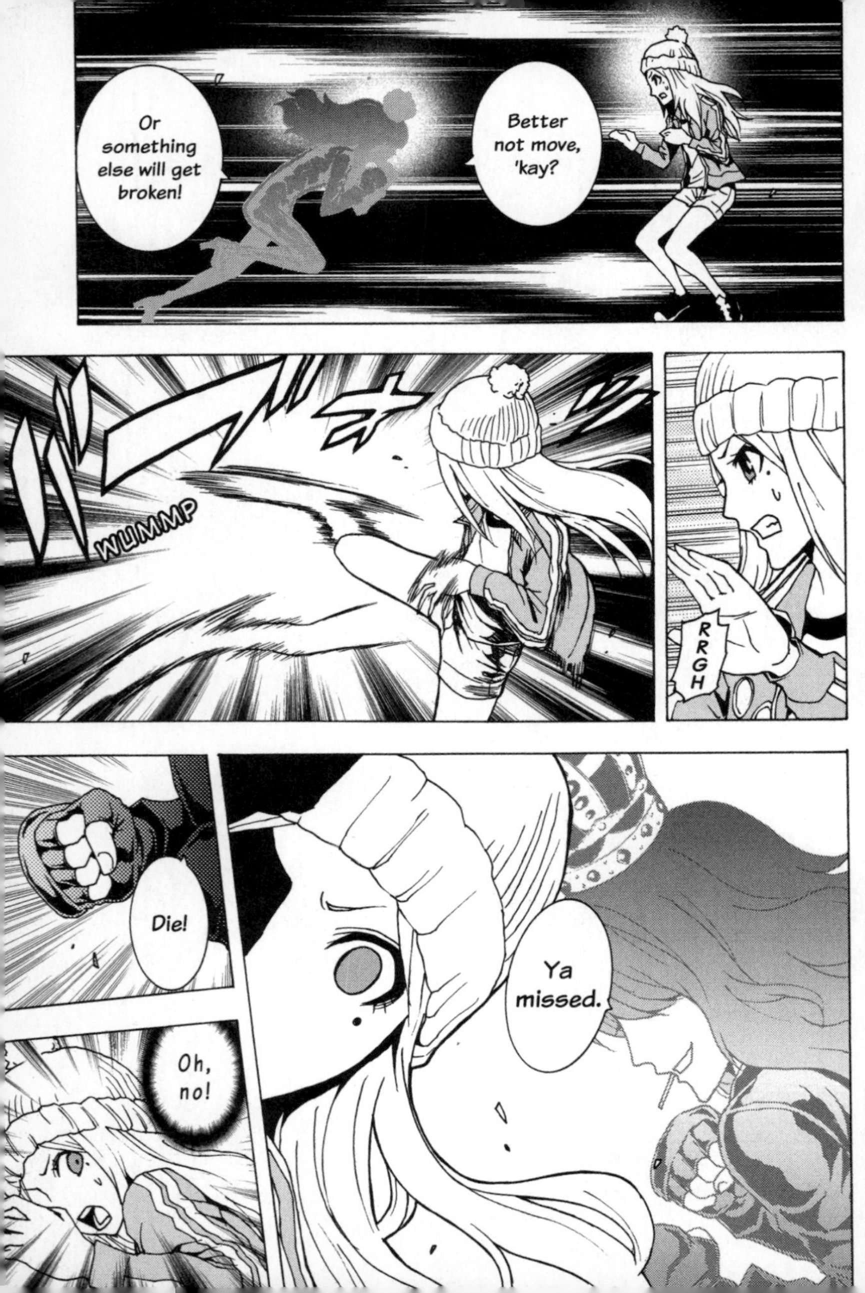
Better not move, 'kay?
Or something else will get broken!
RRGH
WUMMMP
Ya missed.
Die!
Oh, no!

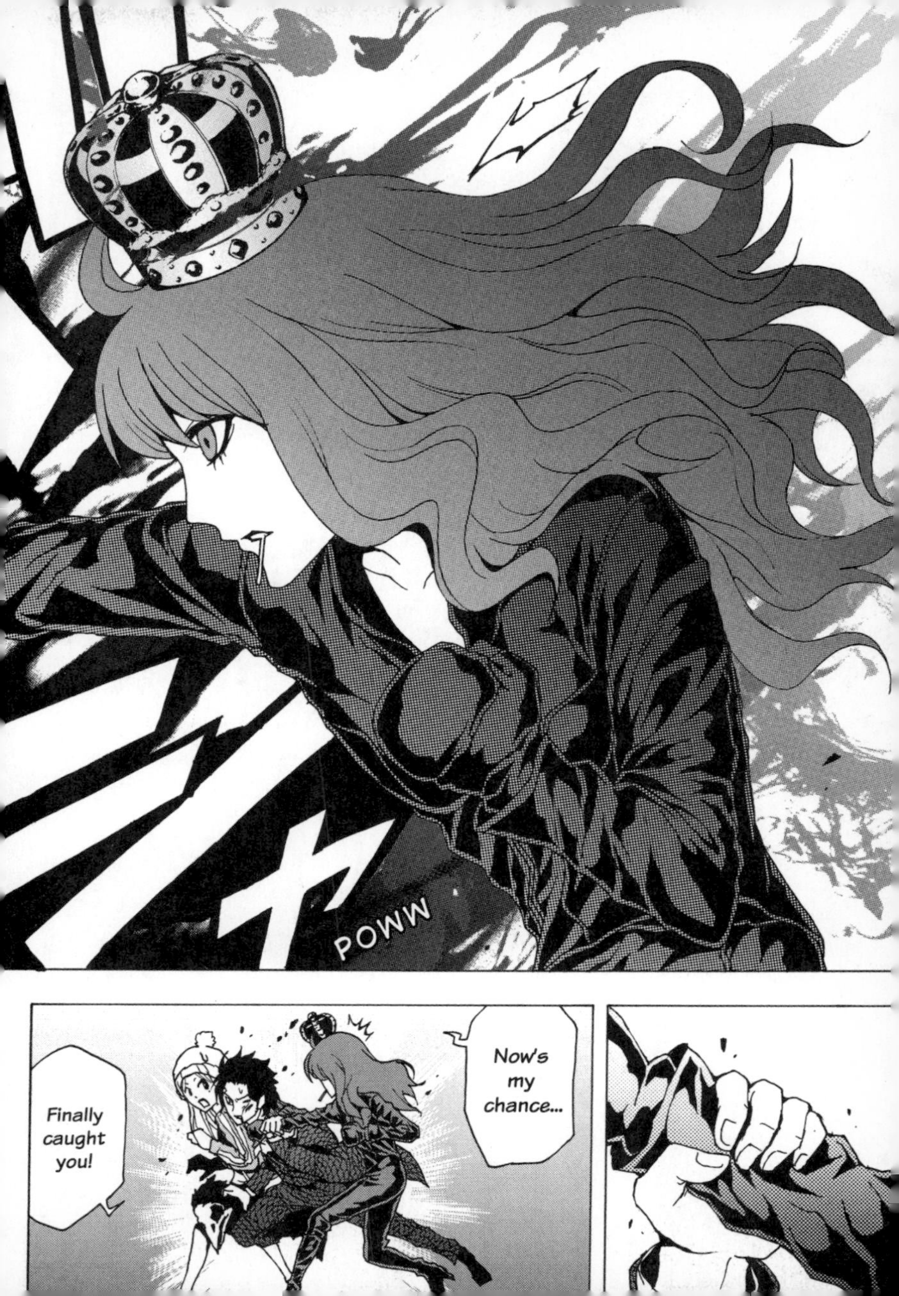
POWW
Now's my chance...
Finally caught you!

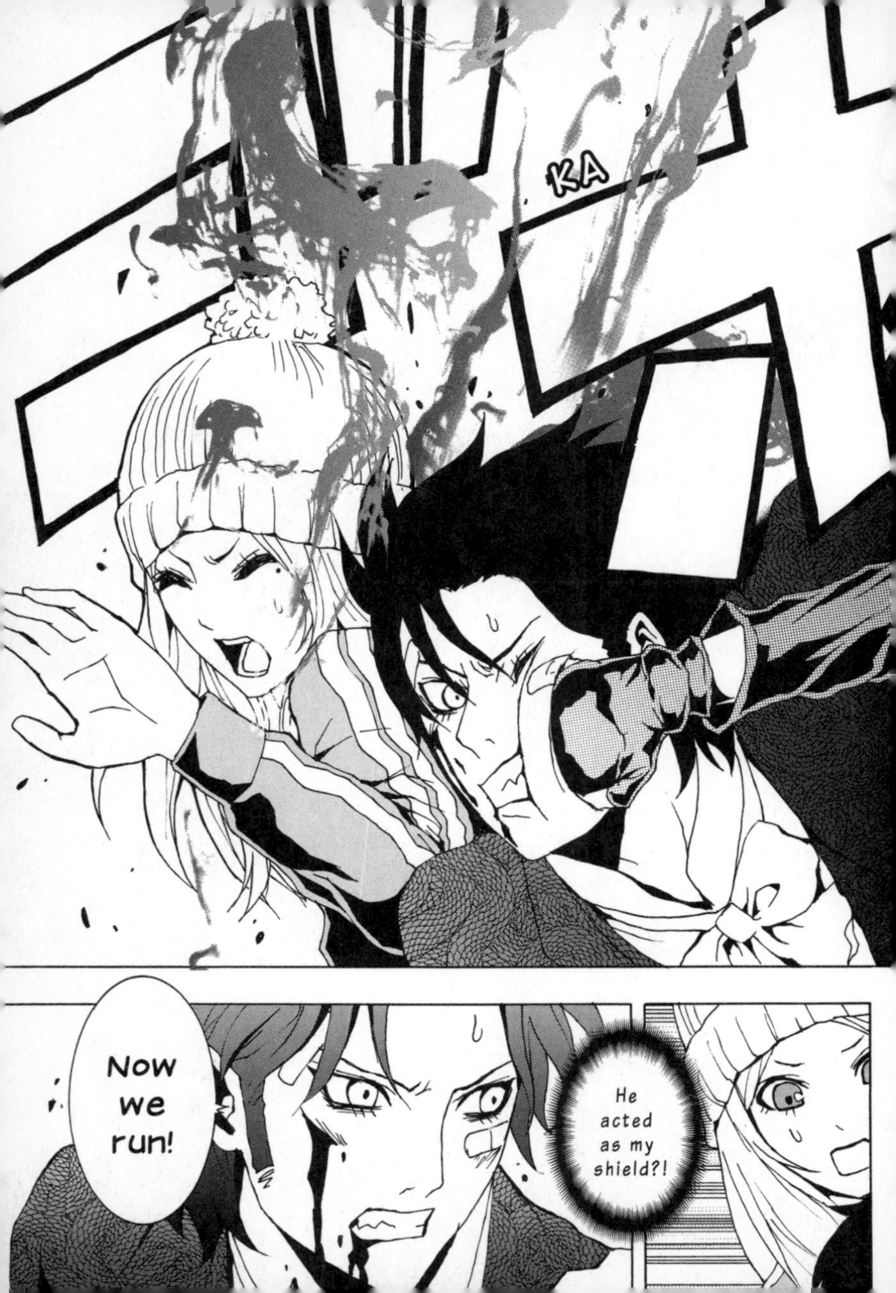
KA
He acted as my shield?!
Now we run!

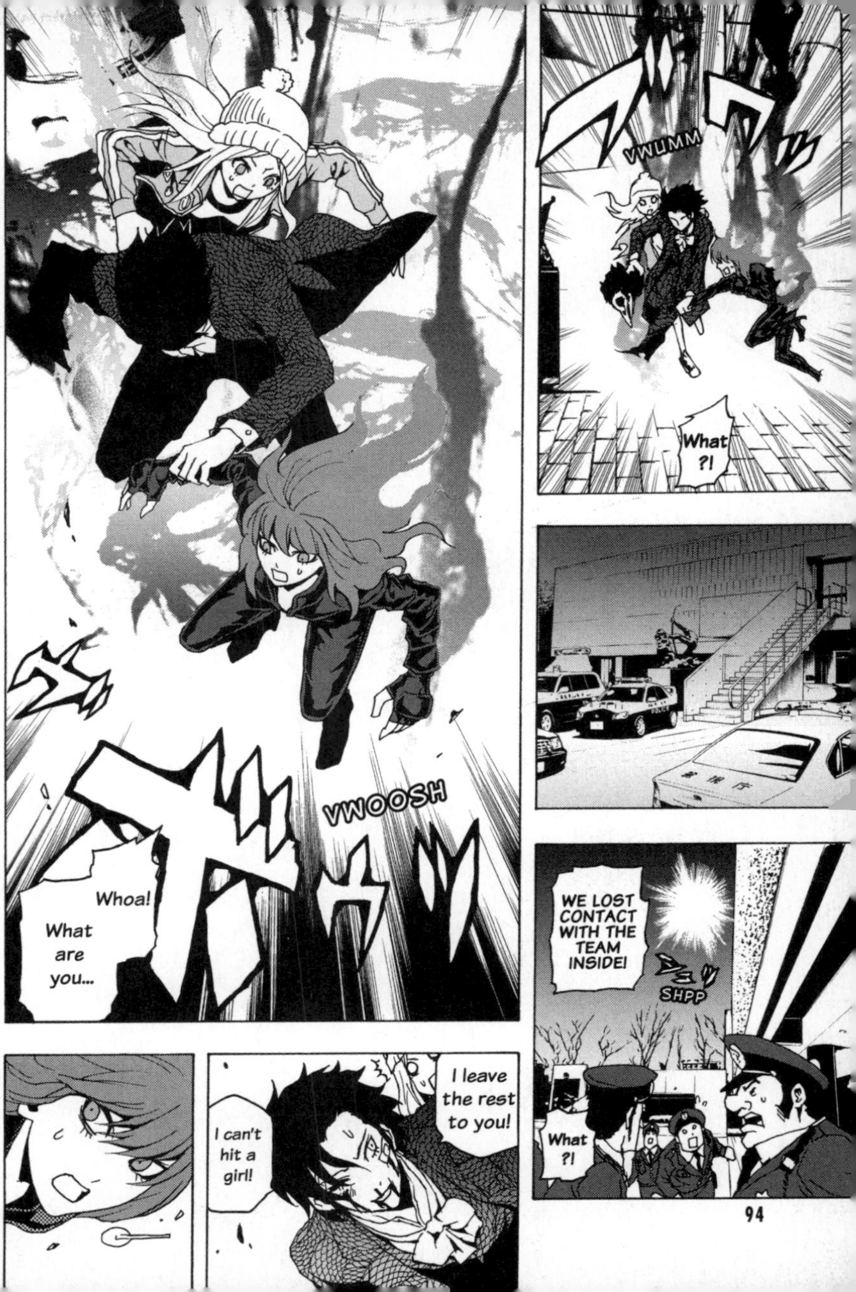
VWUMM
What?!
WE LOST CONTACT WITH THE TEAM INSIDE!
SHPP
What?!
VWOOSH
Whoa!
What are you...
I leave the rest to you!
I can't hit a girl!

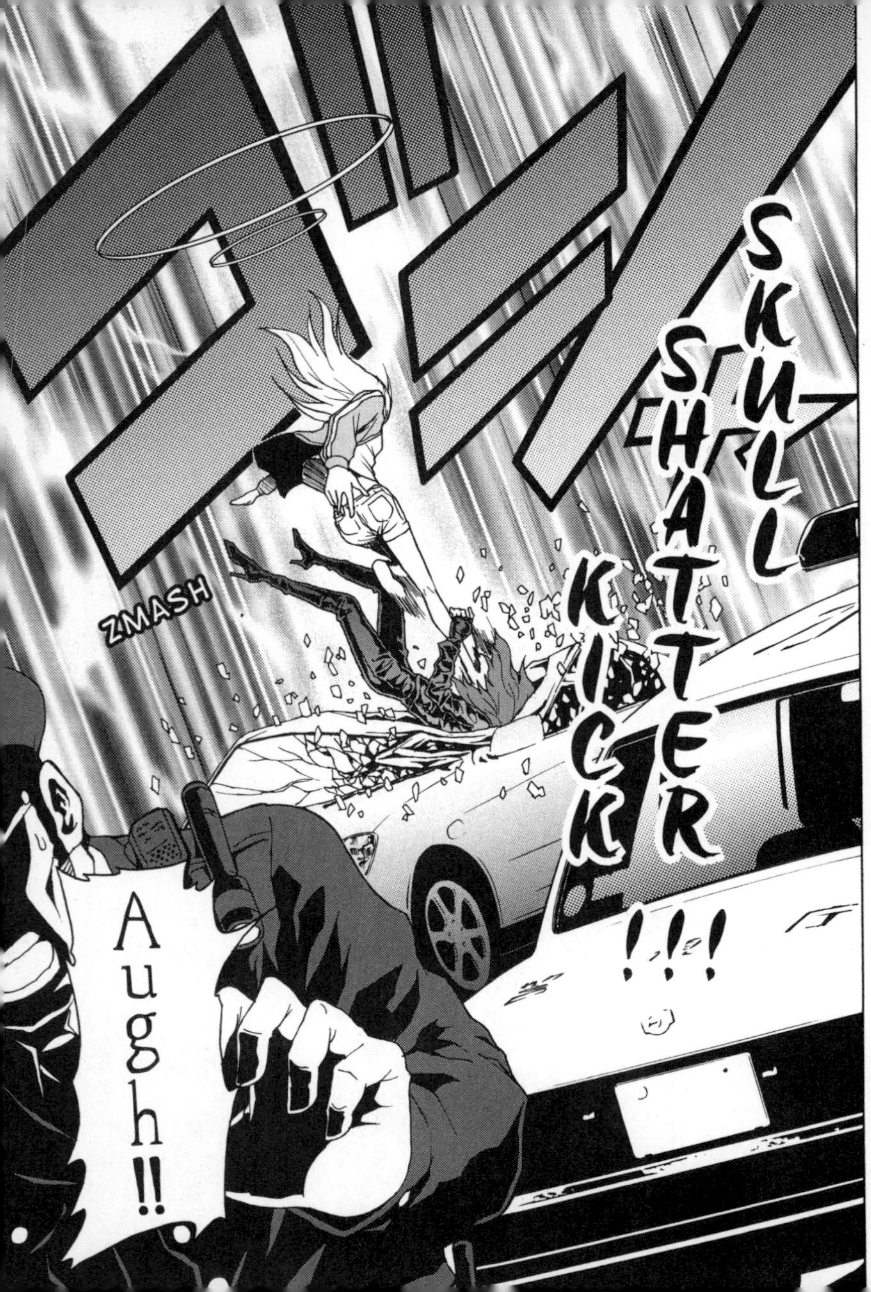
SKULL SHATTER KICK!!!
ZMASH
Augh!!

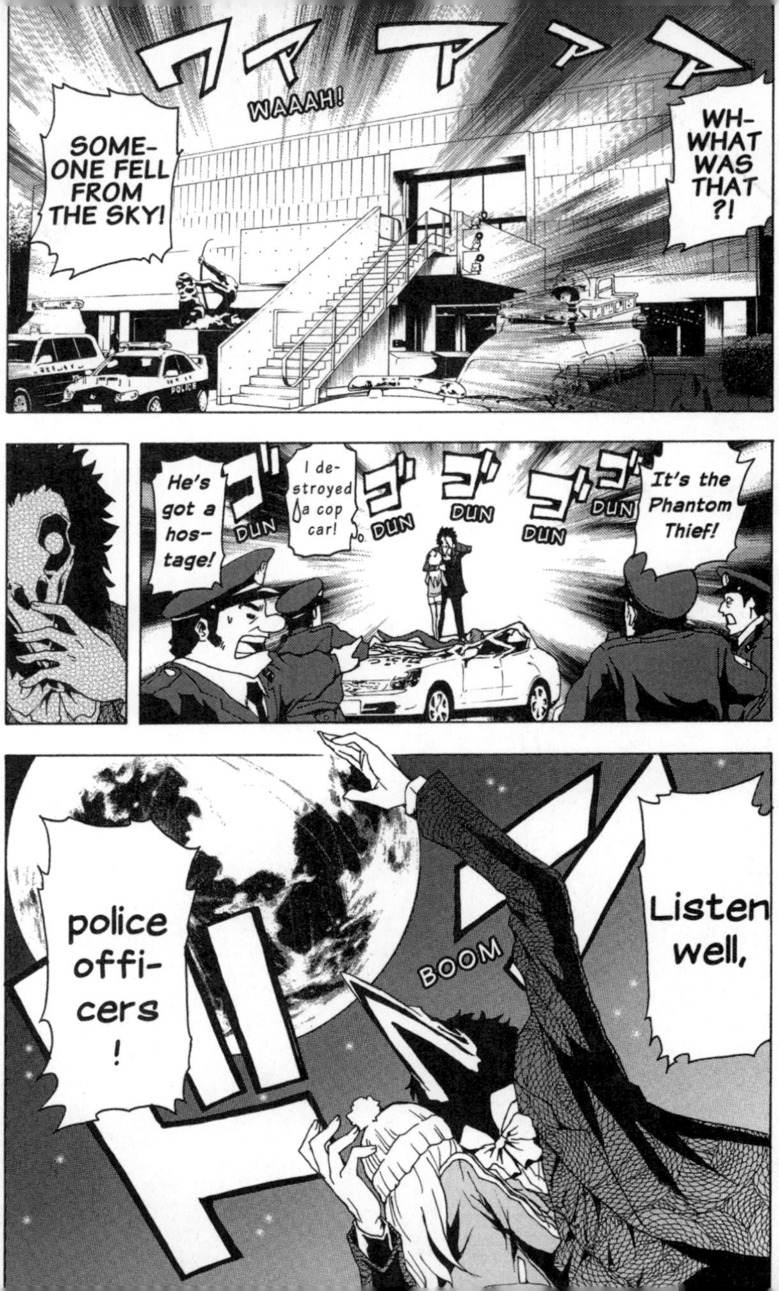
WAAAH!
WH-WHAT WAS THAT?!
SOME-ONE FELL FROM THE SKY!
It's the Phantom Thief!
DUN
DUN
DUN
DUN
I de-stroyed a cop car!
DUN
He's got a hos-tage!
Listen well,
BOOM
police offi-cers!

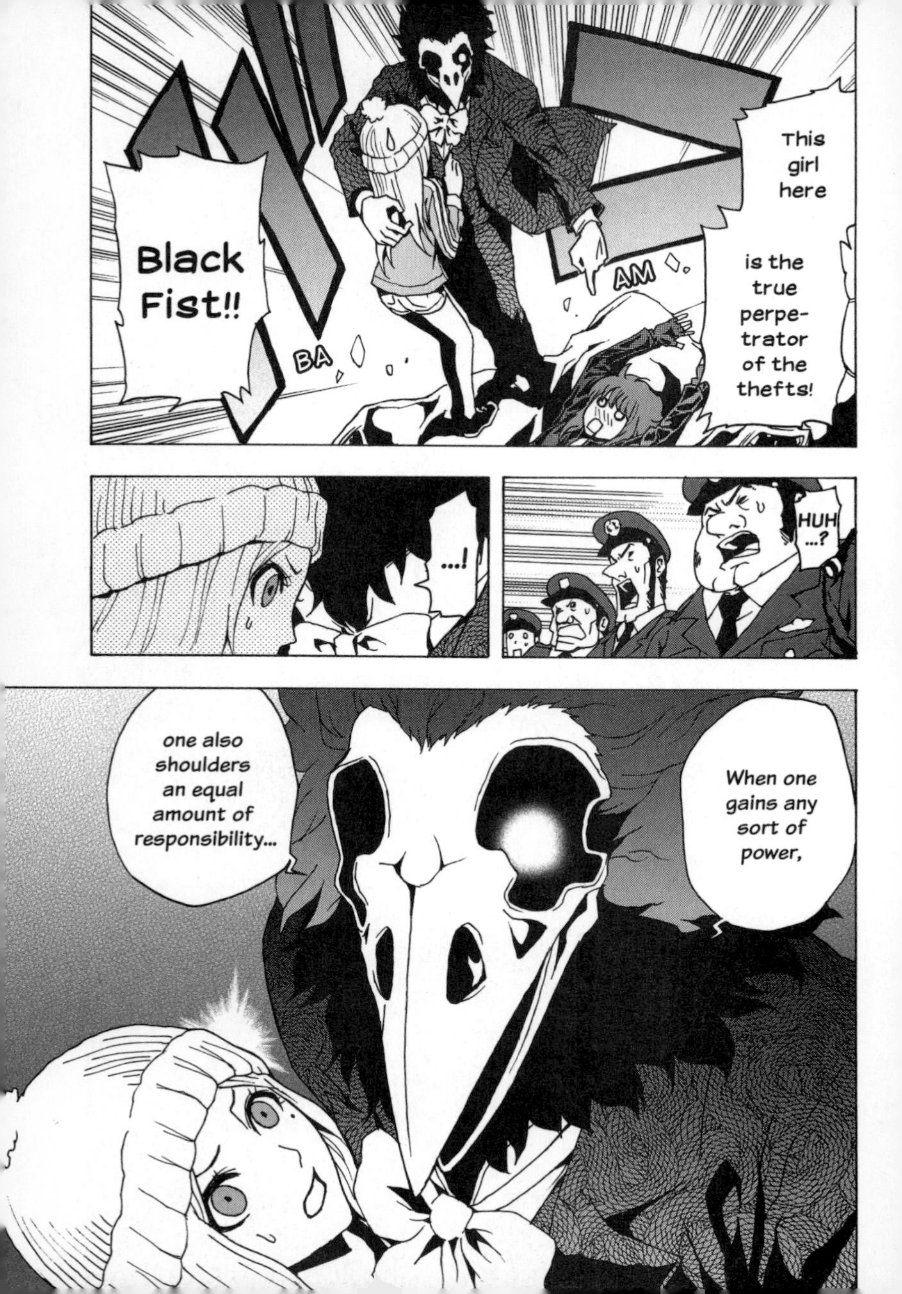
This girl here
is the true perpetrator of the thefts!
Black Fist!!
BA
AM
HUH ...?
...!
When one gains any sort of power,
one also shoulders an equal amount of responsibility...

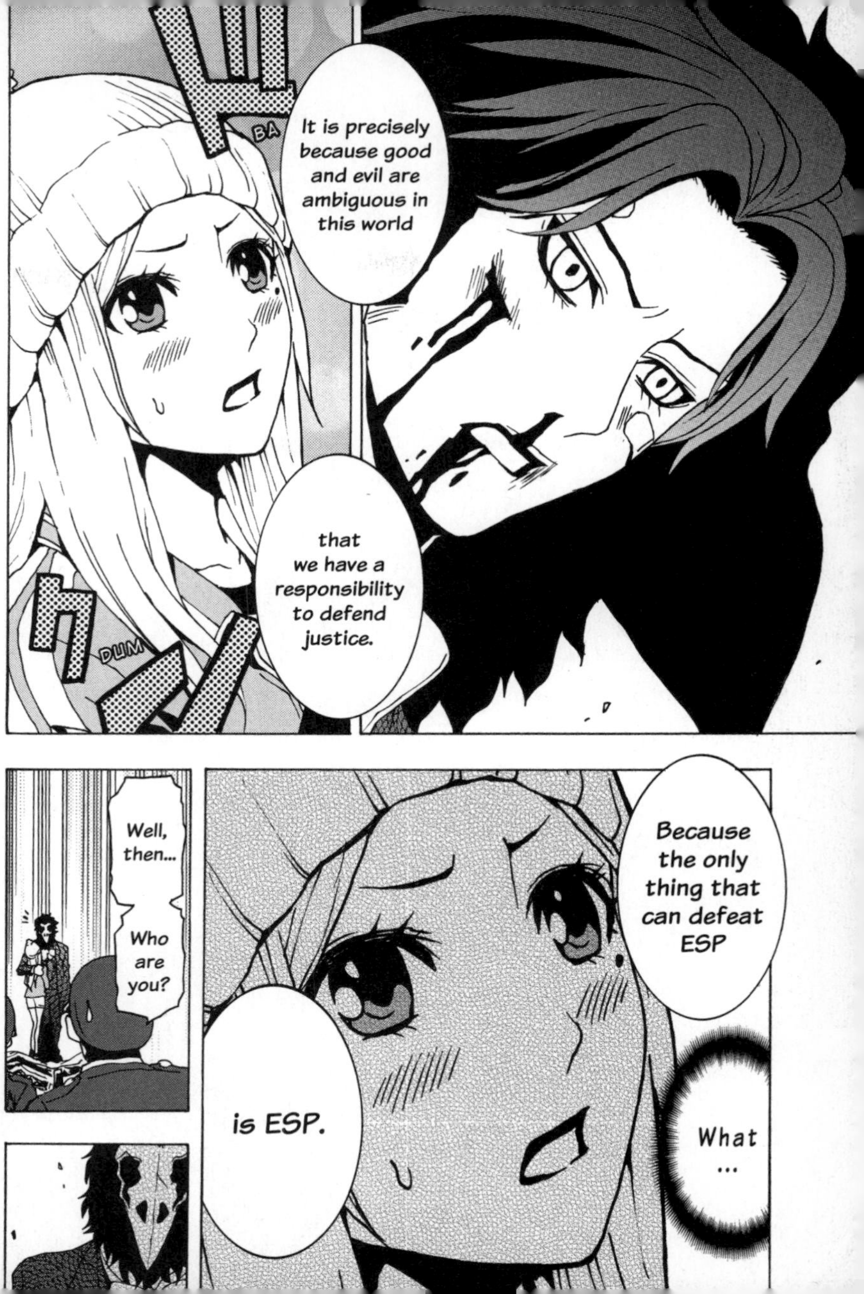
It is precisely because good and evil are ambiguous in this world
that we have a responsibility to defend justice.
BA
DUM
Because the only thing that can defeat ESP
is ESP.
What ...
Well, then...
Who are you?

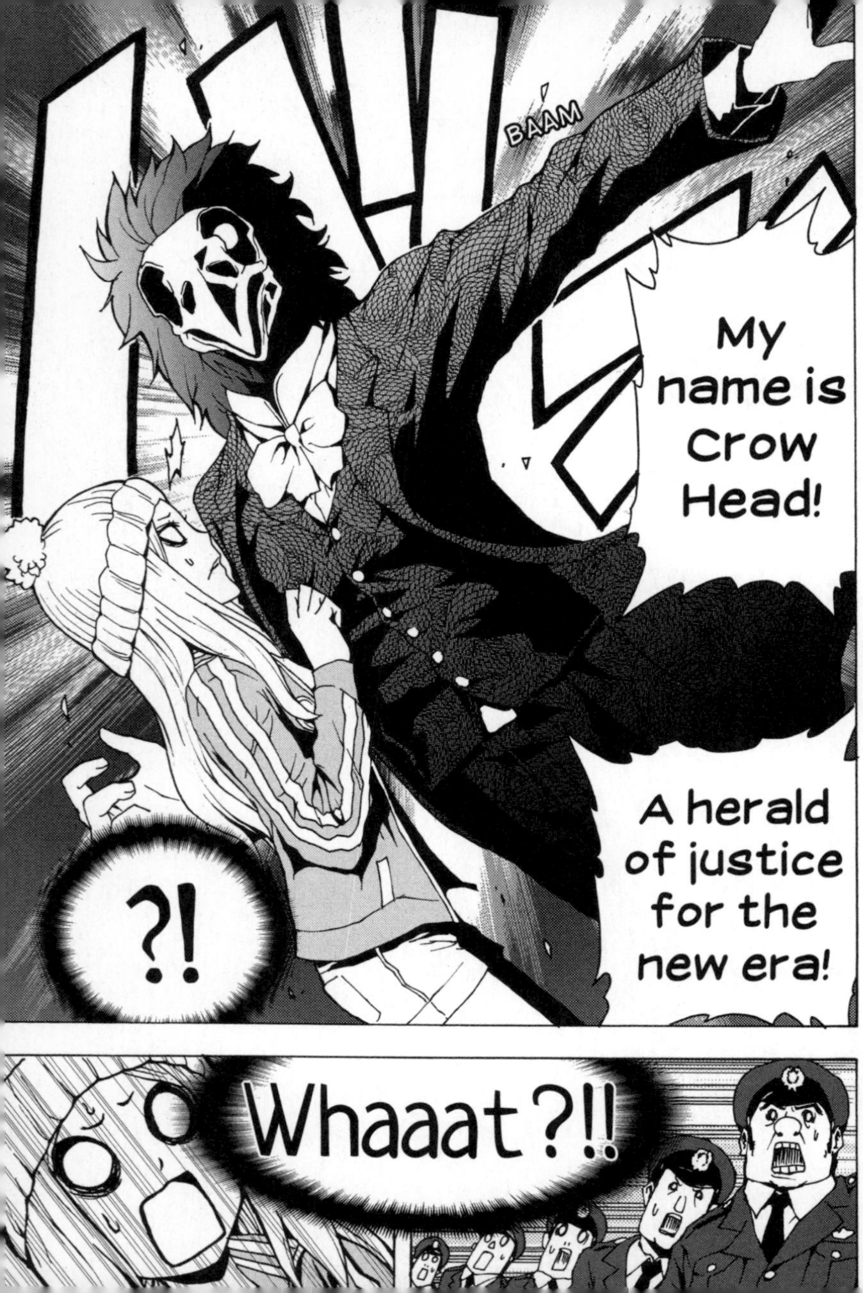
BAAM
My name is Crow Head!
A herald of justice for the new era!
?!
Whaaat?!!

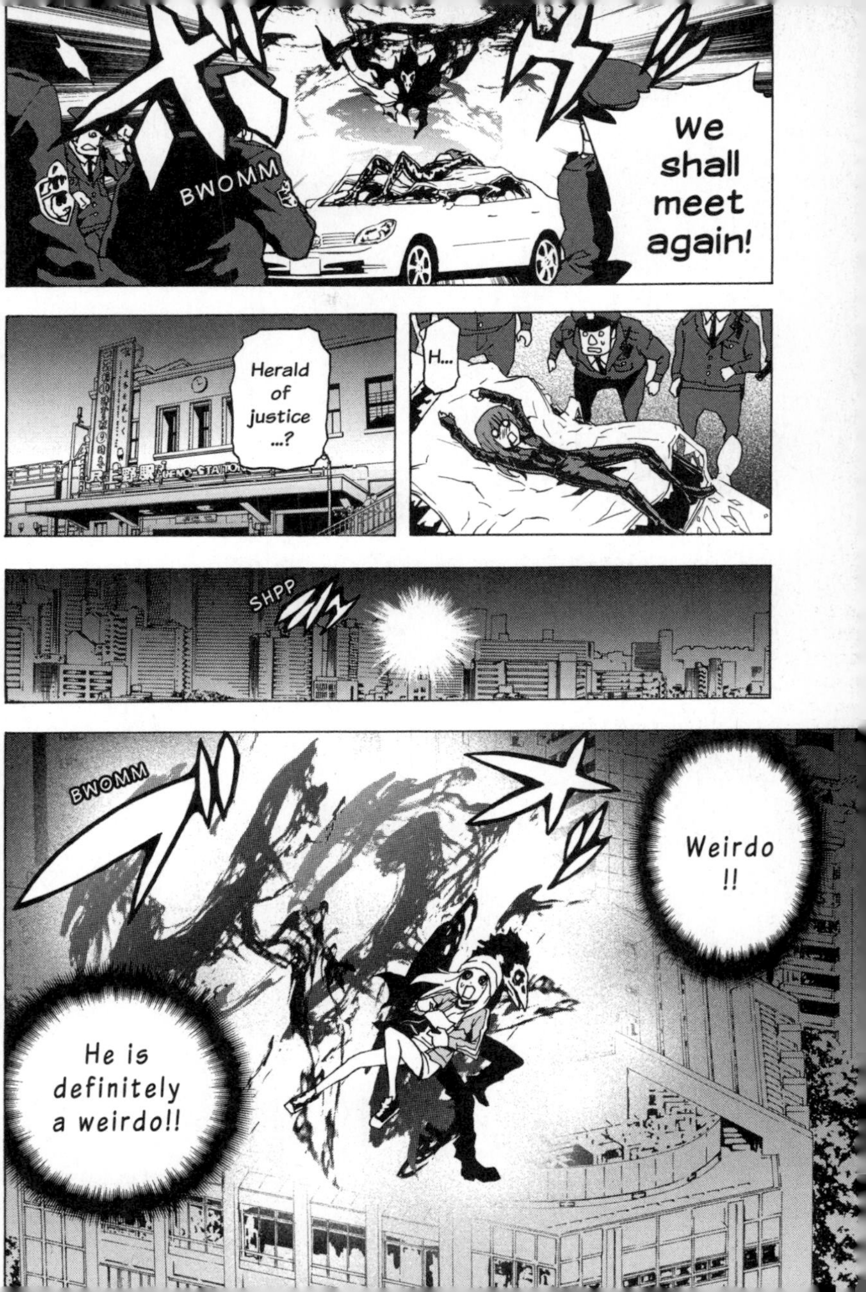
We shall meet again!
BWOMM
H...
Herald of justice ...?
SHPP
Weirdo !!
BWOMM
He is definitely a weirdo!!

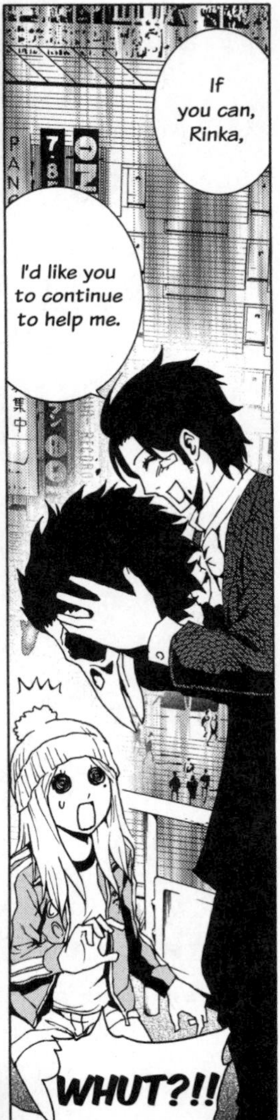
If you can, Rinka,
I'd like you to continue to help me.
WHUT?!!

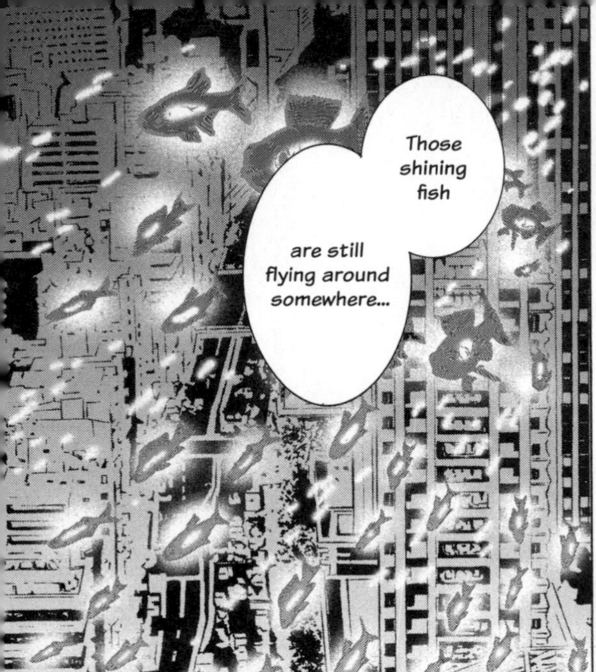
Those shining fish
are still flying around somewhere...
And there might still be others out there...

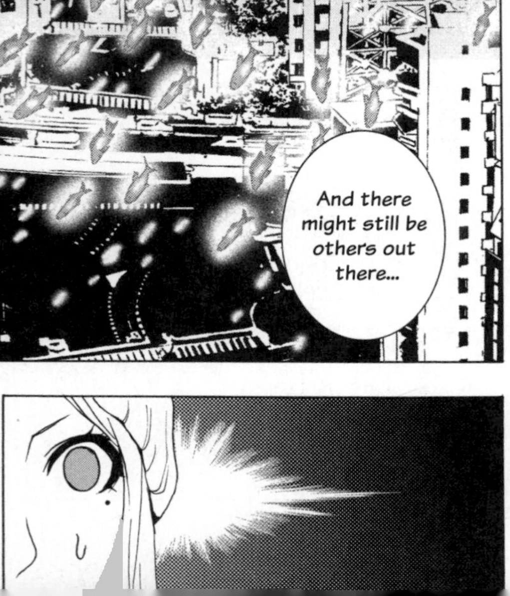

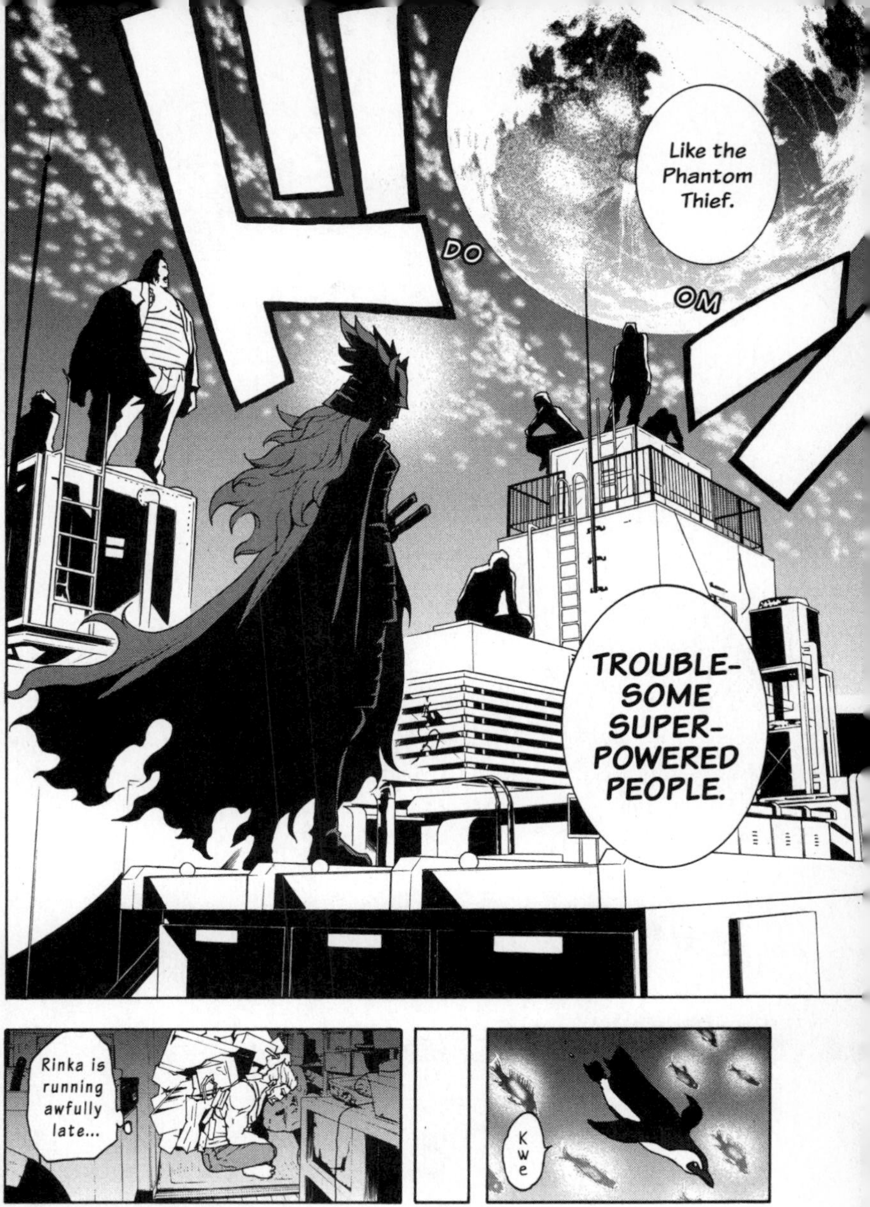
DO
OM
Like the Phantom Thief.
TROUBLE-SOME SUPER-POWERED PEOPLE.
Kwe
Rinka is running awfully late...

SCENE 2 /// END

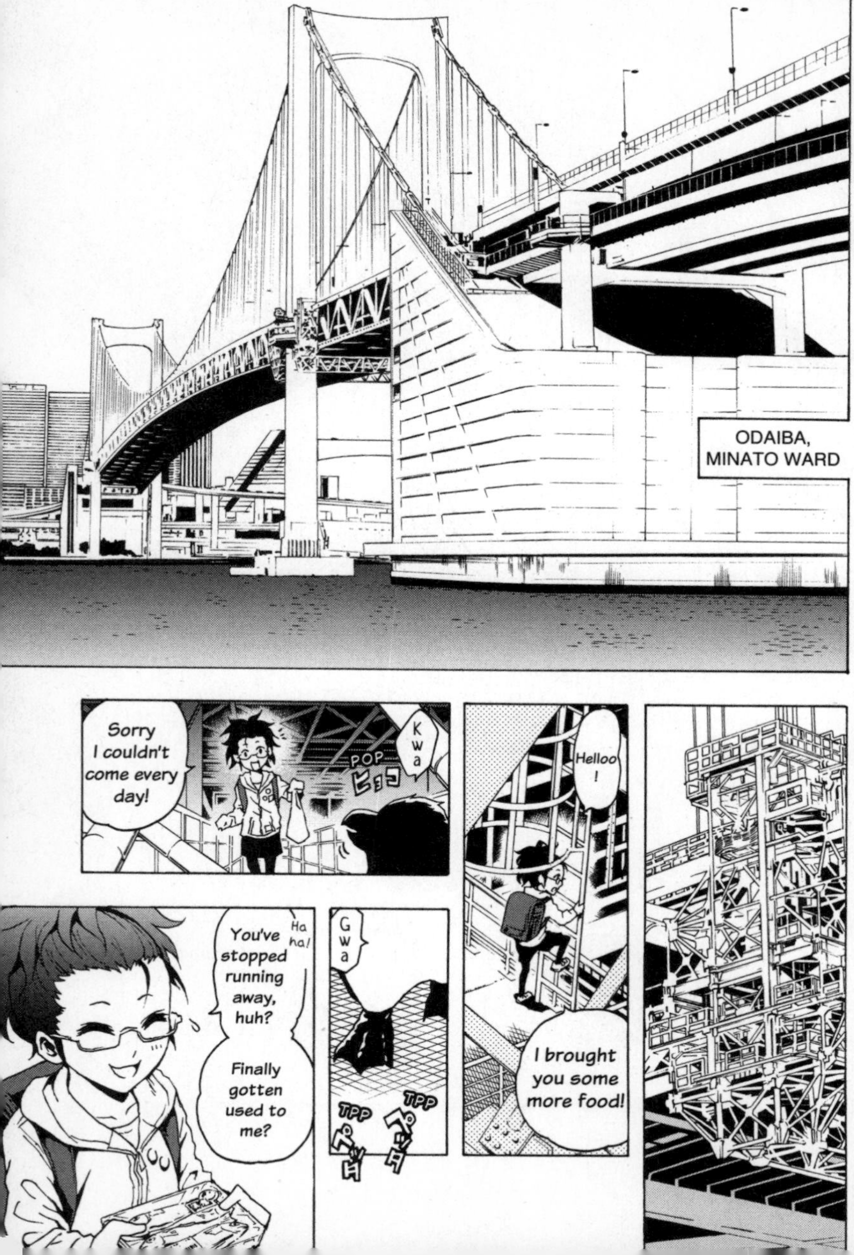
ODAIBA, MINATO WARD
Helloo!
I brought you some more food!
Sorry I couldn't come every day!
Kwa
POP
ヒョコ
Gwa
TPP
TPP
You've stopped running away, huh?
Ha ha!
Finally gotten used to me?

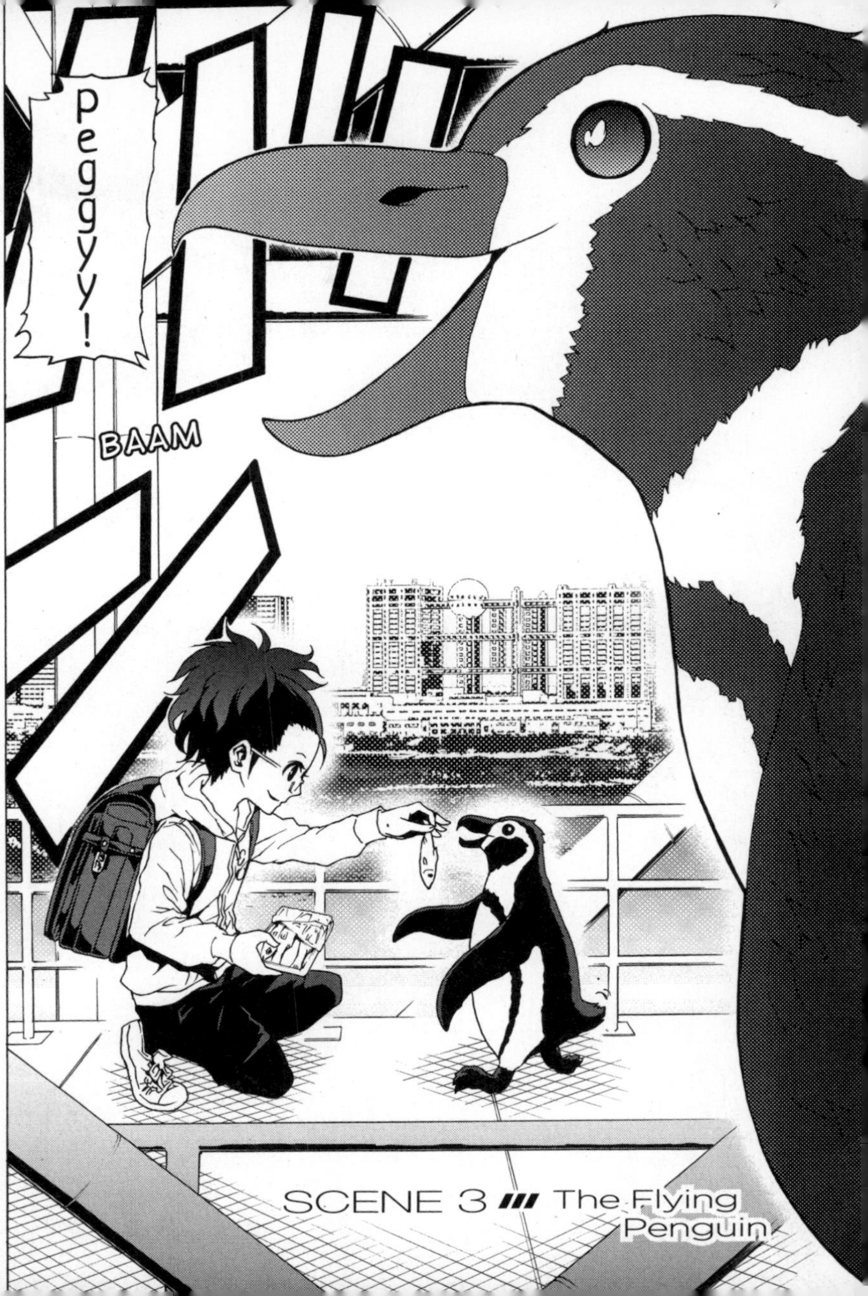
Peggyyy!
BAAM
SCENE 3 /// The Flying Penguin

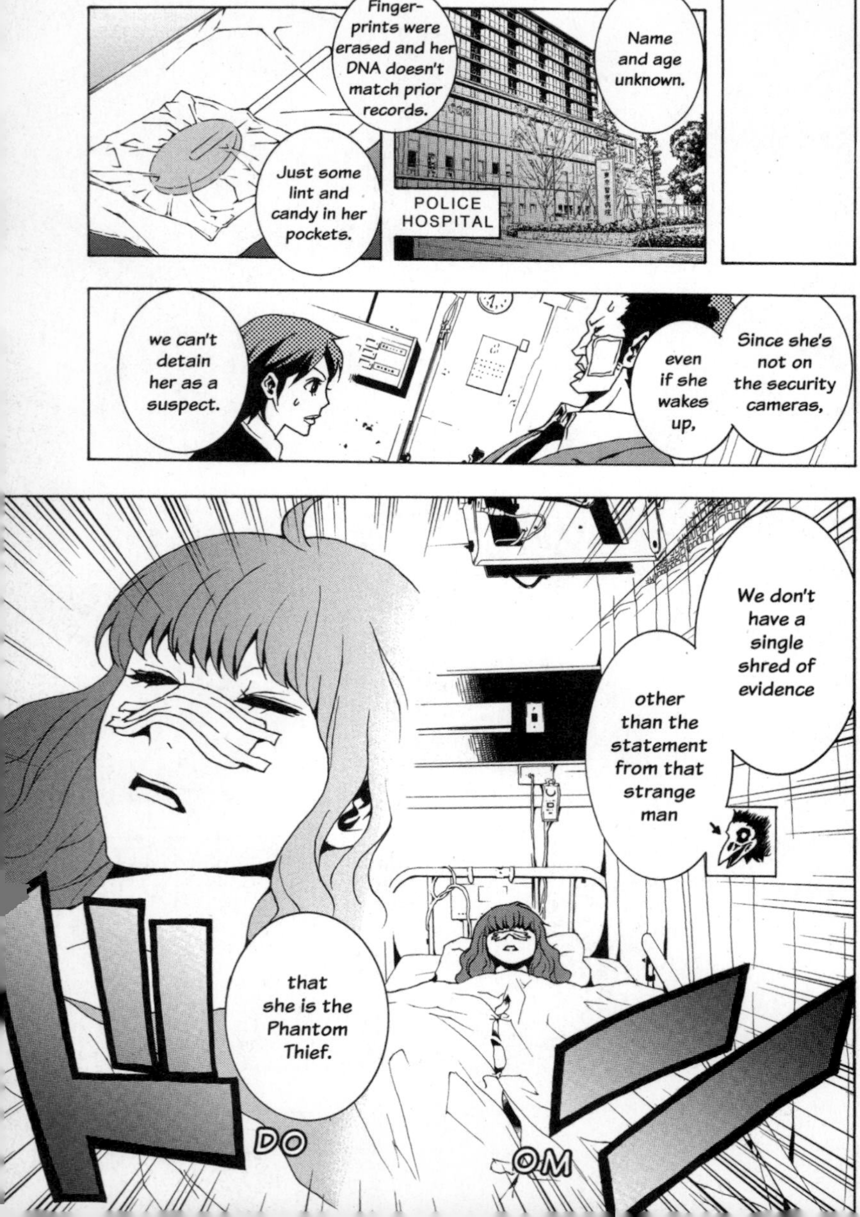
Name and age unknown.
Finger-prints were erased and her DNA doesn't match prior records.
POLICE HOSPITAL
Just some lint and candy in her pockets.
Since she's not on the security cameras,
even if she wakes up,
we can't detain her as a suspect.
We don't have a single shred of evidence
other than the statement from that strange man
that she is the Phantom Thief.
DO
OM

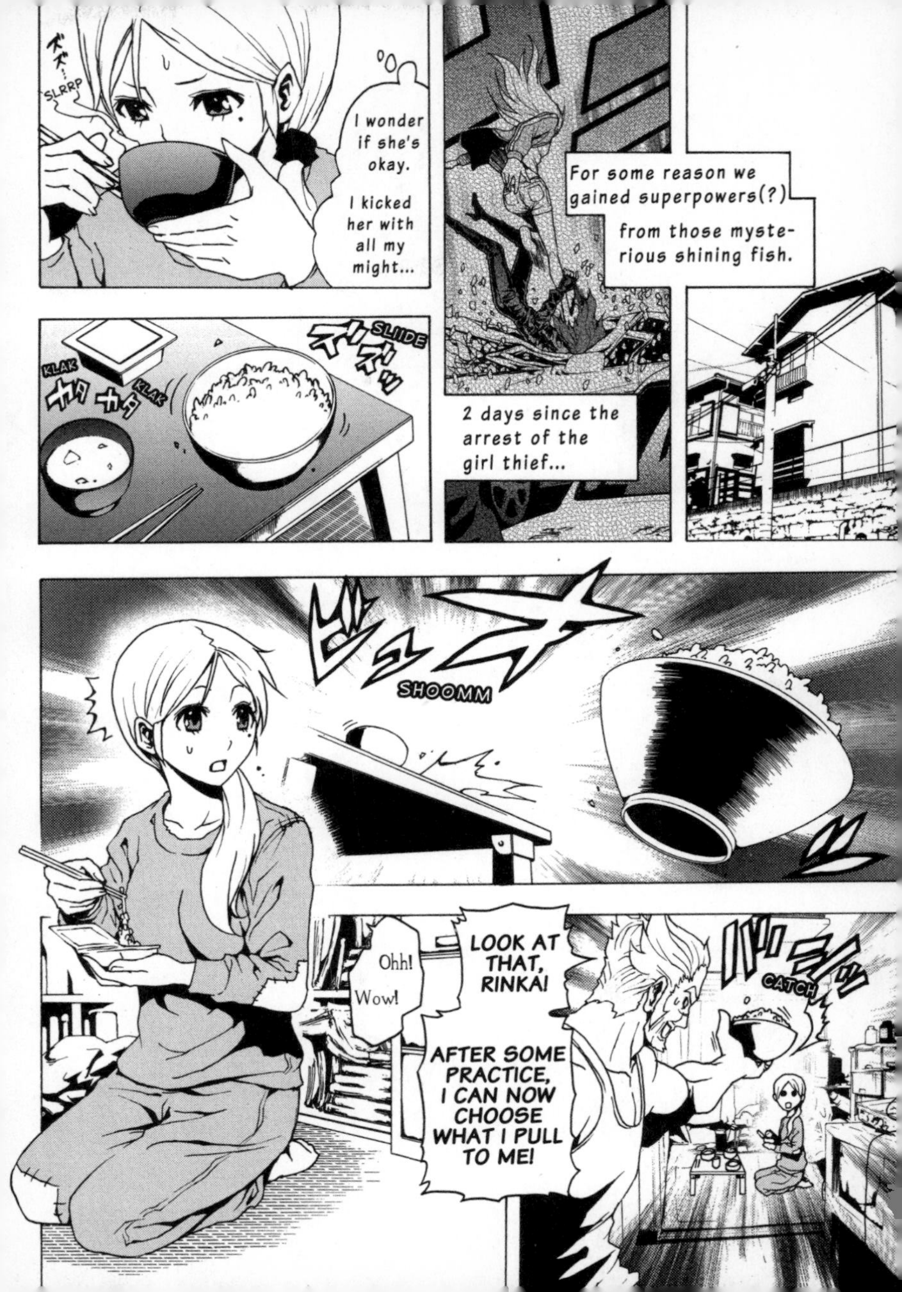
For some reason we gained superpowers(?)
from those mysterious shining fish.
2 days since the arrest of the girl thief...
SLRRP
I wonder if she's okay.
I kicked her with all my might...
SLIIDE
KLAK
KLAK
SHOOMM
CATCH
LOOK AT THAT, RINKA!
AFTER SOME PRACTICE, I CAN NOW CHOOSE WHAT I PULL TO ME!
Ohh!
Wow!

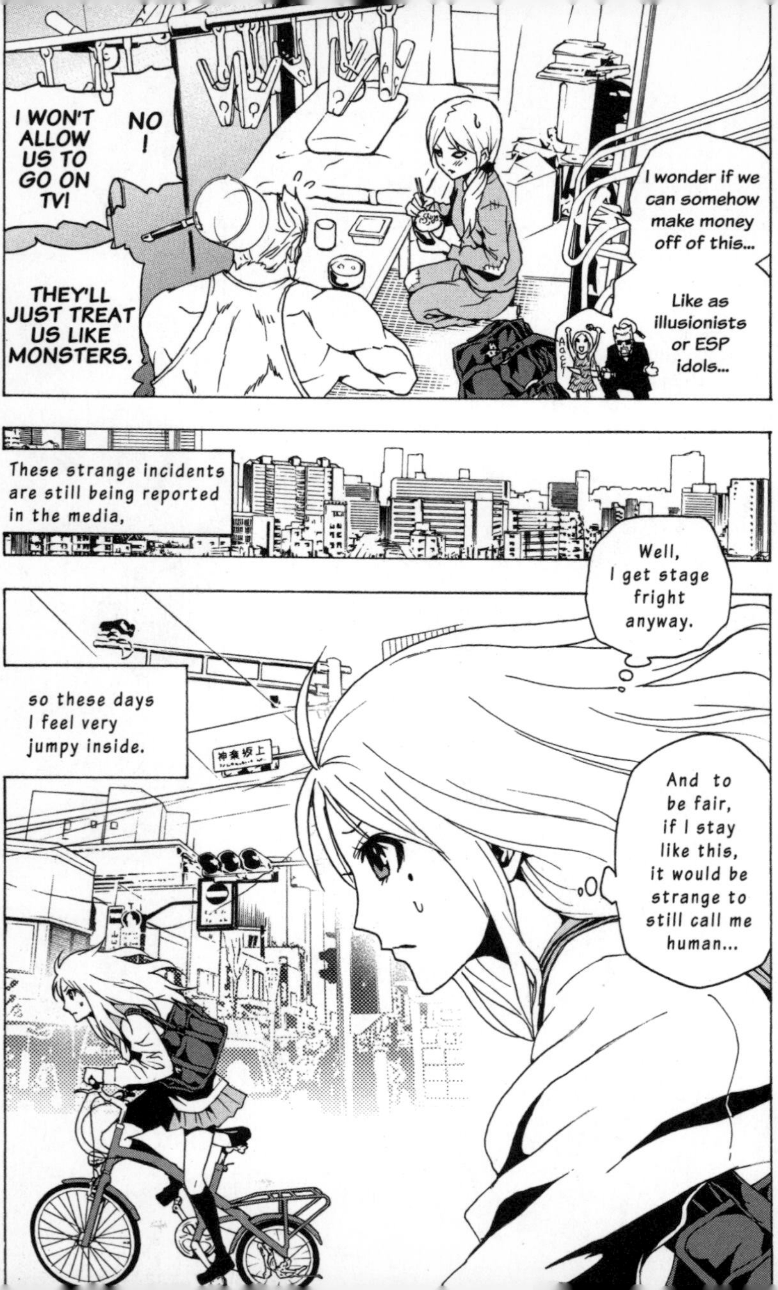
I wonder if we can somehow make money off of this...
Like as illusionists or ESP idols...
NO!
I WON'T ALLOW US TO GO ON TV!
THEY'LL JUST TREAT US LIKE MONSTERS.
These strange incidents are still being reported in the media,
Well, I get stage fright anyway.
And to be fair, if I stay like this, it would be strange to still call me human...
so these days I feel very jumpy inside.
神楽坂上

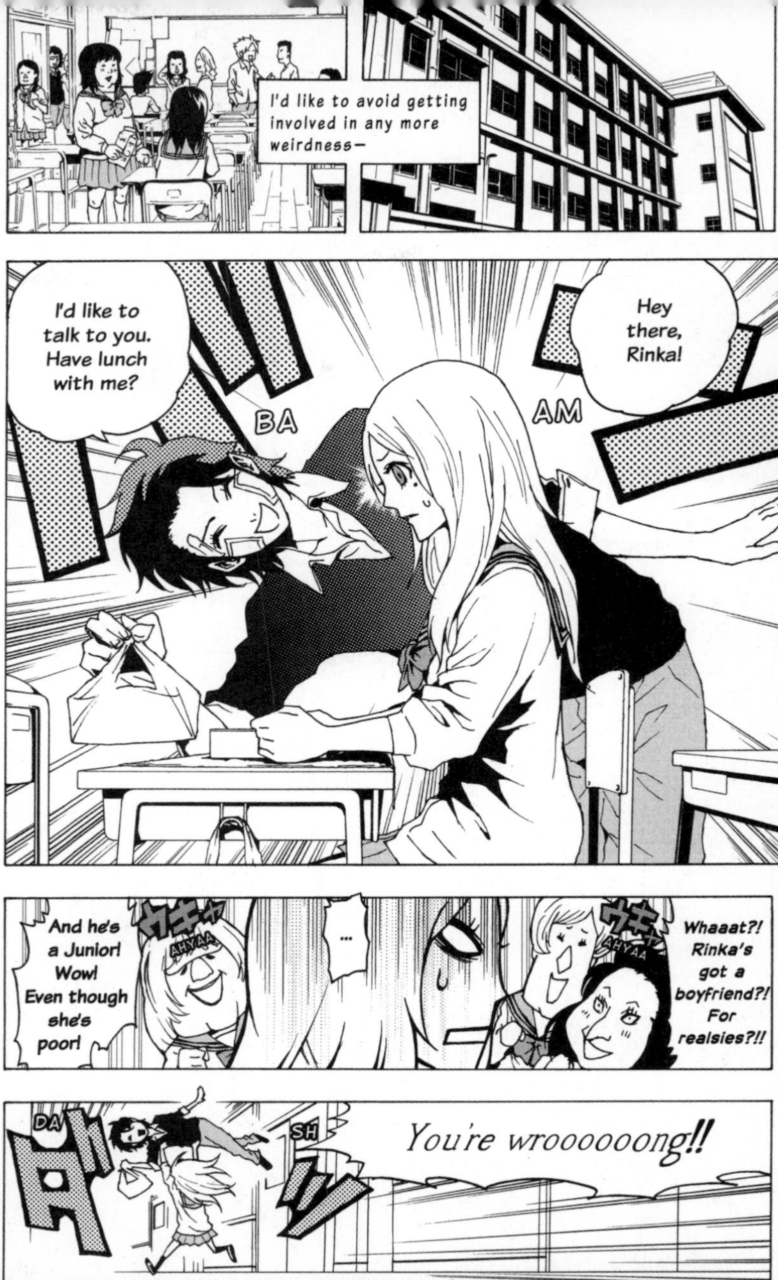
I'd like to avoid getting involved in any more weirdness—
Hey there, Rinka!
BA
AM
I'd like to talk to you. Have lunch with me?
Whaaat?! Rinka's got a boyfriend?! For realsies?!!
AHYAA
...
AHYAA
And he's a Junior! Wow! Even though she's poor!
You're wroooooong!!
SH
DA

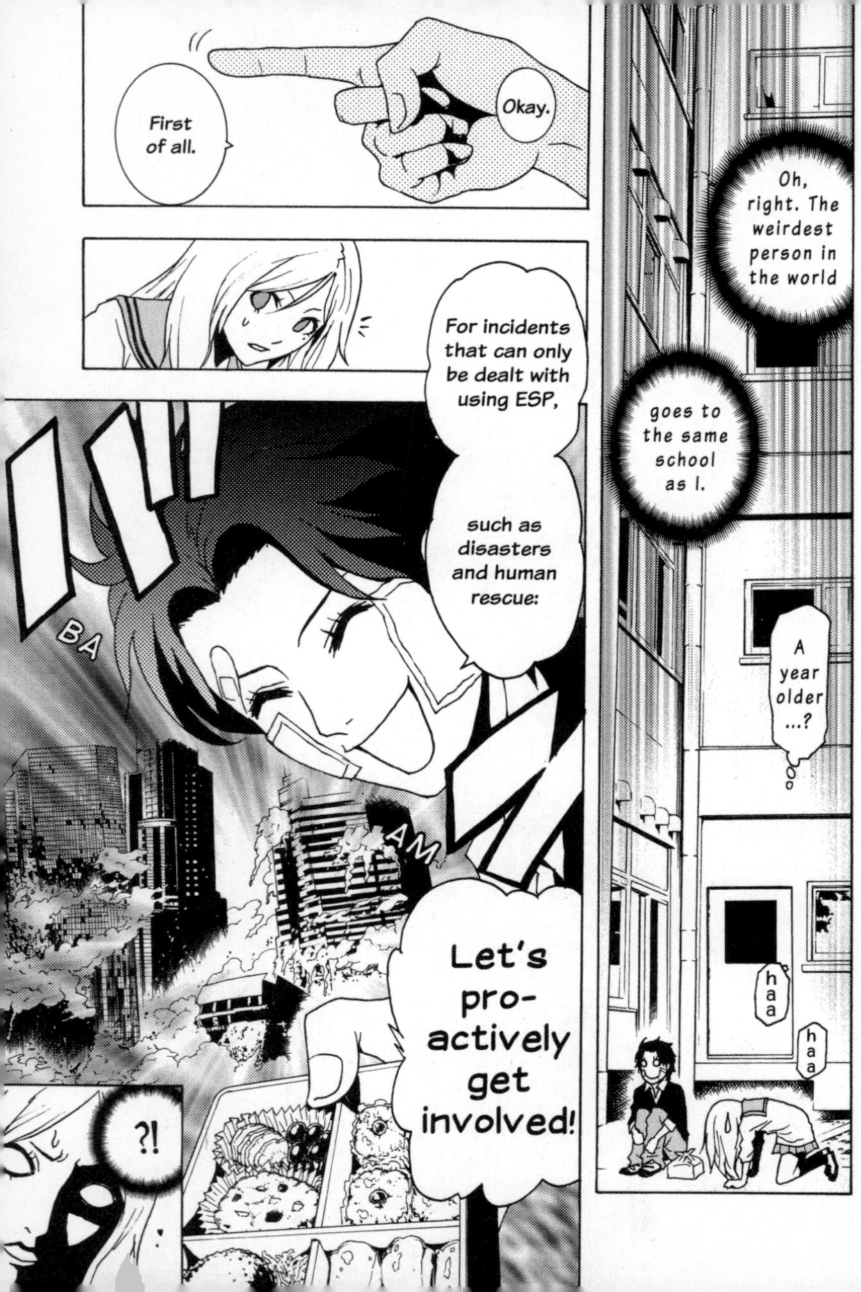
Oh, right. The weirdest person in the world
goes to the same school as I.
A year older ...?
haa
haa
Okay.
First of all.
For incidents that can only be dealt with using ESP,
such as disasters and human rescue:
BA
AM
Let's pro-actively get involved!
?!

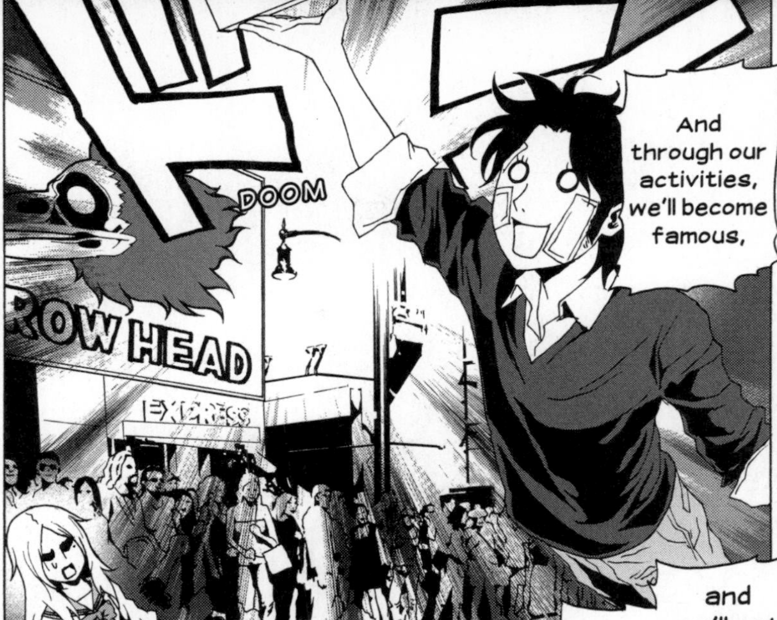
And through our activities, we'll become famous,
DOOM
ROW HEAD
EXPRESS
and we'll get support from the masses
and the media will be our allies!
HOORAAY
Huhn ?!

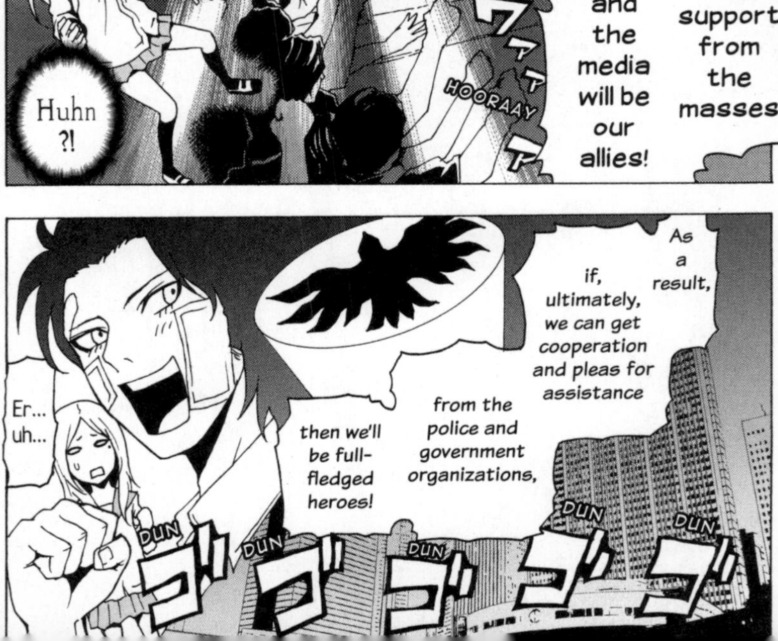
As a result,
if, ultimately, we can get cooperation and pleas for assistance
from the police and government organizations,
then we'll be full-fledged heroes!
Er... uh...
DUN
DUN
DUN
DUN
DUN

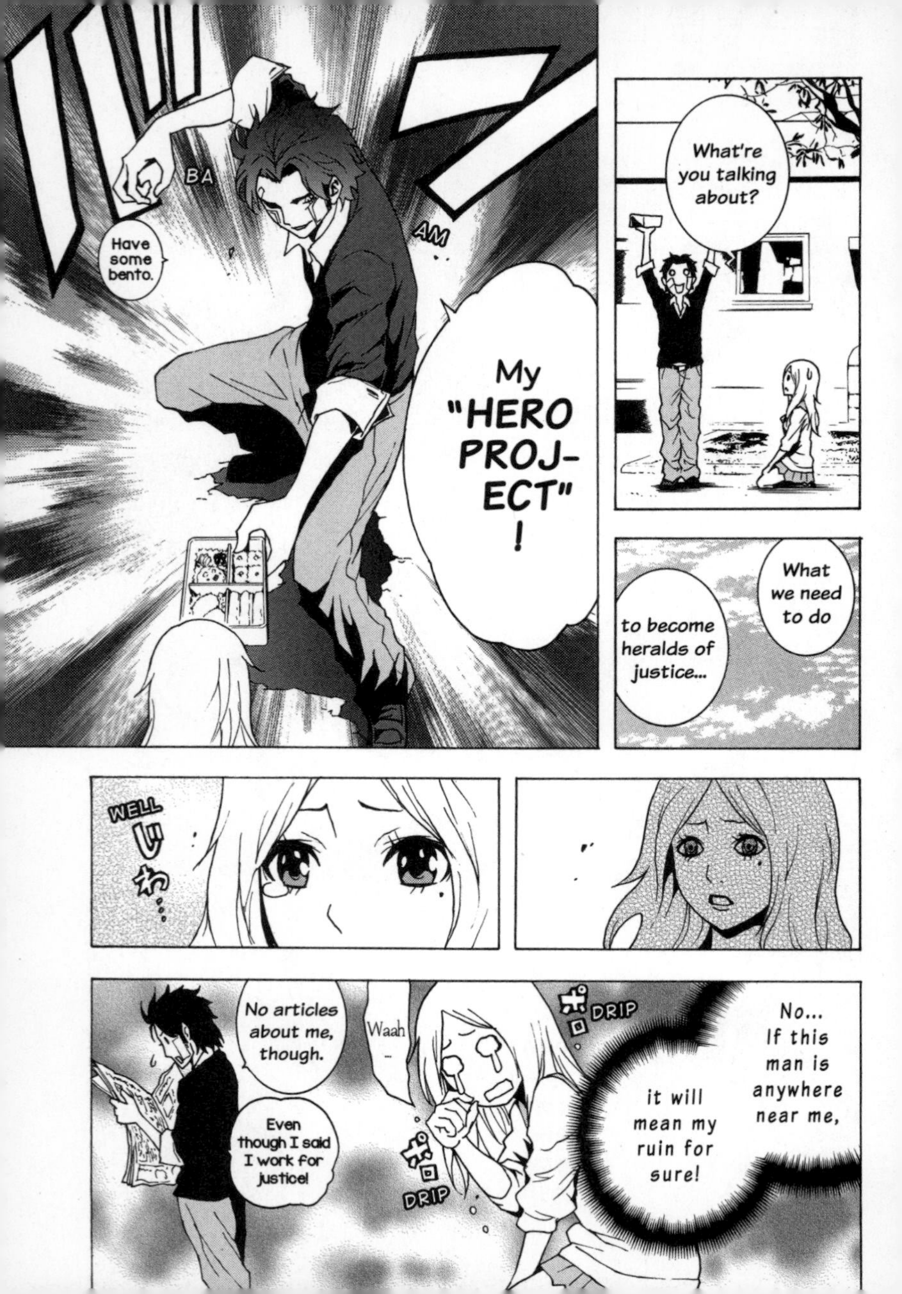
What're you talking about?
What we need to do
to become heralds of justice...
My "HERO PROJECT"!
BA
AM
Have some bento.
WELL
じわ…
No... If this man is anywhere near me,
it will mean my ruin for sure!
ポロ DRIP
ポロ DRIP
Waah...
No articles about me, though.
Even though I said I work for justice!

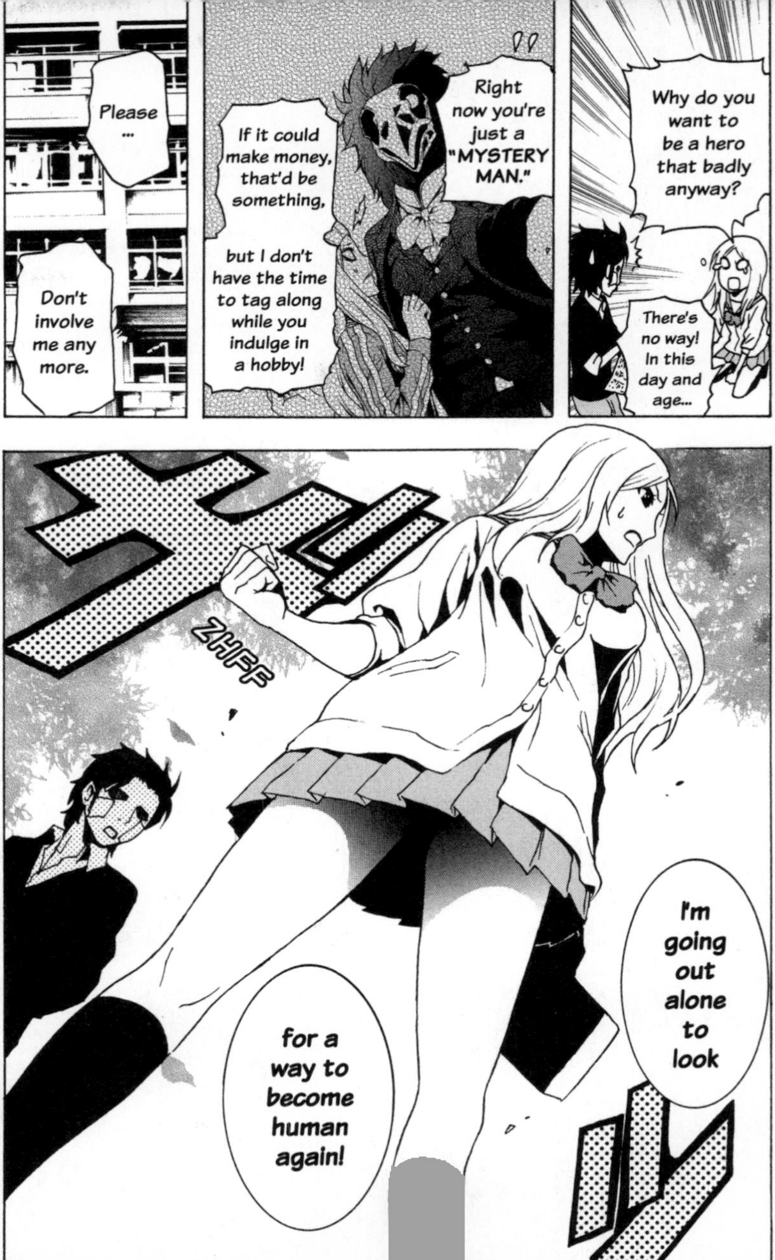
Why do you want to be a hero that badly anyway?
There's no way! In this day and age...
Right now you're just a "MYSTERY MAN."
If it could make money, that'd be something,
but I don't have the time to tag along while you indulge in a hobby!
Please ...
Don't involve me any more.
ZHFF
I'm going out alone to look
for a way to become human again!

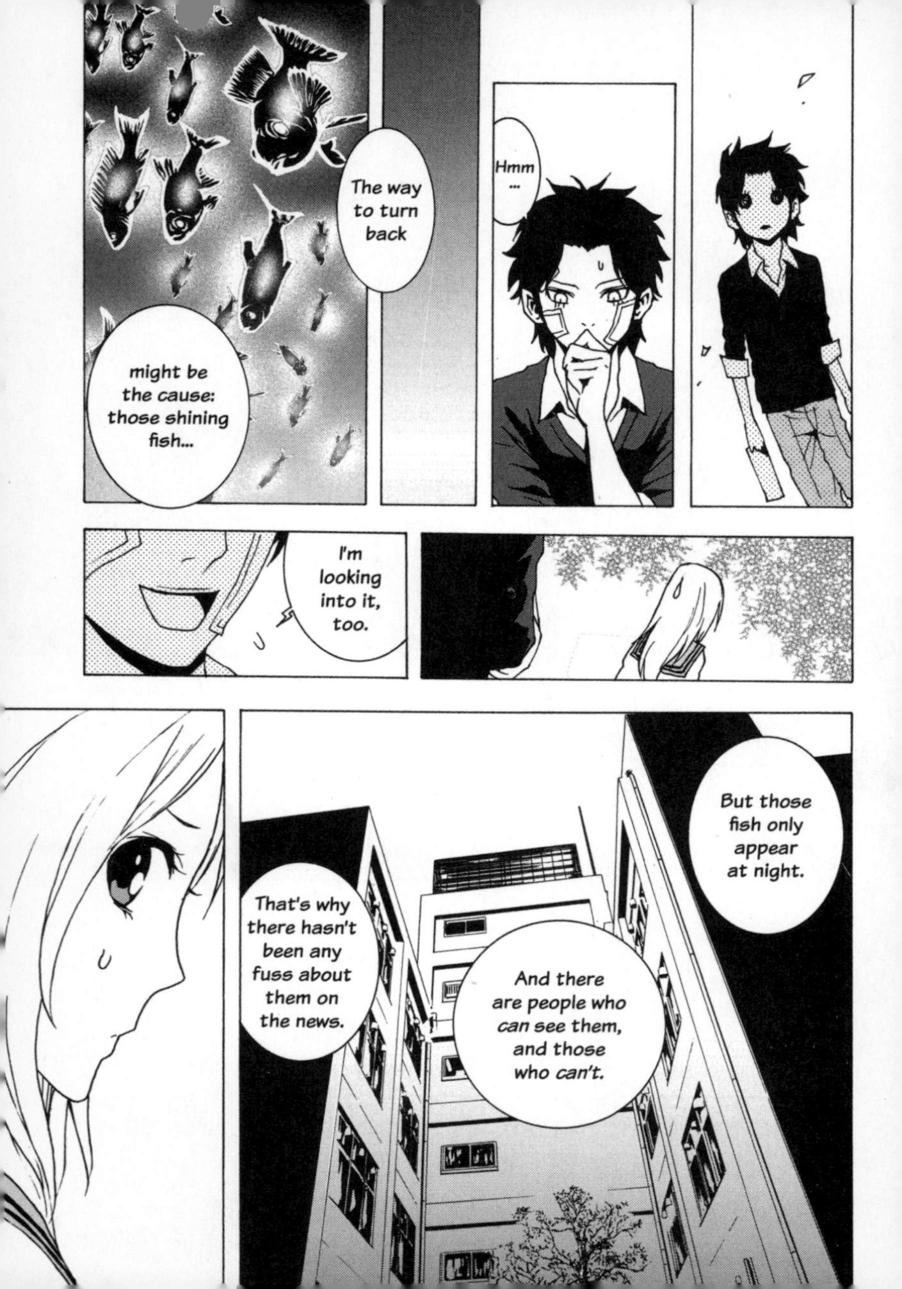
Hmm ...
The way to turn back
might be the cause: those shining fish...
I'm looking into it, too.
But those fish only appear at night.
That's why there hasn't been any fuss about them on the news.
And there are people who *can* see them, and those who *can't*.

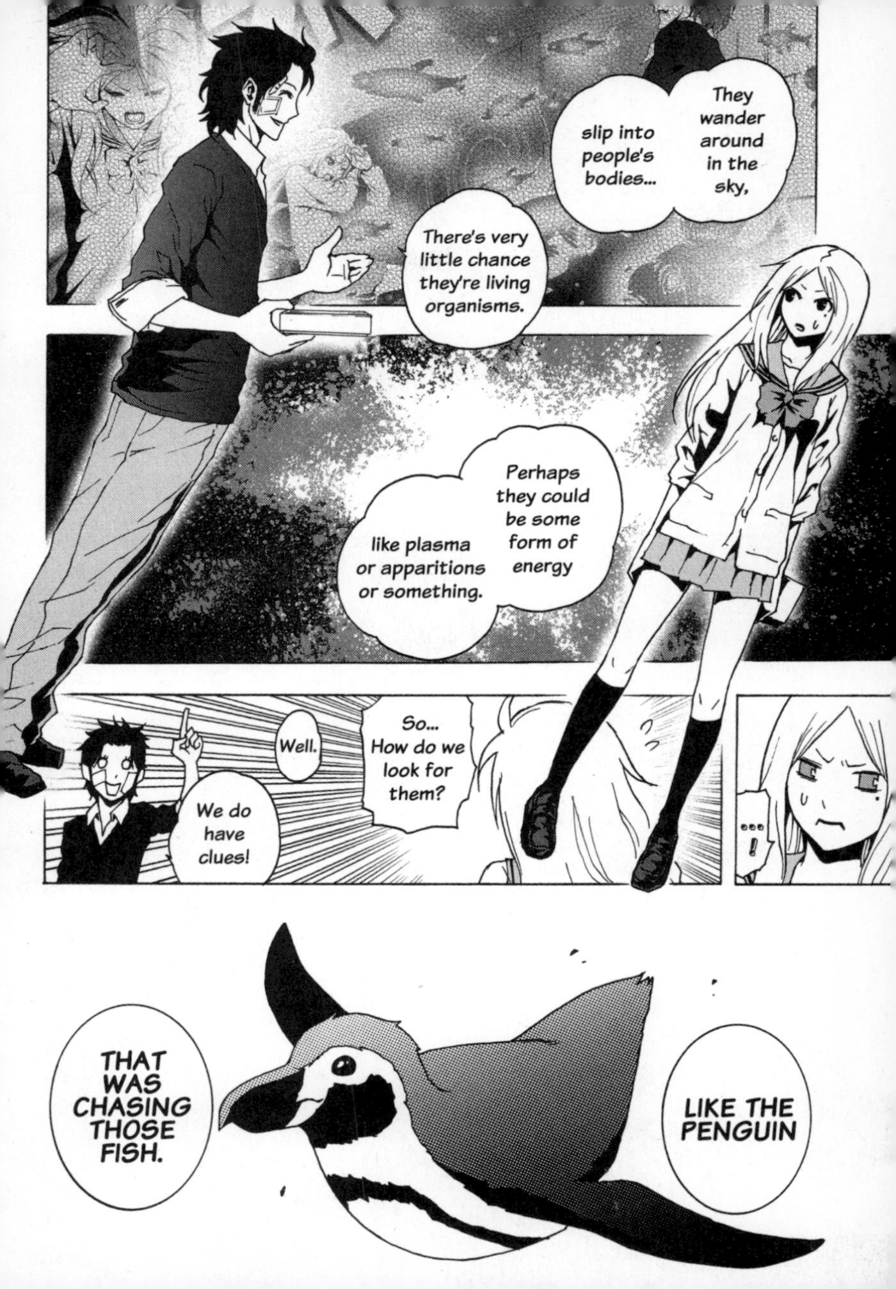
They wander around in the sky,
slip into people's bodies...
There's very little chance they're living organisms.
Perhaps they could be some form of energy
like plasma or apparitions or something.
...!
So... How do we look for them?
Well.
We do have clues!
LIKE THE PENGUIN
THAT WAS CHASING THOSE FISH.

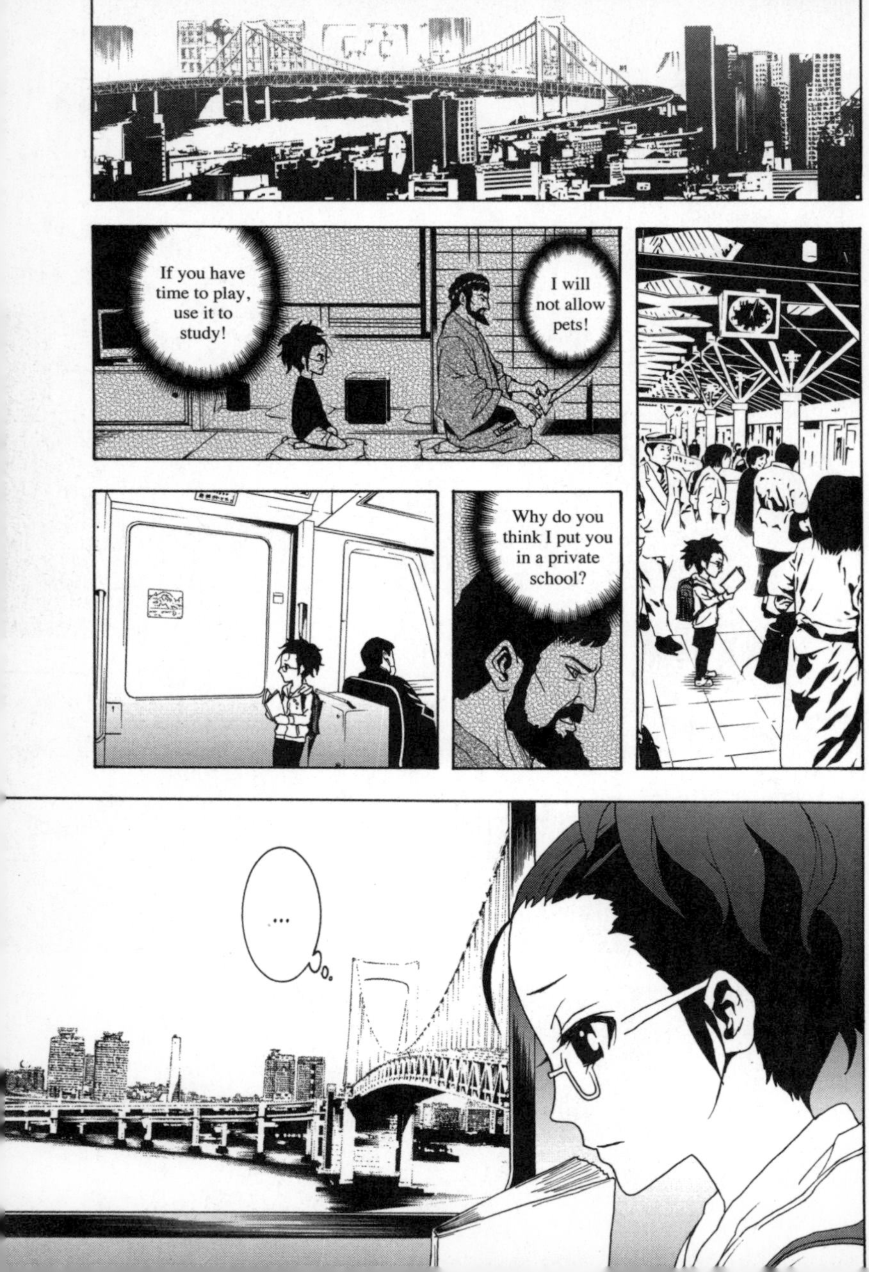
I will not allow pets!
If you have time to play, use it to study!
Why do you think I put you in a private school?
...

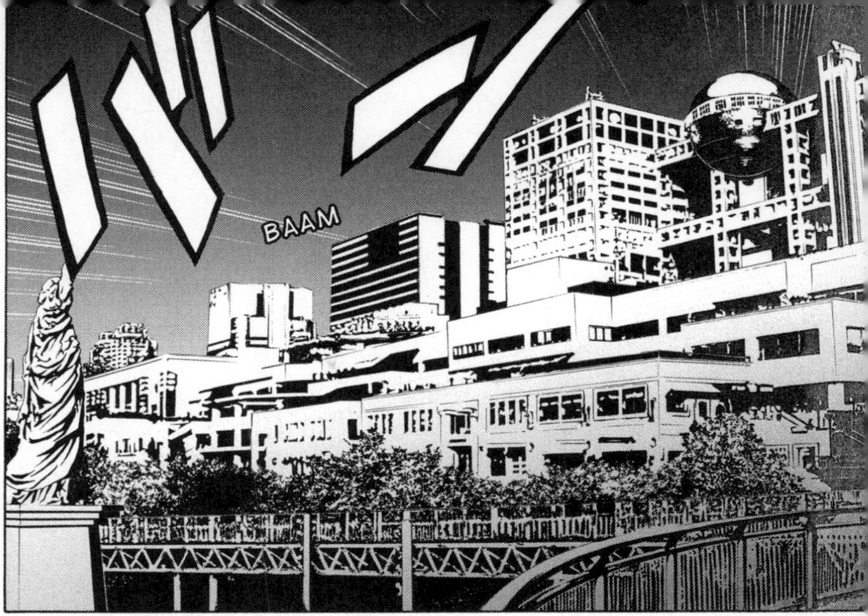
BAAM

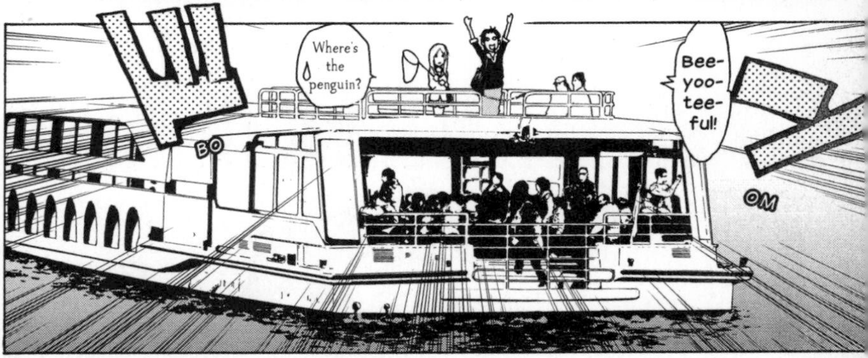
Bee-yoo-tee-ful!
Where's the penguin?
BO
OM

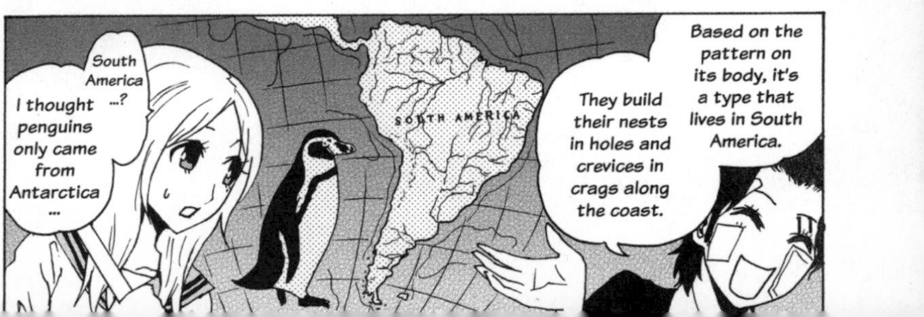
Based on the pattern on its body, it's a type that lives in South America.
They build their nests in holes and crevices in crags along the coast.
SOUTH AMERICA
South America ...?
I thought penguins only came from Antarctica ...

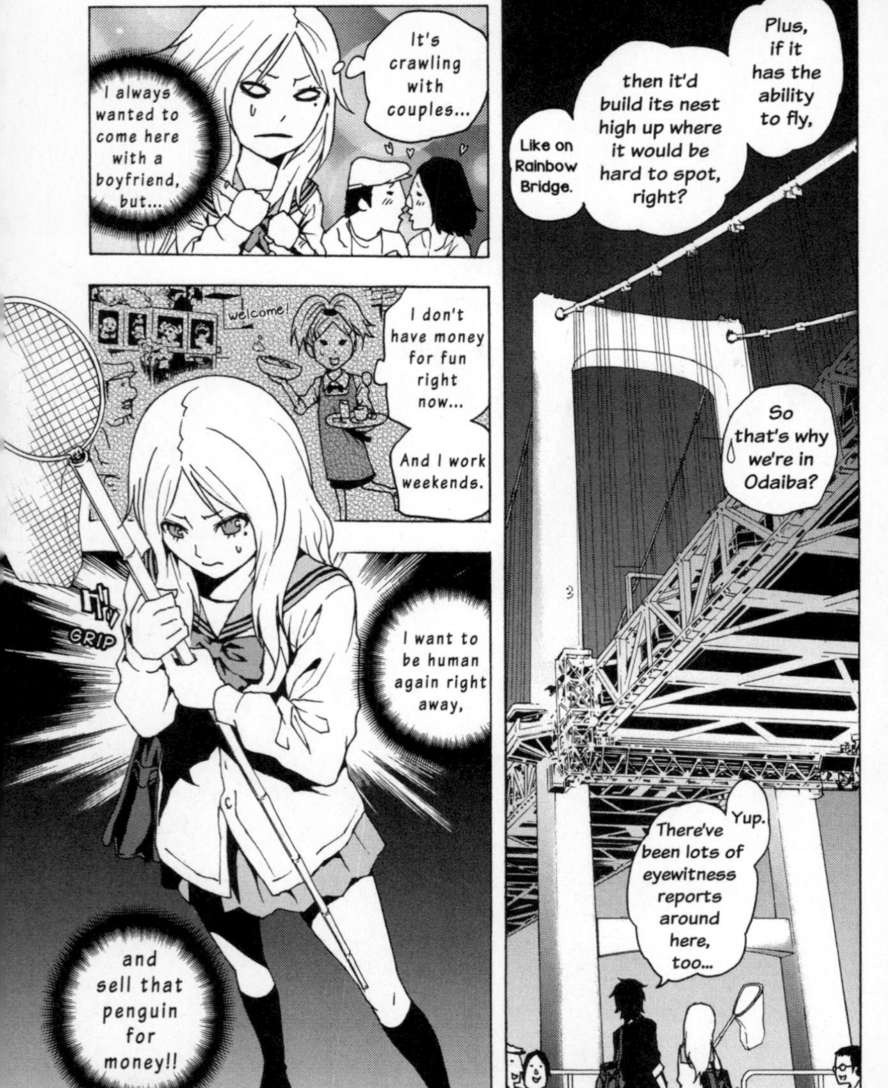
Plus, if it has the ability to fly,
then it'd build its nest high up where it would be hard to spot, right?
Like on Rainbow Bridge.
So that's why we're in Odaiba?
Yup.
There've been lots of eyewitness reports around here, too...
It's crawling with couples...
I always wanted to come here with a boyfriend, but...
I don't have money for fun right now...
And I work weekends.
welcome!
I want to be human again right away,
GRIP
and sell that penguin for money!!

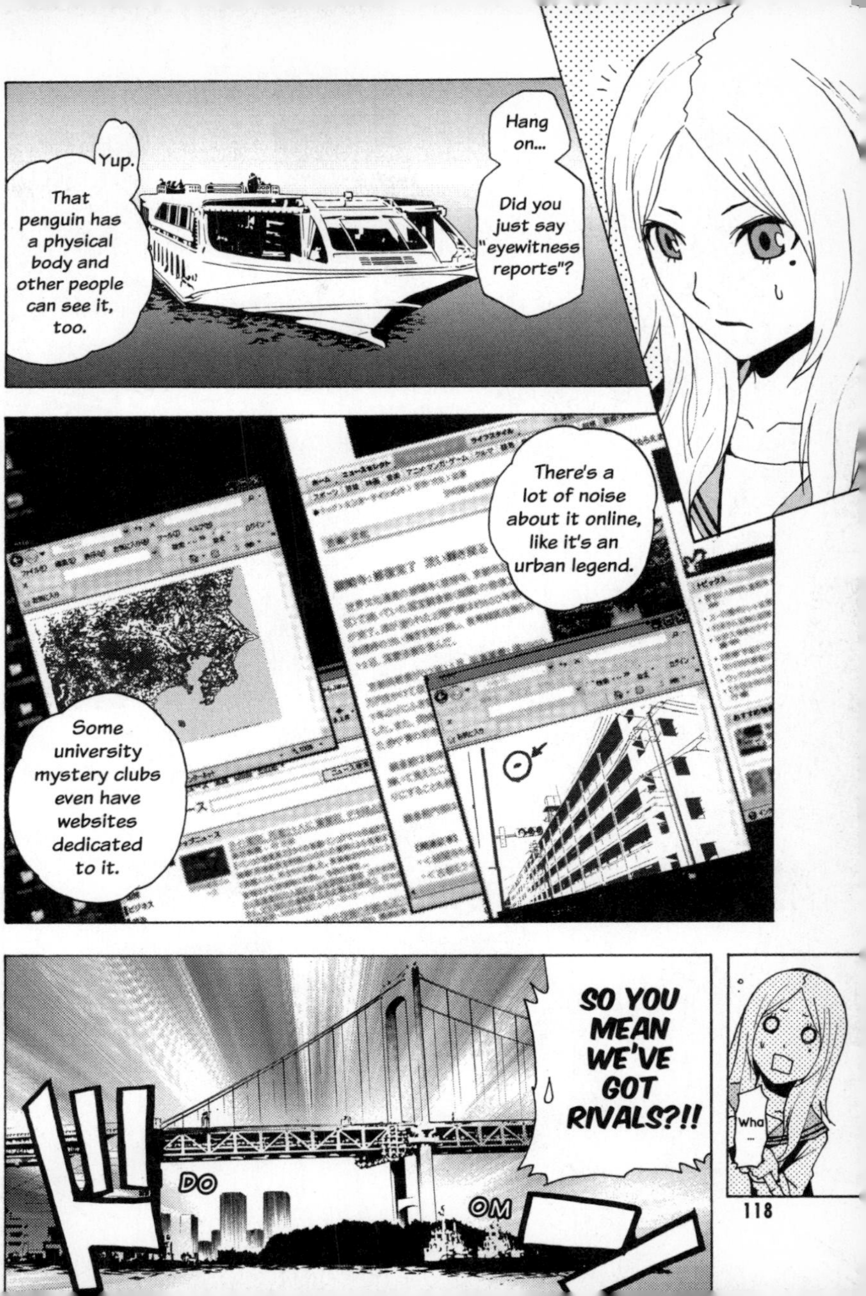
Hang on...
Did you just say "eyewitness reports"?
Yup.
That penguin has a physical body and other people can see it, too.
There's a lot of noise about it online, like it's an urban legend.
Some university mystery clubs even have websites dedicated to it.
Wha...
SO YOU MEAN WE'VE GOT RIVALS?!!
DO
OM

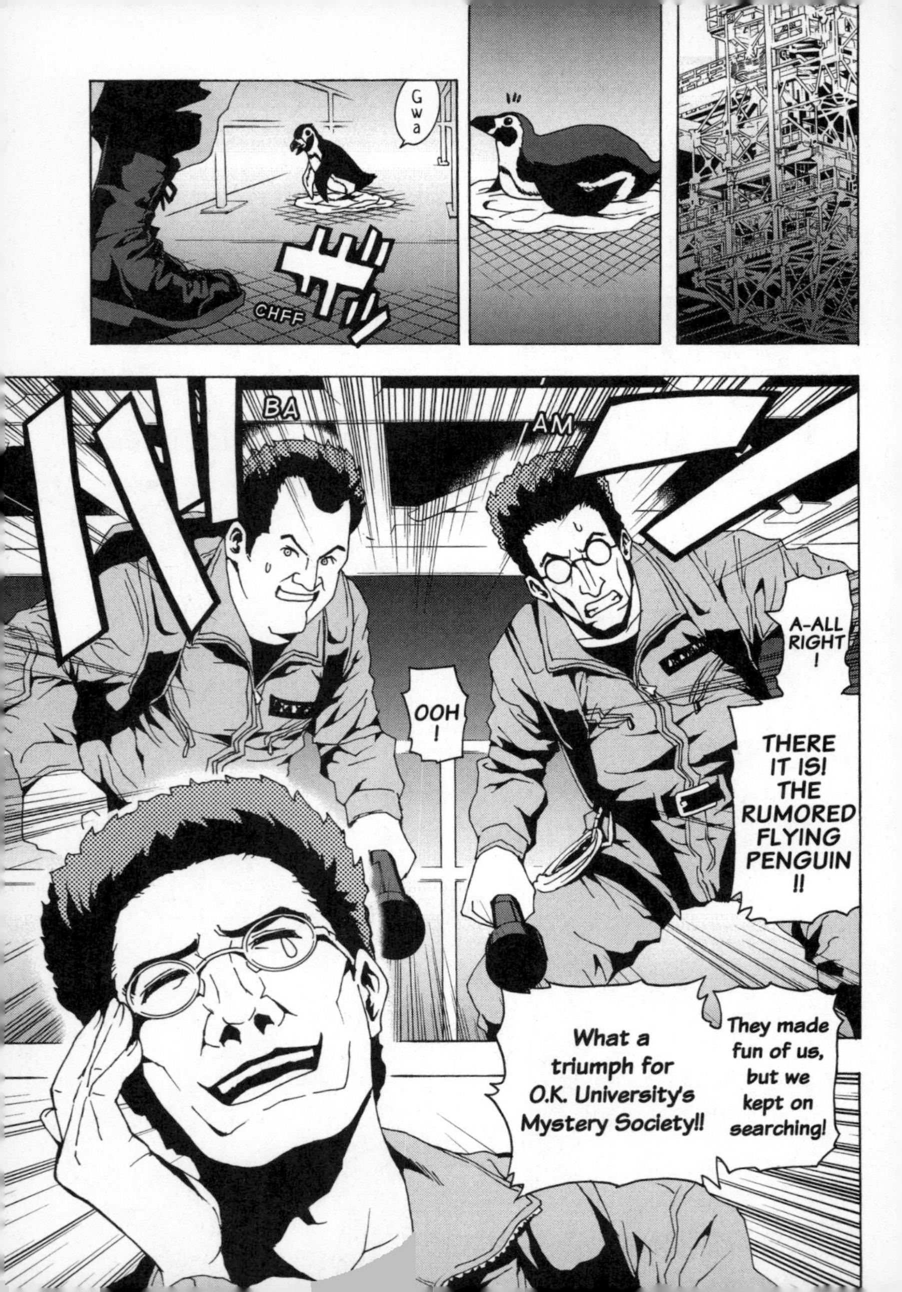
Gwa
CHFF
A-ALL RIGHT!
THERE IT IS! THE RUMORED FLYING PENGUIN!!
OOH!
BA AM
They made fun of us, but we kept on searching!
What a triumph for O.K. University's Mystery Society!!

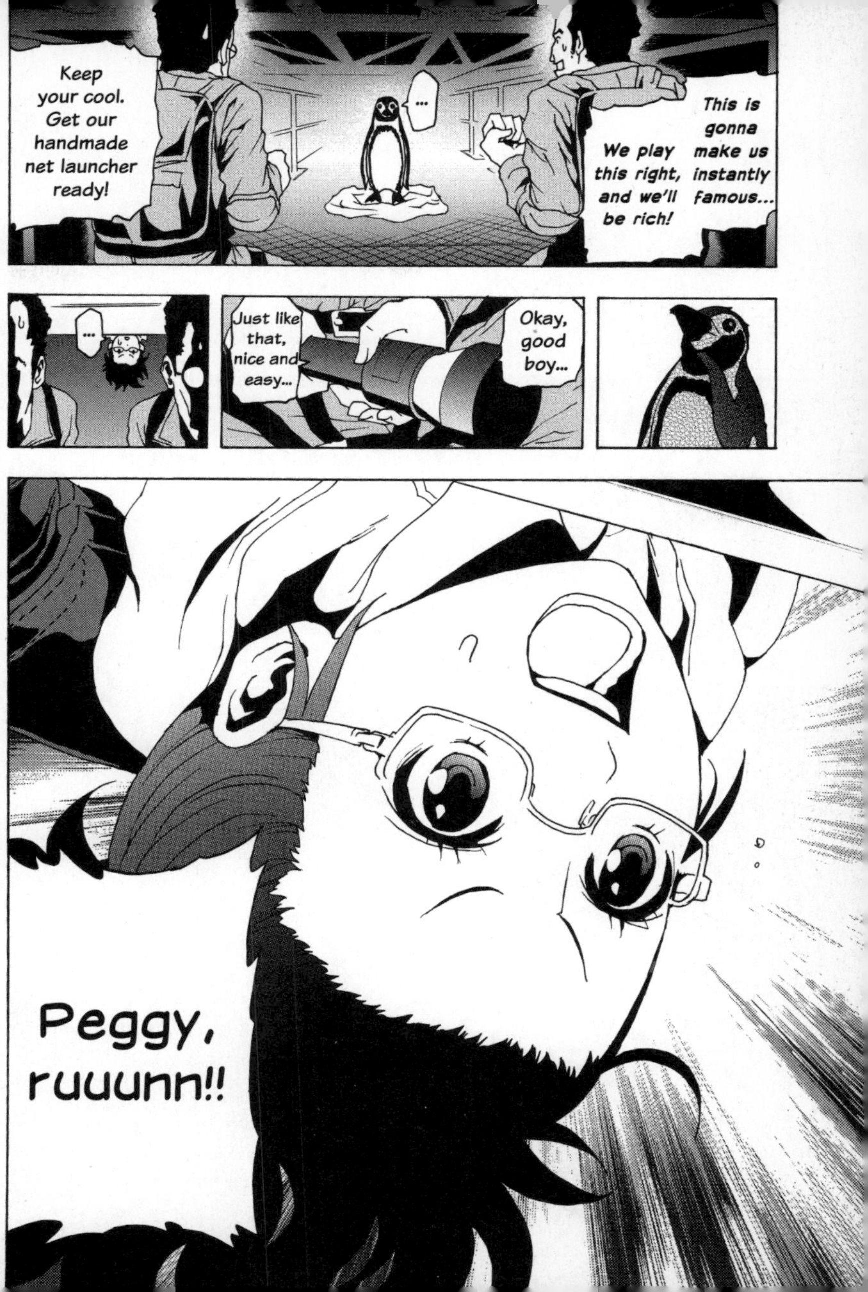
This is gonna make us instantly famous...
We play this right, and we'll be rich!
...
Keep your cool. Get our handmade net launcher ready!
Okay, good boy...
Just like that, nice and easy...
...
Peggy, ruuunn!!

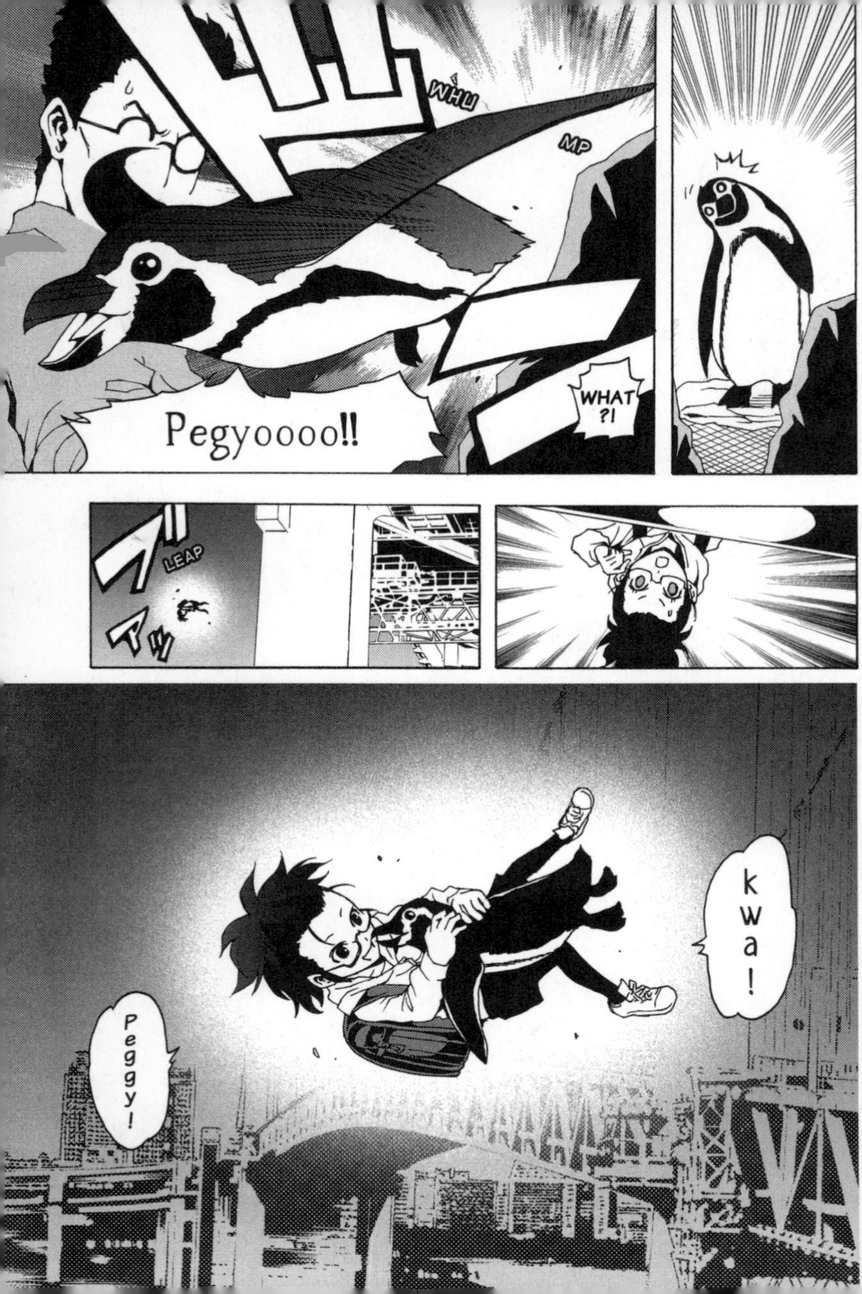
WHU
MP
WHAT ?!
Pegyoooo!!
LEAP
kwa!
Peggy!

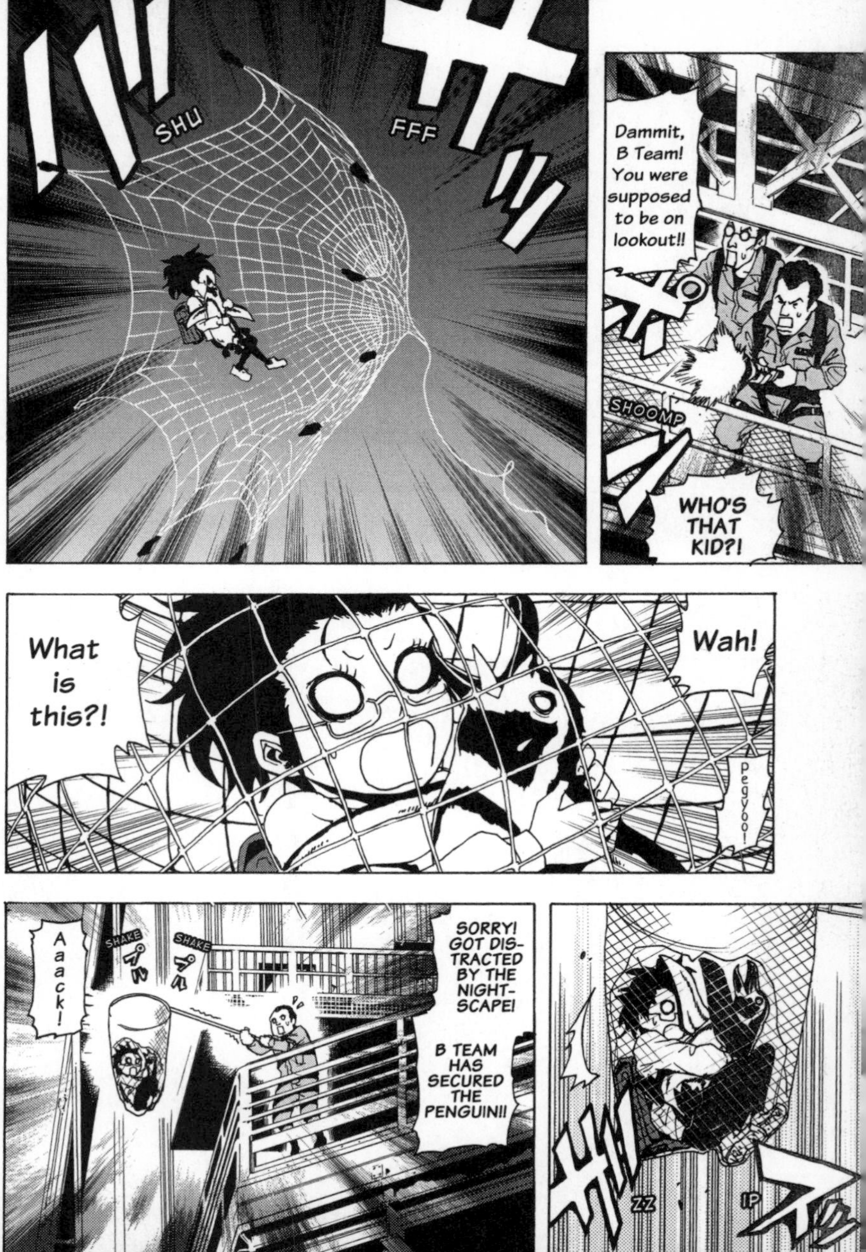
Dammit, B Team! You were supposed to be on lookout!!
SHOOMP
WHO'S THAT KID?!
FFF
SHU
Wah!
pegyoo!
What is this?!
ZZ
IP
SORRY! GOT DIS-TRACTED BY THE NIGHT-SCAPE!
B TEAM HAS SECURED THE PENGUIN!!
SHAKE
SHAKE
Aaack!

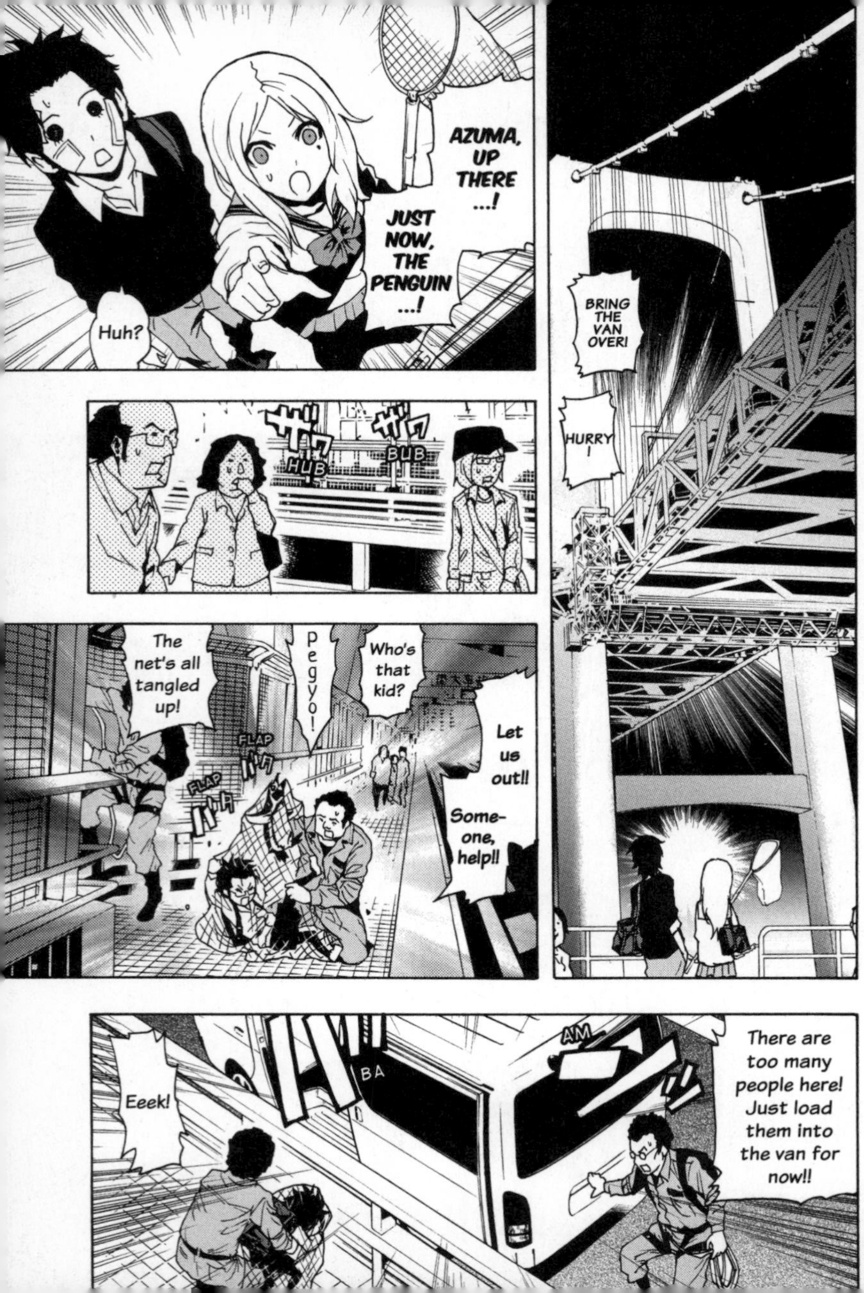
BRING THE VAN OVER!
HURRY!
AZUMA, UP THERE ...!
JUST NOW, THE PENGUIN ...!
Huh?
BUB
HUB
Who's that kid?
Let us out!!
Some-one, help!!
Pegyo!
The net's all tangled up!
FLAP
FLAP
There are too many people here! Just load them into the van for now!!
AM
BA
Eeek!

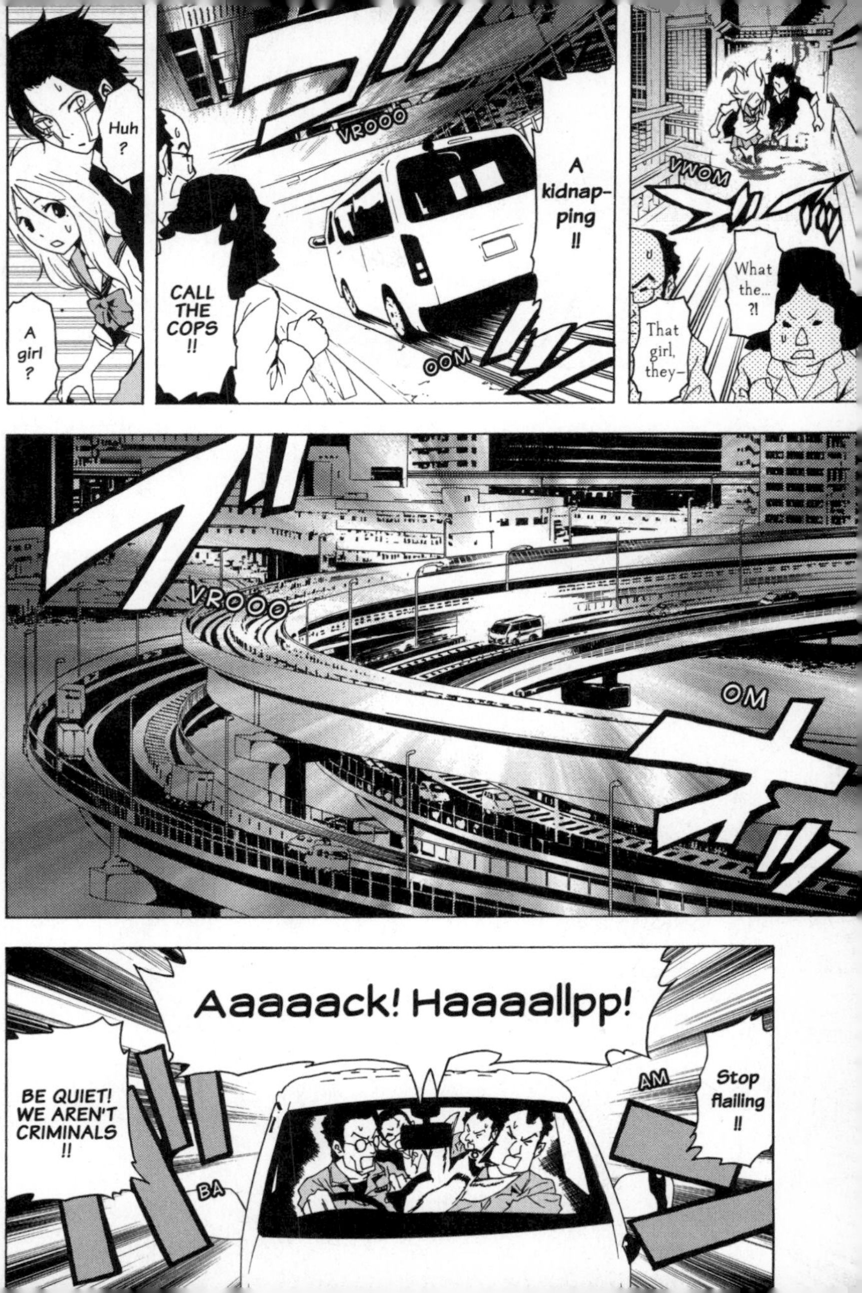
VWOM
What the...?!
That girl, they–
A kidnapping!!
VROOO
CALL THE COPS!!
OOM
Huh?
A girl?
VROOO
OM
Aaaaack! Haaaallpp!
Stop flailing!!
AM
BE QUIET! WE AREN'T CRIMINALS!!
BA

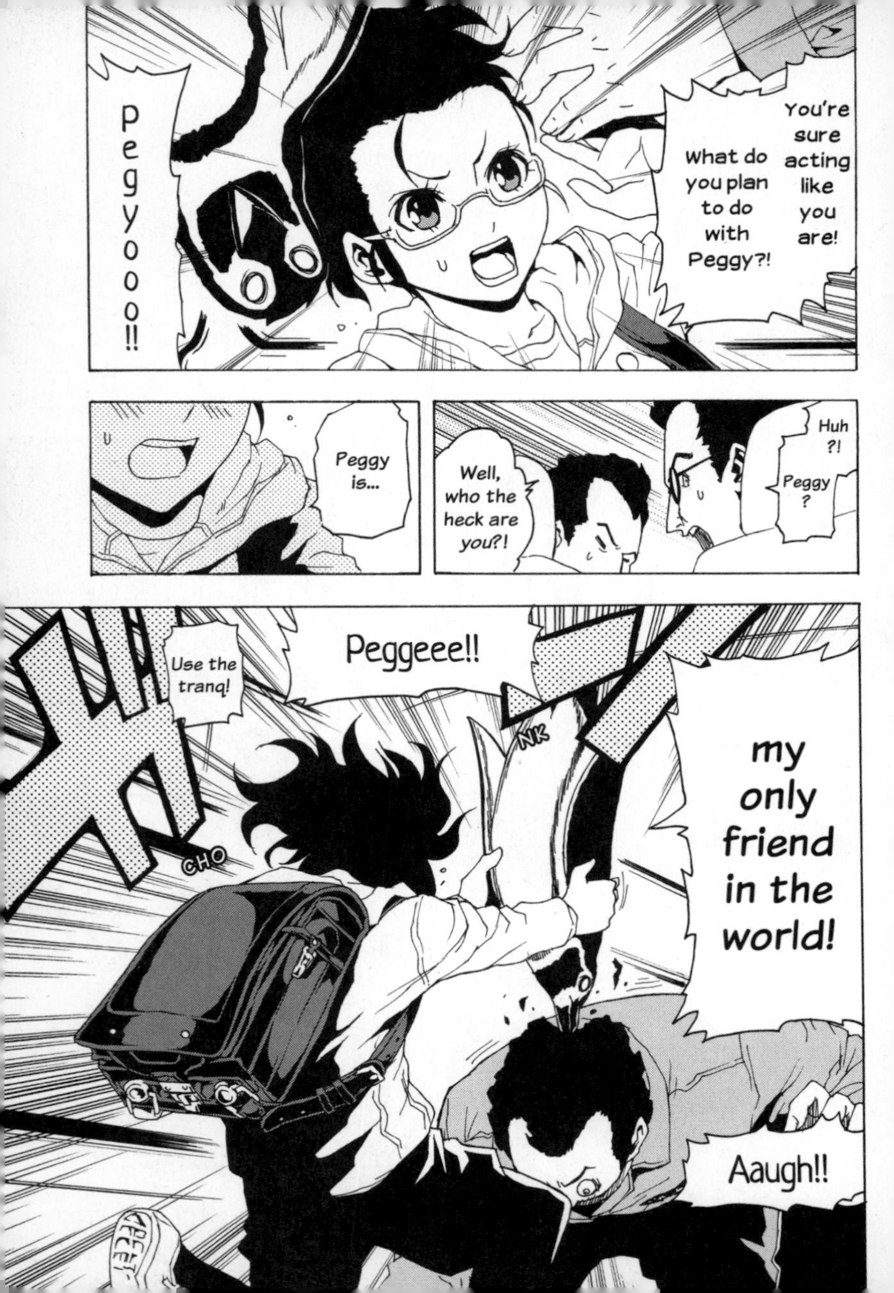
You're sure acting like you are!
What do you plan to do with Peggy?!
Pegyoooo!!
Huh?!
Peggy?
Well, who the heck are you?!
Peggy is...
Peggeee!!
my only friend in the world!
Use the tranq!
NK
CHO
Aaugh!!

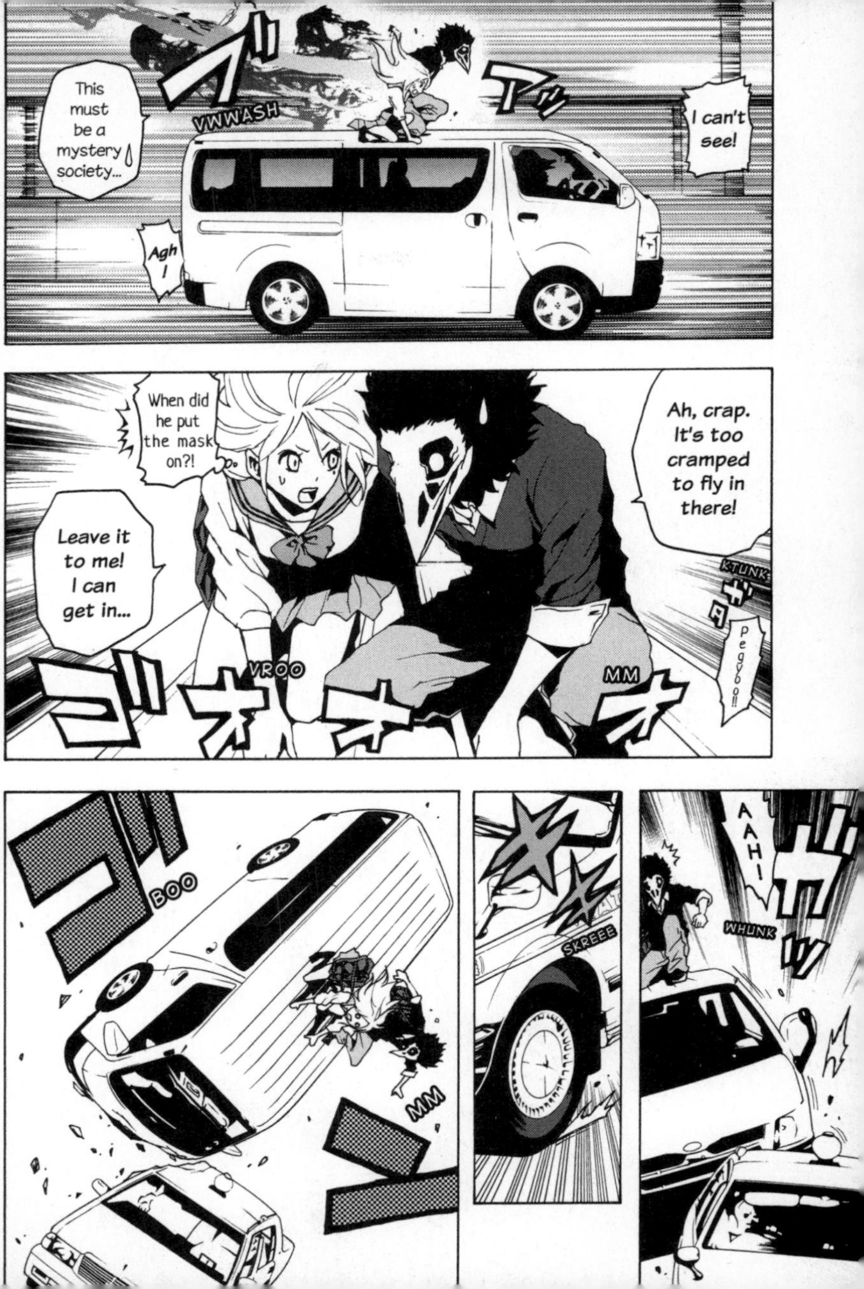
I can't see!
VWWASH
This must be a mystery society...
Agh!
Ah, crap. It's too cramped to fly in there!
When did he put the mask on?!
KTUNK
Leave it to me! I can get in...
Pegyoo!!
VROO
MM
AAH!
WHUNK
SKREEE
BOO
MM

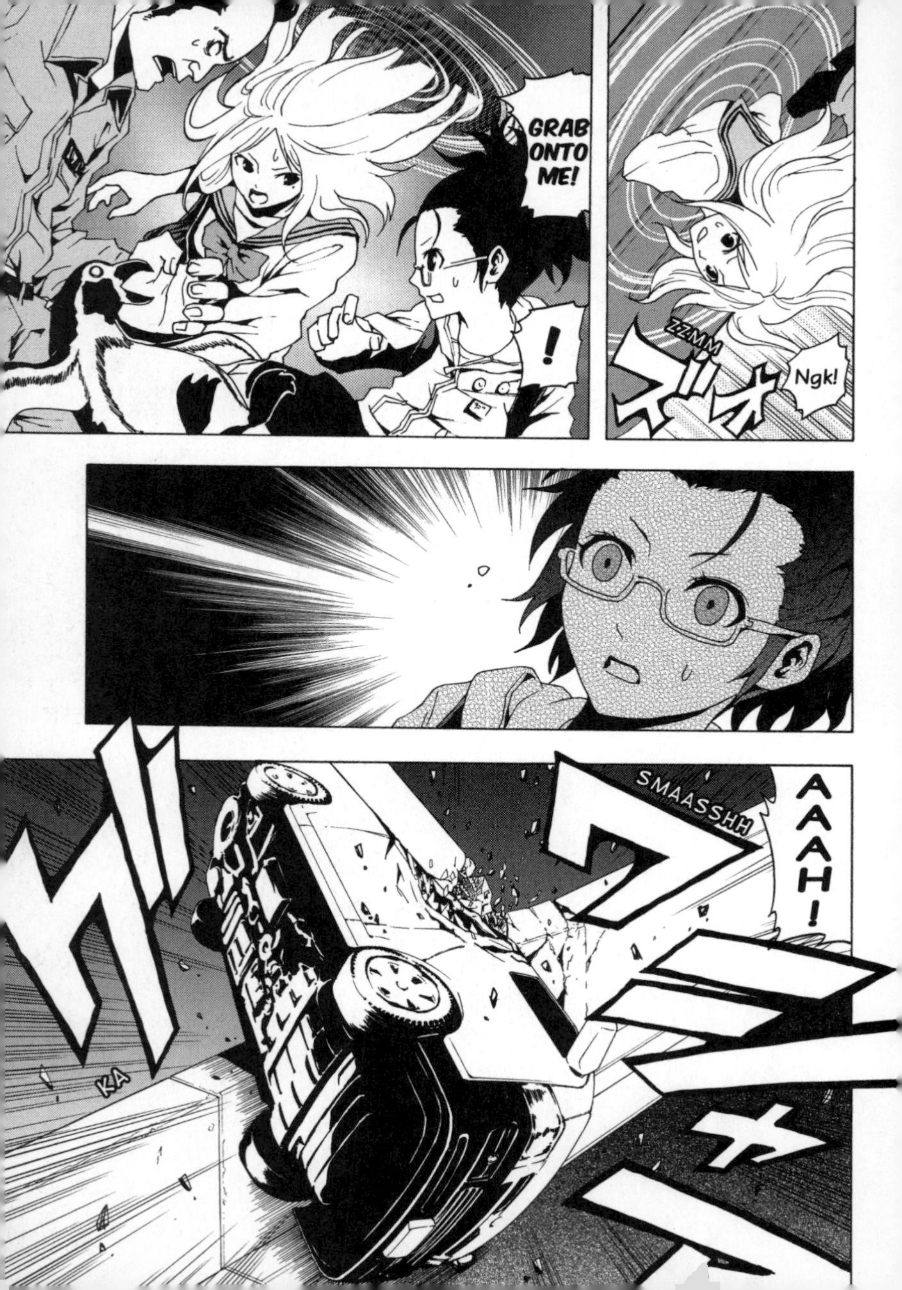
ZZMM
Ngk!
GRAB ONTO ME!
!
AAAH!
SMAASSHH
KA

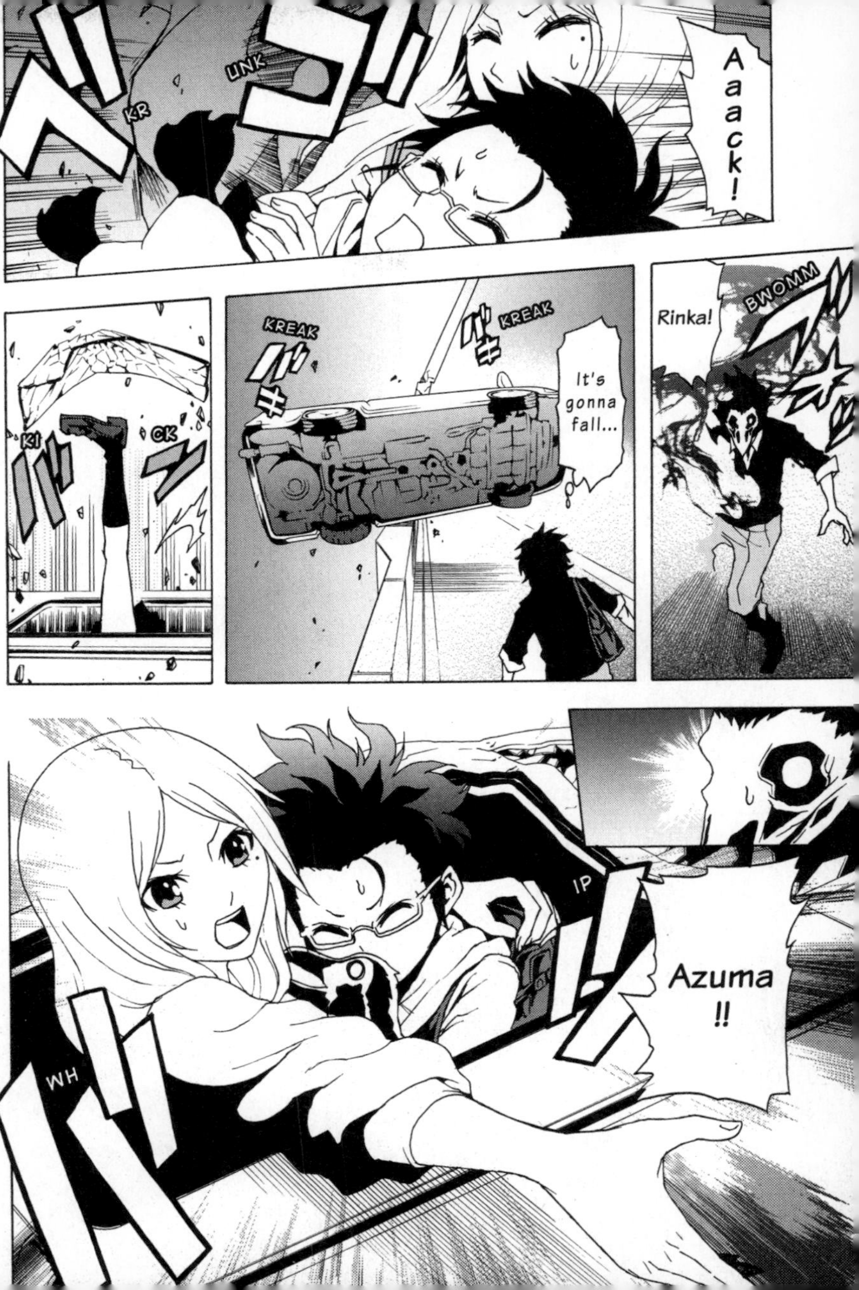
Aaaack!
UNK
KR
BWOMM
Rinka!
KREAK
It's gonna fall...
KREAK
CK
KI
Azuma !!
IP
WH

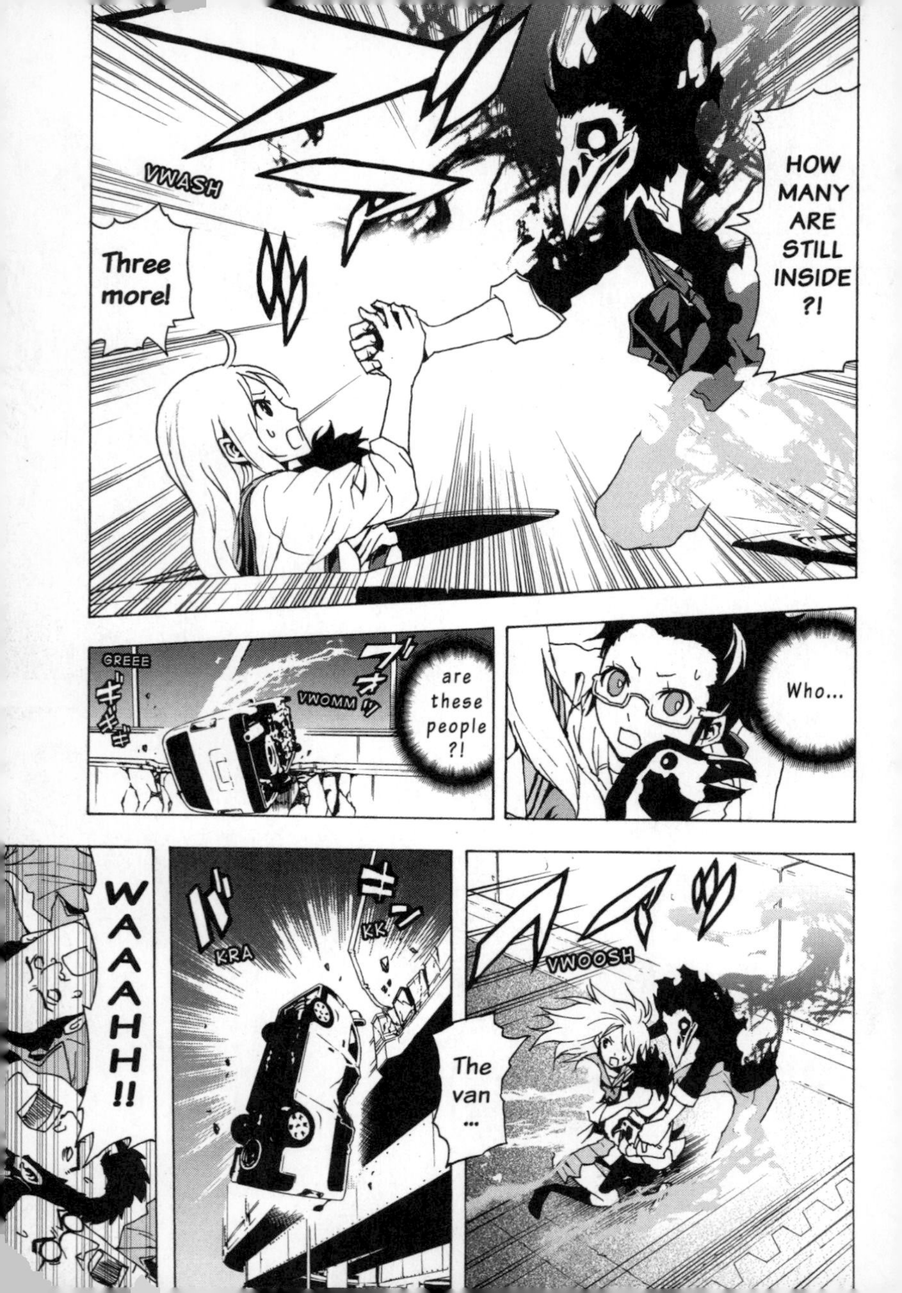
HOW MANY ARE STILL INSIDE ?!
VWASH
Three more!
Who...
are these people ?!
VWOMM
GREEE
VWOOSH
The van ...
KK
KRA
WAAAAHH!!

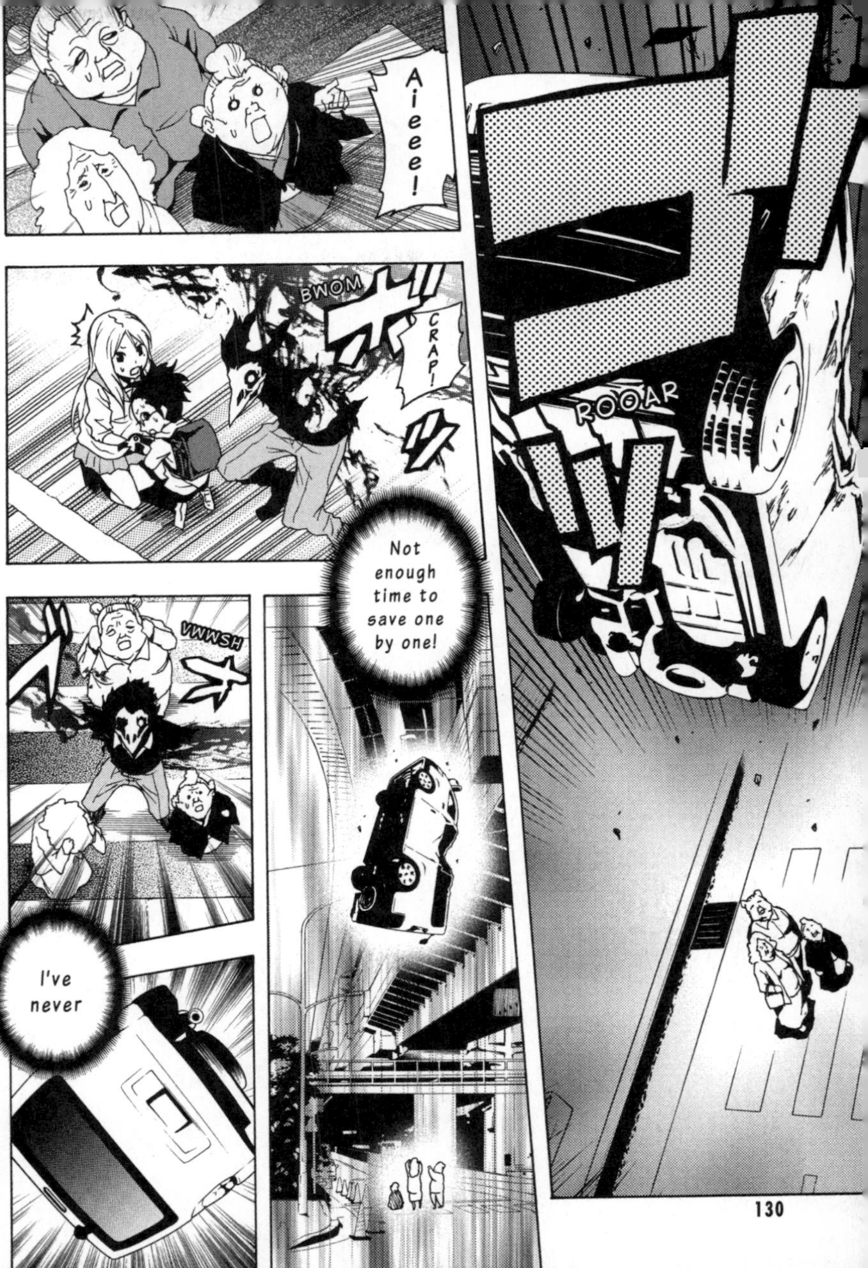
ROOAR
Aieee!
BWOM
CRAP!
Not enough time to save one by one!
VWNSH
I've never

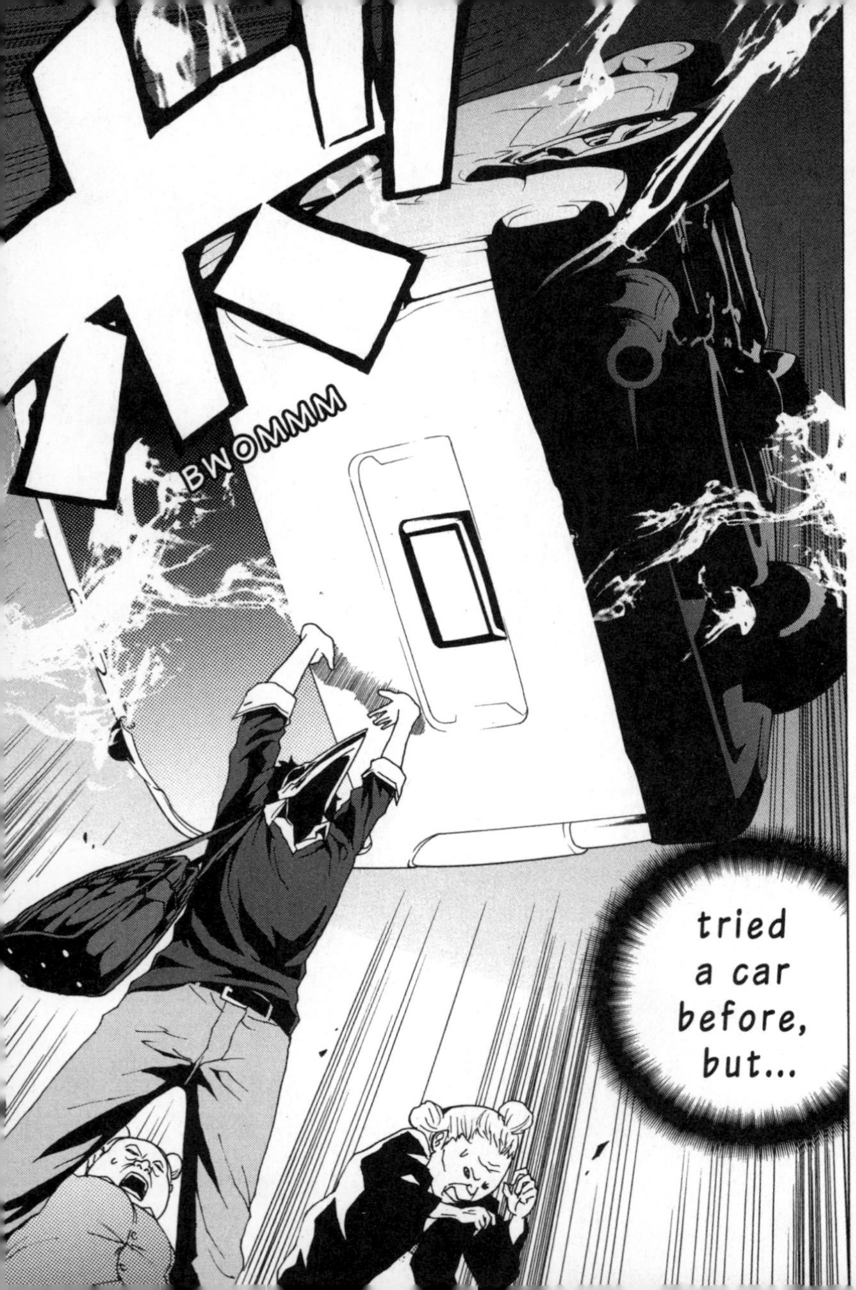
BWOMMM
tried a car before, but...

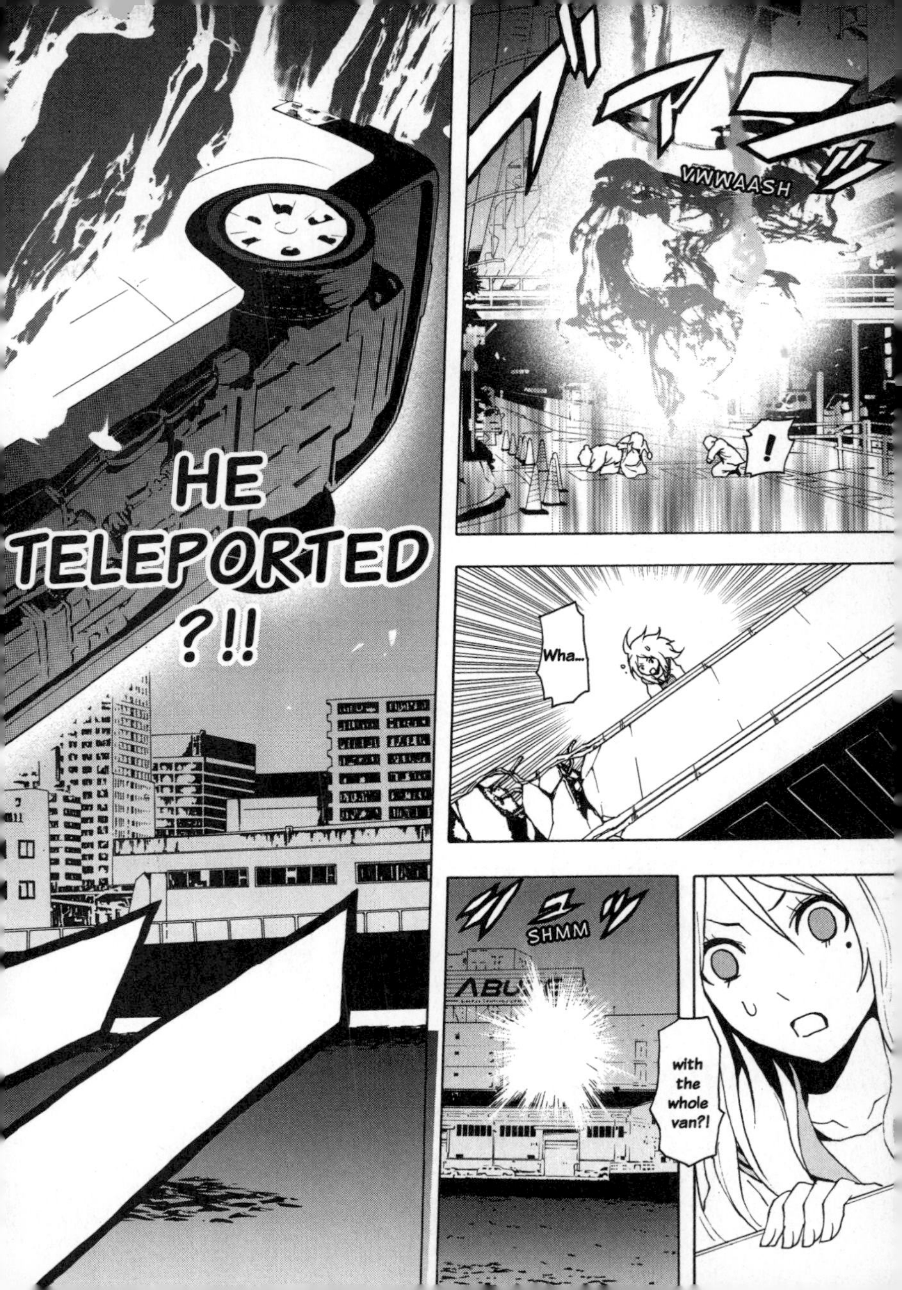
VWWAASH
!
Wha...
with the whole van?!
SHMM
HE TELEPORTED ?!!

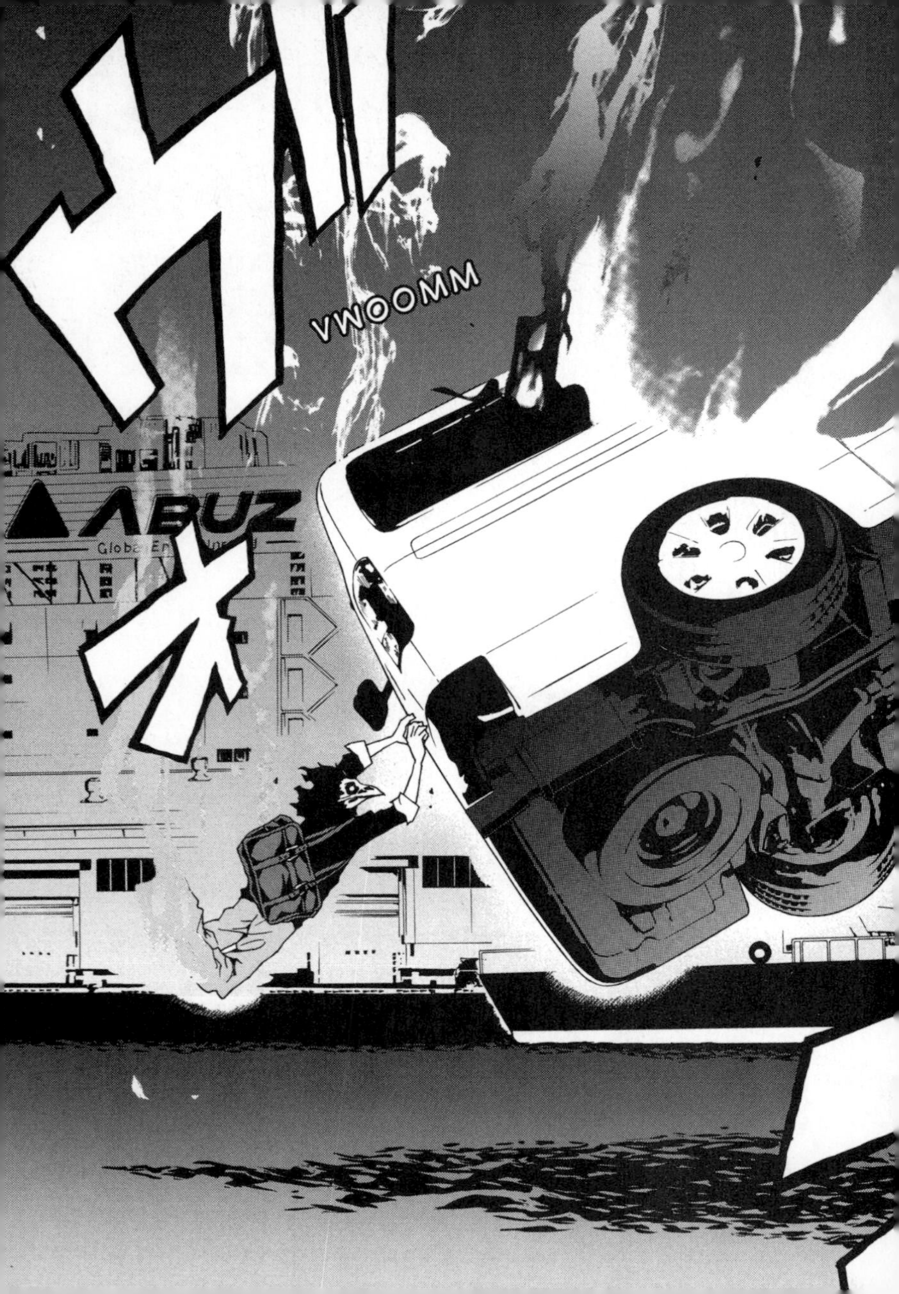
VWOOMM
ABUZ

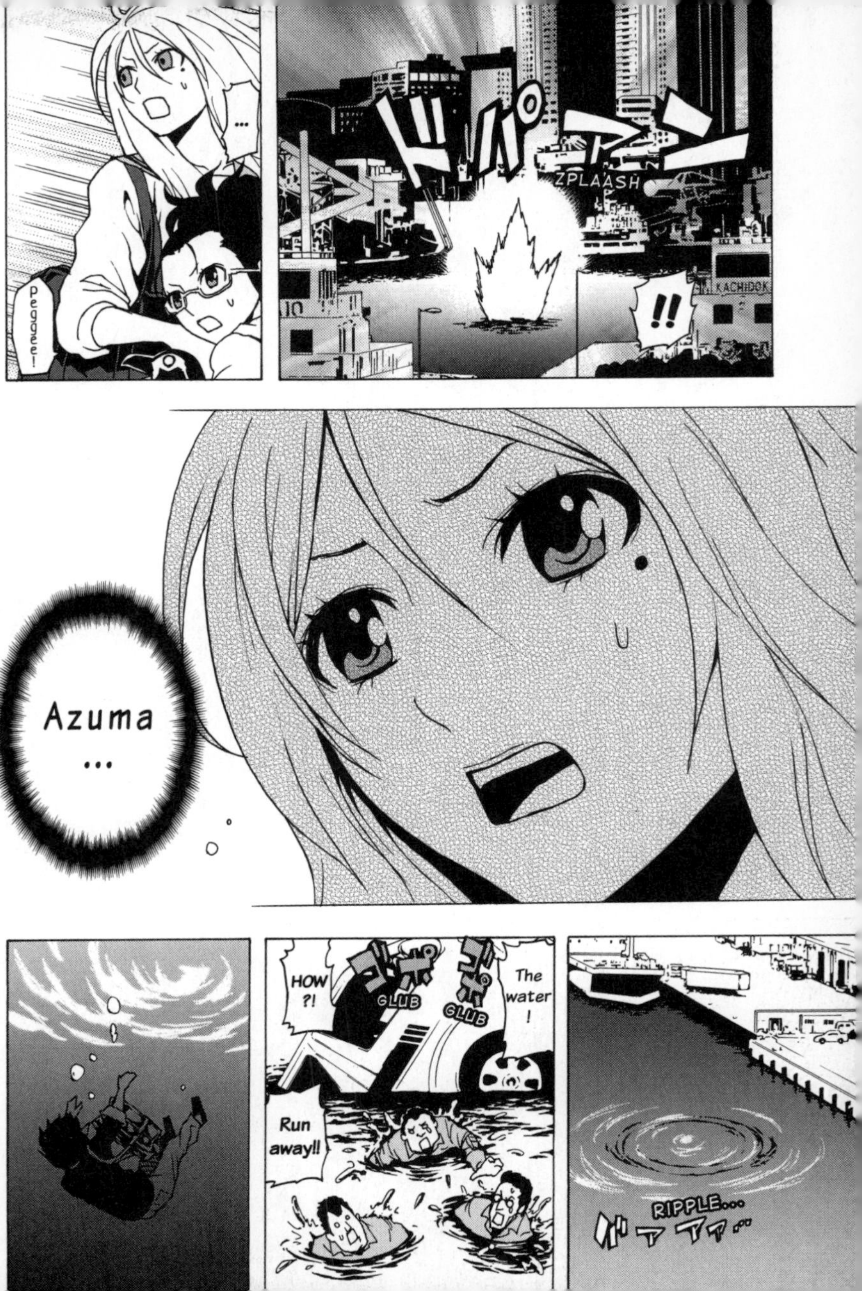

ZPLAASH
!!
...
Peggee!
Azuma ...
RIPPLE...
The water !
GLUB
GLUB
HOW ?!
Run away!!

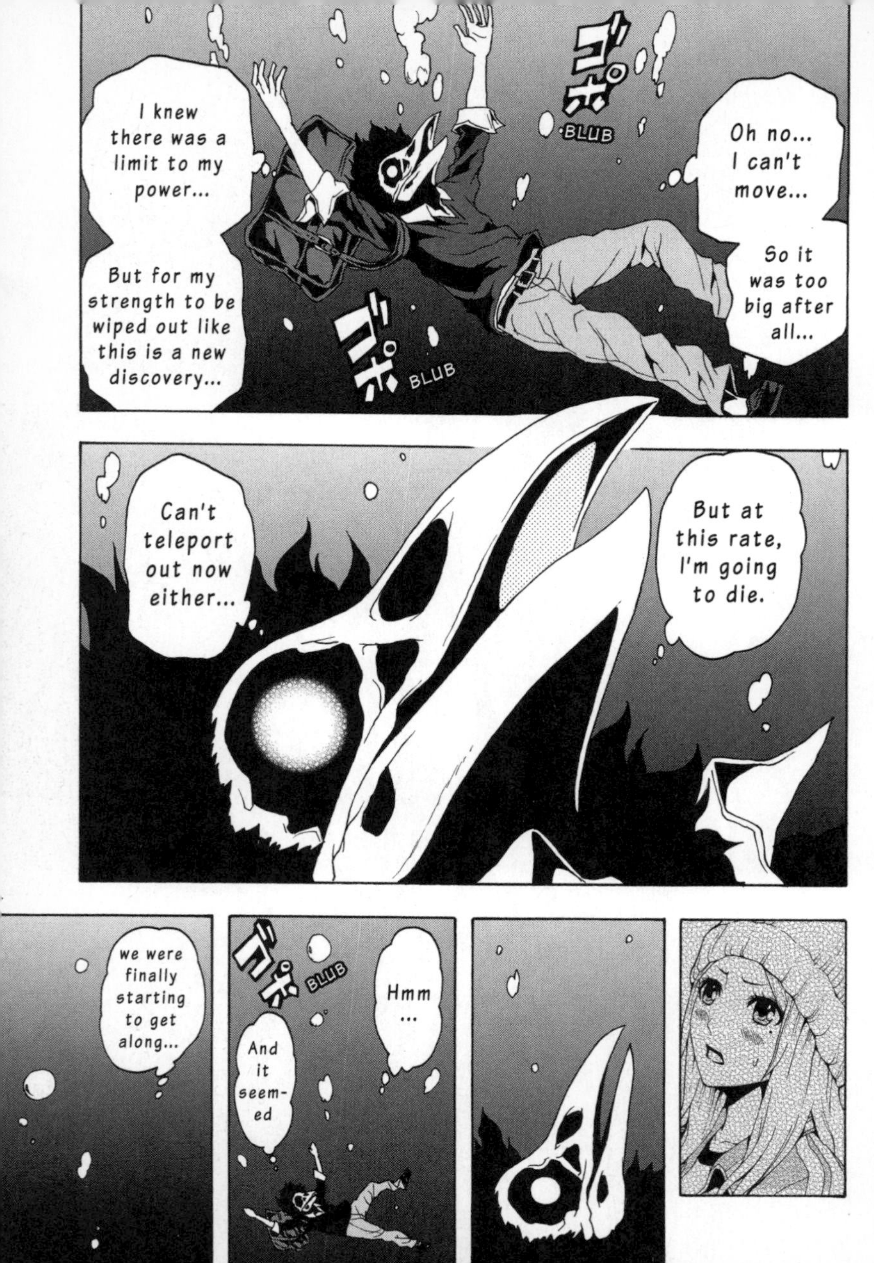
ゴポ
BLUB
Oh no... I can't move...
So it was too big after all...
I knew there was a limit to my power...
But for my strength to be wiped out like this is a new discovery...
ゴポ
BLUB
But at this rate, I'm going to die.
Can't teleport out now either...
Hmm ...
And it seem-ed
ゴポ
BLUB
we were finally starting to get along...

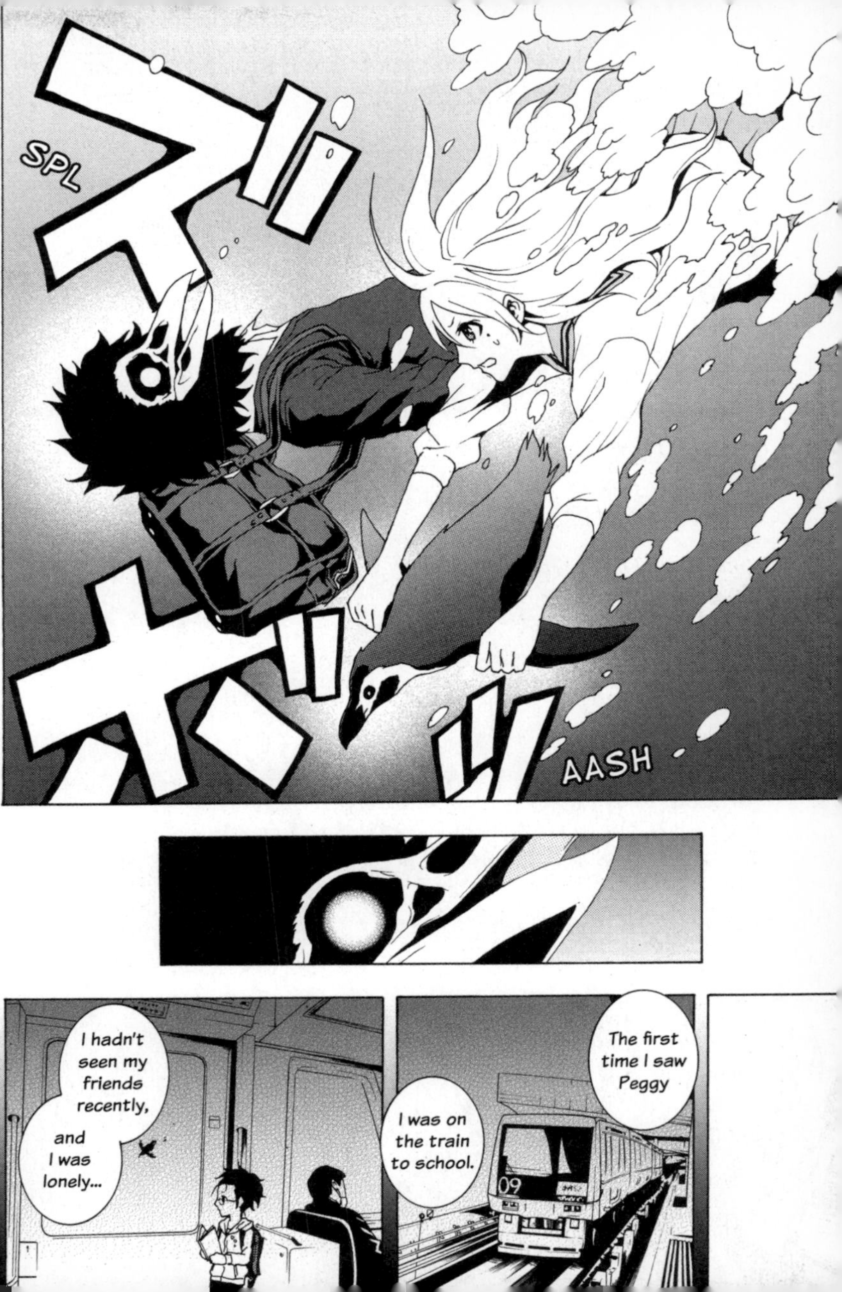
SPL
AASH
The first time I saw Peggy
I was on the train to school.
I hadn't seen my friends recently,
and I was lonely...

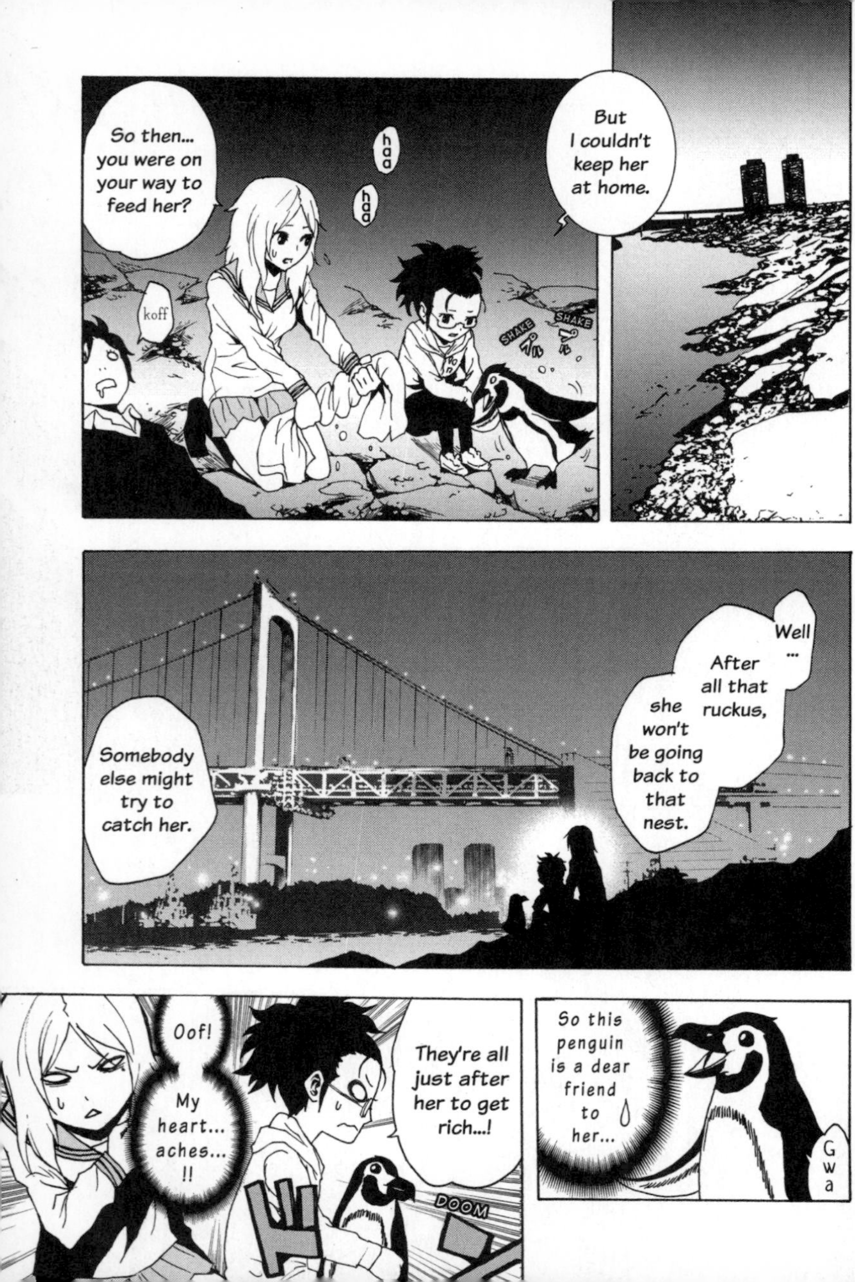
But I couldn't keep her at home.
So then... you were on your way to feed her?
haa
haa
koff
SHAKE
SHAKE
Well...
After all that ruckus, she won't be going back to that nest.
Somebody else might try to catch her.
So this penguin is a dear friend to her...
Gwa
They're all just after her to get rich...!
Oof! My heart... aches... !!
DOOM

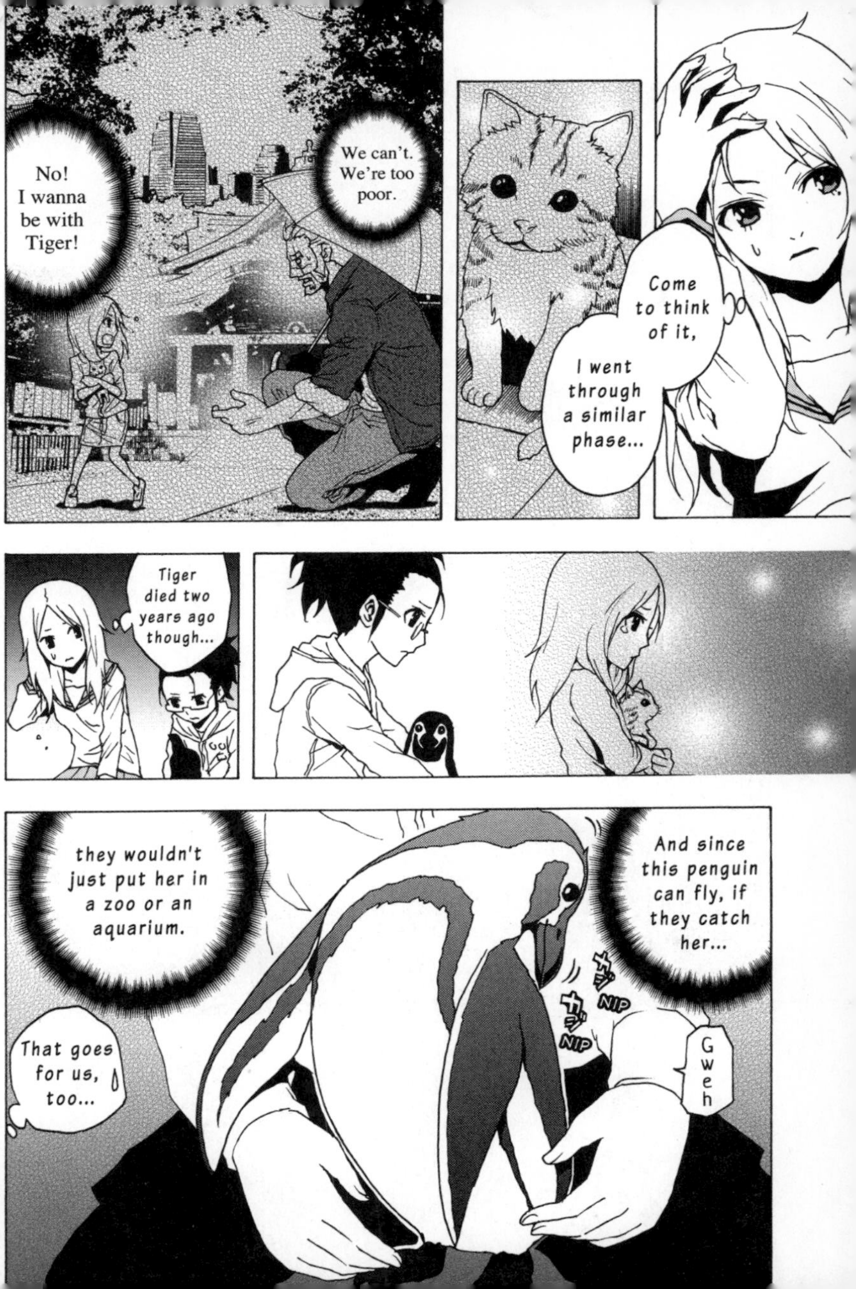
Come to think of it,
I went through a similar phase...
We can't. We're too poor.
No! I wanna be with Tiger!
Tiger died two years ago though...
And since this penguin can fly, if they catch her...
they wouldn't just put her in a zoo or an aquarium.
Gweh
NIP
NIP
That goes for us, too...

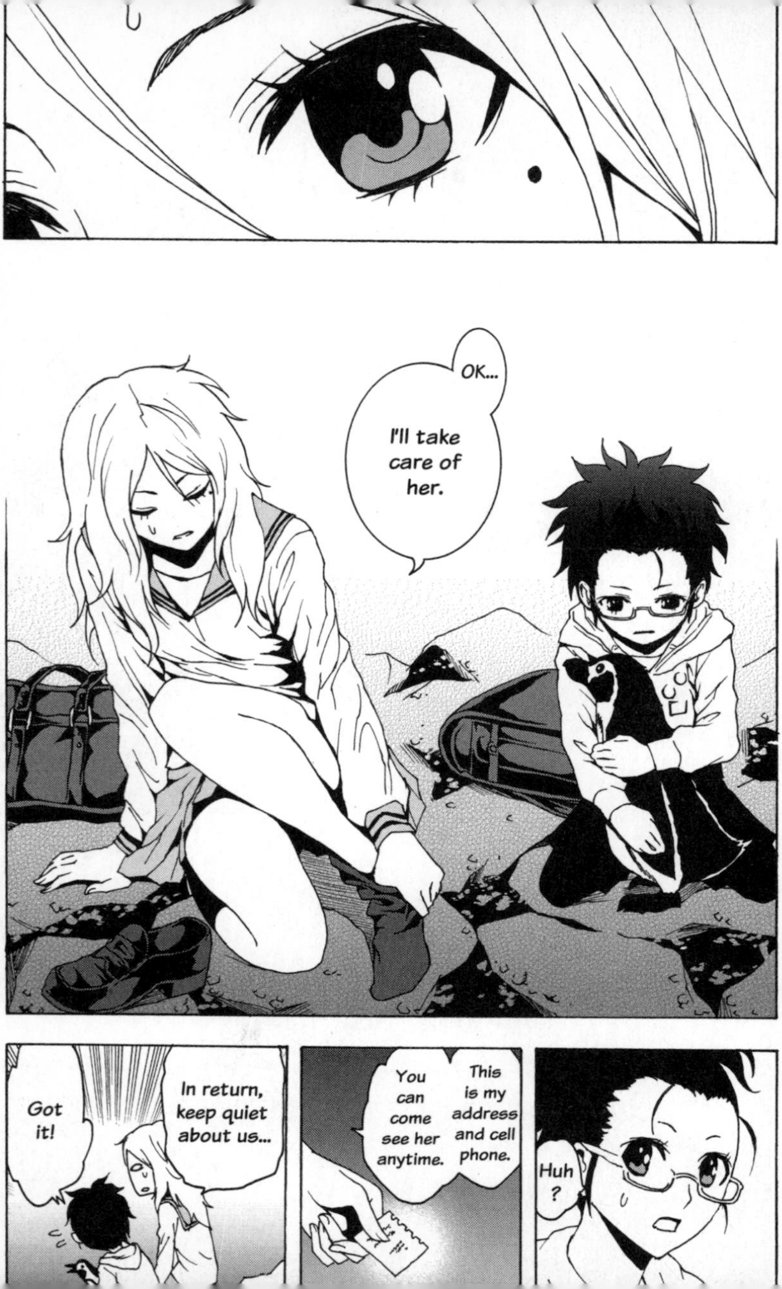
OK...
I'll take care of her.
Huh?
This is my address and cell phone.
You can come see her anytime.
In return, keep quiet about us...
Got it!

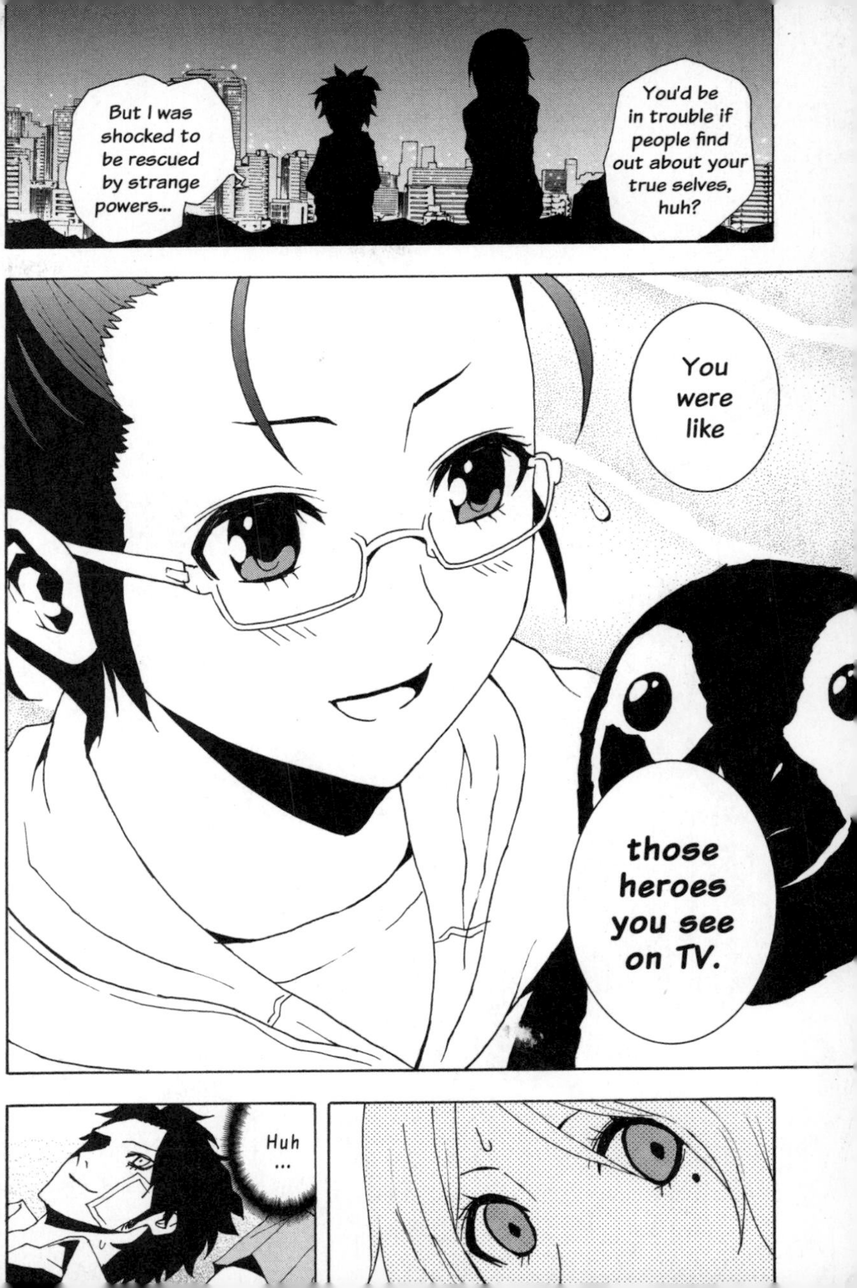
You'd be in trouble if people find out about your true selves, huh?
But I was shocked to be rescued by strange powers...
You were like
those heroes you see on TV.
Huh ...

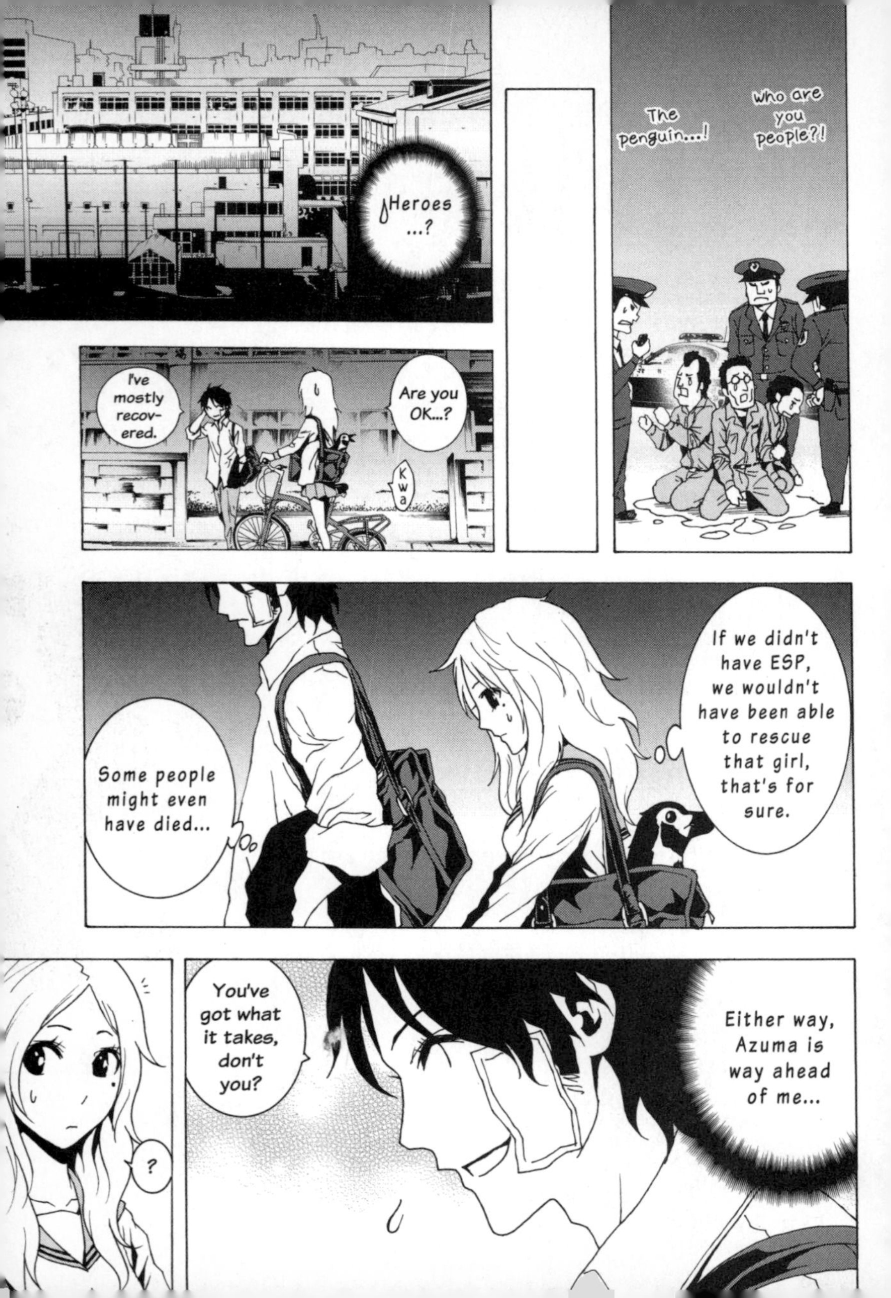
who are you people?!
The penguin...!
Heroes ...?
Are you OK...?
Kwa
I've mostly recov- ered.
If we didn't have ESP, we wouldn't have been able to rescue that girl, that's for sure.
Some people might even have died...
Either way, Azuma is way ahead of me...
You've got what it takes, don't you?
?

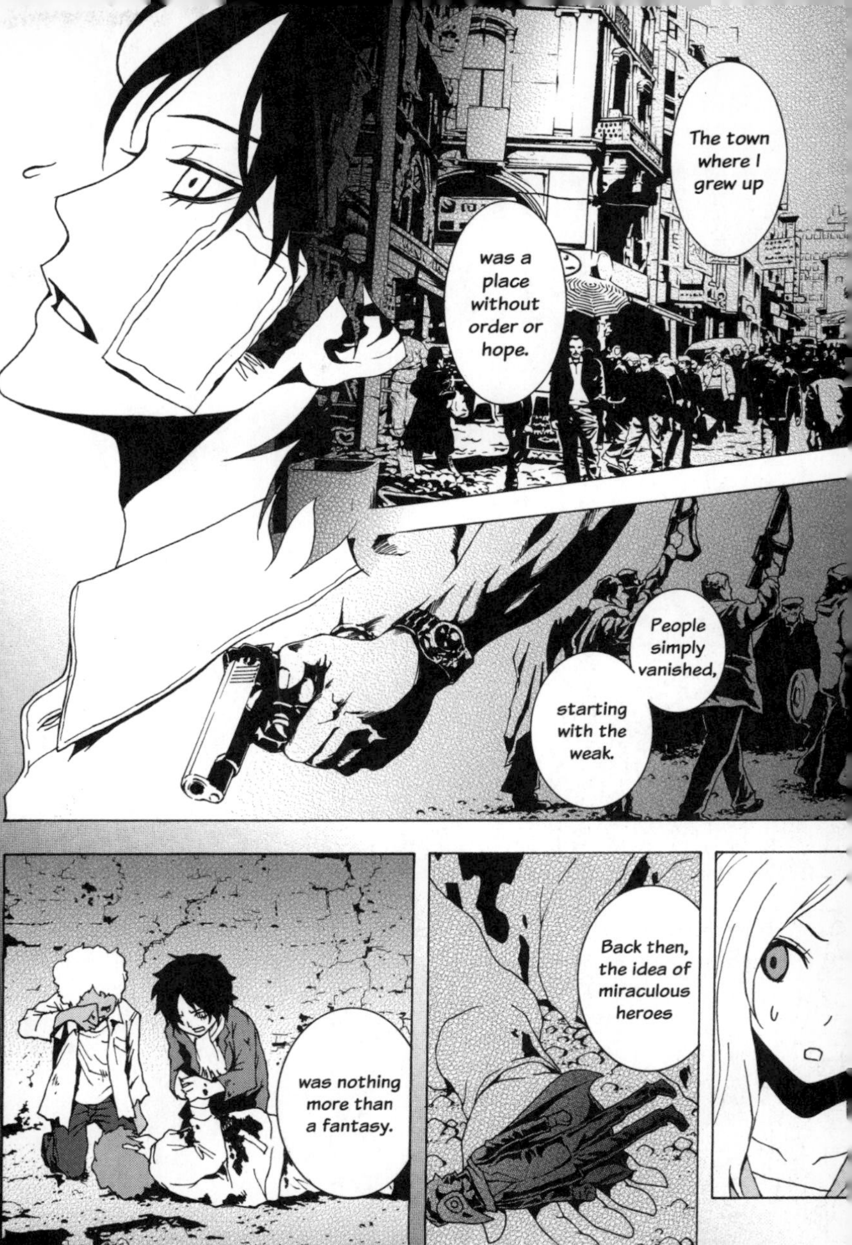
The town where I grew up
was a place without order or hope.
People simply vanished,
starting with the weak.
Back then, the idea of miraculous heroes
was nothing more than a fantasy.

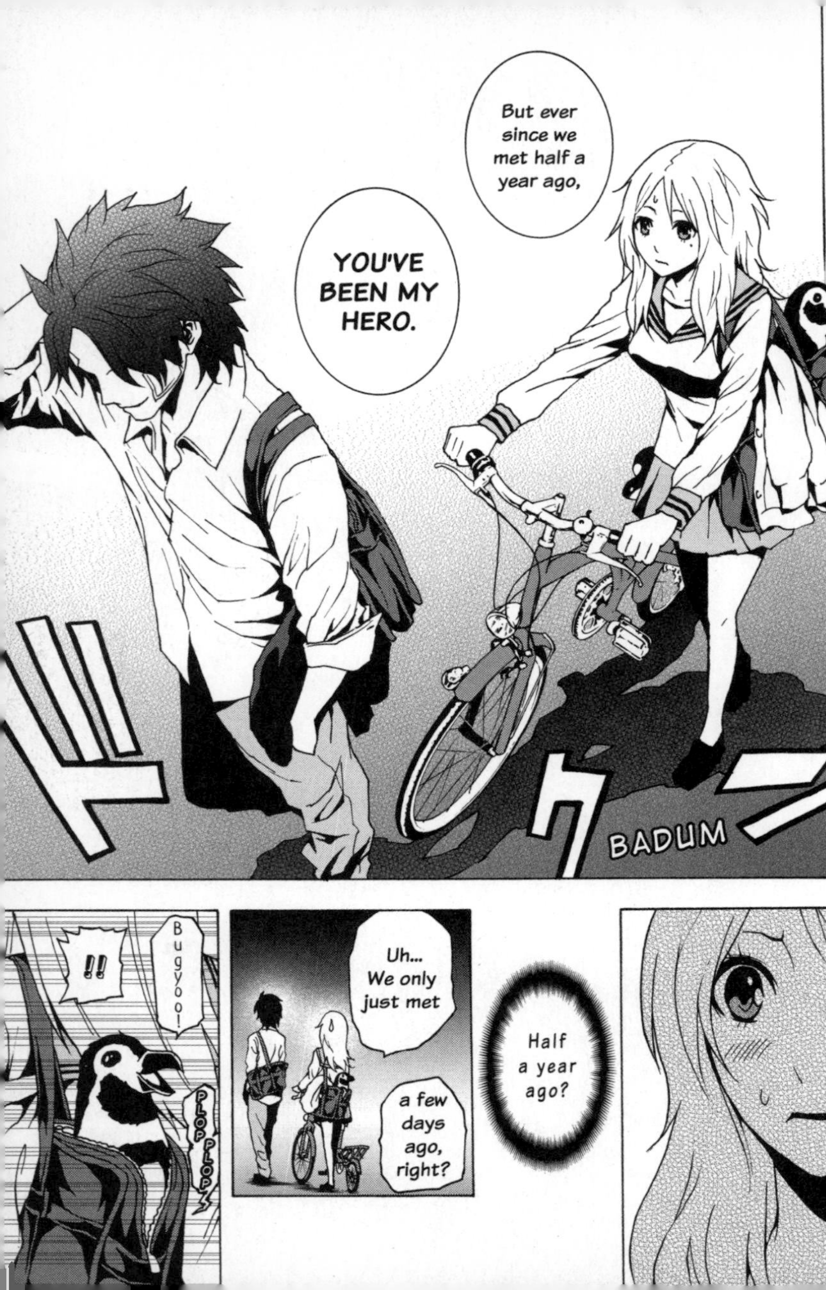

But ever since we met half a year ago,
YOU'VE BEEN MY HERO.
BADUM
Half a year ago?
Uh... We only just met
a few days ago, right?
!!
Bugyoo!
PLOP PLOP

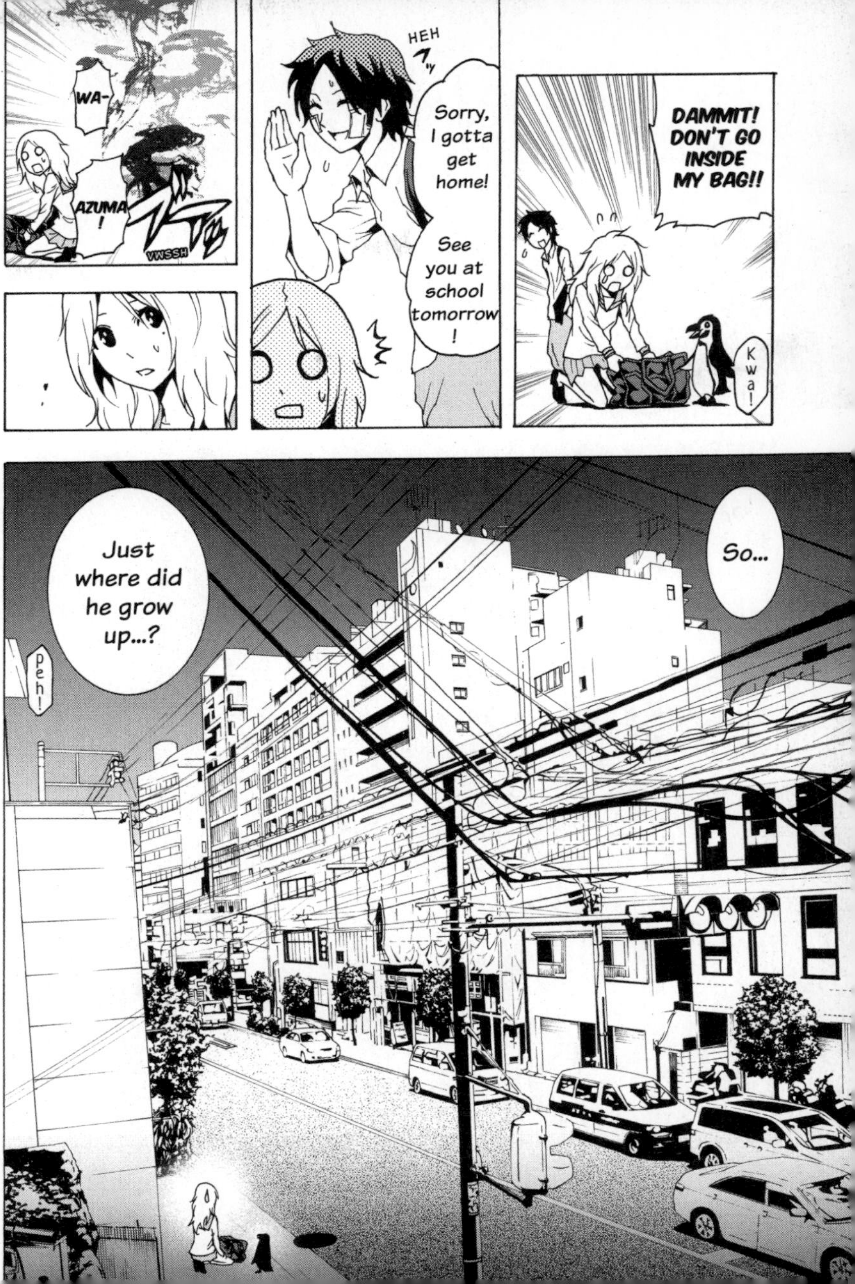
DAMMIT! DON'T GO INSIDE MY BAG!!
Kwa!
HEH
Sorry, I gotta get home!
See you at school tomorrow!
WA-
AZUMA!
VWSSH
So...
Just where did he grow up...?
peh!

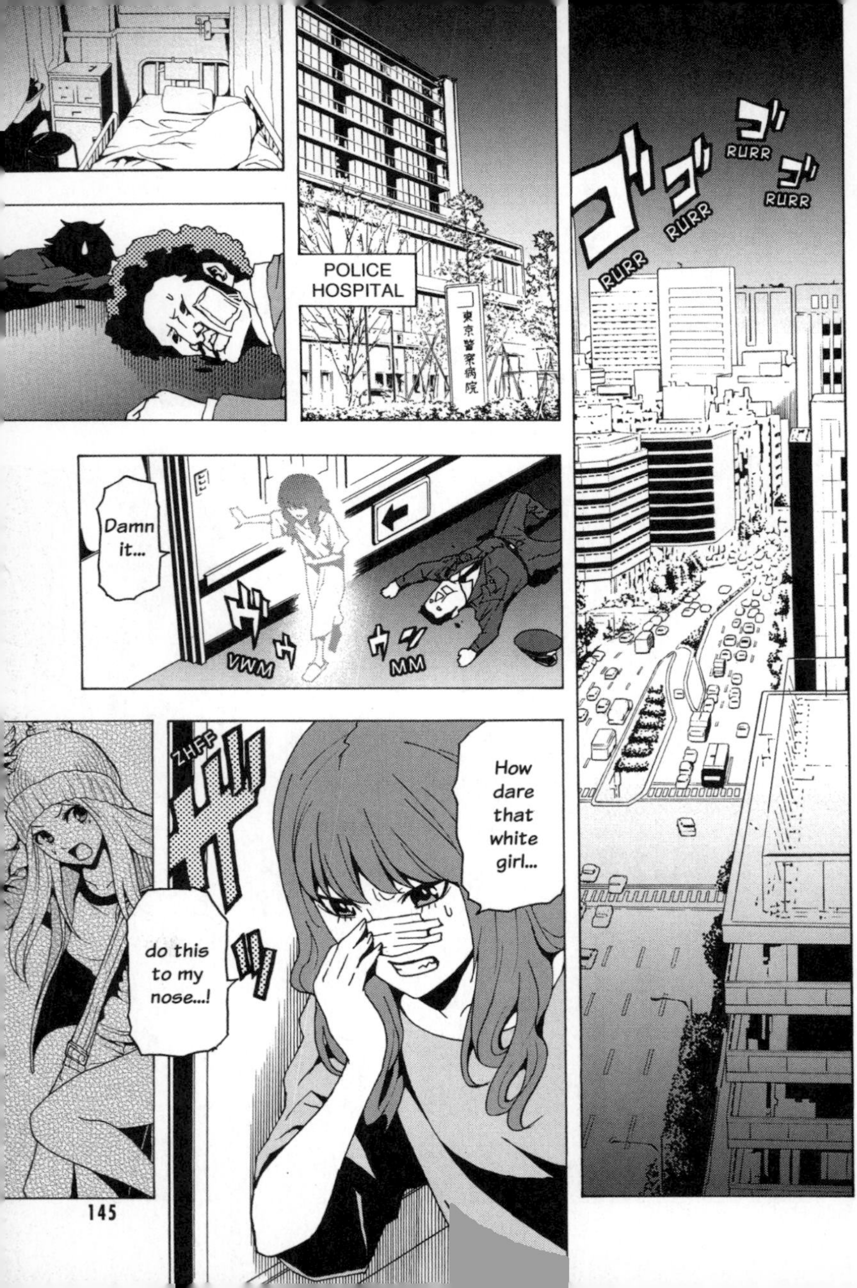
RURR
RURR
RURR
RURR
RURR
POLICE HOSPITAL
東京警察病院
Damn it...
VWM
MM
How dare that white girl...
ZHFF
do this to my nose...!

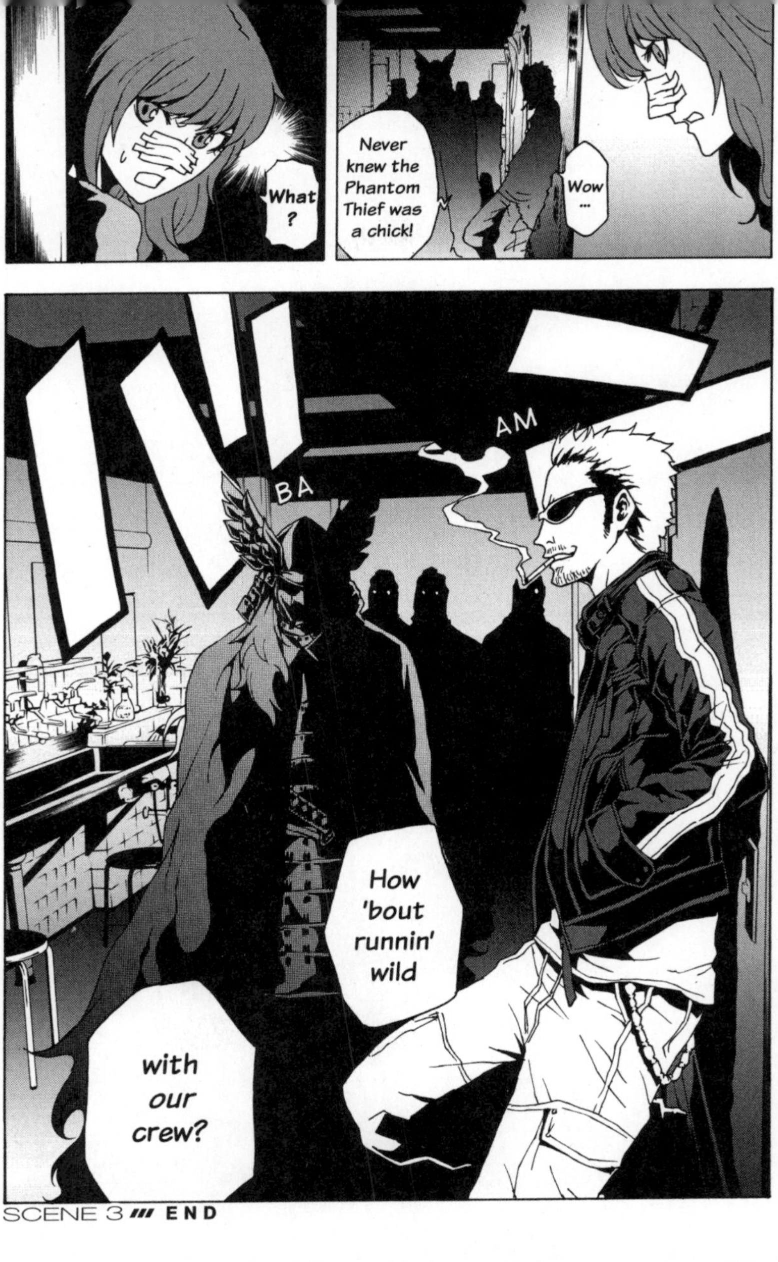
Wow ...
Never knew the Phantom Thief was a chick!
What?
BA
AM
How 'bout runnin' wild
with our crew?

SCENE 3 /// END

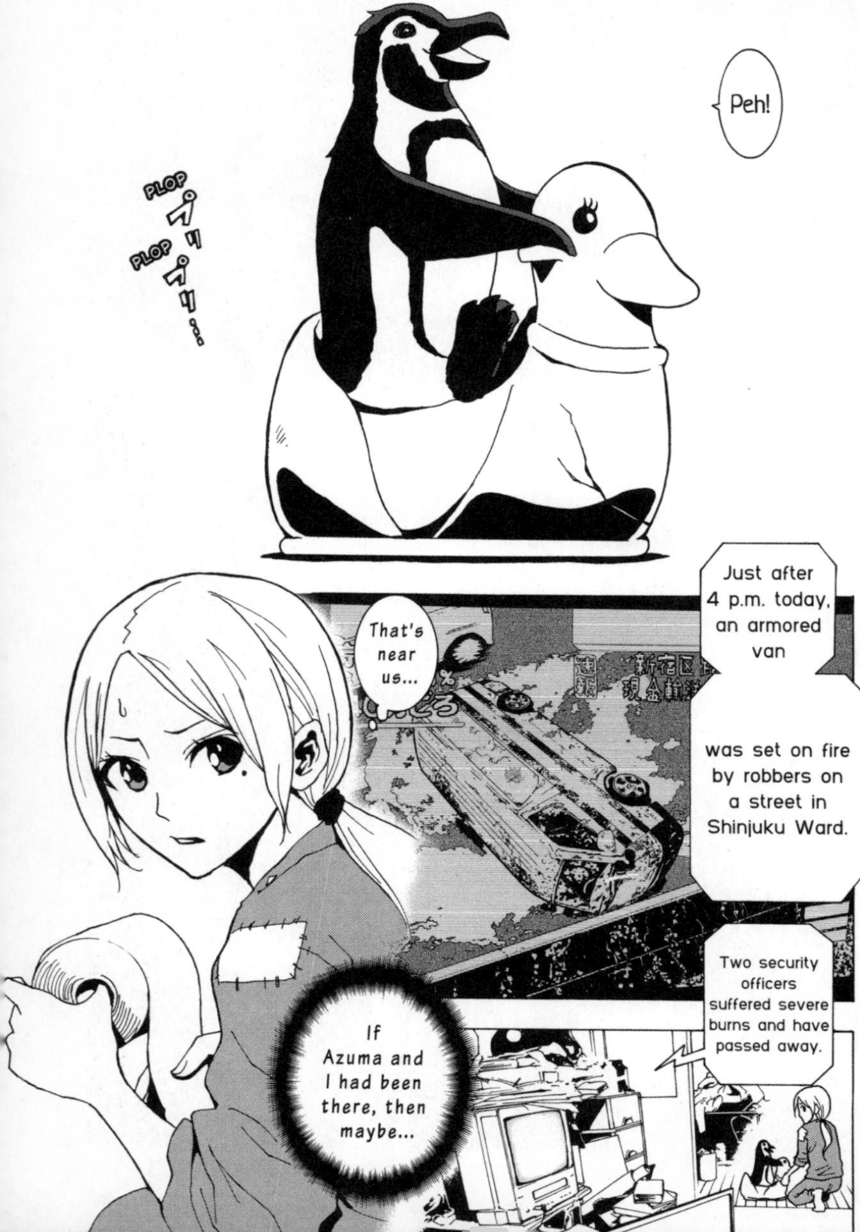
Peh!
PLOP
PLOP
Just after 4 p.m. today, an armored van
was set on fire by robbers on a street in Shinjuku Ward.
That's near us...
Two security officers suffered severe burns and have passed away.
If Azuma and I had been there, then maybe...

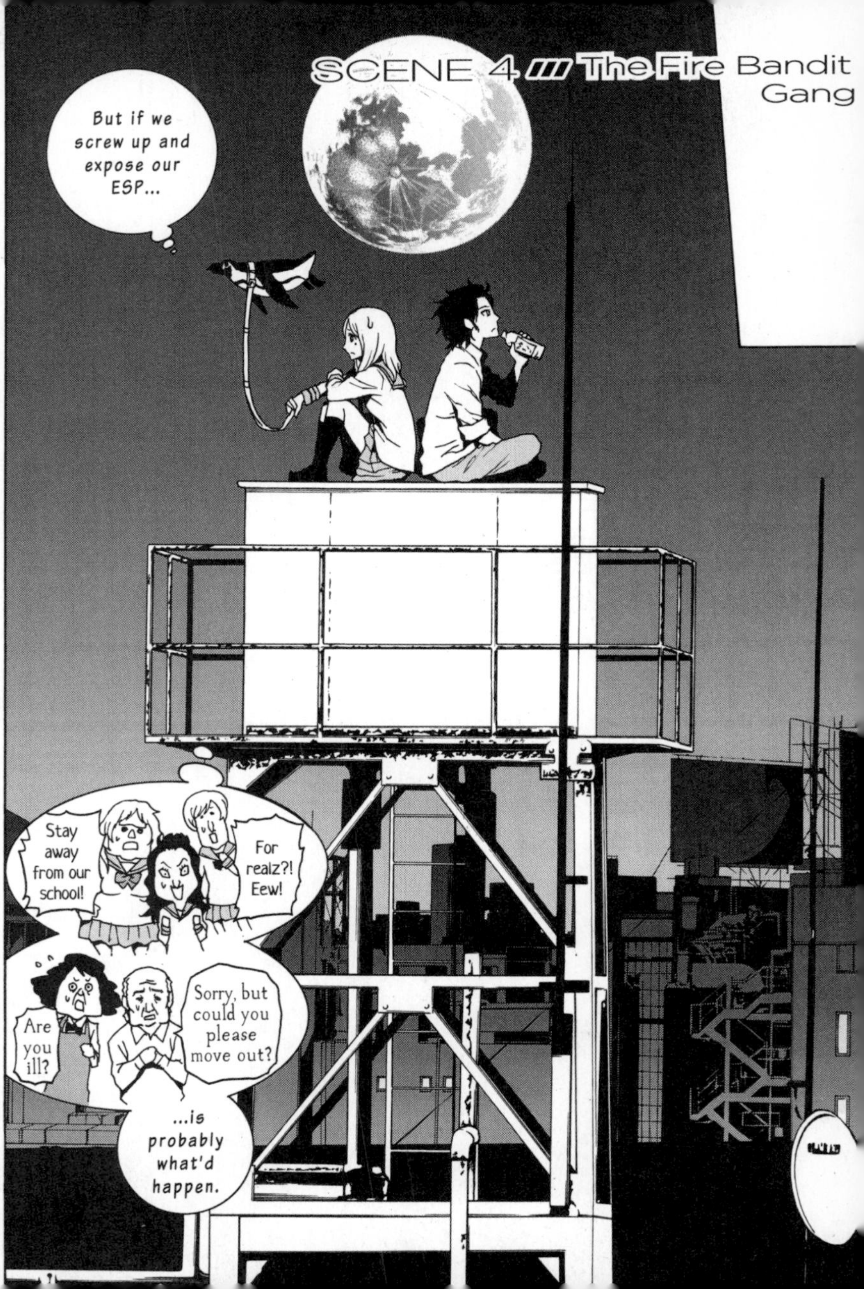
SCENE 4 /// The Fire Bandit Gang
But if we screw up and expose our ESP...
For realz?! Eew!
Stay away from our school!
Sorry, but could you please move out?
Are you ill?
...is probably what'd happen.

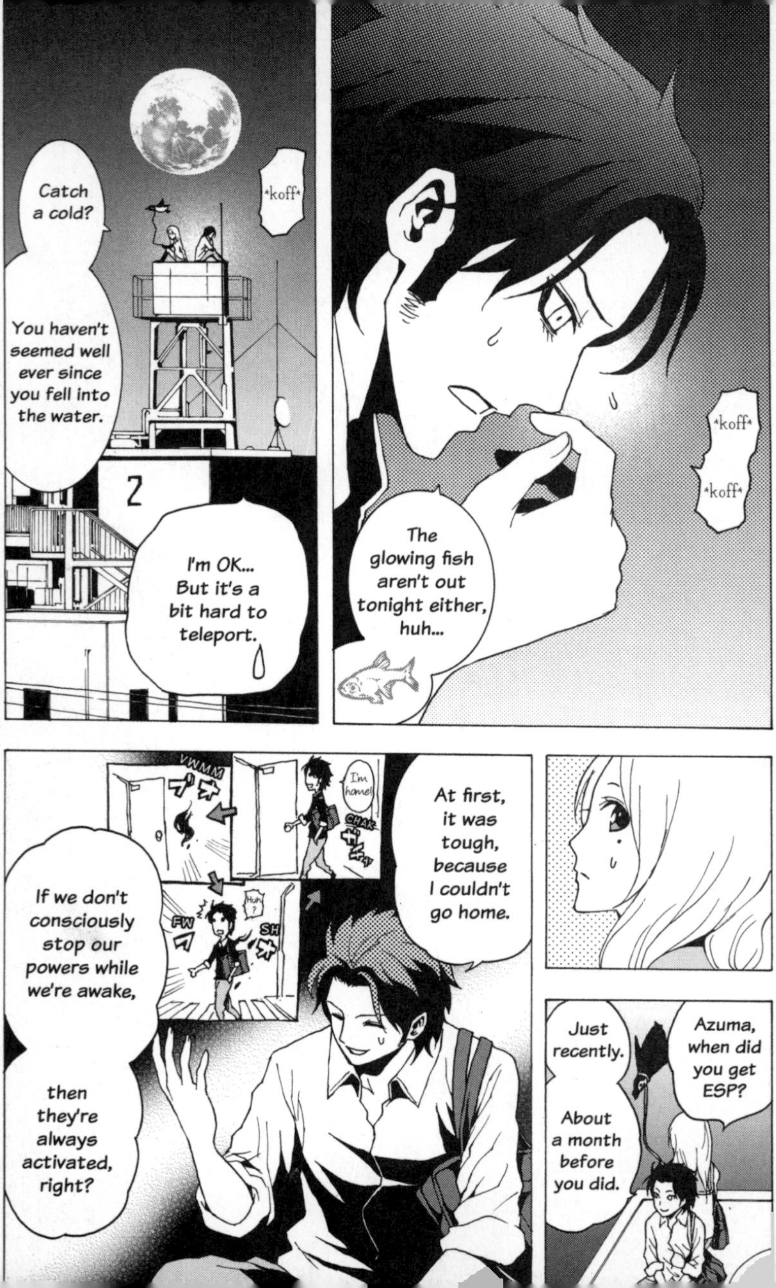
koff
koff
The glowing fish aren't out tonight either, huh...
koff
Catch a cold?
You haven't seemed well ever since you fell into the water.
I'm OK... But it's a bit hard to teleport.
Azuma, when did you get ESP?
Just recently.
About a month before you did.
At first, it was tough, because I couldn't go home.
I'm home!
CHAK
VWMM
Huh?
SH
FW
If we don't consciously stop our powers while we're awake,
then they're always activated, right?

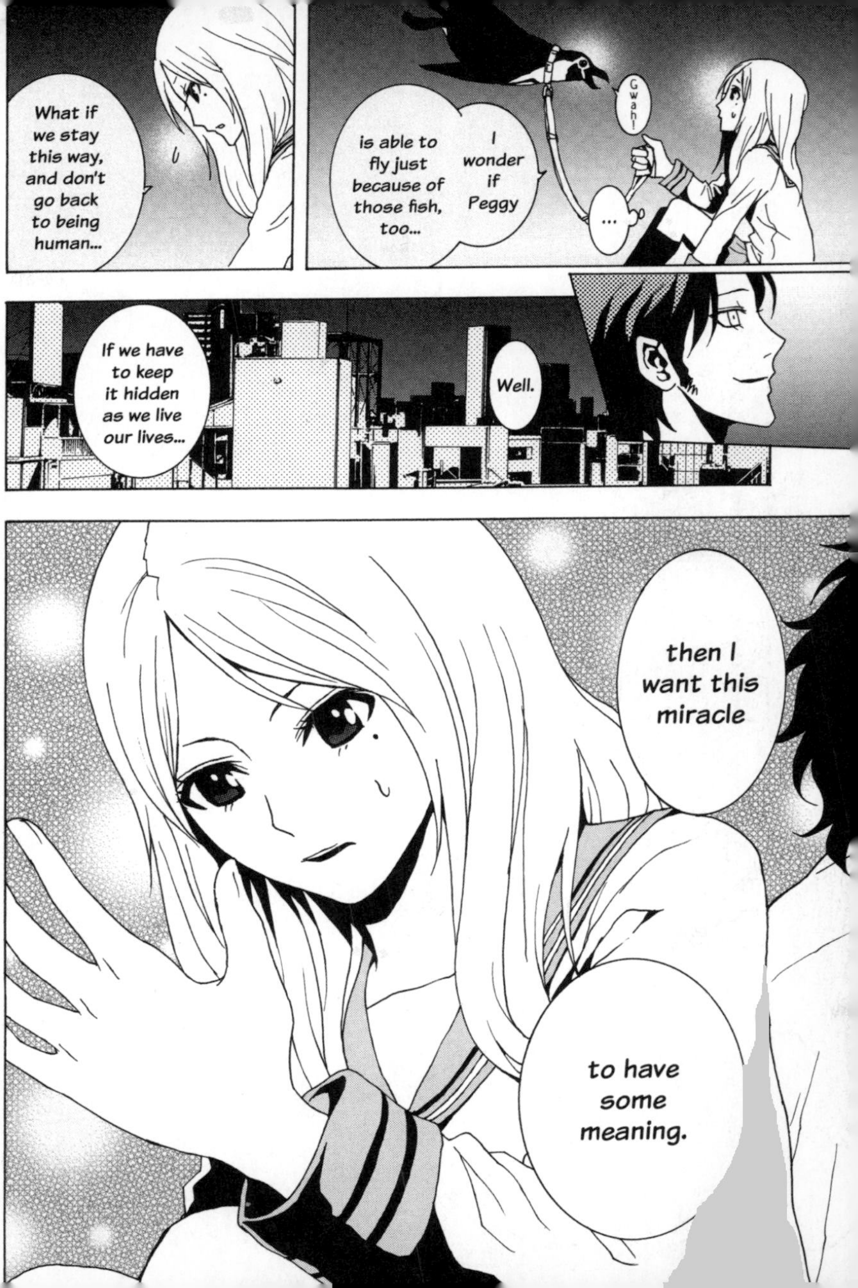

Gwah!
I wonder if Peggy
is able to fly just because of those fish, too...
...
What if we stay this way, and don't go back to being human...
Well.
If we have to keep it hidden as we live our lives...
then I want this miracle
to have some meaning.

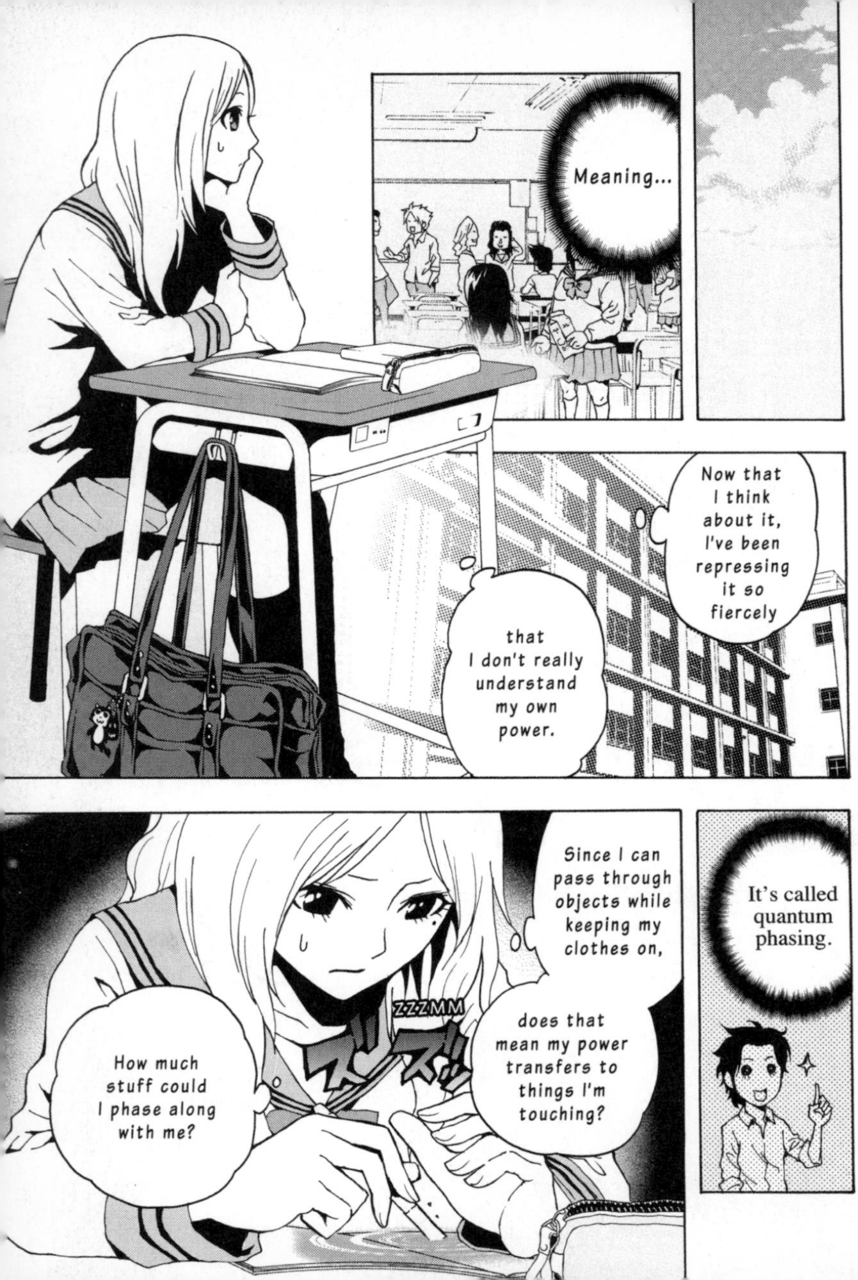

Meaning...
Now that I think about it, I've been repressing it so fiercely
that I don't really understand my own power.
It's called quantum phasing.
Since I can pass through objects while keeping my clothes on,
does that mean my power transfers to things I'm touching?
ZZZMM
How much stuff could I phase along with me?

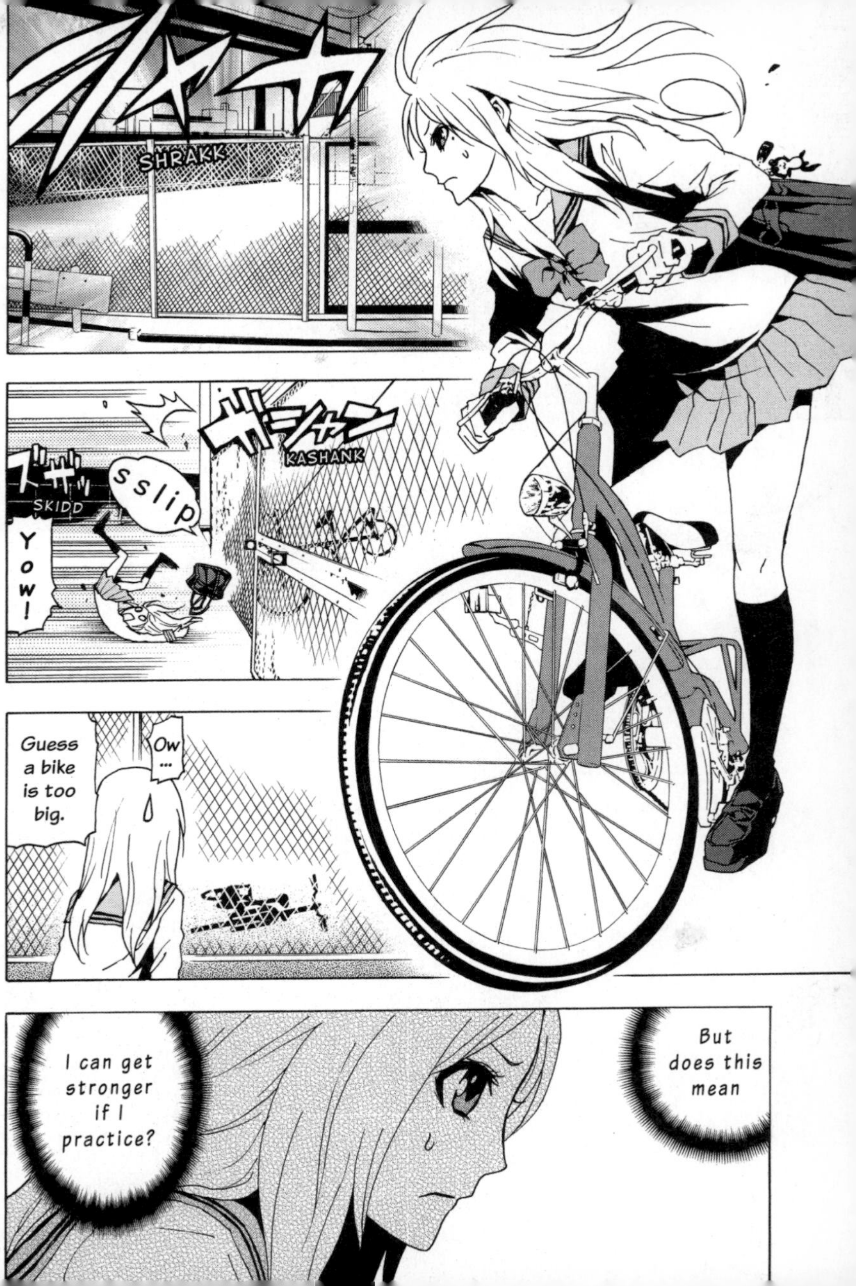
SHRAKK
KASHANK
sslip
SKIDD
Yow!
Ow ...
Guess a bike is too big.
But does this mean
I can get stronger if I practice?

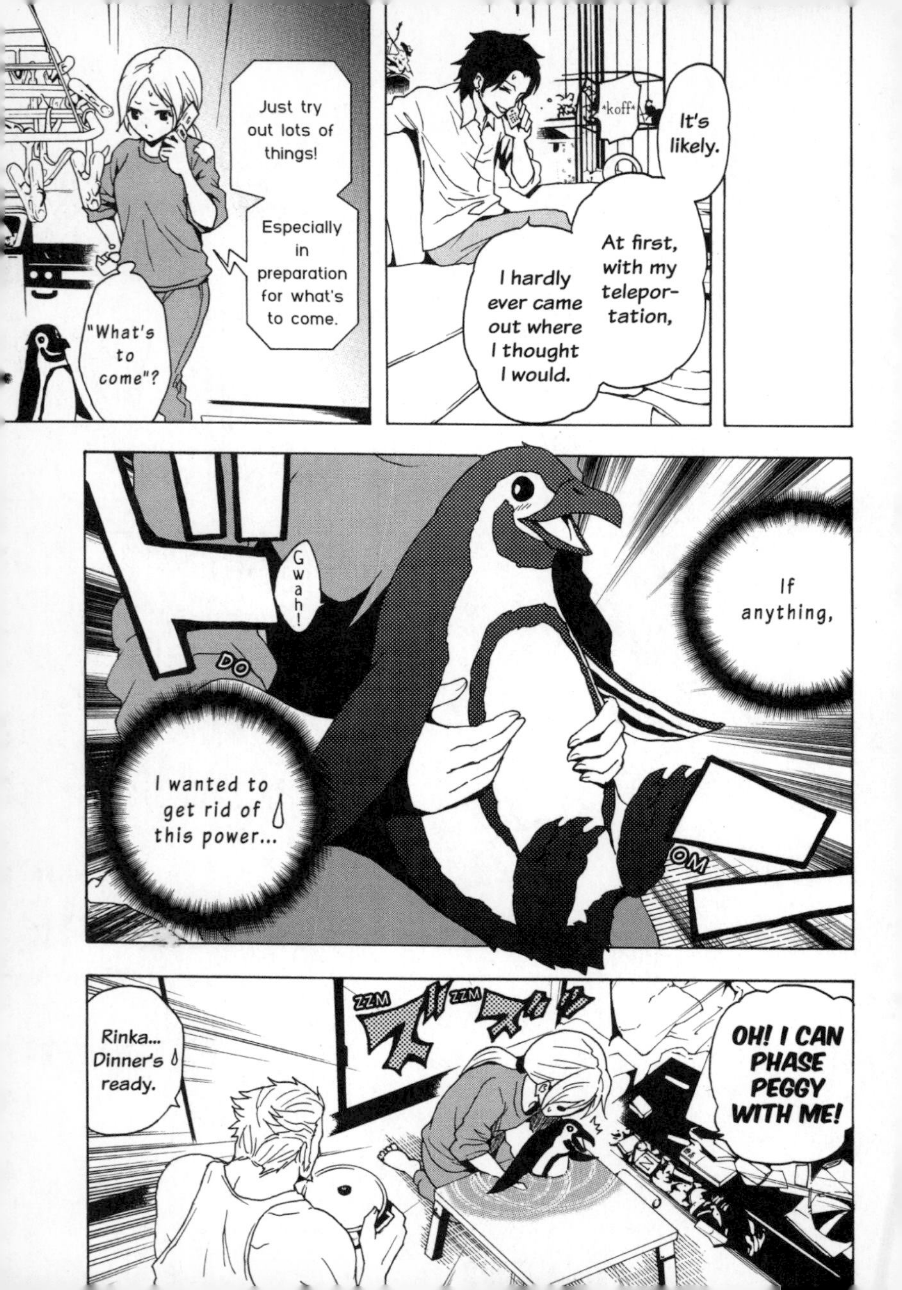
koff
It's likely.
At first, with my teleportation,
I hardly ever came out where I thought I would.
Just try out lots of things!
Especially in preparation for what's to come.
"What's to come"?
If anything,
Gwah!
DO
OM
I wanted to get rid of this power...
OH! I CAN PHASE PEGGY WITH ME!
ZZM
ZZM
Rinka... Dinner's ready.

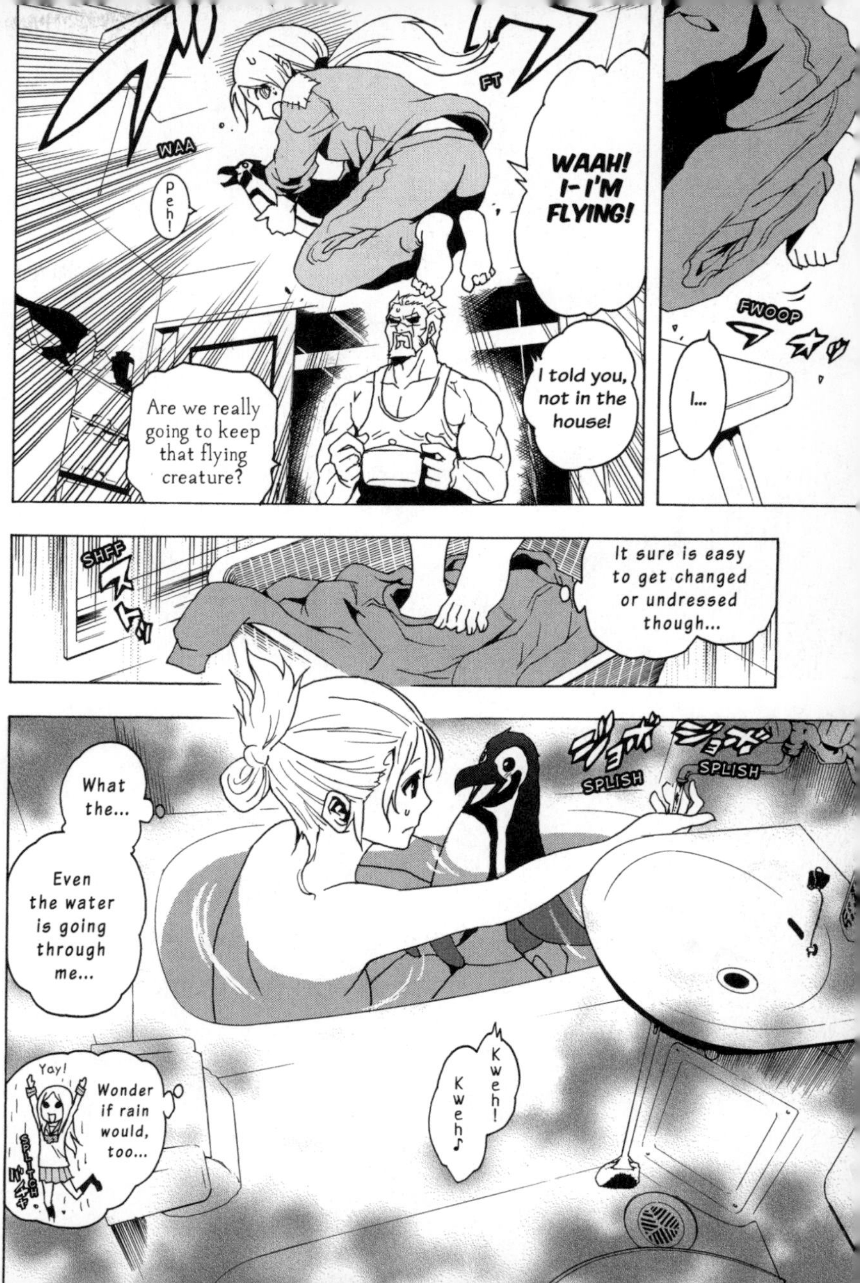
FWOOP
I...
FT
WAAH! I-I'M FLYING!
WAA
Peh!
I told you, not in the house!
Are we really going to keep that flying creature?
It sure is easy to get changed or undressed though...
SHFF
SPLISH
SPLISH
What the...
Even the water is going through me...
Kweh! Kweh♪
Yay!
Wonder if rain would, too...
SPLITCH

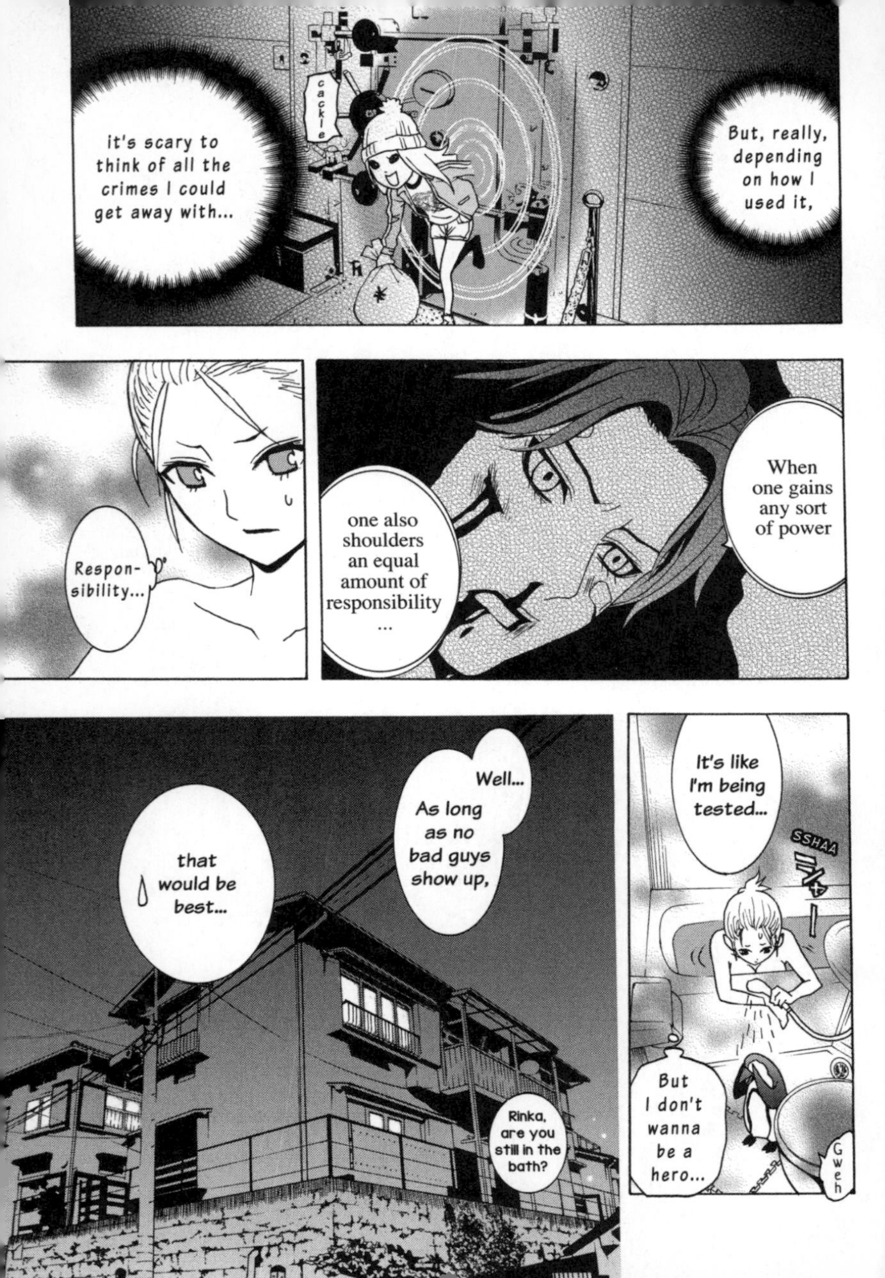
But, really, depending on how I used it,
cackle
it's scary to think of all the crimes I could get away with...
When one gains any sort of power
one also shoulders an equal amount of responsibility ...
Respon-sibility...
It's like I'm being tested...
SSHAA
But I don't wanna be a hero...
Gweh
Well... As long as no bad guys show up,
that would be best...
Rinka, are you still in the bath?

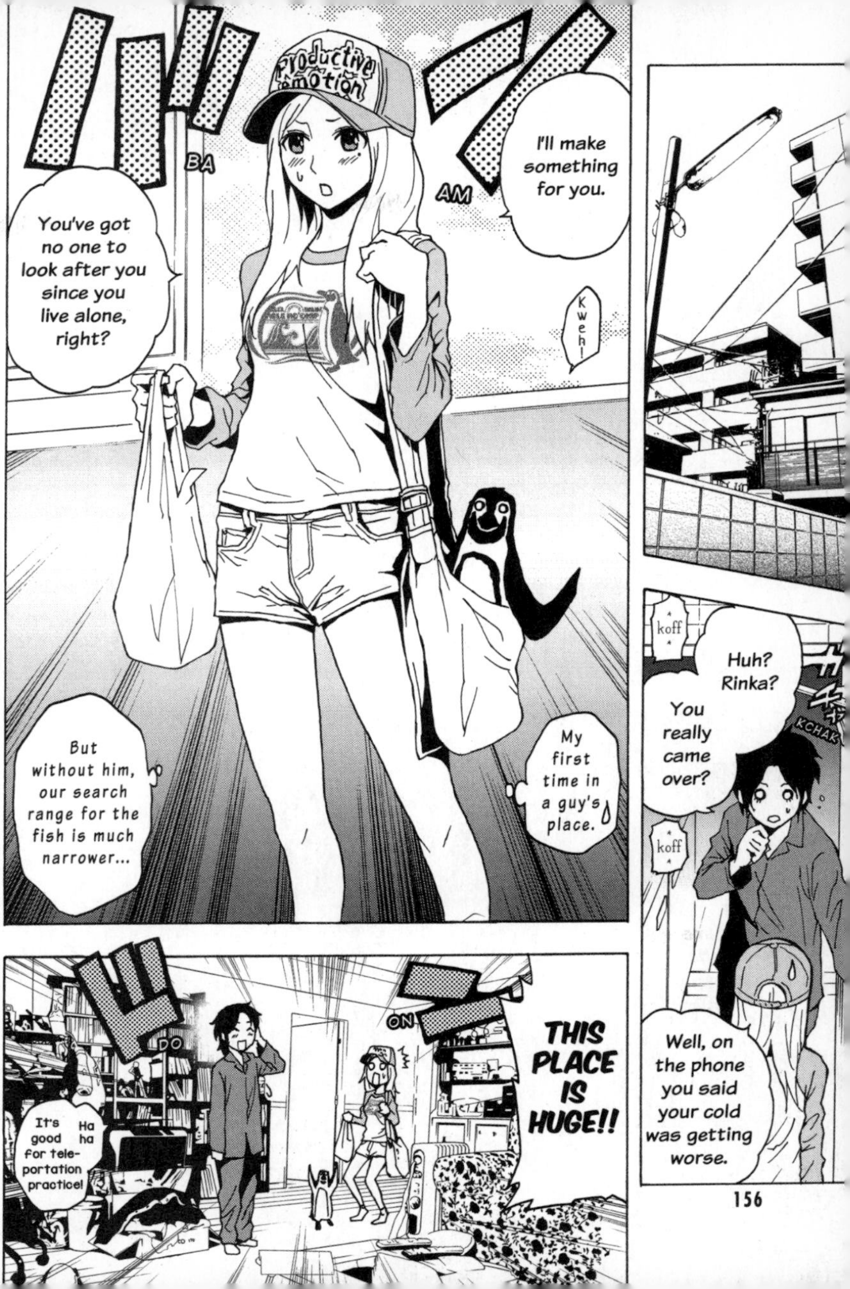
koff
Huh? Rinka?
KCHAK
You really came over?
koff
Well, on the phone you said your cold was getting worse.
BA
AM
I'll make something for you.
You've got no one to look after you since you live alone, right?
Kweh!
My first time in a guy's place.
But without him, our search range for the fish is much narrower...
DO
ON
THIS PLACE IS HUGE!!
Ha ha
It's good for tele-portation practice!

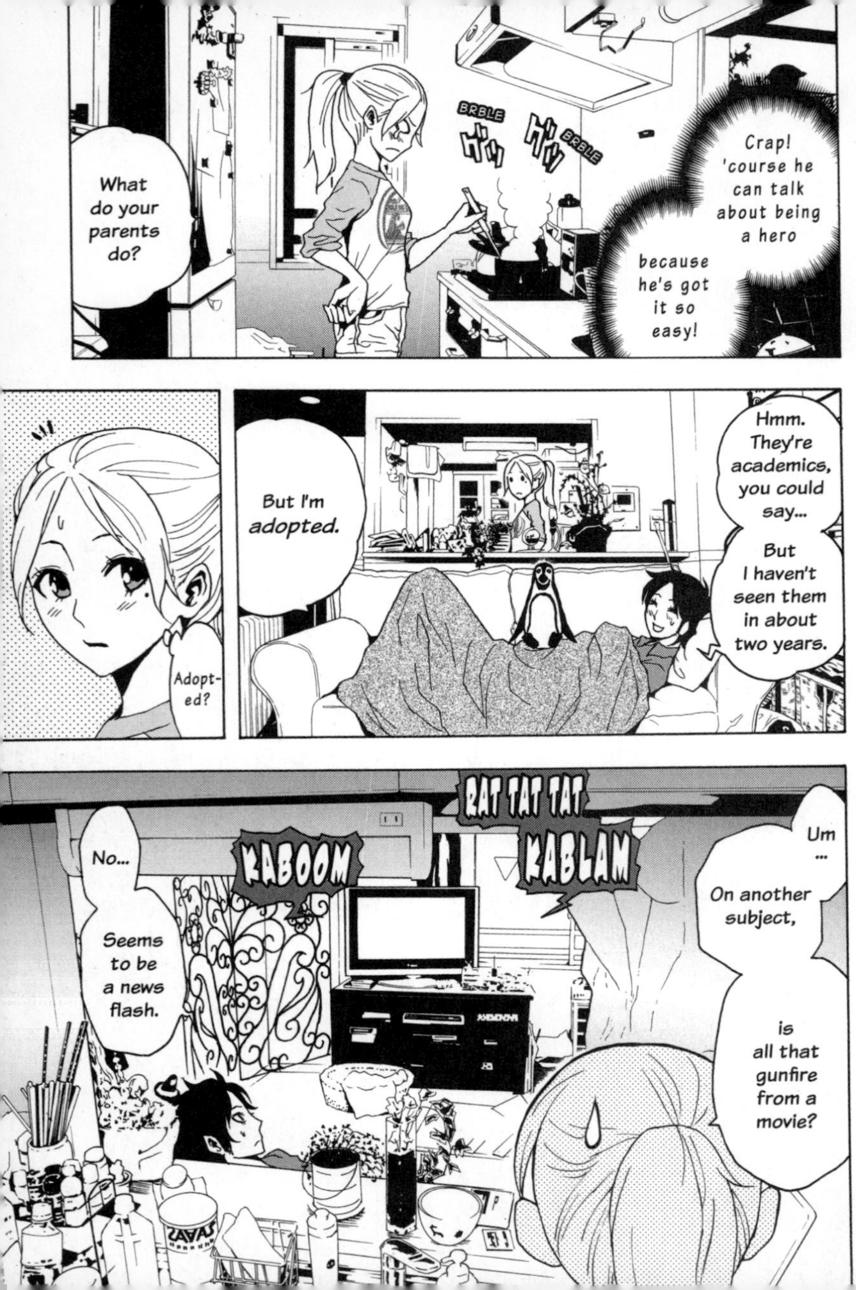
Crap! 'course he can talk about being a hero
because he's got it so easy!
BRBLE
BRBLE
What do your parents do?
Hmm. They're academics, you could say...
But I haven't seen them in about two years.
But I'm adopted.
Adopt-ed?
RAT TAT TAT
KABLAM
Um ...
On another subject,
is all that gunfire from a movie?
KABOOM
No...
Seems to be a news flash.

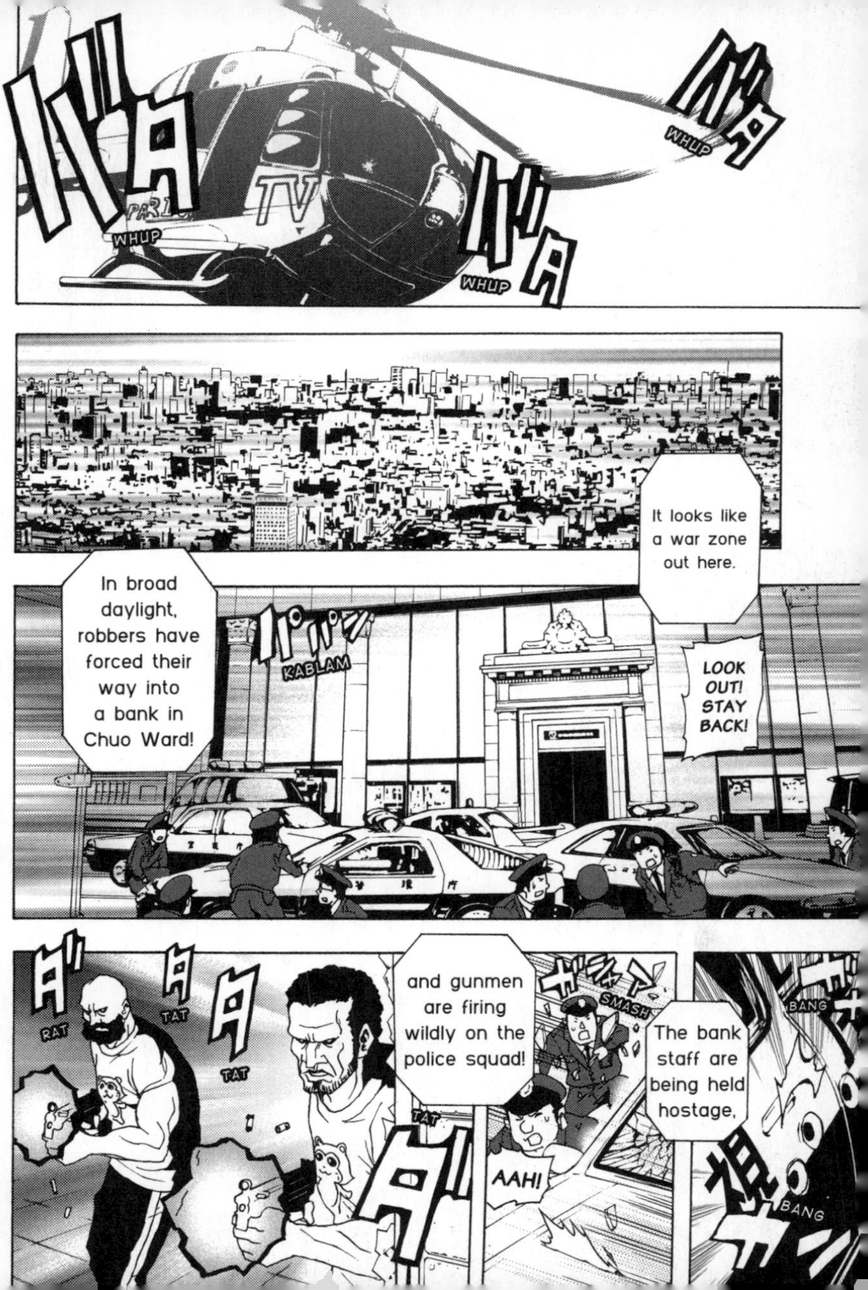
WHUP
TV
WHUP
WHUP
It looks like a war zone out here.
In broad daylight, robbers have forced their way into a bank in Chuo Ward!
KABLAM
LOOK OUT! STAY BACK!
BANG
BANG
and gunmen are firing wildly on the police squad!
SMASH
The bank staff are being held hostage,
TAT
AAH!
RAT
TAT
TAT

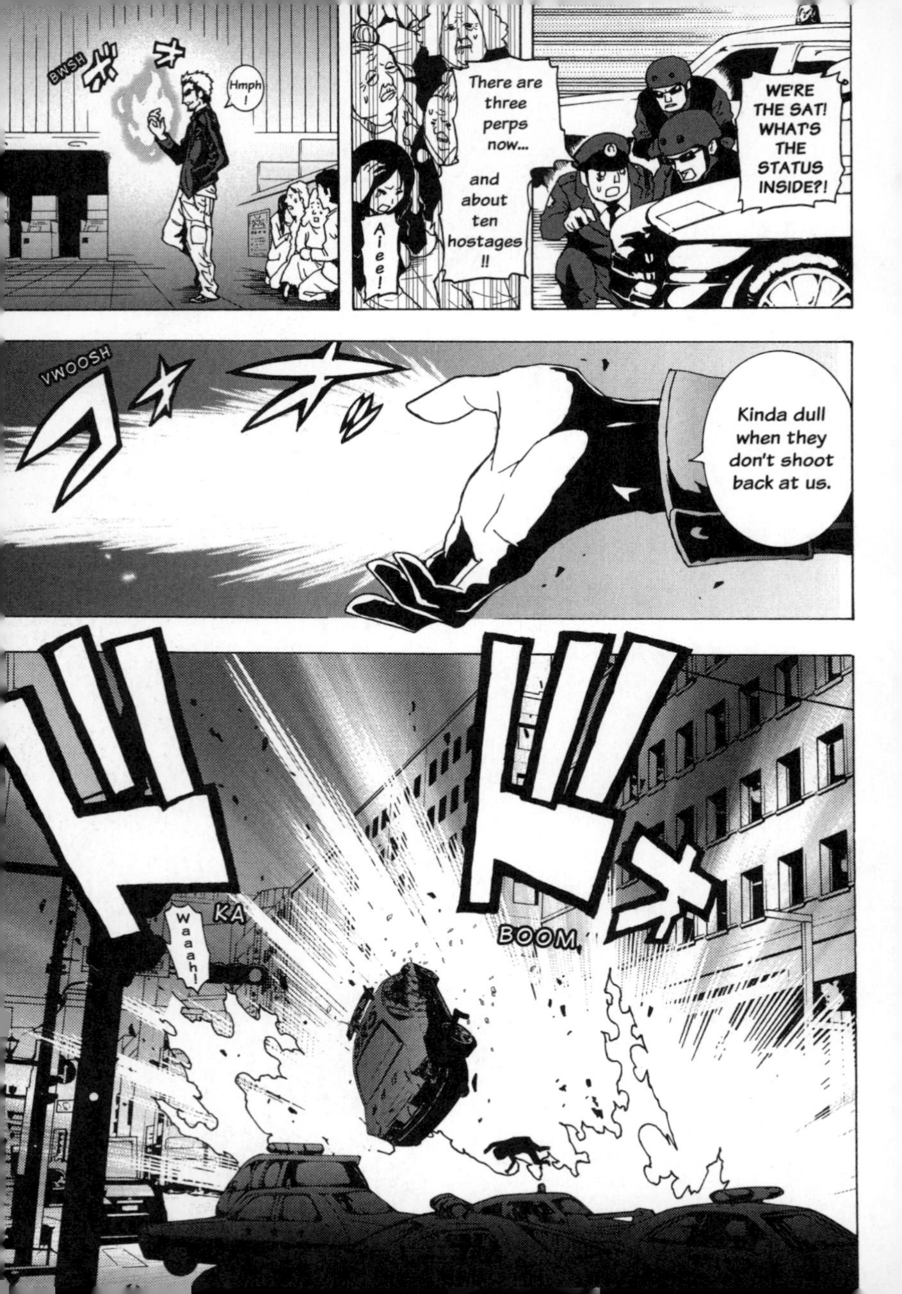
WE'RE THE SAT! WHAT'S THE STATUS INSIDE?!
There are three perps now...
and about ten hostages!!
Aieee!
BWSH
Hmph!
VWOOSH
Kinda dull when they don't shoot back at us.
BOOM
KA
Waaah!

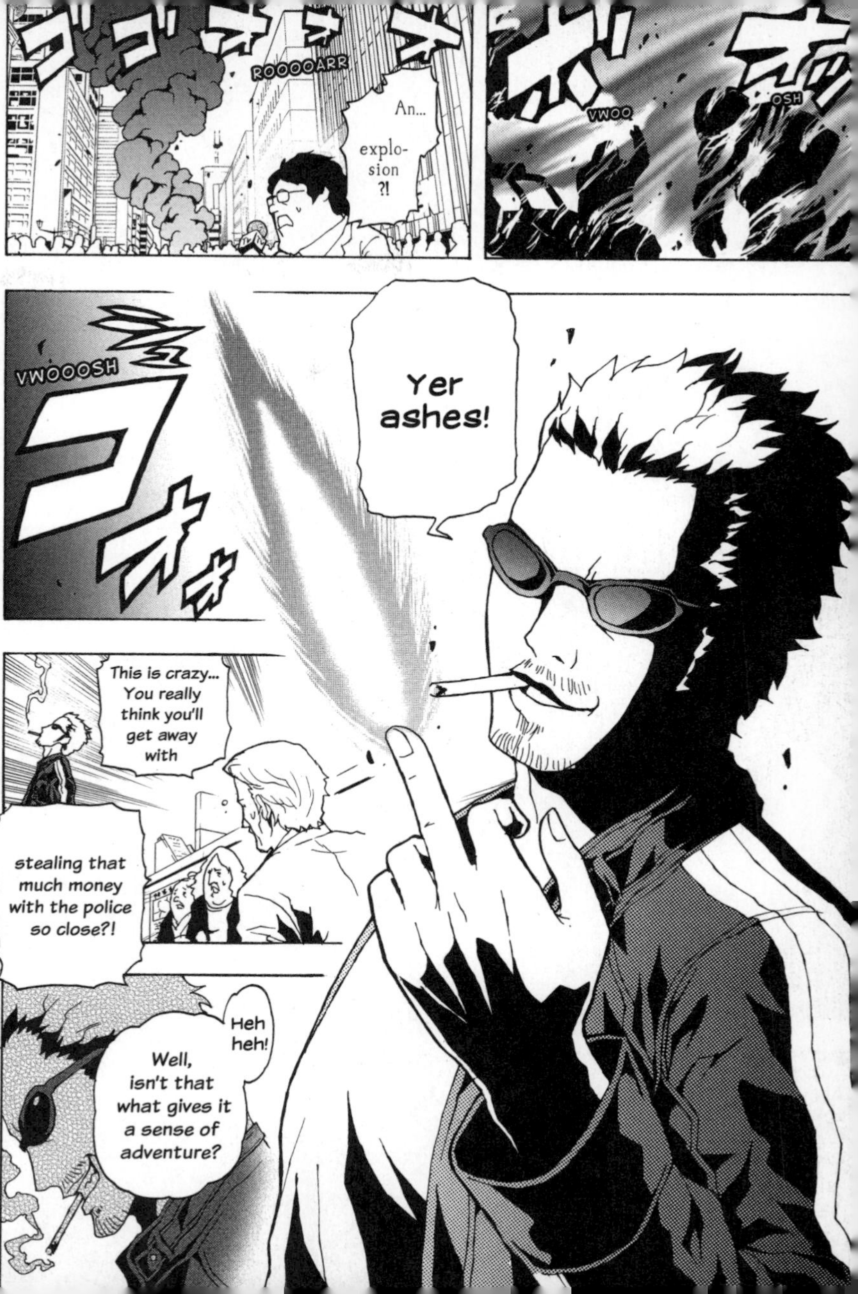
VWOO
OSH
ROOOOARR
An... explosion?!
Yer ashes!
VWOOOSH
This is crazy... You really think you'll get away with
stealing that much money with the police so close?!
Heh heh!
Well, isn't that what gives it a sense of adventure?

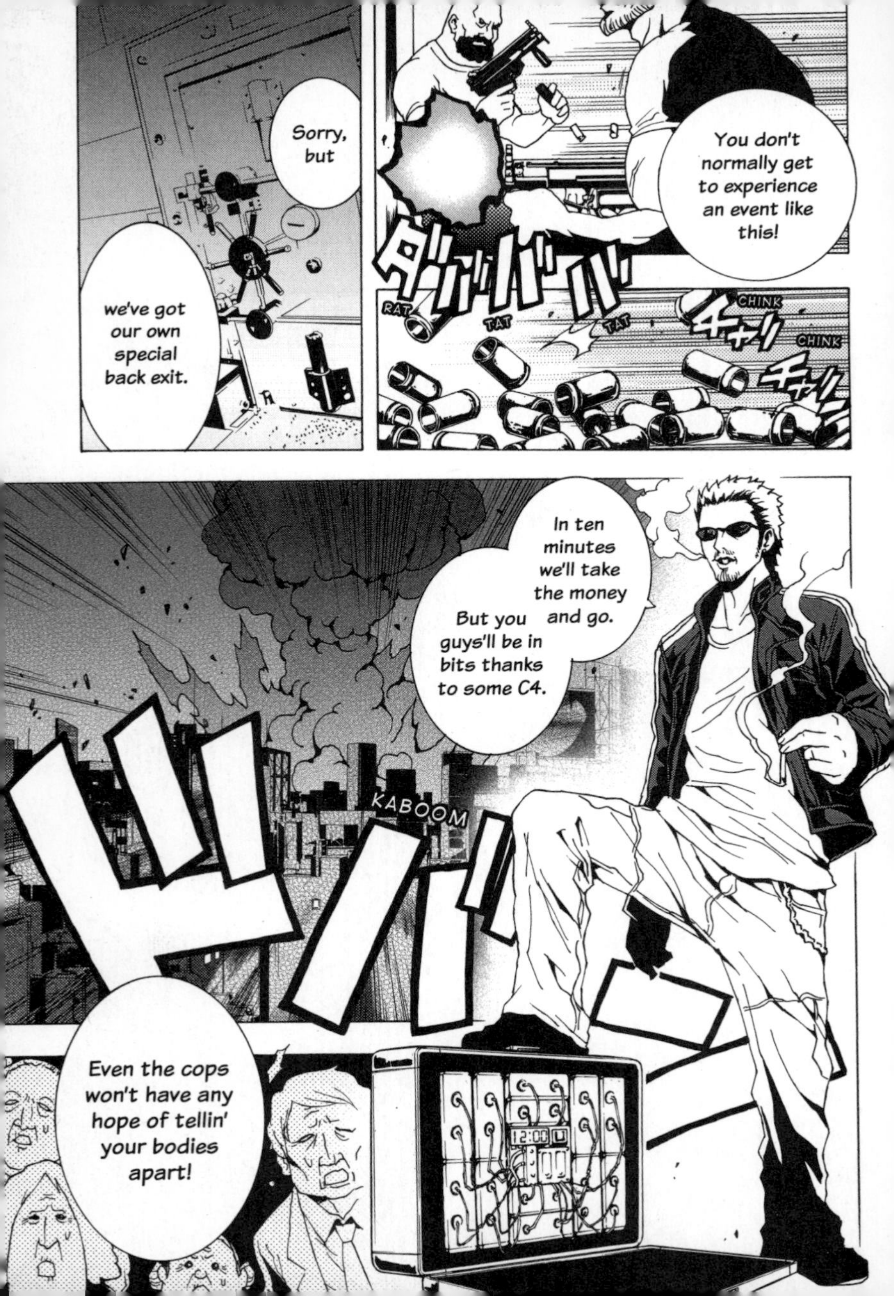
You don't normally get to experience an event like this!
RAT
TAT
TAT
CHINK
CHINK
Sorry, but
we've got our own special back exit.
In ten minutes we'll take the money and go.
But you guys'll be in bits thanks to some C4.
KABOOM
12:00
Even the cops won't have any hope of tellin' your bodies apart!

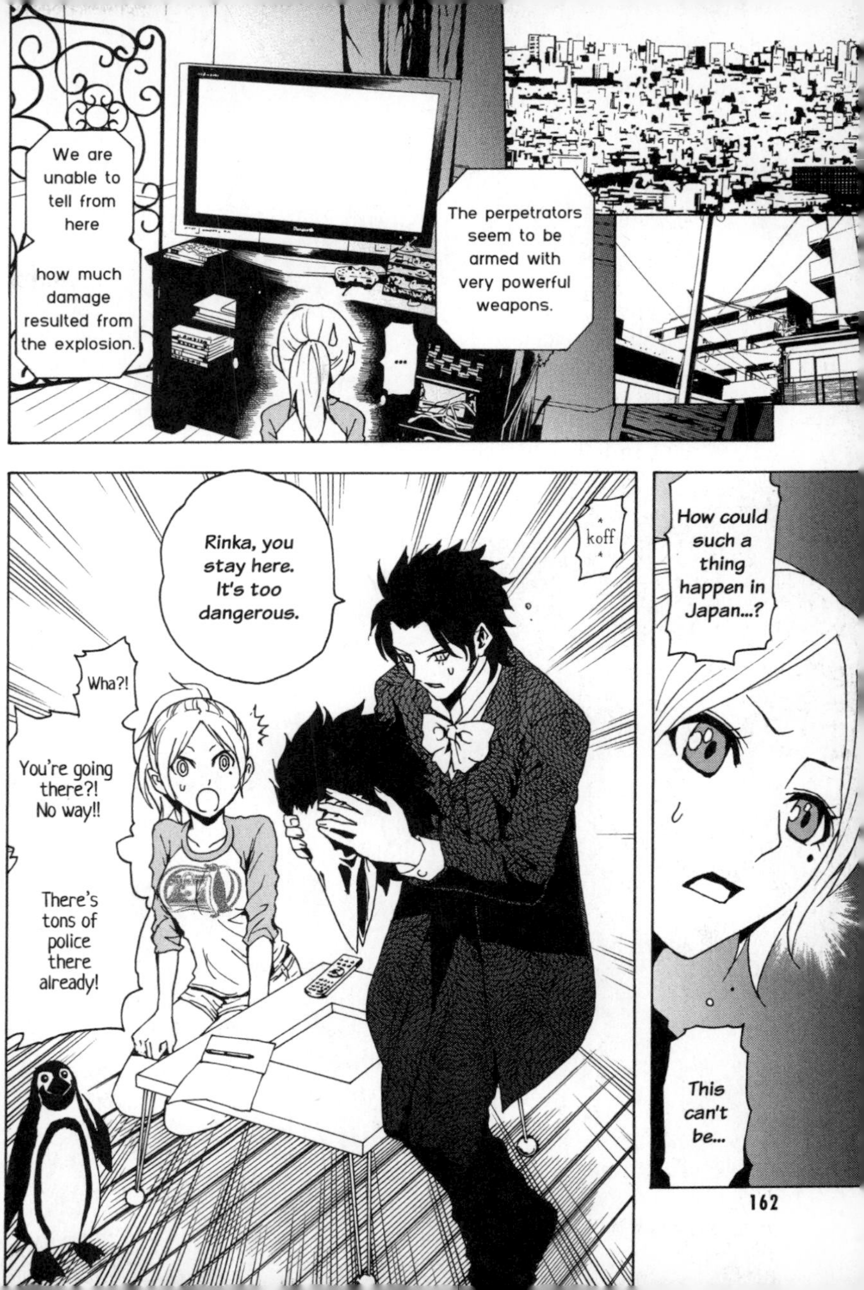
We are unable to tell from here how much damage resulted from the explosion.
The perpetrators seem to be armed with very powerful weapons.
...
How could such a thing happen in Japan...?
This can't be...
koff
Rinka, you stay here. It's too dangerous.
Wha?!
You're going there?! No way!!
There's tons of police there already!

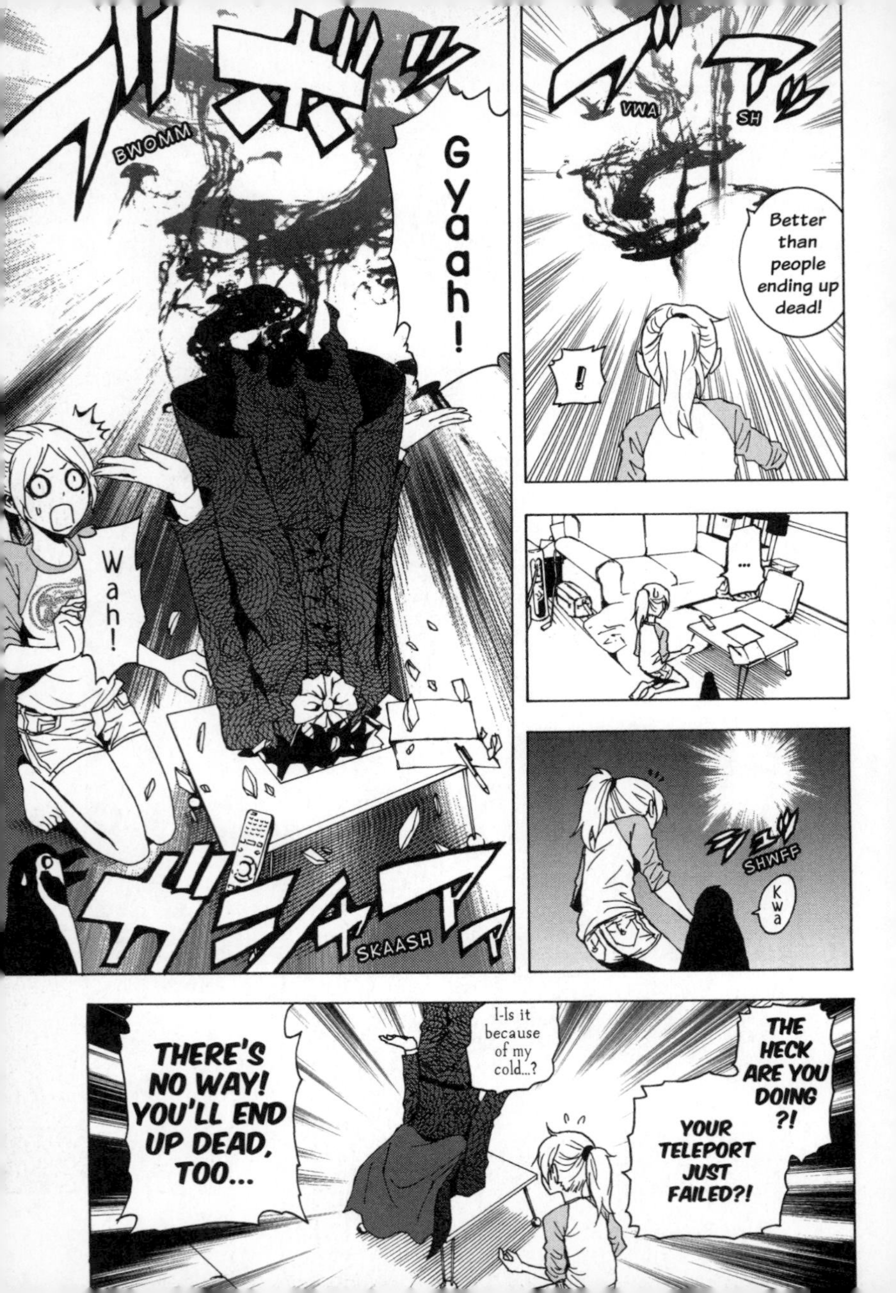
VWA SH
Better than people ending up dead!
!
...
SHWFF
Kwa
BWOMM
Gyaah!
Wah!
SKAASH
THE HECK ARE YOU DOING?!
YOUR TELEPORT JUST FAILED?!
I-Is it because of my cold...?
THERE'S NO WAY! YOU'LL END UP DEAD, TOO...

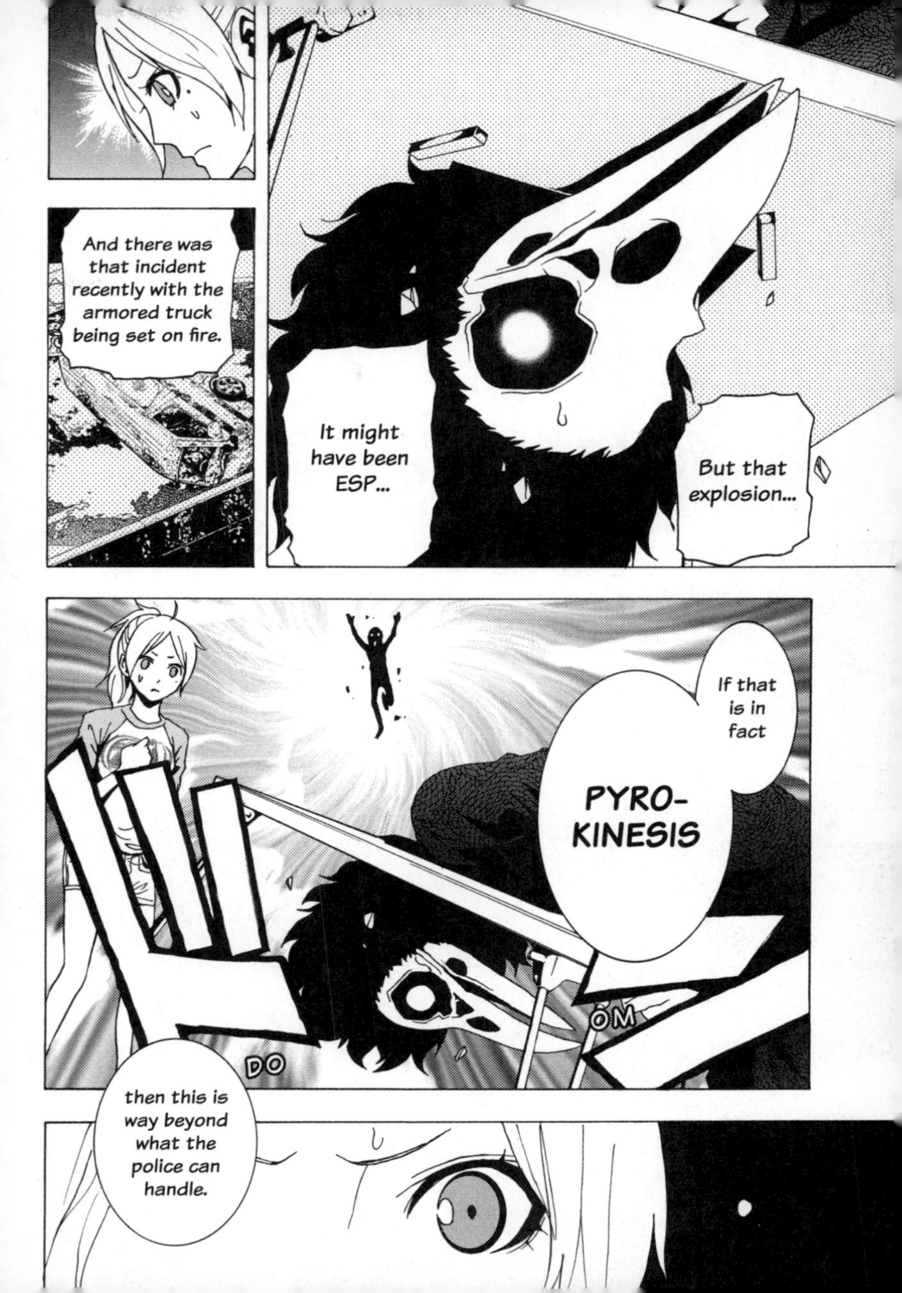
But that explosion...
It might have been ESP...
And there was that incident recently with the armored truck being set on fire.
If that is in fact
PYRO-KINESIS
OM
DO
then this is way beyond what the police can handle.

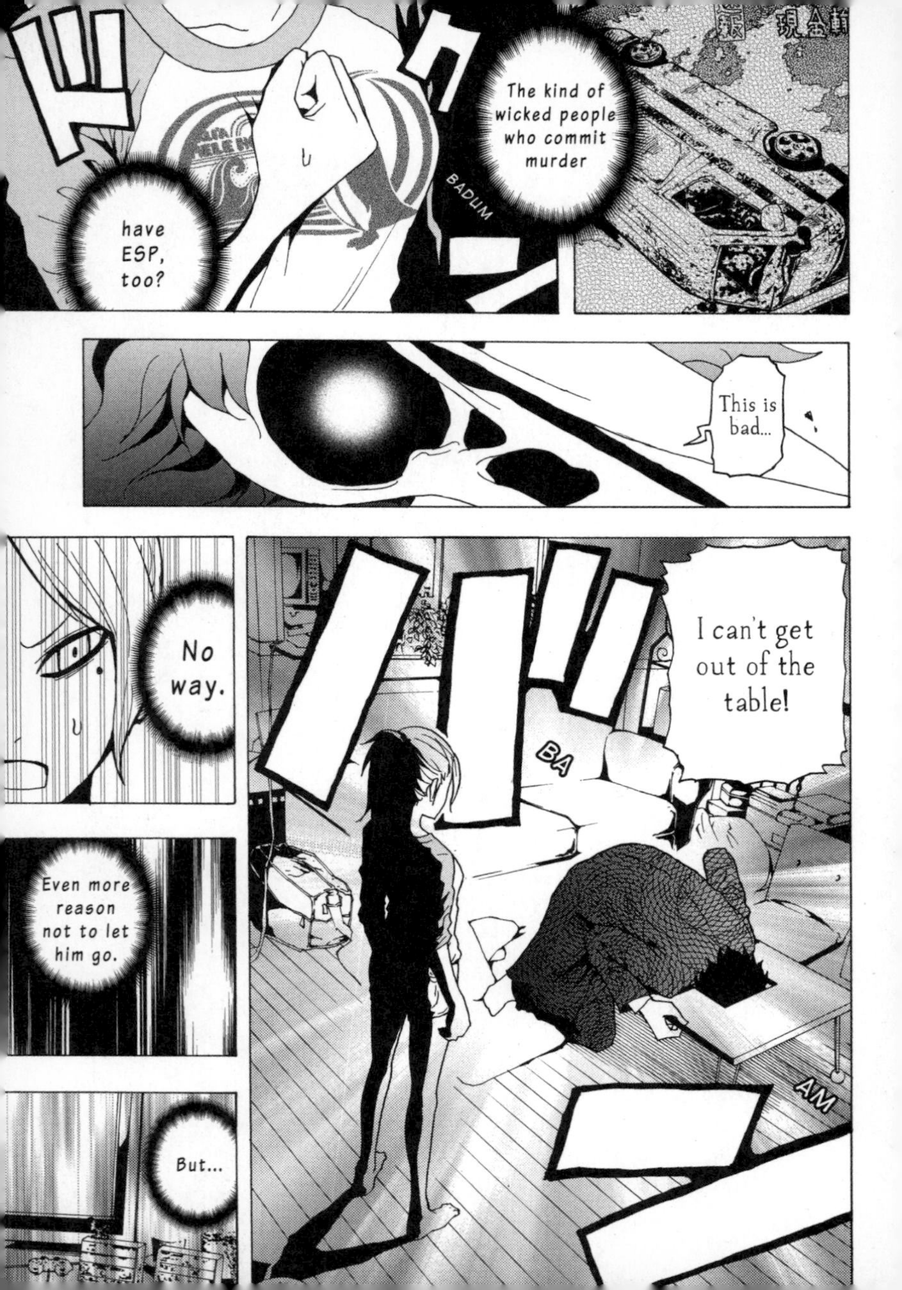
The kind of wicked people who commit murder
BADUM
have ESP, too?
This is bad...
I can't get out of the table!
BA
AM
No way.
Even more reason not to let him go.
But...

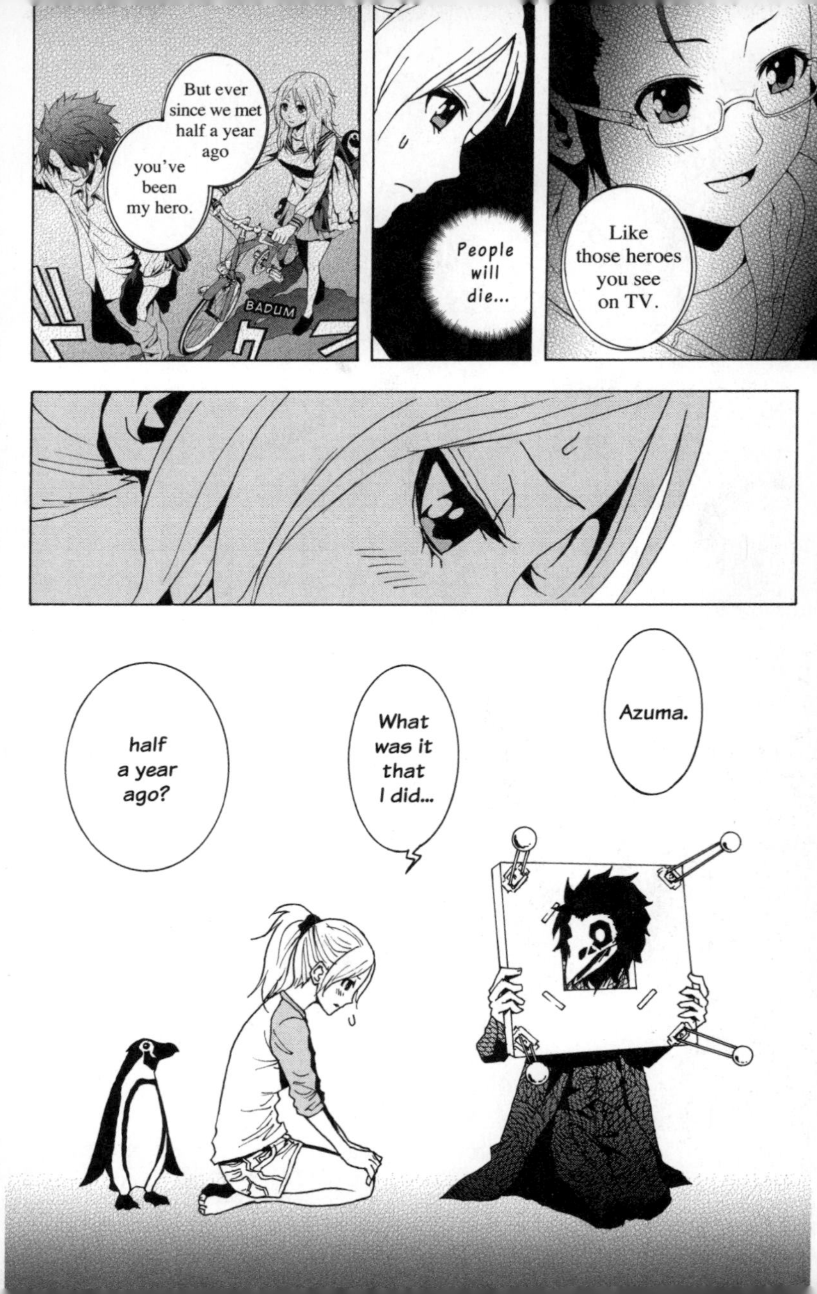
Like those heroes you see on TV.
People will die...
But ever since we met half a year ago
you've been my hero.
BADUM
Azuma.
What was it that I did...
half a year ago?

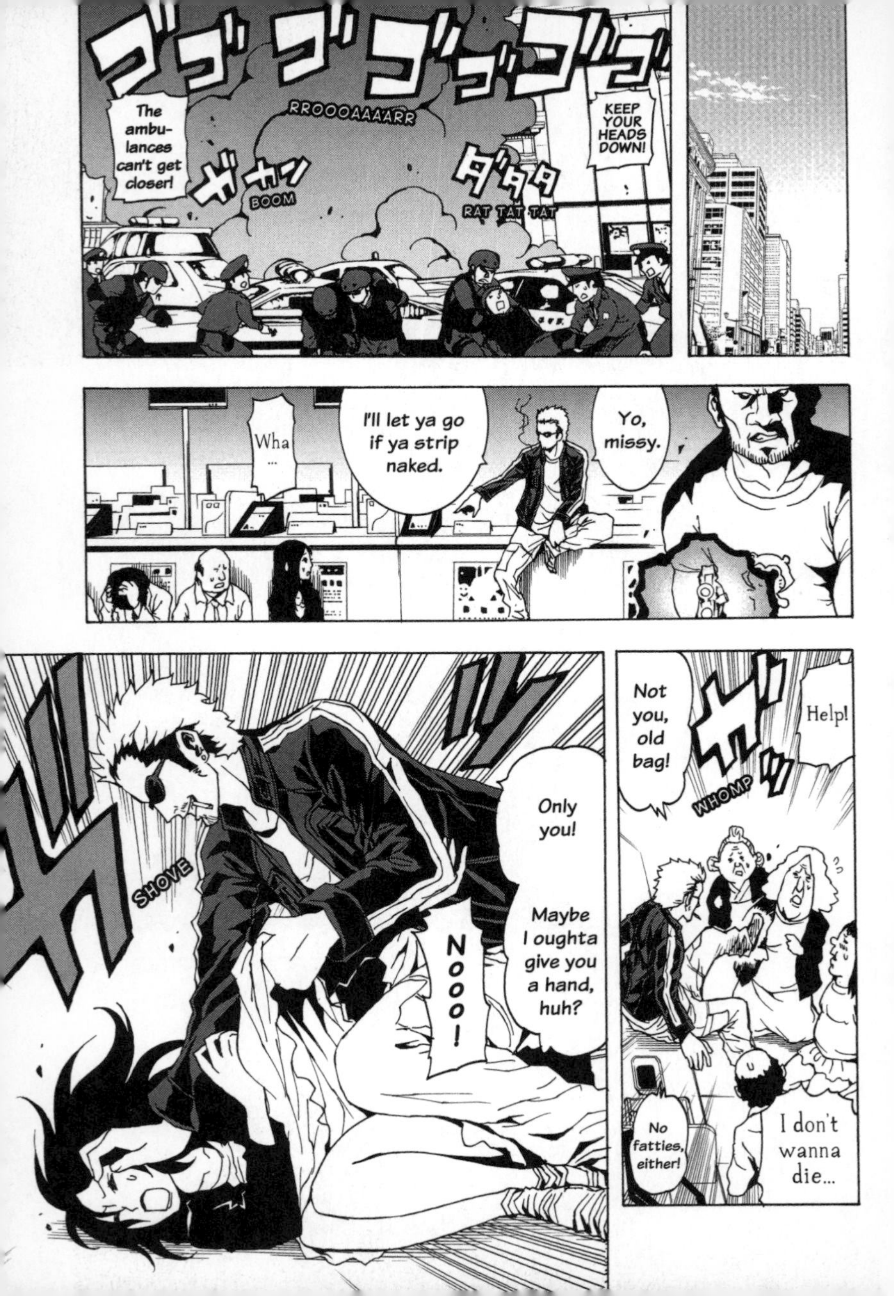
KEEP YOUR HEADS DOWN!
RRROOOAAAARR
RAT TAT TAT
BOOM
The ambulances can't get closer!
Yo, missy.
I'll let ya go if ya strip naked.
Wha ...
Help!
Not you, old bag!
WHOMP
I don't wanna die...
No fatties, either!
Only you!
Maybe I oughta give you a hand, huh?
NOOOO!
SHOVE

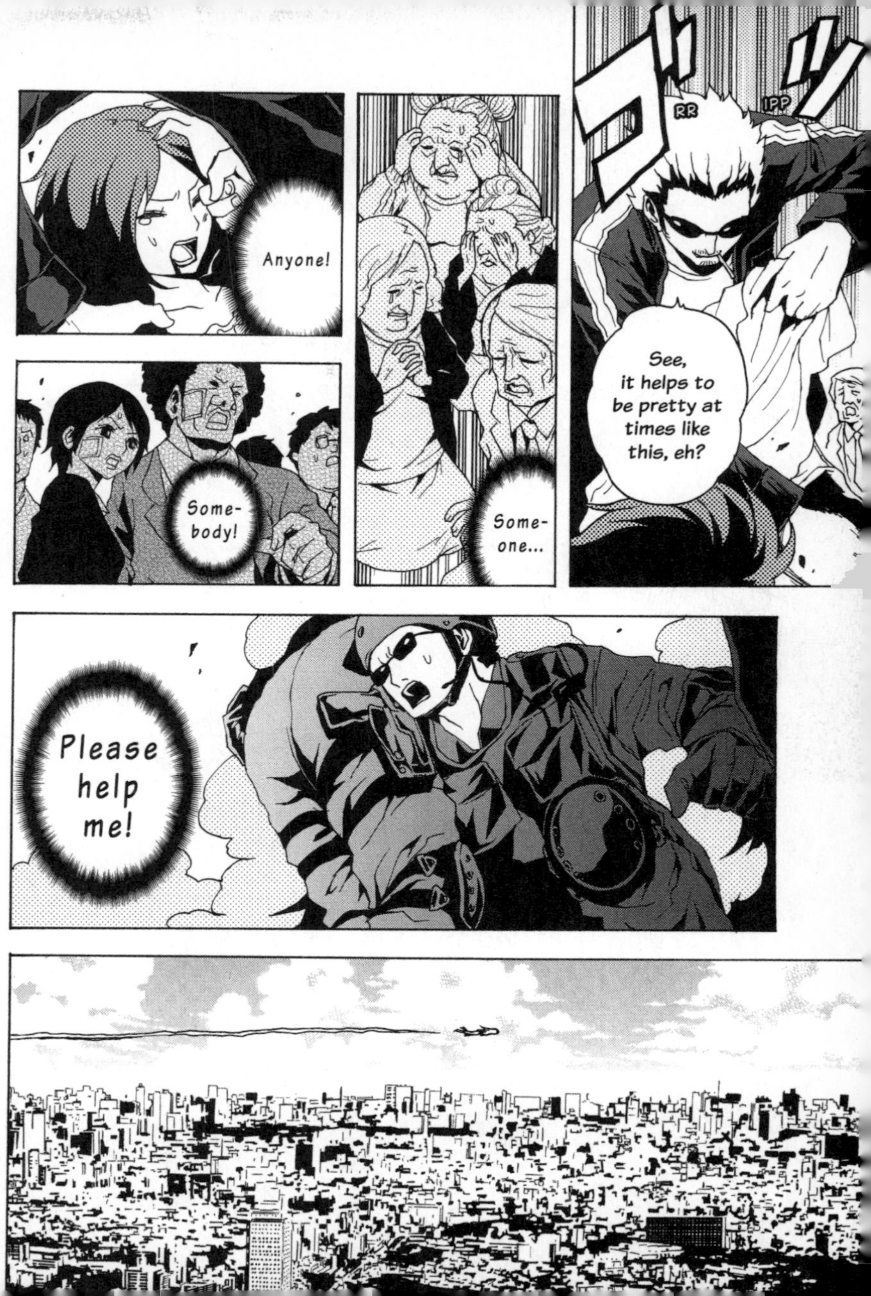
RR
IPP
See, it helps to be pretty at times like this, eh?
Some-one...
Anyone!
Some-body!
Please help me!

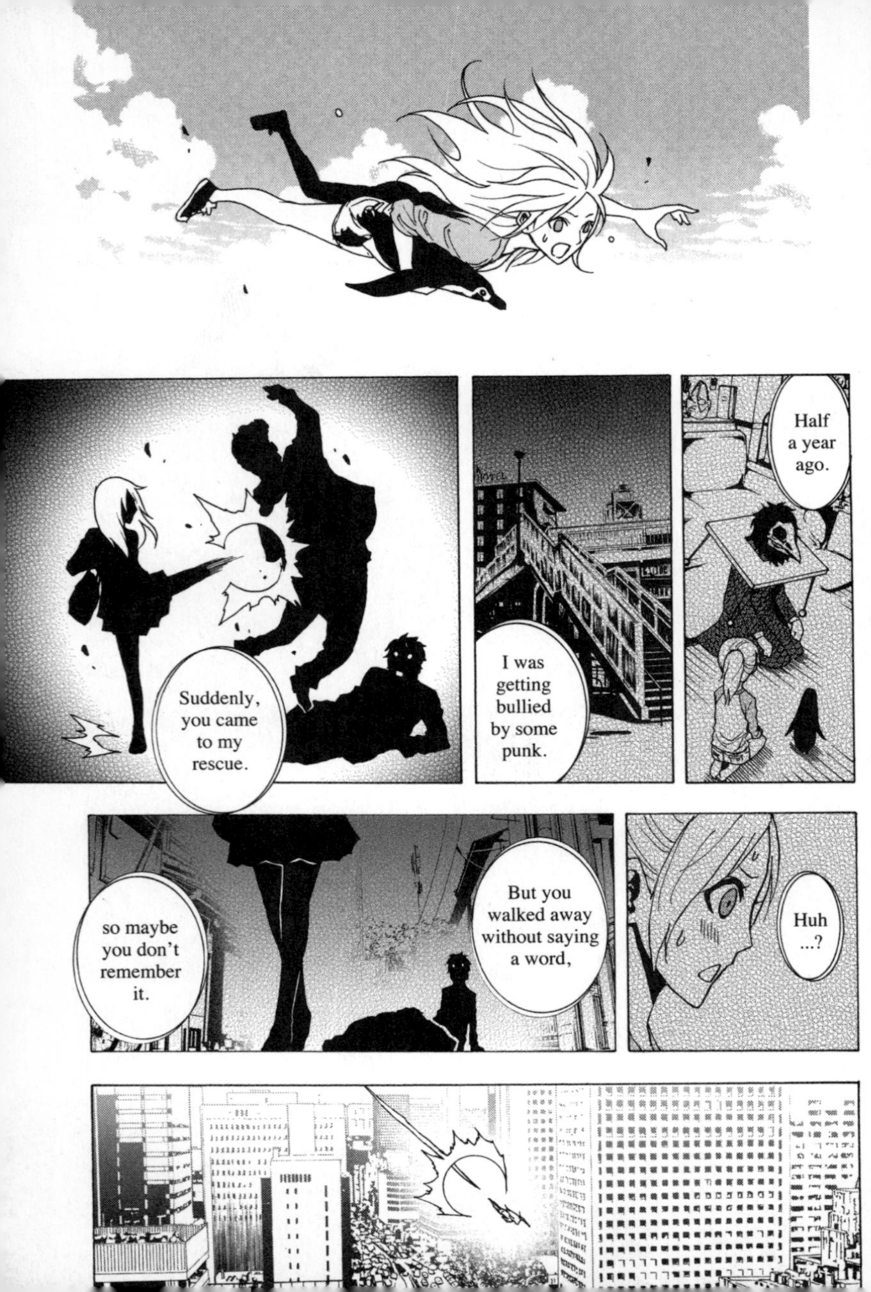

Half a year ago.
I was getting bullied by some punk.
Suddenly, you came to my rescue.
Huh ...?
But you walked away without saying a word,
so maybe you don't remember it.

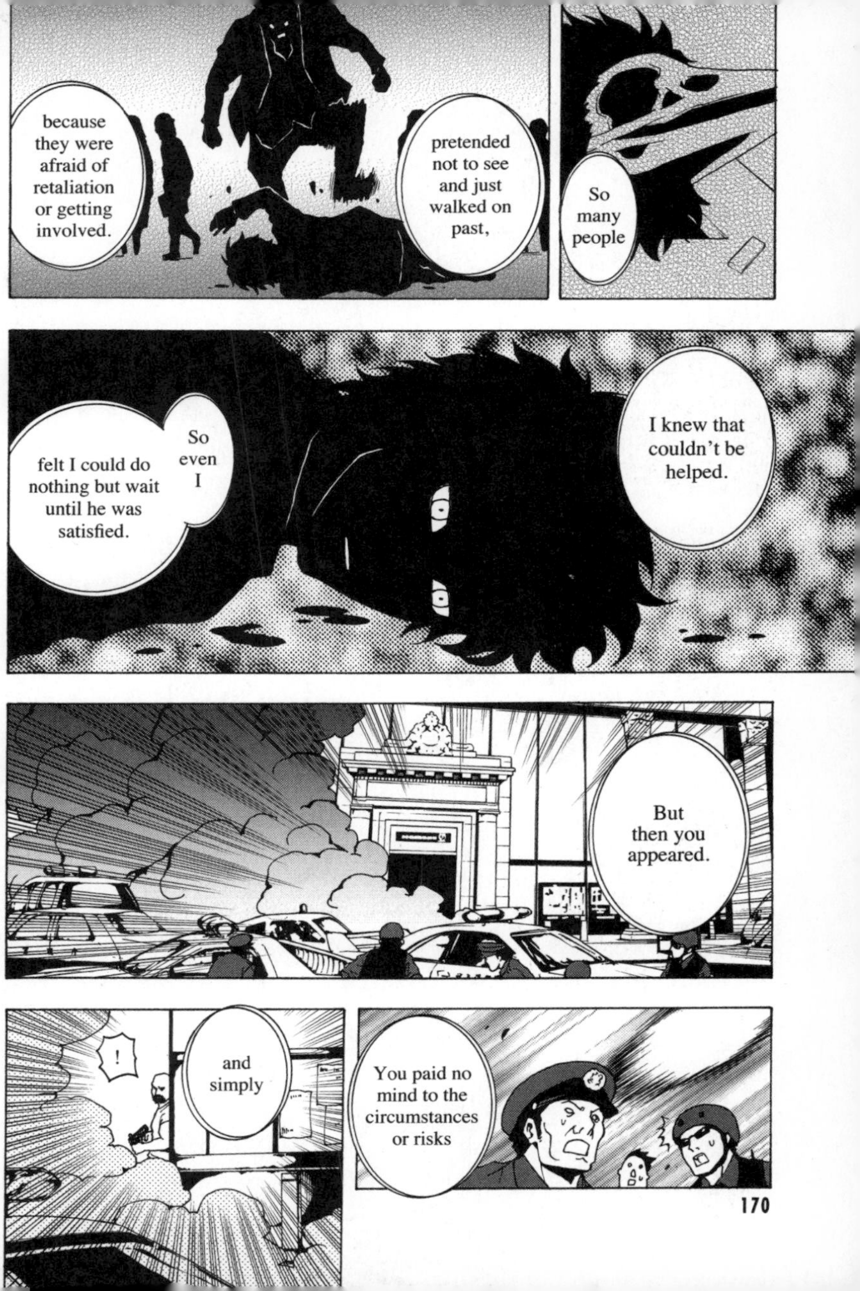
So many people
pretended not to see and just walked on past,
because they were afraid of retaliation or getting involved.
I knew that couldn't be helped.
So even I
felt I could do nothing but wait until he was satisfied.
But then you appeared.
You paid no mind to the circumstances or risks
and simply
!

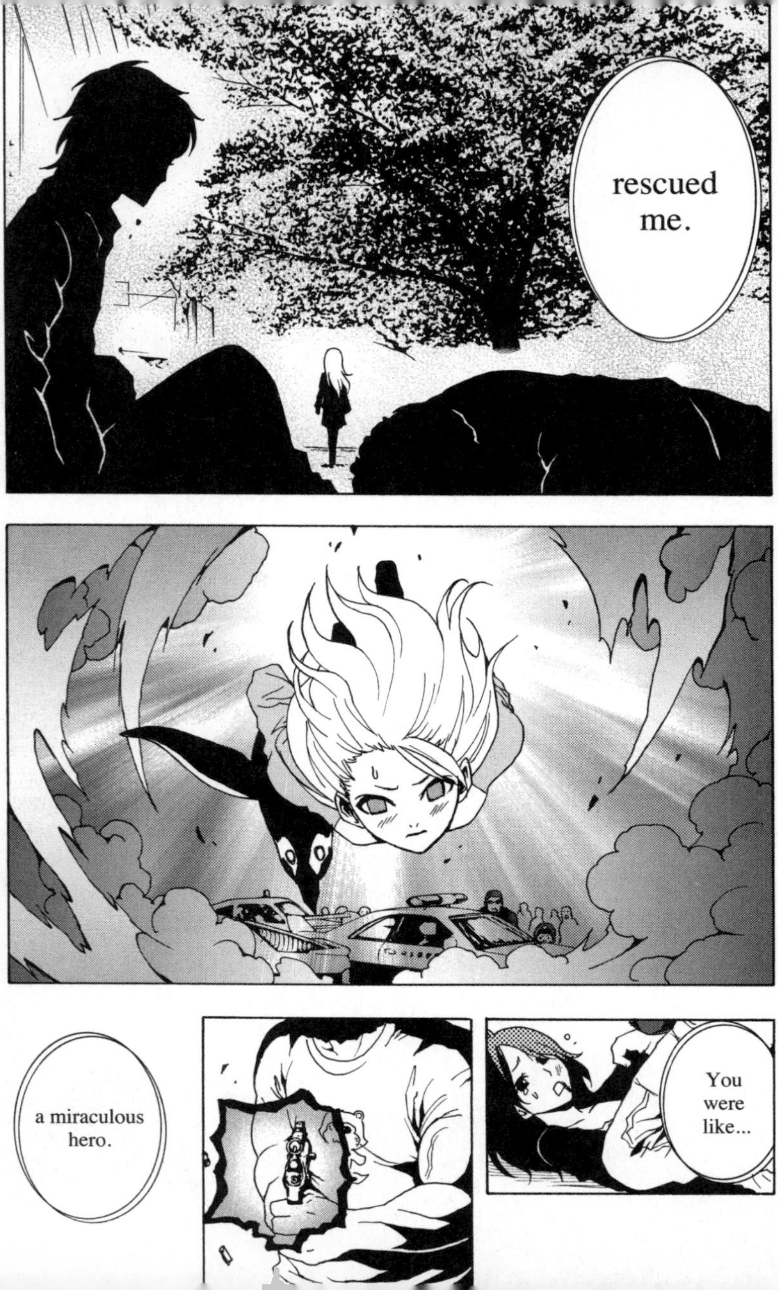
rescued me.
You were like...
a miraculous hero.

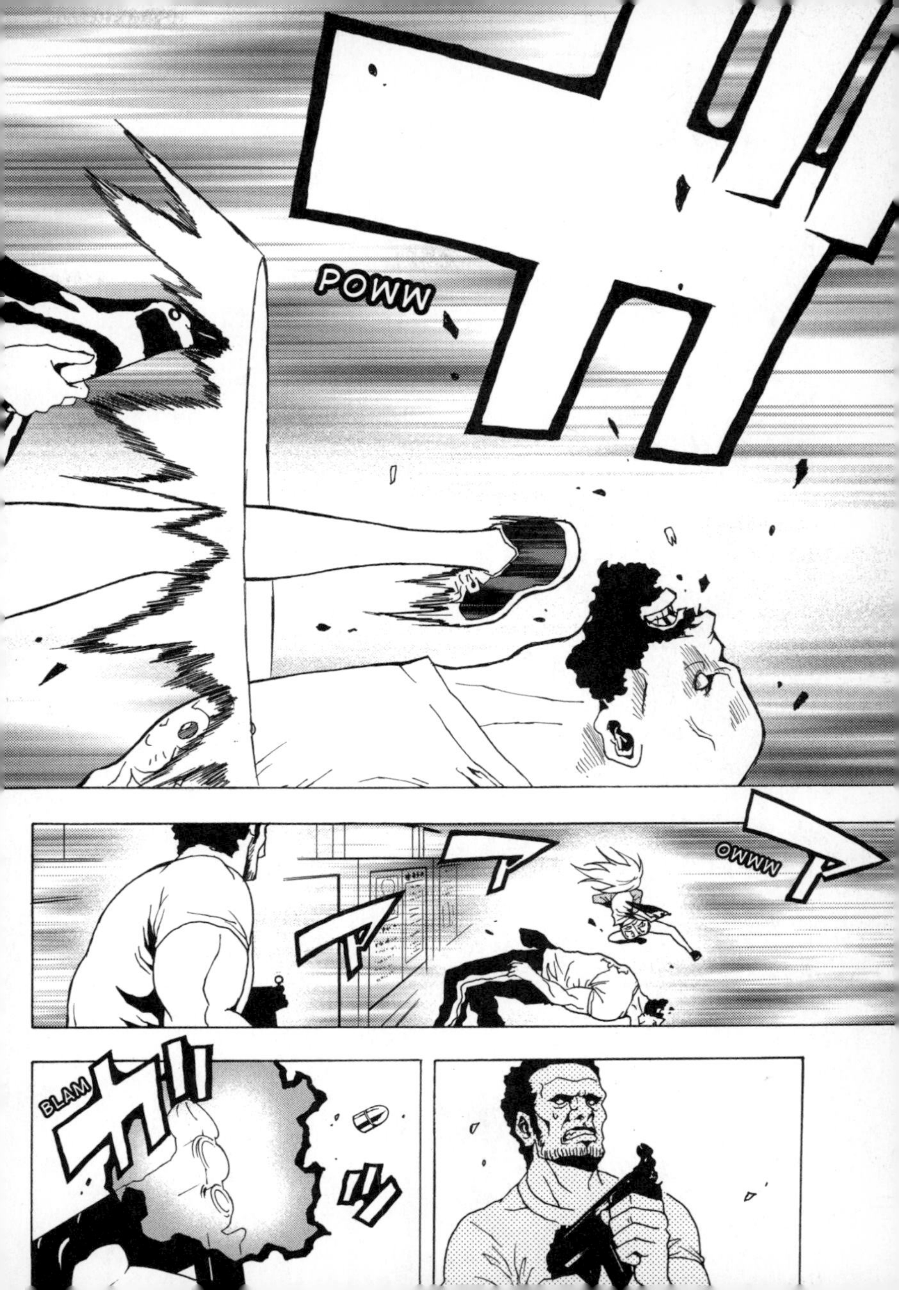
POWW
OWWW
BLAM

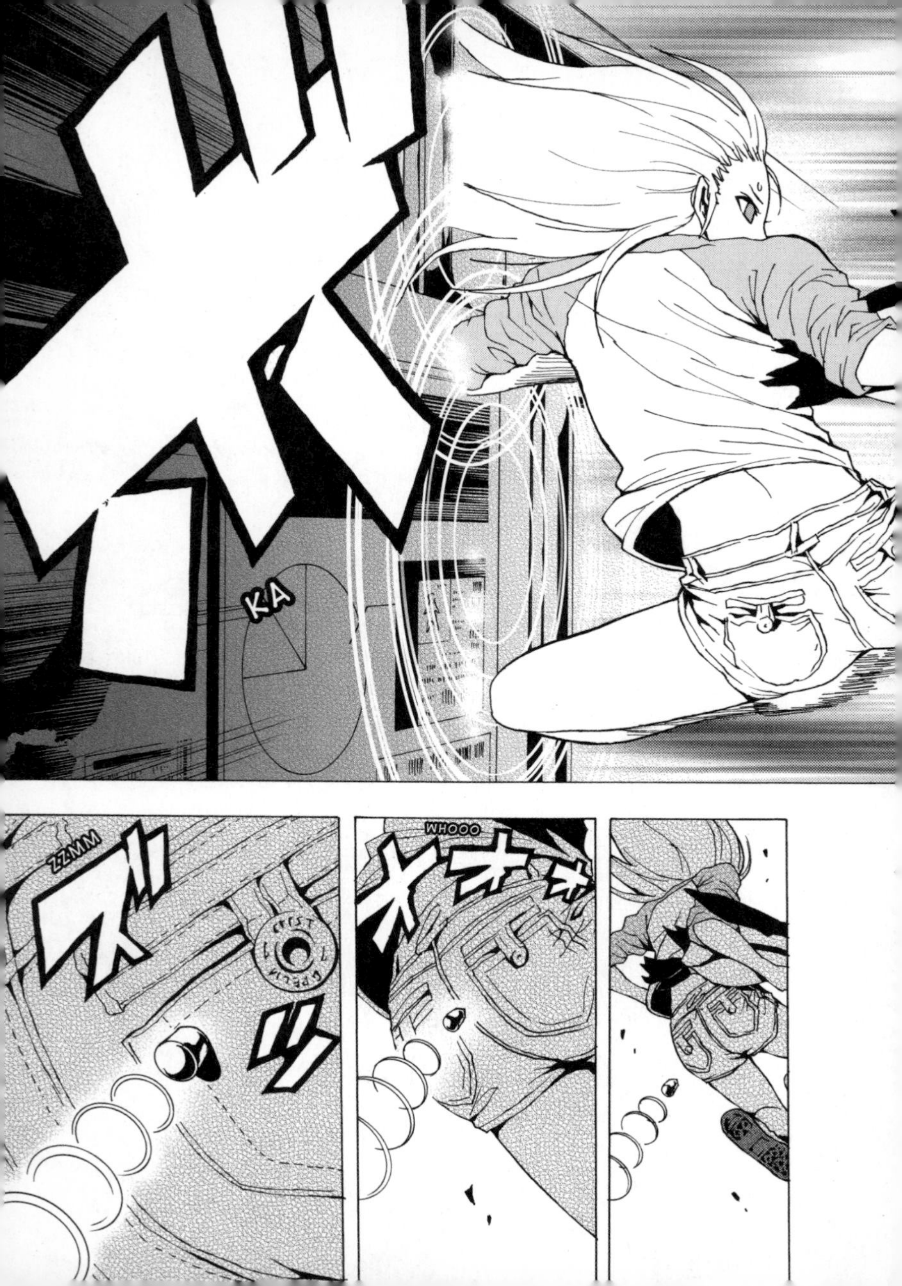
KA
WHOOO
ZZMM

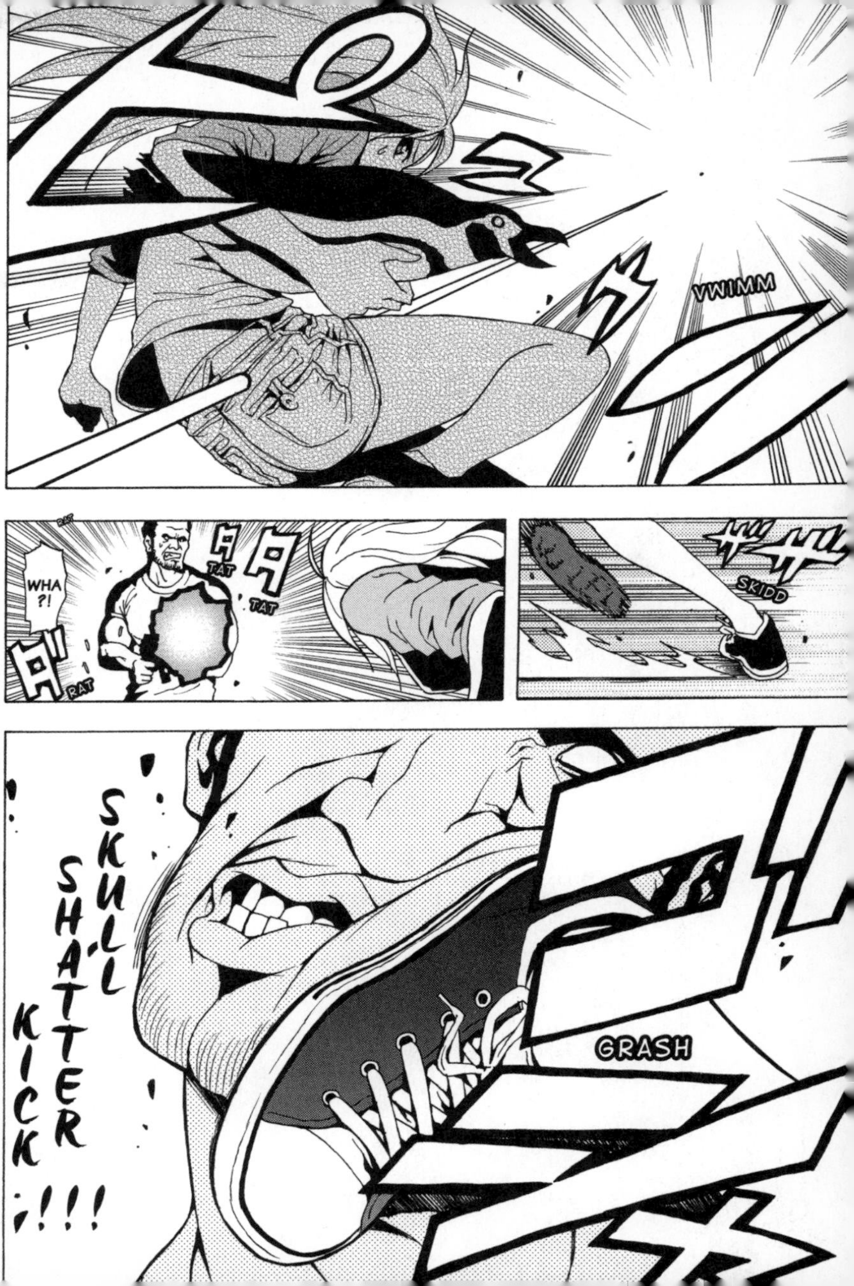
VWIMM
SKIDD
TAT
TAT
RAT
WHA ?!
RAT
GRASH
SKULL-SHATTER KICK ¡!!!

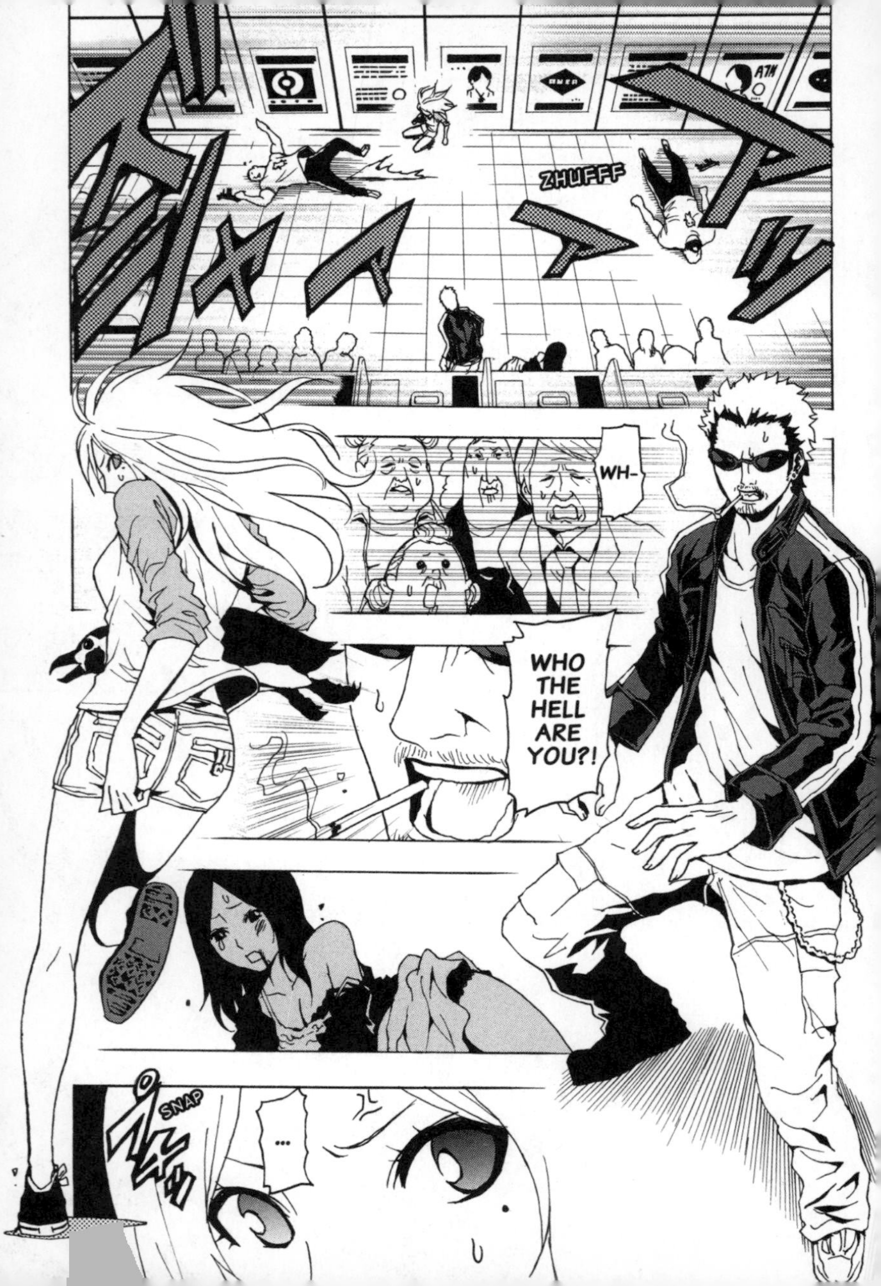
ZHUFFF
WH-
WHO THE HELL ARE YOU?!
SNAP
...

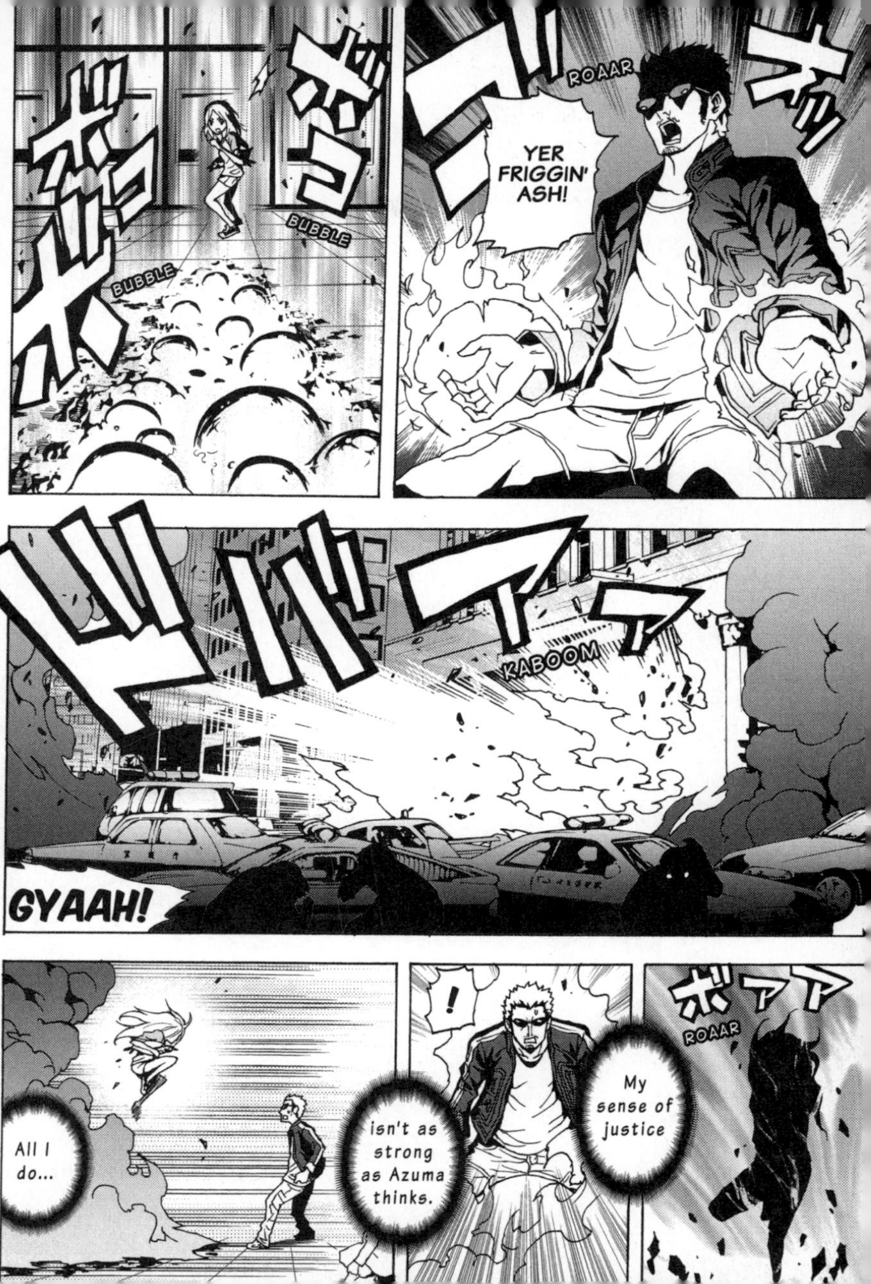
ROAAR
YER FRIGGIN' ASH!
BUBBLE
BUBBLE
KABOOM
GYAAH!
ROAAR
!
My sense of justice
isn't as strong as Azuma thinks.
All I do...

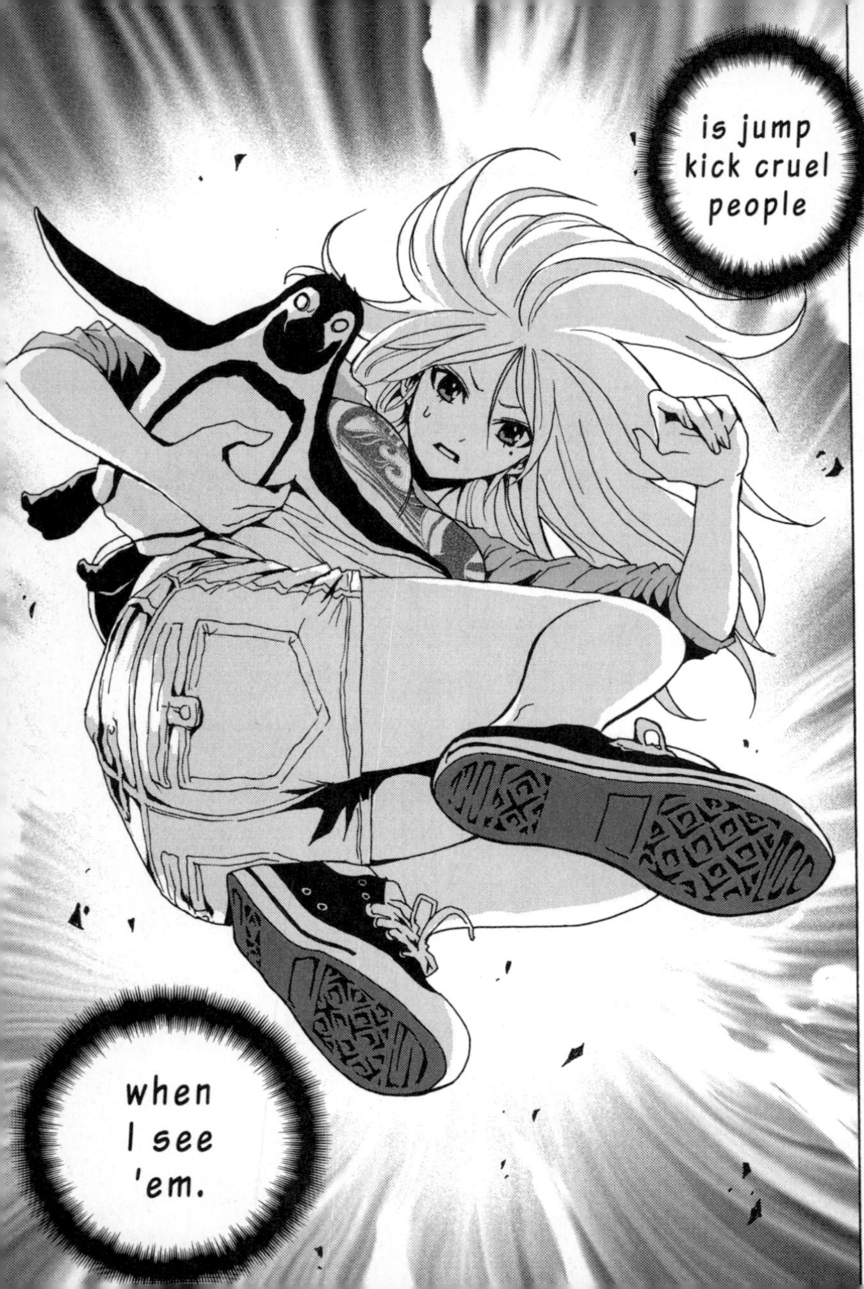
is jump kick cruel people
when I see 'em.

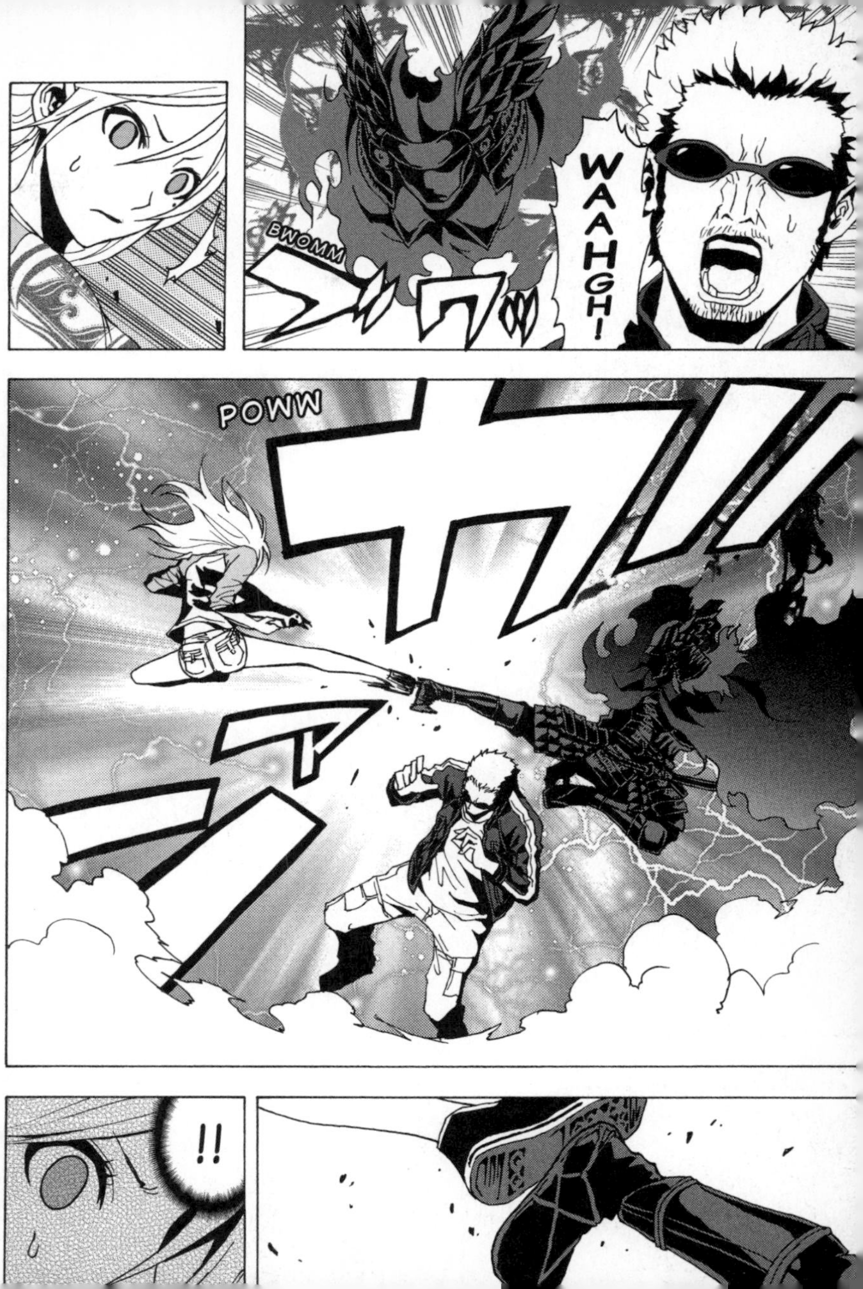
WAAHGH!
BWOMM
POWW
!!

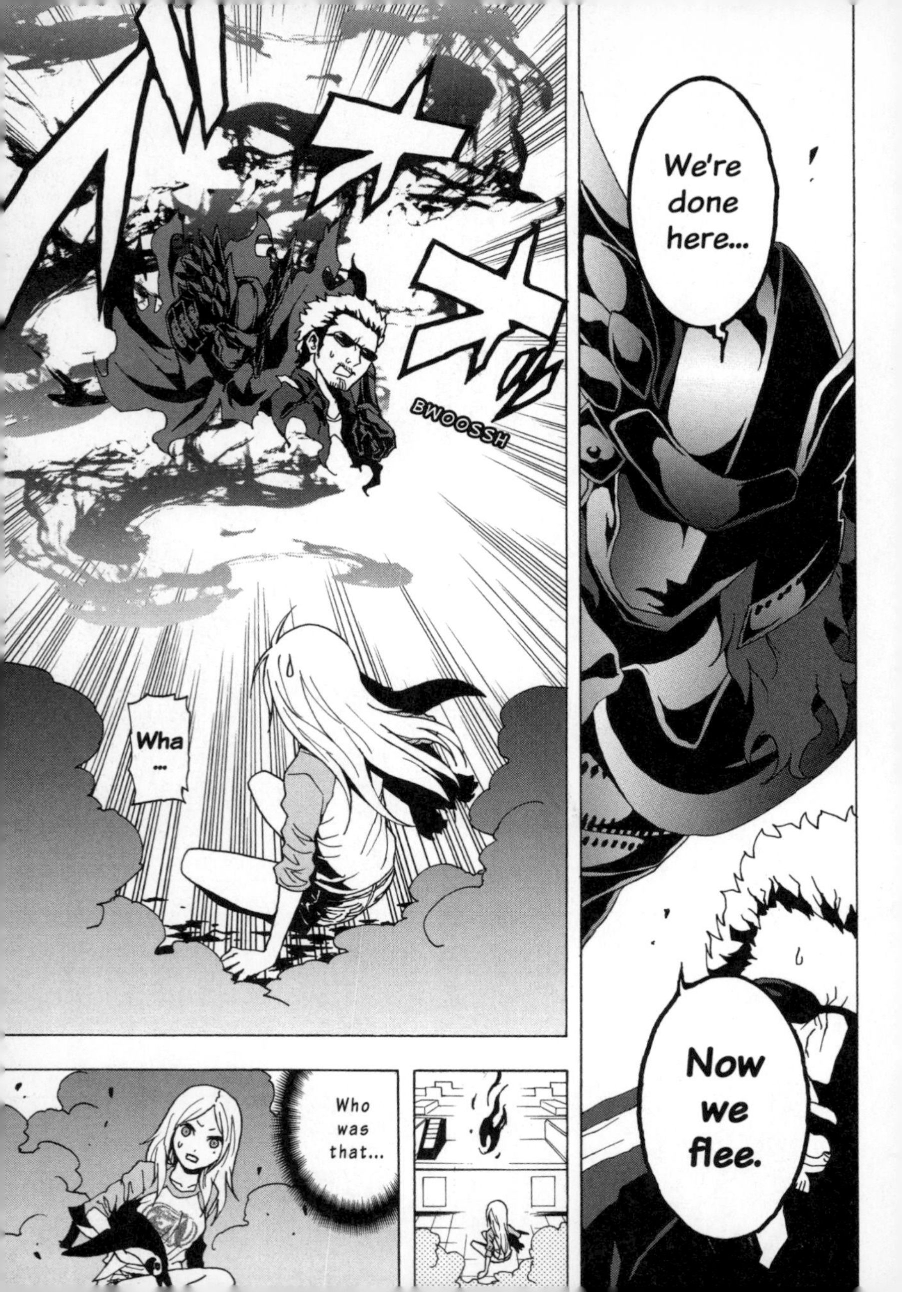
We're done here...
Now we flee.
BWOOSSH
Wha ...
Who was that...

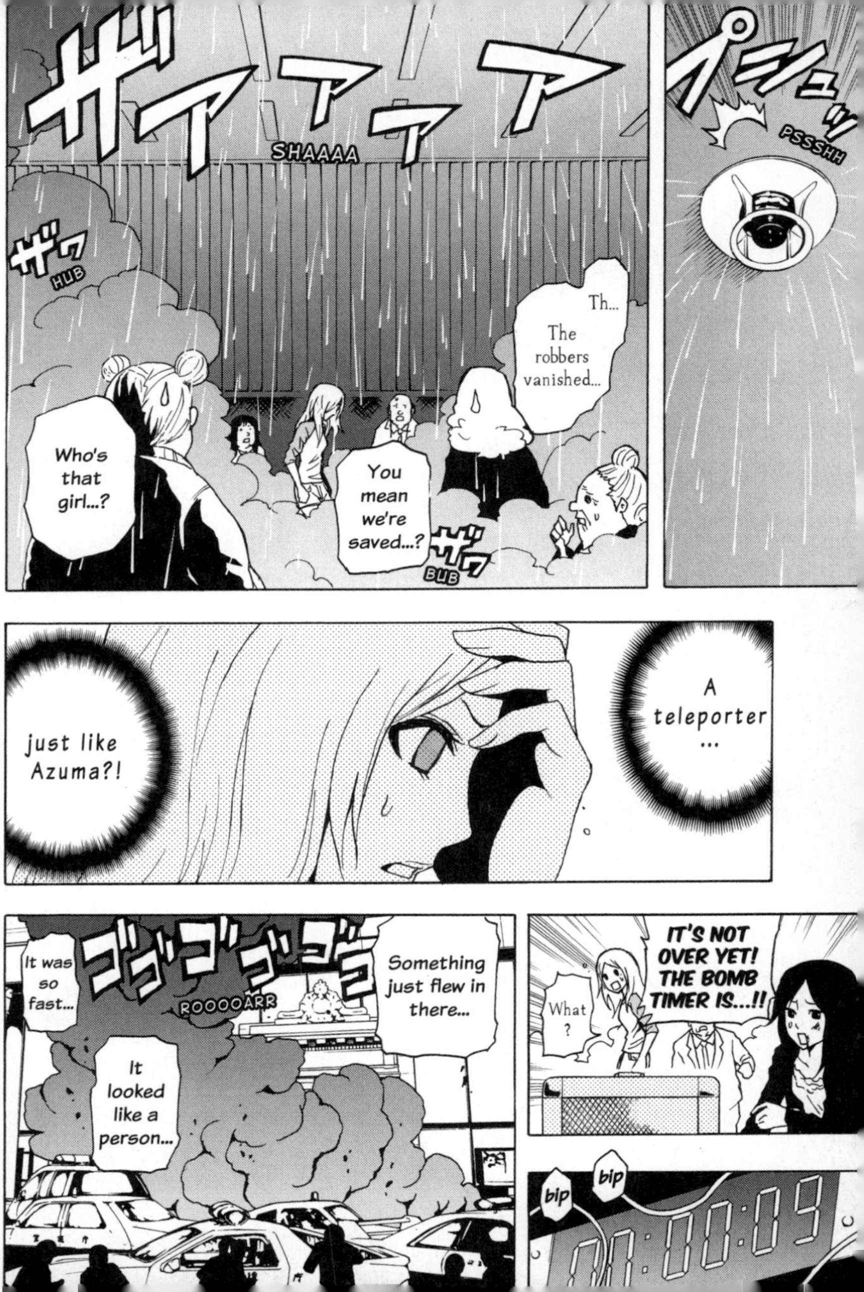
パシュッ
PSSSHH
ザァァァァ
SHAAAA
Th...
The robbers vanished...
ザワ
HUB
You mean we're saved...?
ザワ
BUB
Who's that girl...?
A teleporter...
just like Azuma?!
IT'S NOT OVER YET! THE BOMB TIMER IS...!!
What?
bip
bip
Something just flew in there...
ゴゴゴゴ
ROOOOARR
It was so fast...
It looked like a person...

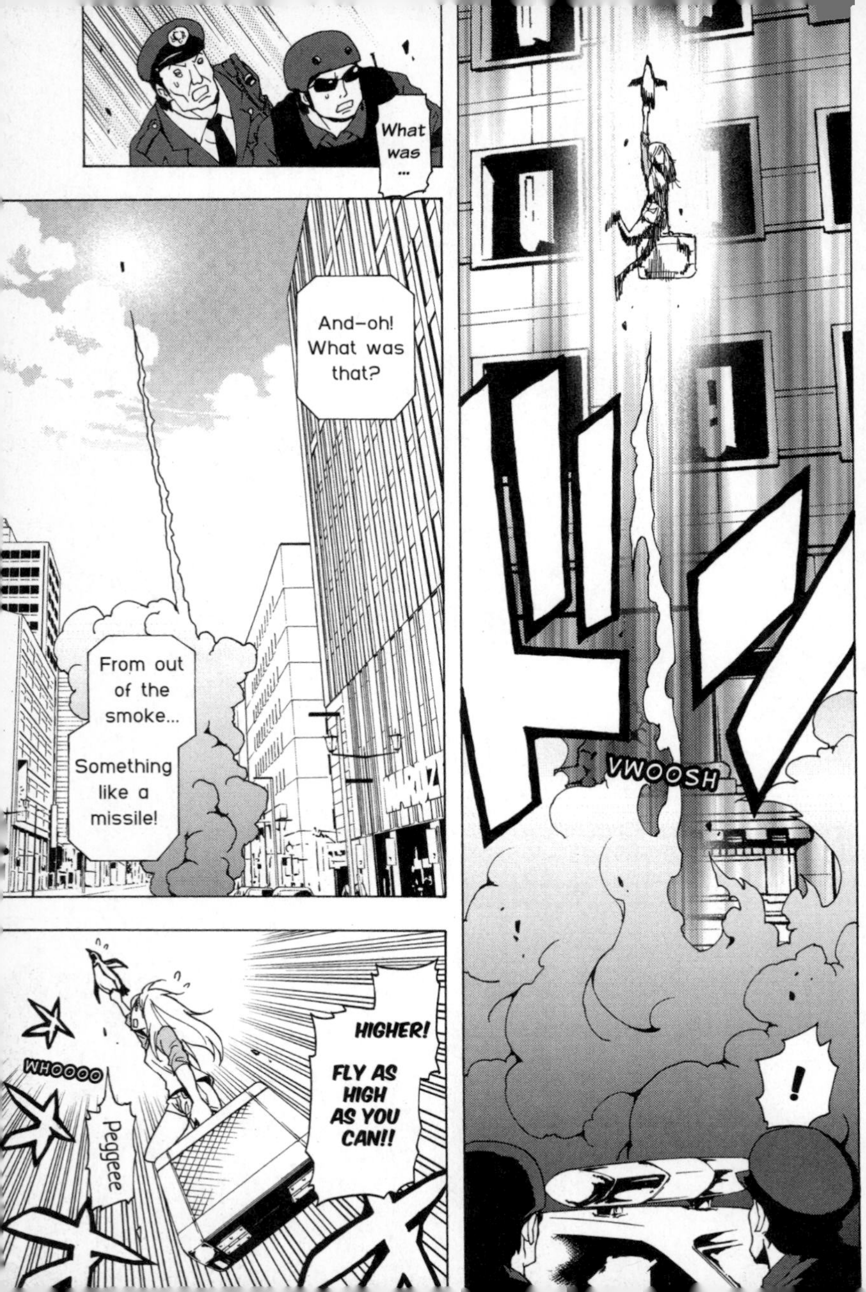
VWOOSH
!
What was ...
And-oh! What was that?
From out of the smoke...
Something like a missile!
HIGHER!
FLY AS HIGH AS YOU CAN!!
WHOOOO
Peggeee

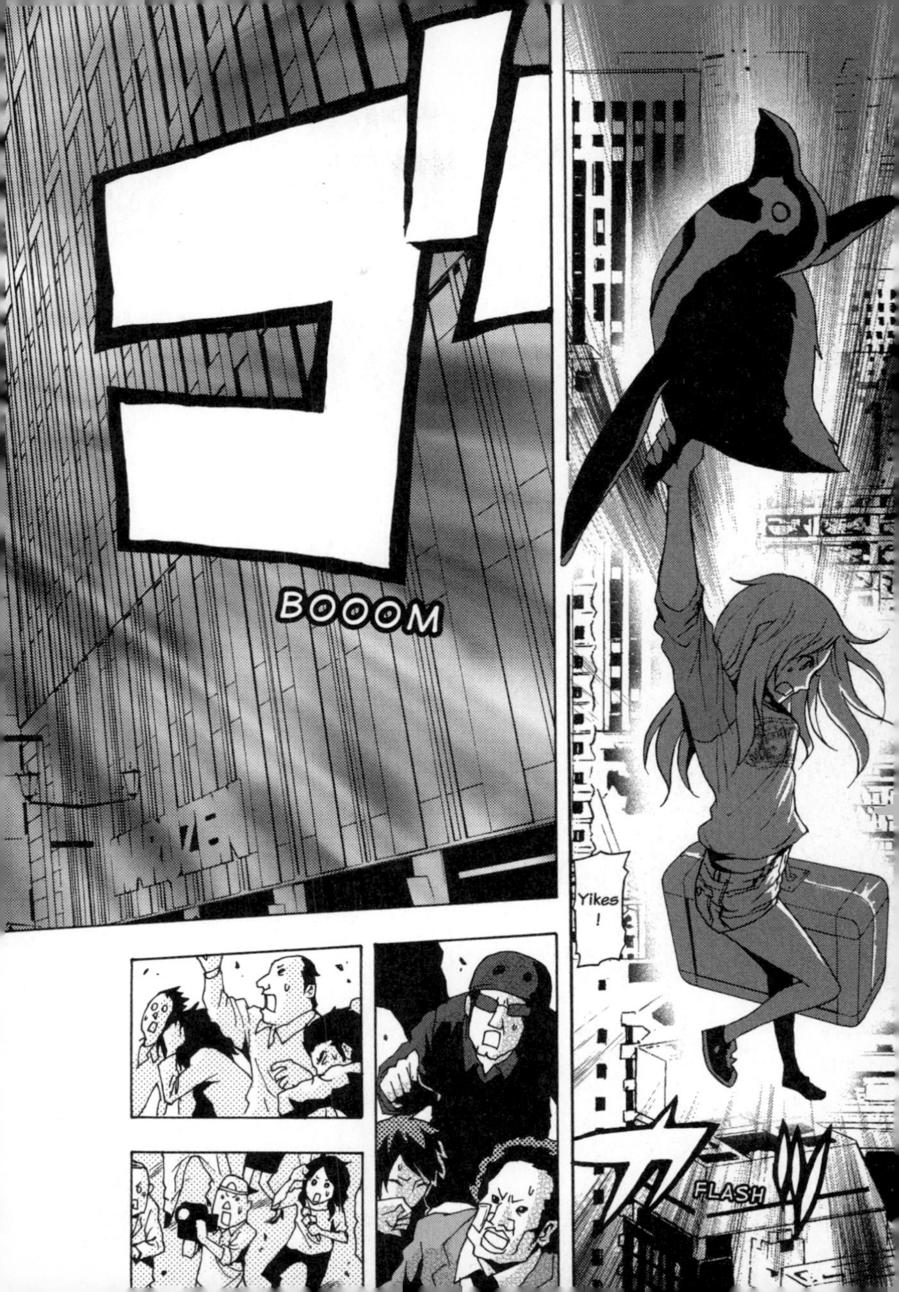
Yikes!
FLASH
BOOOM

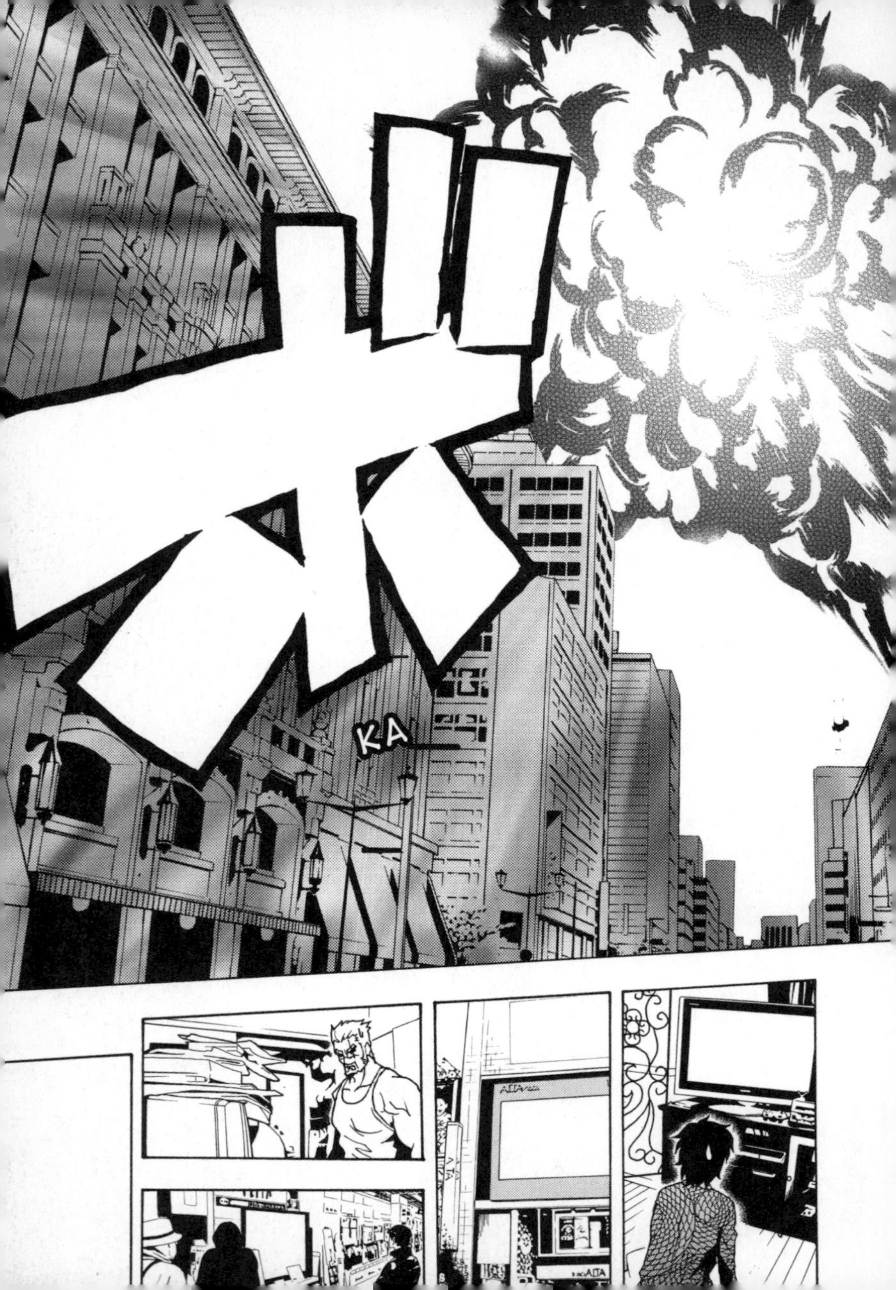
KA

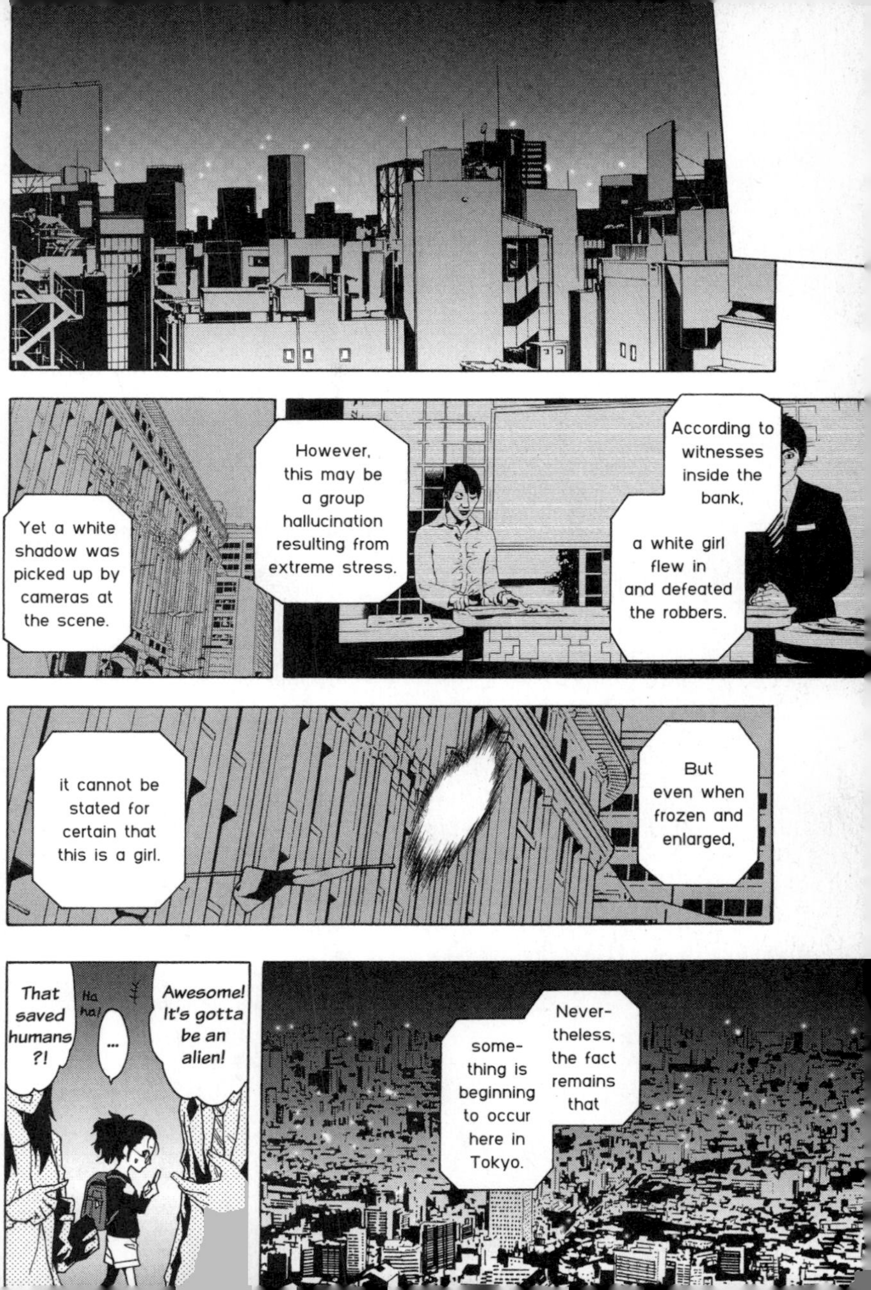
According to witnesses inside the bank,
a white girl flew in and defeated the robbers.
However, this may be a group hallucination resulting from extreme stress.
Yet a white shadow was picked up by cameras at the scene.
But even when frozen and enlarged,
it cannot be stated for certain that this is a girl.
Never-theless, the fact remains that
some-thing is beginning to occur here in Tokyo.
Awesome! It's gotta be an alien!
...
Ha ha!
That saved humans?!

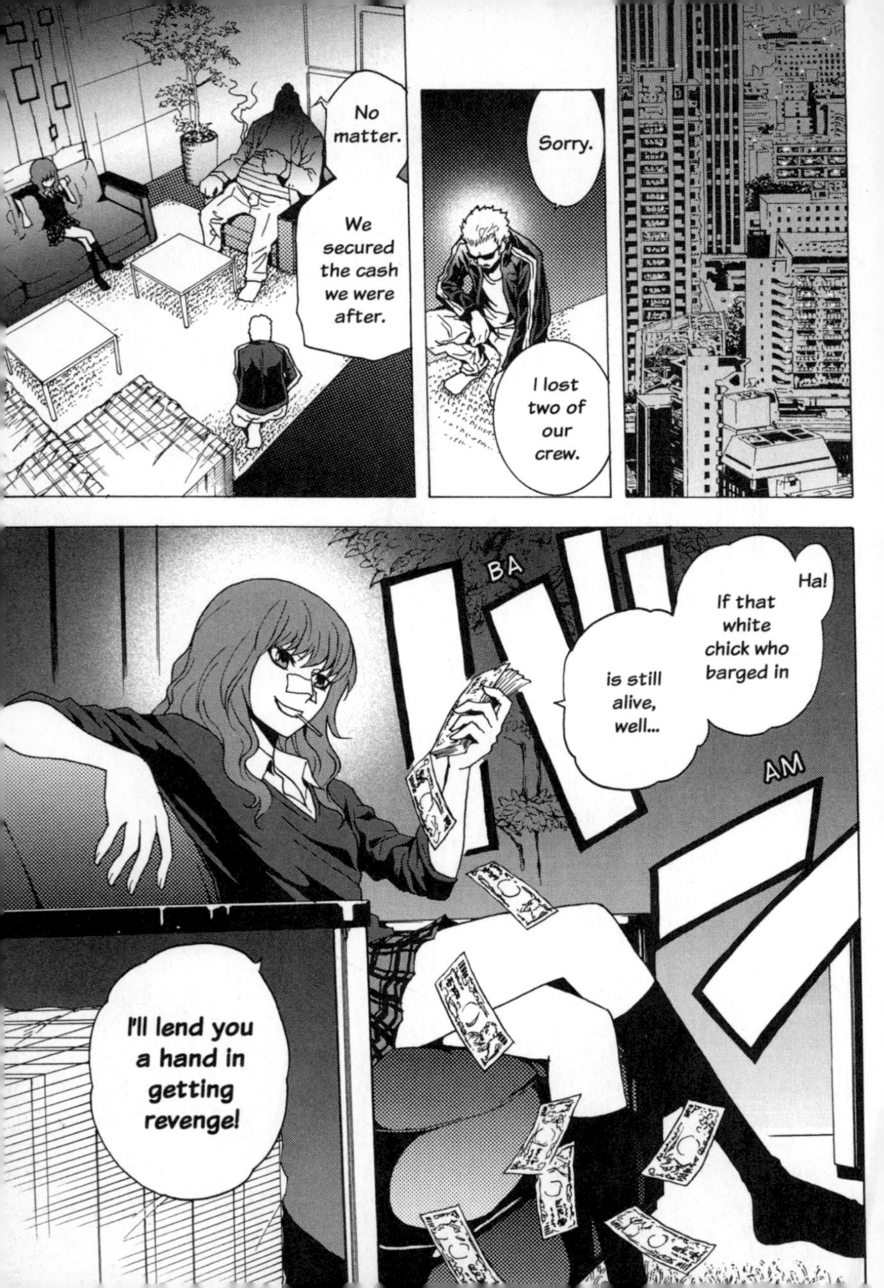
Sorry.
I lost two of our crew.
No matter.
We secured the cash we were after.
BA
AM
Ha!
If that white chick who barged in
is still alive, well...
I'll lend you a hand in getting revenge!

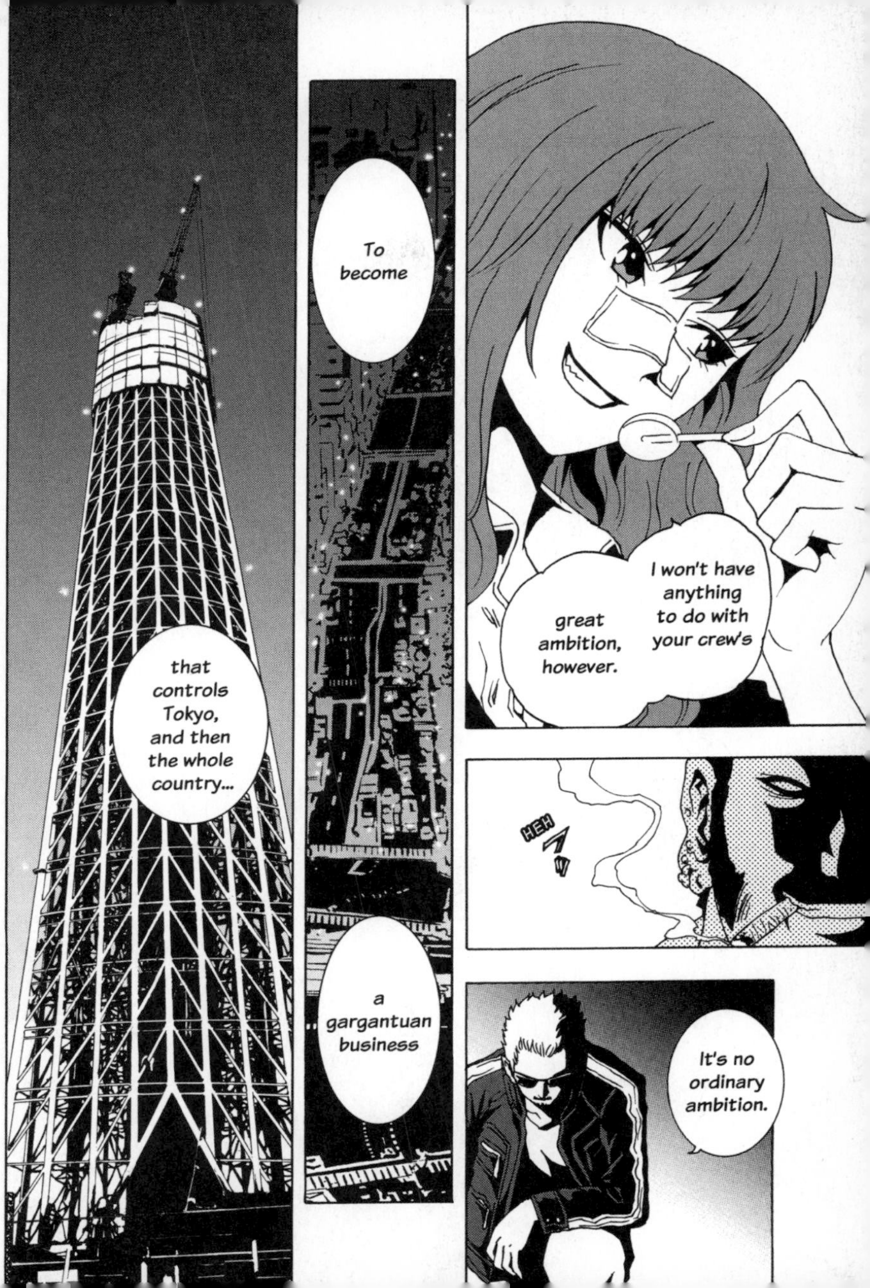
I won't have anything to do with your crew's great ambition, however.
HEH
It's no ordinary ambition.
To become
a gargantuan business
that controls Tokyo, and then the whole country...

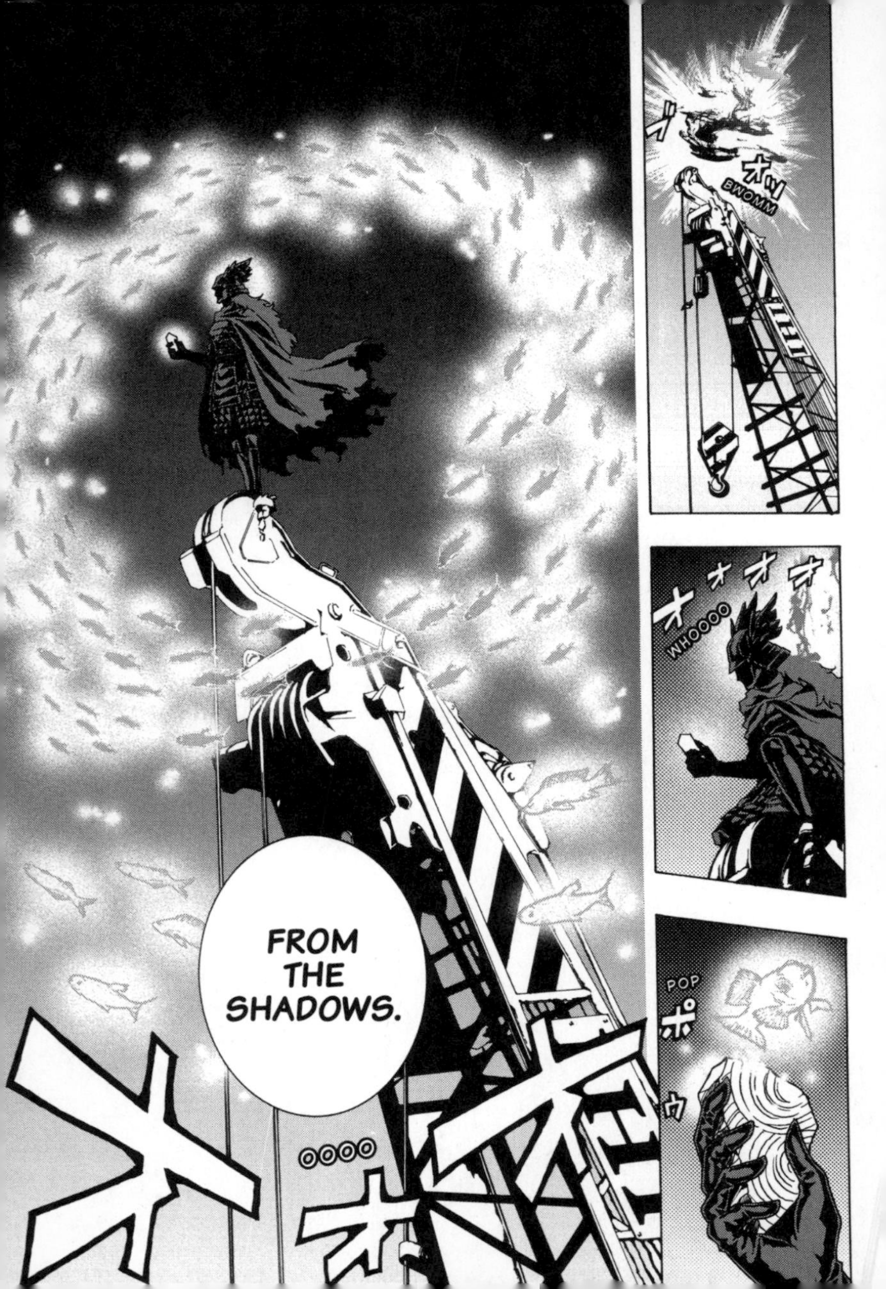
BWOMM
WHOOOO
POP
FROM THE SHADOWS.
OOOO

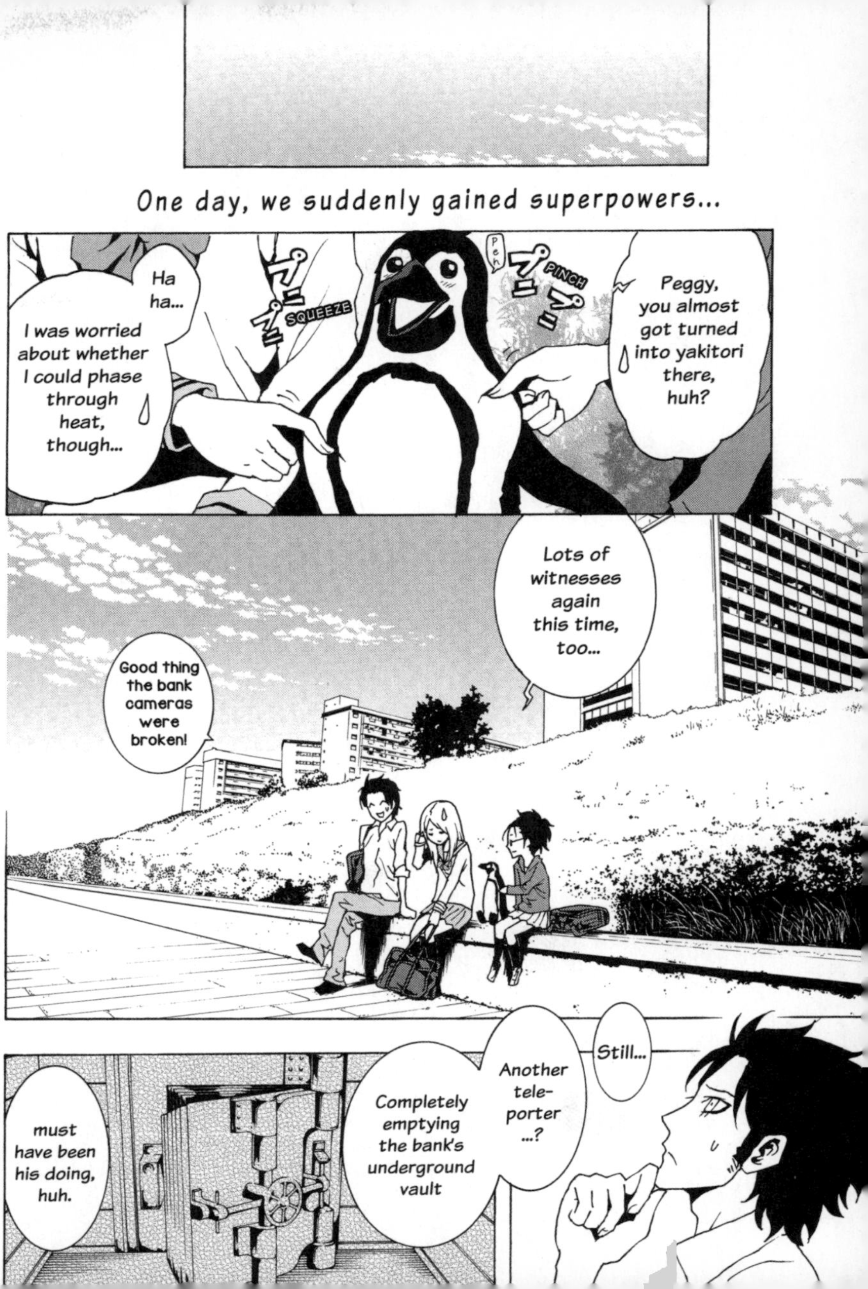
One day, we suddenly gained superpowers...
Peggy, you almost got turned into yakitori there, huh?
PINCH
Peh
SQUEEZE
Ha ha... I was worried about whether I could phase through heat, though...
Lots of witnesses again this time, too...
Good thing the bank cameras were broken!
Still...
Another tele-porter ...?
Completely emptying the bank's underground vault
must have been his doing, huh.

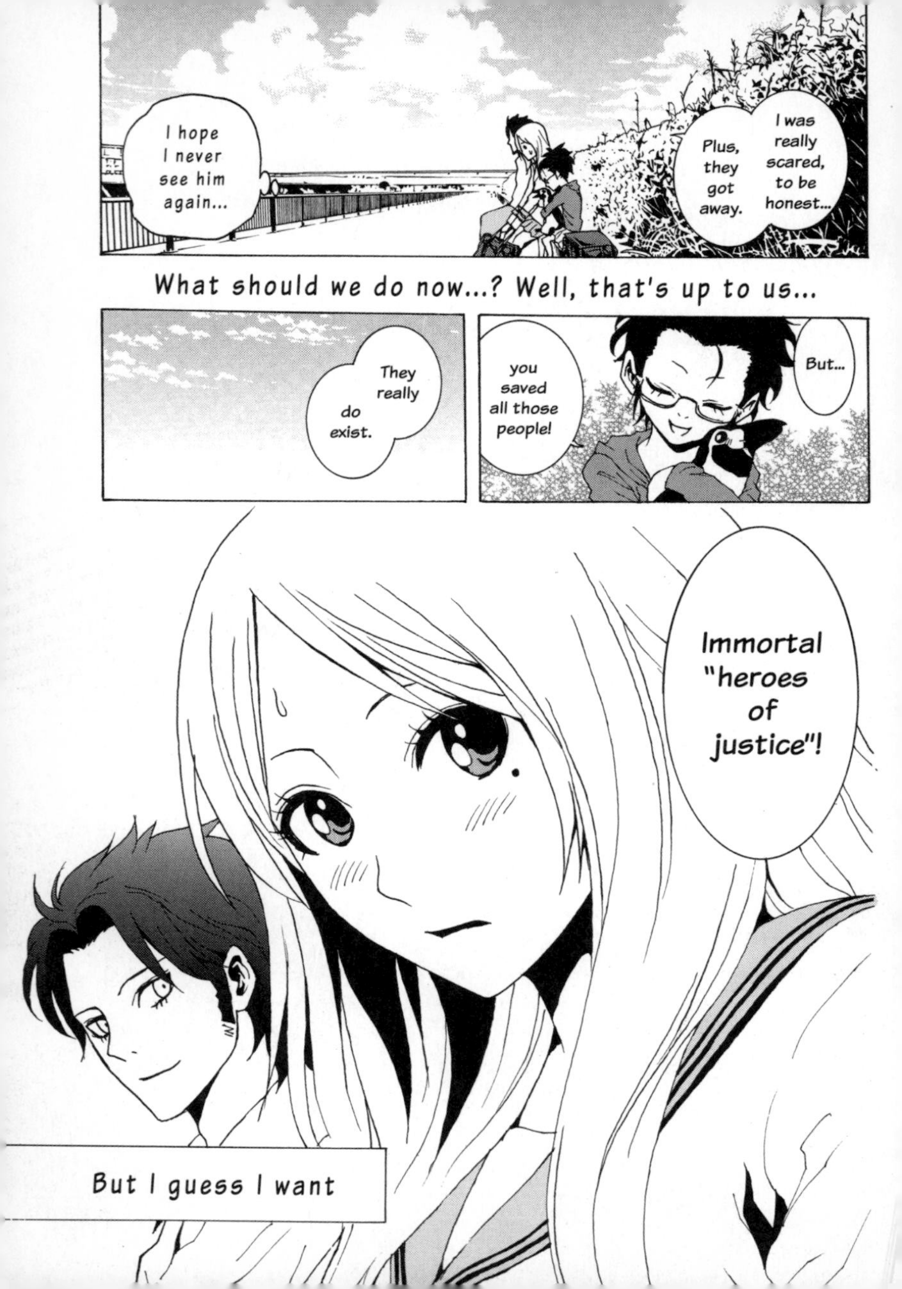
I was really scared, to be honest...
Plus, they got away.
I hope I never see him again...
What should we do now...? Well, that's up to us...
But...
you saved all those people!
They really do exist.
Immortal "heroes of justice"!
But I guess I want

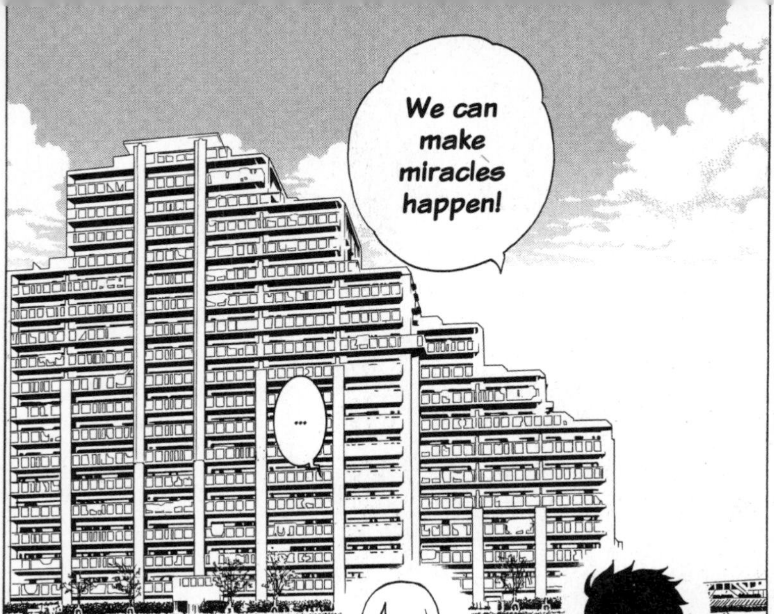
We can make miracles happen!
...

to do my best and move forward

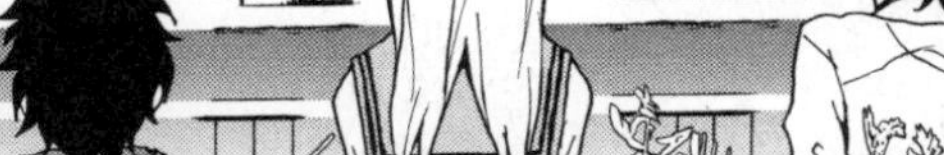
Made this for you.
White Crow
I DON'T WANT IT!

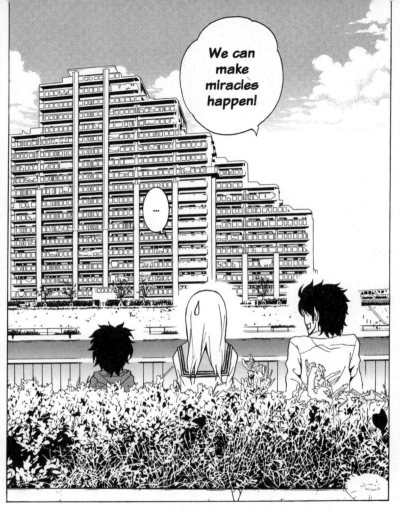

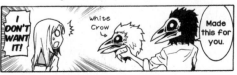

SCENE 4 /// END

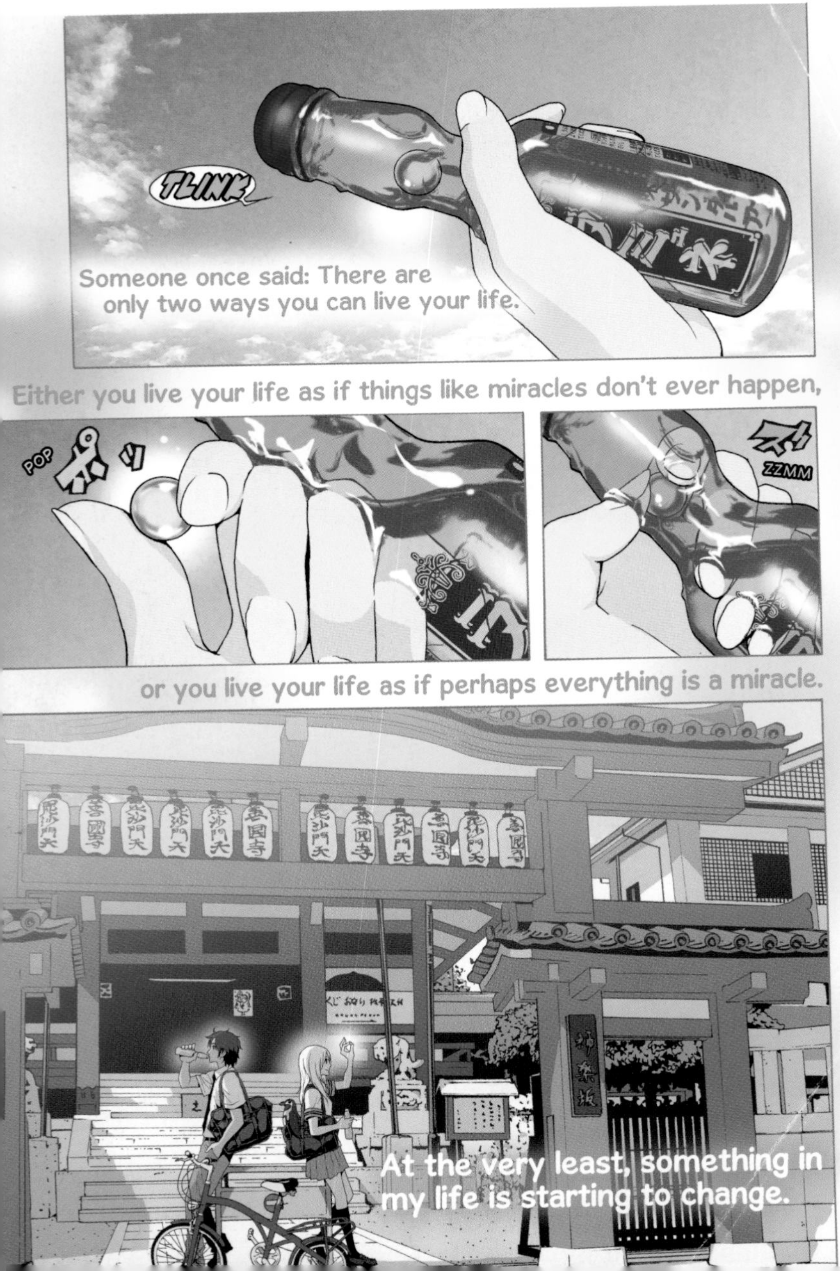
TLINK
Someone once said: There are only two ways you can live your life.
Either you live your life as if things like miracles don't ever happen,
ZZMM
POP
or you live your life as if perhaps everything is a miracle.
At the very least, something in my life is starting to change.

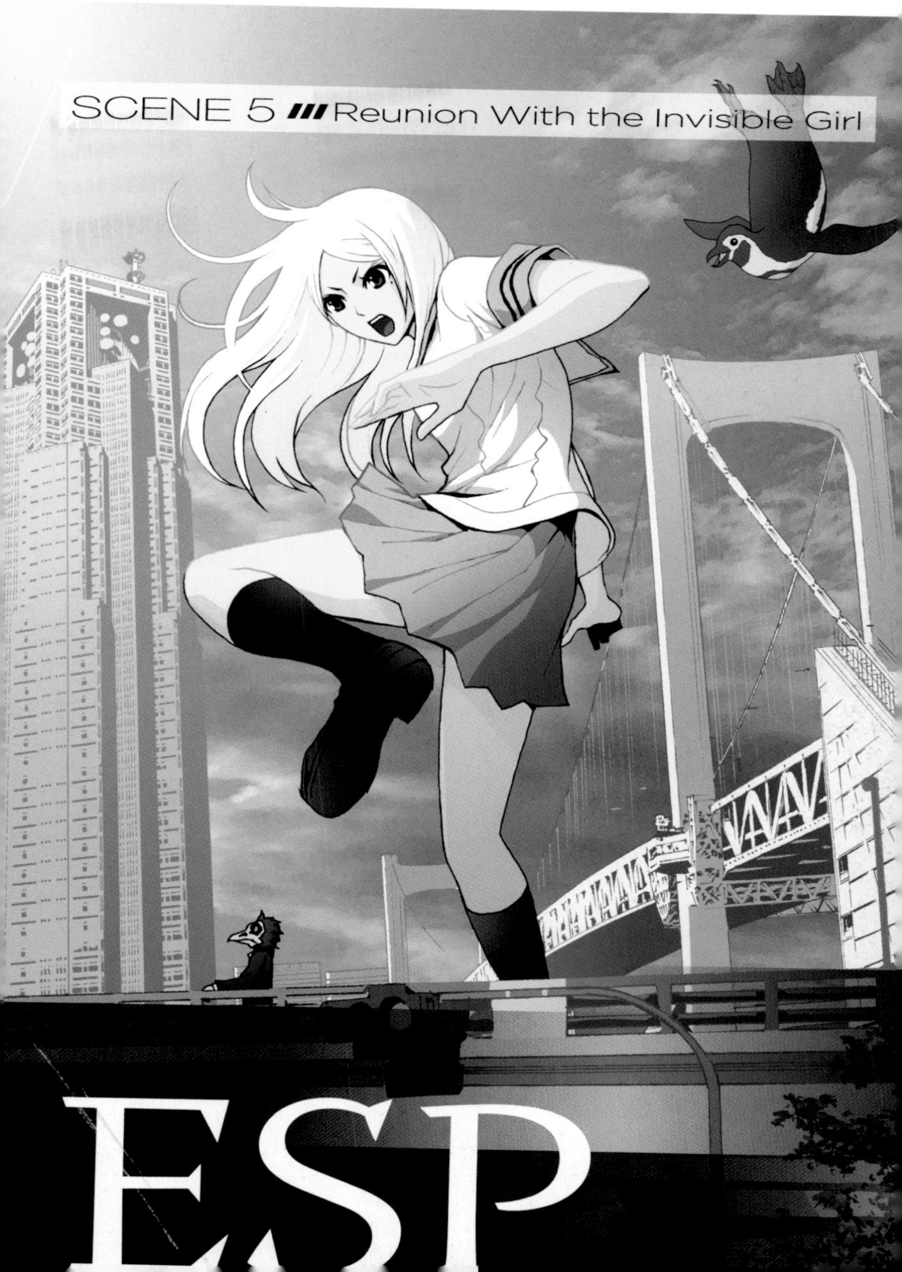
SCENE 5 /// Reunion With the Invisible Girl
ESP

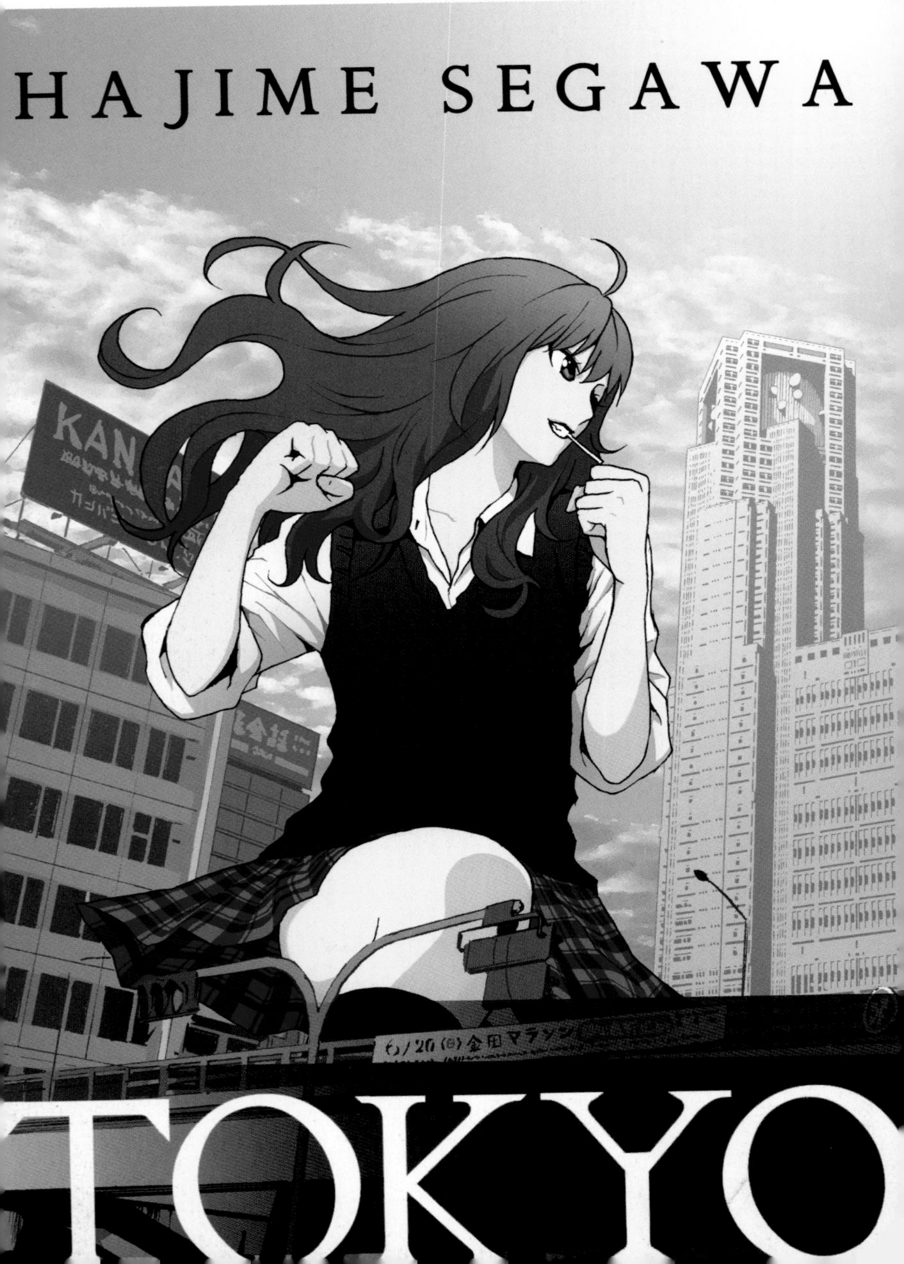
HAJIME SEGAWA
TOKYO

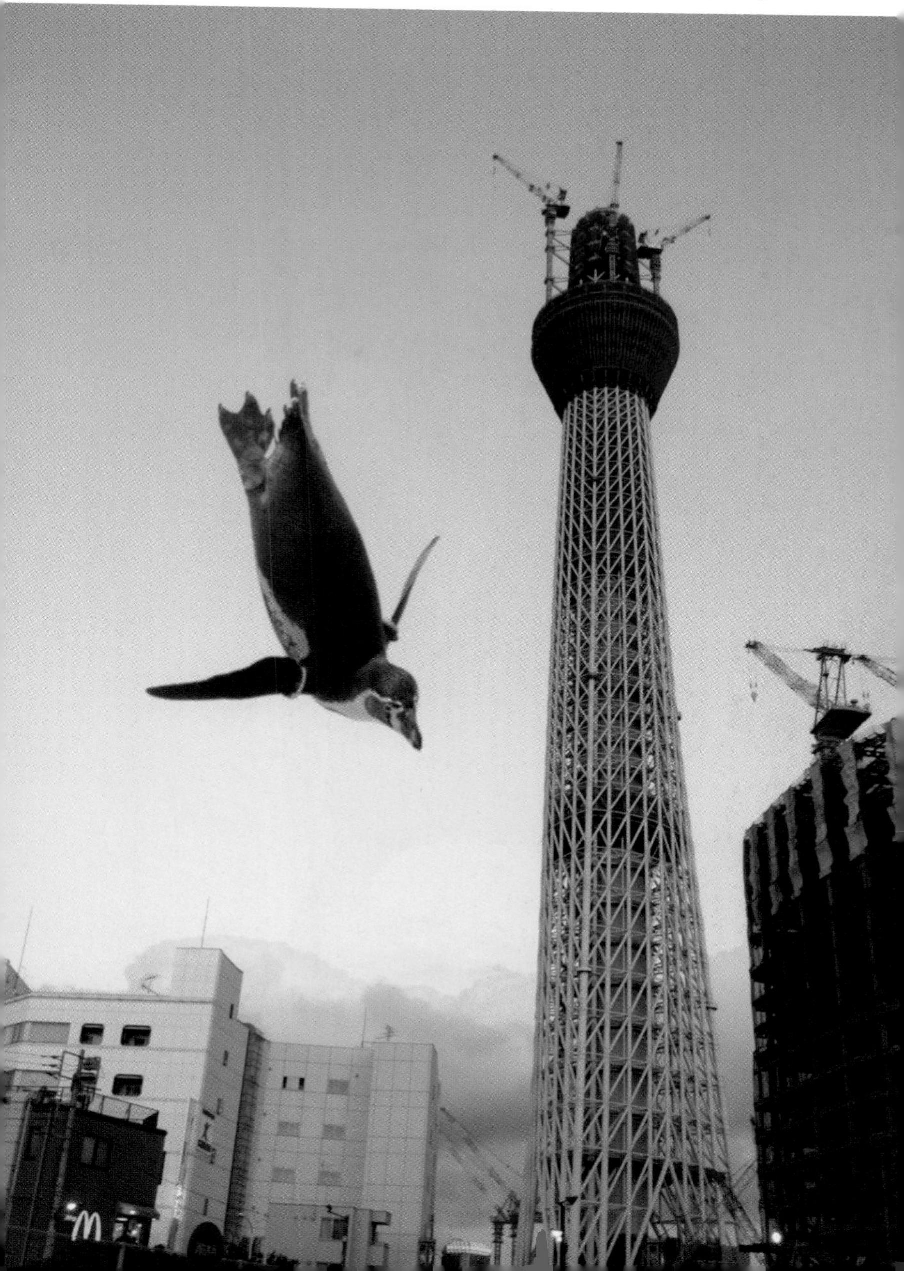

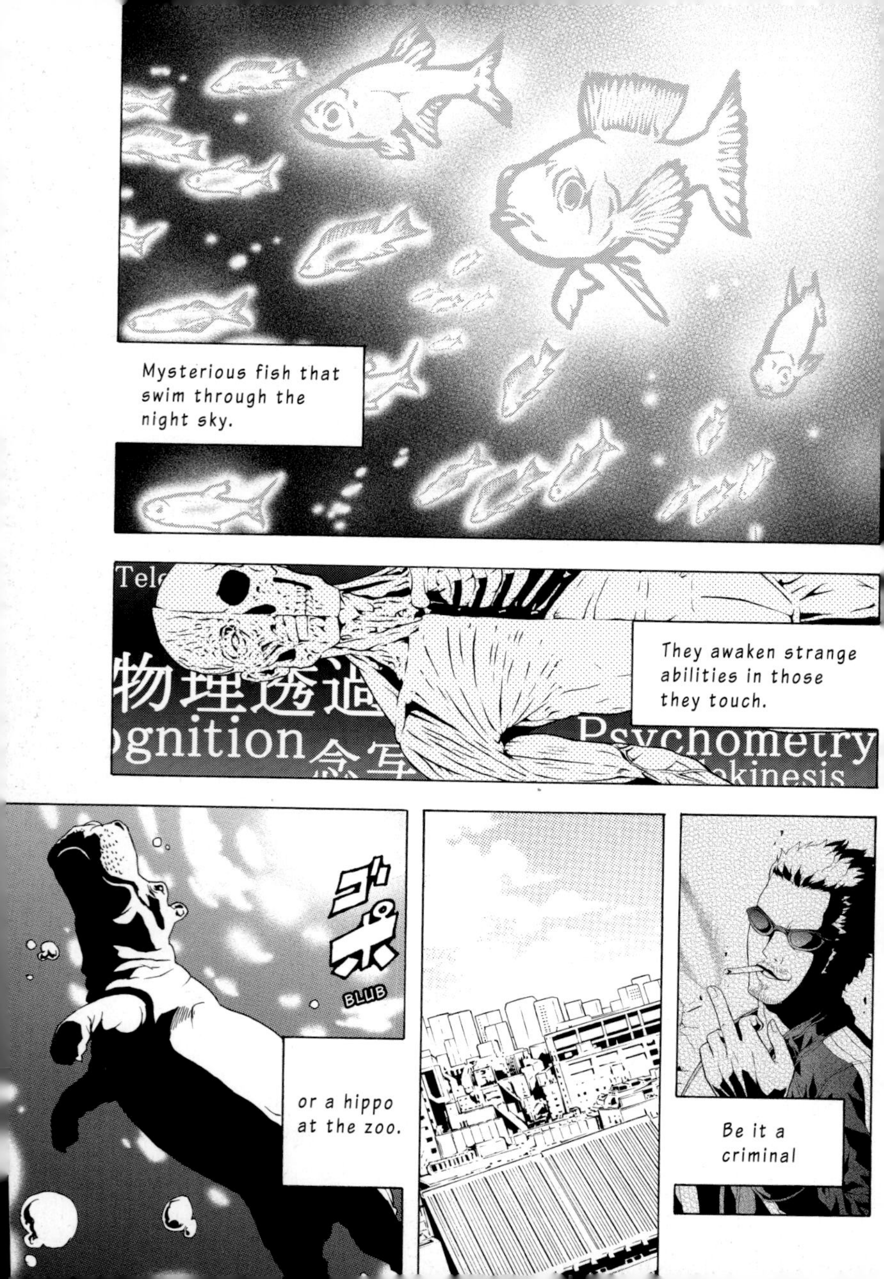
Mysterious fish that swim through the night sky.
Tele
They awaken strange abilities in those they touch.
Psychometry
物理透過
ognition
Be it a criminal
ゴポ
BLUB
or a hippo at the zoo.

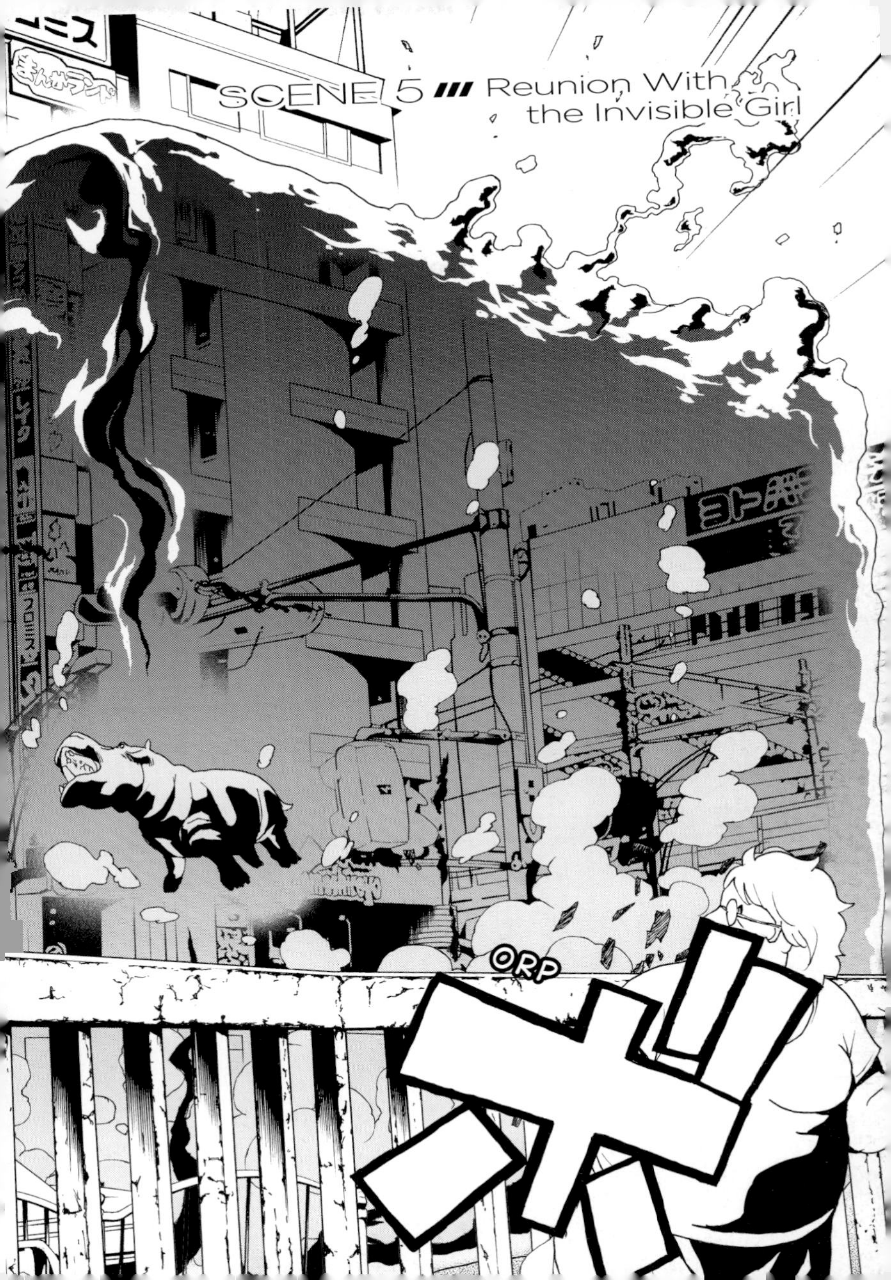
SCENE 5 /// Reunion With the Invisible Girl
ORP

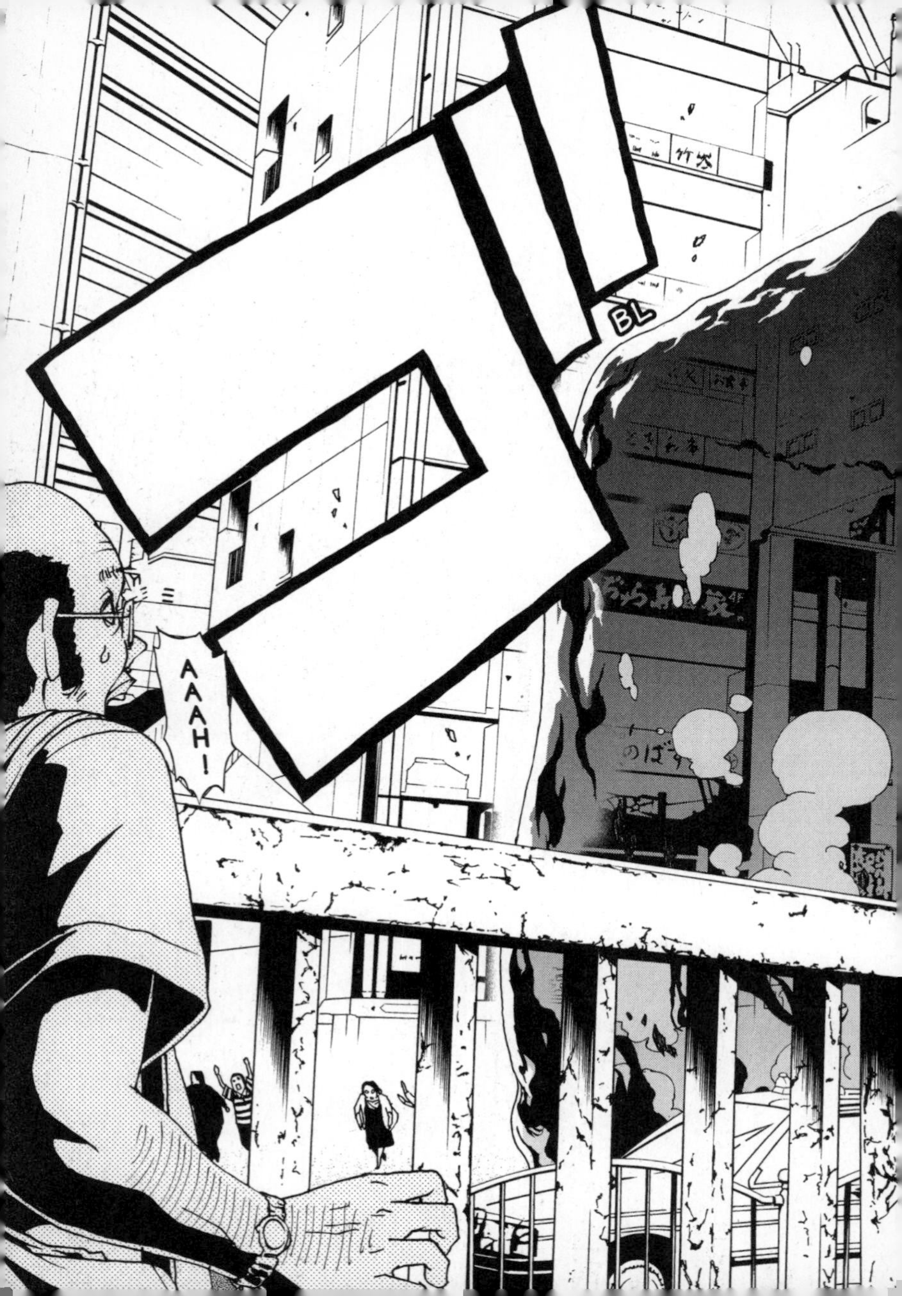
BL
AAAH!

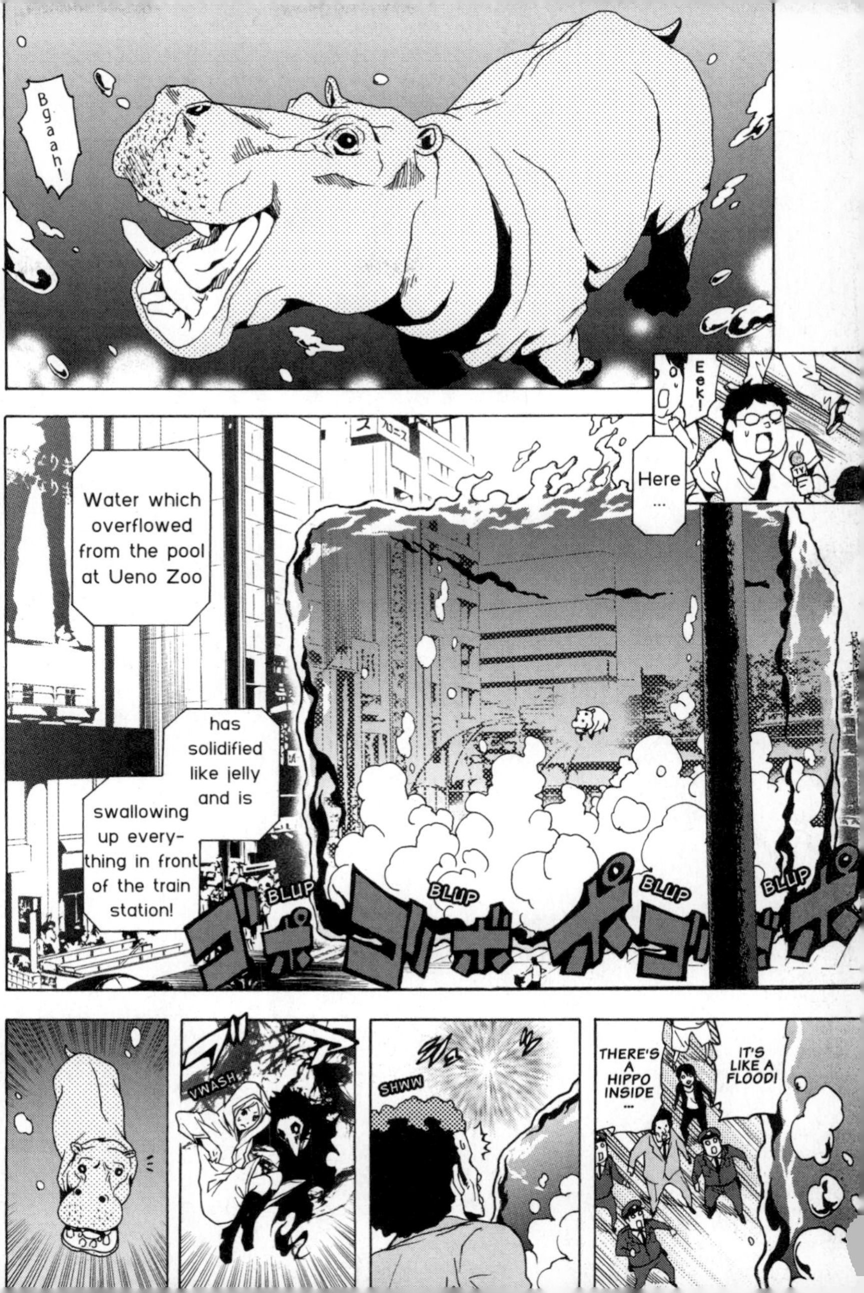
Bgaah!
Eek!
Here ...
Water which overflowed from the pool at Ueno Zoo
has solidified like jelly and is
swallowing up every-thing in front of the train station!
BLUP
BLUP
BLUP
BLUP
IT'S LIKE A FLOOD!
THERE'S A HIPPO INSIDE ...
SHWW
VWASH

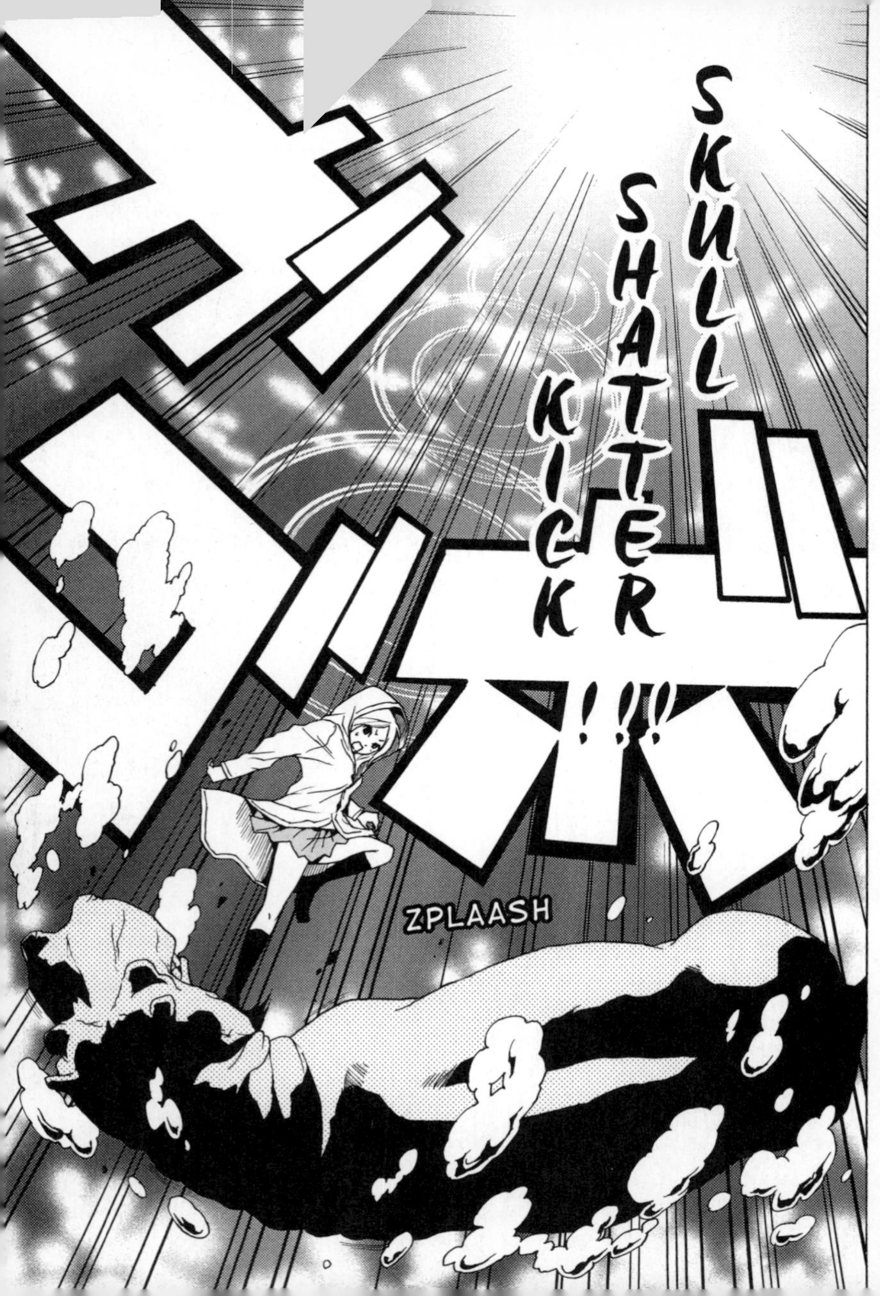
SKULL SHATTER KICK!!!!
ZPLAASH

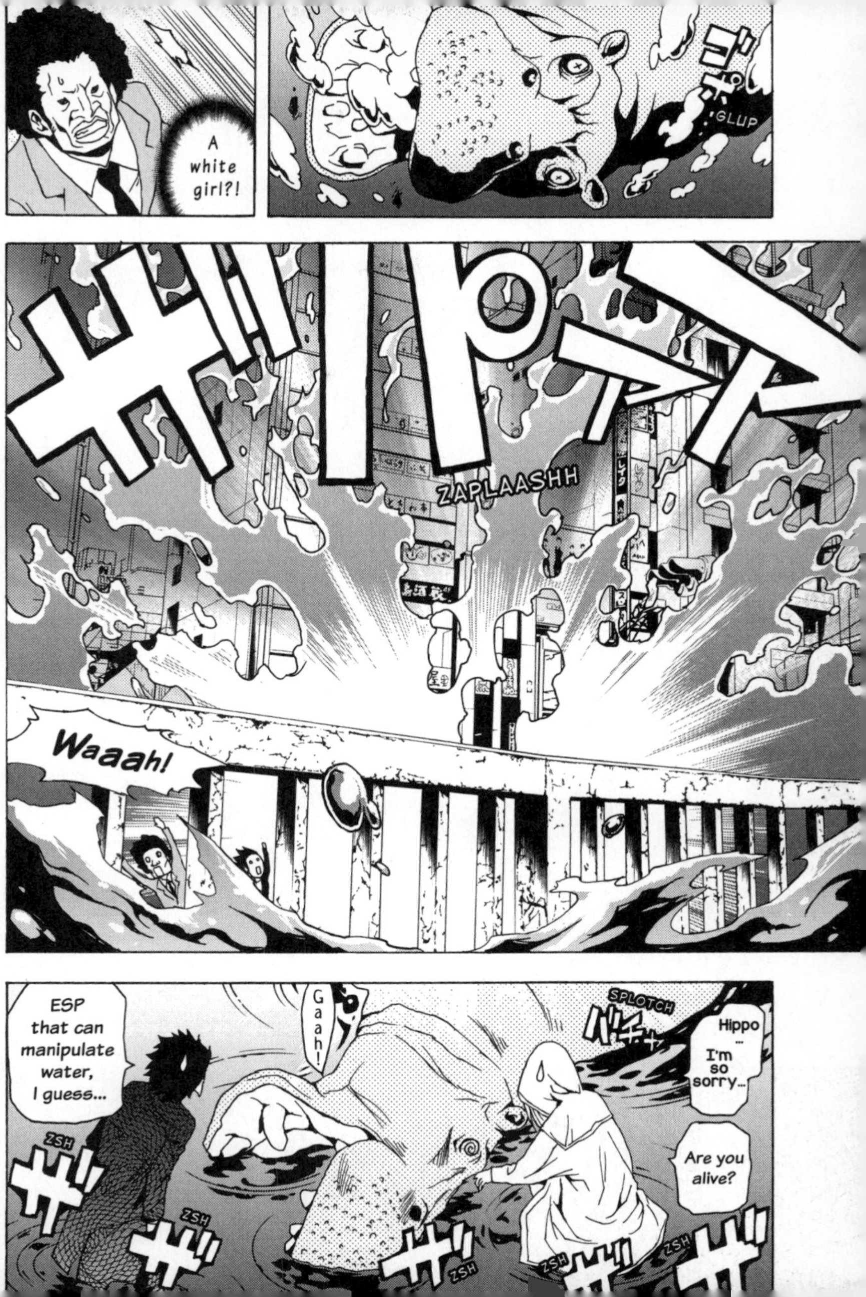
GLUP
A white girl?!
ZAPLAASHH
Waaah!
SPLOTCH
Hippo... I'm so sorry...
Are you alive?
Gaaah!
ESP that can manipulate water, I guess...
ZSH
ZSH
ZSH
ZSH

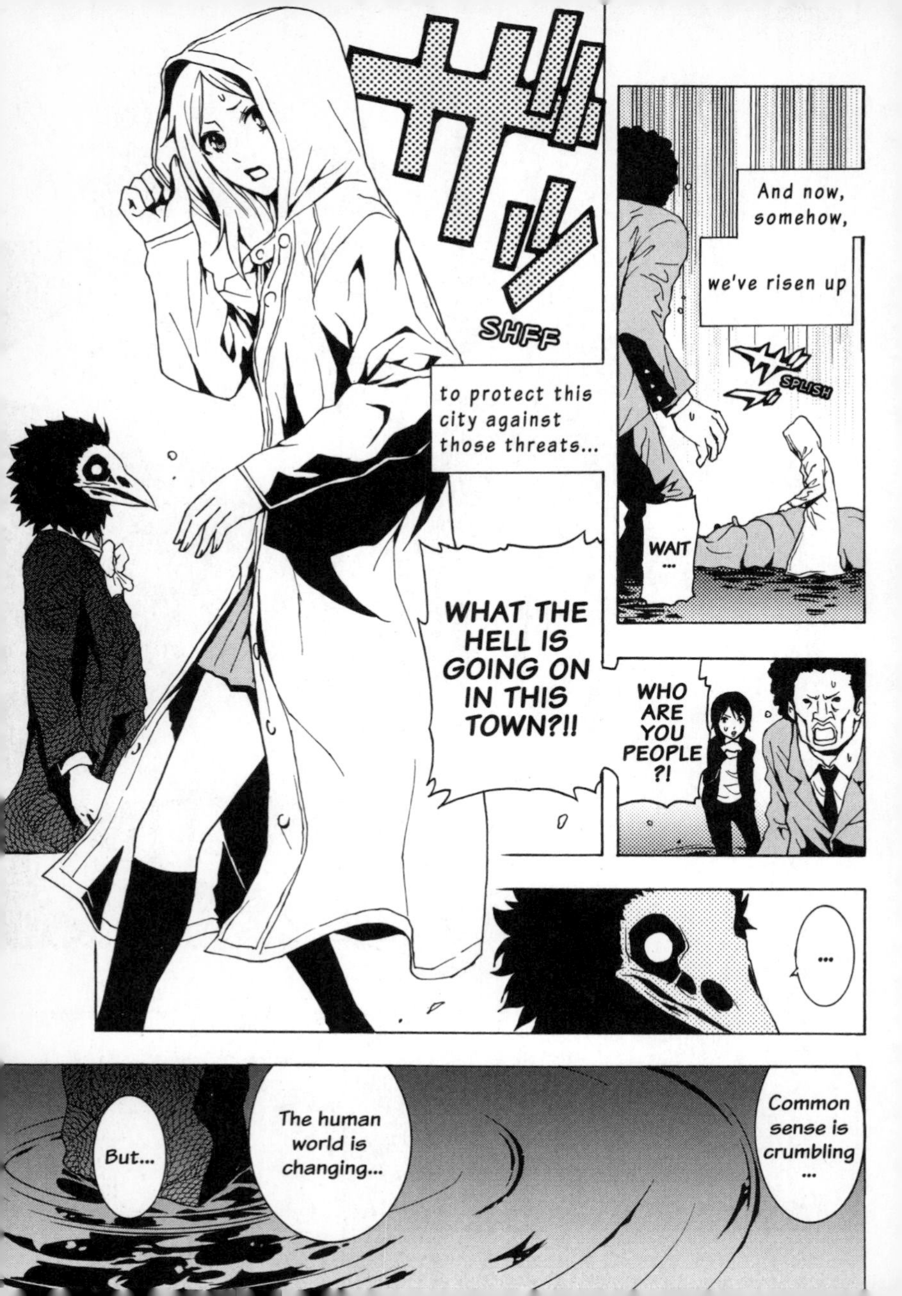
And now, somehow,
we've risen up
SPLISH
WAIT ...
SHFF
to protect this city against those threats...
WHAT THE HELL IS GOING ON IN THIS TOWN?!!
WHO ARE YOU PEOPLE ?!
...
Common sense is crumbling ...
The human world is changing...
But...

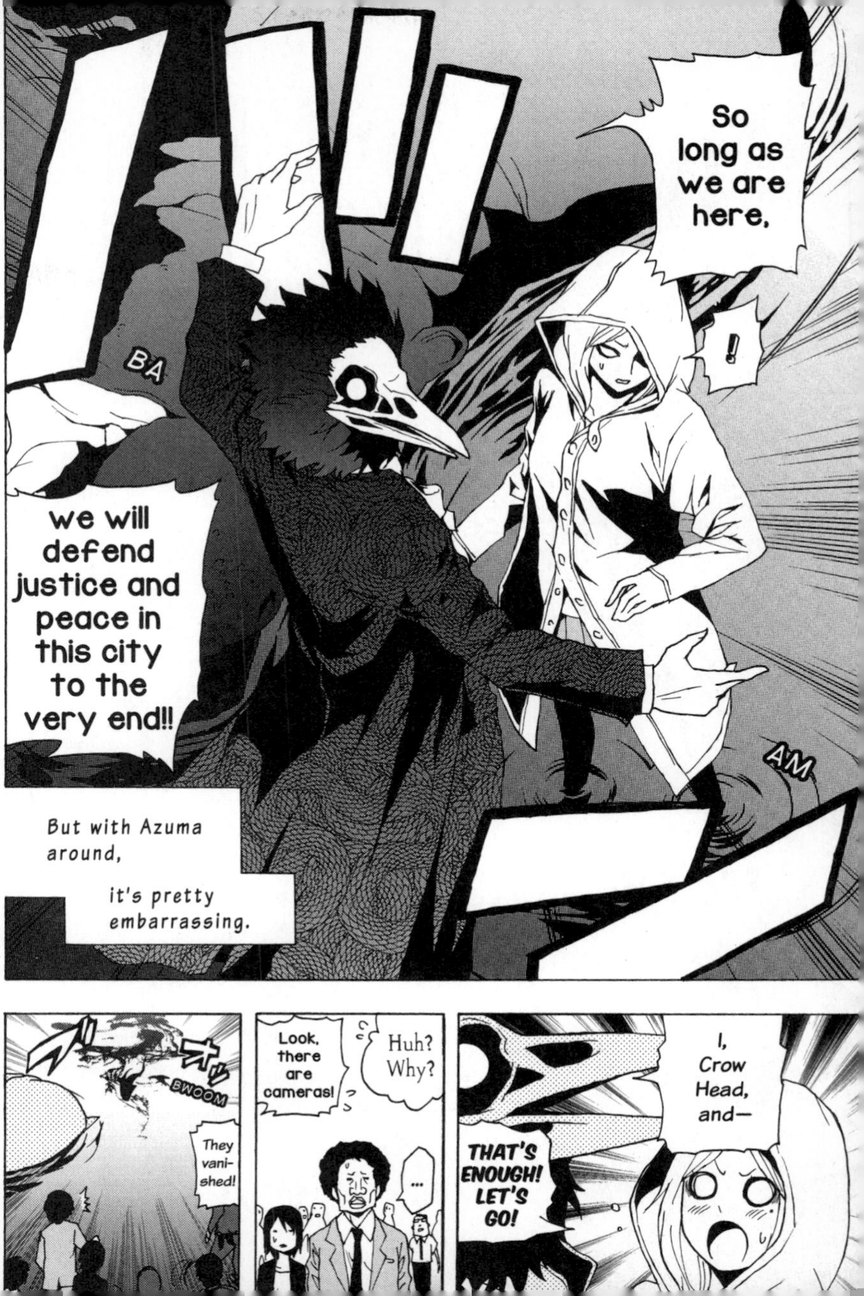
So long as we are here,
!
BA
AM
we will defend justice and peace in this city to the very end!!
But with Azuma around,
it's pretty embarrassing.
I, Crow Head, and—
THAT'S ENOUGH! LET'S GO!
Look, there are cameras!
Huh? Why?
...
BWOOM
They vanished!

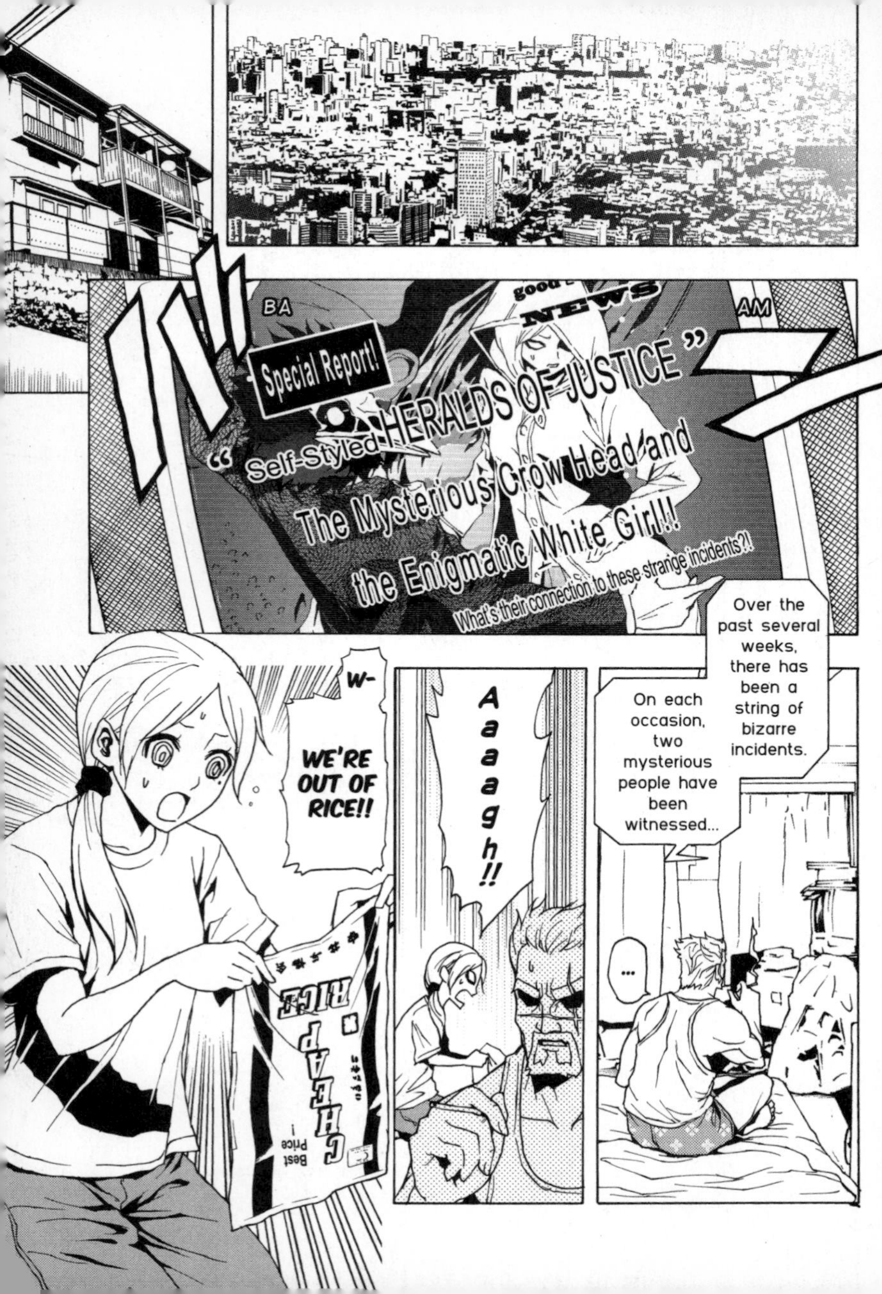
BA
AM
Special Report!
"Self-Styled HERALDS OF JUSTICE"
The Mysterious Crow Head and
the Enigmatic White Girl!!
What's their connection to these strange incidents?!
Over the past several weeks, there has been a string of bizarre incidents.
On each occasion, two mysterious people have been witnessed...
...
Aaaaagh!!
W-
WE'RE OUT OF RICE!!
CHEAP RICE
Best Price!

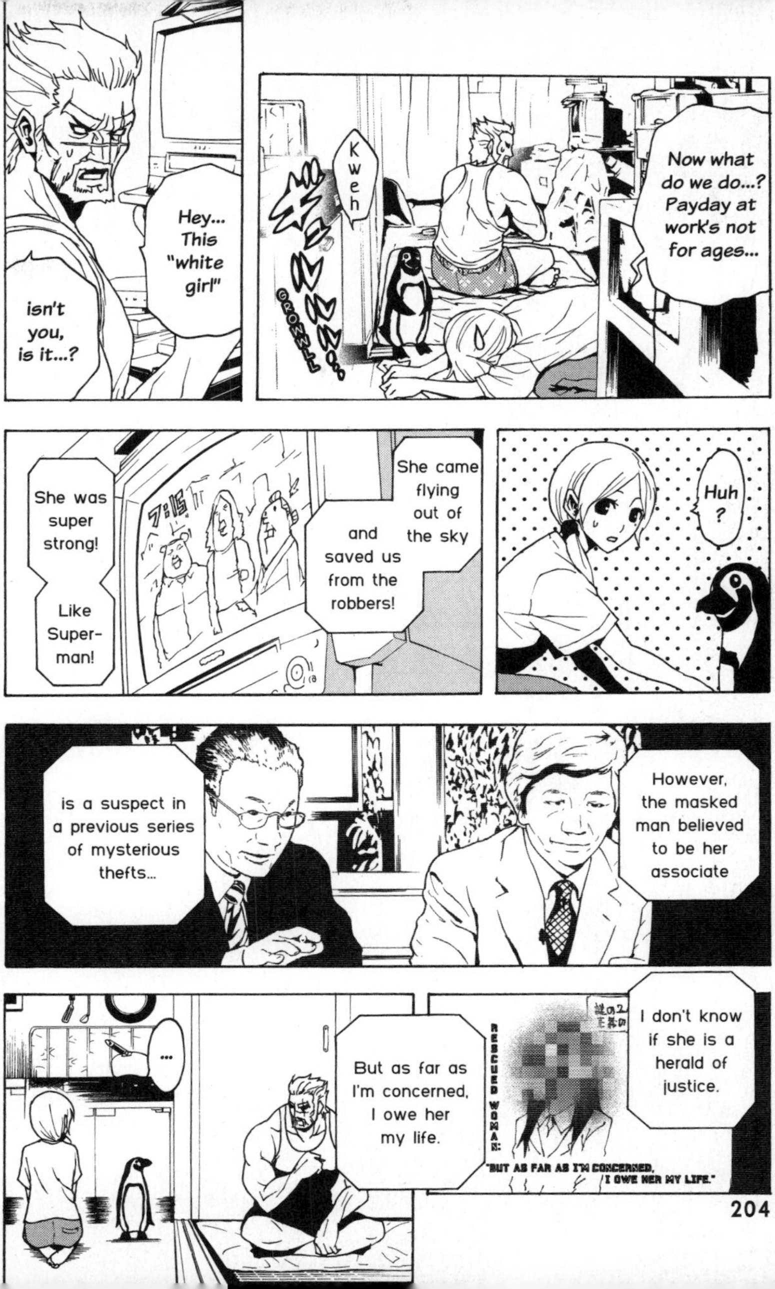
Now what do we do...? Payday at work's not for ages...
Kweh
GROWLL
Hey... This "white girl"
isn't you, is it...?
Huh?
She came flying out of the sky
and saved us from the robbers!
She was super strong!
Like Superman!
However, the masked man believed to be her associate
is a suspect in a previous series of mysterious thefts...
I don't know if she is a herald of justice.
RESCUED WOMAN:
"BUT AS FAR AS I'M CONCERNED, I OWE HER MY LIFE."
But as far as I'm concerned, I owe her my life.
...

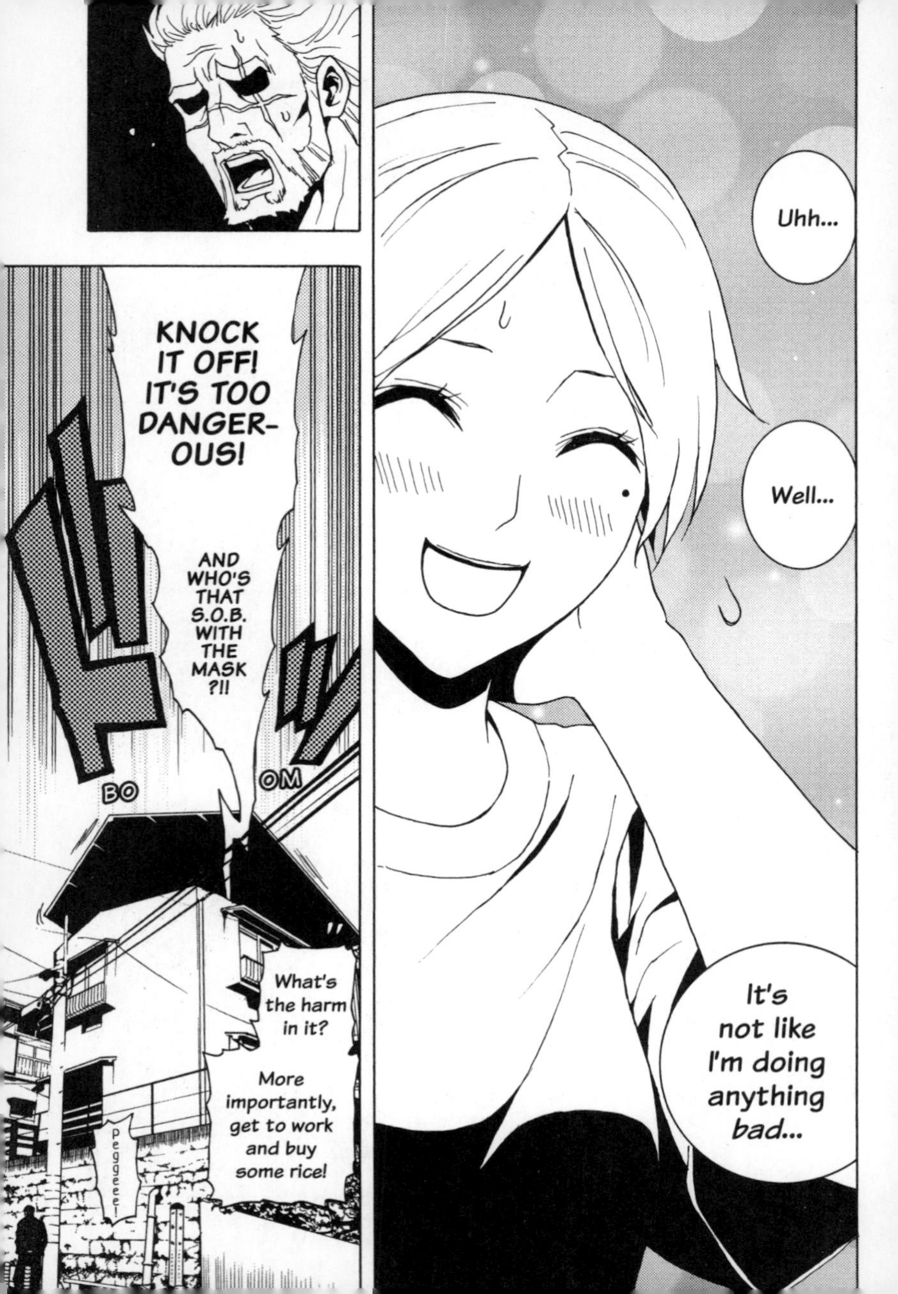
Uhh...
Well...
It's not like I'm doing anything bad...
KNOCK IT OFF! IT'S TOO DANGER-OUS!
AND WHO'S THAT S.O.B. WITH THE MASK ?!!
BO OM
What's the harm in it?
More importantly, get to work and buy some rice!
Peggeee!

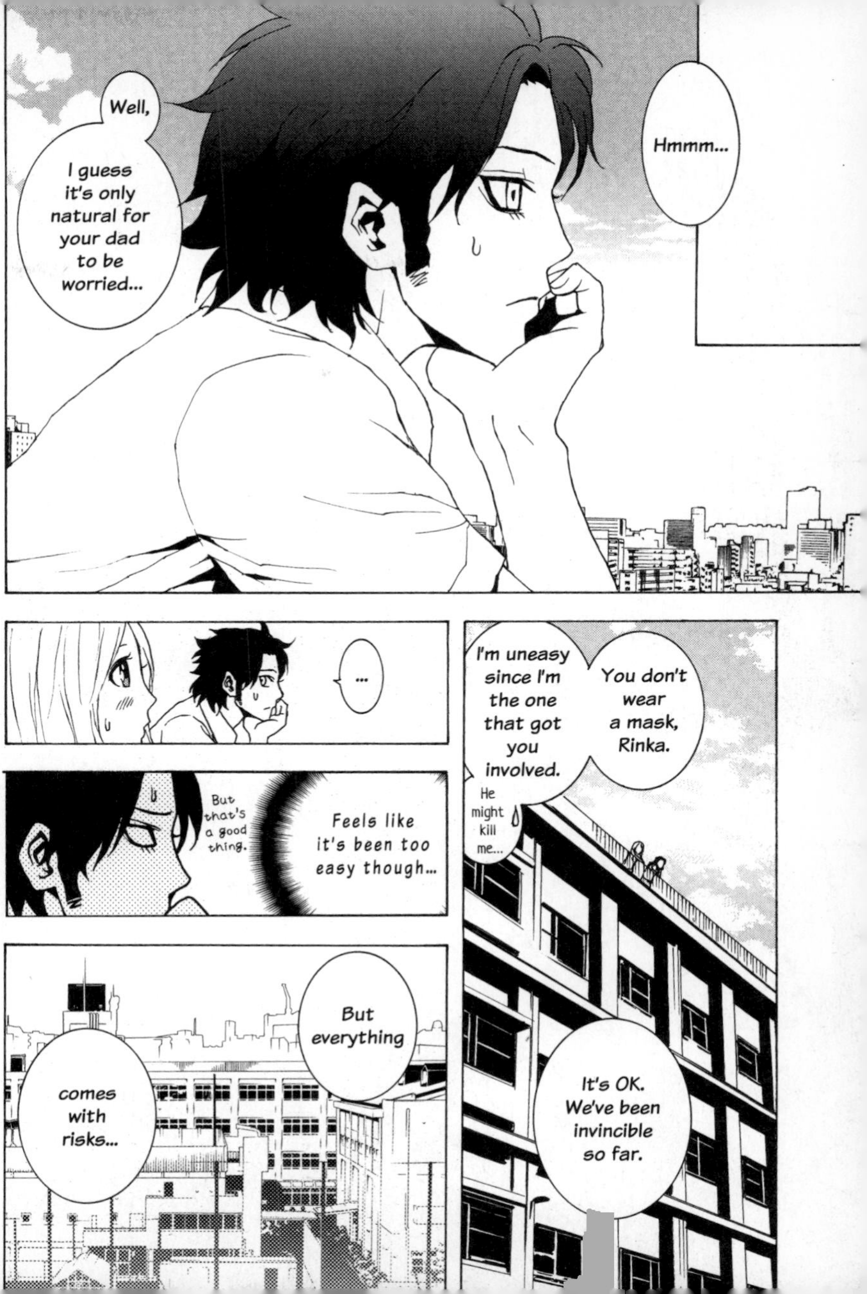
Hmmm...
Well,
I guess it's only natural for your dad to be worried...
You don't wear a mask, Rinka.
I'm uneasy since I'm the one that got you involved.
He might kill me...
It's OK. We've been invincible so far.
...
Feels like it's been too easy though...
But that's a good thing.
But everything
comes with risks...

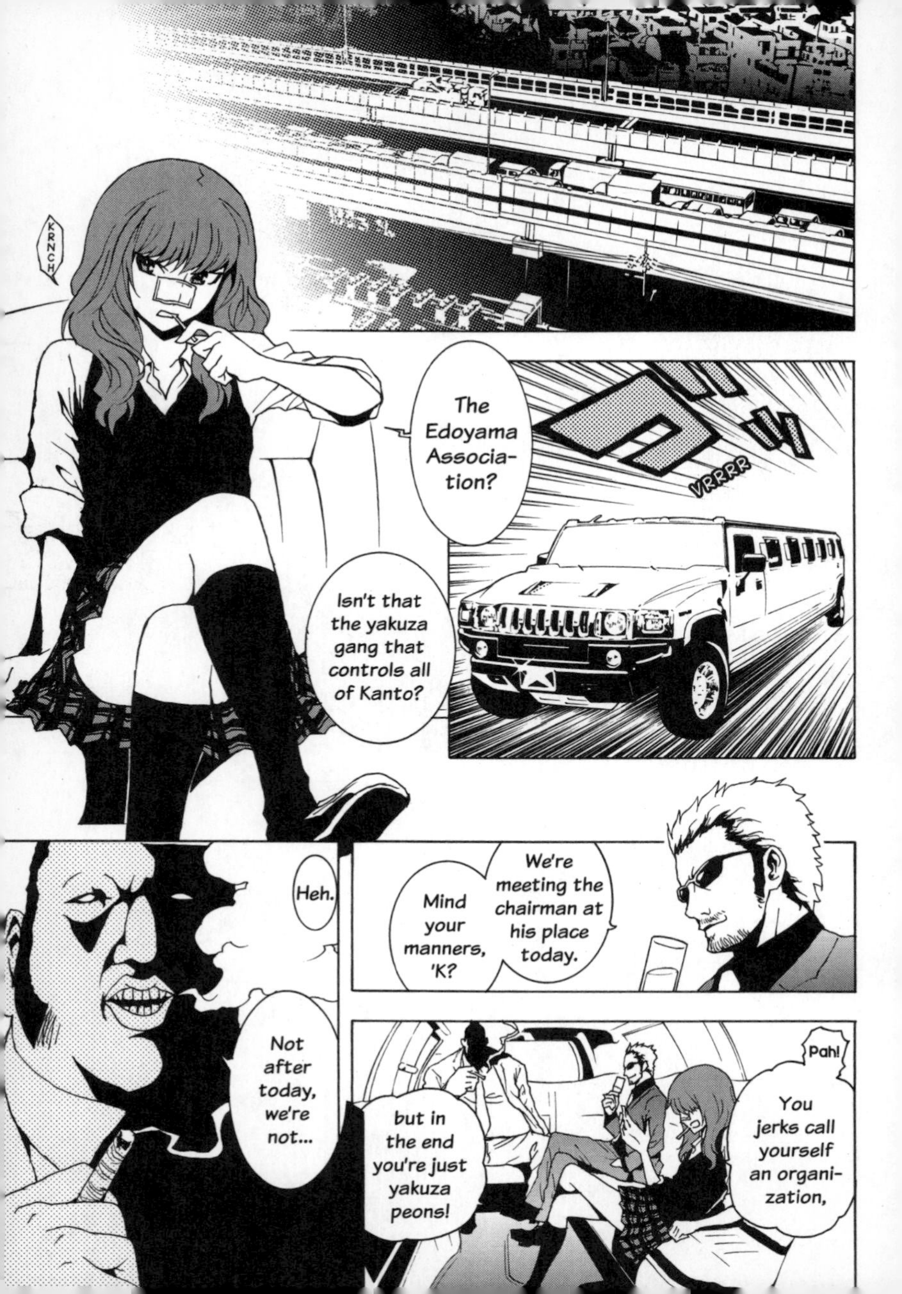
VRRRR
KRNCH
The Edoyama Association?
Isn't that the yakuza gang that controls all of Kanto?
We're meeting the chairman at his place today.
Mind your manners, 'K?
Pah!
You jerks call yourself an organization,
but in the end you're just yakuza peons!
Heh.
Not after today, we're not...

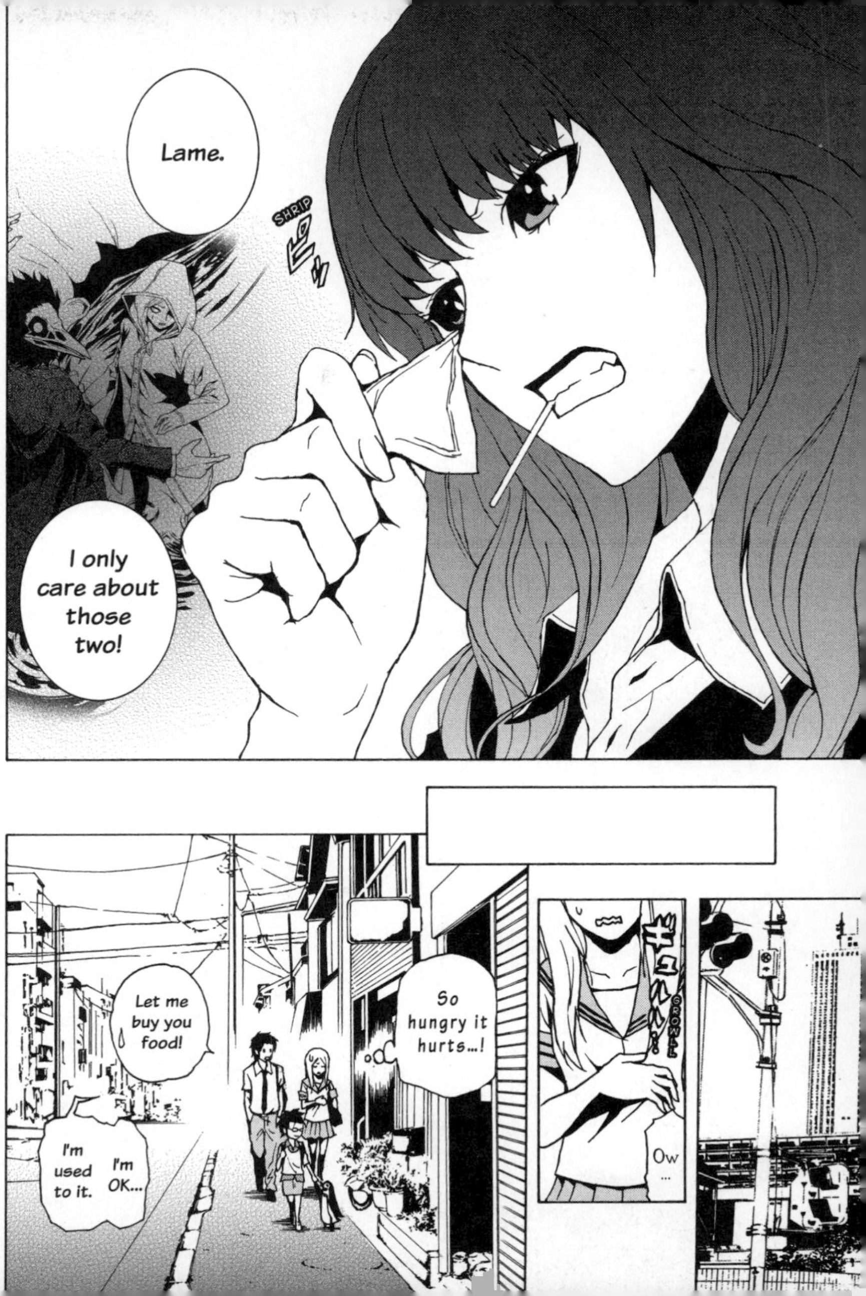
Lame.
SHRIP
I only care about those two!
GROWL
Ow ...
So hungry it hurts...!
Let me buy you food!
I'm OK...
I'm used to it.

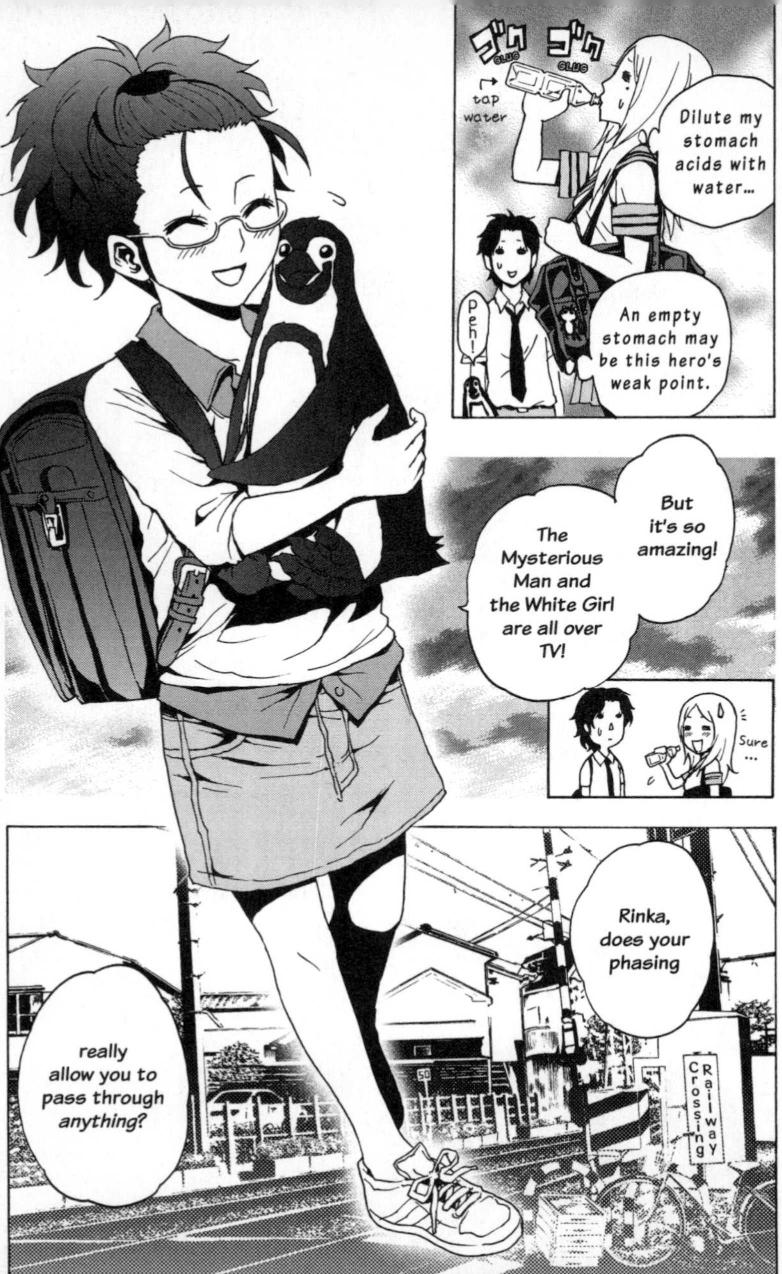
ゴク ゴク
GLUG GLUG
tap water
Dilute my stomach acids with water...
Peh!
An empty stomach may be this hero's weak point.
But it's so amazing!
The Mysterious Man and the White Girl are all over TV!
Sure...
Rinka, does your phasing
really allow you to pass through *anything*?
Railway Crossing

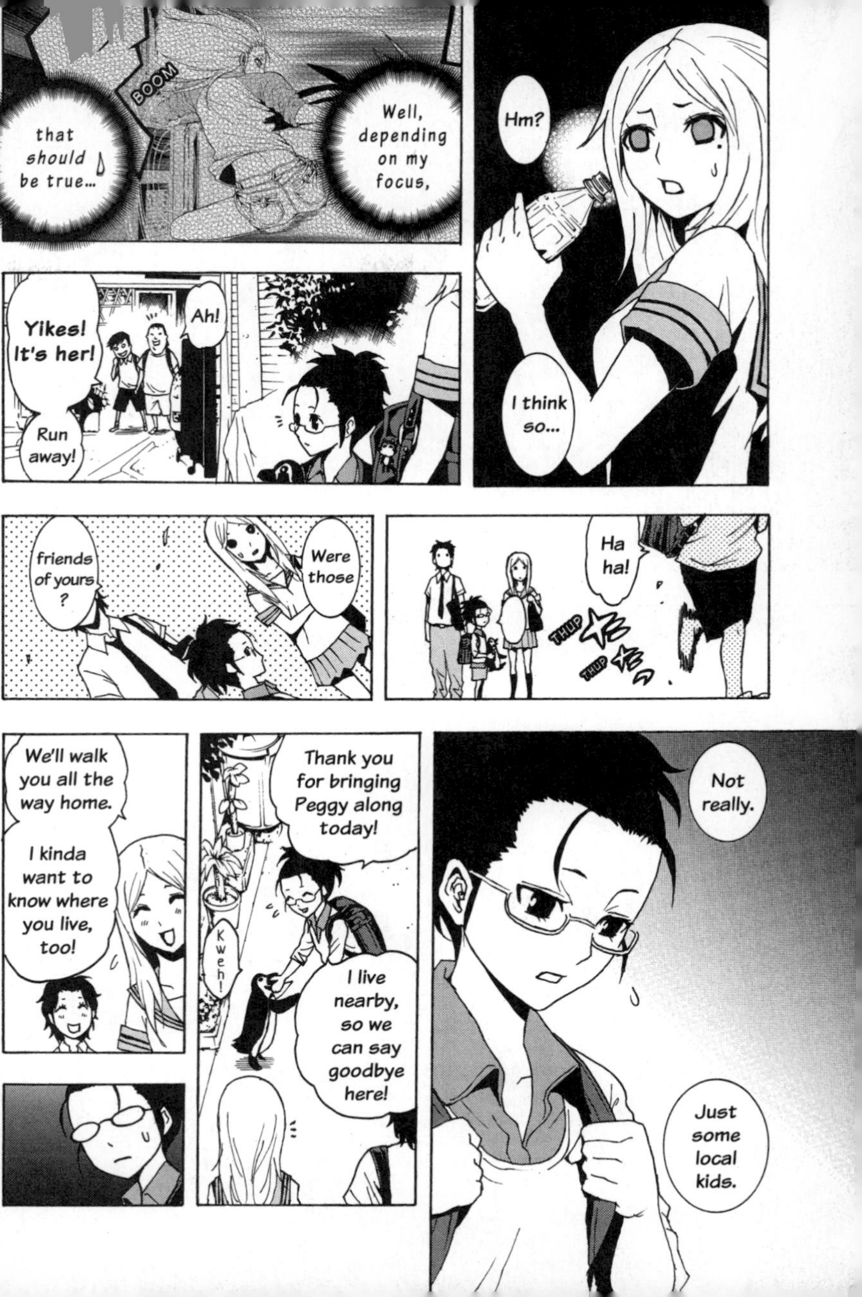
Hm?
I think so...
Well, depending on my focus,
that should be true...
BOOM
Ah!
Yikes! It's her!
Run away!
Ha ha!
THUP
THUP
Were those
friends of yours?
Not really.
Just some local kids.
Thank you for bringing Peggy along today!
Kweh!
I live nearby, so we can say goodbye here!
We'll walk you all the way home.
I kinda want to know where you live, too!

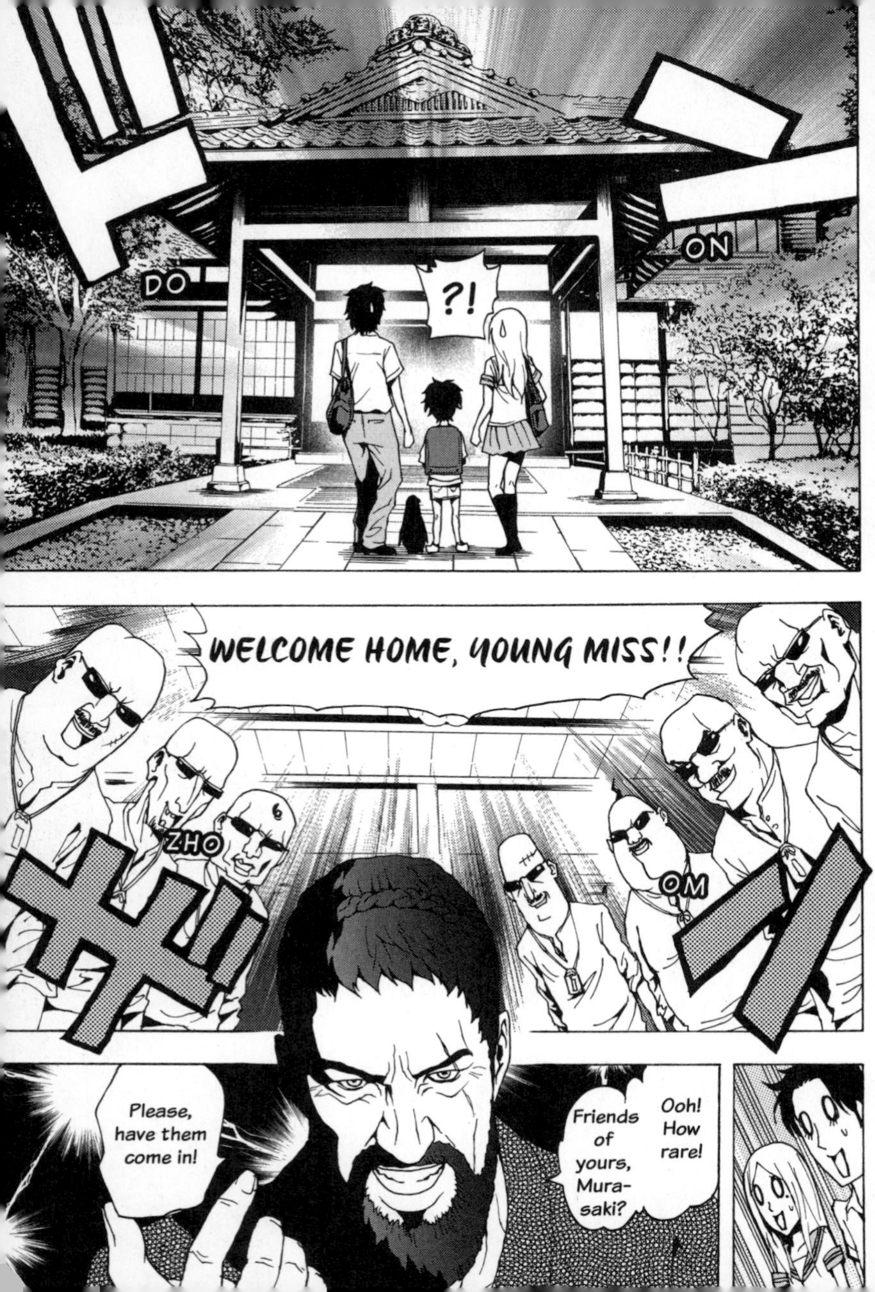
DO
ON
?!
WELCOME HOME, YOUNG MISS!!
ZHO
OM
Ooh! How rare!
Friends of yours, Mura-saki?
Please, have them come in!

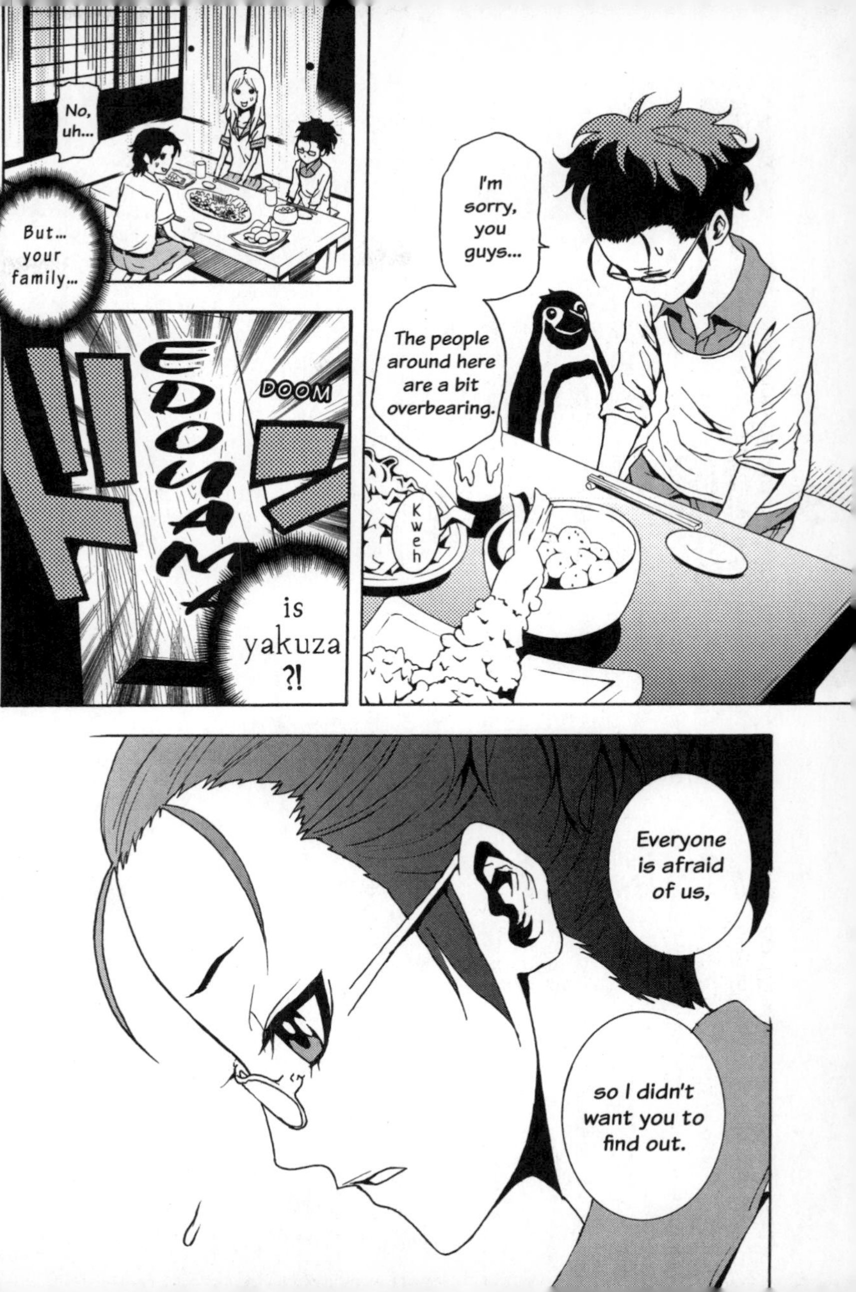
I'm sorry, you guys...
The people around here are a bit overbearing.
Kweh
No, uh...
But... your family...
EDOUAMA
DOOM
is yakuza ?!
Everyone is afraid of us,
so I didn't want you to find out.

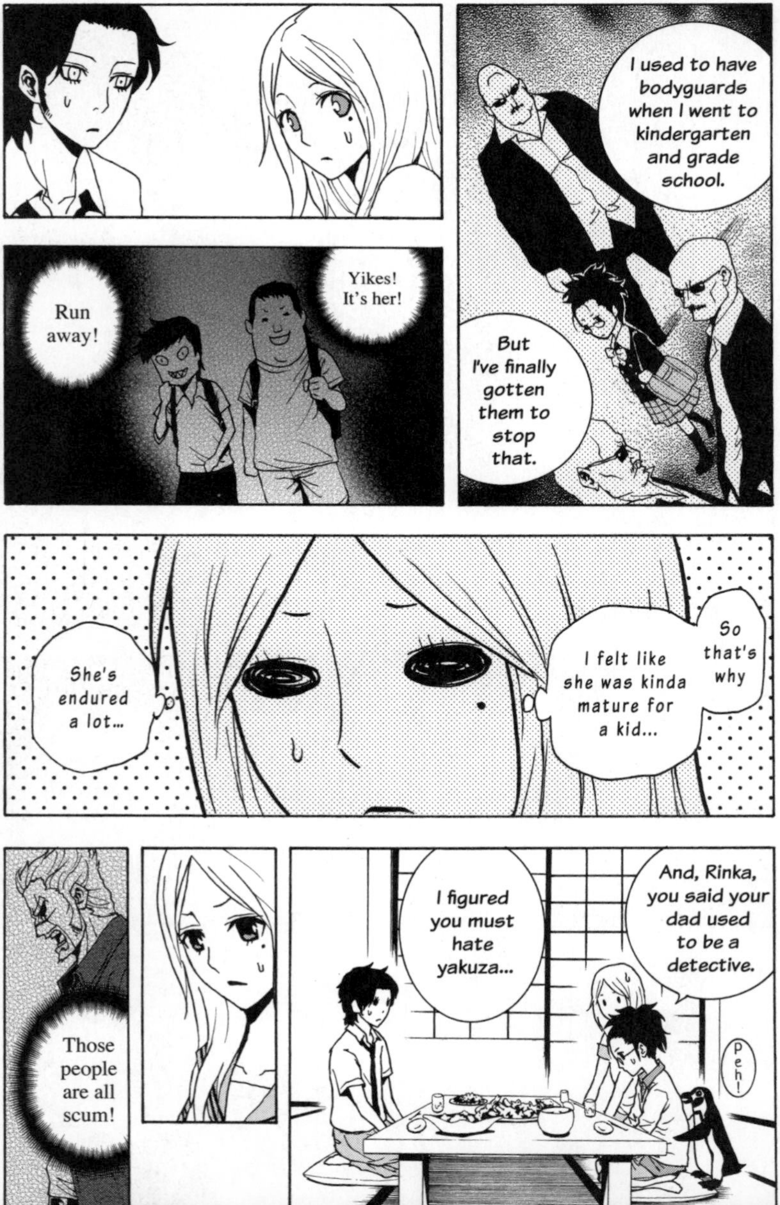
I used to have bodyguards when I went to kindergarten and grade school.
But I've finally gotten them to stop that.
Yikes! It's her!
Run away!
So that's why
I felt like she was kinda mature for a kid...
She's endured a lot...
And, Rinka, you said your dad used to be a detective.
I figured you must hate yakuza...
Peh!
Those people are all scum!

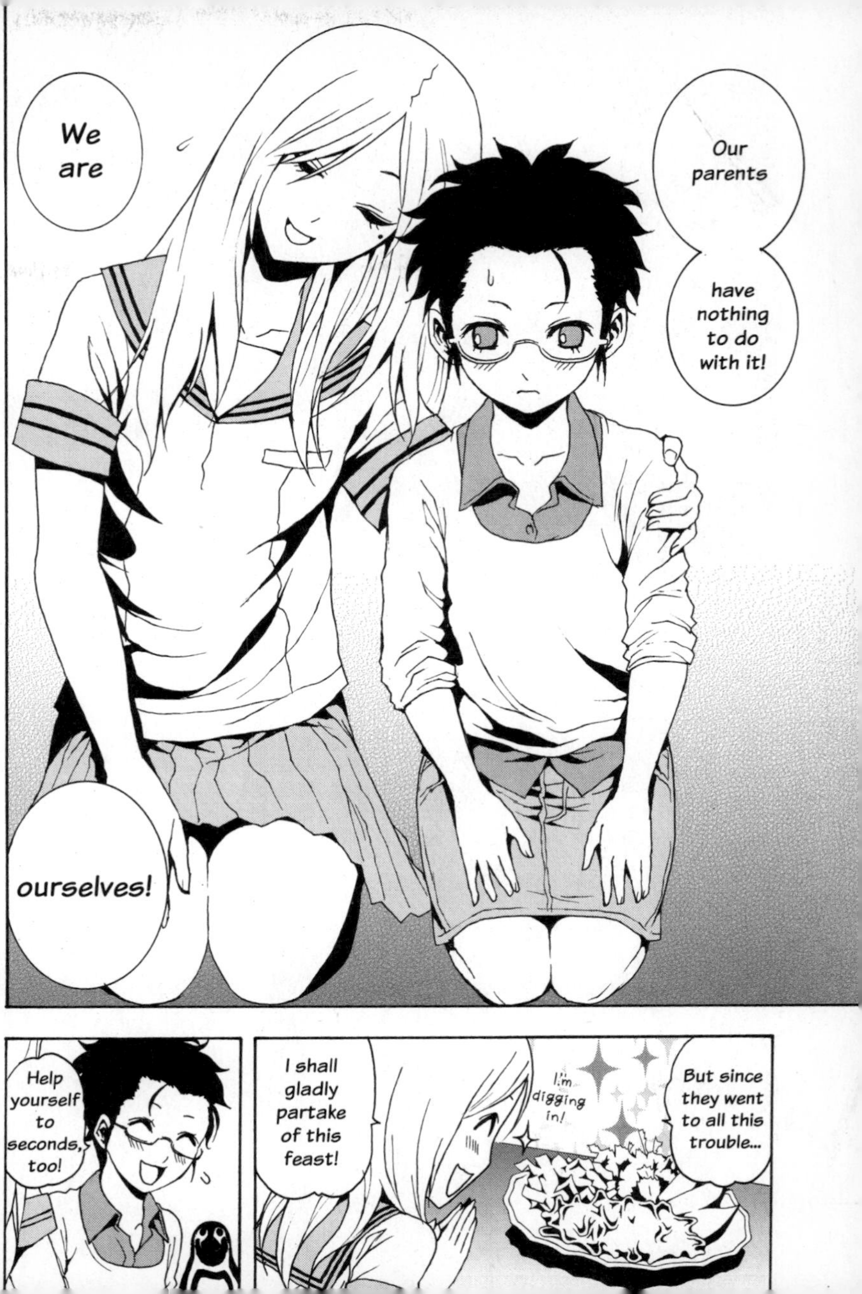

Our parents
have nothing to do with it!
We are
ourselves!
But since they went to all this trouble...
I'm digging in!
I shall gladly partake of this feast!
Help yourself to seconds, too!

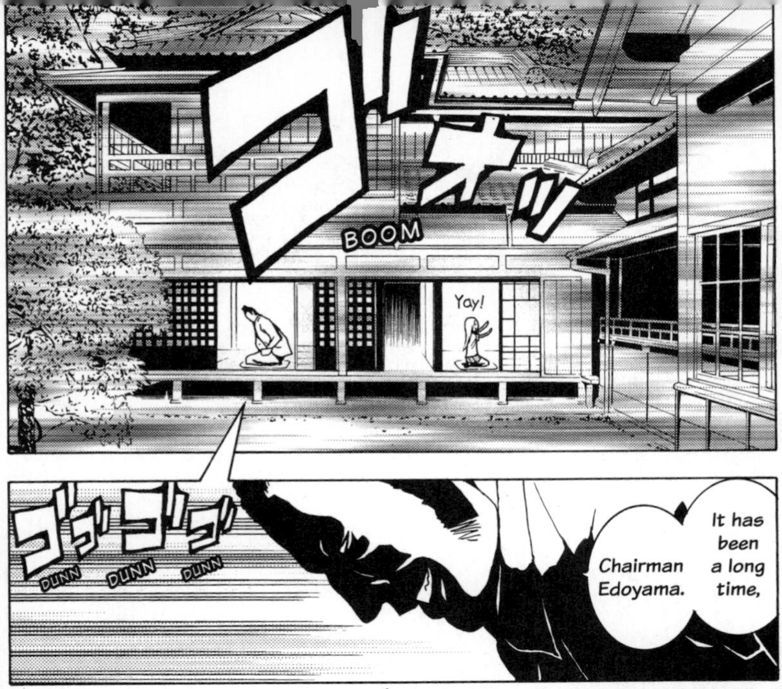
BOOM
Yay!
DUNN DUNN DUNN
It has been a long time, Chairman Edoyama.

* "Hotokeda" literally translates to "The Buddha."

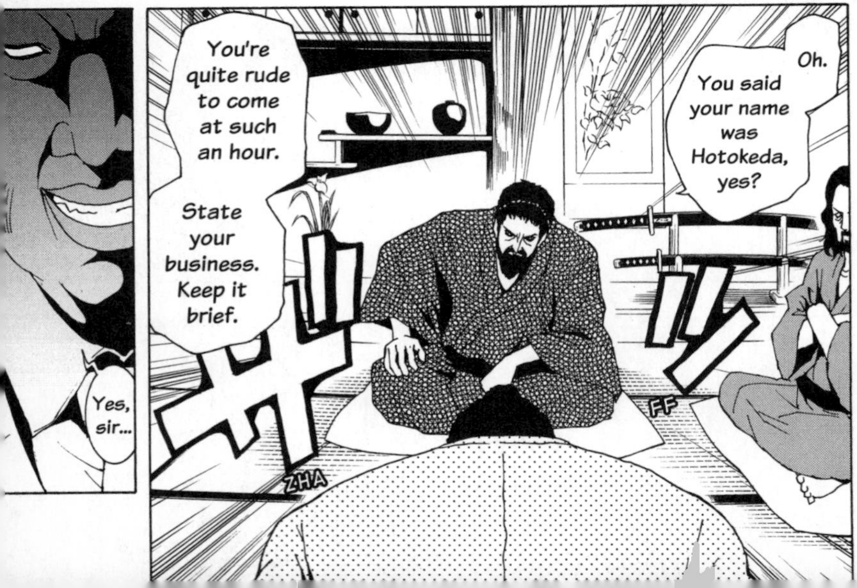
Oh.
You said your name was Hotokeda, yes?
You're quite rude to come at such an hour.
State your business. Keep it brief.
FF
ZHA
Yes, sir...

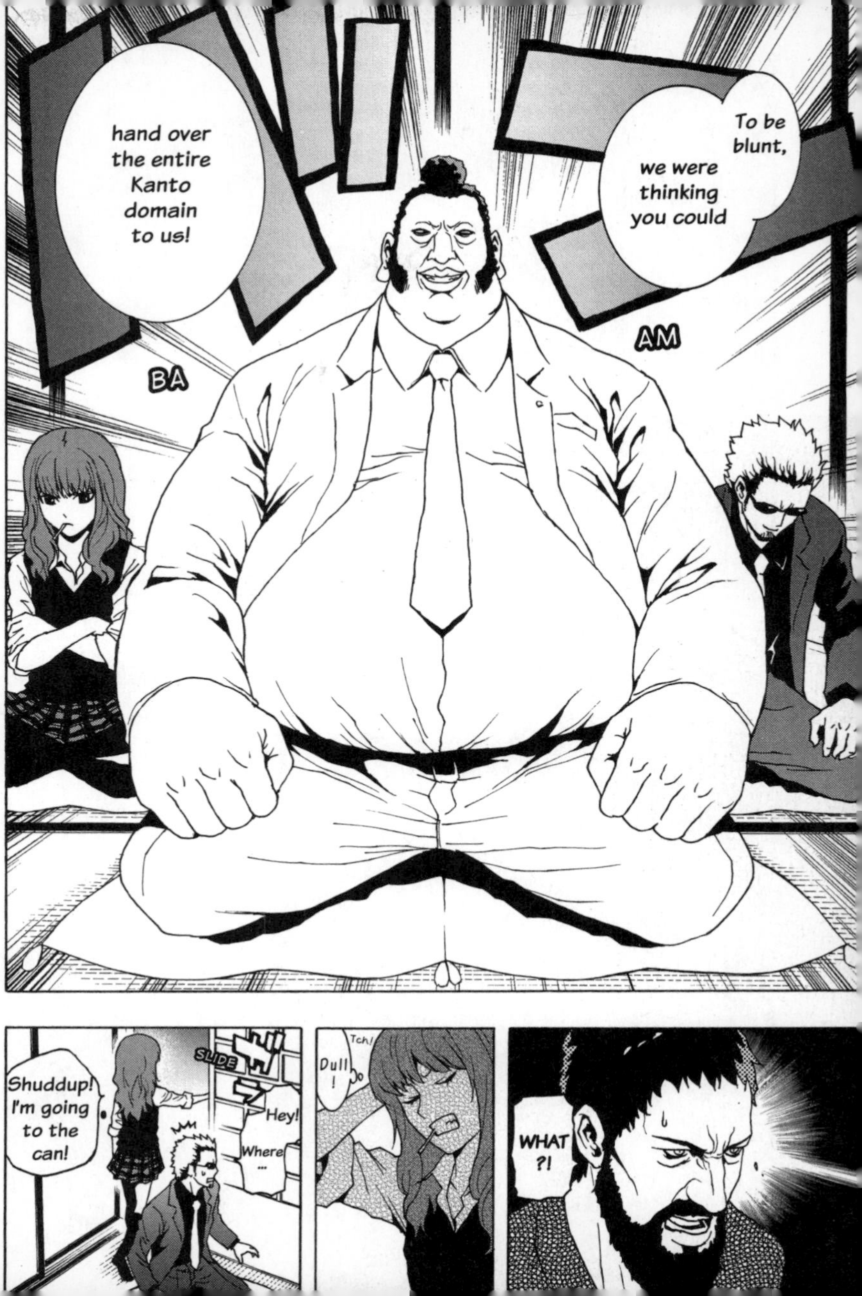
To be blunt,
we were thinking you could
hand over the entire Kanto domain to us!
BA AM
WHAT ?!
Tch!
Dull !
SLIDE
Hey!
Where ...
Shuddup! I'm going to the can!

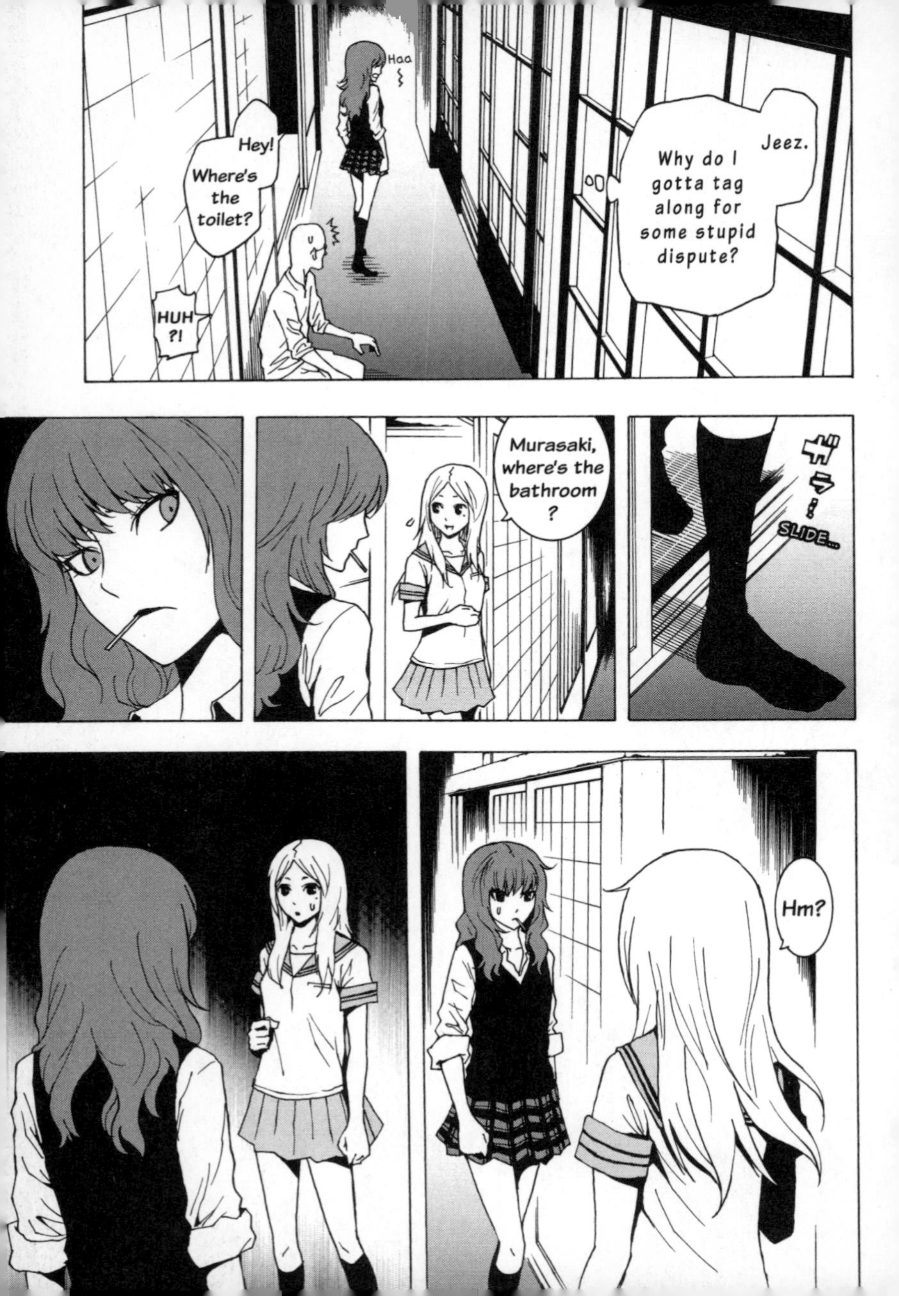
Jeez.
Why do I gotta tag along for some stupid dispute?
Haa
Hey! Where's the toilet?
HUH ?!
SLIDE...
Murasaki, where's the bathroom ?
Hm?

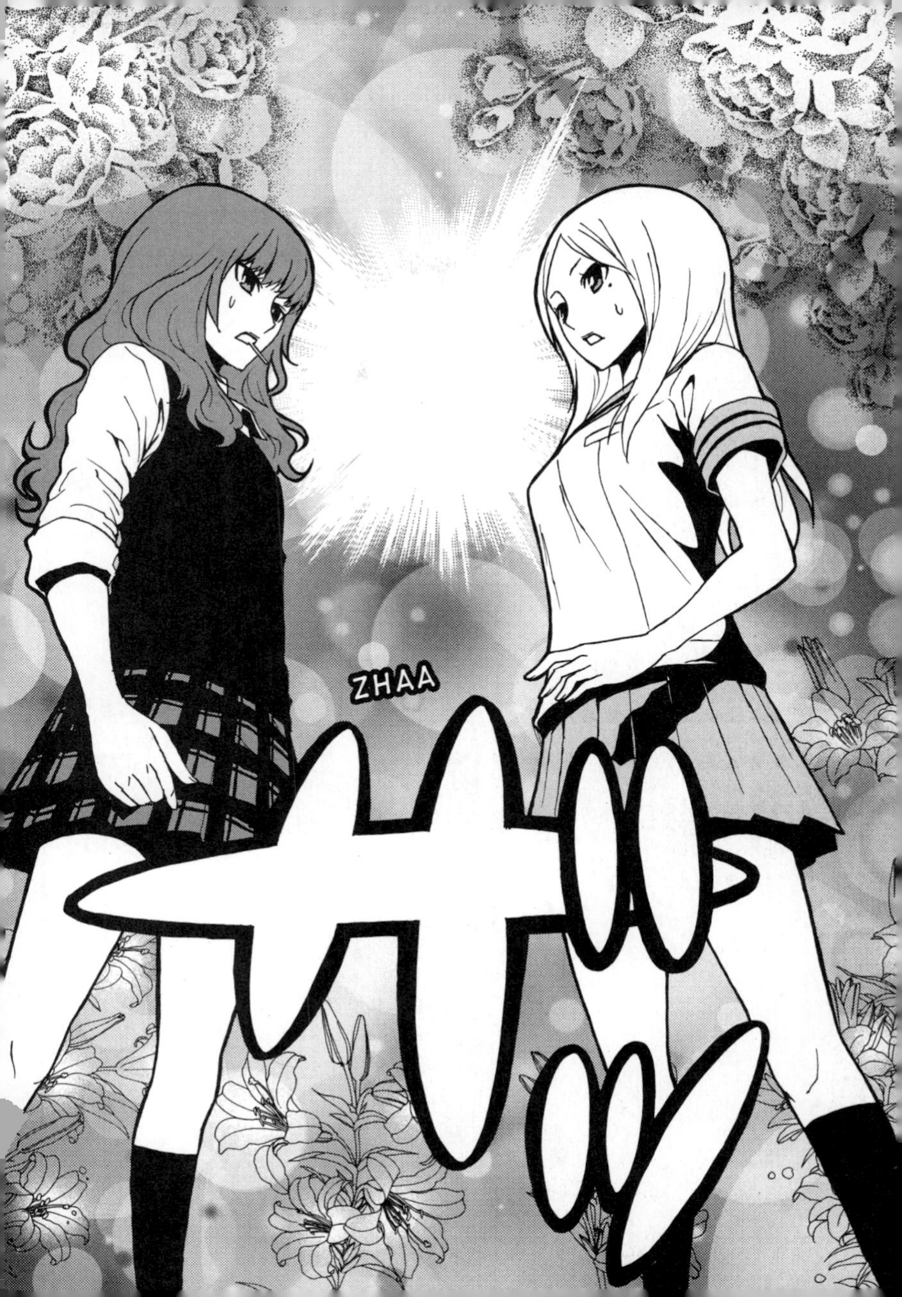
ZHAA
ザッ

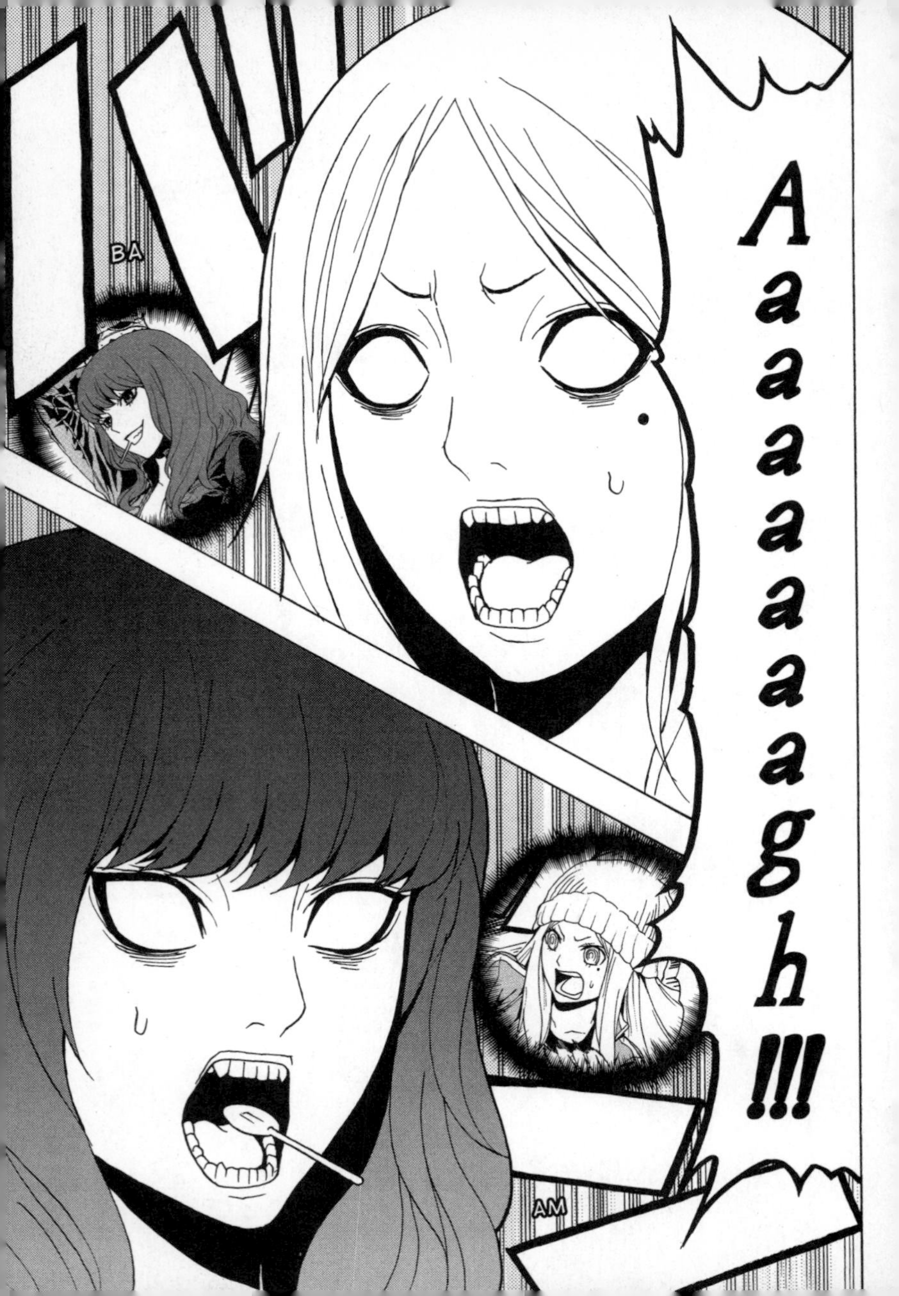
BA
Aaaaaaaaaagh!!!
AM

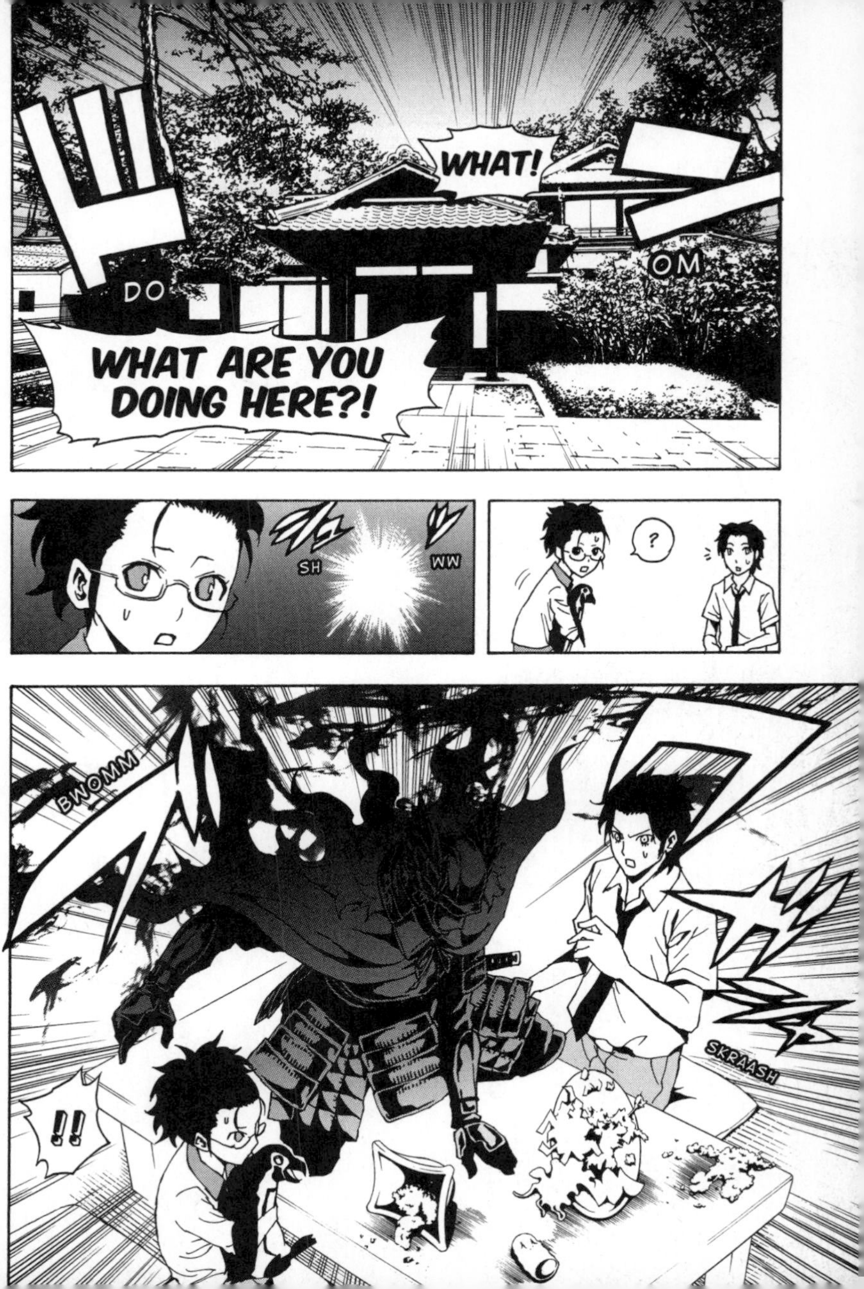
WHAT!
OM
DO
WHAT ARE YOU DOING HERE?!
?
WW
SH
SKRAASH
BWOMM
!!

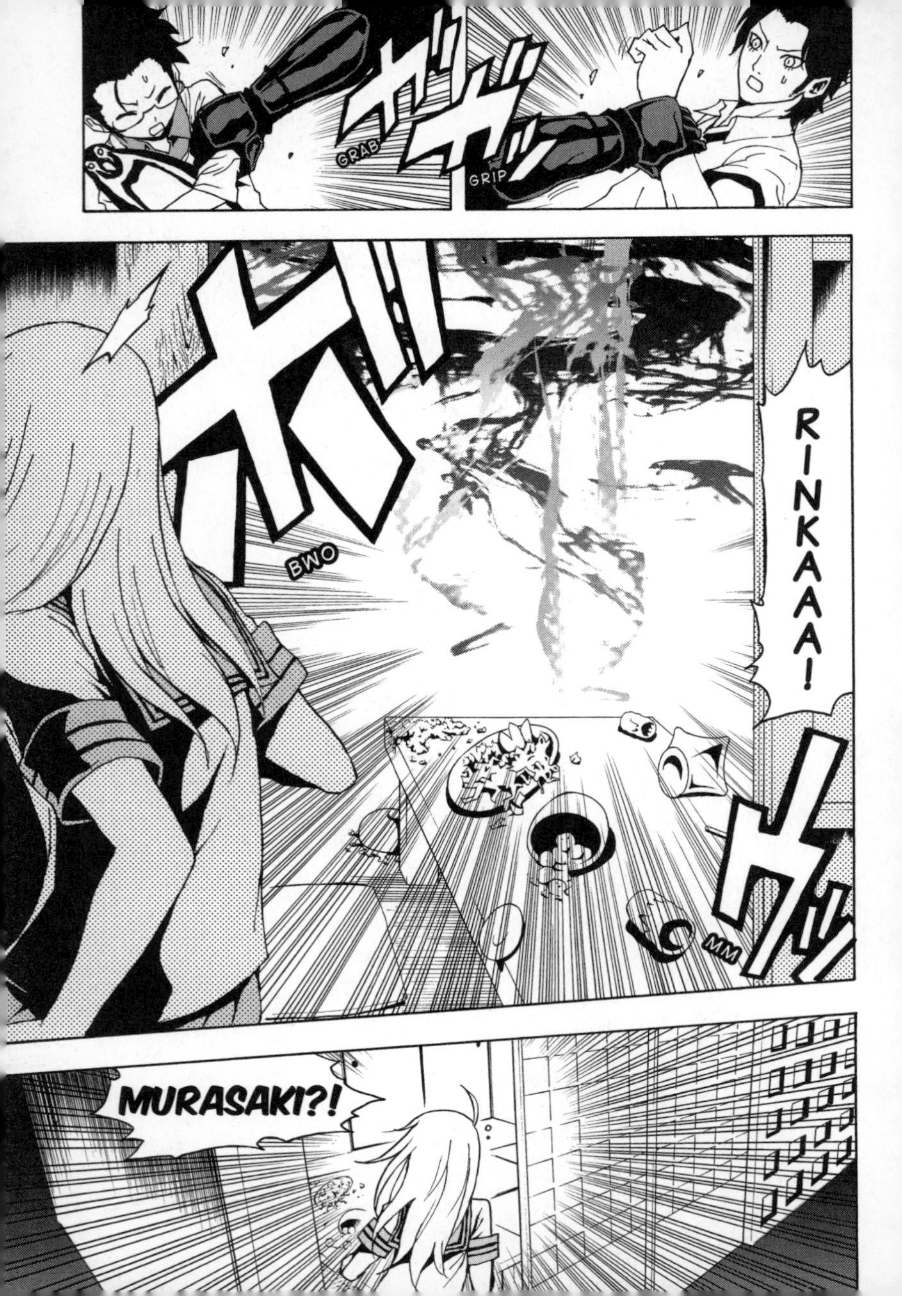
GRIP
GRAB
RINKAAAA!
BWO
MM
MURASAKI?!

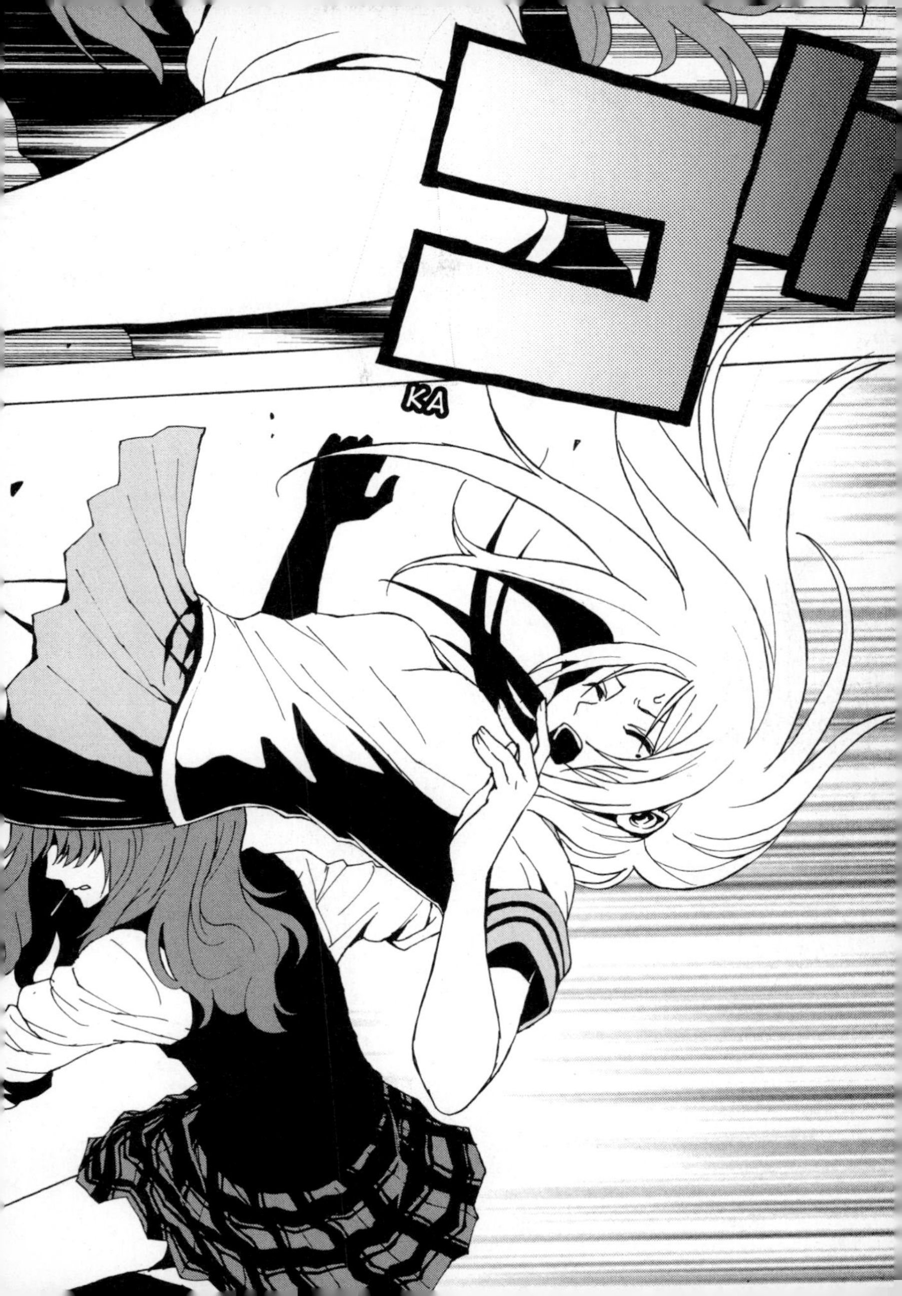
KA

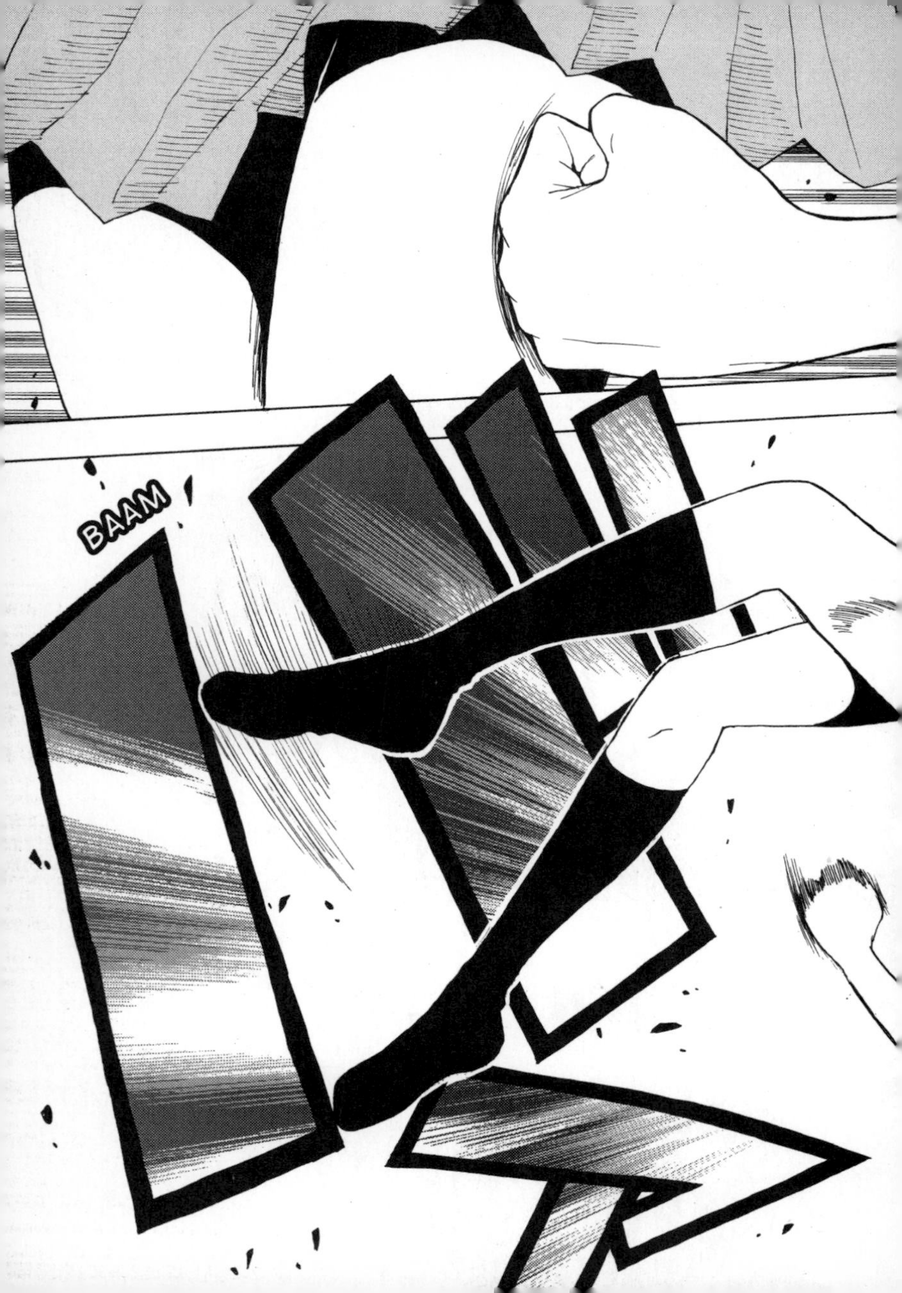
BAAM

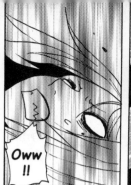

Oww!!

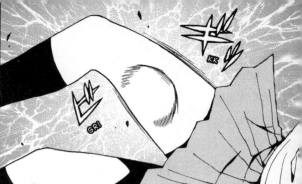

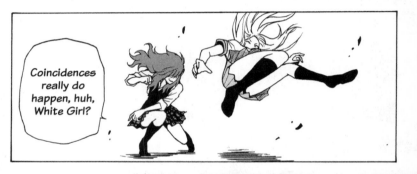

Coincidences really do happen, huh, White Girl?

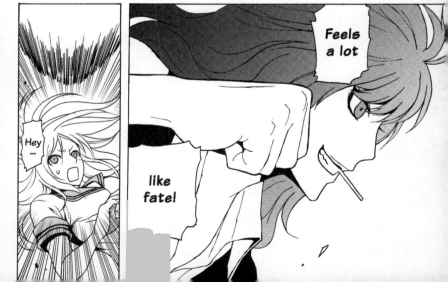

Hey...

Feels a lot

like fate!

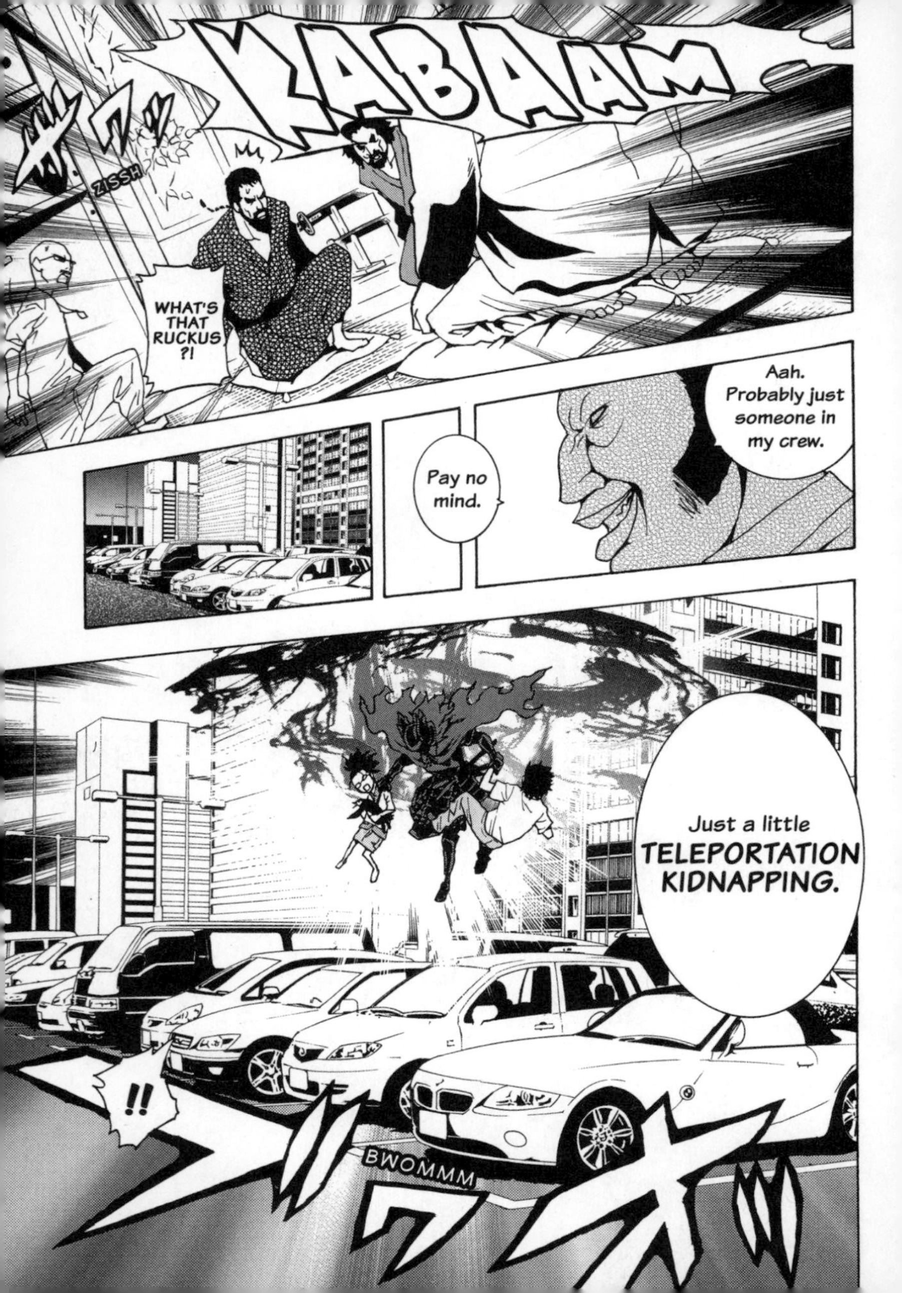
KABAAM
ZISSH
WHAT'S THAT RUCKUS ?!
Aah. Probably just someone in my crew.
Pay no mind.
Just a little TELEPORTATION KIDNAPPING.
!!
BWOMMM

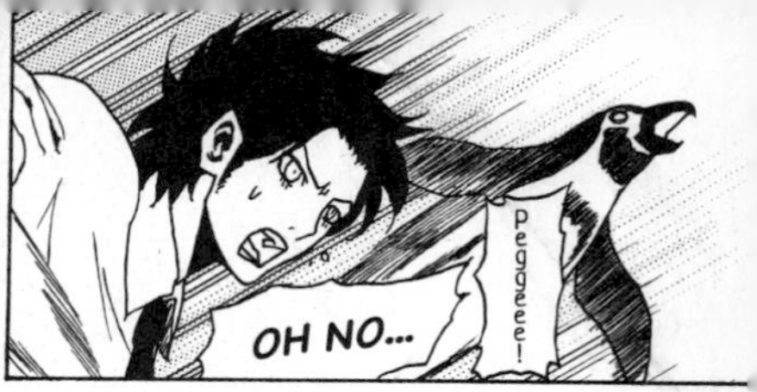
OH NO...
Peggeee!
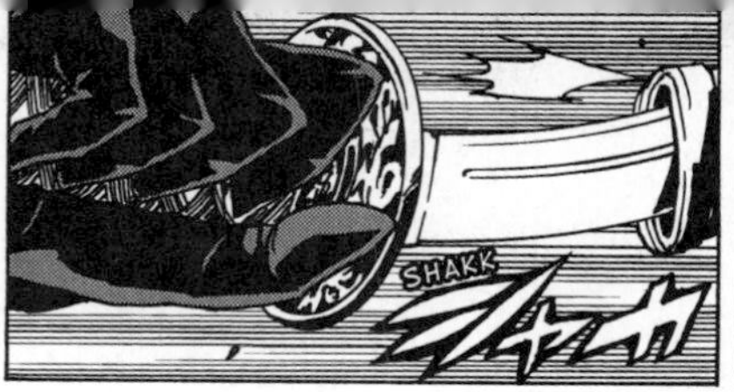
SHAKK
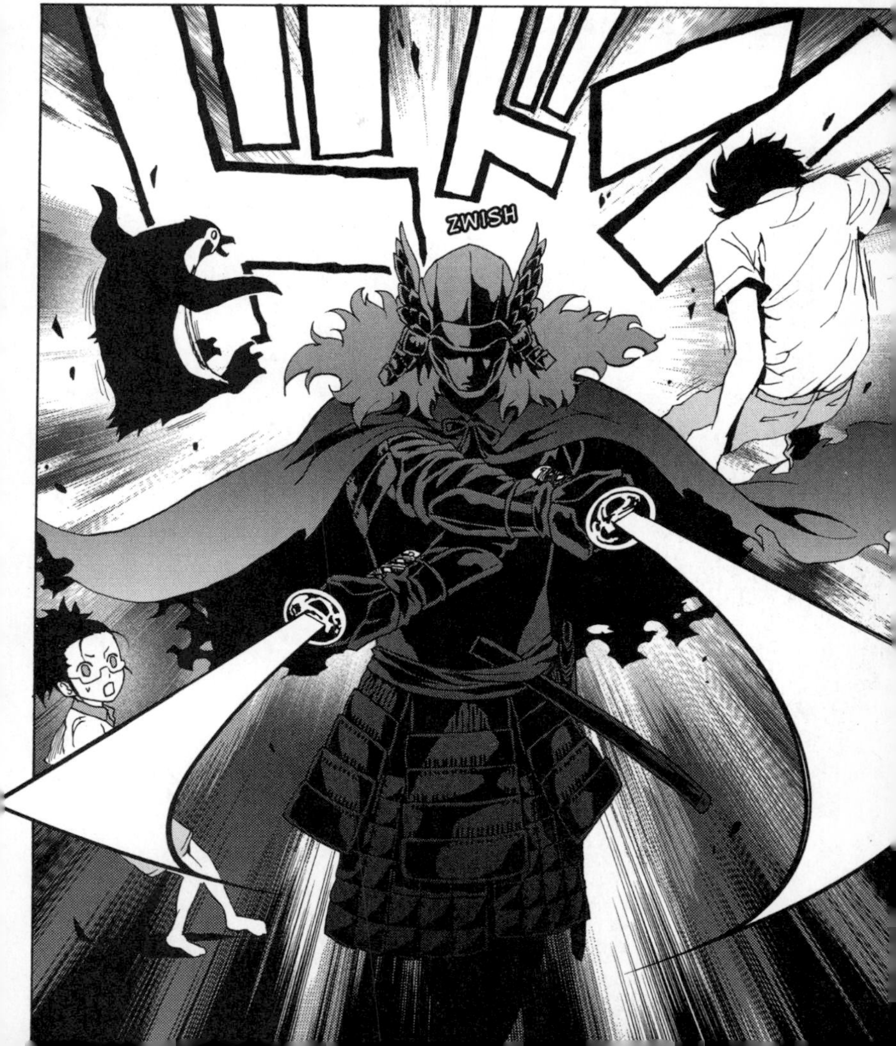
ZWISH

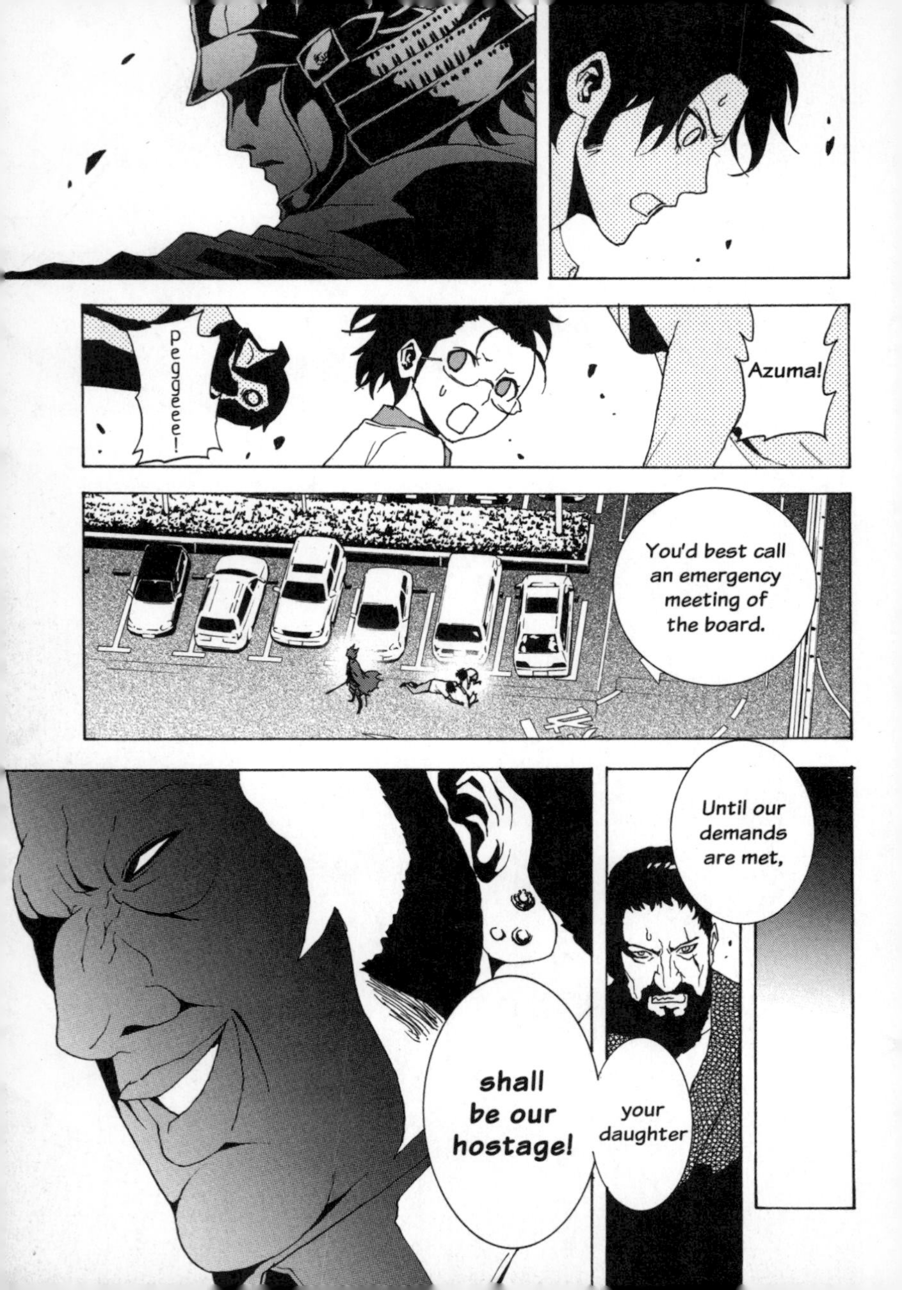
Azuma!
Peggeee!
You'd best call an emergency meeting of the board.
Until our demands are met,
your daughter
shall be our hostage!

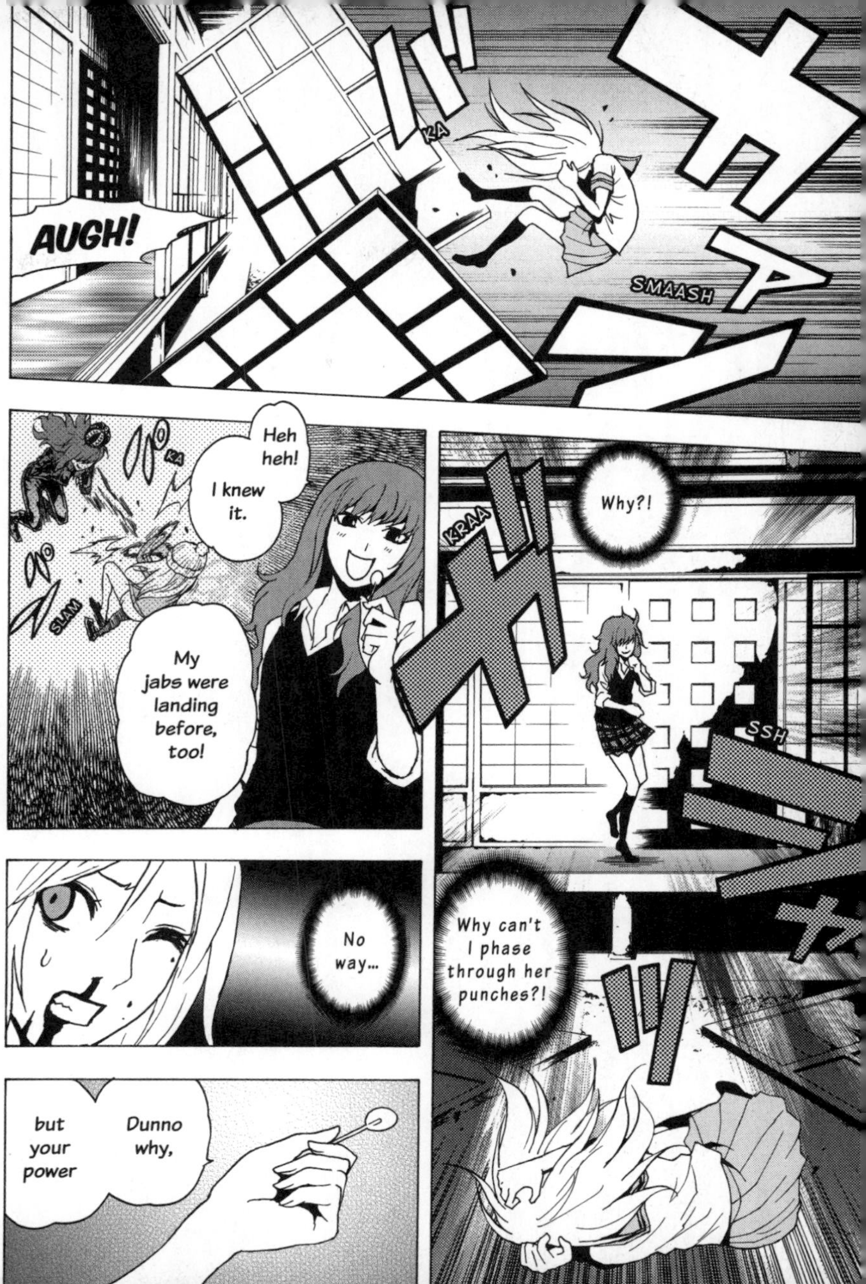
KA
SMAASH
AUGH!
KRAA
Why?!
SSH
Heh heh!
I knew it.
KA
SLAM
My jabs were landing before, too!
Why can't I phase through her punches?!
No way...
Dunno why,
but your power

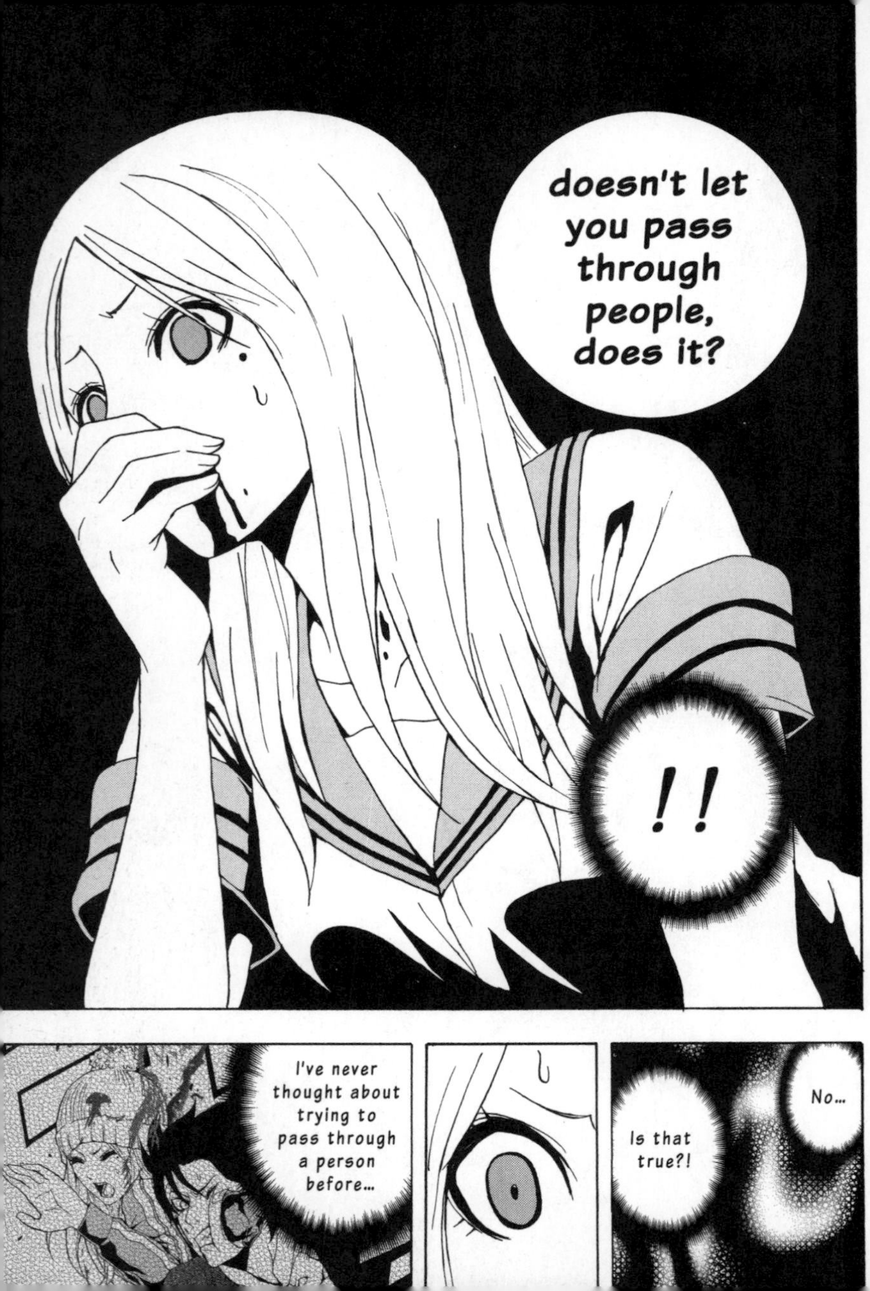
doesn't let you pass through people, does it?
!!
No...
Is that true?!
I've never thought about trying to pass through a person before...

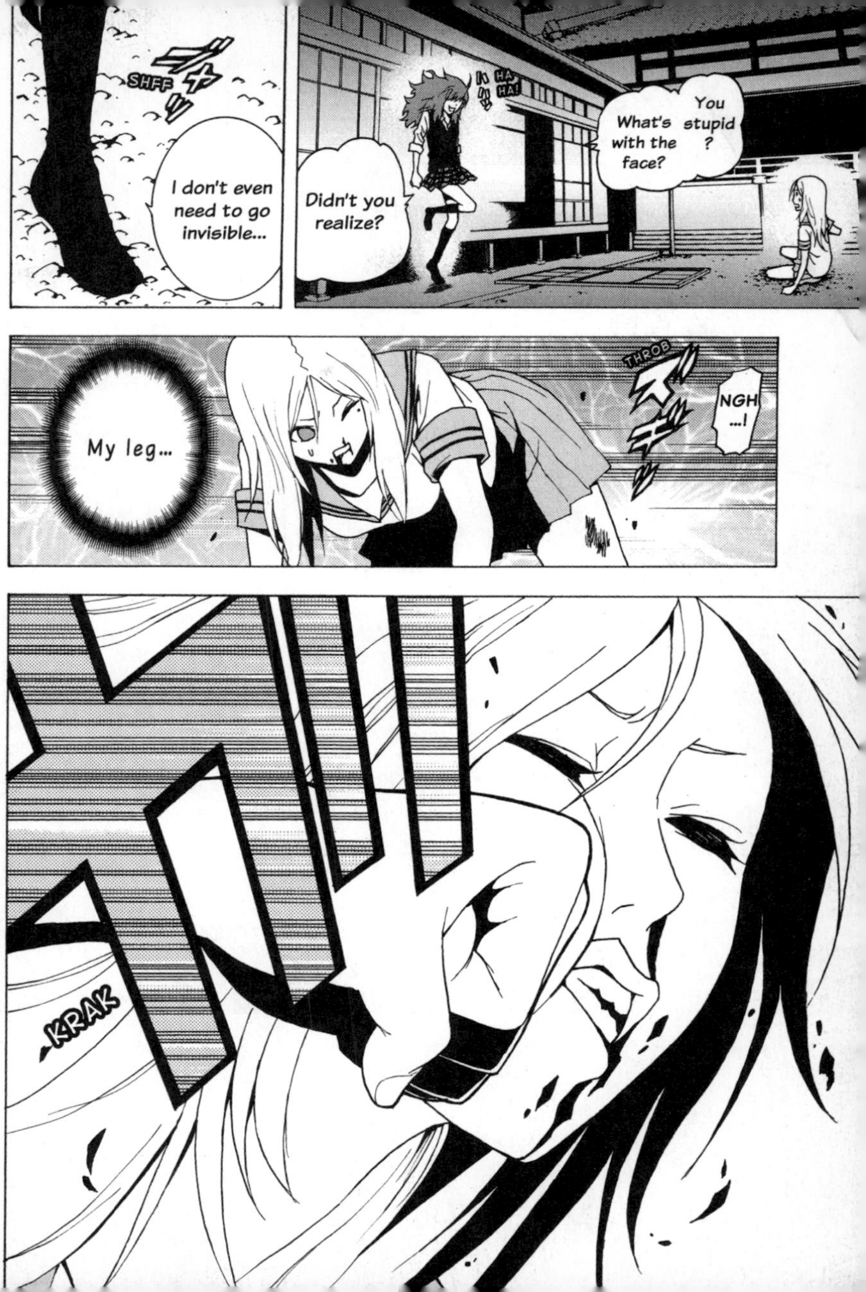

You stupid?
What's with the face?
HA HA!
Didn't you realize?
SHFF
I don't even need to go invisible...
THROB
NGH...!
My leg...
KRAK

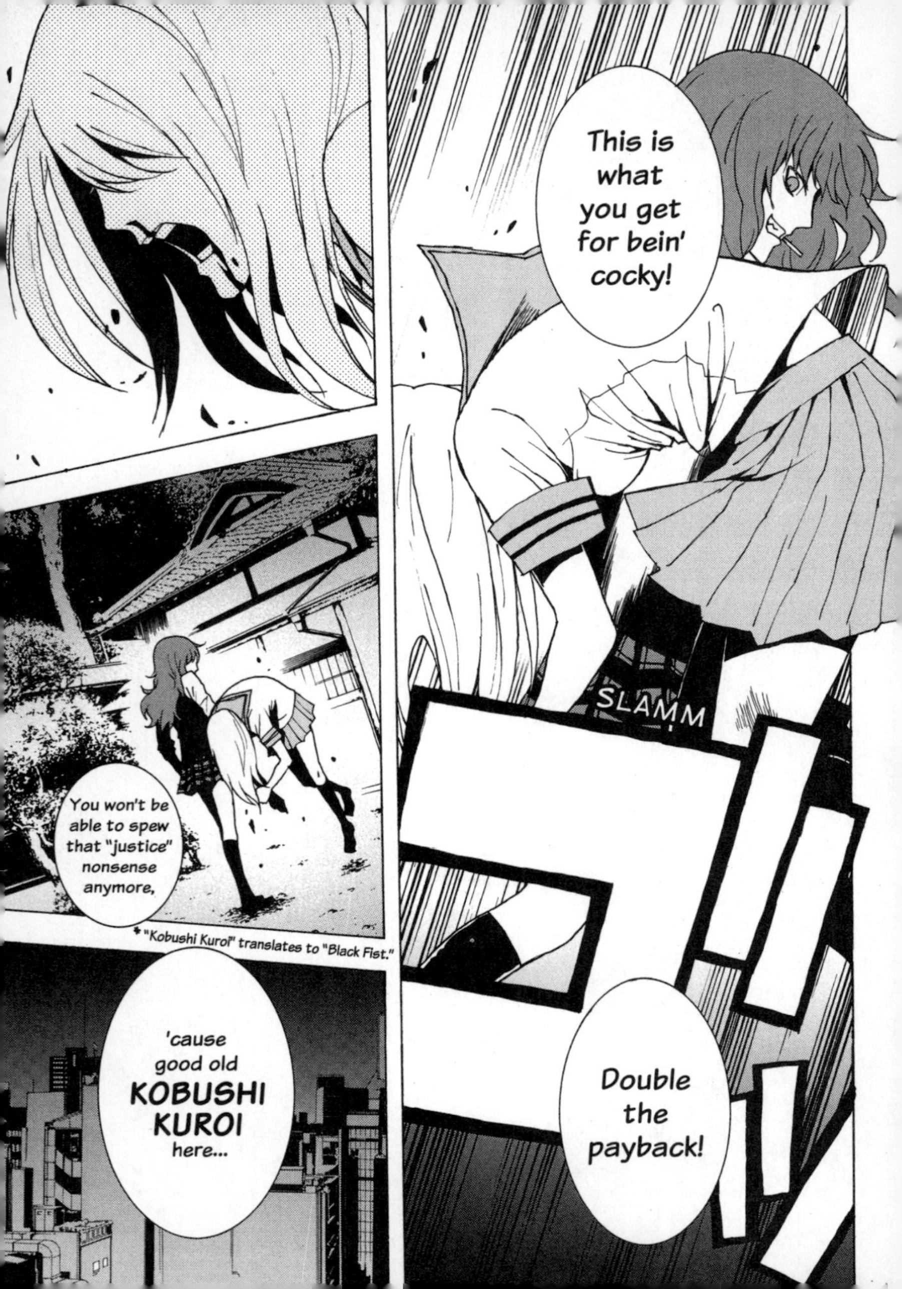
You won't be able to spew that "justice" nonsense anymore,
'cause good old KOBUSHI KUROI here...
This is what you get for bein' cocky!
SLAMM
Double the payback!

* "Kobushi Kuroi" translates to "Black Fist."

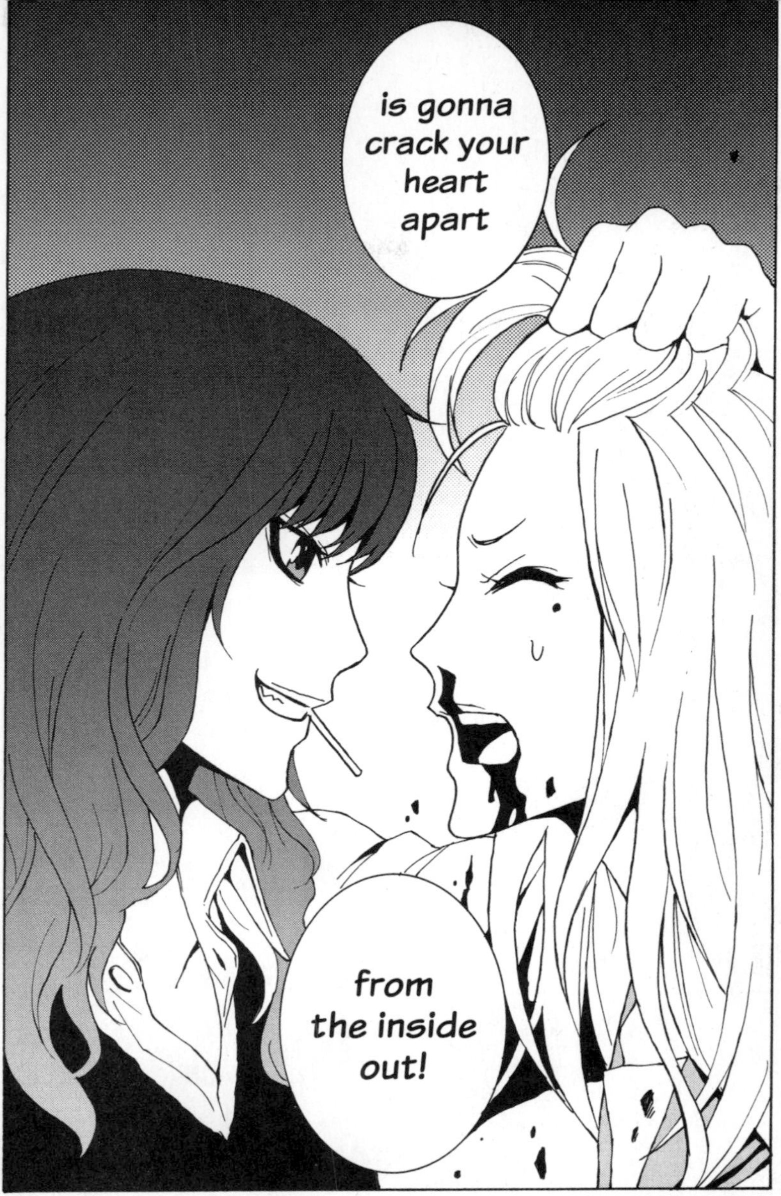
is gonna crack your heart apart
from the inside out!

SCENE 5 /// END

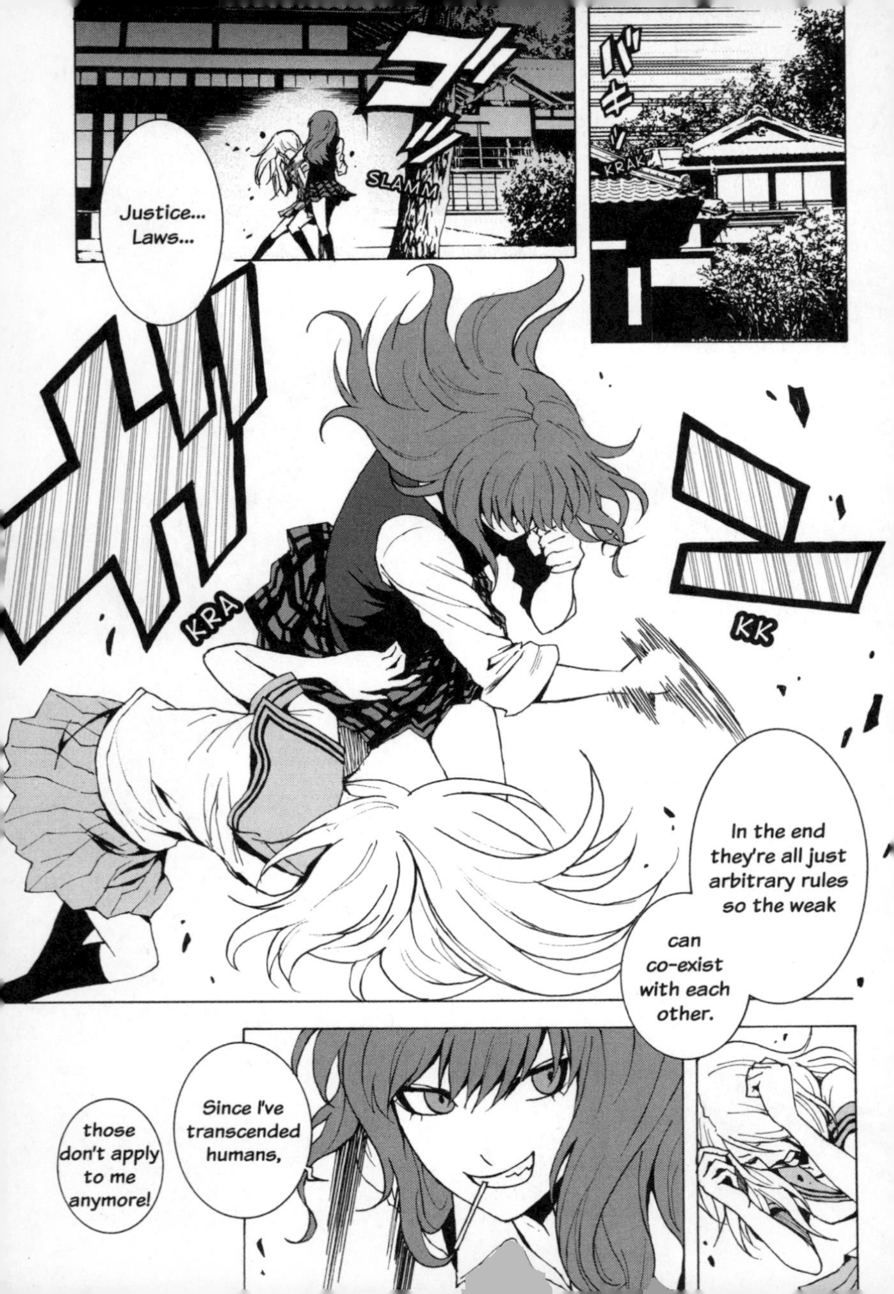
KRAK
SLAMM
Justice... Laws...
KK
KRA
In the end they're all just arbitrary rules so the weak
can co-exist with each other.
Since I've transcended humans,
those don't apply to me anymore!

SCENE 6 /// The Teleporter: Counterattack

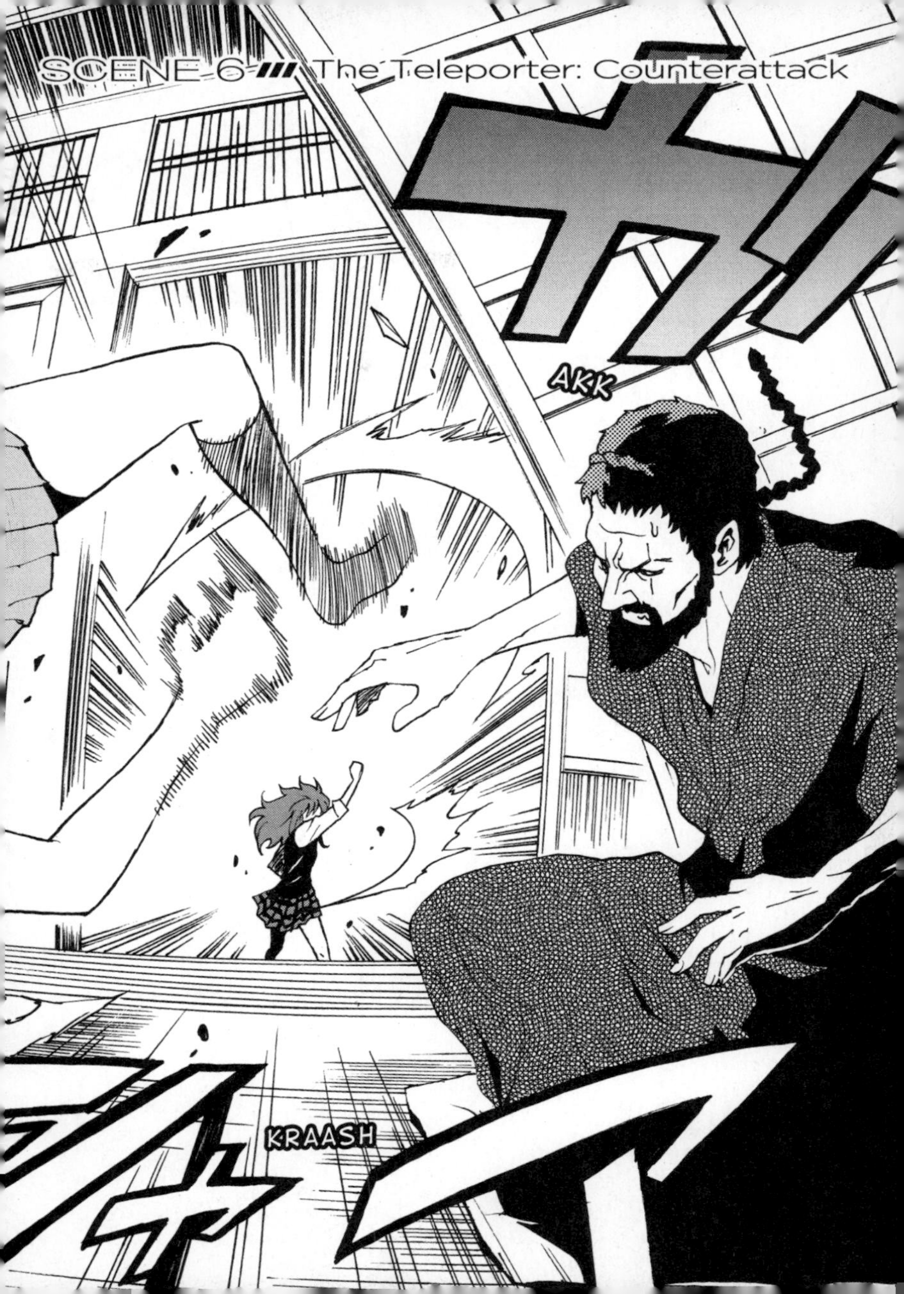
AKK
KRAASH

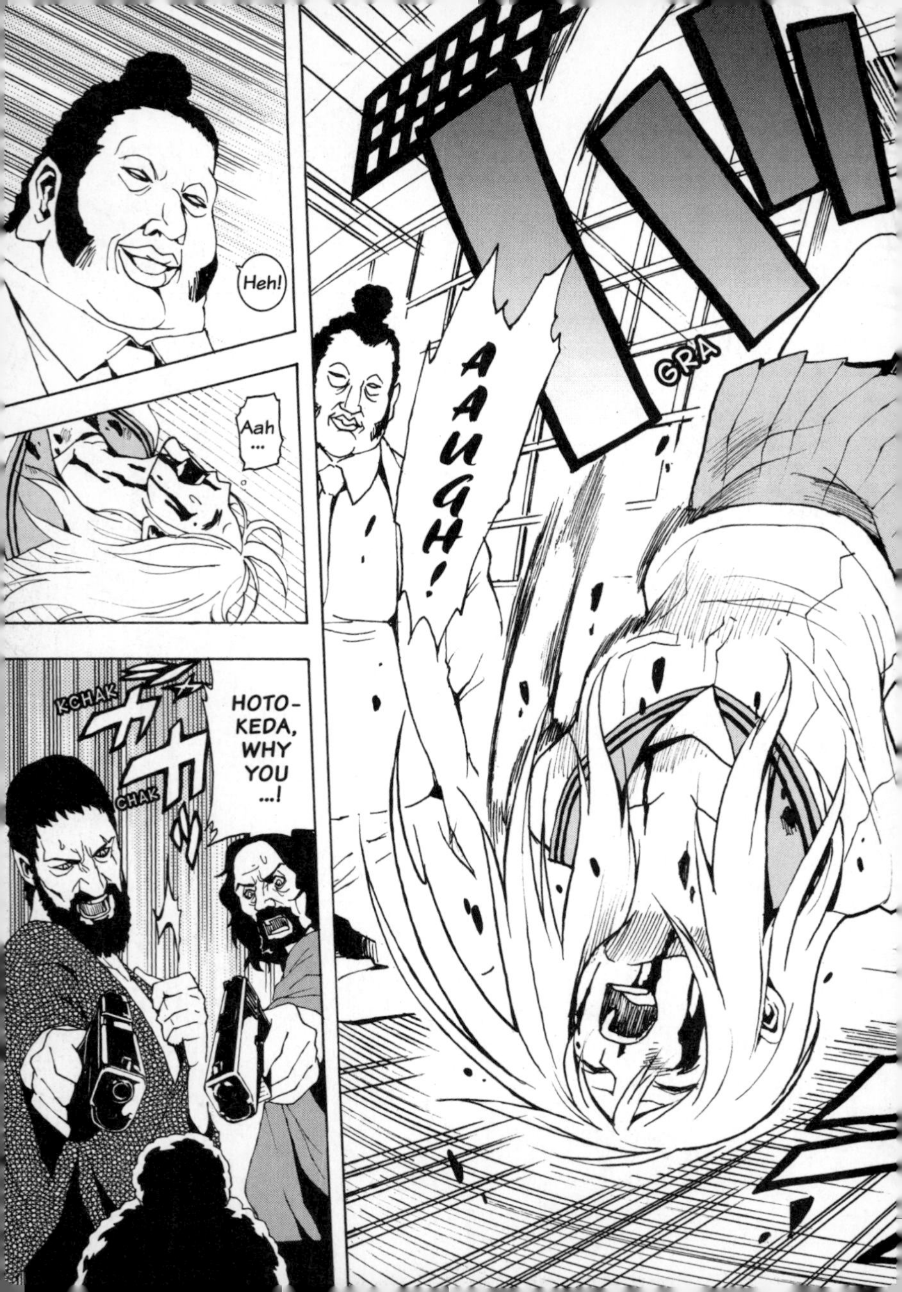
AAUGH!
GRA
Heh!
Aah ...
HOTO-KEDA, WHY YOU ...!
KCHAK
CHAK

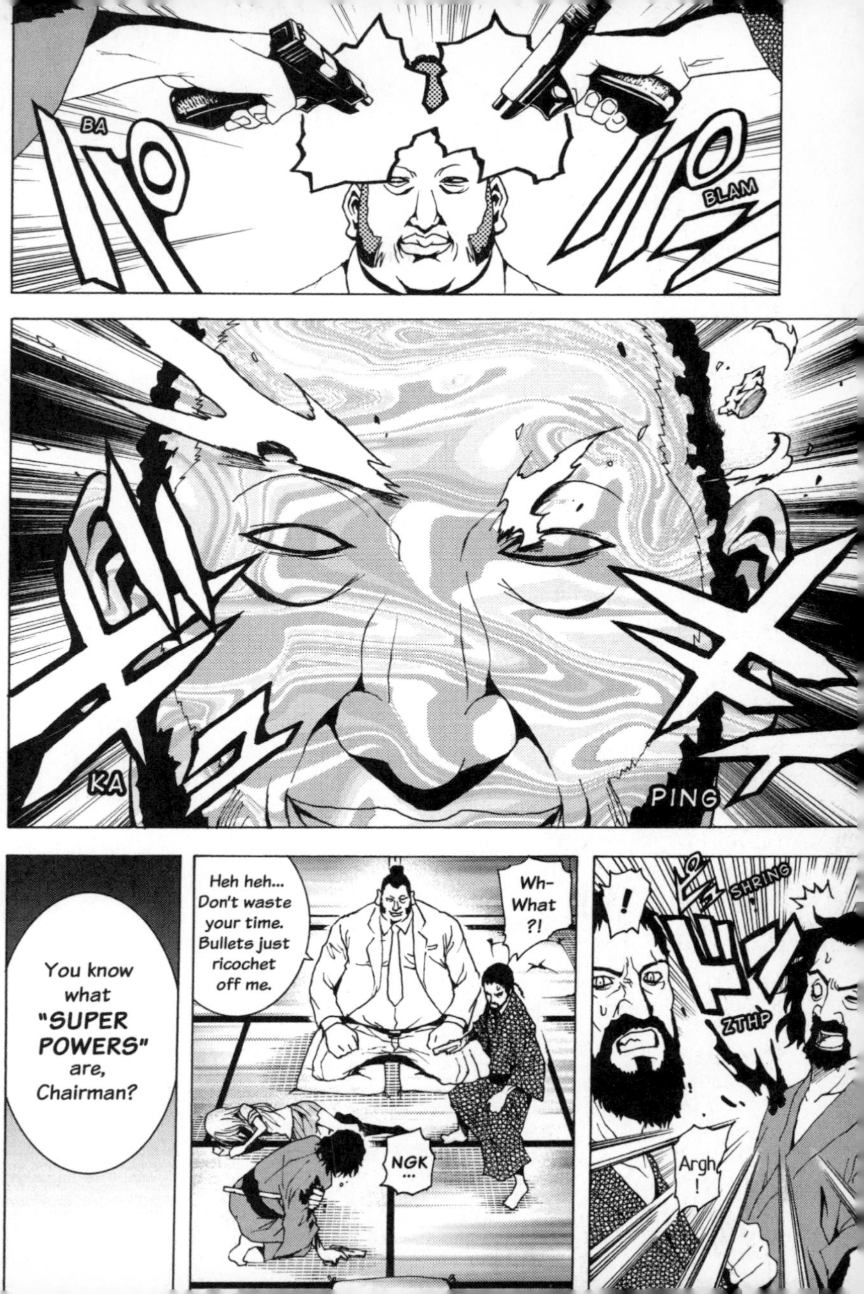
BA
BLAM
KA
PING
SHRING
!
ZTHP
Argh!
Wh-What?!
Heh heh... Don't waste your time. Bullets just ricochet off me.
NGK...
You know what "SUPER POWERS" are, Chairman?

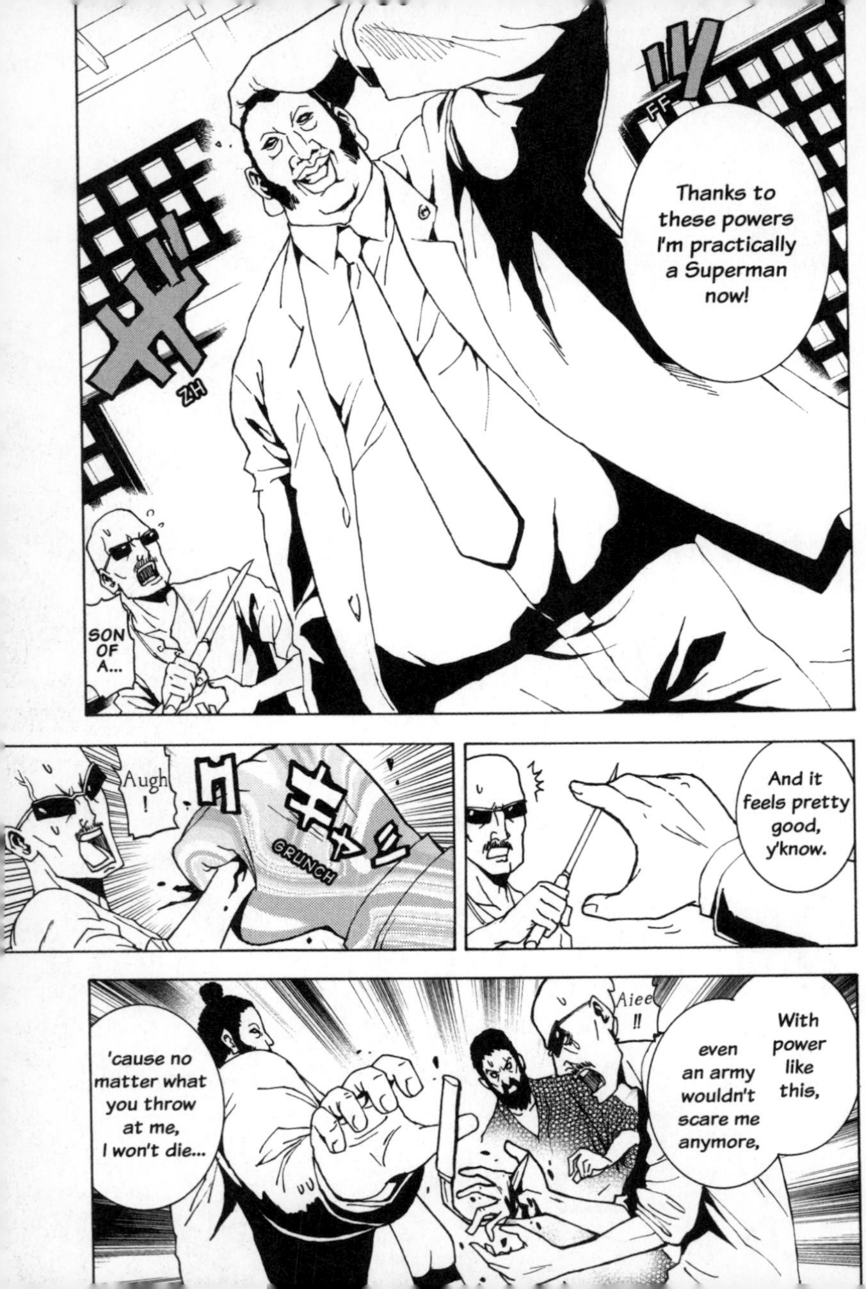
FF
Thanks to these powers I'm practically a Superman now!
ZAH
SON OF A...
And it feels pretty good, y'know.
Augh!
GRUNCH
With power like this,
even an army wouldn't scare me anymore,
Aiee!!
'cause no matter what you throw at me, I won't die...

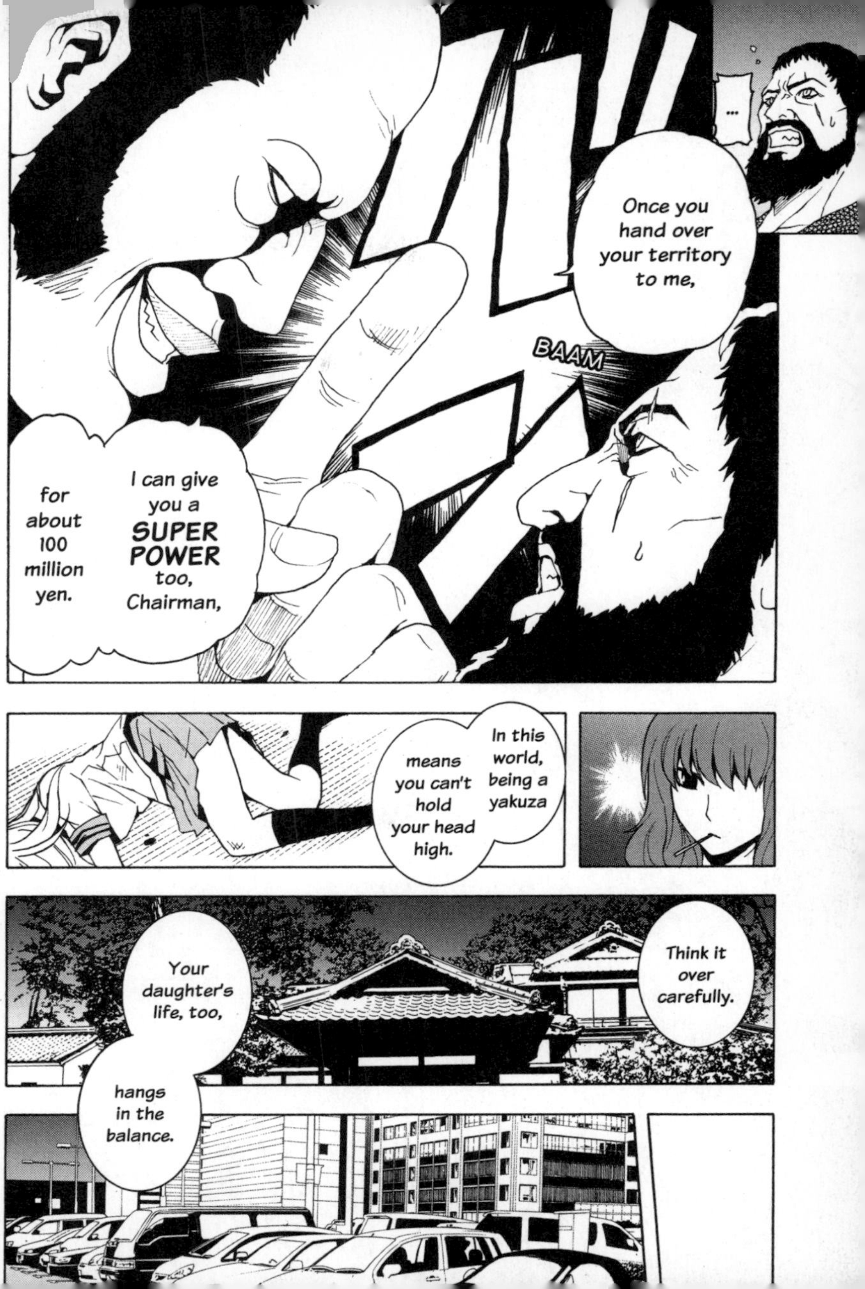
...
Once you hand over your territory to me,
BAAM
I can give you a SUPER POWER too, Chairman,
for about 100 million yen.
In this world, being a yakuza
means you can't hold your head high.
Think it over carefully.
Your daughter's life, too,
hangs in the balance.

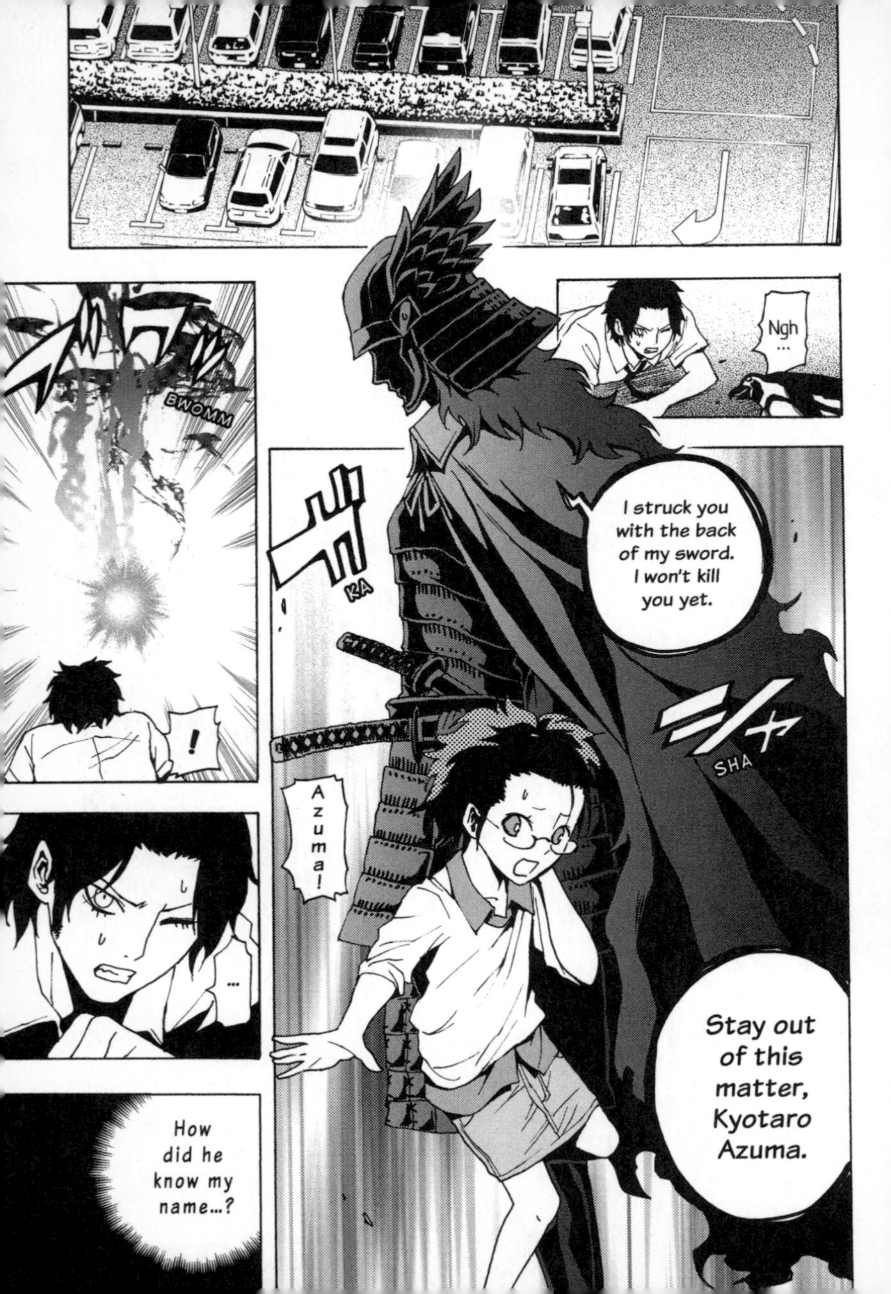
Ngh ...
I struck you with the back of my sword. I won't kill you yet.
KA
SHA
Azuma!
Stay out of this matter, Kyotaro Azuma.
BWOMM
!
...
How did he know my name...?

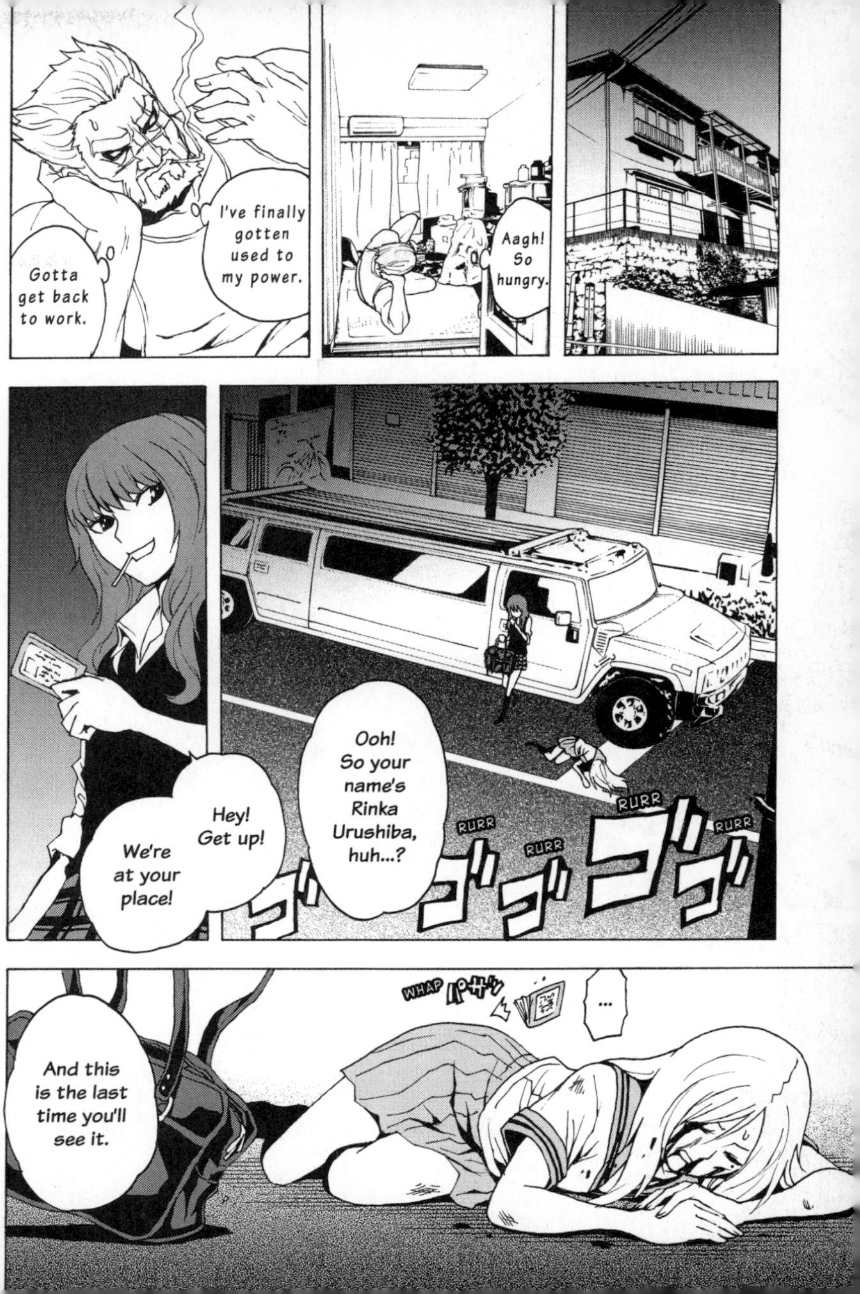
Aagh! So hungry.
I've finally gotten used to my power.
Gotta get back to work.
Ooh! So your name's Rinka Urushiba, huh...?
RURR
RURR
RURR
RURR
Hey! Get up!
We're at your place!
...
WHAP
And this is the last time you'll see it.

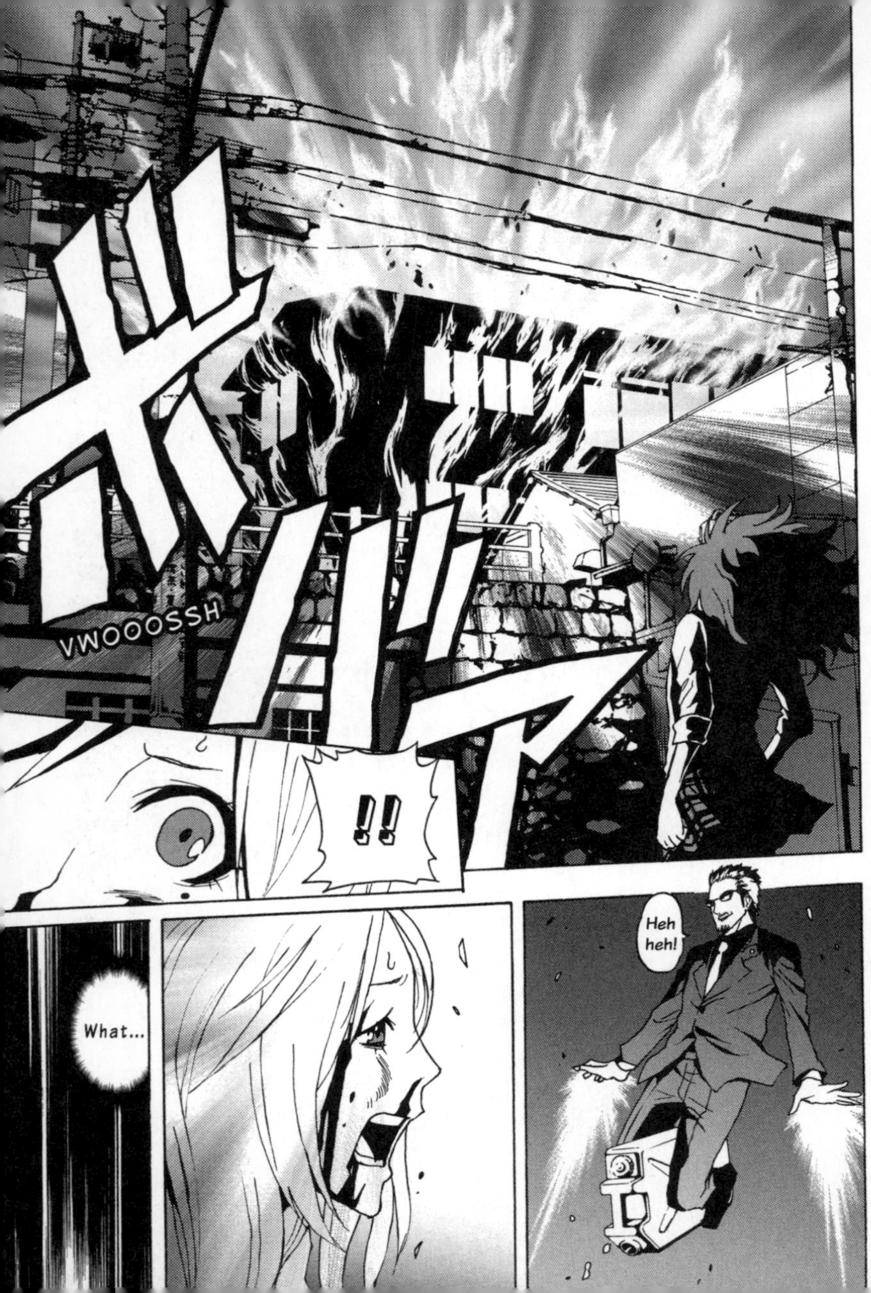
VWOOOSSH
!!
Heh heh!
What...

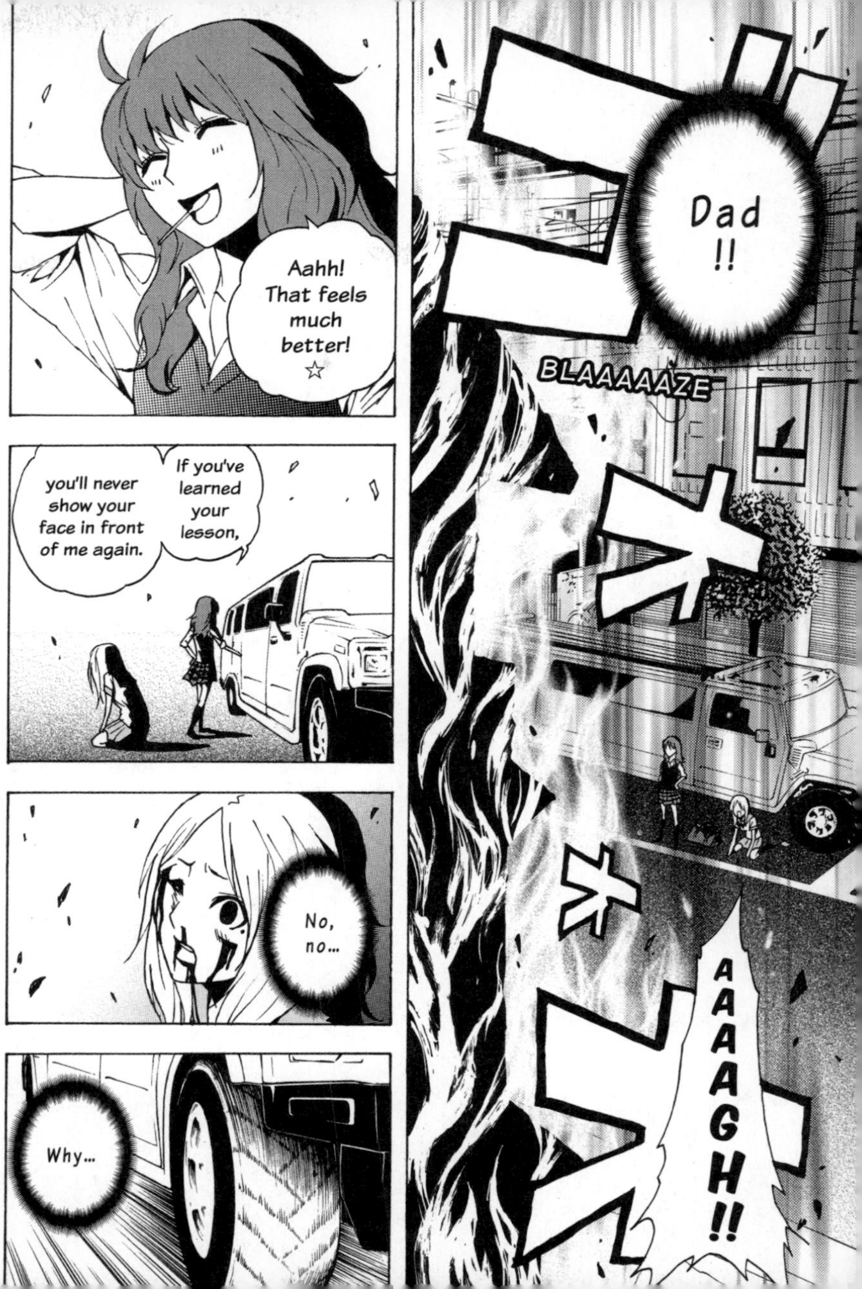
Dad !!
BLAAAAAAZE
AAAAAGH!!
Aahh! That feels much better! ☆
If you've learned your lesson,
you'll never show your face in front of me again.
No, no...
Why...

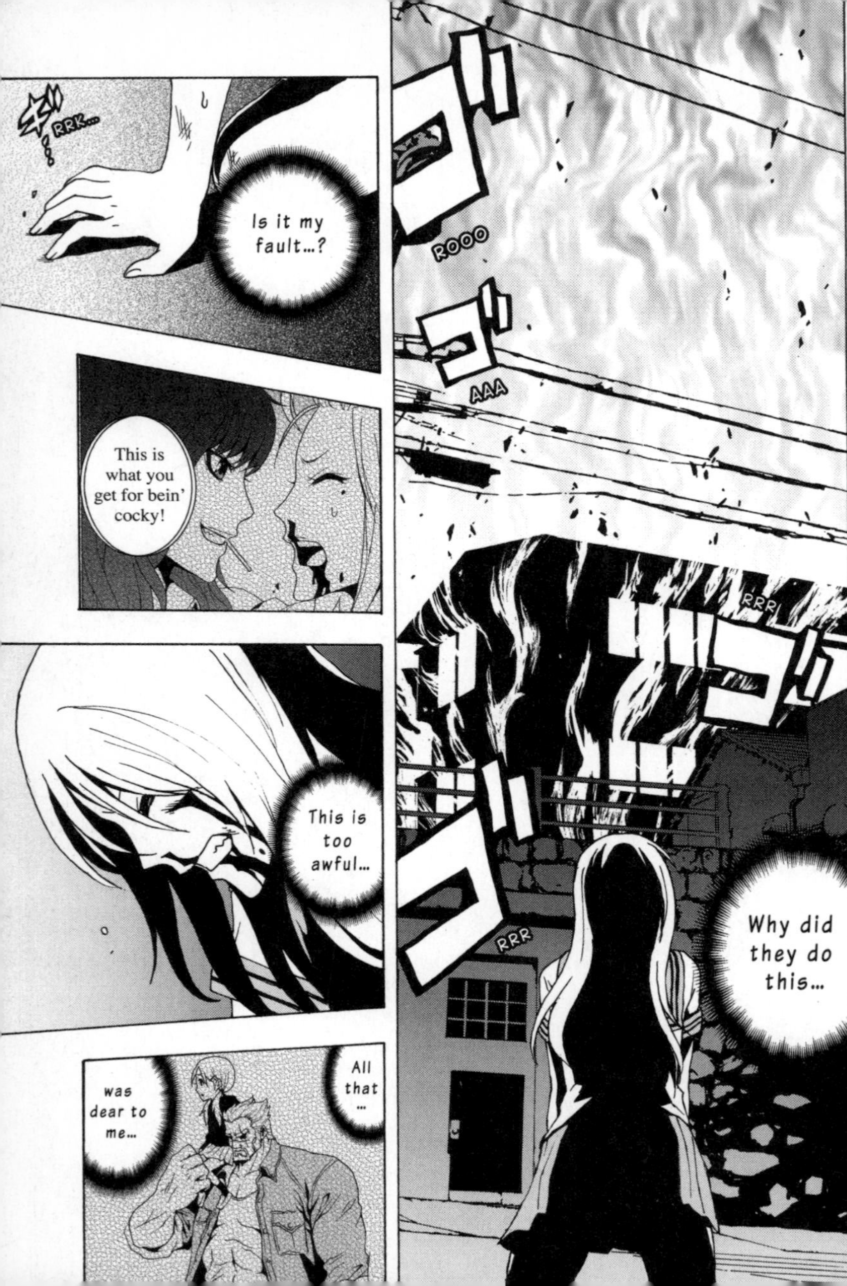
ROOO
AAA
RRR
Why did they do this...
RRR
RRK...
Is it my fault...?
This is what you get for bein' cocky!
This is too awful...
All that...
was dear to me...

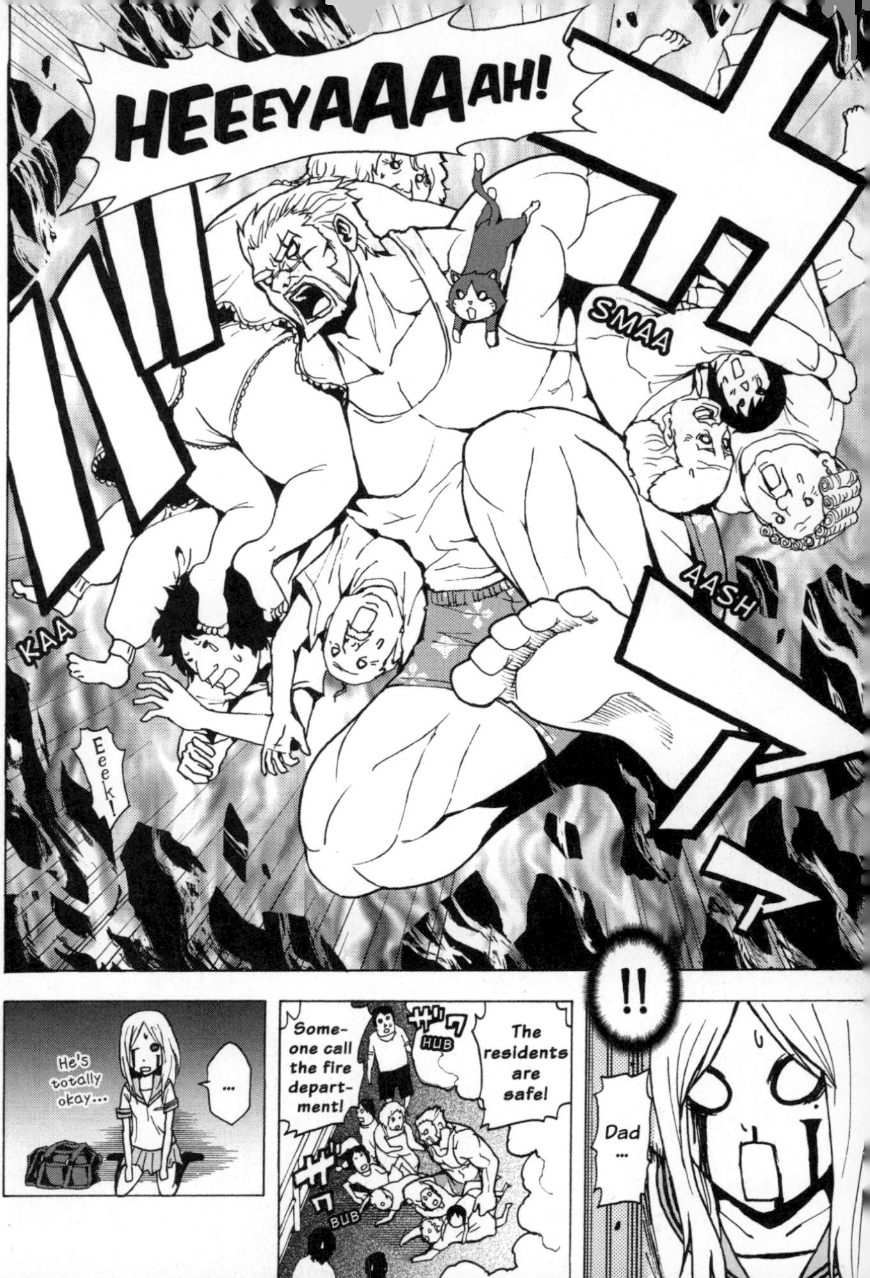
HEEEYAAAAAH!
SMAA
AASH
KAA
Eeeek!
!!
Dad ...
The residents are safe!
HUB
Some-one call the fire depart-ment!
BUB
...
He's totally okay...

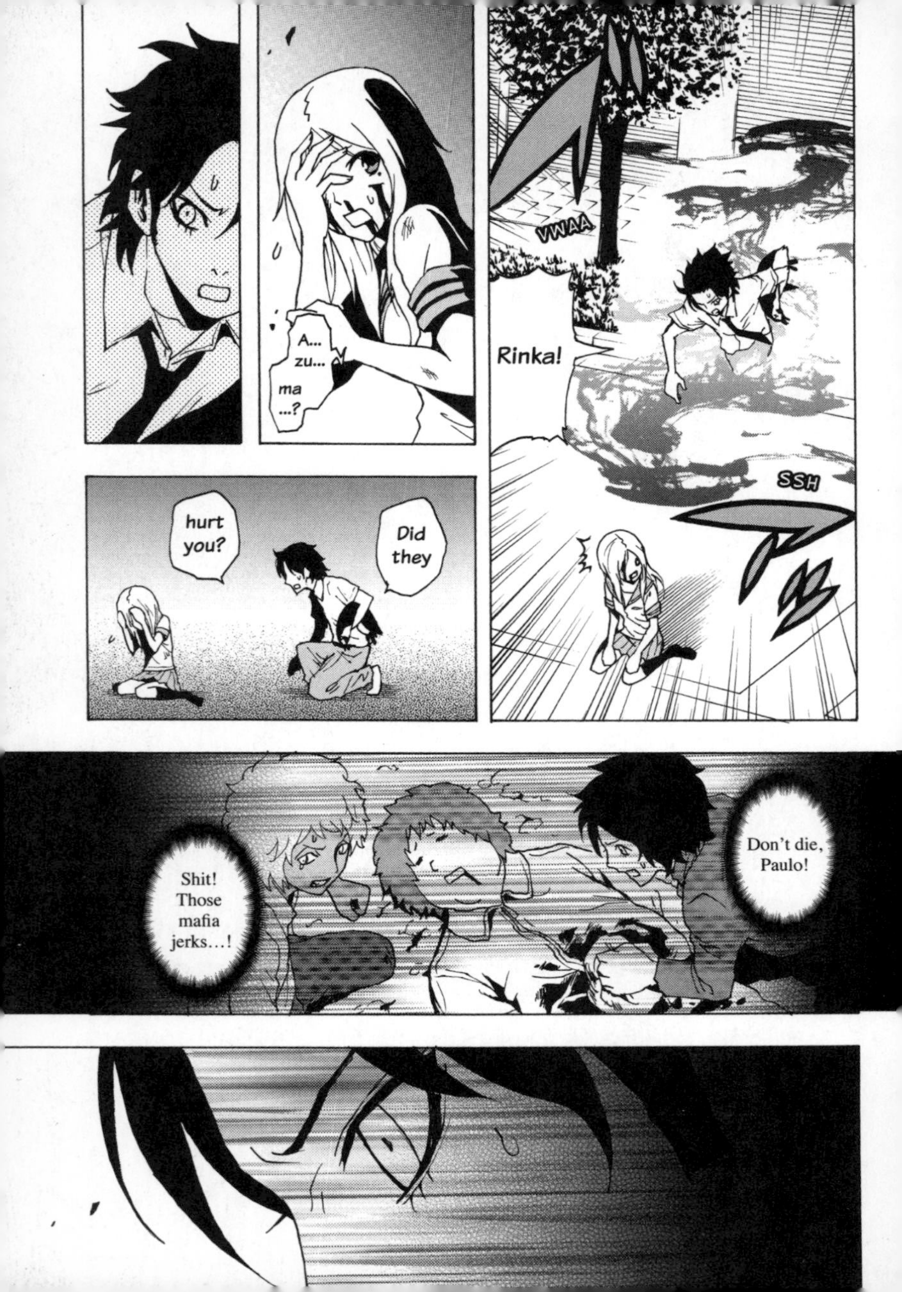

VWAA
Rinka!
SSH
A... zu... ma ...?
Did they
hurt you?
Don't die, Paulo!
Shit! Those mafia jerks…!

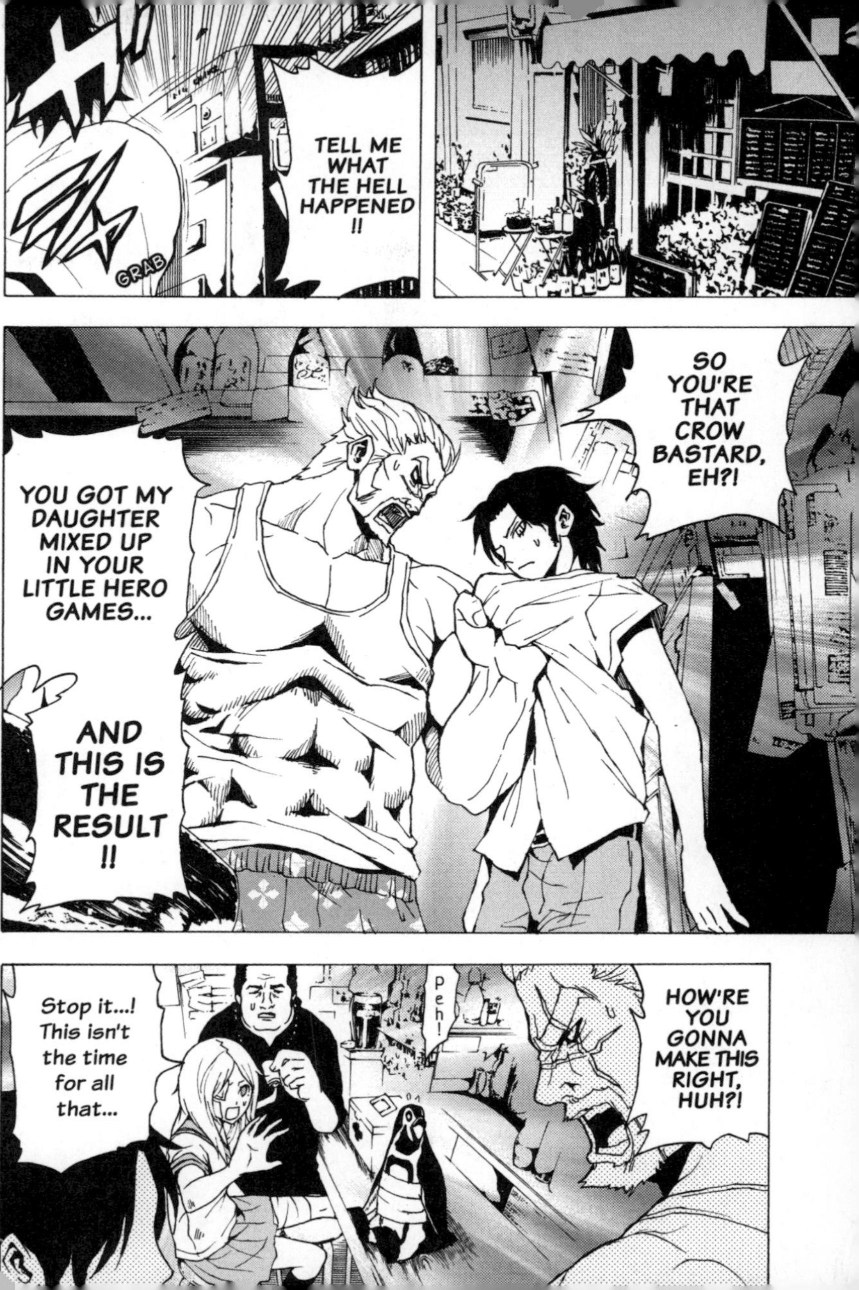
TELL ME WHAT THE HELL HAPPENED !!
GRAB
SO YOU'RE THAT CROW BASTARD, EH?!
YOU GOT MY DAUGHTER MIXED UP IN YOUR LITTLE HERO GAMES...
AND THIS IS THE RESULT !!
HOW'RE YOU GONNA MAKE THIS RIGHT, HUH?!
Peh!
Stop it...! This isn't the time for all that...

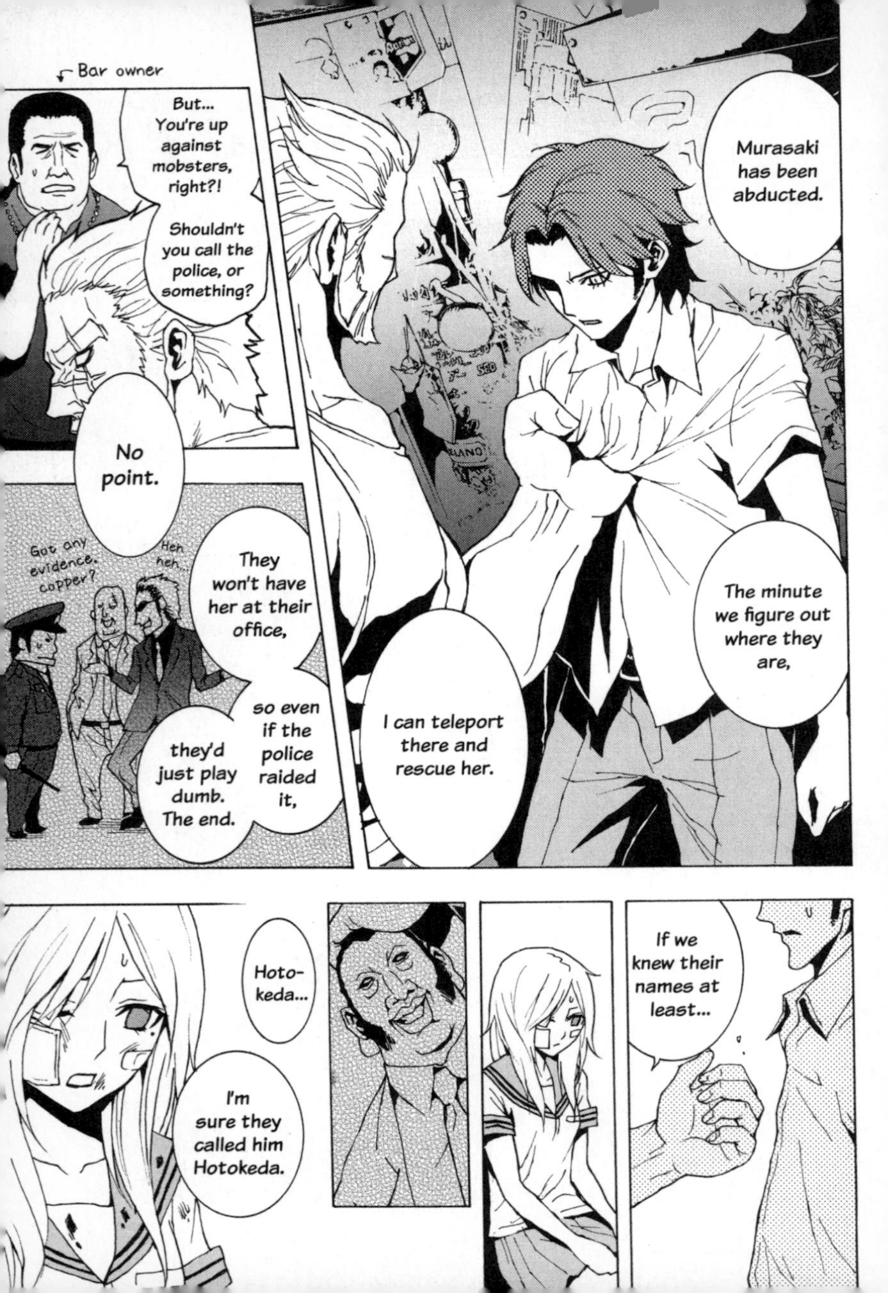
Murasaki has been abducted.
The minute we figure out where they are,
I can teleport there and rescue her.
Bar owner
But... You're up against mobsters, right?!
Shouldn't you call the police, or something?
No point.
They won't have her at their office,
so even if the police raided it,
they'd just play dumb. The end.
Got any evidence, copper?
Heh heh...
If we knew their names at least...
Hoto-keda...
I'm sure they called him Hotokeda.

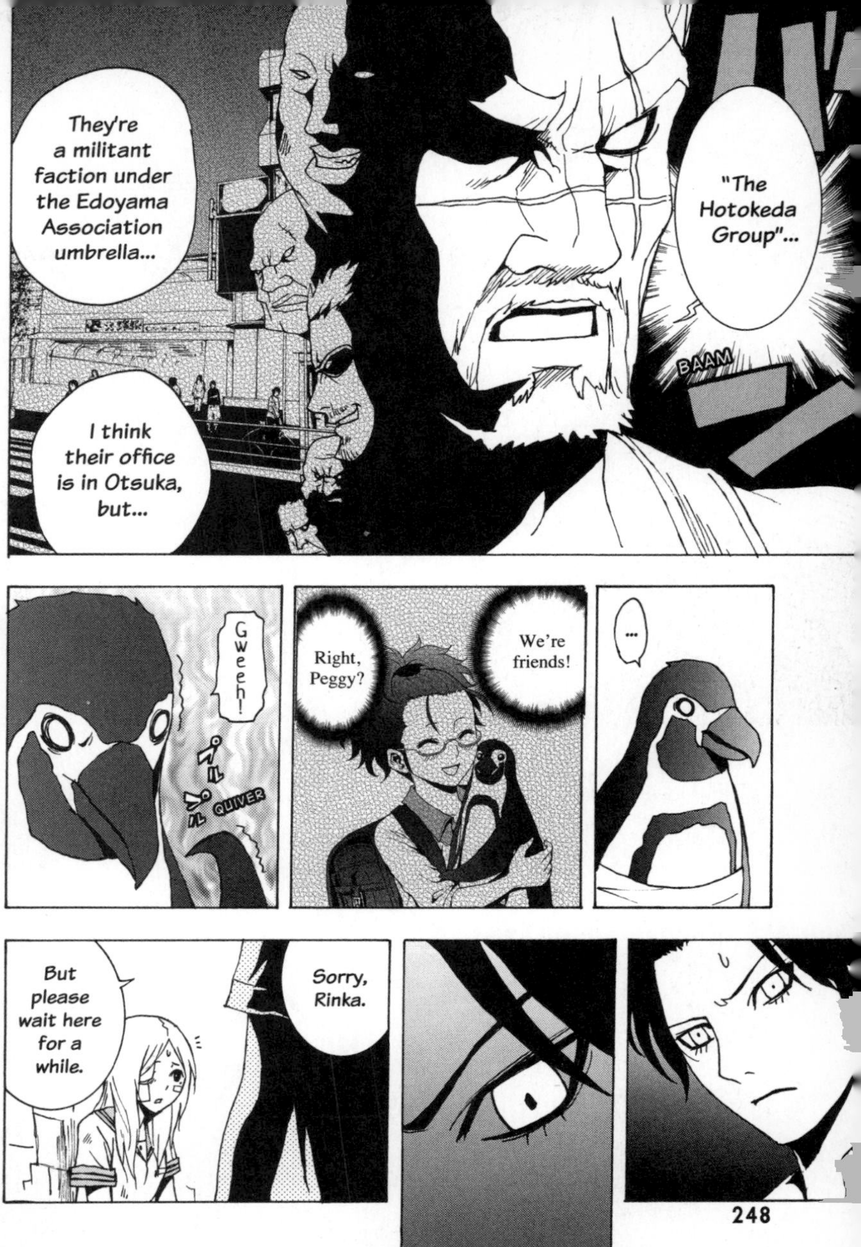
"The Hotokeda Group"...
BAAM
They're a militant faction under the Edoyama Association umbrella...
I think their office is in Otsuka, but...
...
We're friends!
Right, Peggy?
Gweeh!
QUIVER
Sorry, Rinka.
But please wait here for a while.

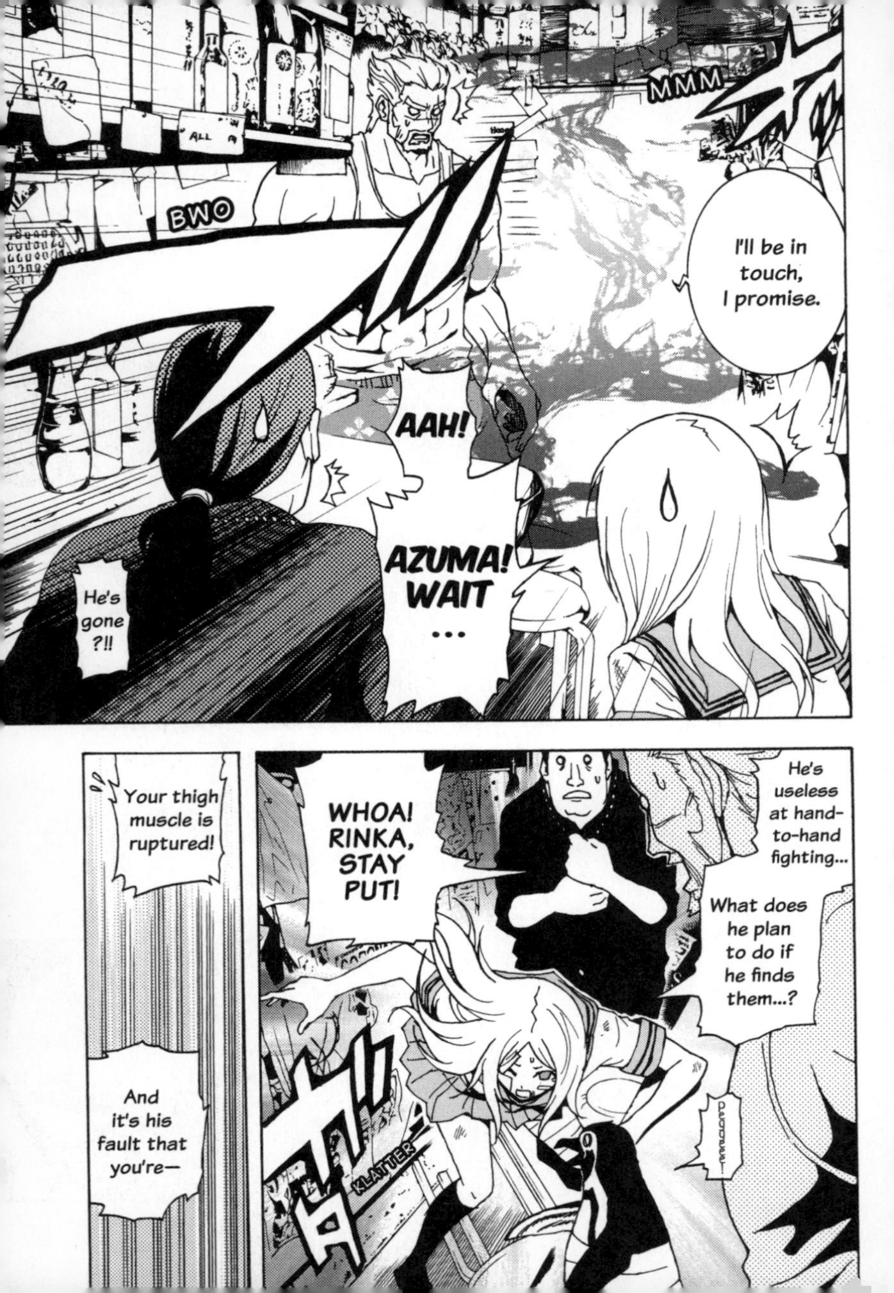
MMM
I'll be in touch, I promise.
BWO
AAH!
AZUMA! WAIT ...
He's gone ?!!
He's useless at hand-to-hand fighting...
What does he plan to do if he finds them...?
WHOA! RINKA, STAY PUT!
KLATTER
Your thigh muscle is ruptured!
And it's his fault that you're—

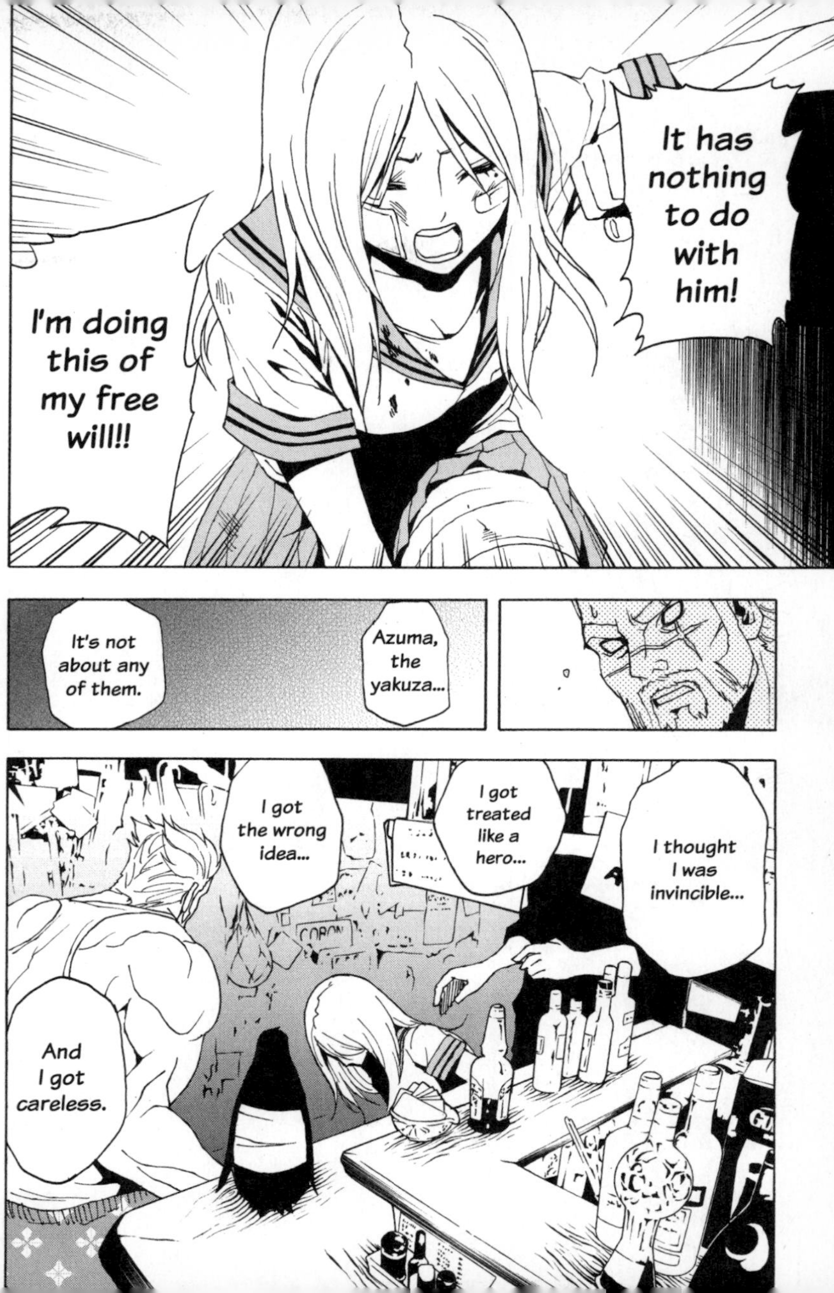

It has nothing to do with him!
I'm doing this of my free will!!
Azuma, the yakuza...
It's not about any of them.
I thought I was invincible...
I got treated like a hero...
I got the wrong idea...
And I got careless.

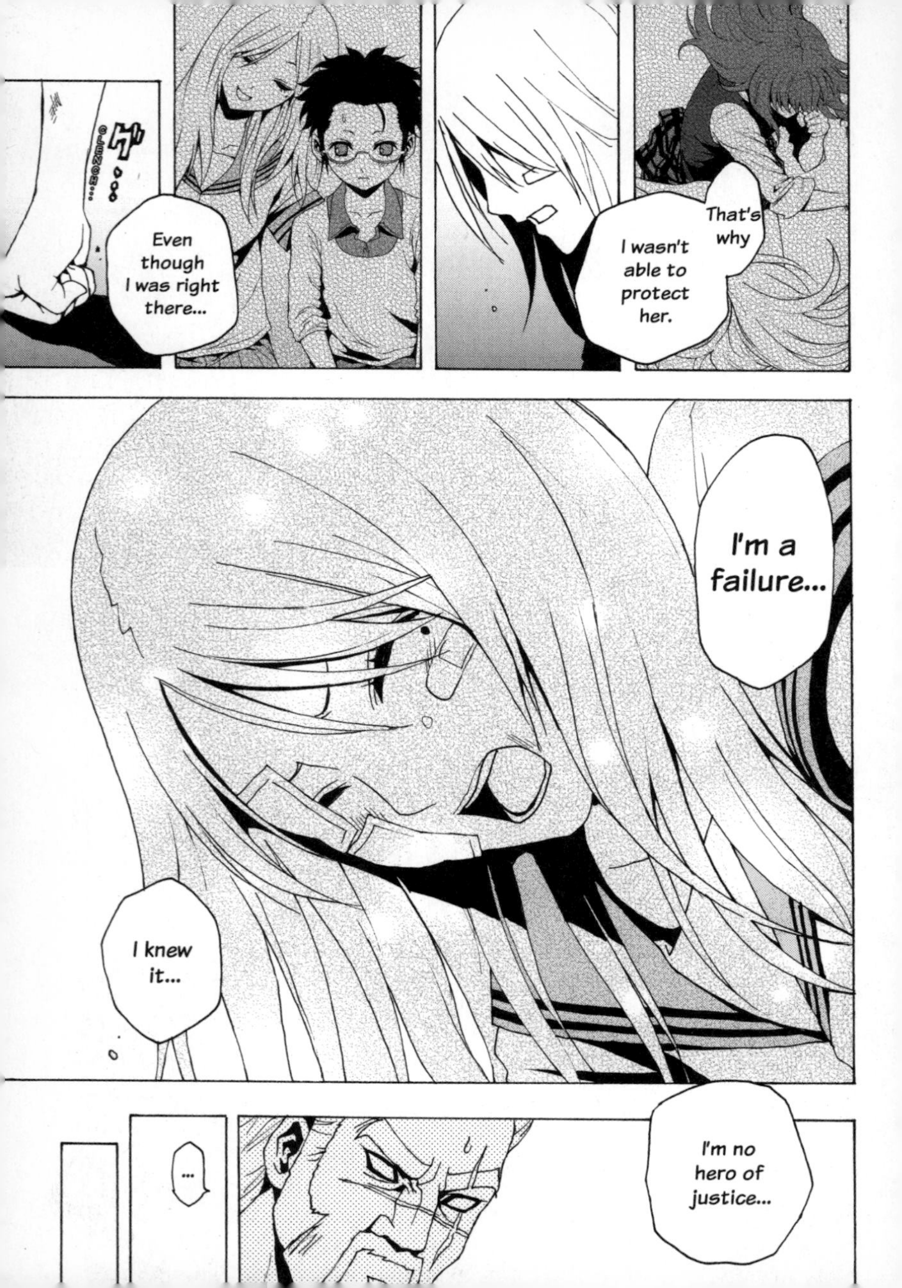
That's why
I wasn't able to protect her.
Even though I was right there...
グ
CLENCH...
I'm a failure...
I knew it...
I'm no hero of justice...
...

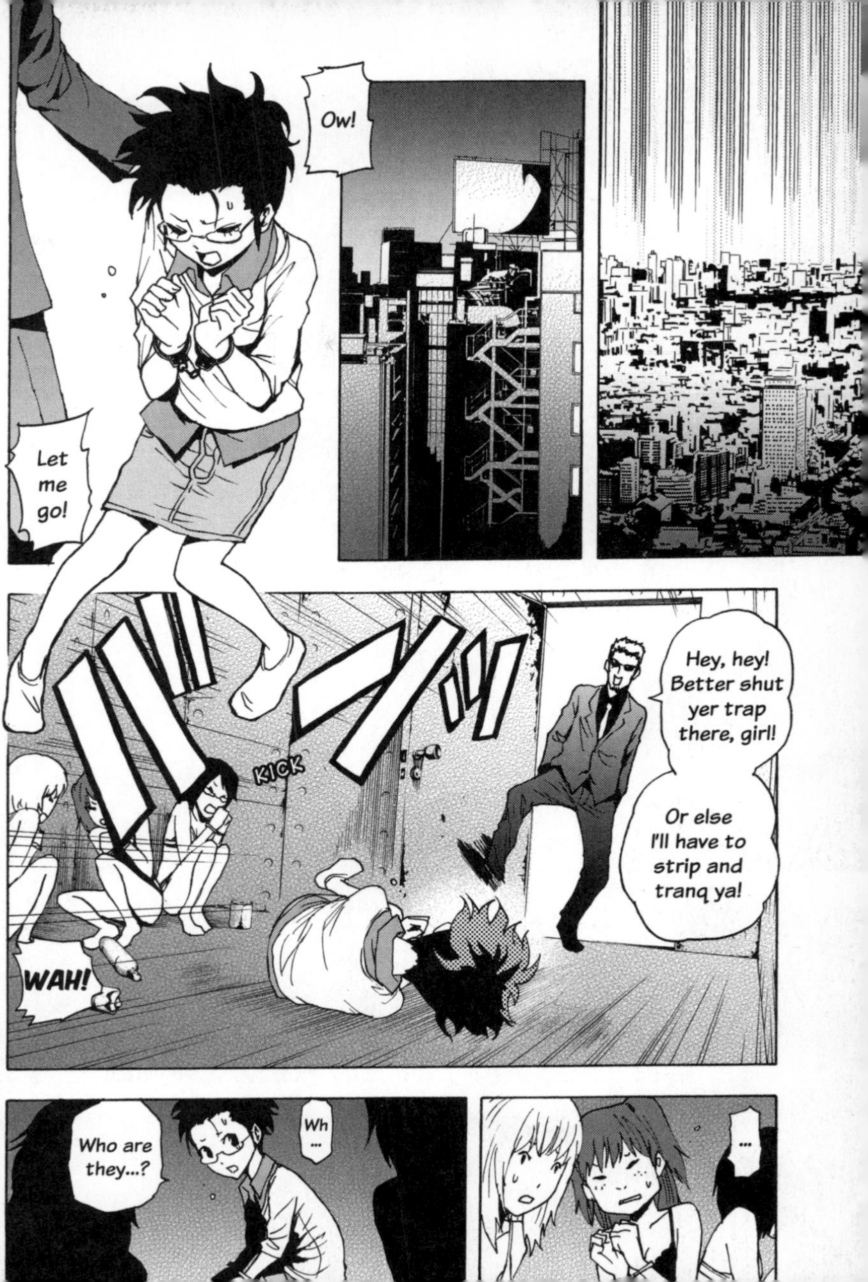
Ow!
Let me go!
Hey, hey! Better shut yer trap there, girl!
Or else I'll have to strip and tranq ya!
KICK
WAH!
...
Wh ...
Who are they...?

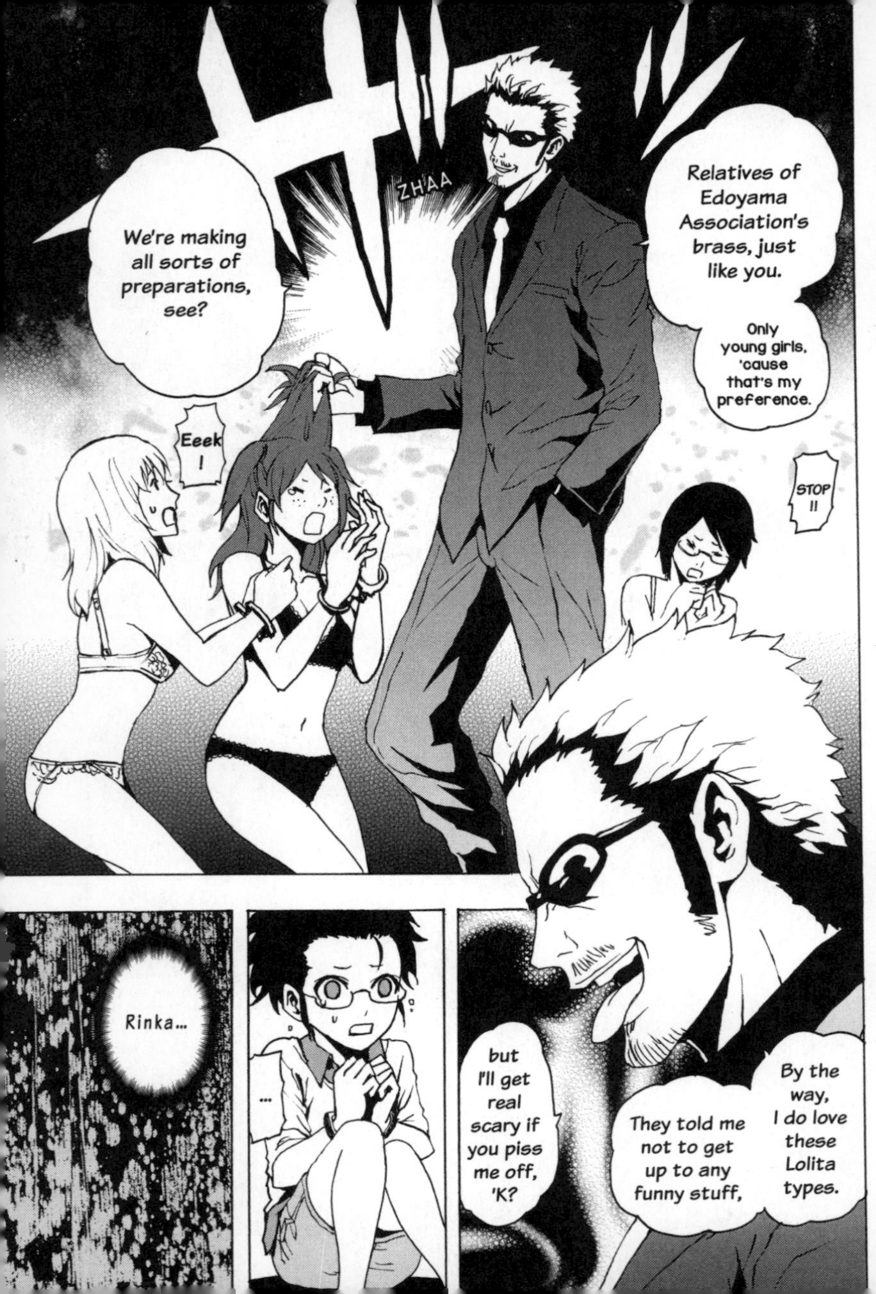
Relatives of Edoyama Association's brass, just like you.
Only young girls, 'cause that's my preference.
ZHAA
We're making all sorts of preparations, see?
STOP!!
Eeek!
By the way, I do love these Lolita types.
They told me not to get up to any funny stuff,
but I'll get real scary if you piss me off, 'K?
...
Rinka...

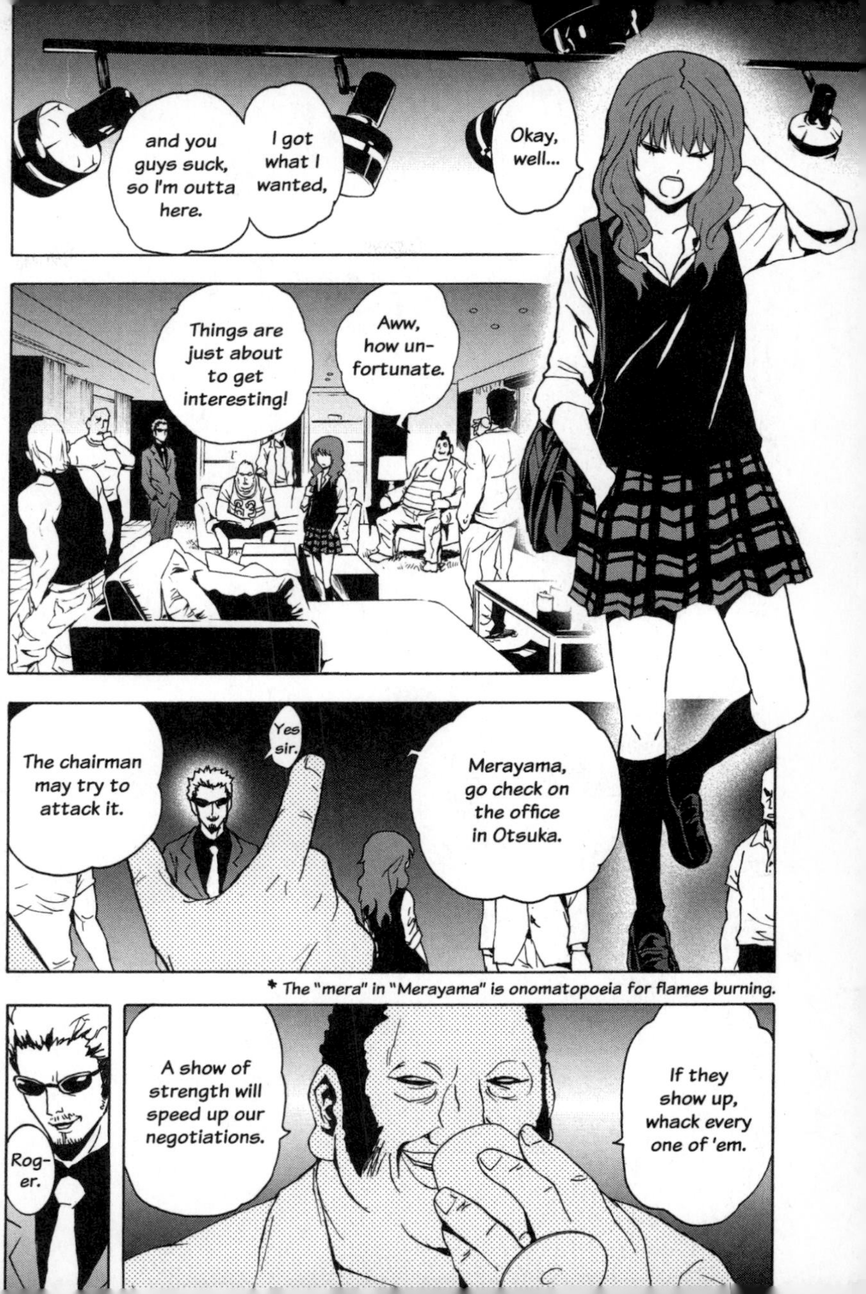
Okay, well...
I got what I wanted,
and you guys suck, so I'm outta here.
Aww, how unfortunate.
Things are just about to get interesting!
Merayama, go check on the office in Otsuka.
Yes sir.
The chairman may try to attack it.
If they show up, whack every one of 'em.
A show of strength will speed up our negotiations.
Roger.

* The "mera" in "Merayama" is onomatopoeia for flames burning.

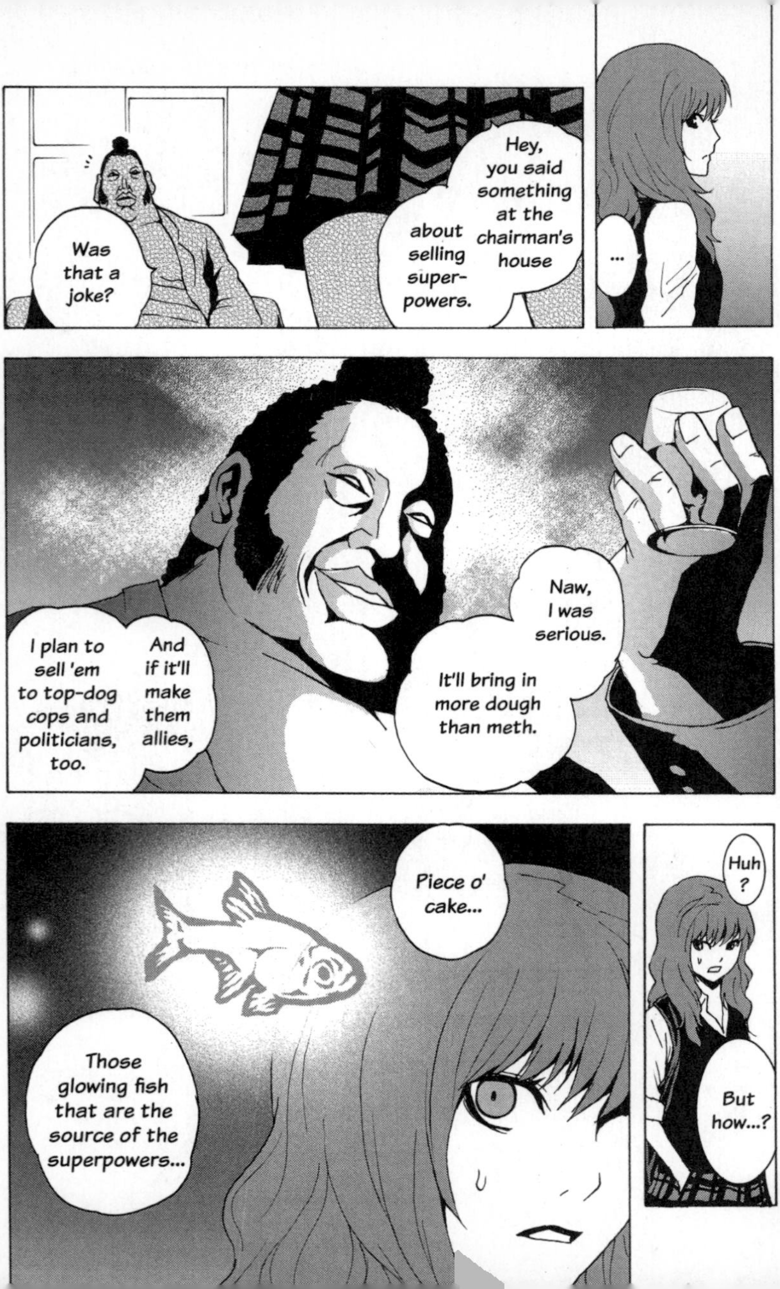
...
Hey, you said something at the chairman's house
about selling super-powers.
Was that a joke?
Naw, I was serious.
It'll bring in more dough than meth.
And if it'll make them allies,
I plan to sell 'em to top-dog cops and politicians, too.
Huh?
But how...?
Piece o' cake...
Those glowing fish that are the source of the superpowers...

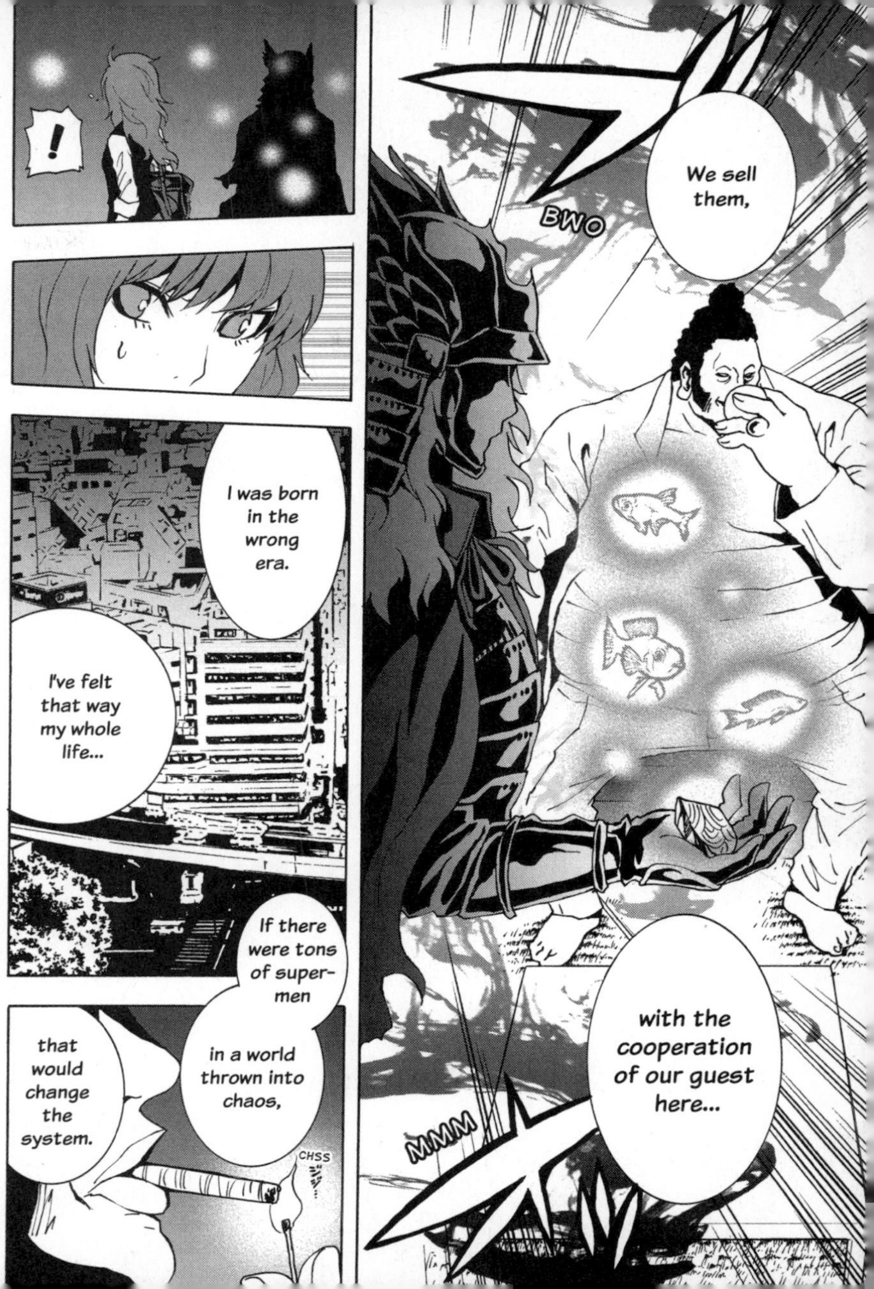
We sell them,
BWO
with the cooperation of our guest here...
MMM
!
I was born in the wrong era.
I've felt that way my whole life...
If there were tons of super-men
in a world thrown into chaos,
that would change the system.
CHSS

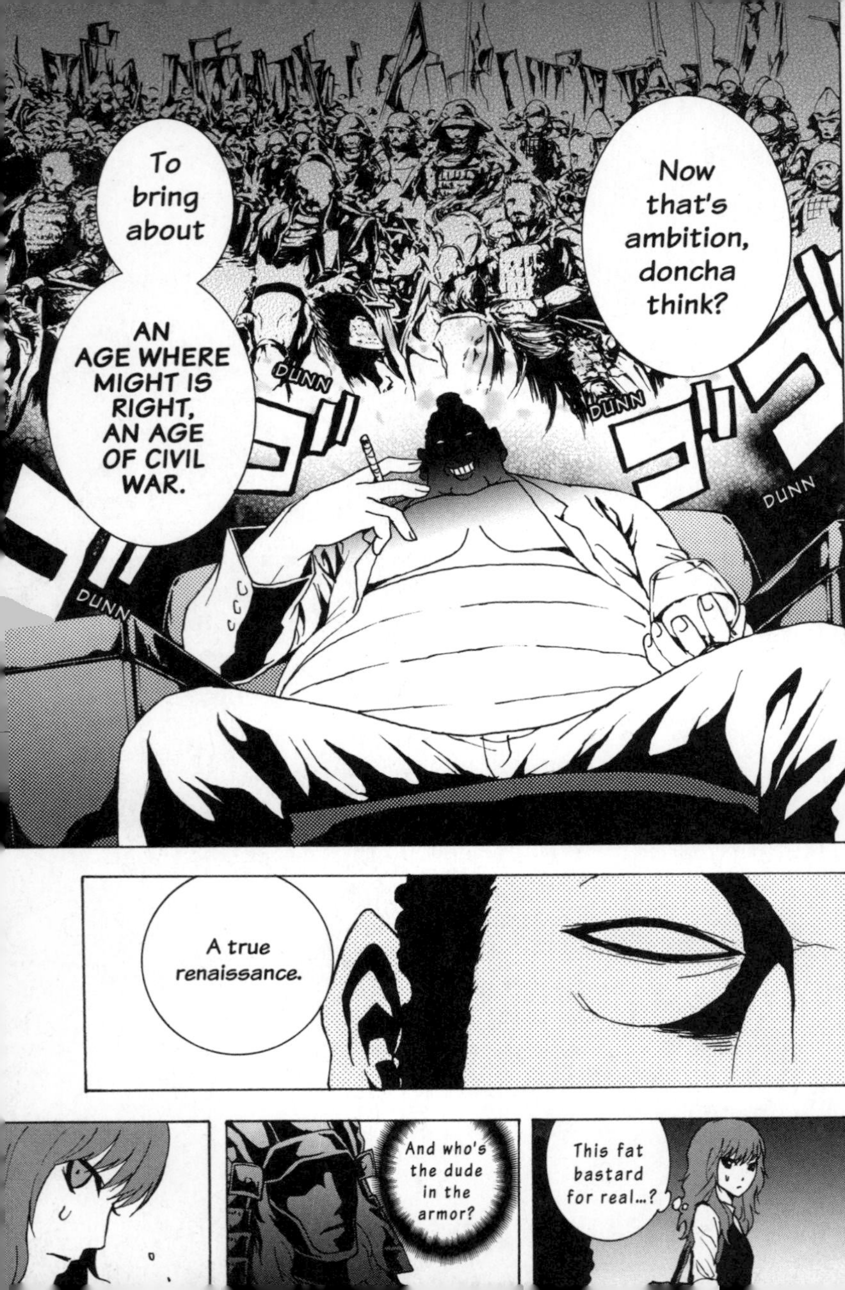
To bring about
AN AGE WHERE MIGHT IS RIGHT, AN AGE OF CIVIL WAR.
Now that's ambition, doncha think?
DUNN
DUNN
DUNN
DUNN
A true renaissance.
This fat bastard for real...?
And who's the dude in the armor?

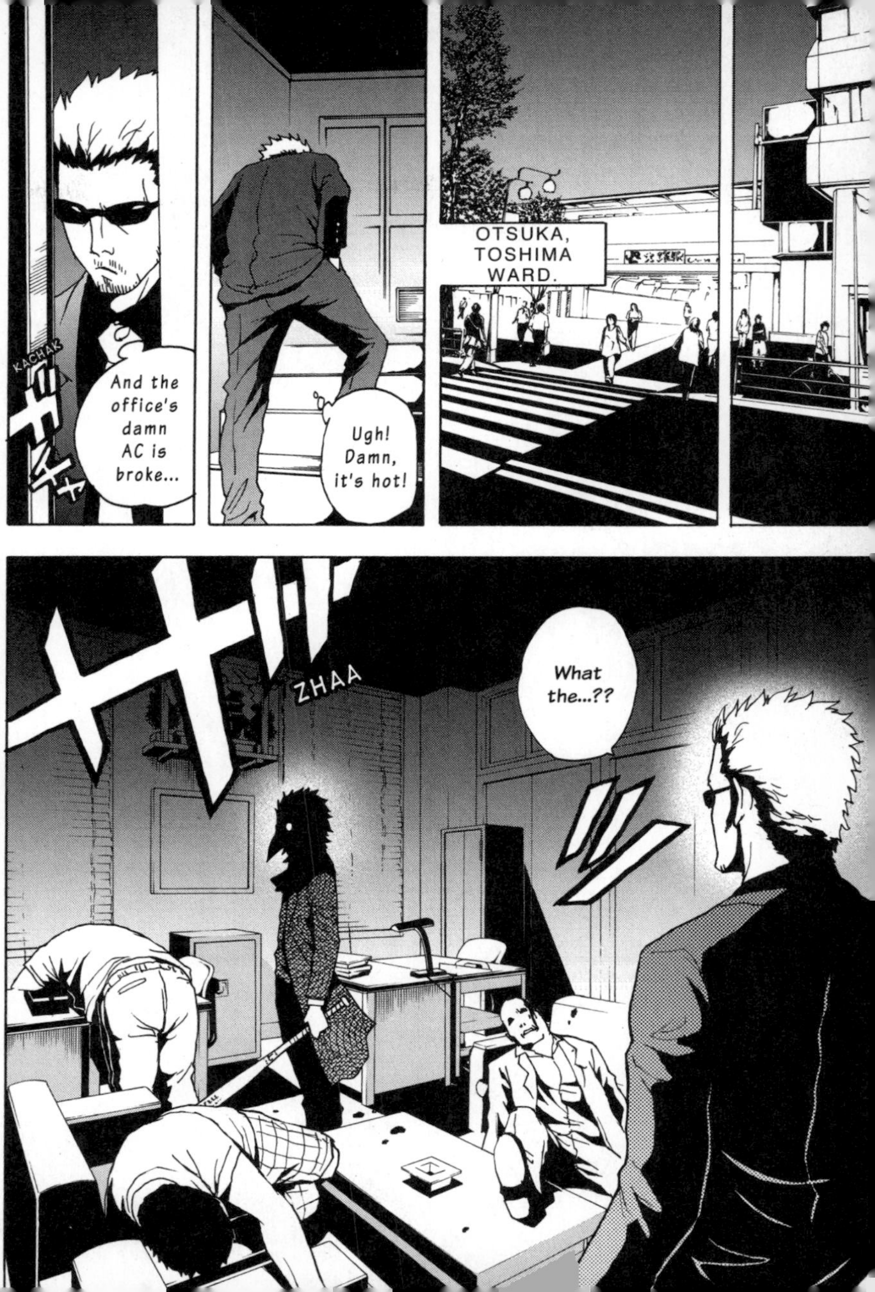
OTSUKA, TOSHIMA WARD.
Ugh! Damn, it's hot!
KACHAK
And the office's damn AC is broke...
ZHAA
What the...??

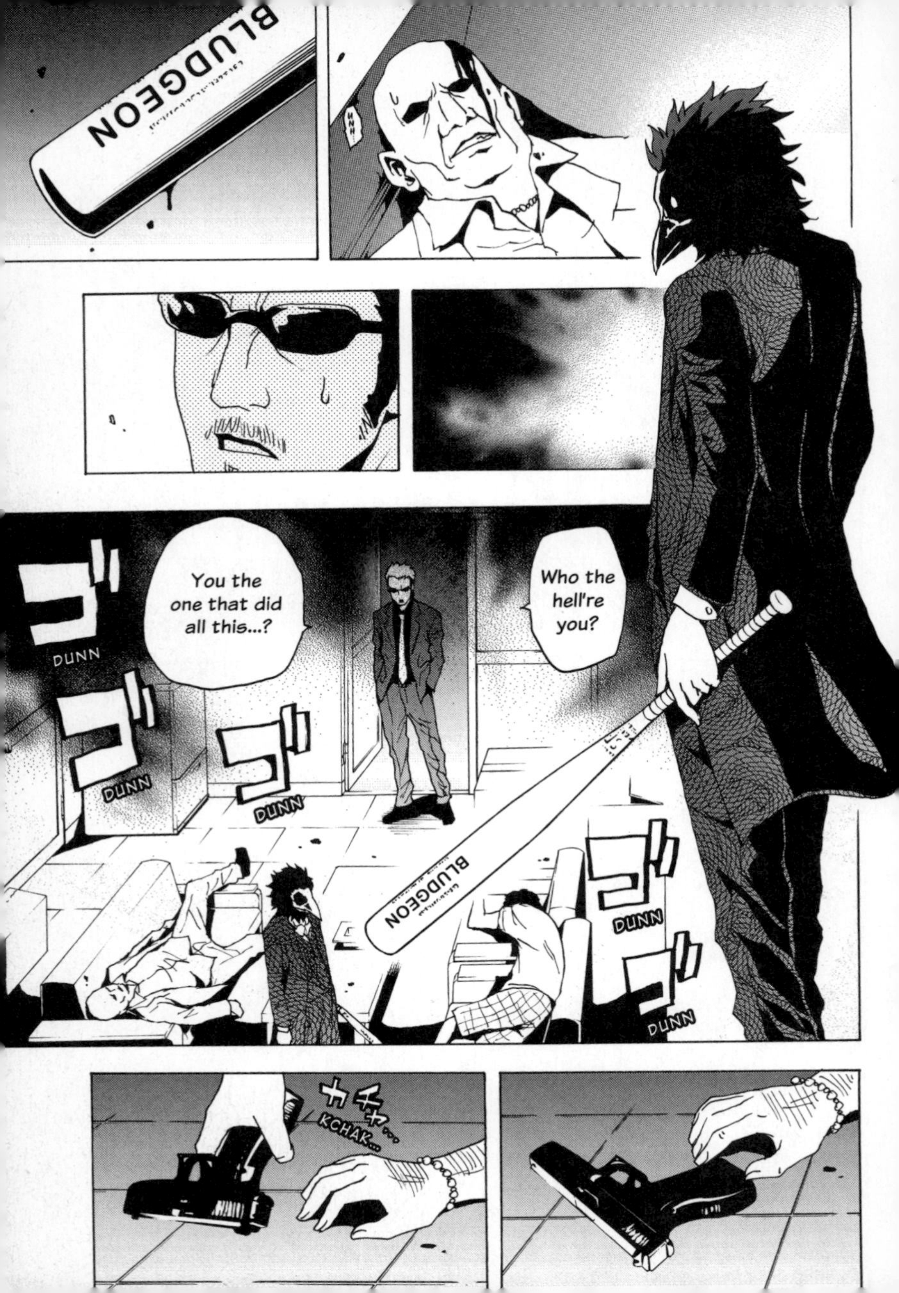
UNH...
BLUDGEON
Who the hell're you?
You the one that did all this...?
DUNN
DUNN
DUNN
DUNN
DUNN
BLUDGEON
KCHAK...

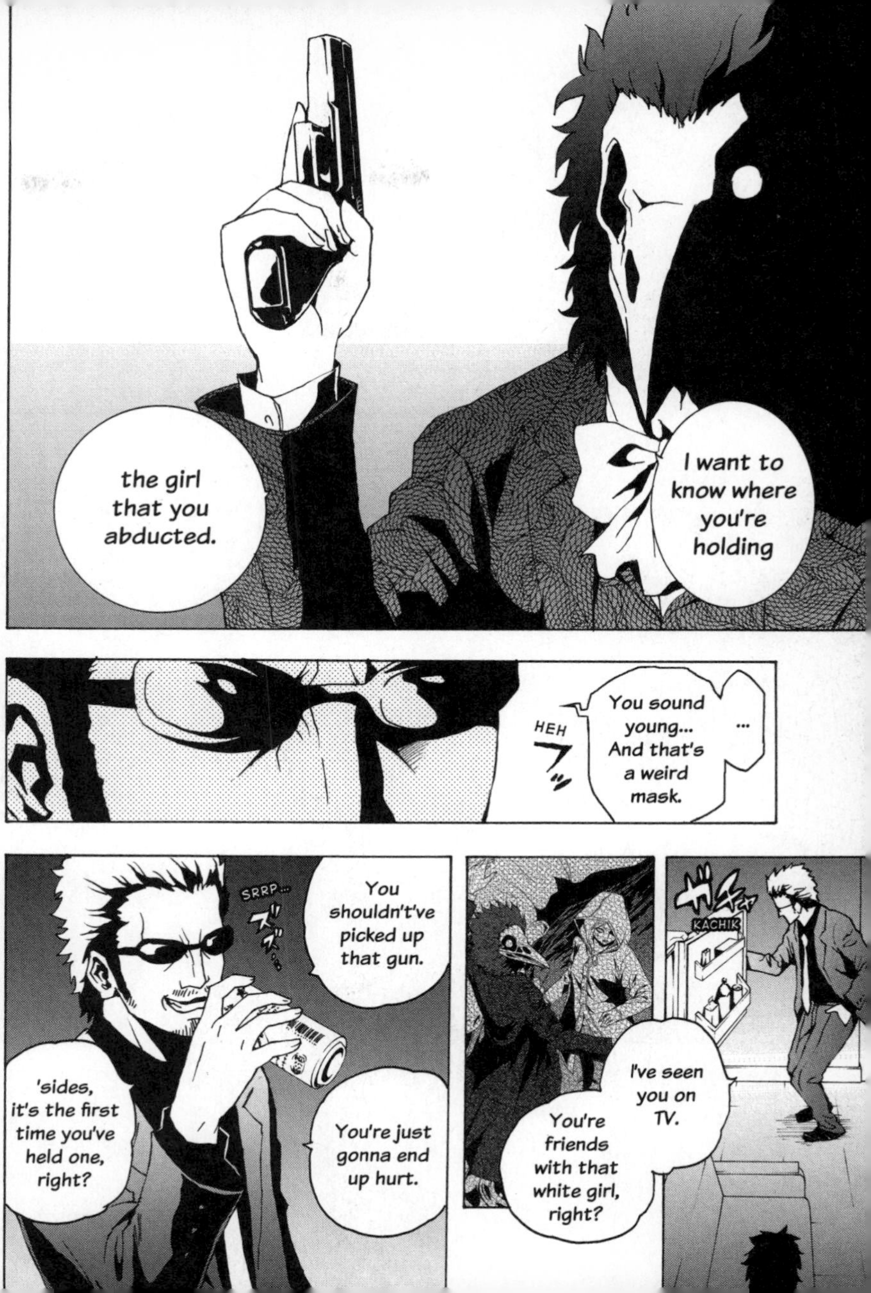
I want to know where you're holding
the girl that you abducted.
...
You sound young... And that's a weird mask.
HEH
KACHIK
I've seen you on TV.
You're friends with that white girl, right?
SRRP...
You shouldn't've picked up that gun.
You're just gonna end up hurt.
'sides, it's the first time you've held one, right?

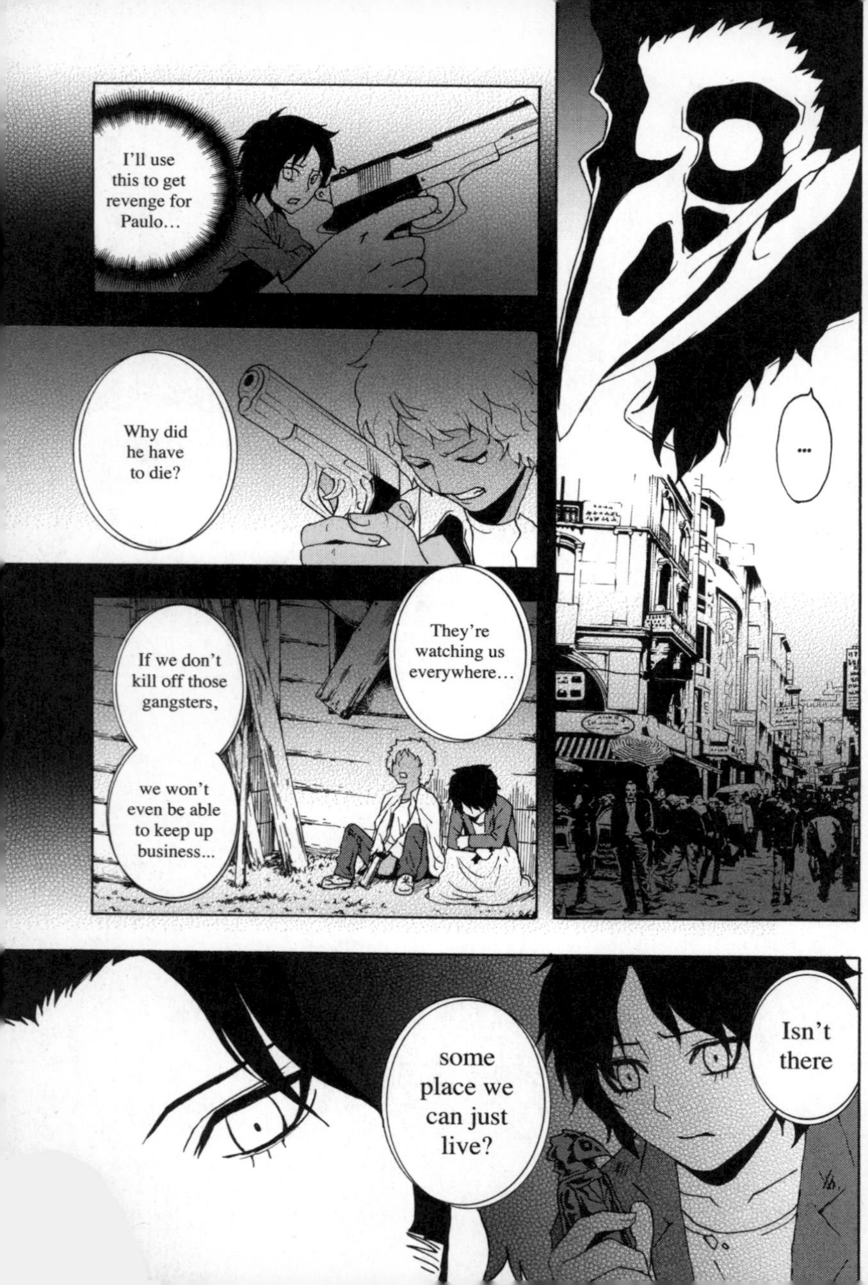
...
I'll use this to get revenge for Paulo…
Why did he have to die?
They're watching us everywhere…
If we don't kill off those gangsters,
we won't even be able to keep up business...
Isn't there
some place we can just live?

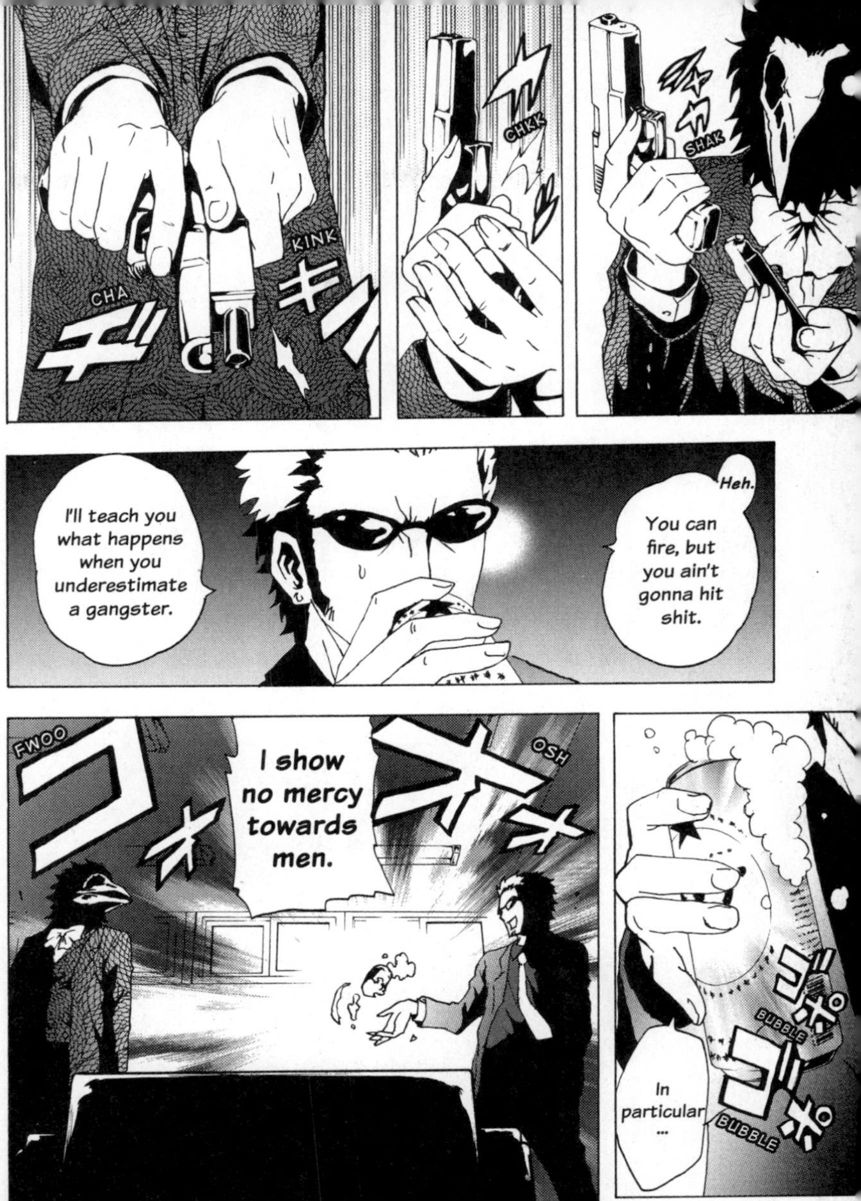
SHAK
CHKK
KINK
CHA
Heh.
You can fire, but you ain't gonna hit shit.
I'll teach you what happens when you underestimate a gangster.
BUBBLE
BUBBLE
In particular...
I show no mercy towards men.
FWOO
OSH

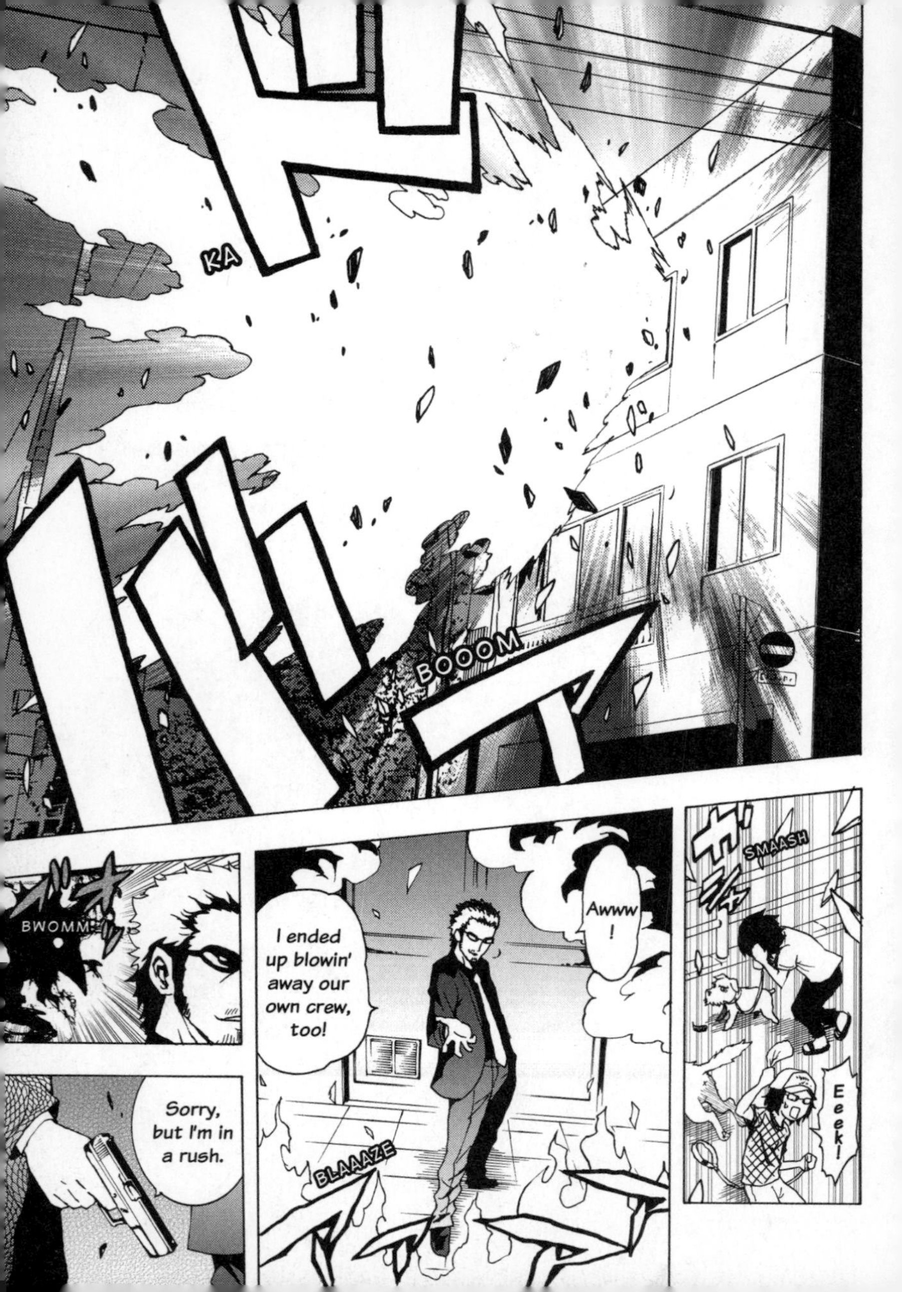
KA
BOOOM
SMAASH
Eeek!
Awww!
I ended up blowin' away our own crew, too!
BLAAAZE
BWOMM
Sorry, but I'm in a rush.

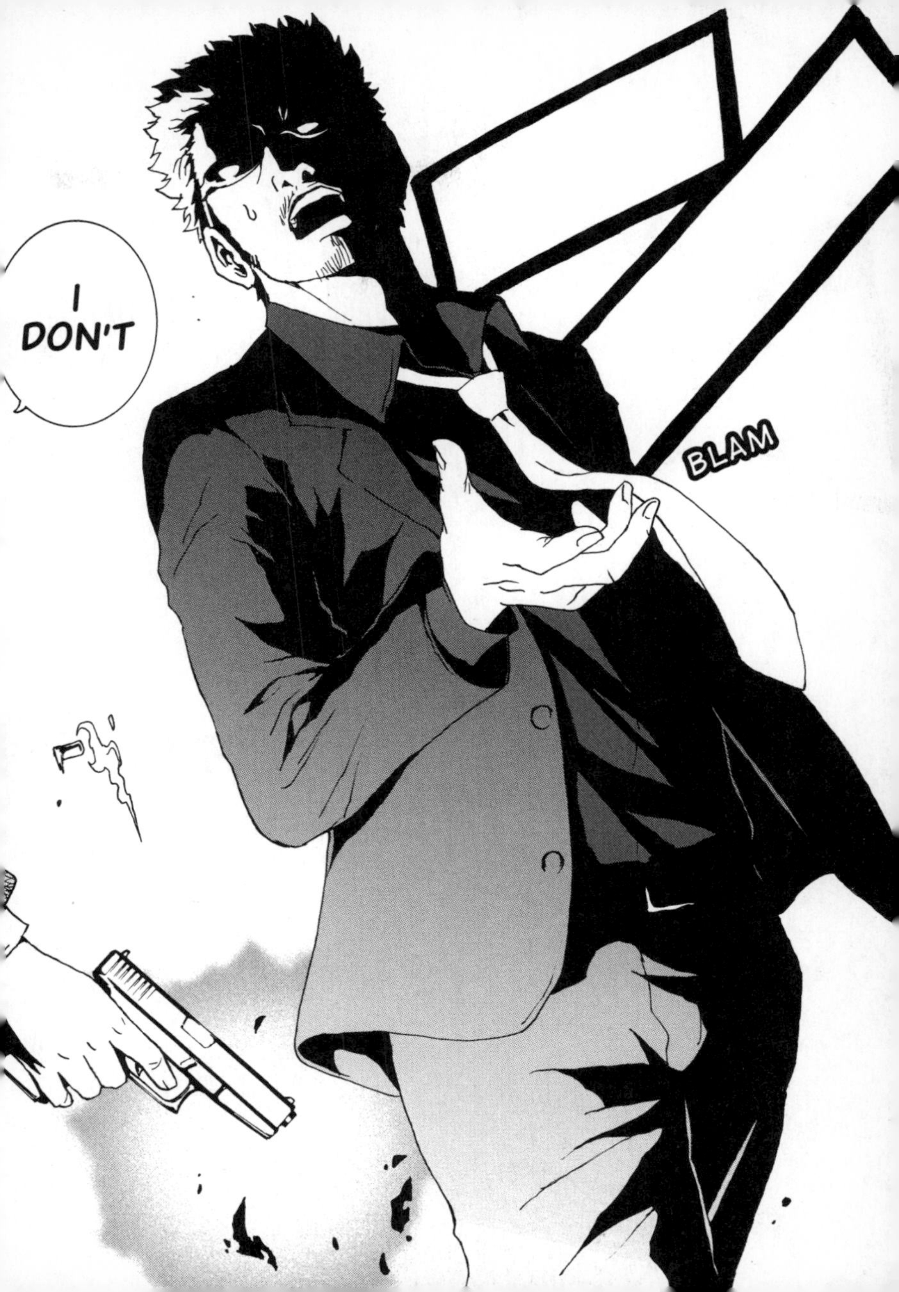
I DON'T
BLAM

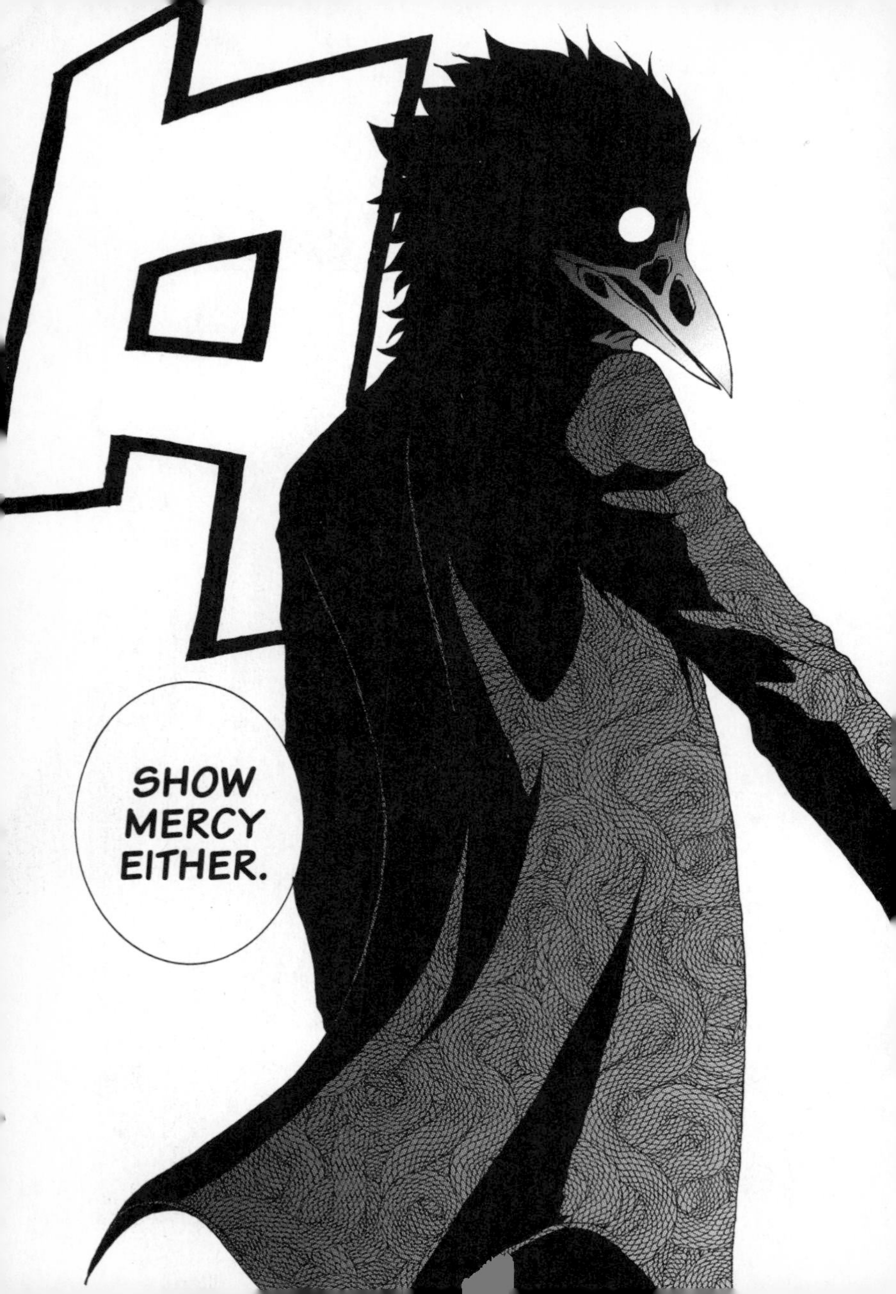
SHOW MERCY EITHER.

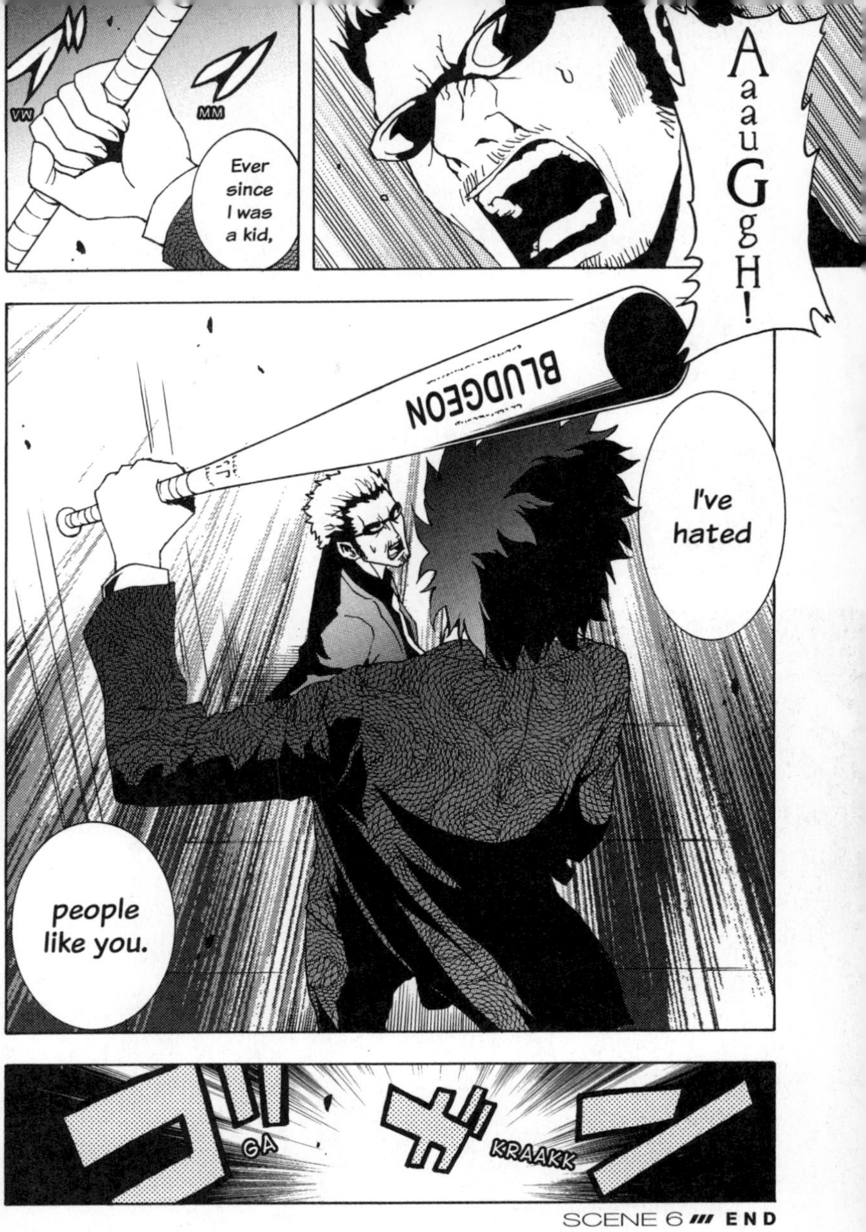
AaauGgH!
VW
MM
Ever since I was a kid,
BLUDGEON
I've hated
people like you.
GA
KRAAKK

SCENE 6 /// END

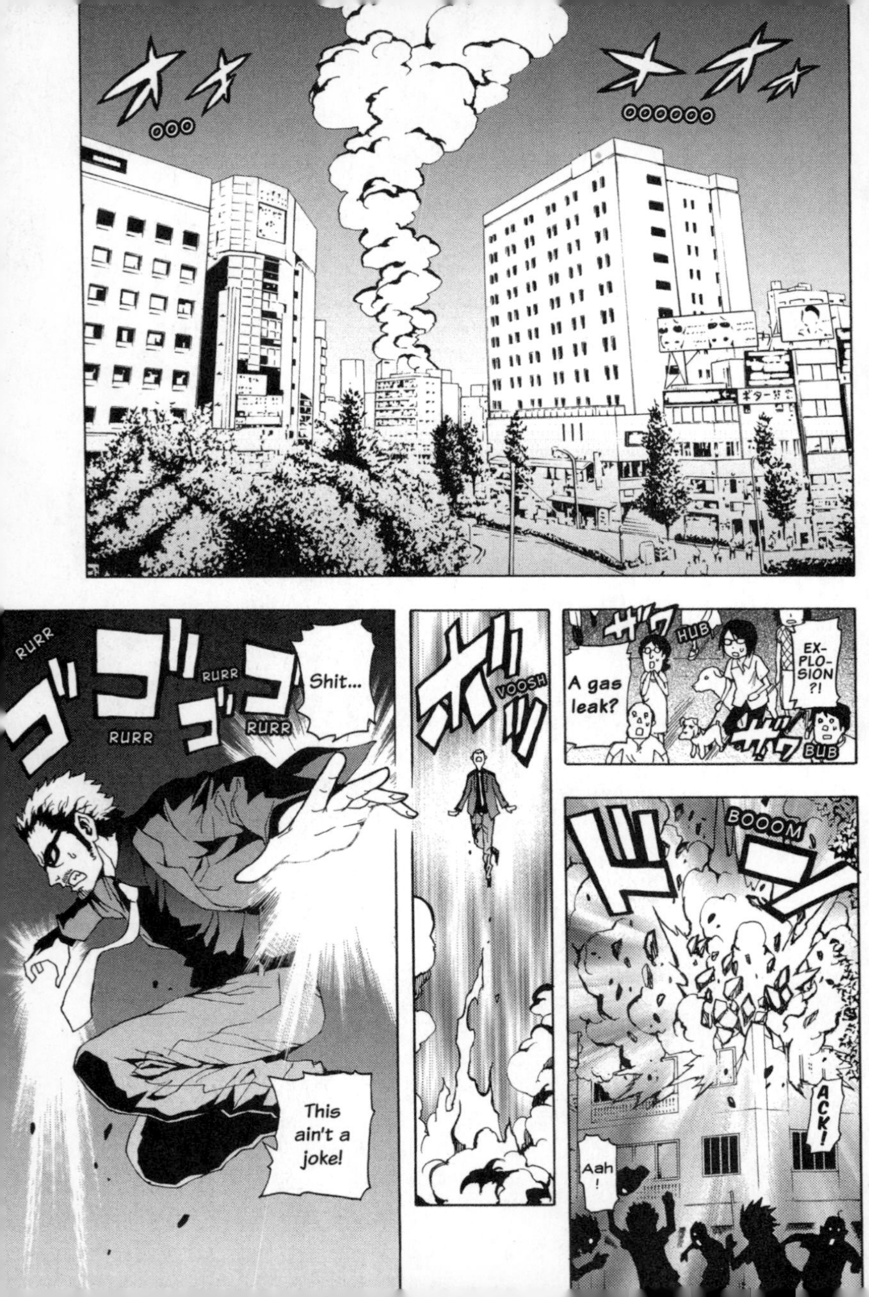
OOOOOOO
OOO
EX-PLO-SION?!
HUB
A gas leak?
BUB
BOOOM
ACK!
Aah!
VOOSH
RURR
RURR
RURR
RURR
Shit...
This ain't a joke!

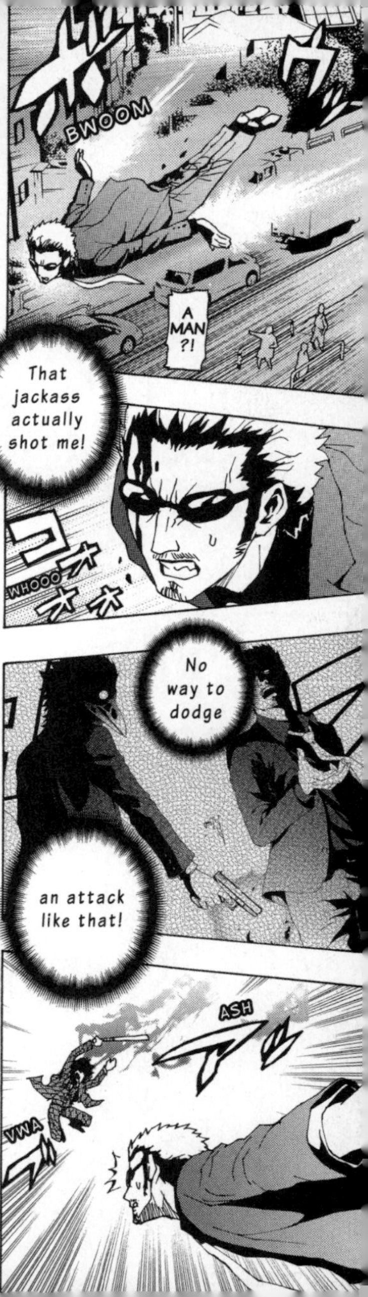
BWOOM
A MAN ?!
That jackass actually shot me!
WHOOO
No way to dodge
an attack like that!
ASH
VWA
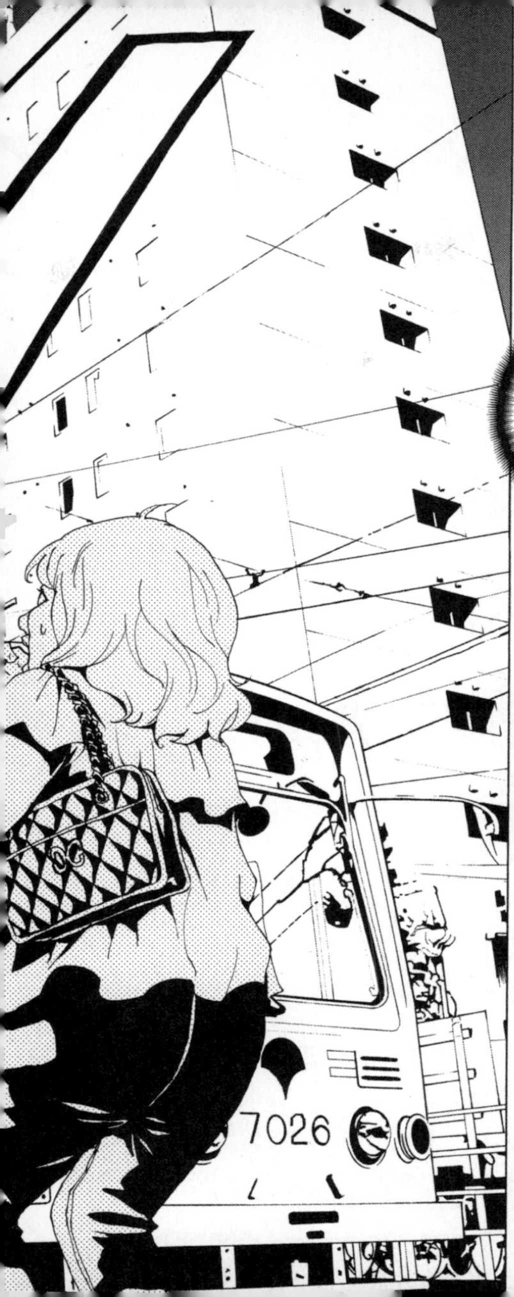
7026

SCENE 7 /// Hard Knocks Heroine

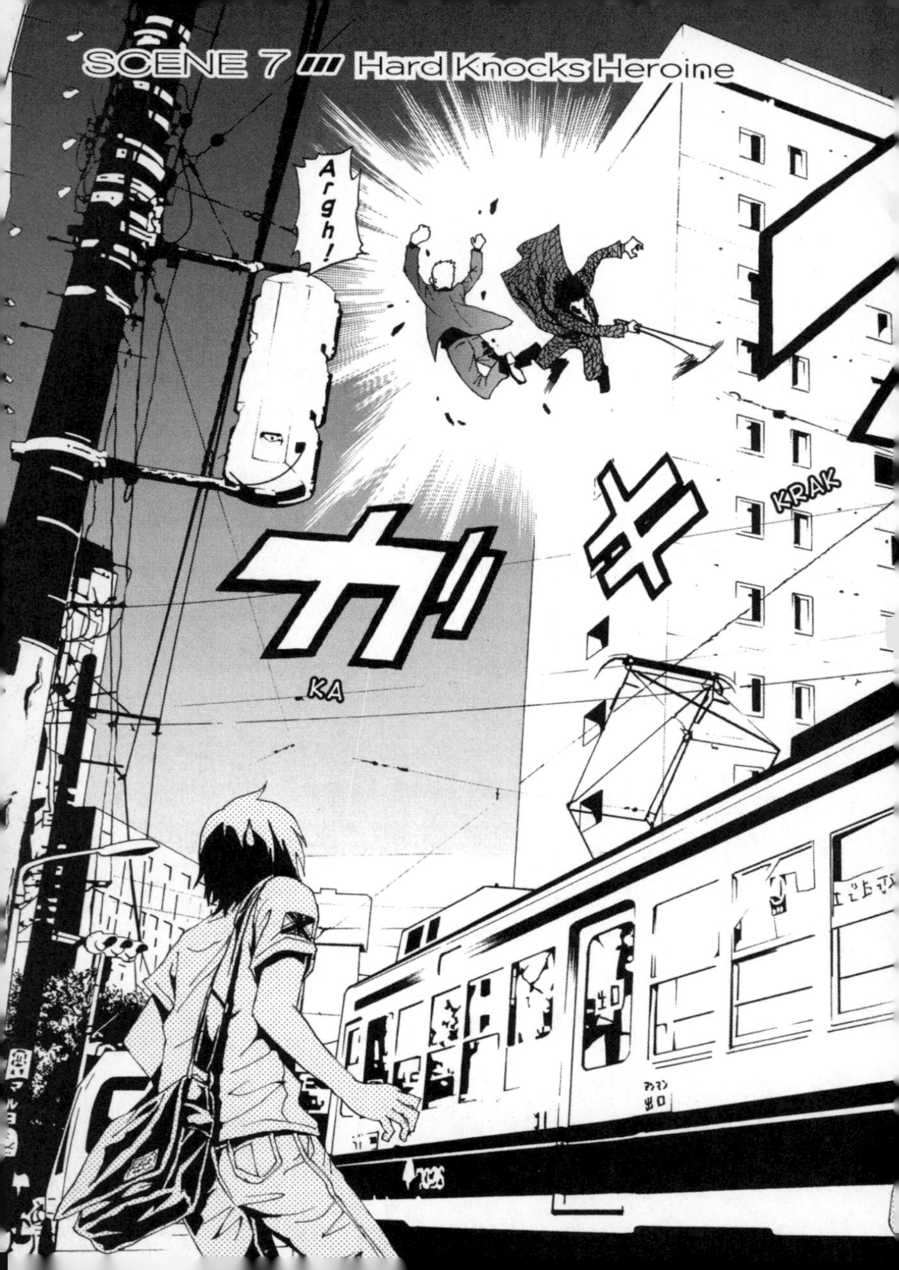
Argh!
KRAK
KA

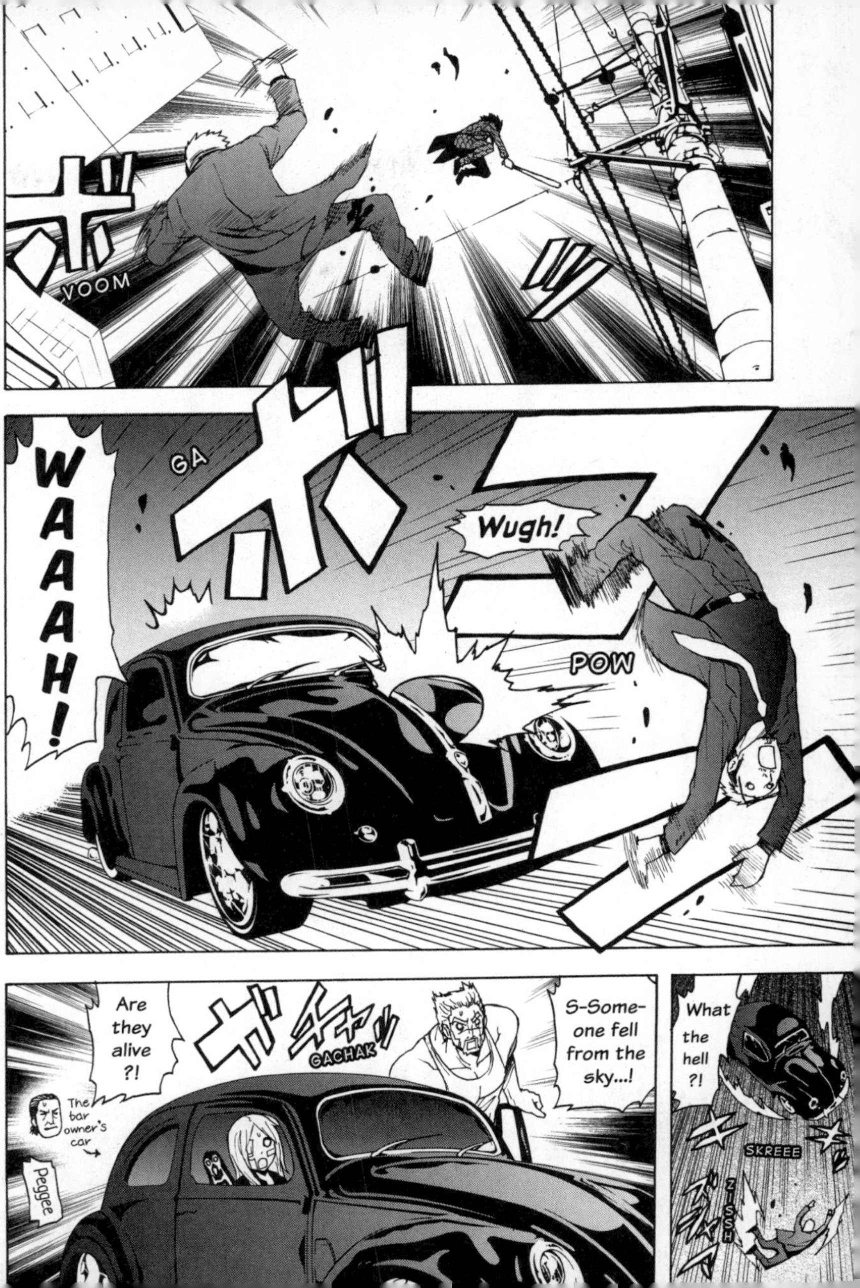
VOOM
Wugh!
GA
POW
WAAAAH!
What the hell?!
SKREEE
ZISSH
S-Some-one fell from the sky...!
GACHAK
Are they alive?!
The bar owner's car
Peggee

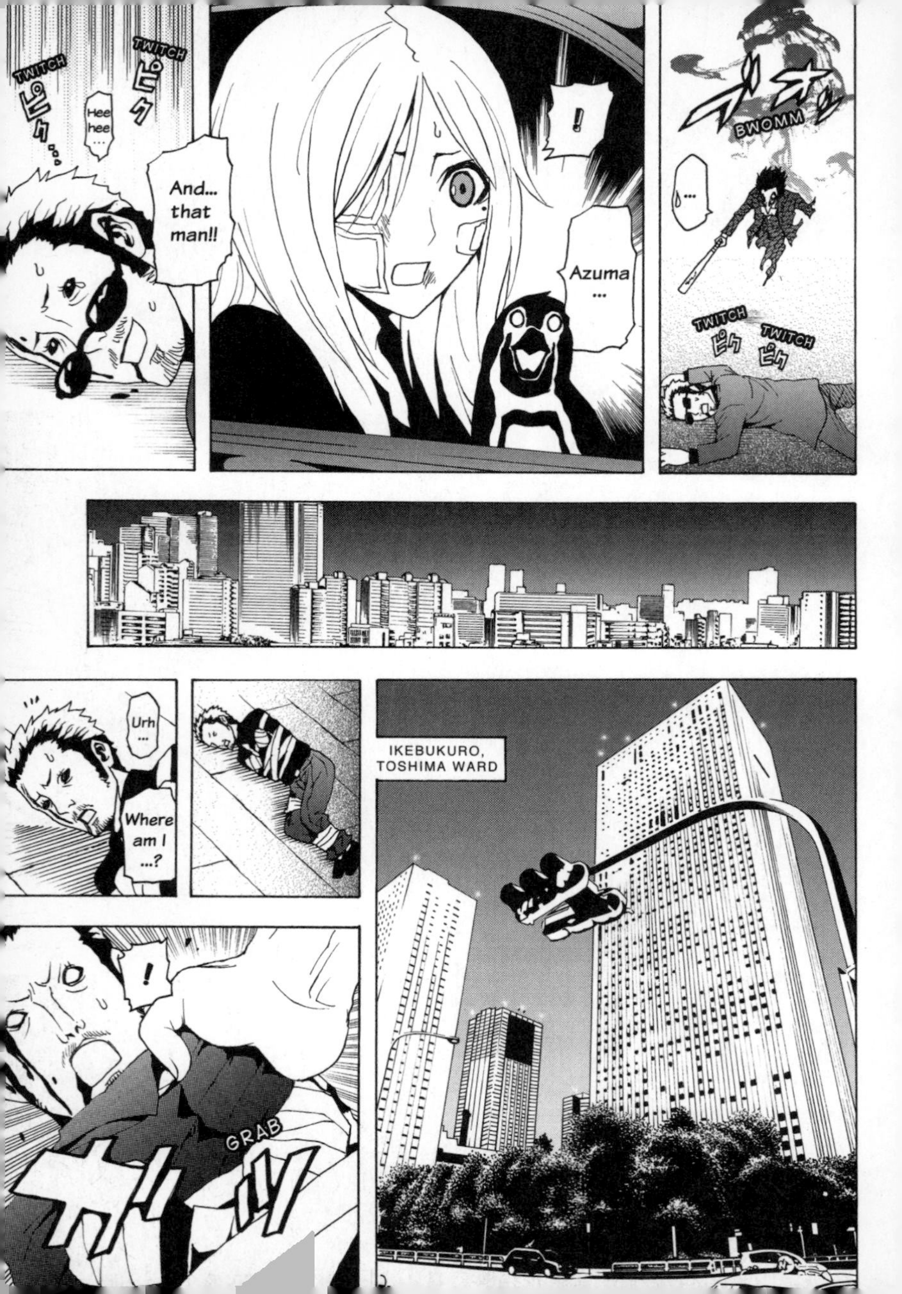
BWOMM
...
TWITCH
TWITCH
!
Azuma ...
And... that man!!
TWITCH
TWITCH
Hee hee ...
IKEBUKURO, TOSHIMA WARD
Urh ...
Where am I ...?
!
GRAB

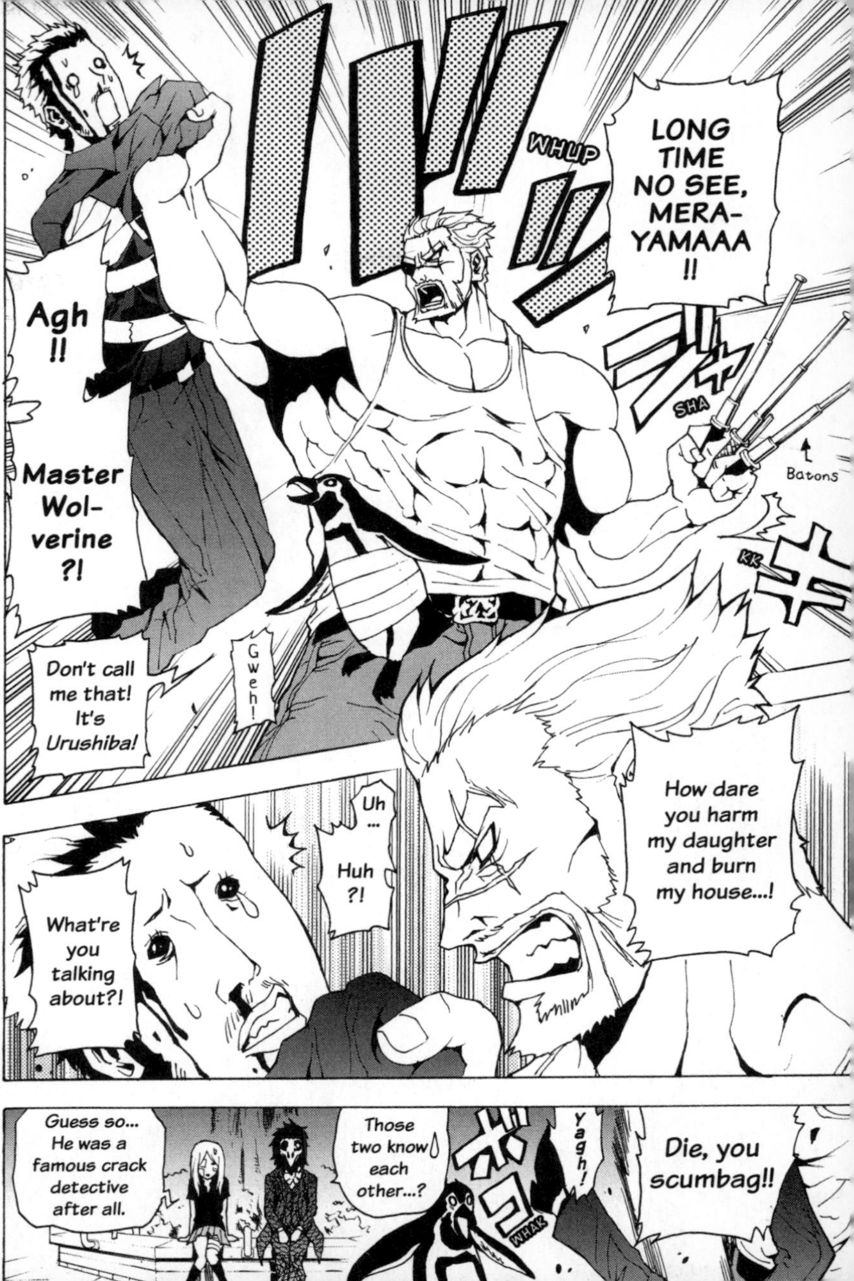
WHUP
LONG TIME NO SEE, MERA-YAMAAA!!
SHA
Batons
Agh!!
Master Wol-verine?!
KK
Gweh!
Don't call me that! It's Urushiba!
How dare you harm my daughter and burn my house...!
Uh... Huh?!
What're you talking about?!
Die, you scumbag!!
Yagh!
WHAK
Those two know each other...?
Guess so... He was a famous crack detective after all.

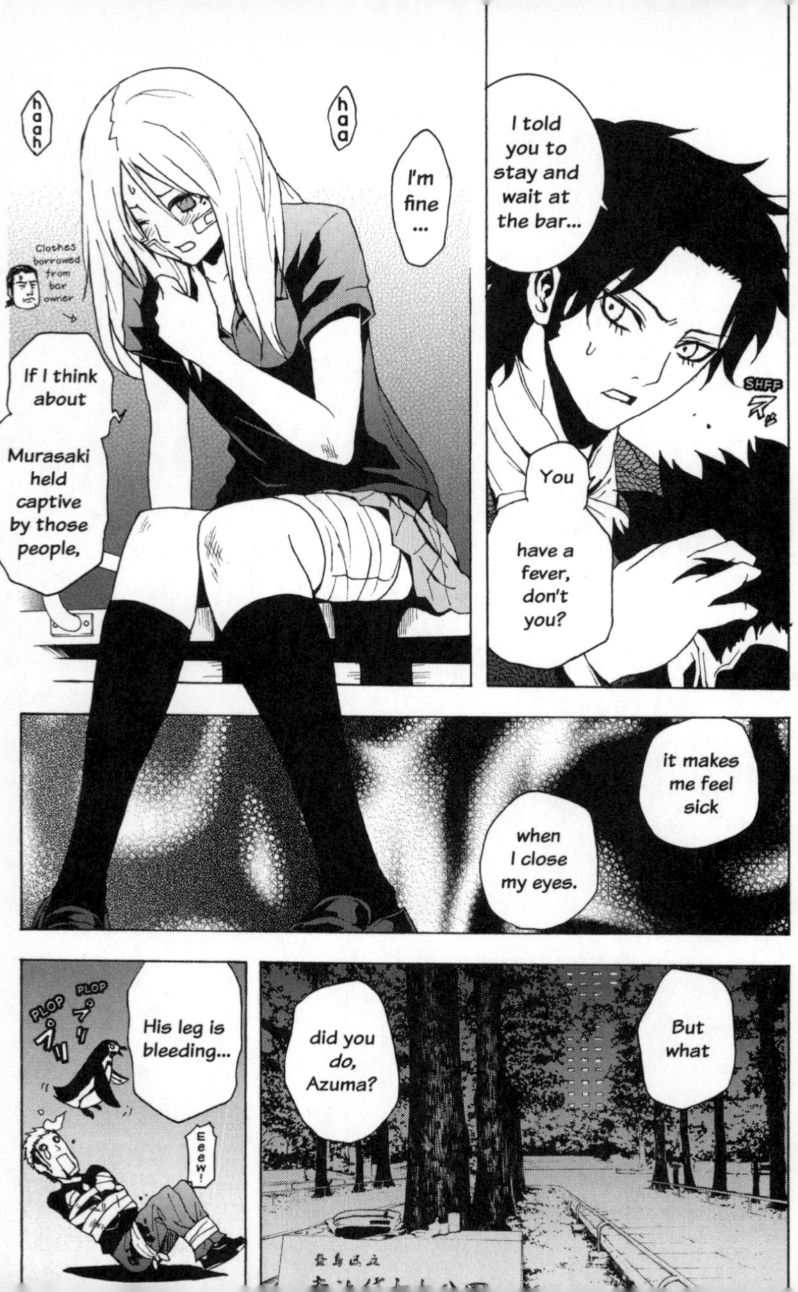
I told you to stay and wait at the bar...
SHFF
You
have a fever, don't you?
haa
haah
I'm fine ...
Clothes borrowed from bar owner
If I think about
Murasaki held captive by those people,
it makes me feel sick
when I close my eyes.
But what
did you do, Azuma?
His leg is bleeding...
PLOP PLOP
Eeew!

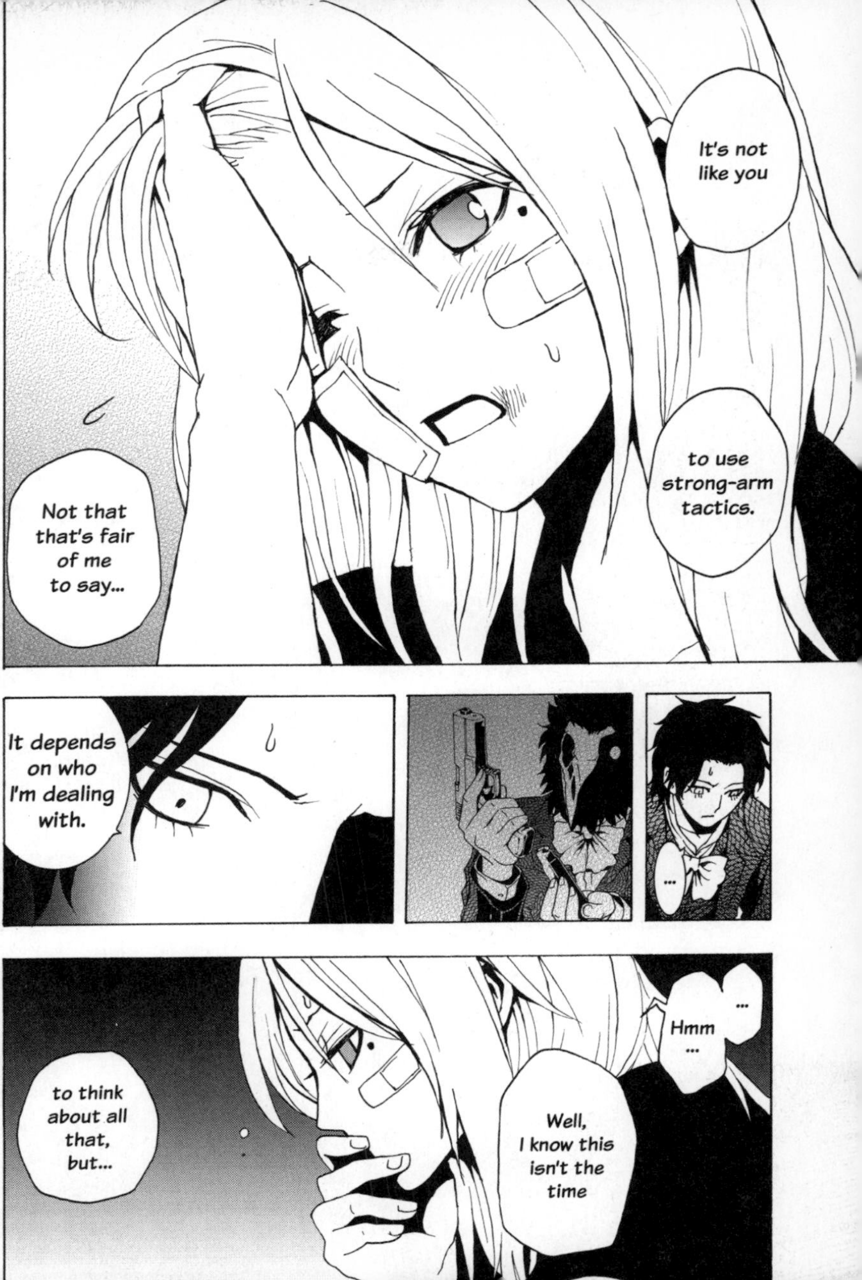
It's not like you
to use strong-arm tactics.
Not that that's fair of me to say...
...
It depends on who I'm dealing with.
... Hmm ...
Well, I know this isn't the time
to think about all that, but...

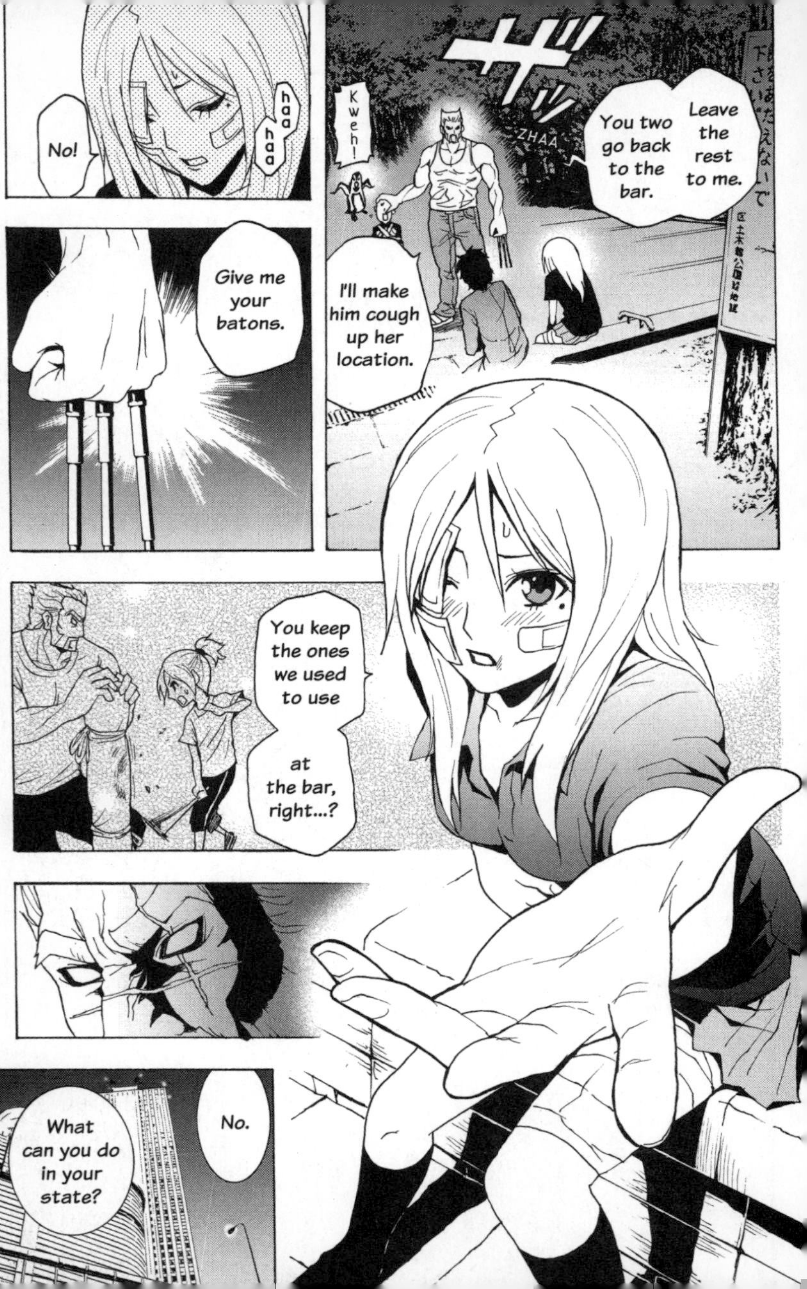

ザッ
ZHAA
Kweh!
Leave the rest to me.
You two go back to the bar.
I'll make him cough up her location.
haa haa
No!
Give me your batons.
You keep the ones we used to use
at the bar, right...?
No.
What can you do in your state?

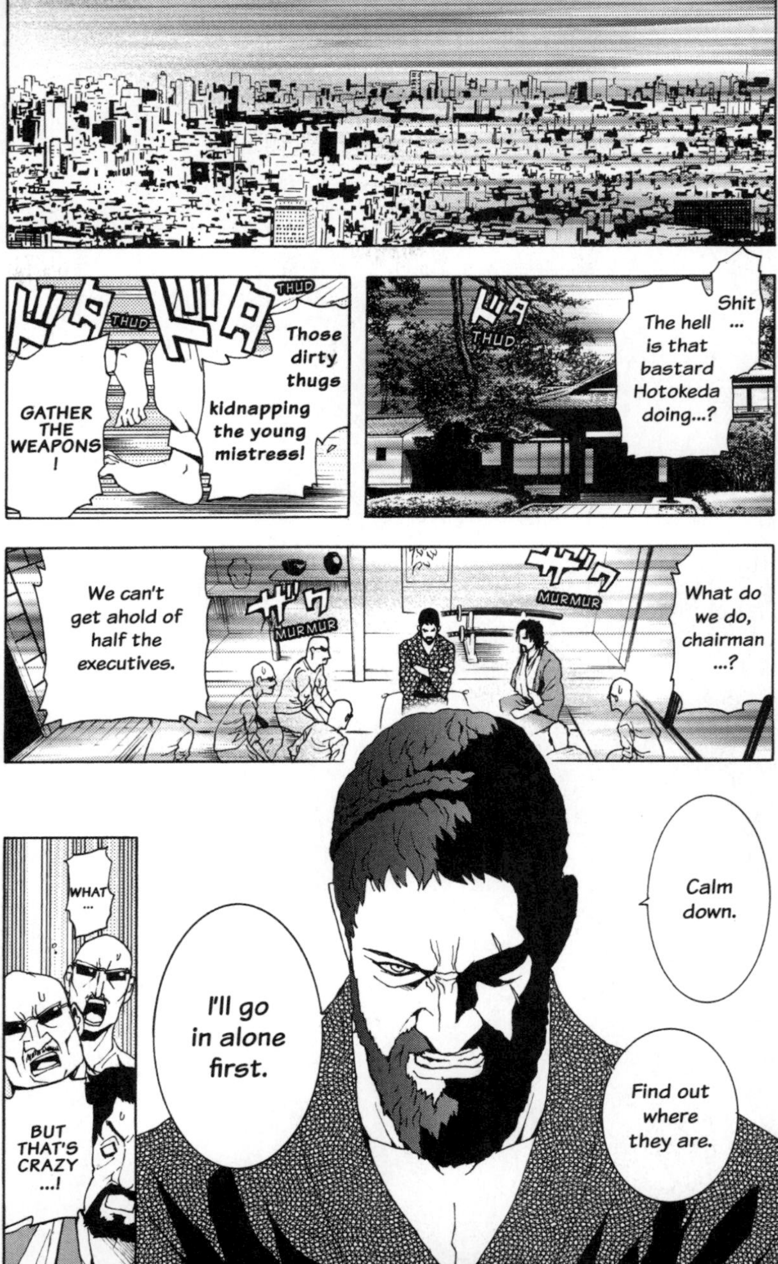
ドタ
THUD
Shit ...
The hell is that bastard Hotokeda doing...?
ドタ ドタ
THUD
THUD
Those dirty thugs kidnapping the young mistress!
GATHER THE WEAPONS!
ザワ
MURMUR
What do we do, chairman ...?
ザワ
MURMUR
We can't get ahold of half the executives.
Calm down.
Find out where they are.
I'll go in alone first.
WHAT ...
BUT THAT'S CRAZY ...!

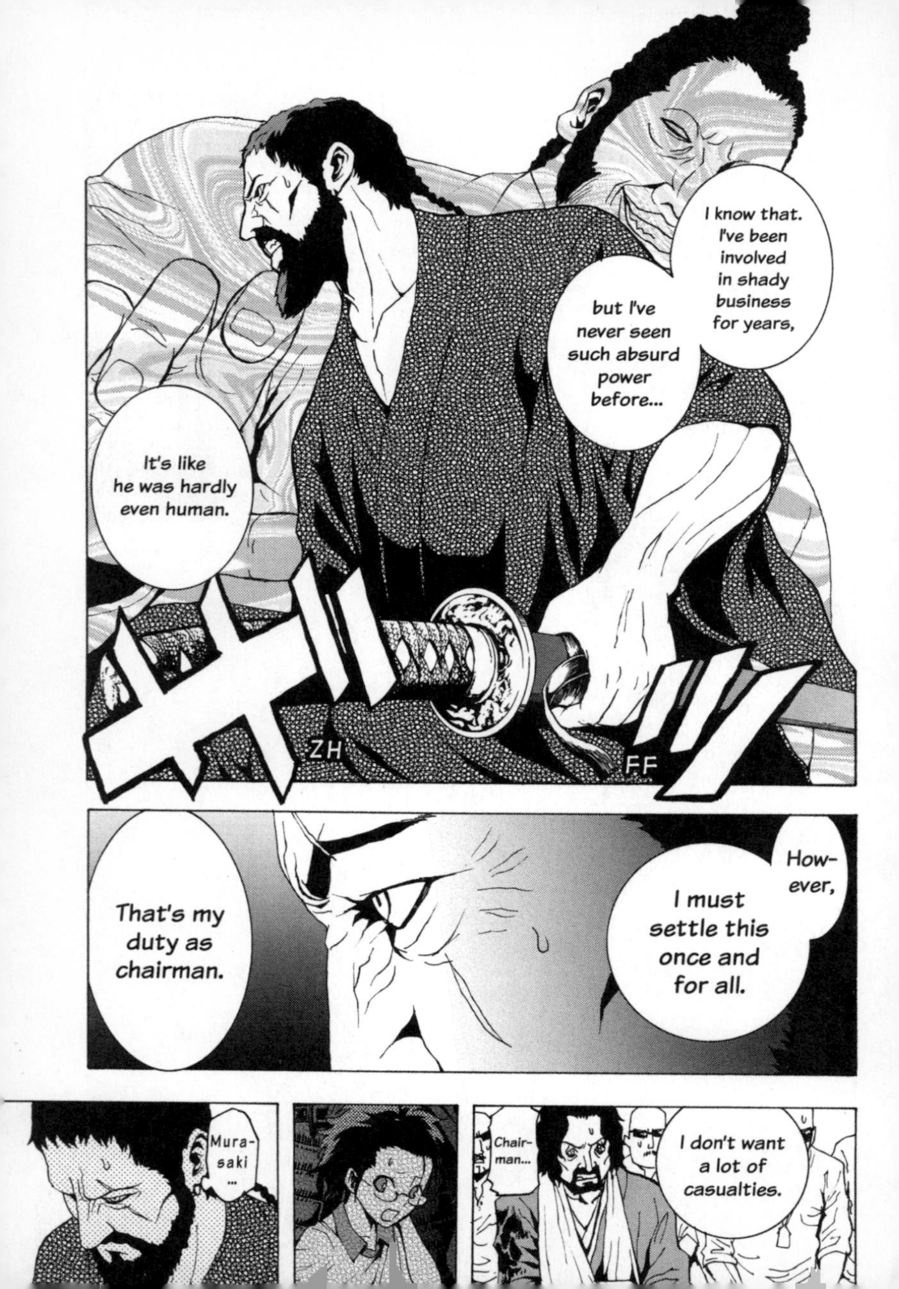
I know that. I've been involved in shady business for years,
but I've never seen such absurd power before...
It's like he was hardly even human.
ZH
FF
How-ever,
I must settle this once and for all.
That's my duty as chairman.
I don't want a lot of casualties.
Chair-man...
Mura-saki ...

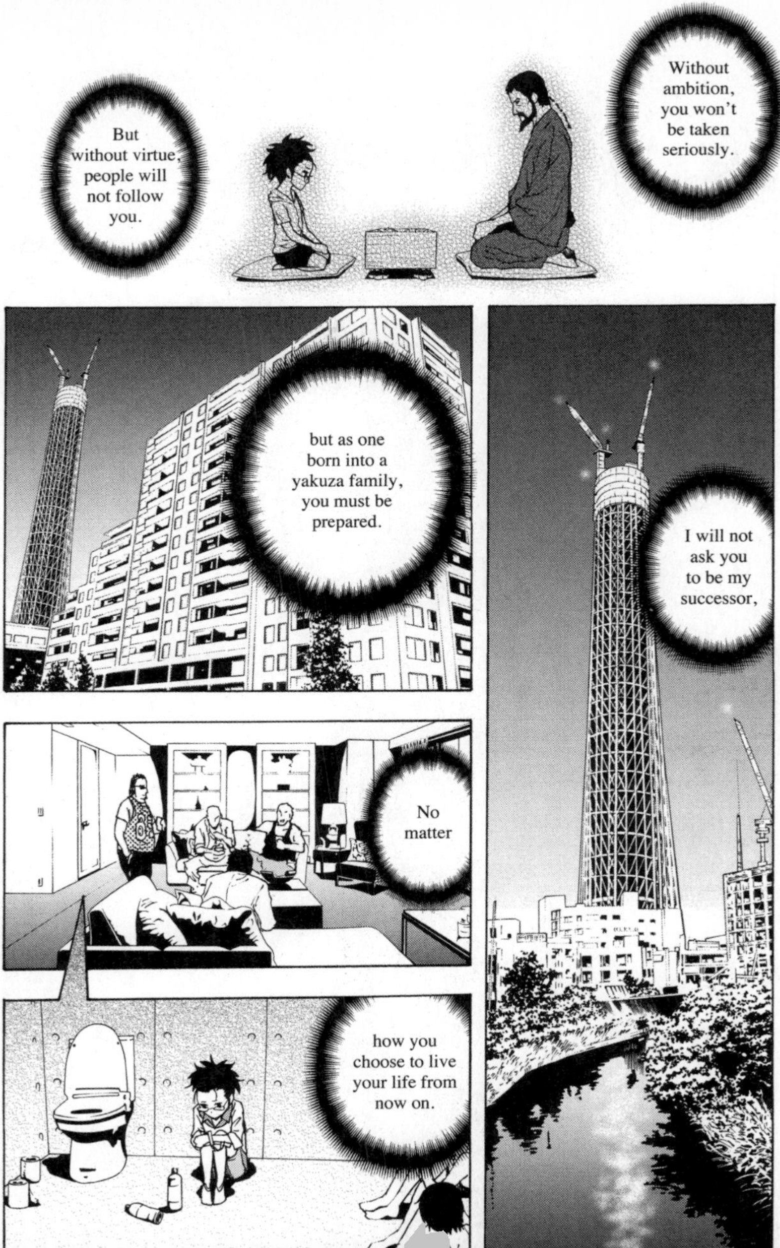
Without ambition, you won't be taken seriously.
But without virtue, people will not follow you.
I will not ask you to be my successor,
but as one born into a yakuza family, you must be prepared.
No matter
how you choose to live your life from now on.

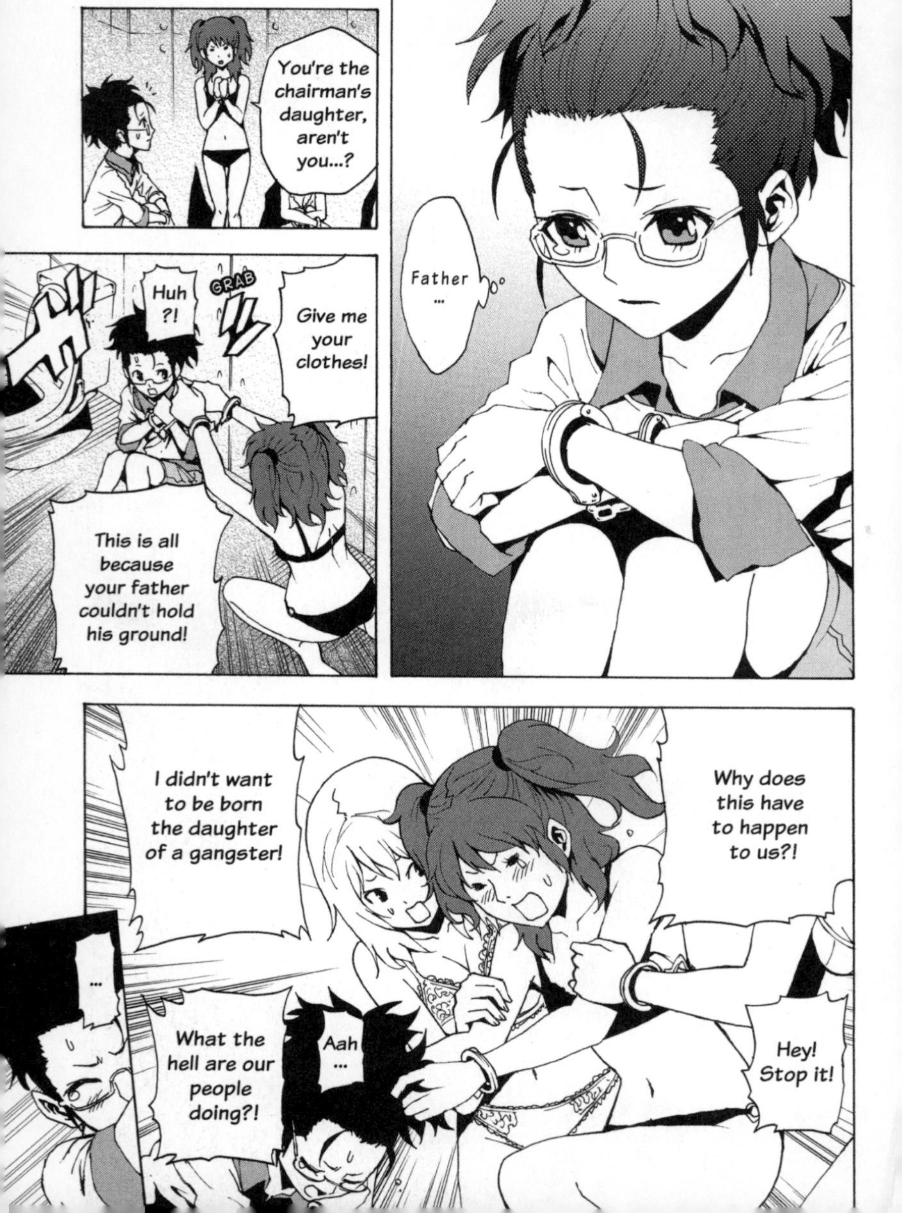
Father ...
You're the chairman's daughter, aren't you...?
Give me your clothes!
GRAB
Huh ?!
This is all because your father couldn't hold his ground!
Why does this have to happen to us?!
I didn't want to be born the daughter of a gangster!
Hey! Stop it!
Aah ...
What the hell are our people doing?!
...

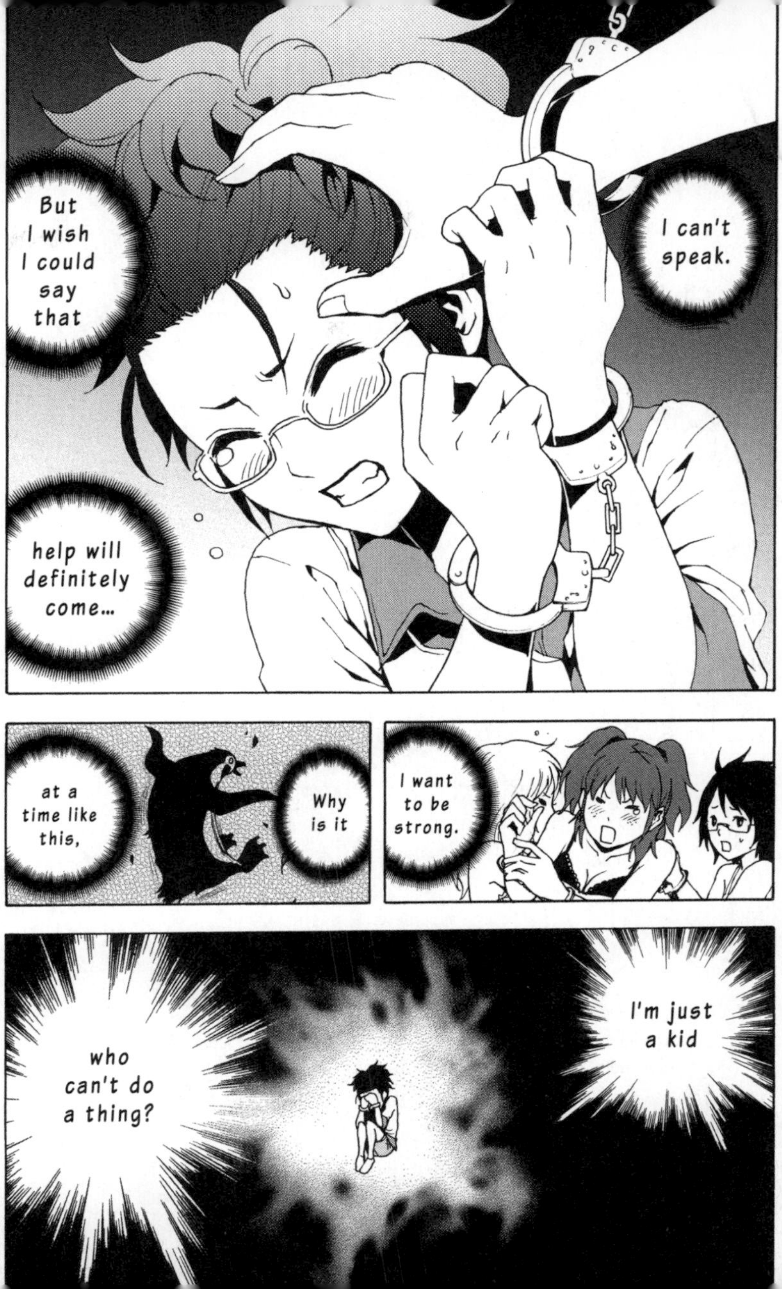
I can't speak.
But I wish I could say that
help will definitely come...
I want to be strong.
Why is it
at a time like this,
I'm just a kid
who can't do a thing?

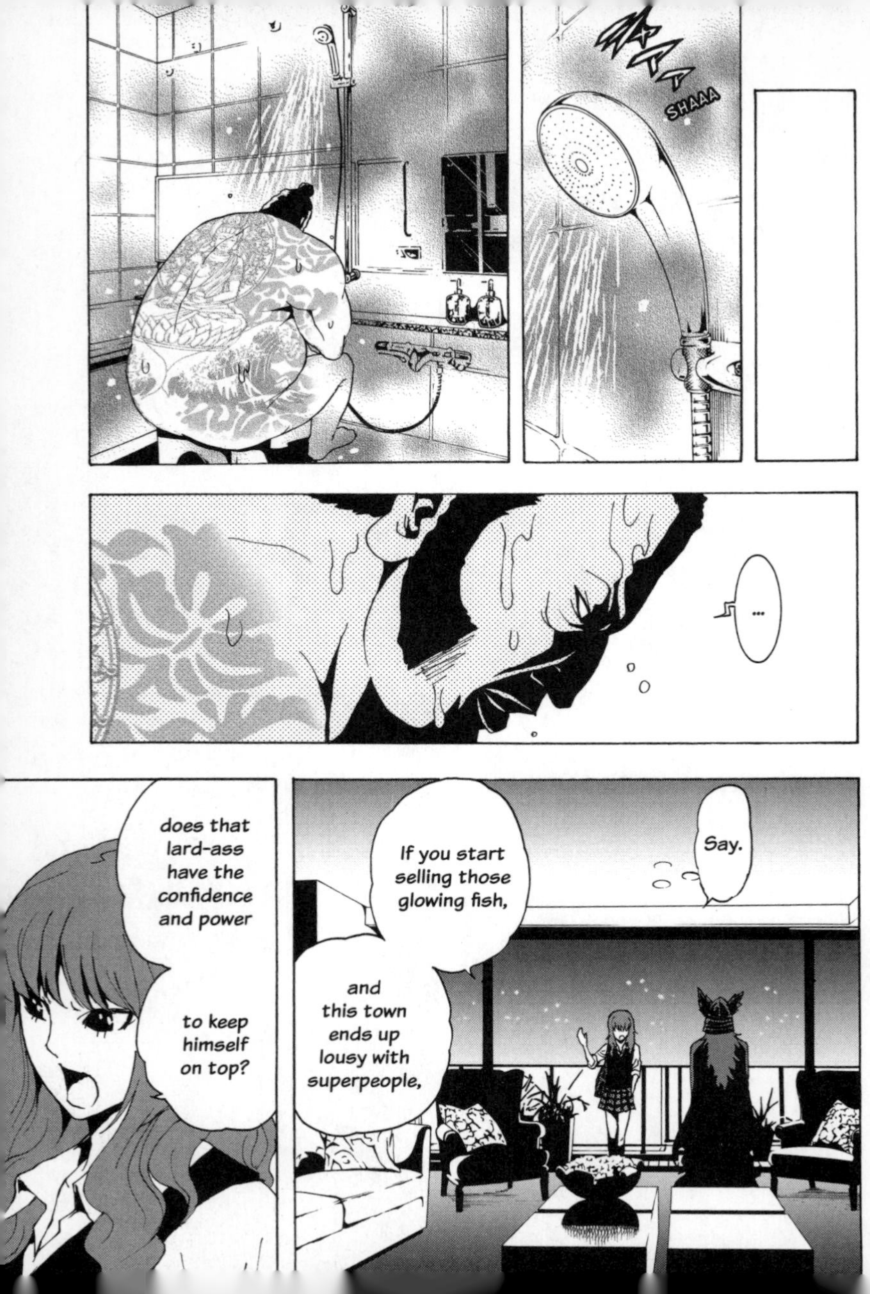
SHAAA
...
Say.
If you start selling those glowing fish,
and this town ends up lousy with superpeople,
does that lard-ass have the confidence and power
to keep himself on top?

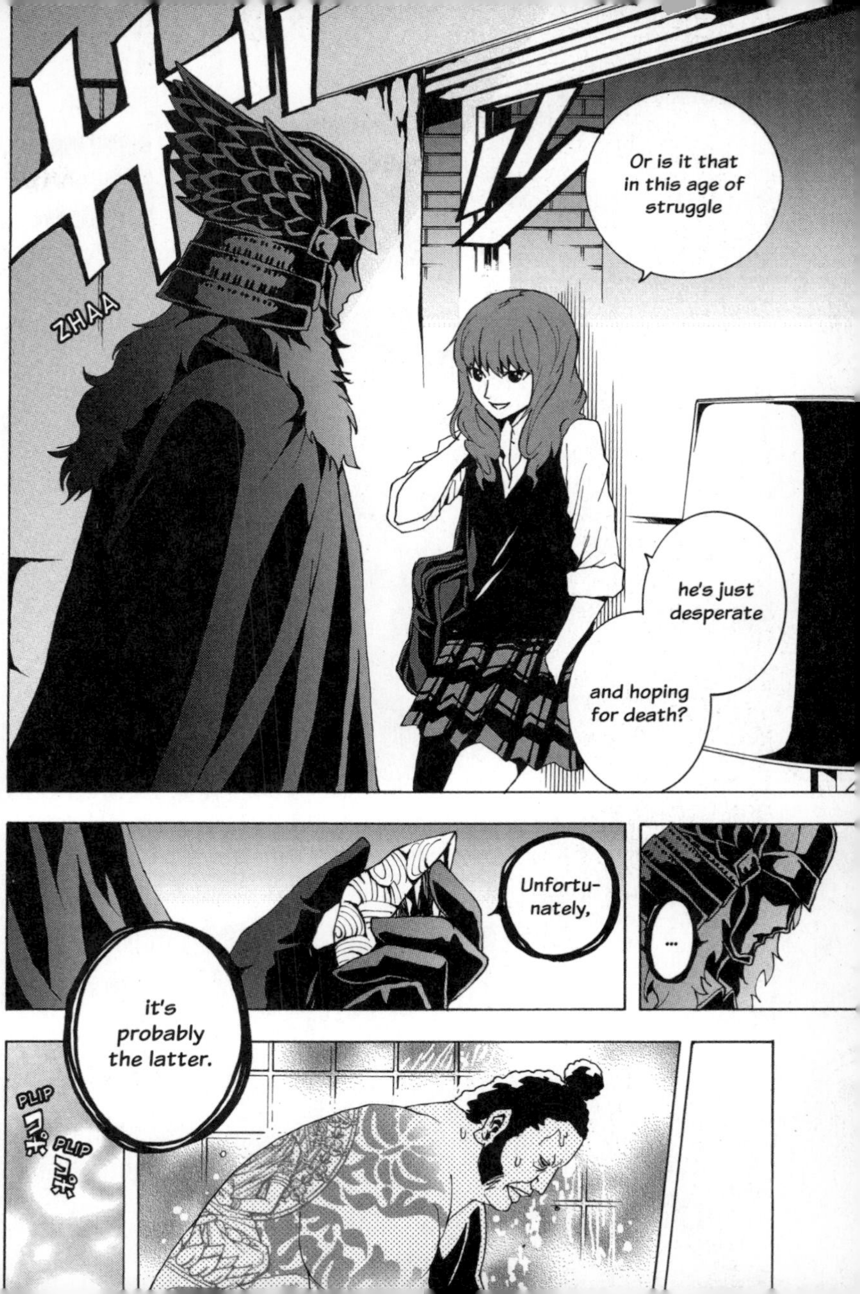
Or is it that in this age of struggle
he's just desperate
and hoping for death?
ZHAA
...
Unfortu-nately,
it's probably the latter.
PLIP
PLIP

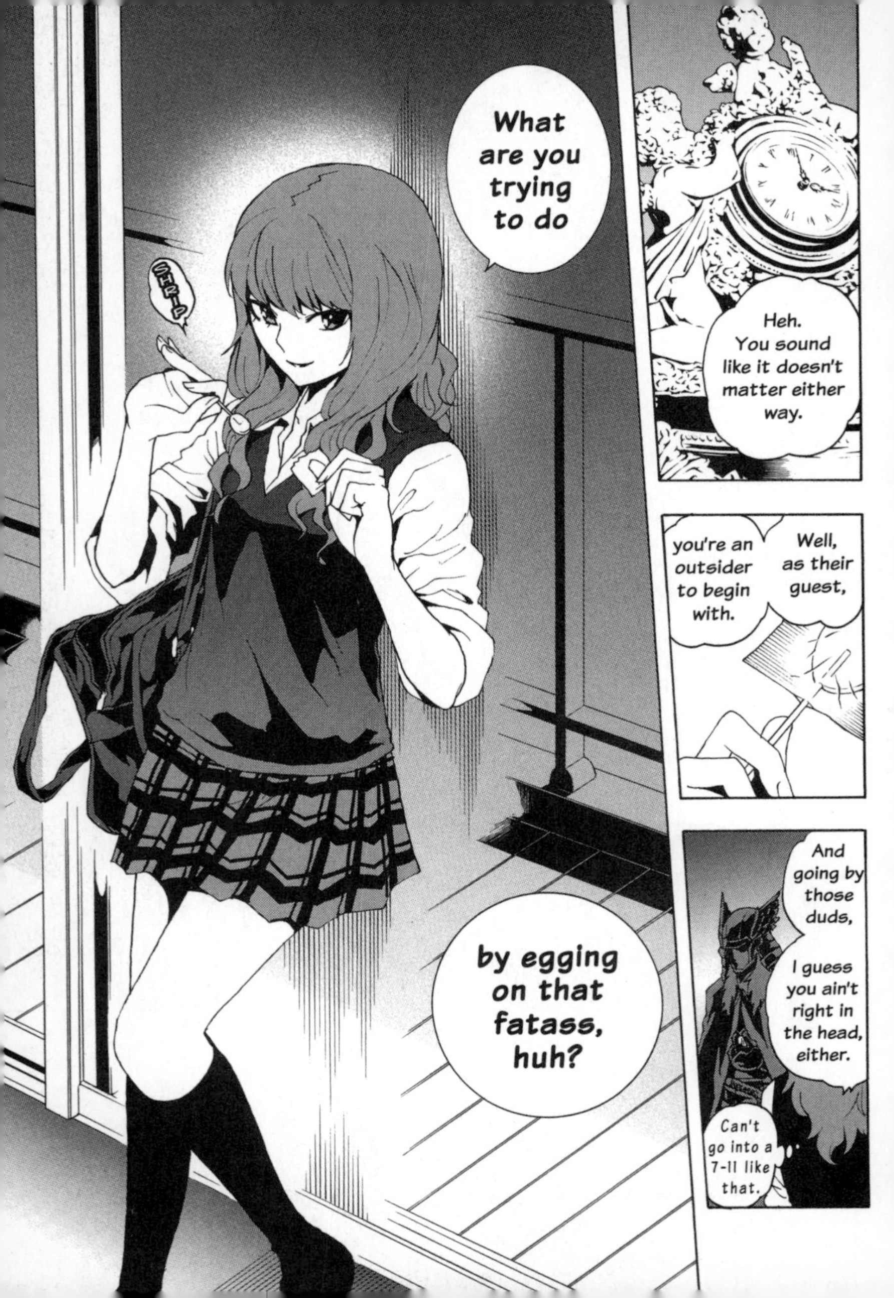
Heh. You sound like it doesn't matter either way.
Well, as their guest,
you're an outsider to begin with.
And going by those duds,
I guess you ain't right in the head, either.
Can't go into a 7-11 like that.
SHRIP
What are you trying to do
by egging on that fatass, huh?

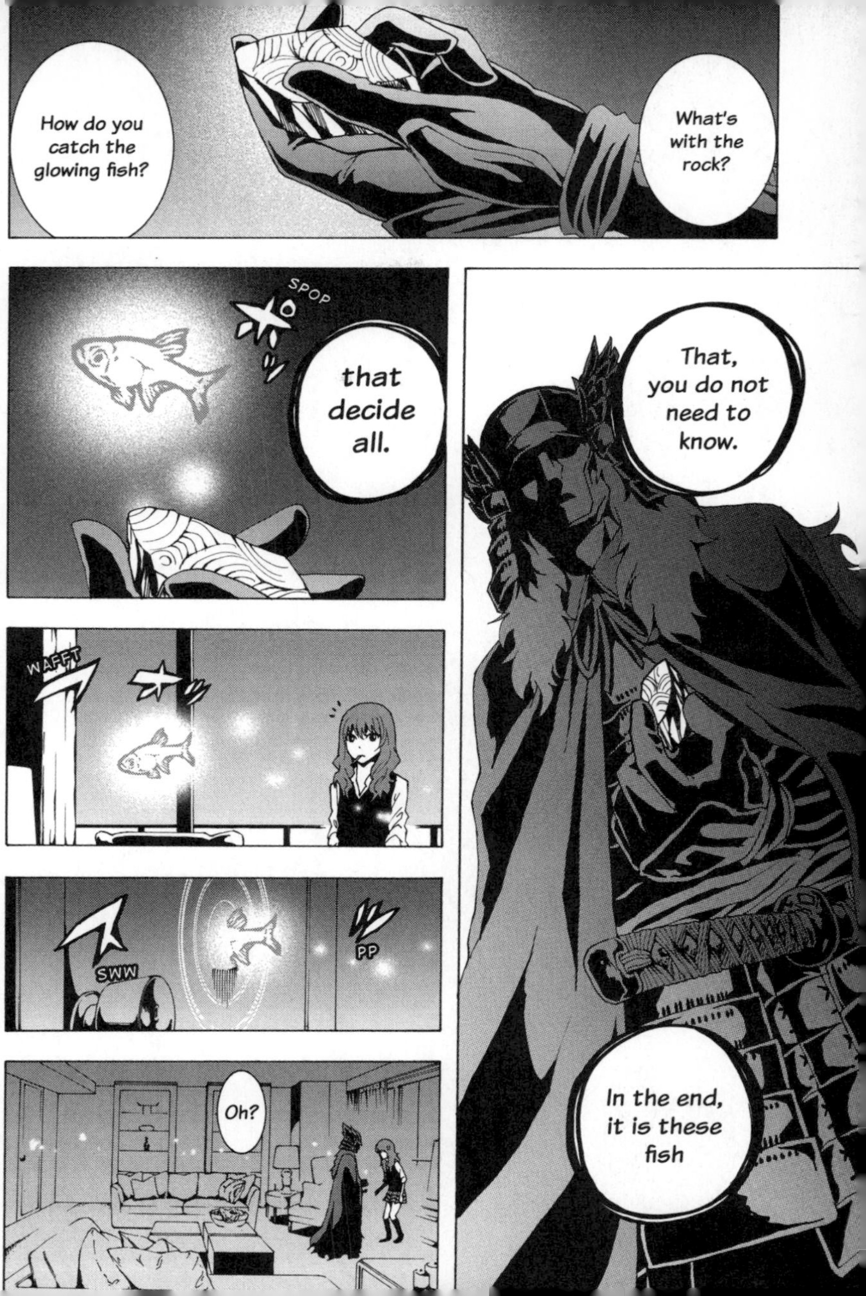
What's with the rock?
How do you catch the glowing fish?
That, you do not need to know.
In the end, it is these fish
SPOP
that decide all.
WAFFT
PP
SWW
Oh?

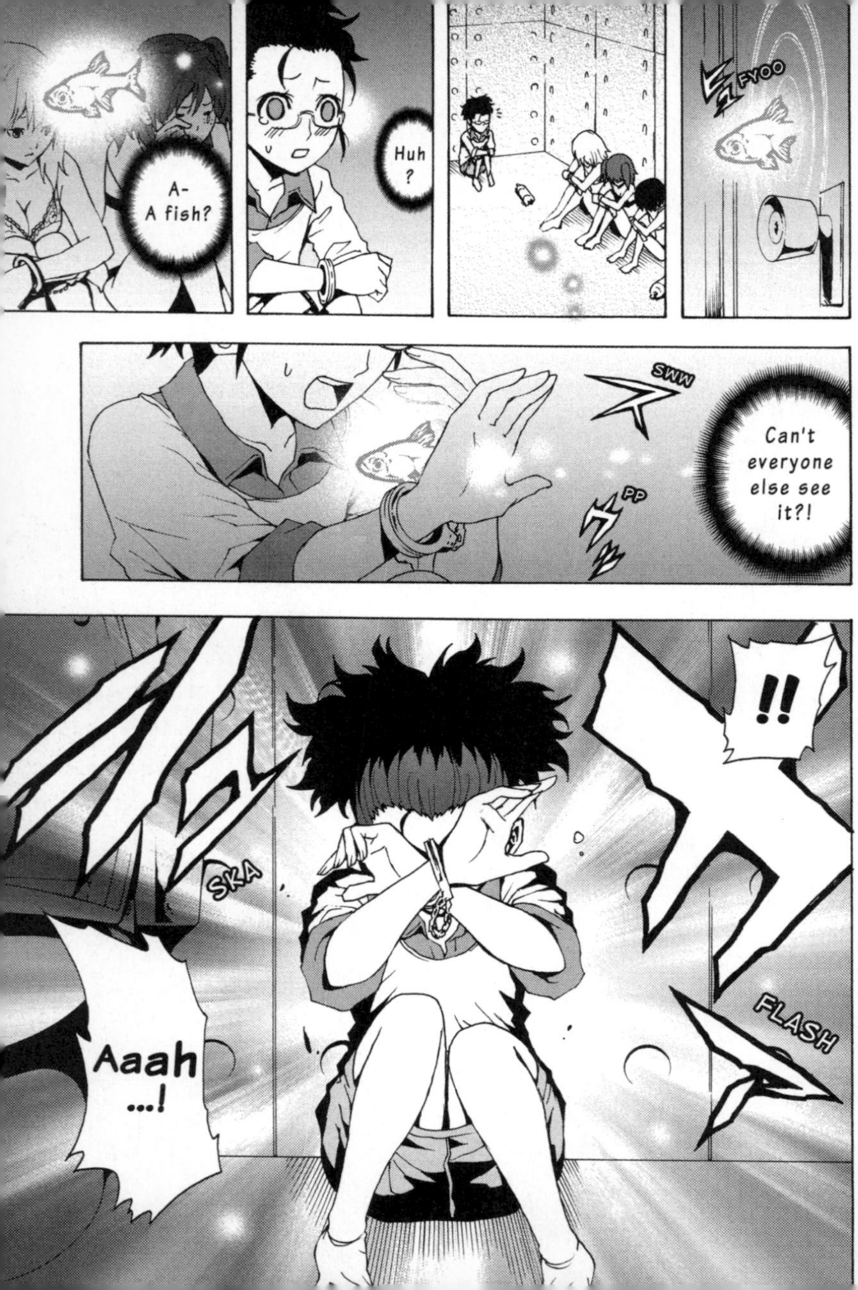
FYOO
Huh
?
A-
A fish?
Can't
everyone
else see
it?!
SWW
PP
!!
FLASH
SKA
Aaah
...!

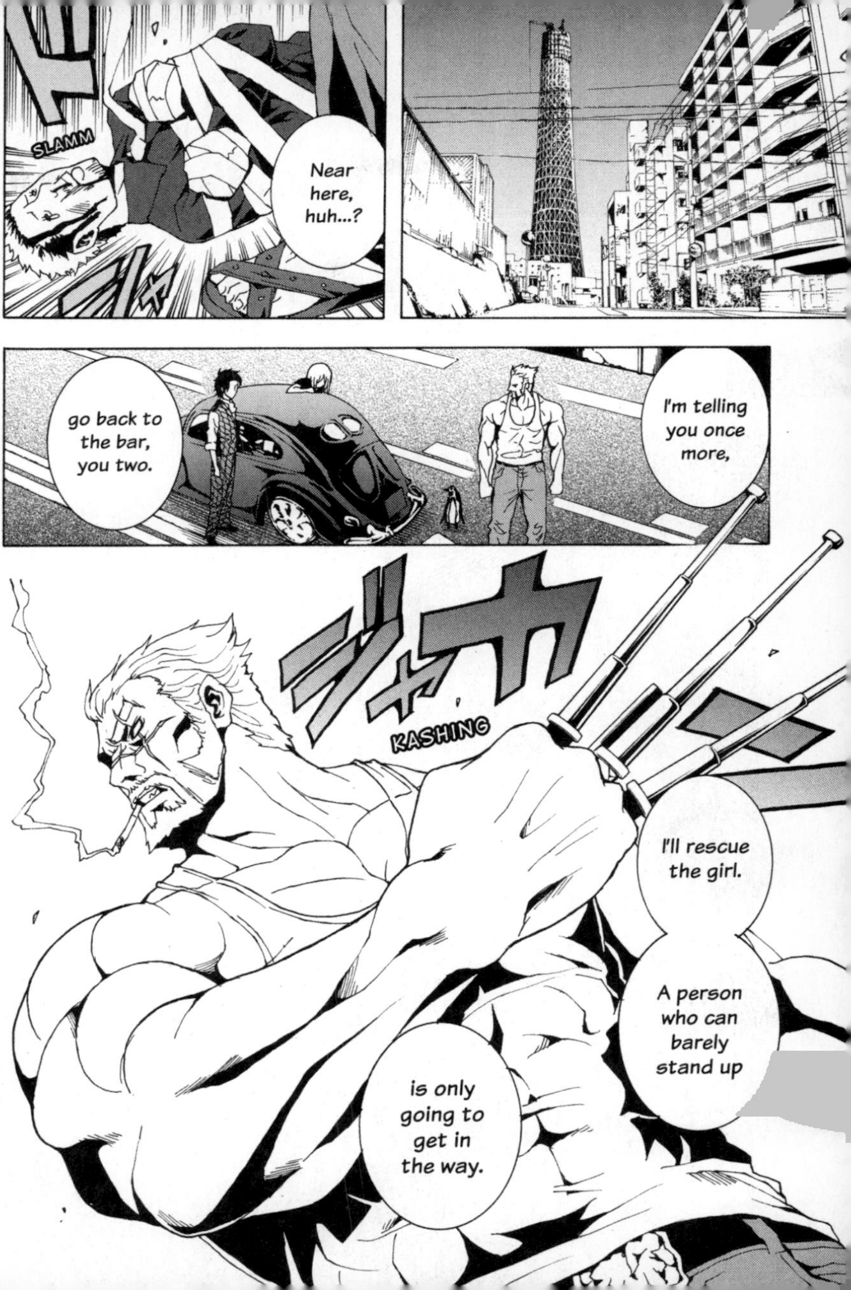
Near here, huh...?
SLAMM
I'm telling you once more,
go back to the bar, you two.
KASHING
I'll rescue the girl.
A person who can barely stand up
is only going to get in the way.

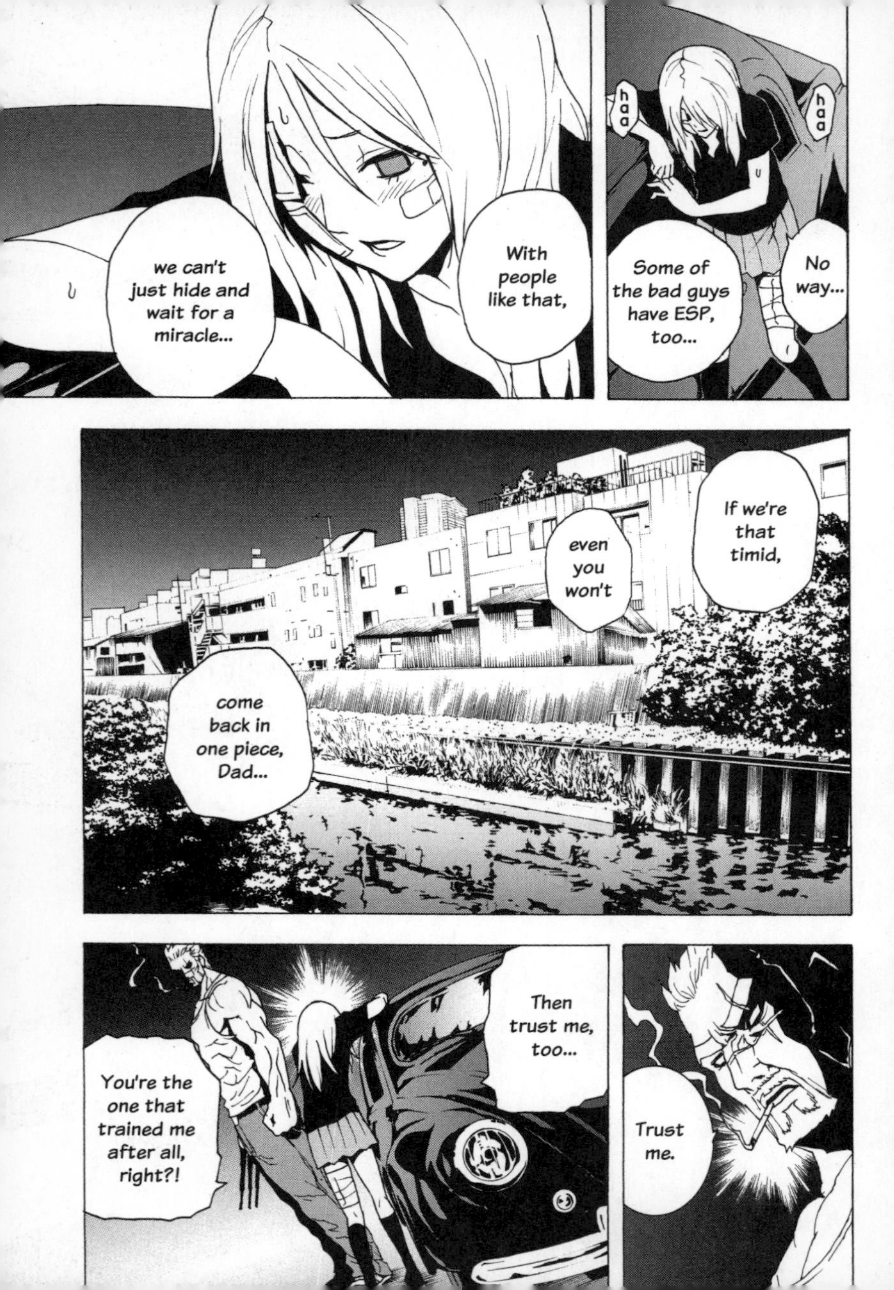
haa
haa
No way...
Some of the bad guys have ESP, too...
With people like that,
we can't just hide and wait for a miracle...
If we're that timid,
even you won't
come back in one piece, Dad...
Trust me.
Then trust me, too...
You're the one that trained me after all, right?!

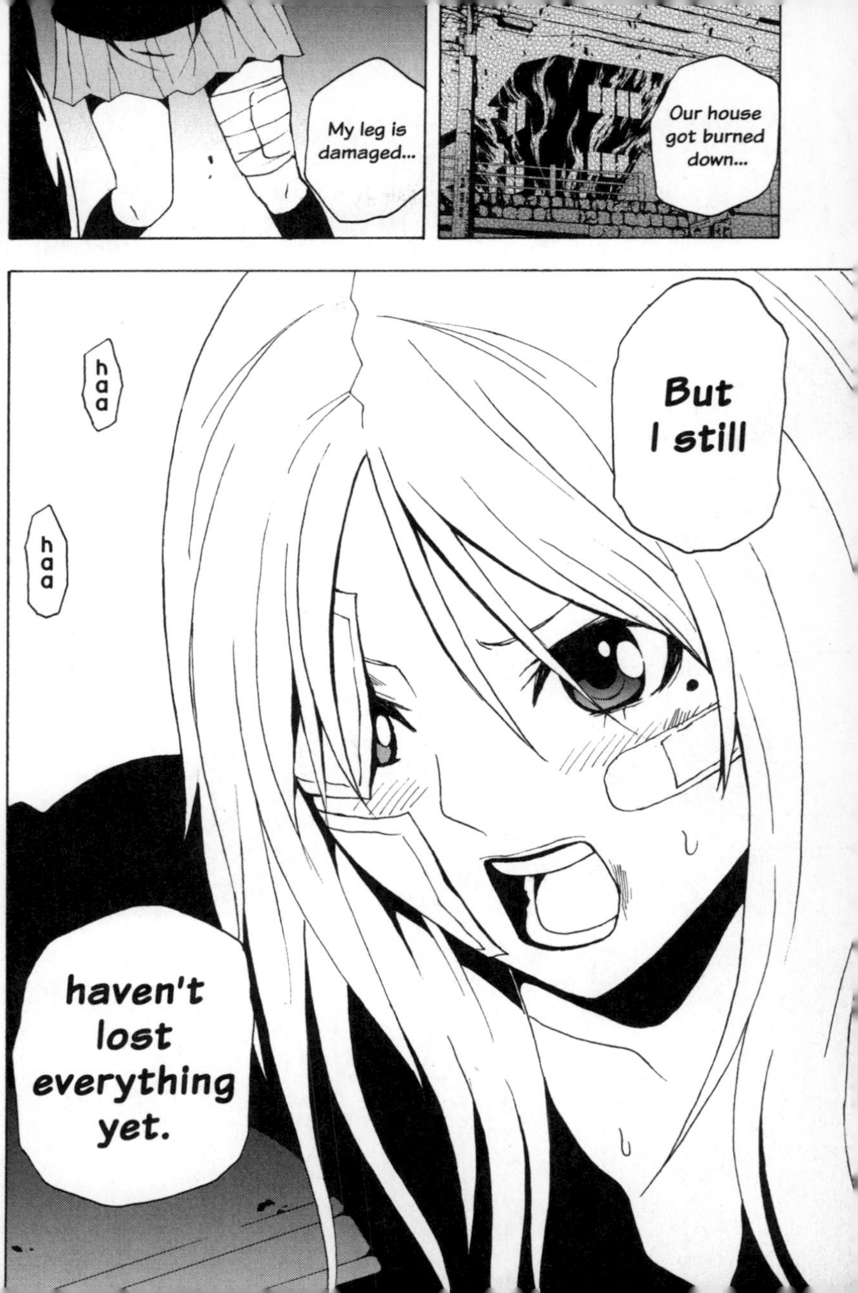
Our house got burned down...
My leg is damaged...
But I still
haa
haa
haven't lost everything yet.

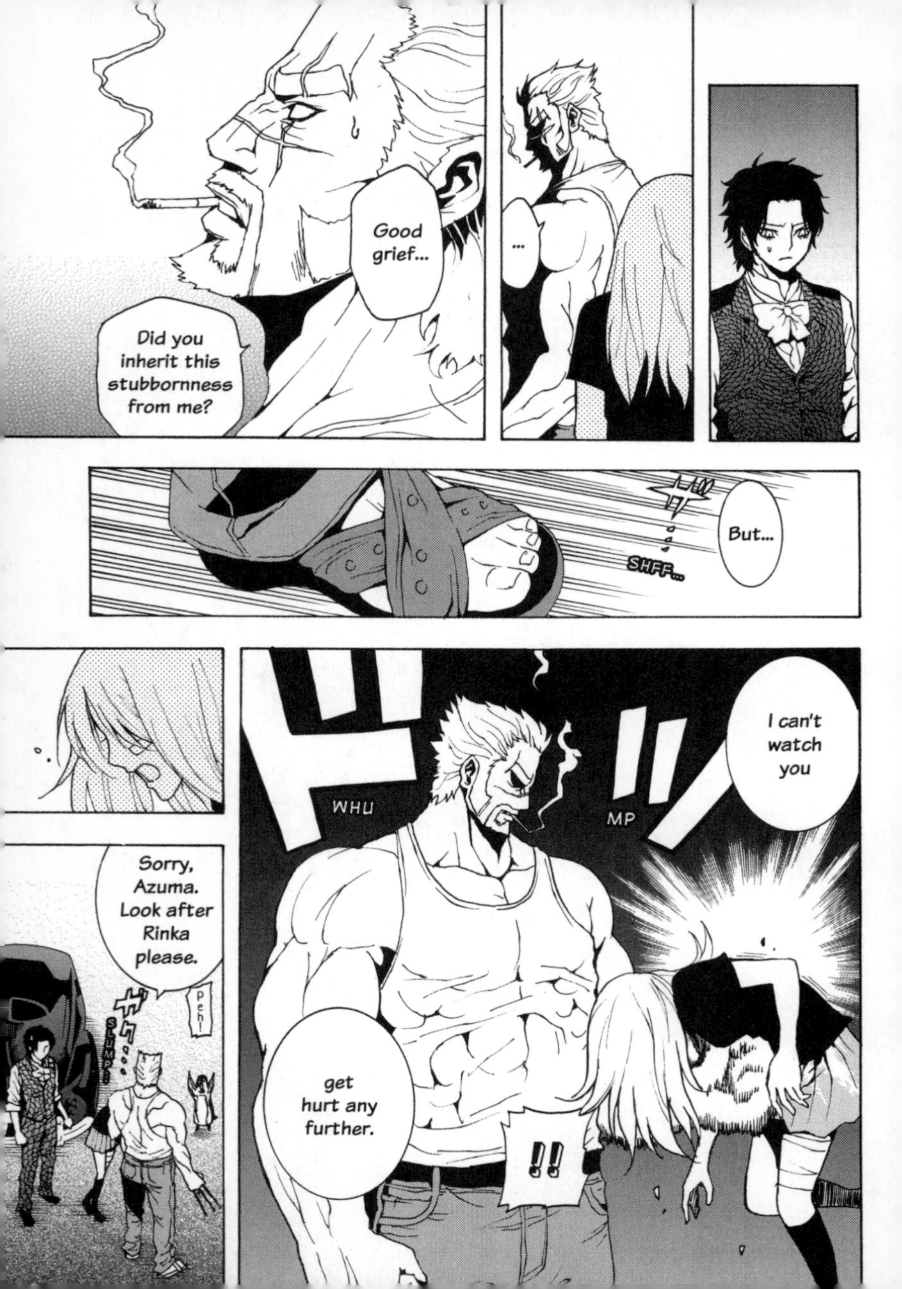
...
Good grief...
Did you inherit this stubbornness from me?
But...
SHFF...
I can't watch you
WHU
MP
get hurt any further.
!!
Sorry, Azuma. Look after Rinka please.
Peh!
SLUMP...

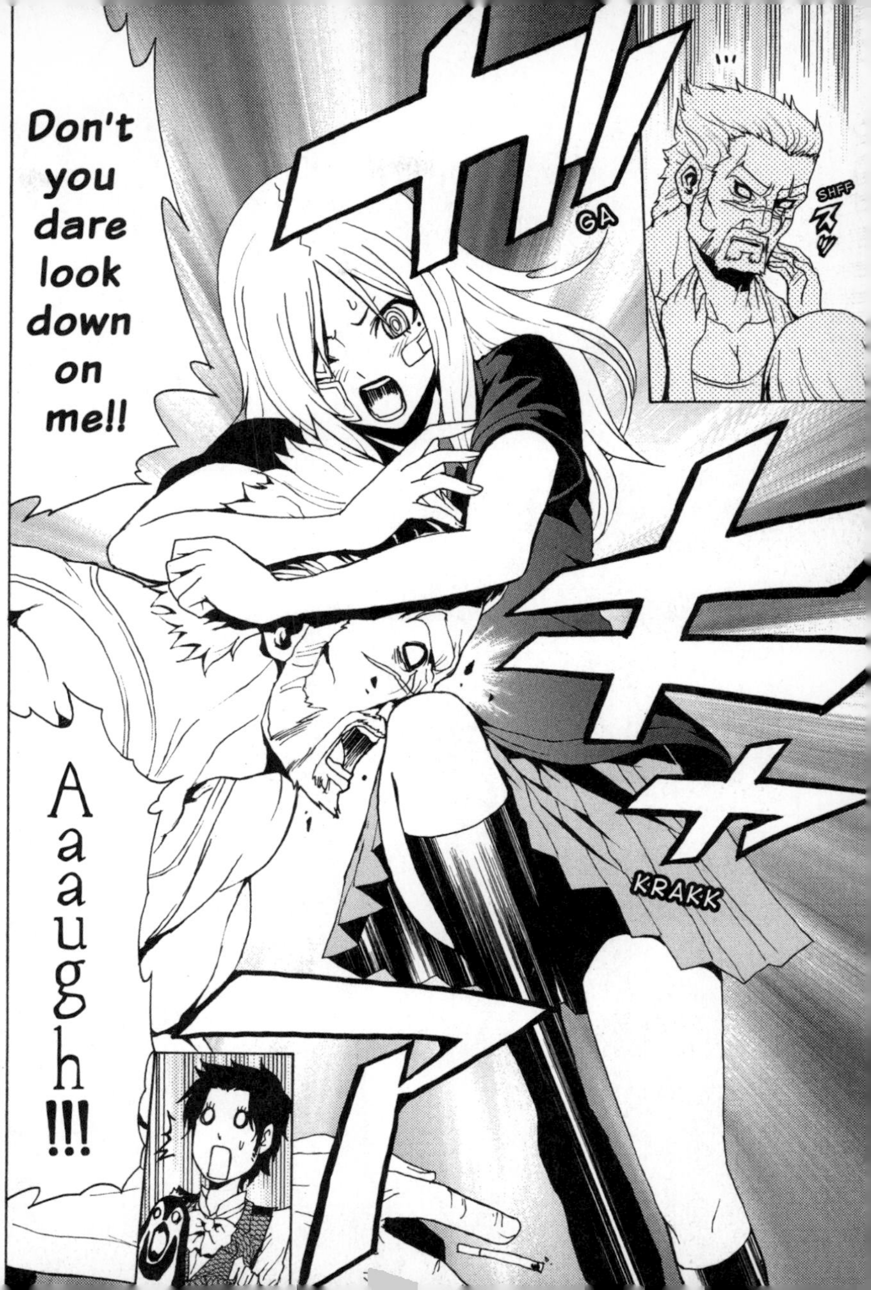
...
SHFF
GA
Don't you dare look down on me!!
KRAKK
Aaaaugh!!!

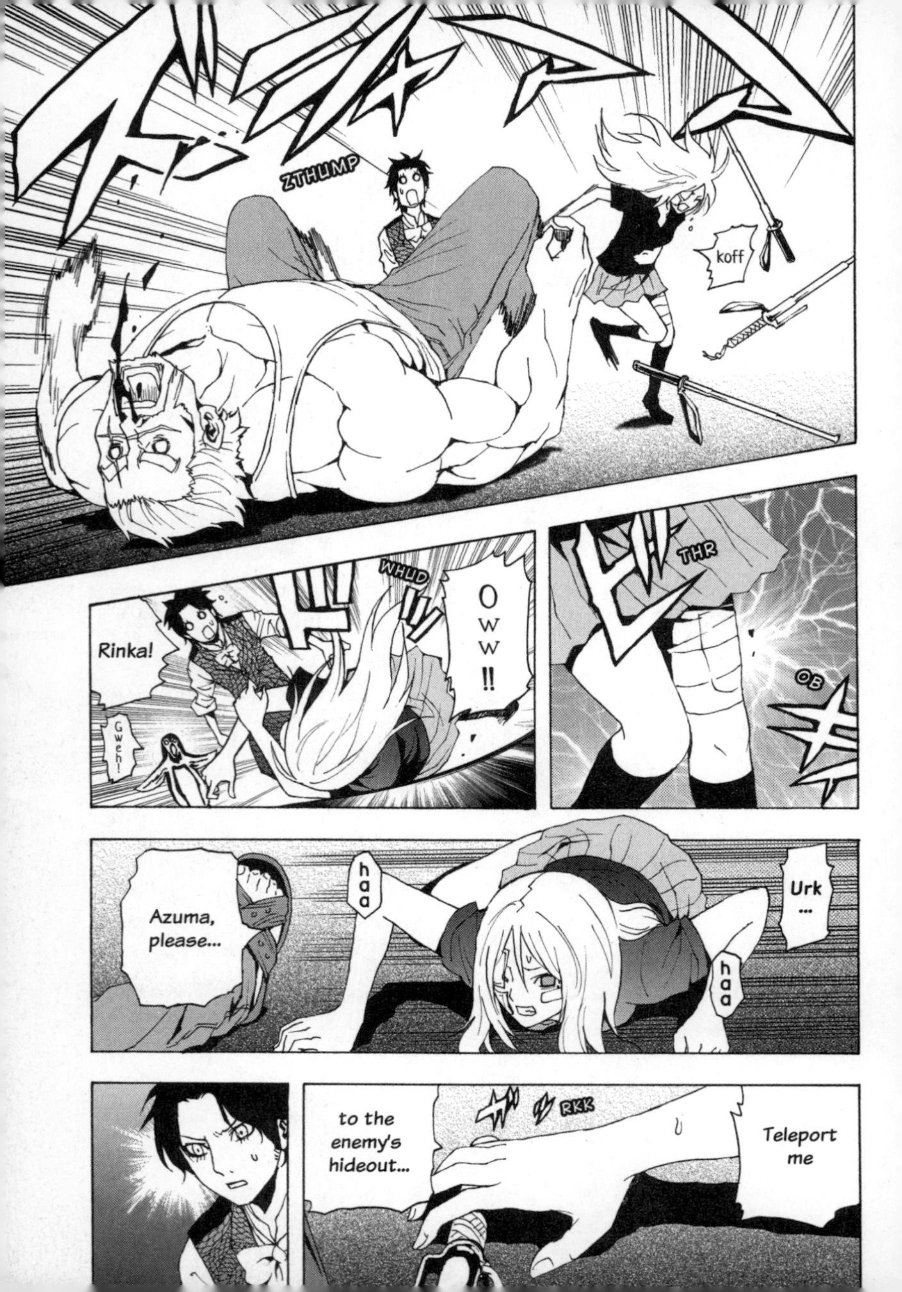
koff
ZTHUMP
THR
OB
Oww!!
WHUD
Rinka!
Gweh!
Urk...
haa
haa
Azuma, please...
Teleport me
RKK
to the enemy's hideout...

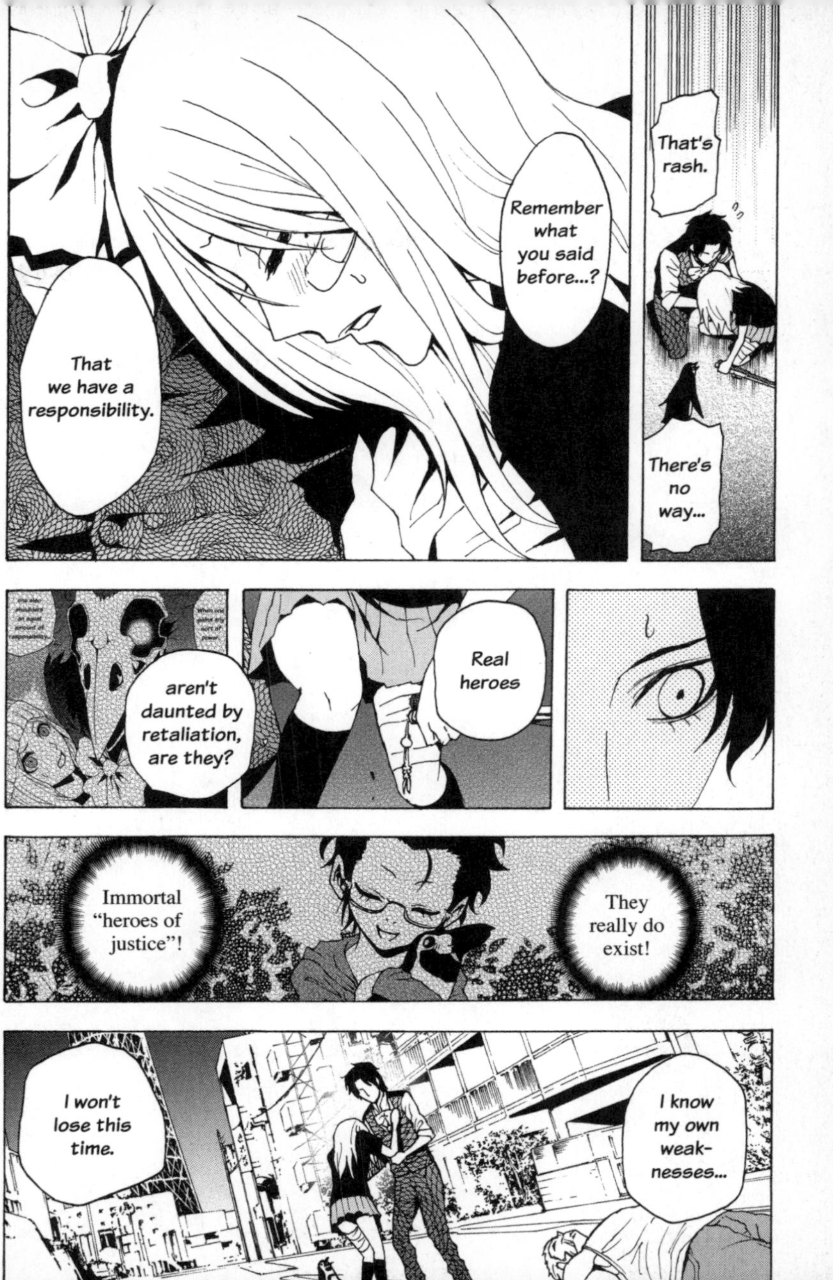
That's rash.
There's no way...
Remember what you said before...?
That we have a responsibility.
Real heroes
aren't daunted by retaliation, are they?
They really do exist!
Immortal "heroes of justice"!
I know my own weak-nesses...
I won't lose this time.

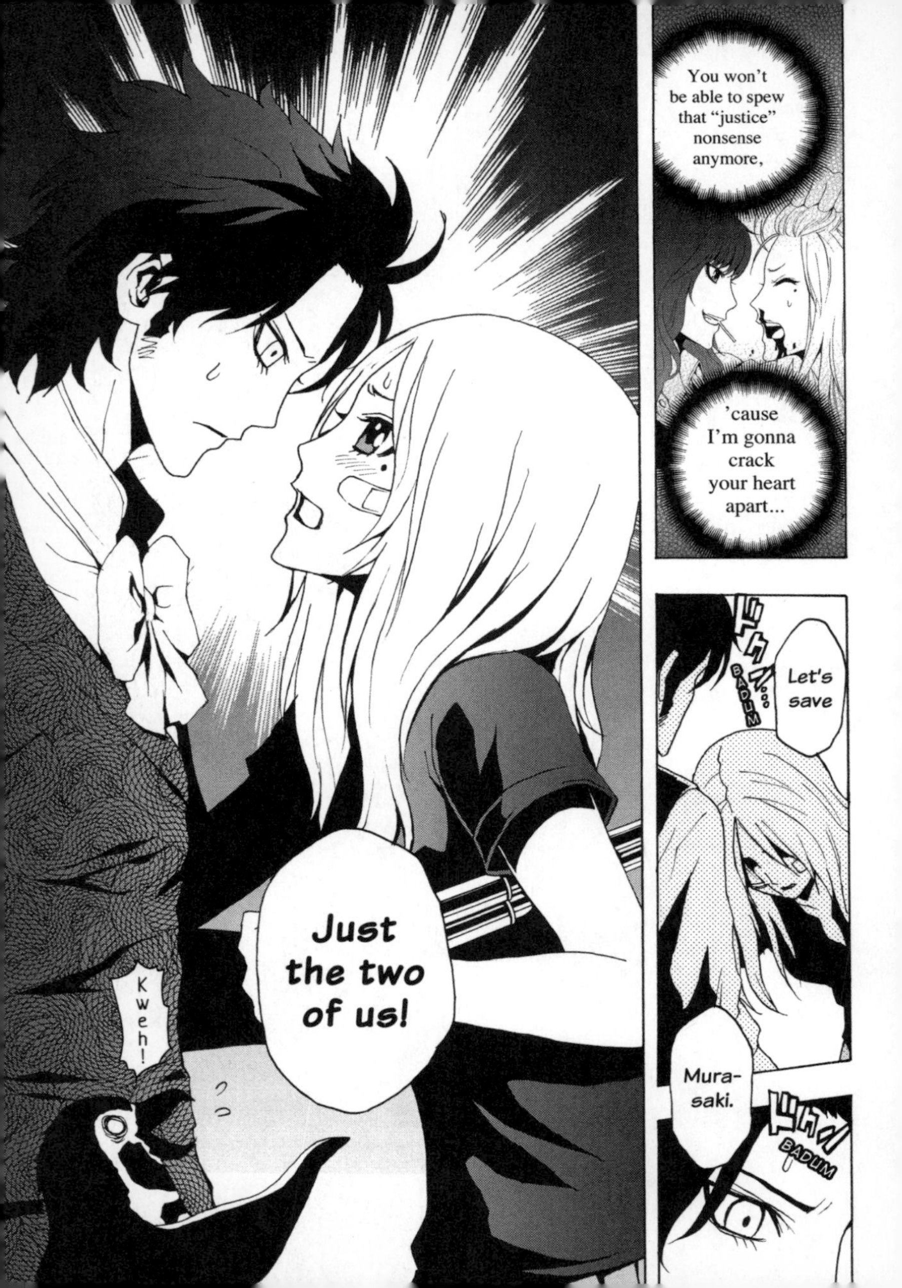
You won't be able to spew that "justice" nonsense anymore,
'cause I'm gonna crack your heart apart...
BADUM
Let's save
Mura-saki.
BADUM
Just the two of us!
Kweh!

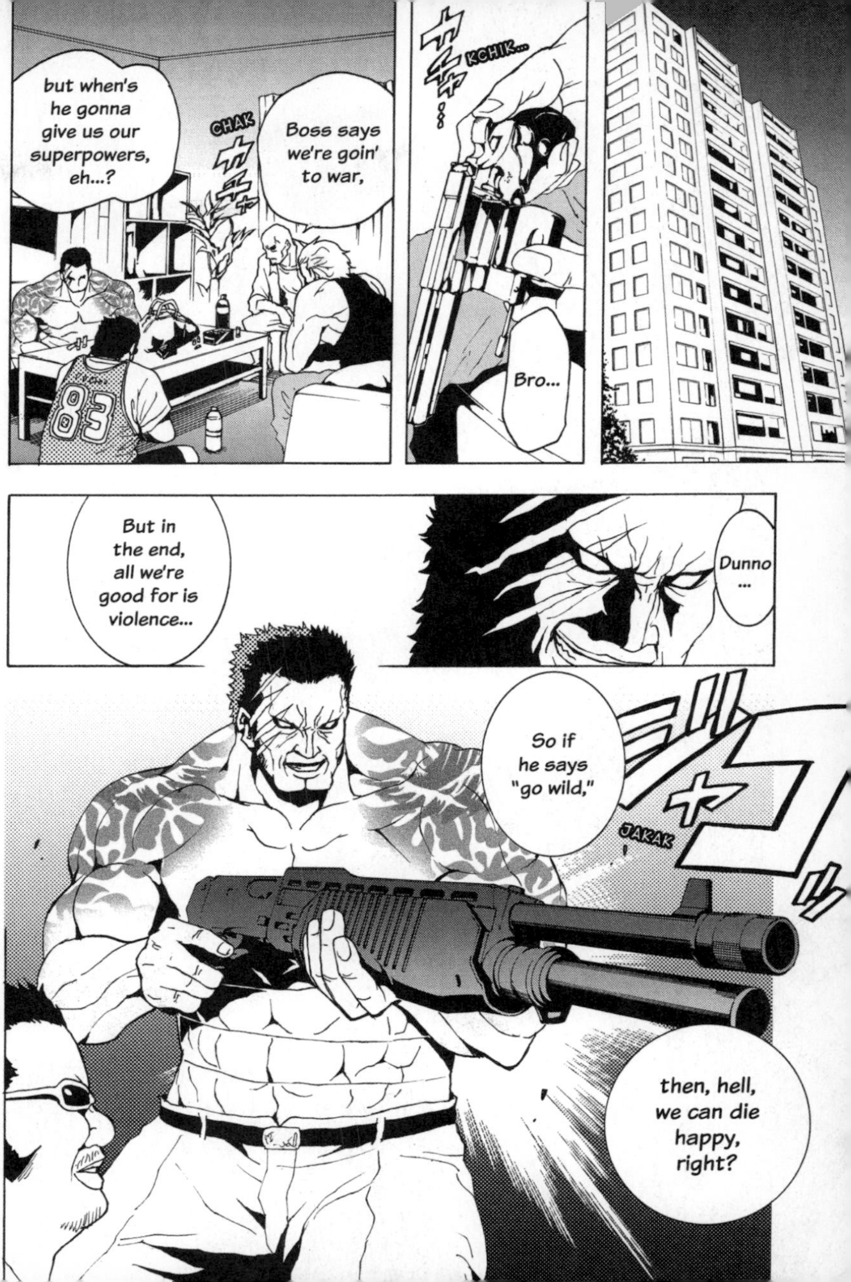
KCHIK...
Bro...
Boss says we're goin' to war,
CHAK
but when's he gonna give us our superpowers, eh...?
Dunno...
But in the end, all we're good for is violence...
JAKAK
So if he says "go wild,"
then, hell, we can die happy, right?

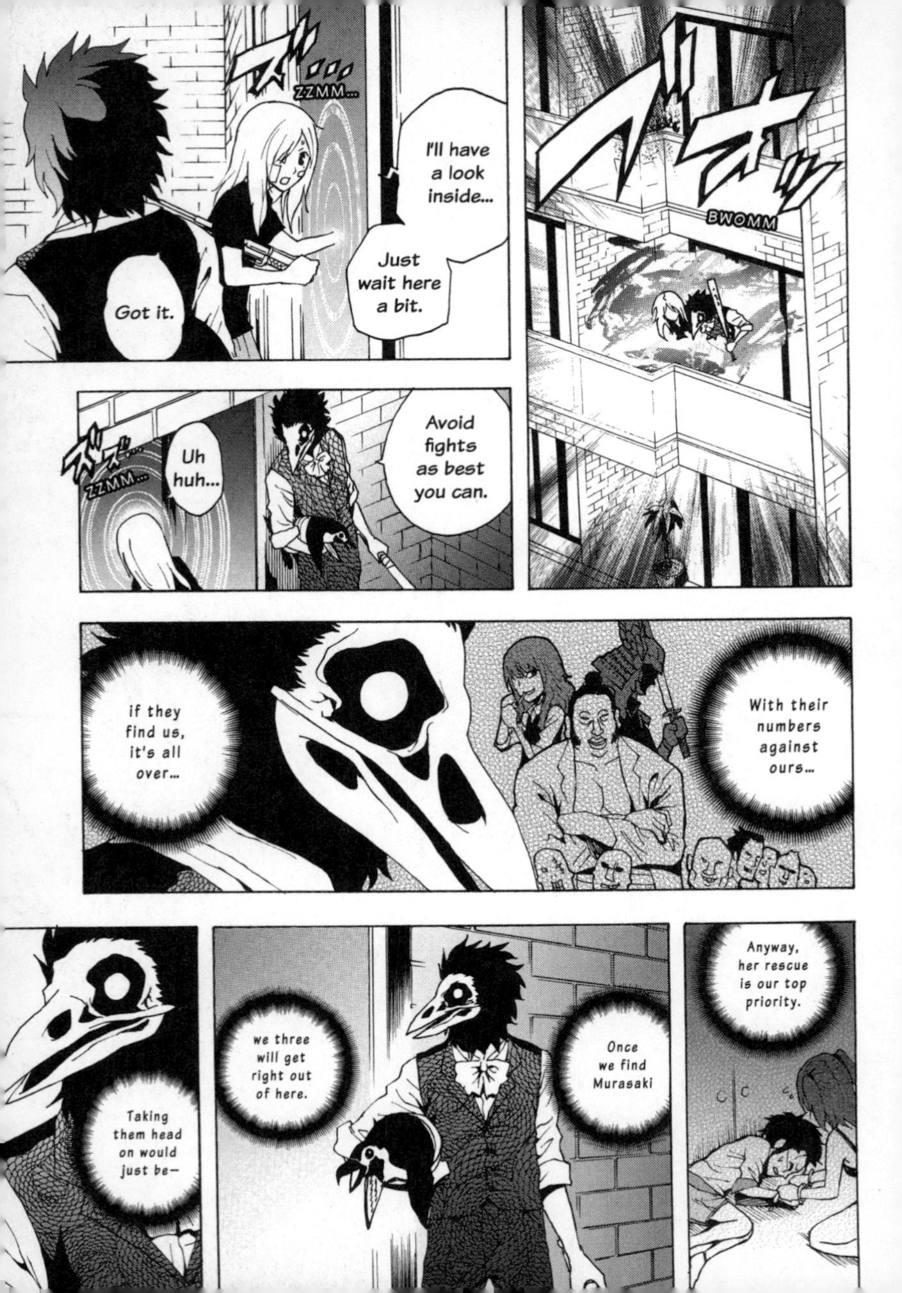
BWOMM
ZZMM...
I'll have a look inside...
Just wait here a bit.
Got it.
Avoid fights as best you can.
Uh huh...
ZZMM...
With their numbers against ours...
if they find us, it's all over...
Anyway, her rescue is our top priority.
Once we find Murasaki
we three will get right out of here.
Taking them head on would just be—

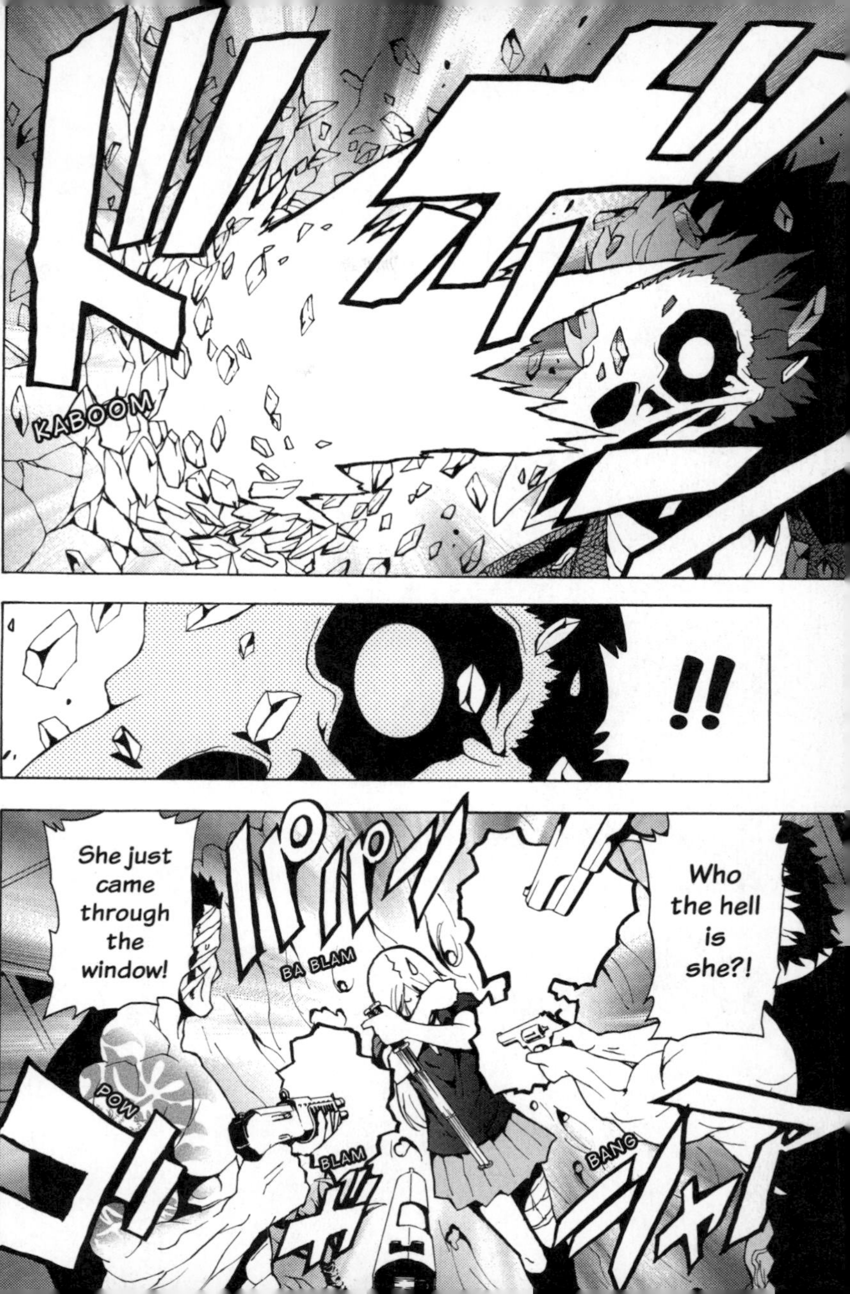
KABOOM
!!
Who the hell is she?!
She just came through the window!
BA BLAM
BANG
BLAM
POW

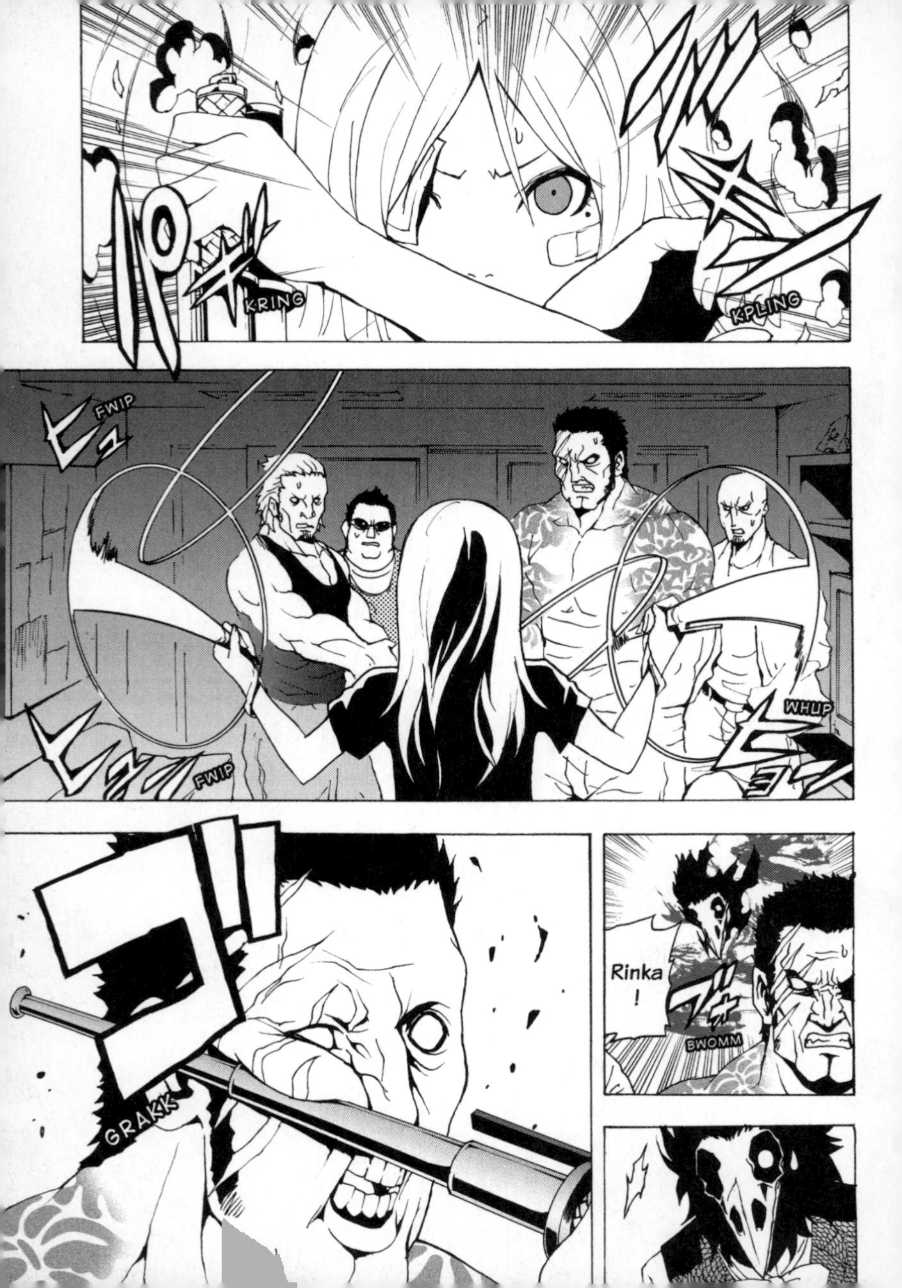
KPLING
KRING
WHUP
FWIP
FWIP
Rinka!
BWOMM
GRAKK

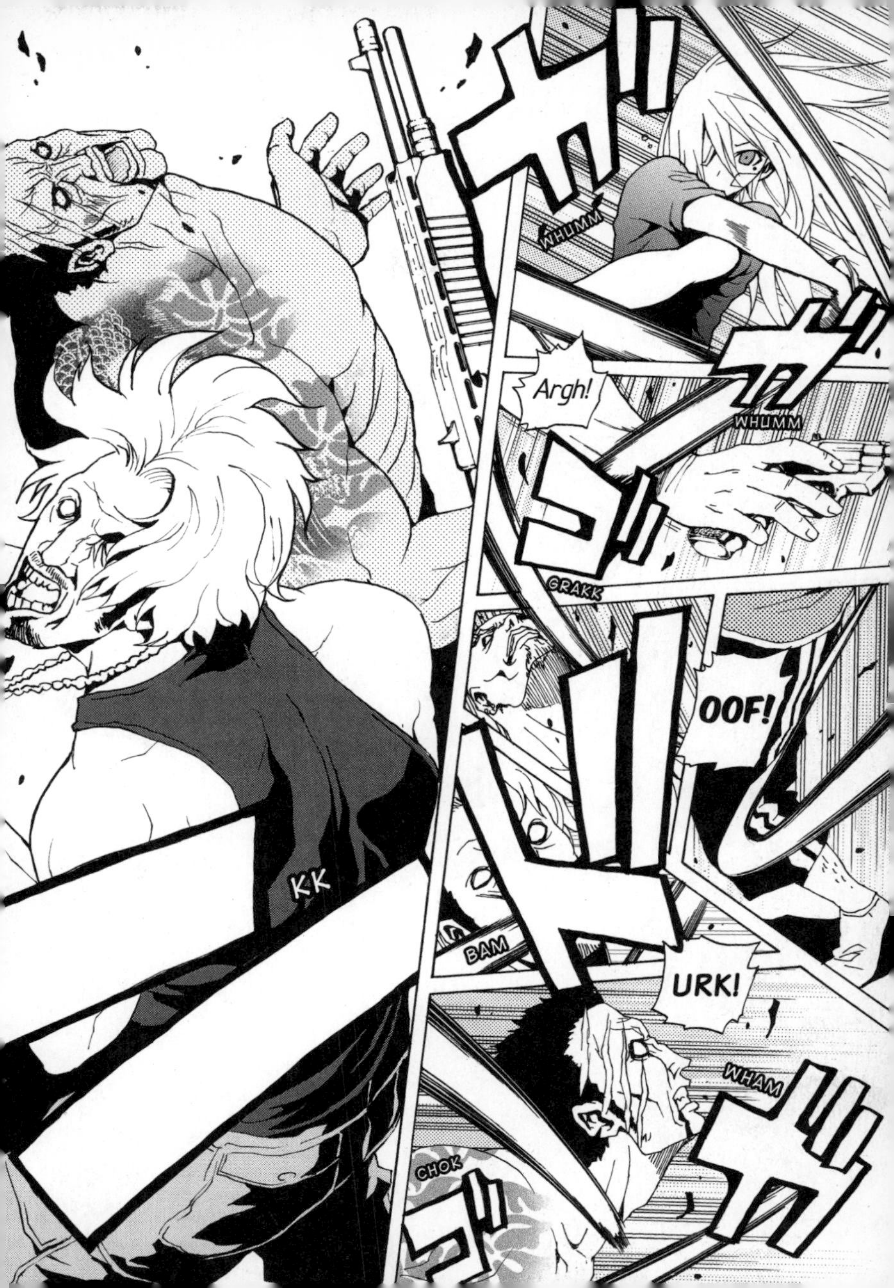
WHUMM
Argh!
WHUMM
GRAKK
OOF!
BAM
URK!
WHAM
CHOK
KK

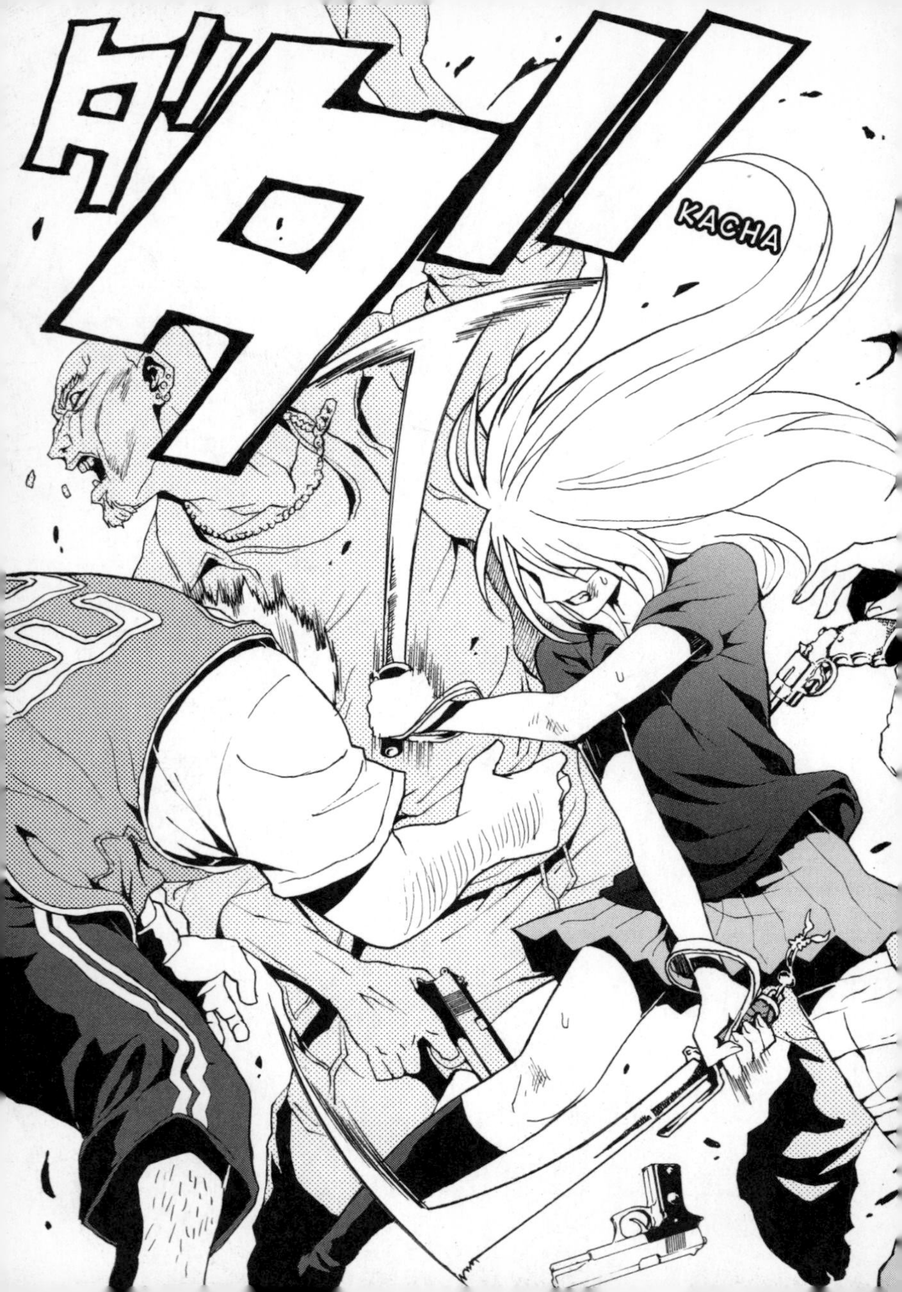
KACHA

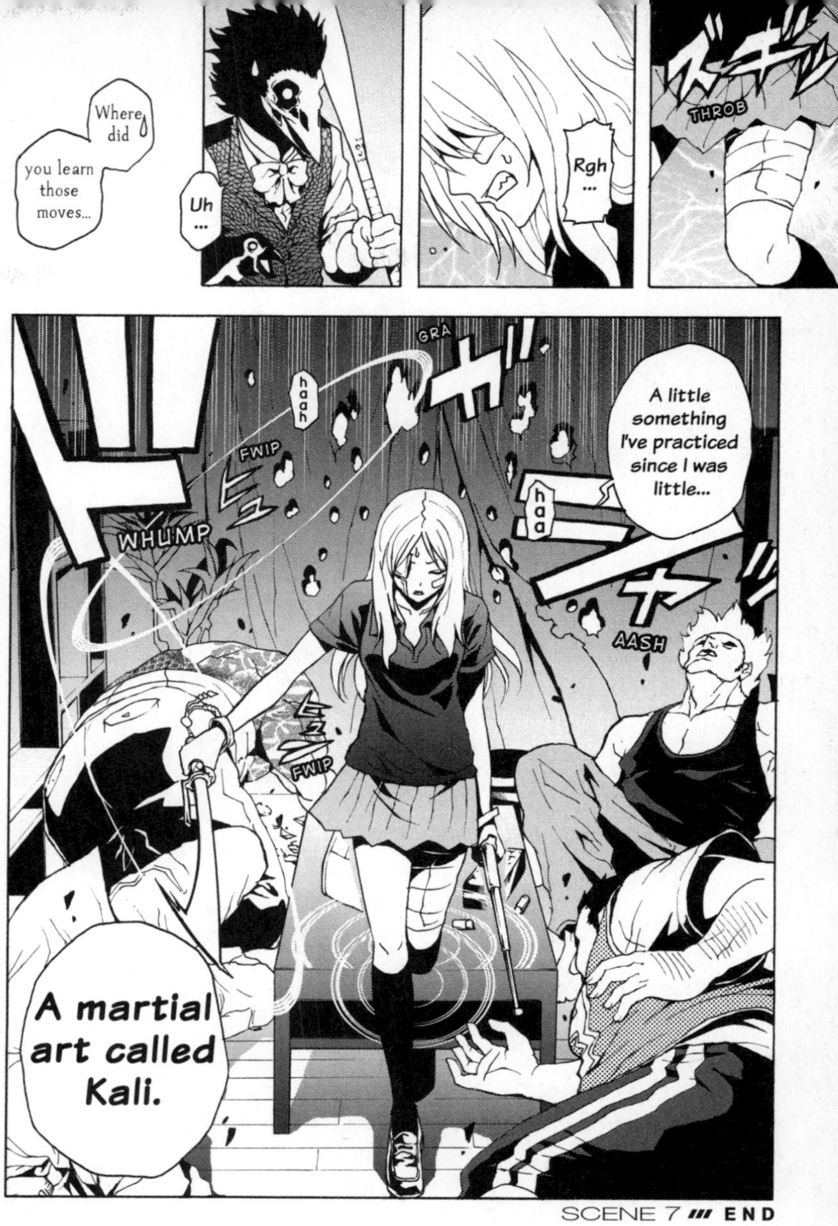
THROB
Rgh ...
Uh ...
Where did you learn those moves...
A little something I've practiced since I was little...
haa
AASH
GRA
haah
FWIP
WHUMP
FWIP
A martial art called Kali.

SCENE 7 /// END

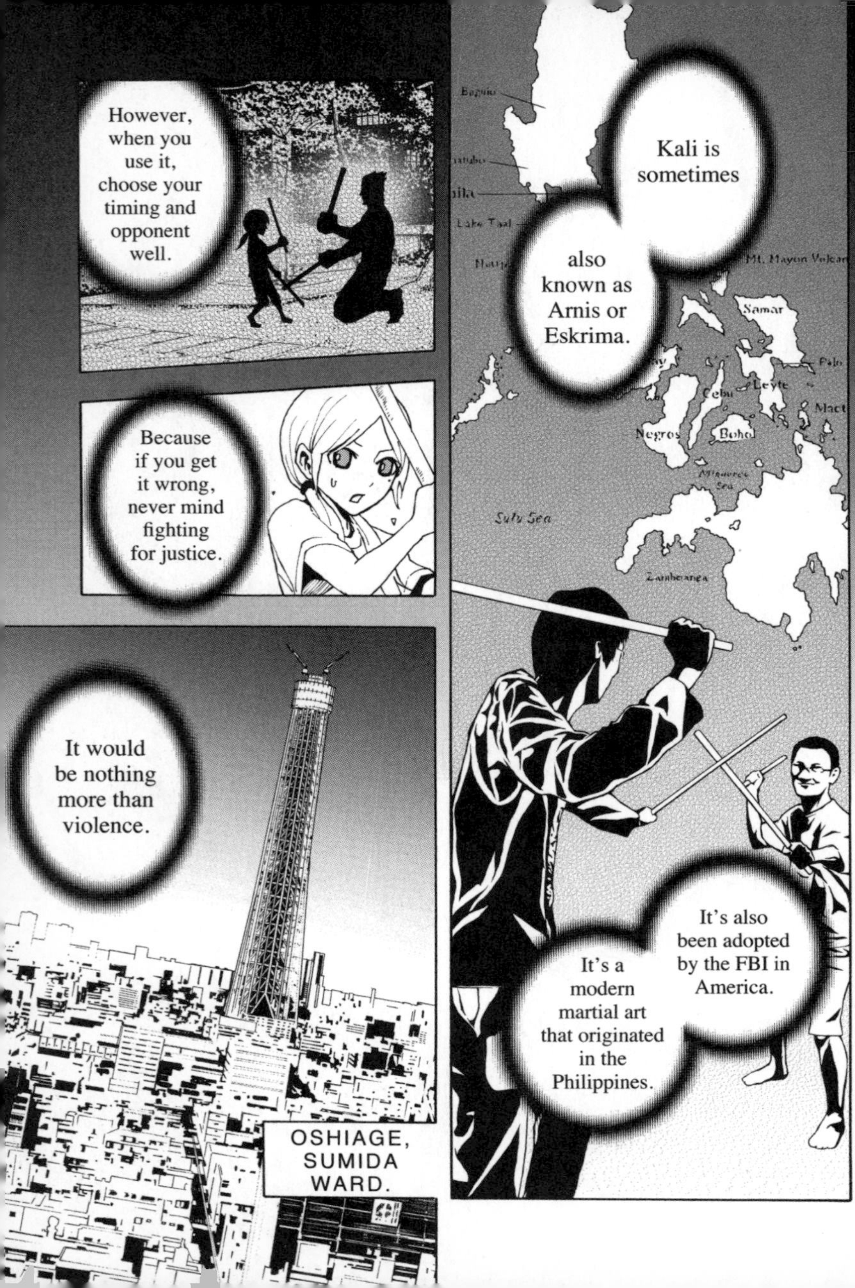

Kali is sometimes
also known as Arnis or Eskrima.
Lake Taal
Mt. Mayon Volcan
Samar
Palo
Leyte
Cebu
Negros
Bohol
Sulu Sea
It's also been adopted by the FBI in America.
It's a modern martial art that originated in the Philippines.
However, when you use it, choose your timing and opponent well.
Because if you get it wrong, never mind fighting for justice.
It would be nothing more than violence.
OSHIAGE, SUMIDA WARD.

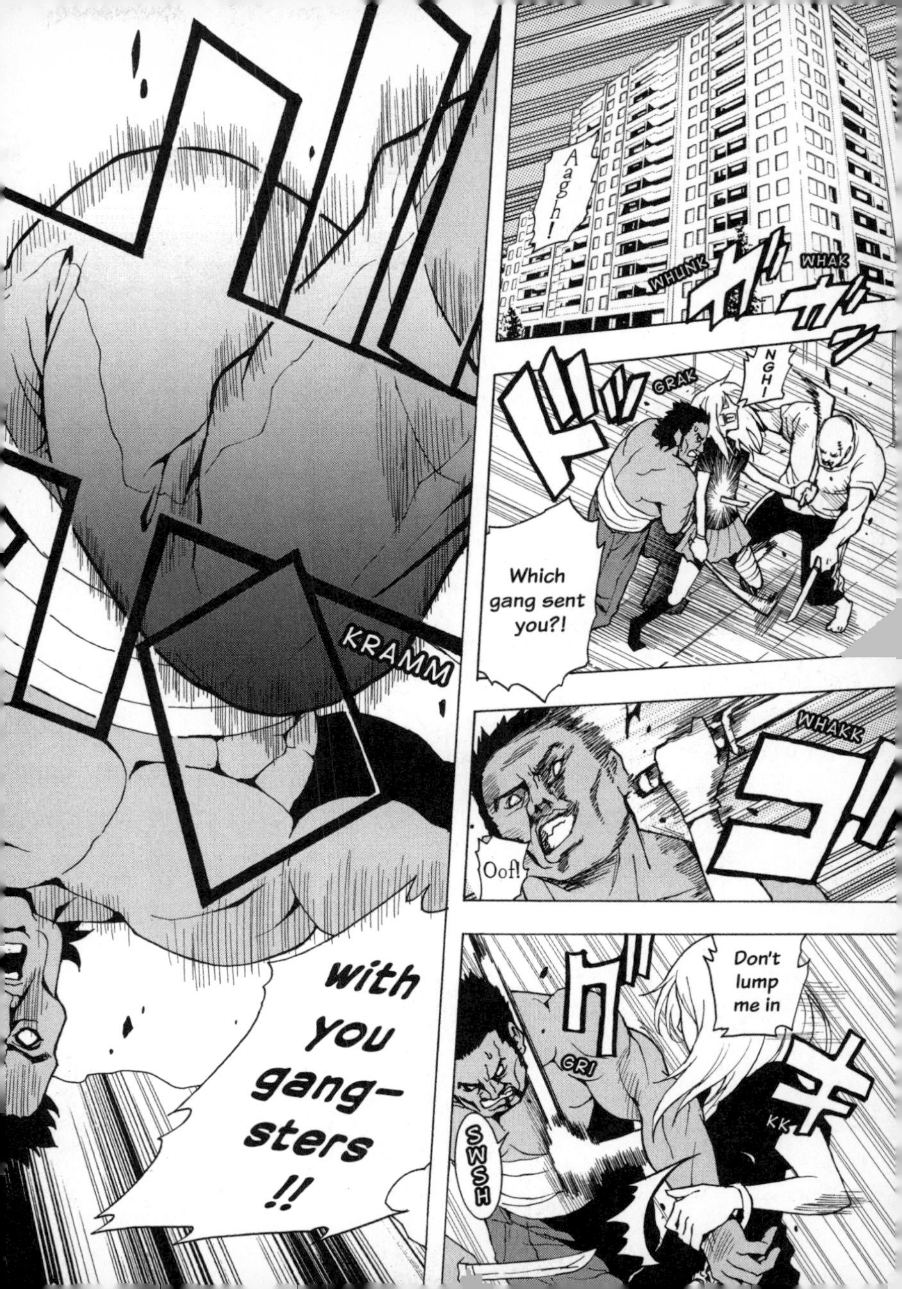
Aagh!
WHAK
WHUNK
NGH!
GRAK
Which gang sent you?!
WHAKK
Oof!
Don't lump me in
GRI
KK
SWSH
KRAMM
with you gang-sters!!

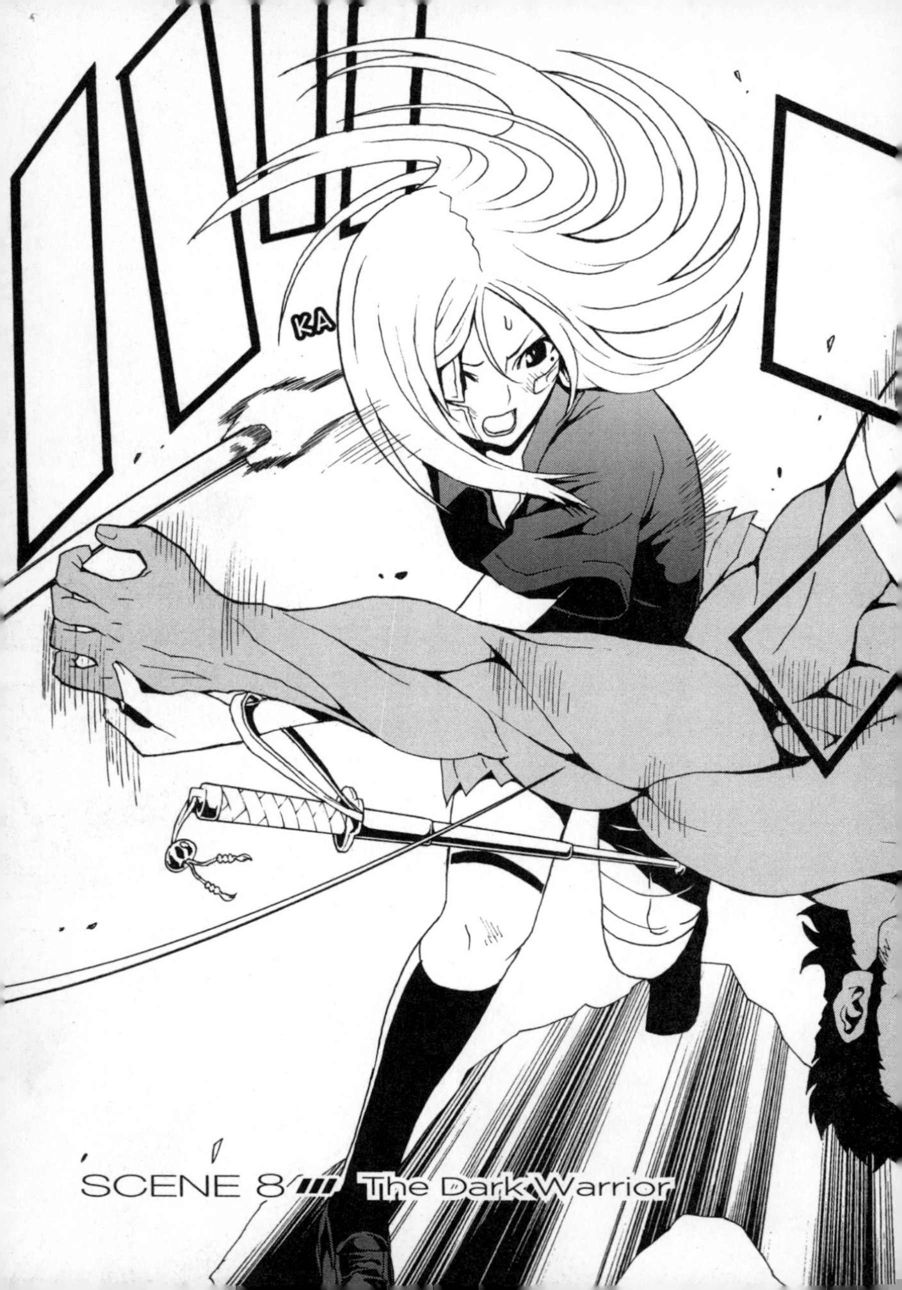
KA

SCENE 8 The Dark Warrior

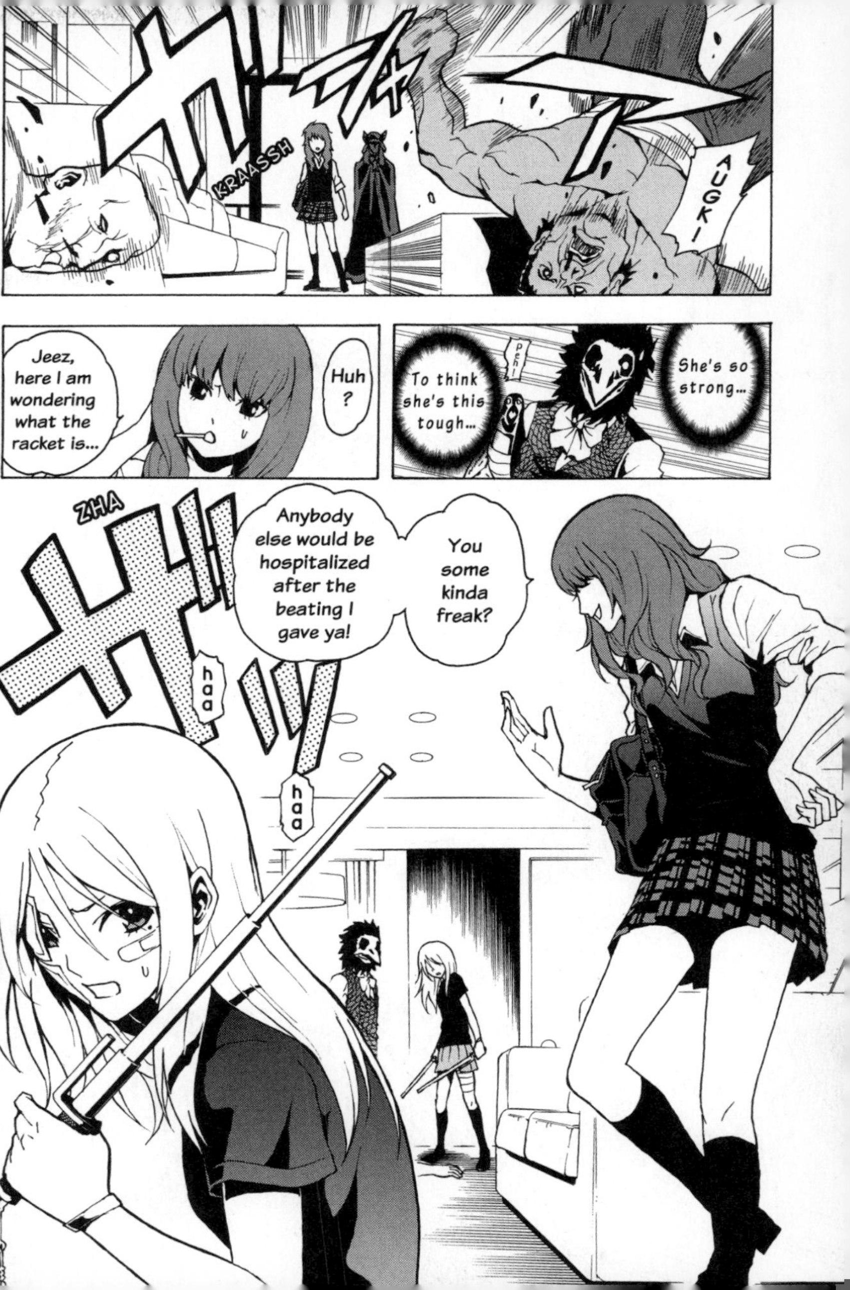
AUGKI
KRAASSH
She's so strong...
Peh!
To think she's this tough...
Huh?
Jeez, here I am wondering what the racket is...
You some kinda freak?
Anybody else would be hospitalized after the beating I gave ya!
ZHA
haa
haa

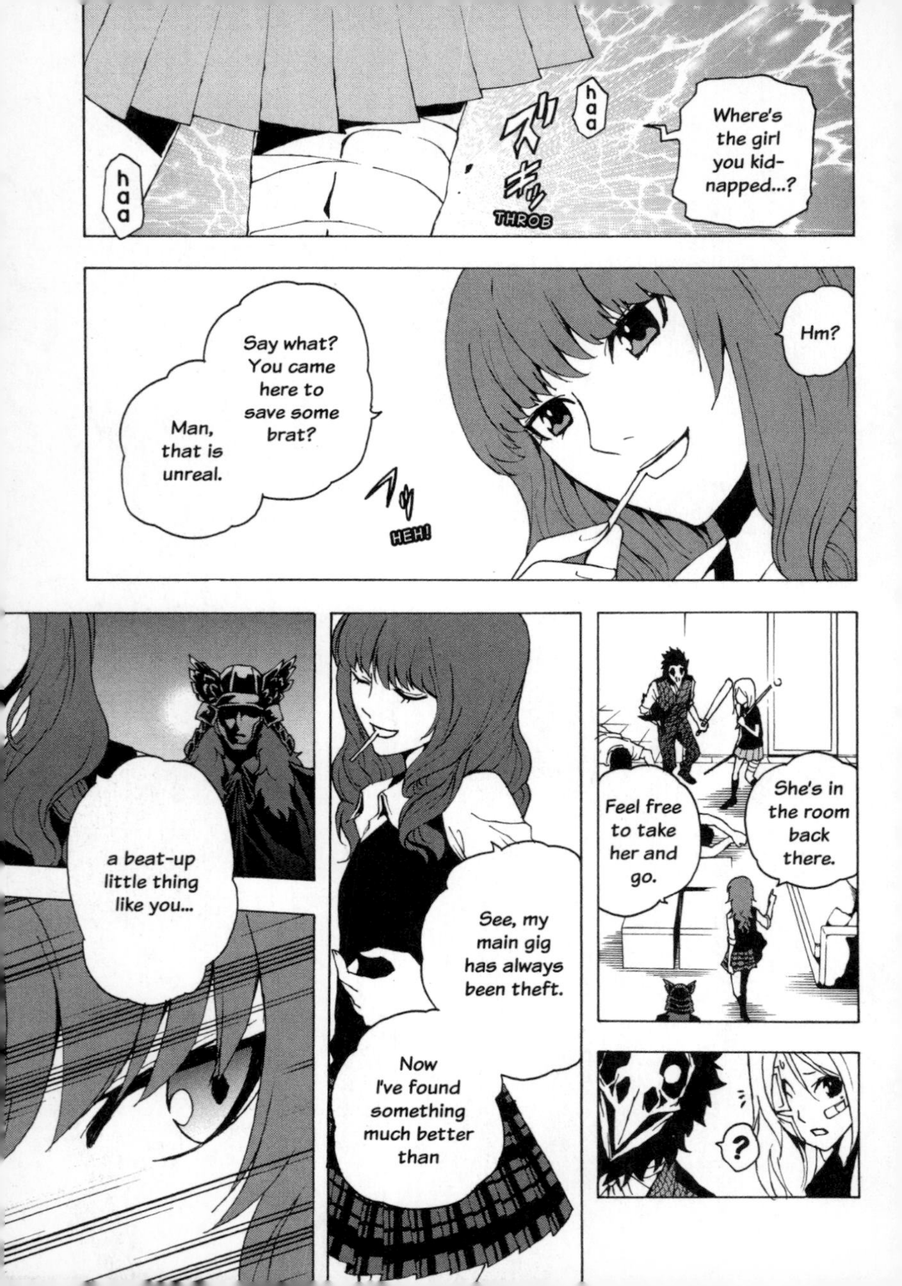
Where's the girl you kid-napped...?
THROB
haa
haa
Hm?
Say what? You came here to save some brat?
Man, that is unreal.
HEH!
She's in the room back there.
Feel free to take her and go.
?
See, my main gig has always been theft.
Now I've found something much better than
a beat-up little thing like you...

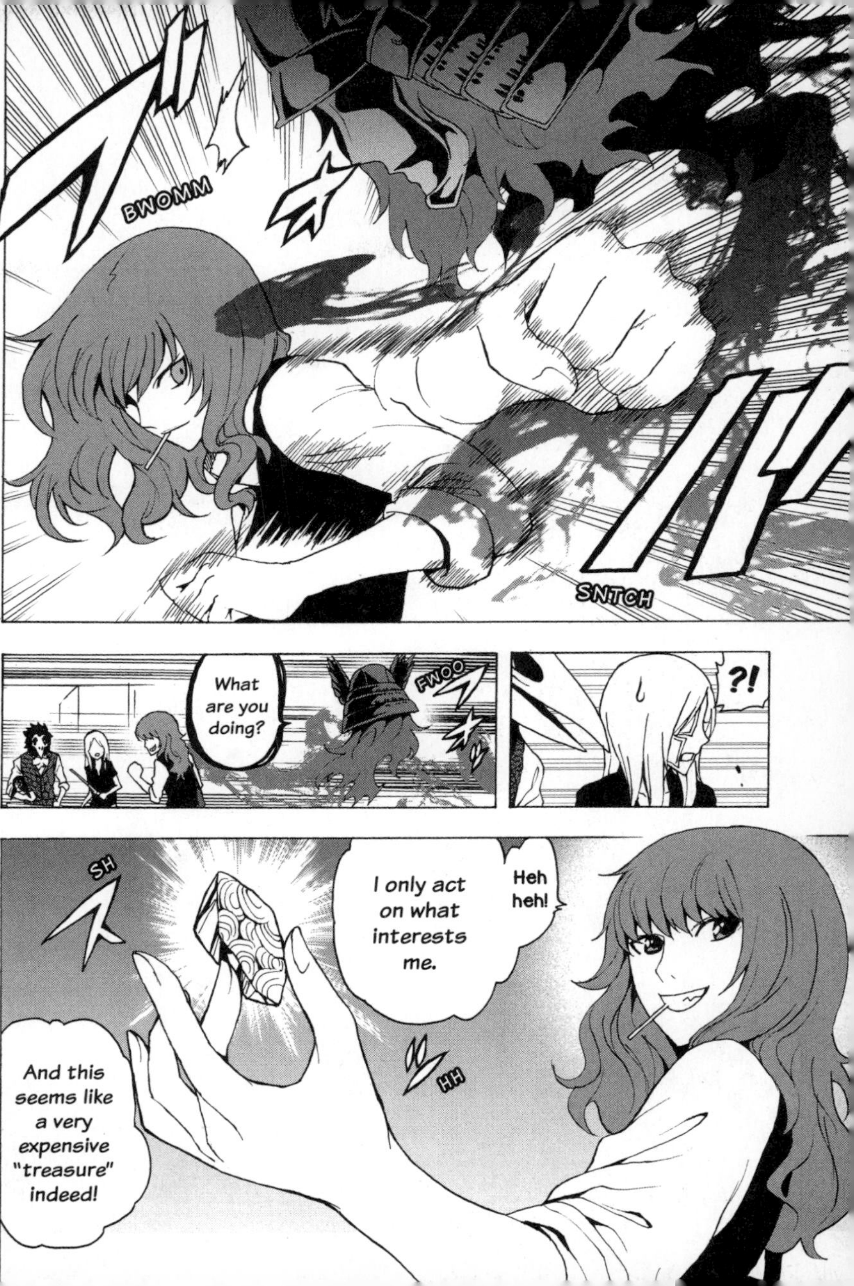
BWOMM
SNTCH
?!
FWOO
What are you doing?
Heh heh!
I only act on what interests me.
SH
HH
And this seems like a very expensive "treasure" indeed!

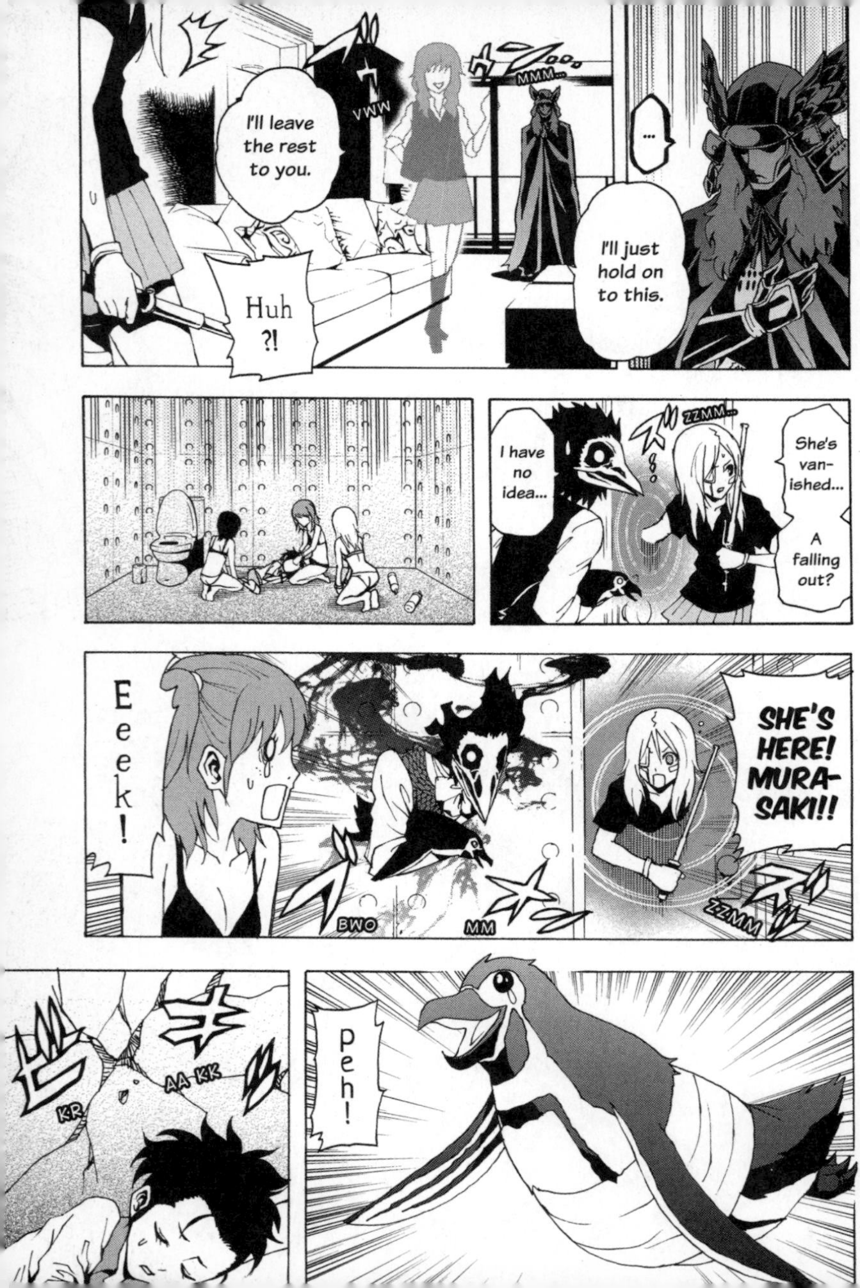
…
MMM...
I'll just hold on to this.
VWW
I'll leave the rest to you.
Huh ?!
She's van-ished...
A falling out?
ZZMM...
I have no idea...
SHE'S HERE! MURA-SAKI!!
ZZMM
BWO MM
Eeek!
peh!
AA KK
KR

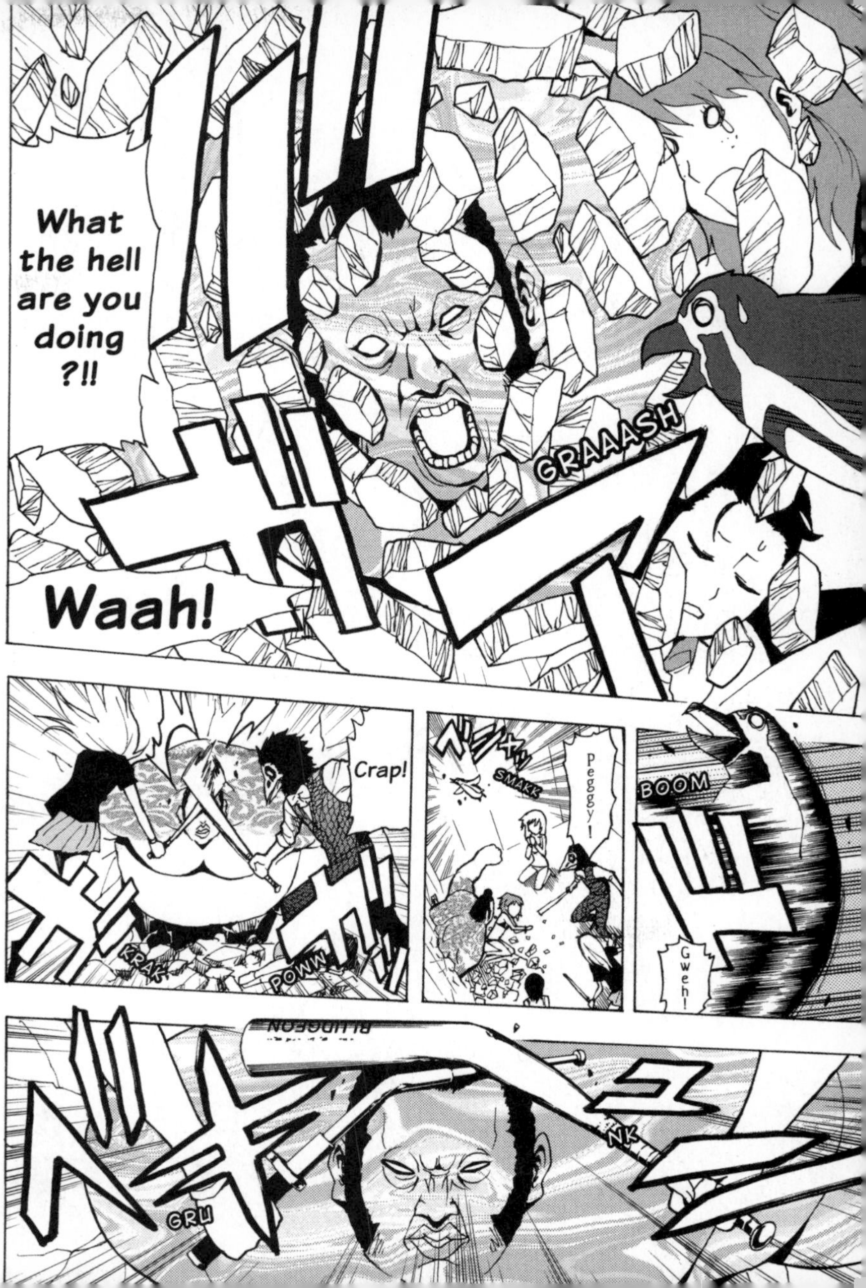
What the hell are you doing?!!
GRAAASH
Waah!
BOOM
Gweh!
SMAKK
Peggy!
Crap!
KRAK
POWW
BLUDGEON
NK
GRU

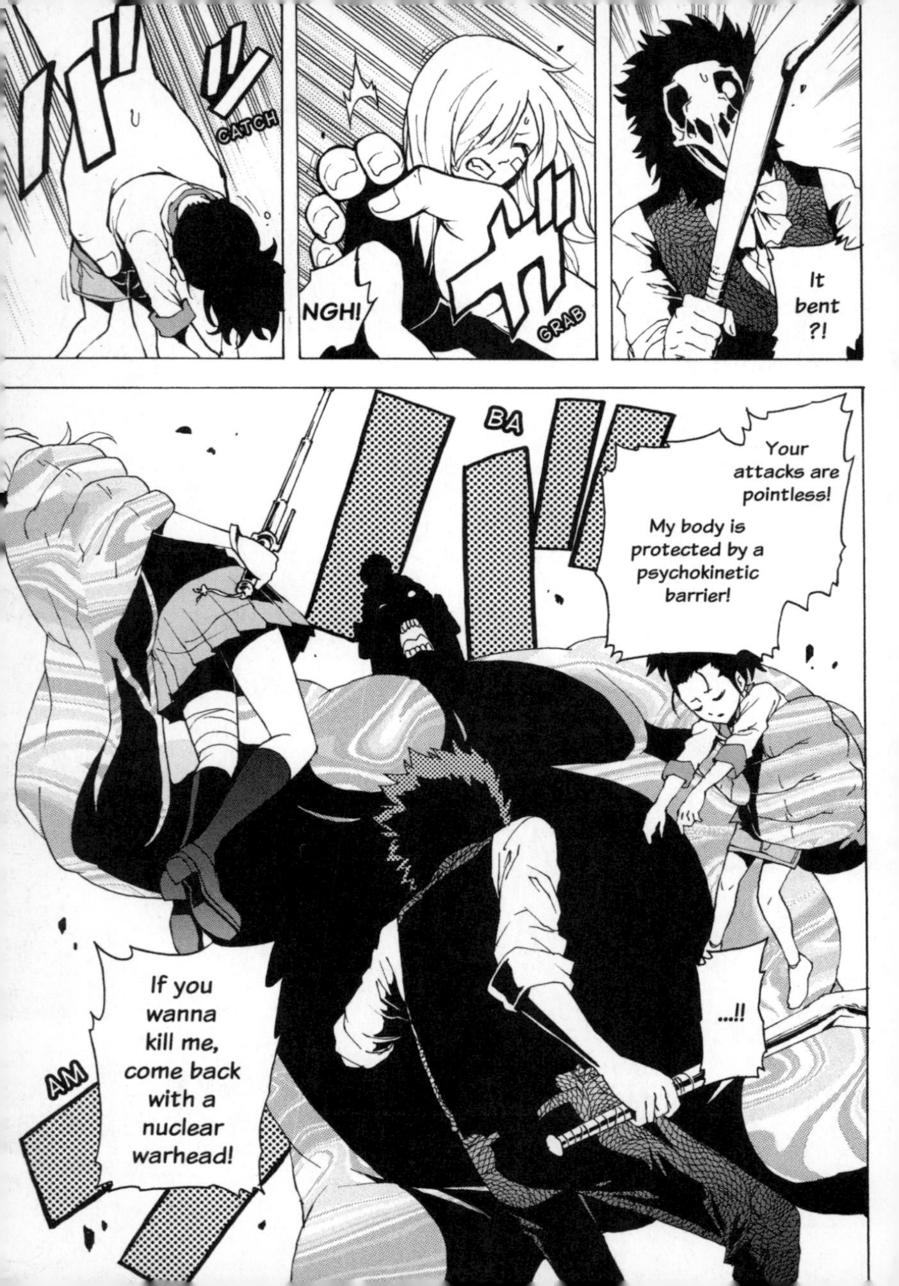
It bent ?!
NGH!
GRAB
CATCH
BA
Your attacks are pointless!
My body is protected by a psychokinetic barrier!
...!!
If you wanna kill me, come back with a nuclear warhead!
AM

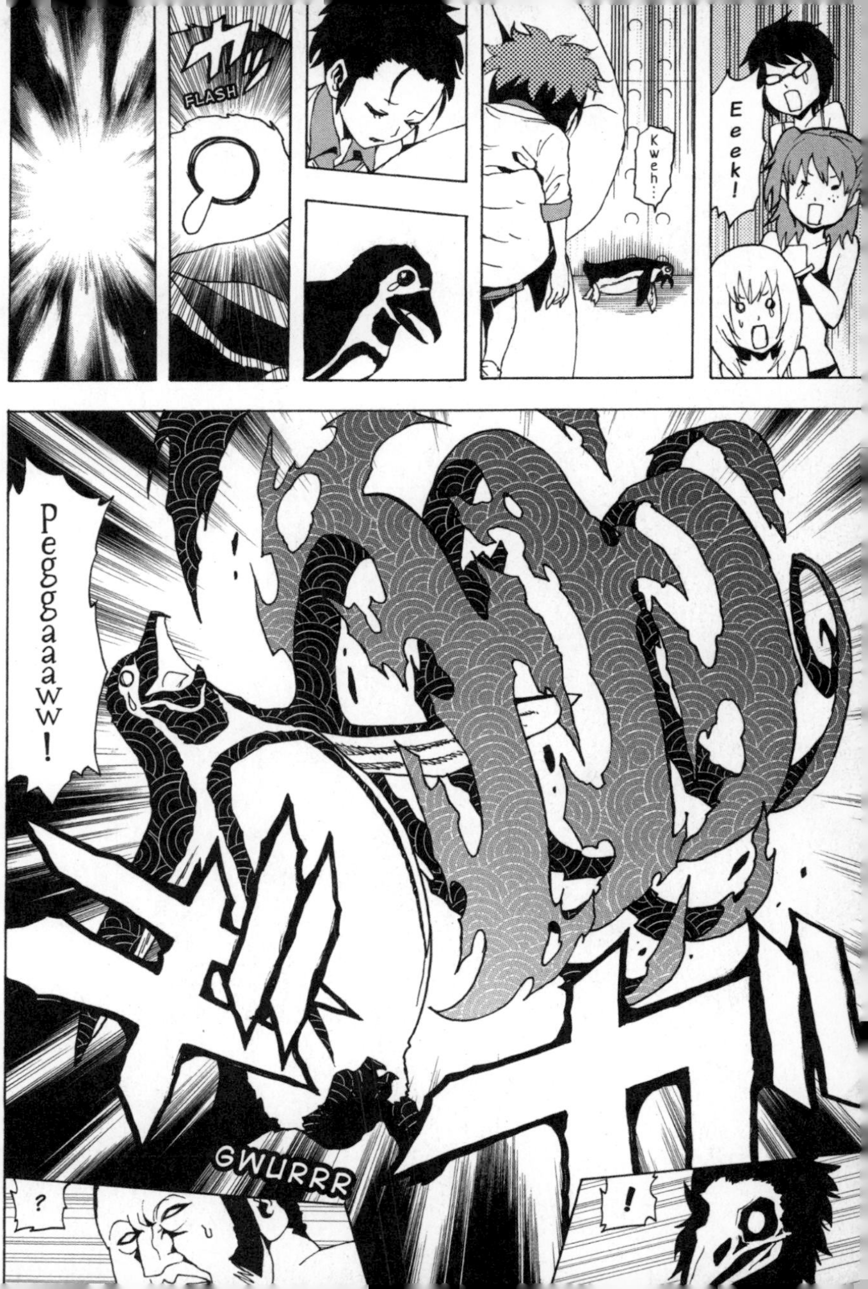
Eeek!
Kweh...
FLASH
Pegggaaaww!
GWURRR
!
?

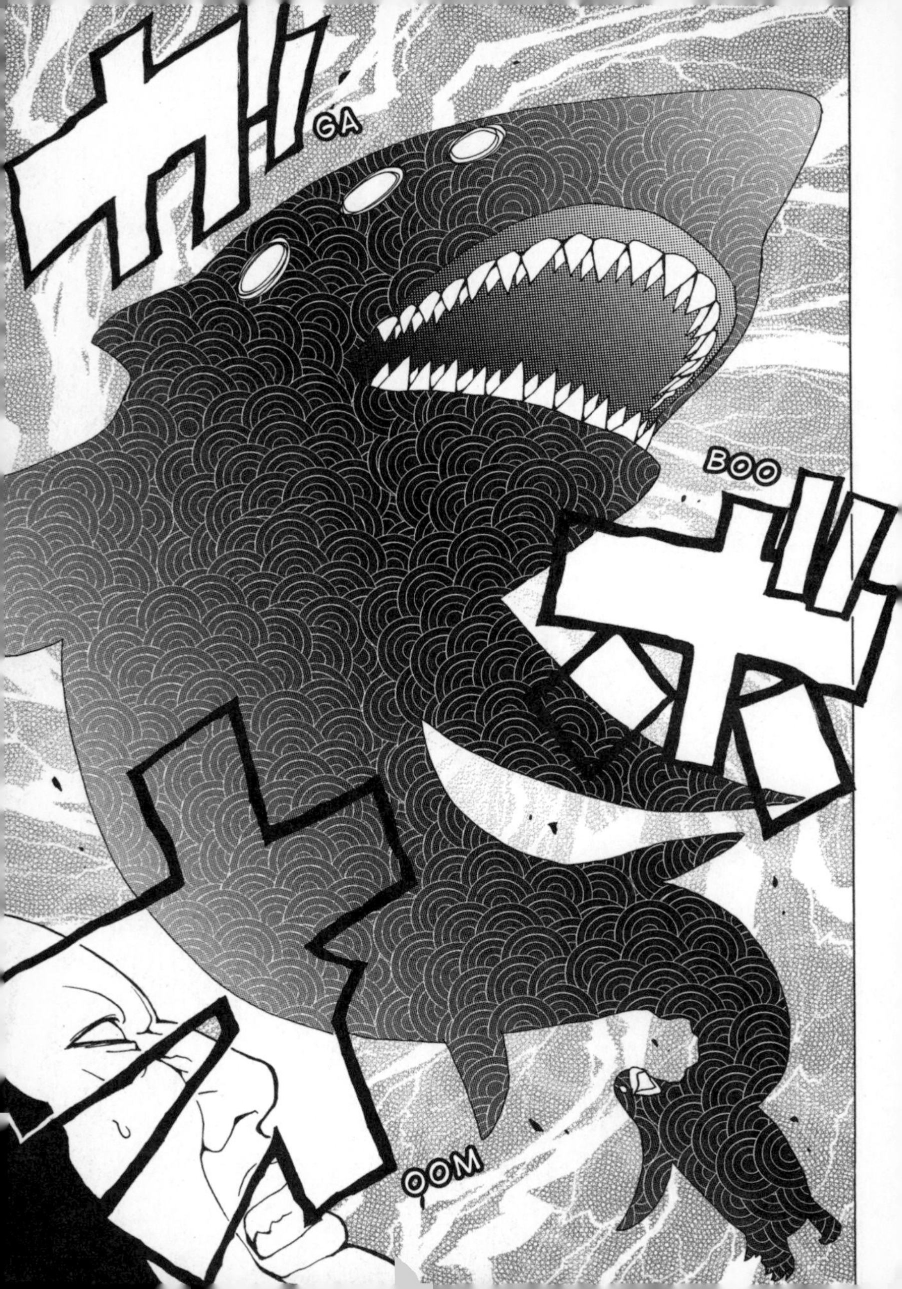
GA
BOO
OOM

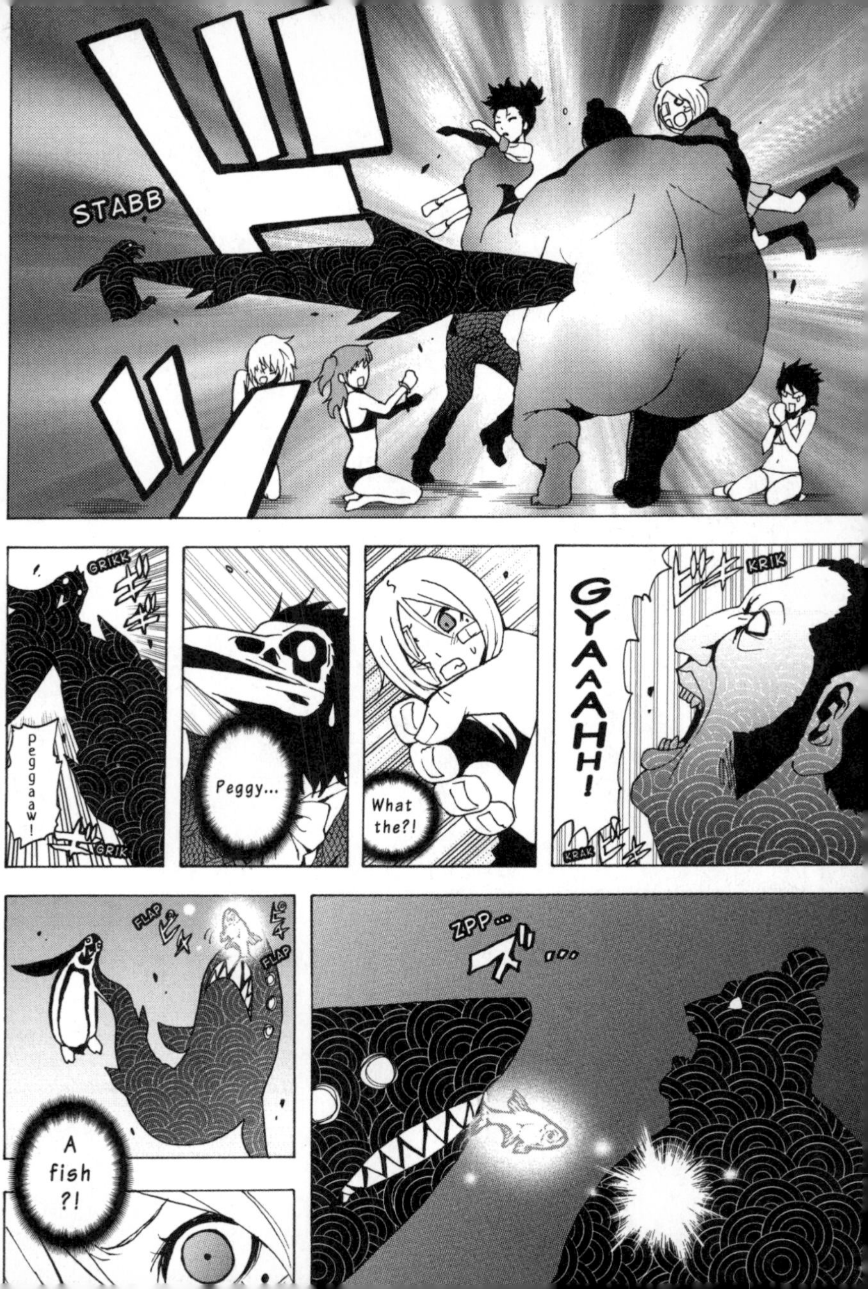
STABB
KRIK
GYAAAHH!
KRAK
What the?!
Peggy...
GRIKK
Peggaaaw!
GRIK
ZPP...
FLAP
FLAP
A fish ?!

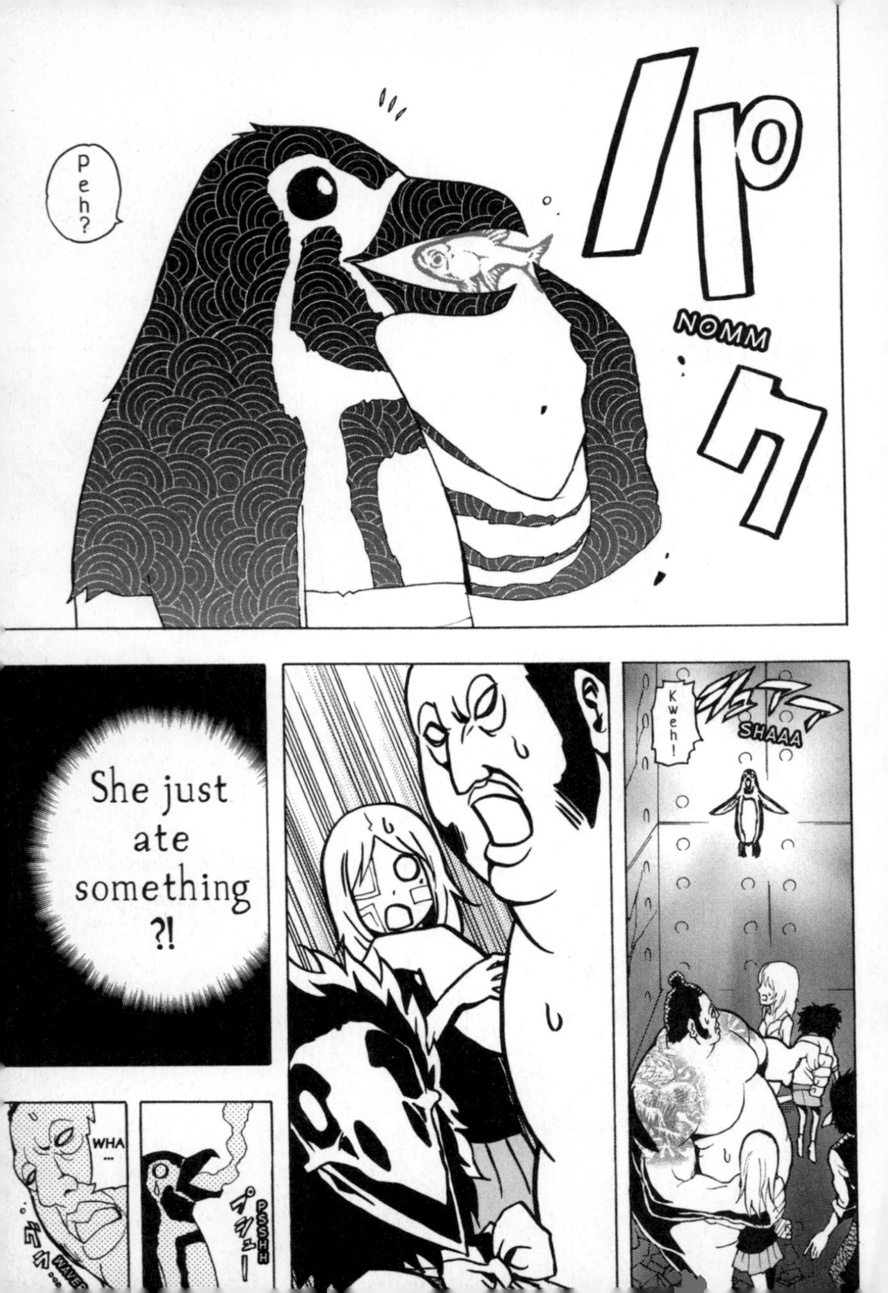
Peh?
パク
NOMM
Kweh!
SHAAA
She just ate something?!
PSSHH
WHA...
WAVE

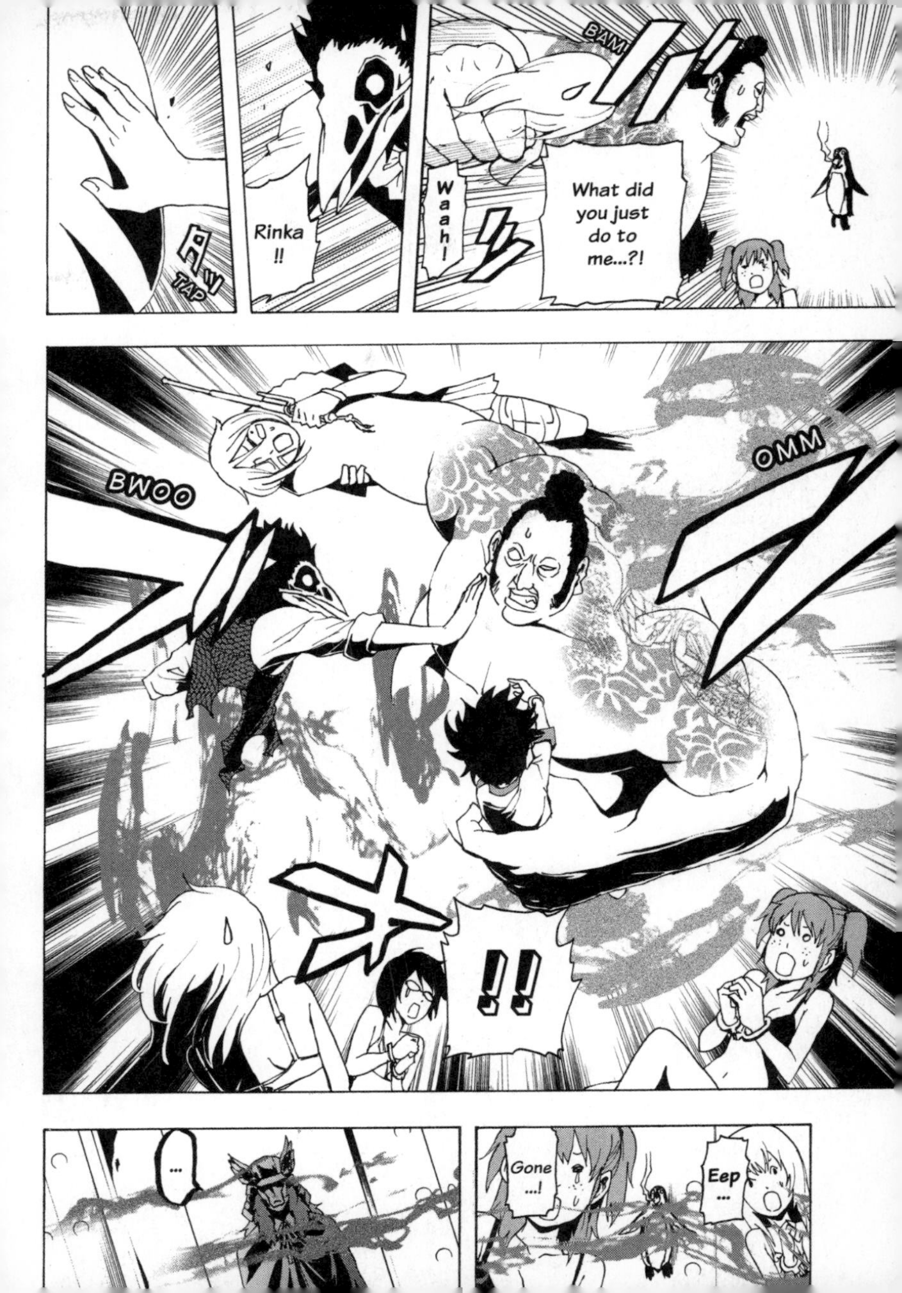
BAM
What did you just do to me...?!
Waah!
Rinka !!
TAP
BWOO
OMM
!!
Eep ...
Gone ...!
...

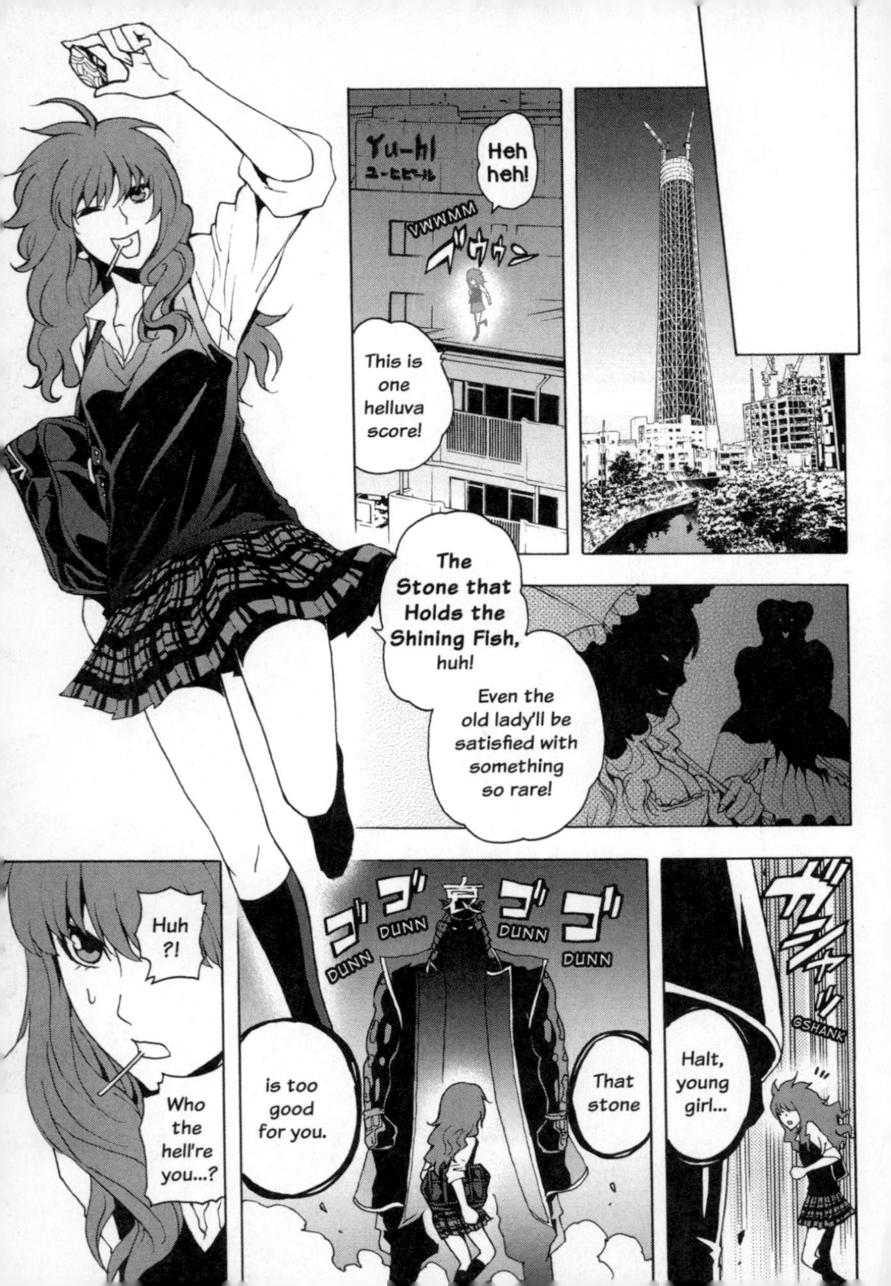
Yu-hi
ユーヒビール
Heh heh!
VWWMM
ブゥゥン
This is one helluva score!
The Stone that Holds the Shining Fish, huh!
Even the old lady'll be satisfied with something so rare!
GSHANK
Halt, young girl...
ゴゴゴゴ
DUNN DUNN DUNN DUNN
That stone
is too good for you.
Huh?!
Who the hell're you...?

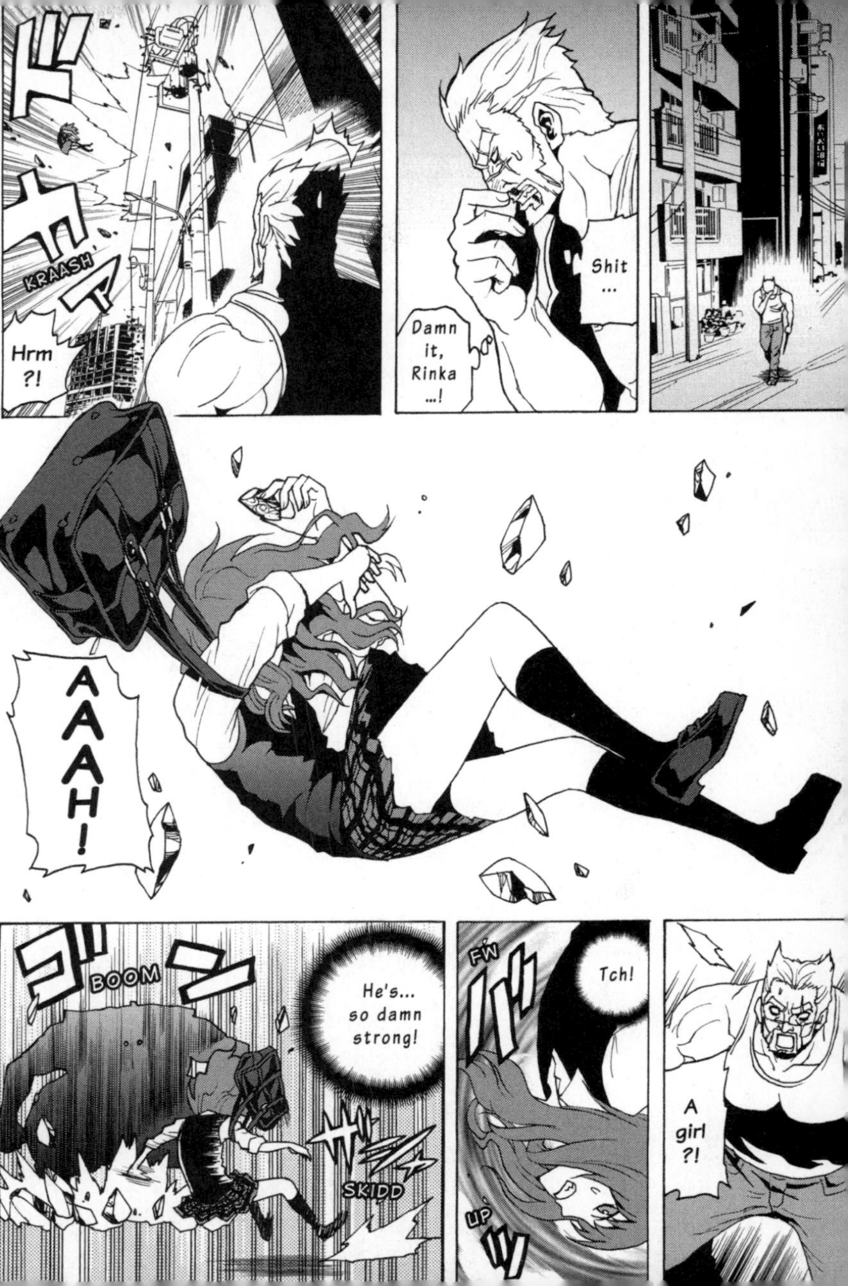
Shit ...
Damn it, Rinka ...!
KRAASH
Hrm ?!
AAAAH!
A girl ?!
Tch!
FW
UP
BOOM
He's... so damn strong!
SKIDD

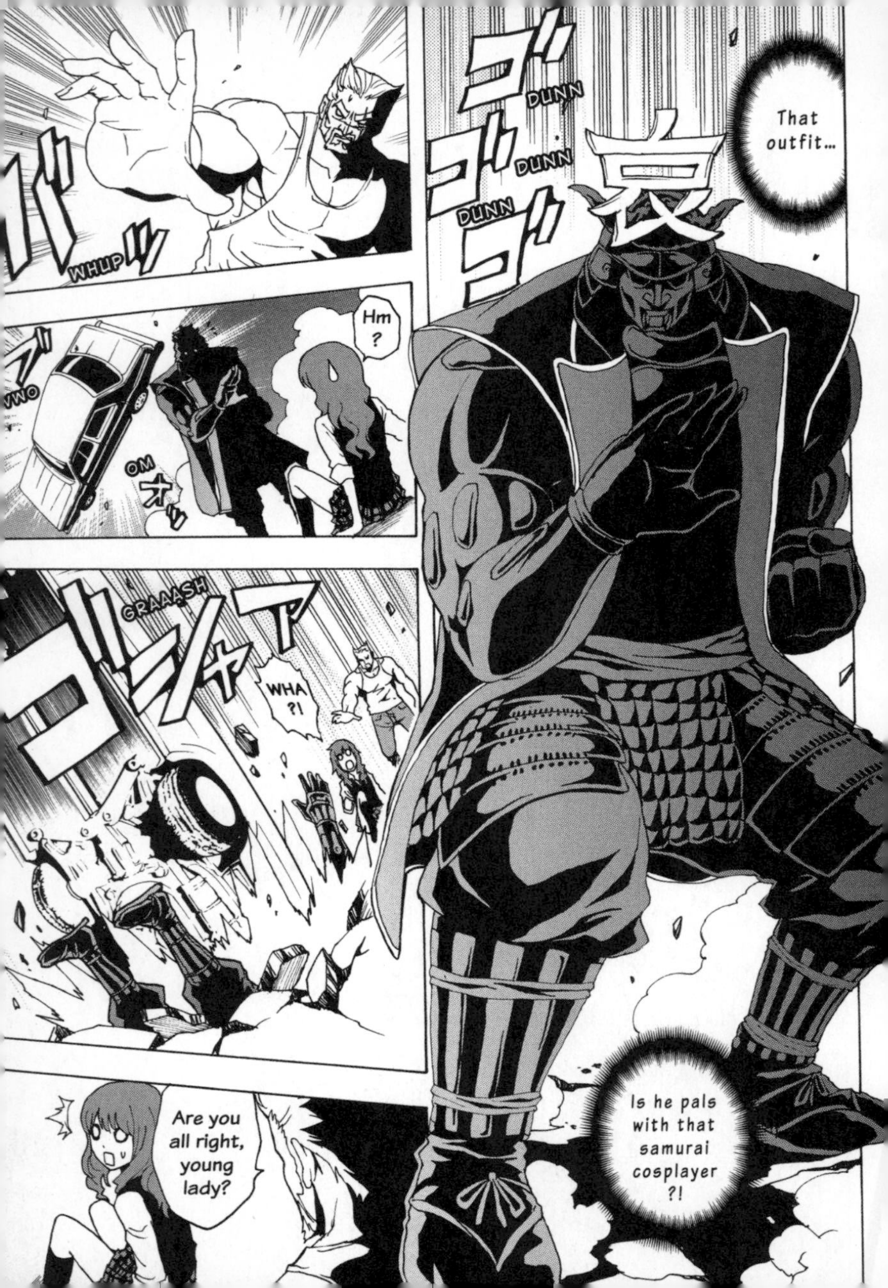
DUNN
DUNN
DUNN
That outfit...
Is he pals with that samurai cosplayer?!
WHUP
Hm?
VVNO
OM
GRAAASH
WHA?!
Are you all right, young lady?

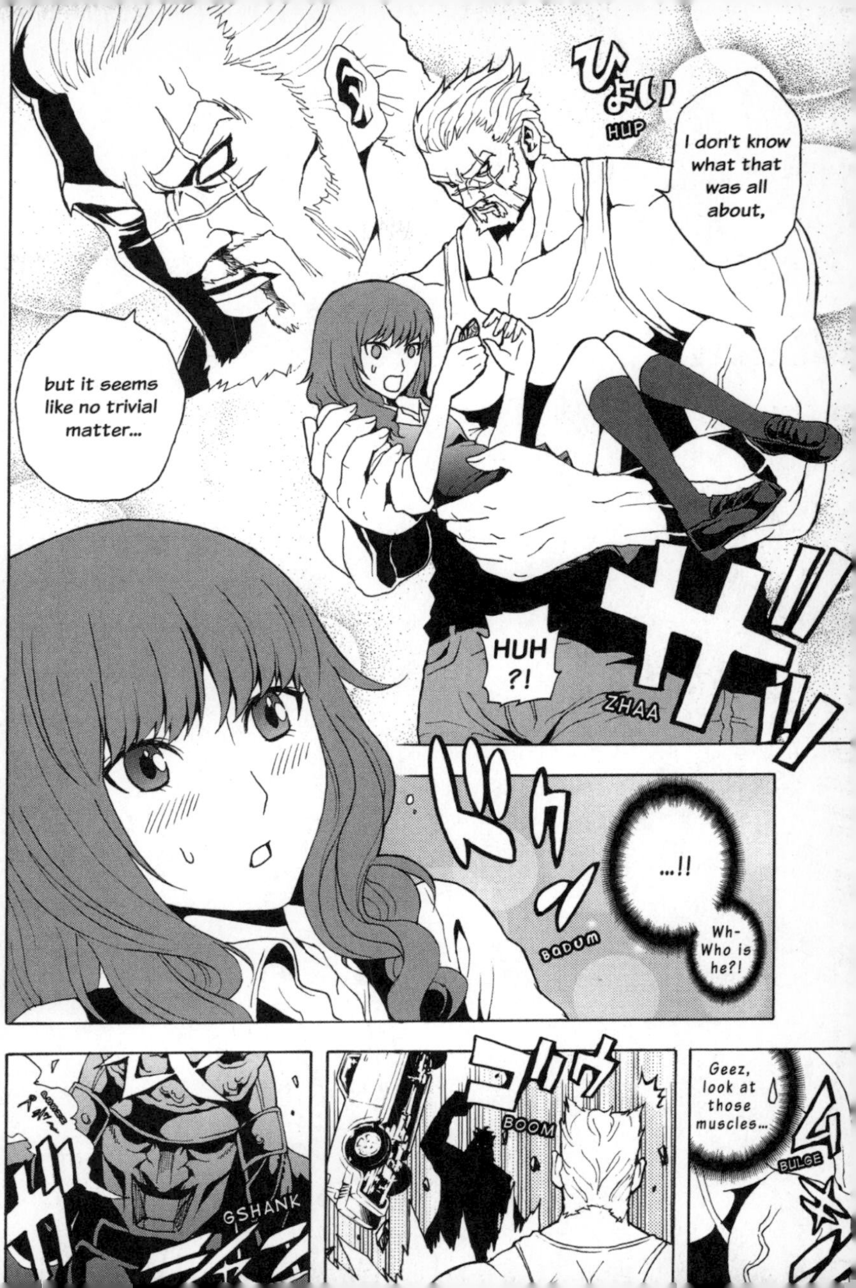

ひょい
HUP
I don't know what that was all about,
but it seems like no trivial matter...
HUH ?!
ZHAA
BADUM
...!!
Wh- Who is he?!
Geez, look at those muscles...
BULGE
BOOM
GSHANK

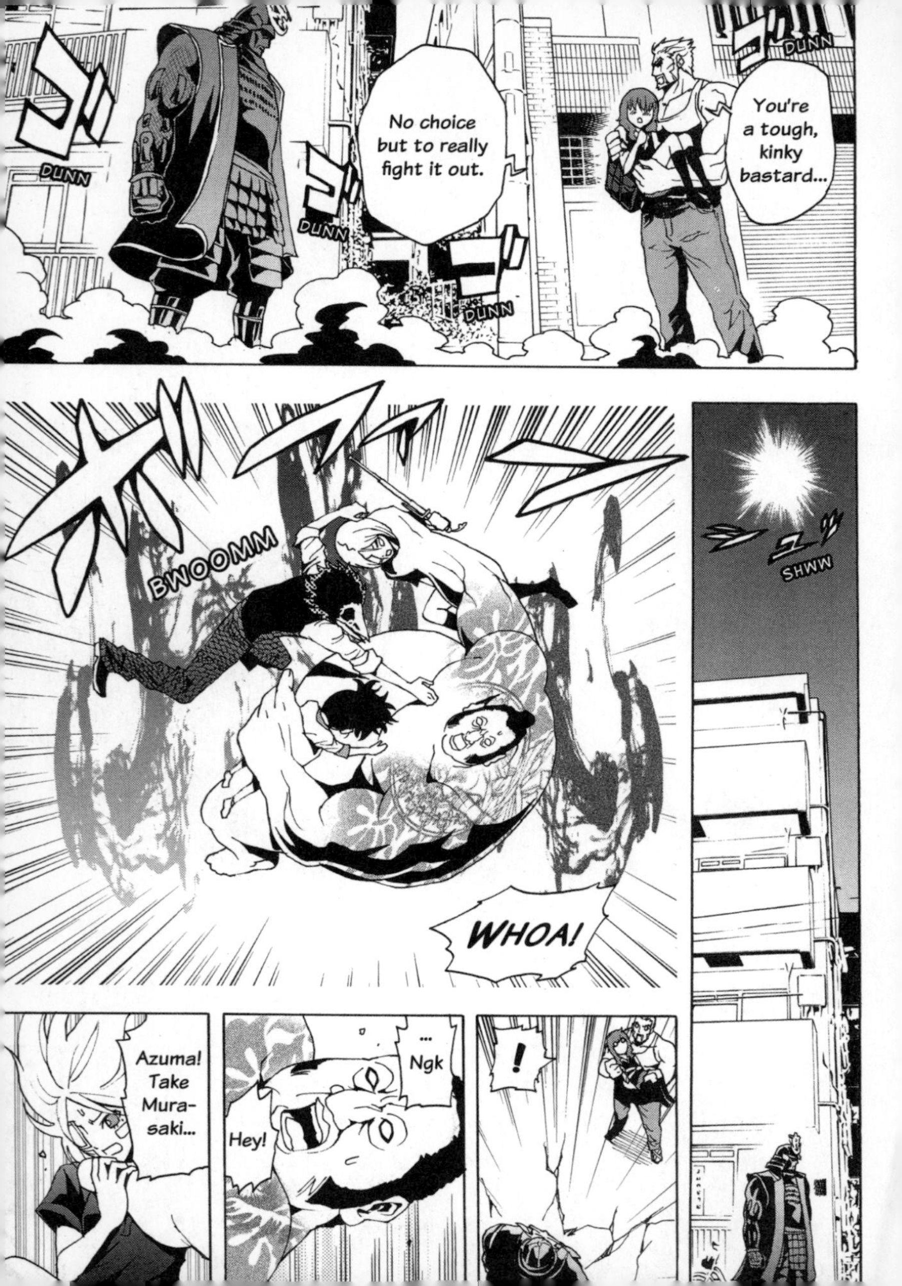
DUNN
You're a tough, kinky bastard...
No choice but to really fight it out.
DUNN
DUNN
DUNN
SHWW
BWOOMM
WHOA!
!
... Ngk
Hey!
Azuma! Take Mura-saki...

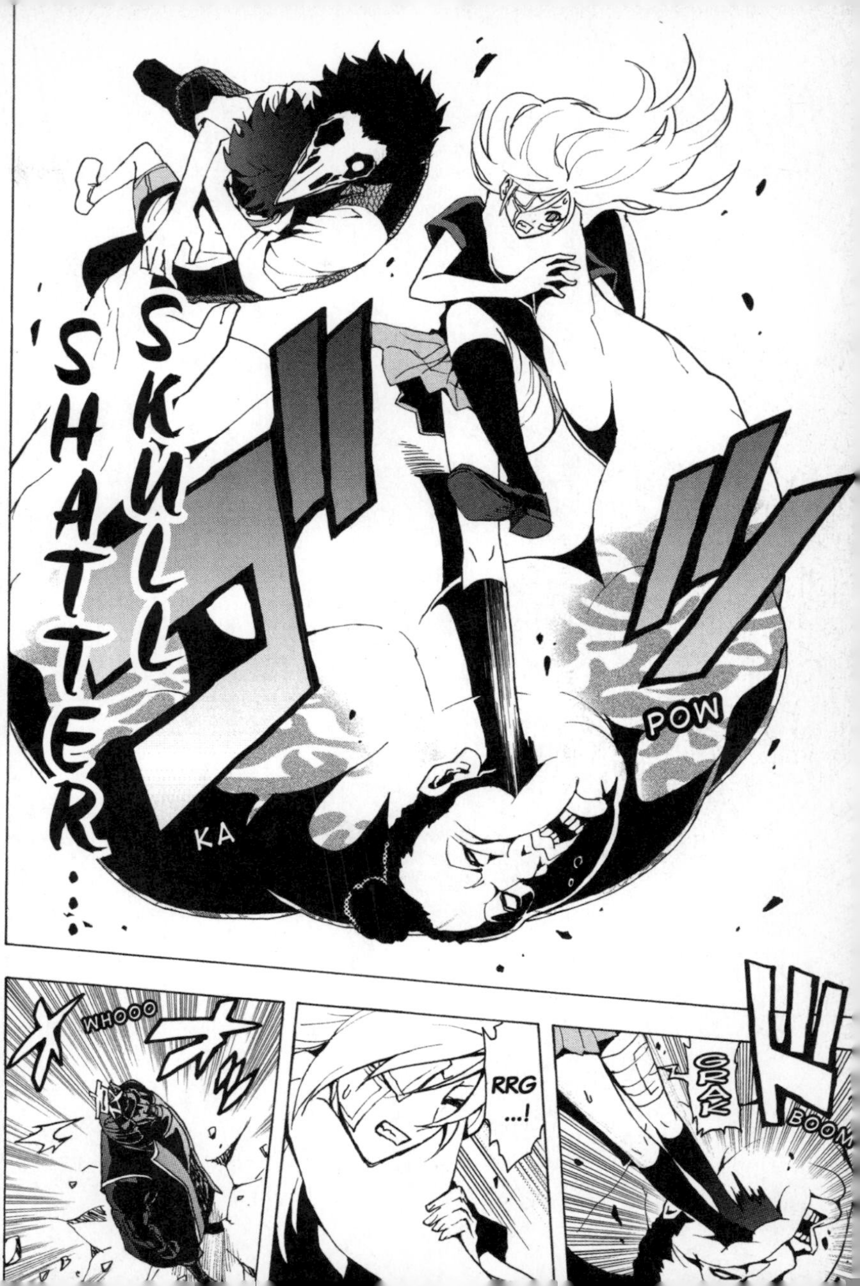
POW
SKULL
SHATTER...
KA
CRAK
BOOM
RRG
...!
WHOOO

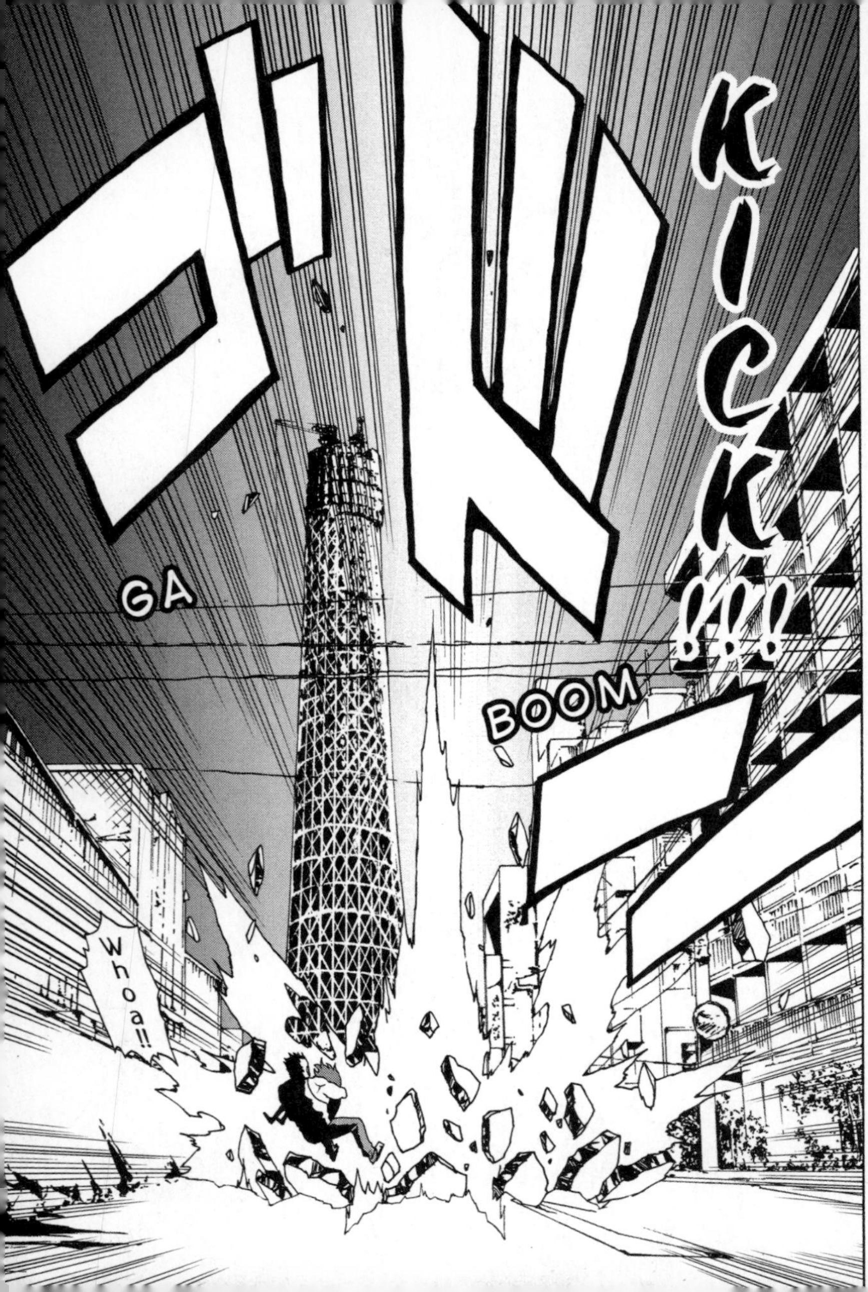
KICK!!!
GA
BOOM
Whoa!!

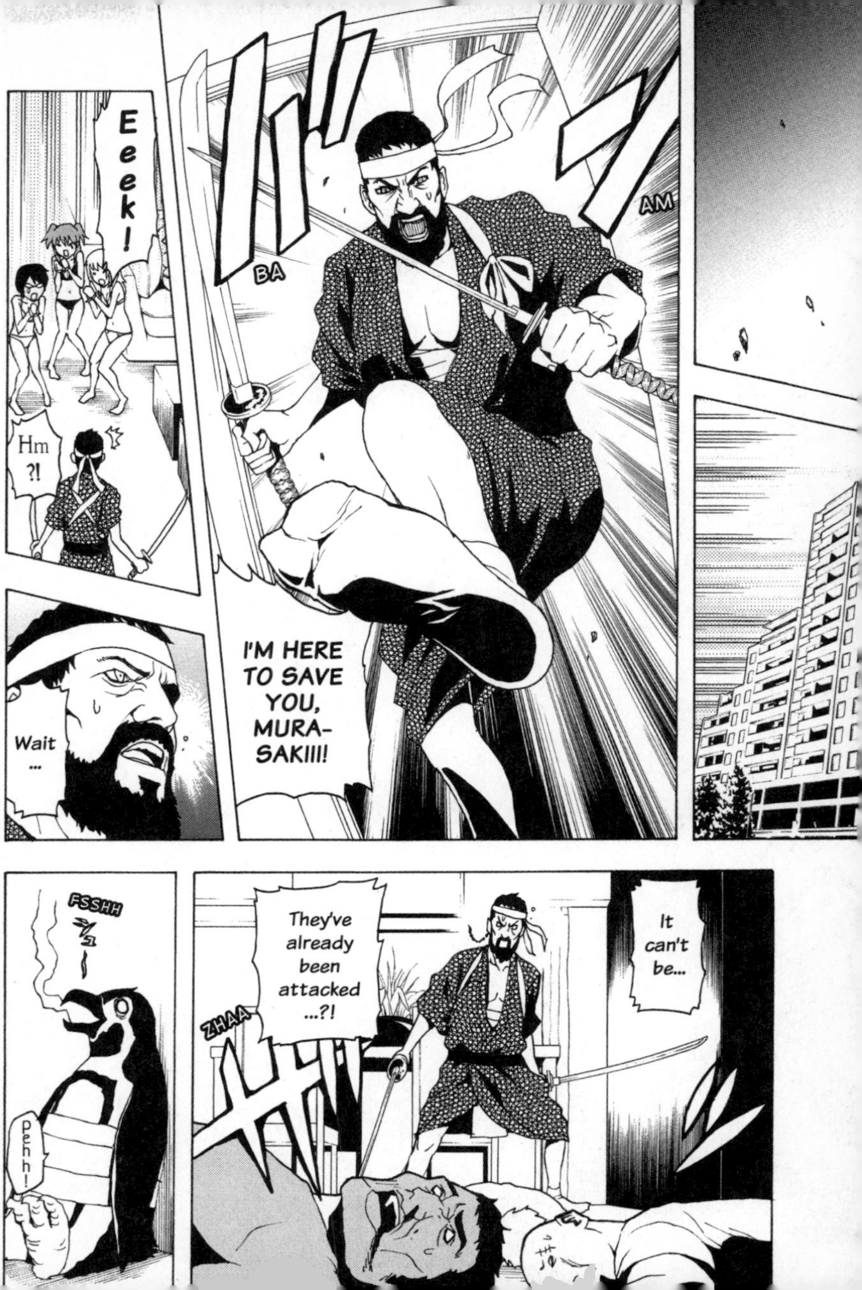
BA
AM
I'M HERE TO SAVE YOU, MURA-SAKIIII!
Eeek!
Hm ?!
Wait ...
It can't be...
They've already been attacked ...?!
ZHAA
FSSHH
Pehh!

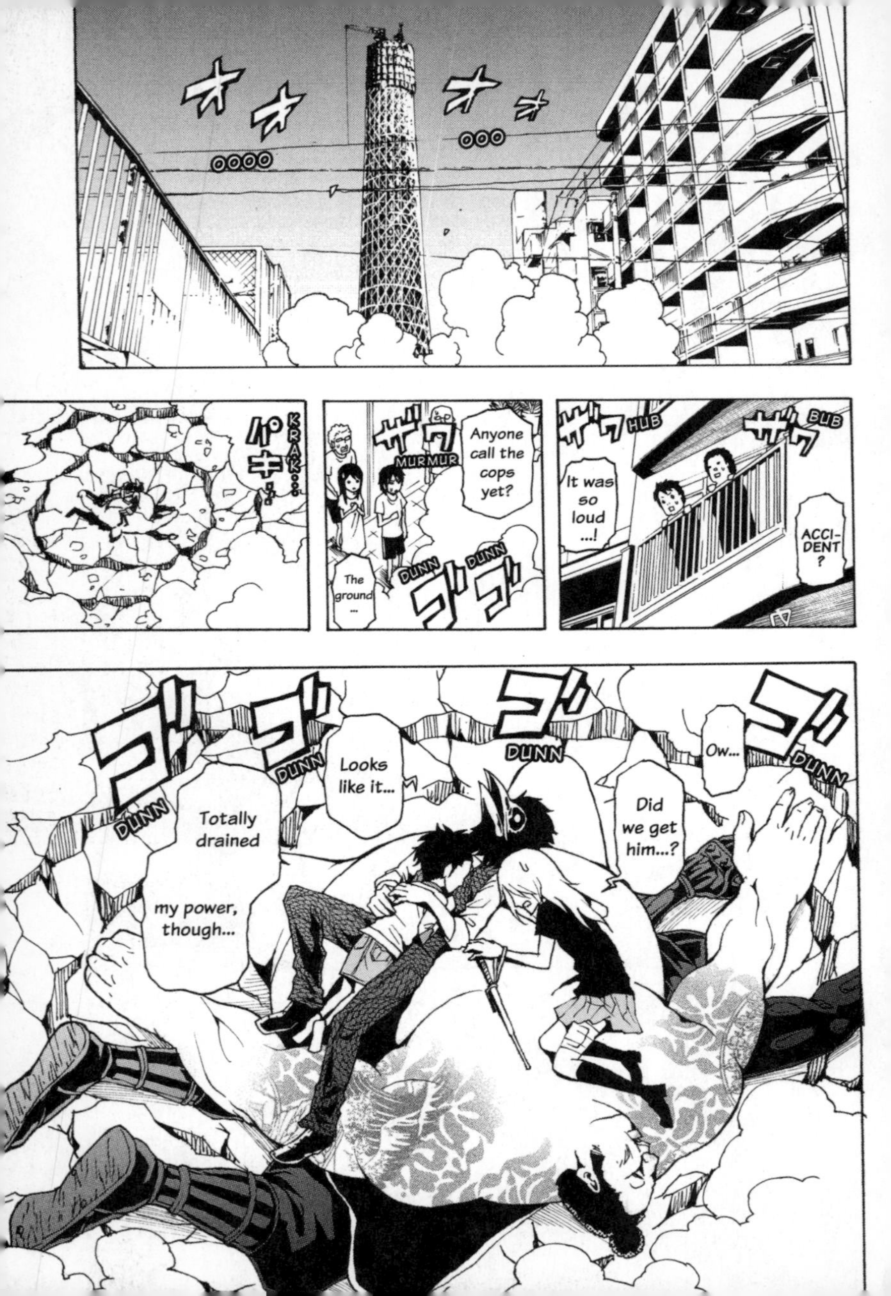
OOO
OOOO
BUB
HUB
ACCI-DENT?
It was so loud ...!
Anyone call the cops yet?
MURMUR
DUNN
DUNN
The ground ...
KRAK...
Ow...
DUNN
Did we get him...?
DUNN
Looks like it...
DUNN
Totally drained
my power, though...
DUNN

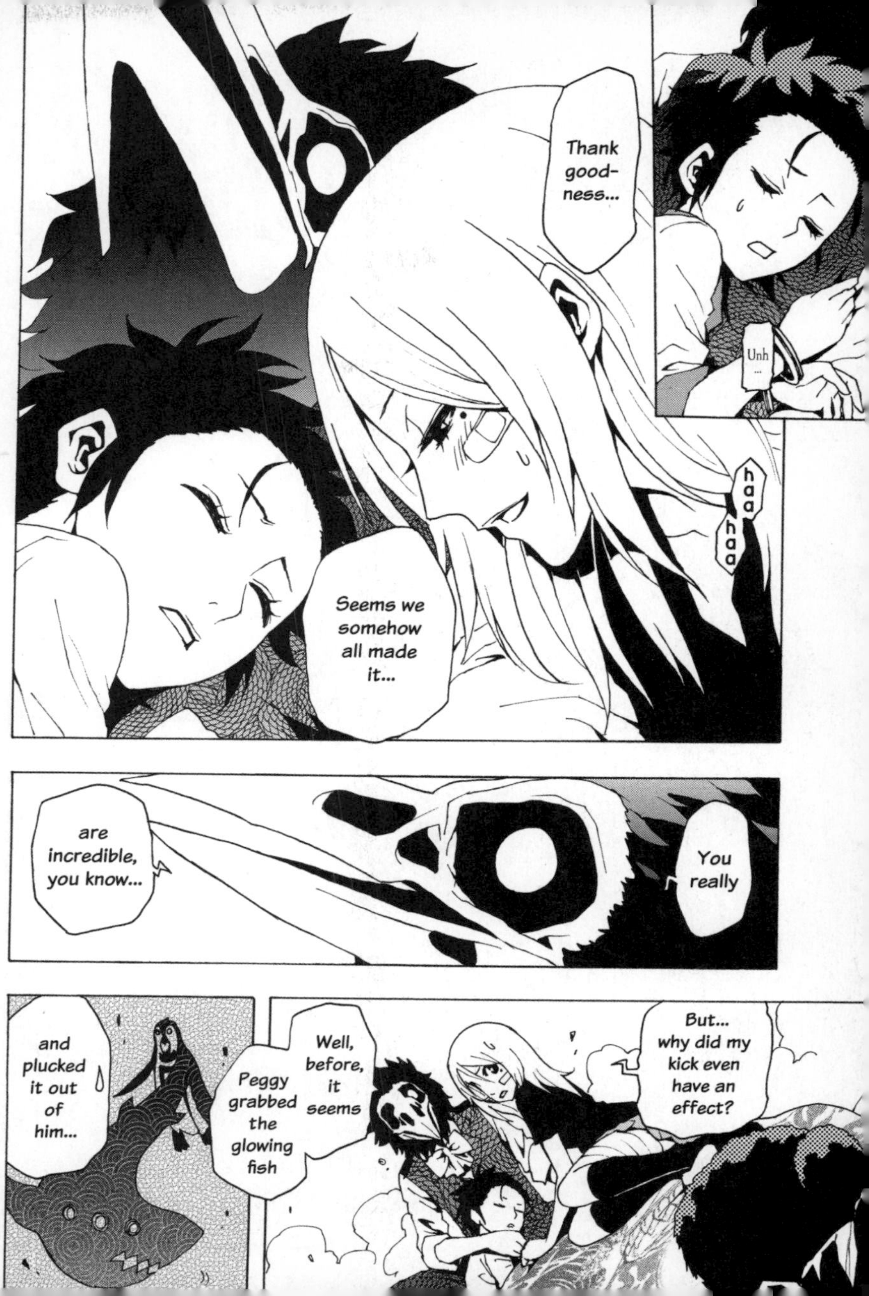
Unh...
Thank goodness...
haa haa
Seems we somehow all made it...
You really
are incredible, you know...
But... why did my kick even have an effect?
Well, before, it seems
Peggy grabbed the glowing fish
and plucked it out of him...

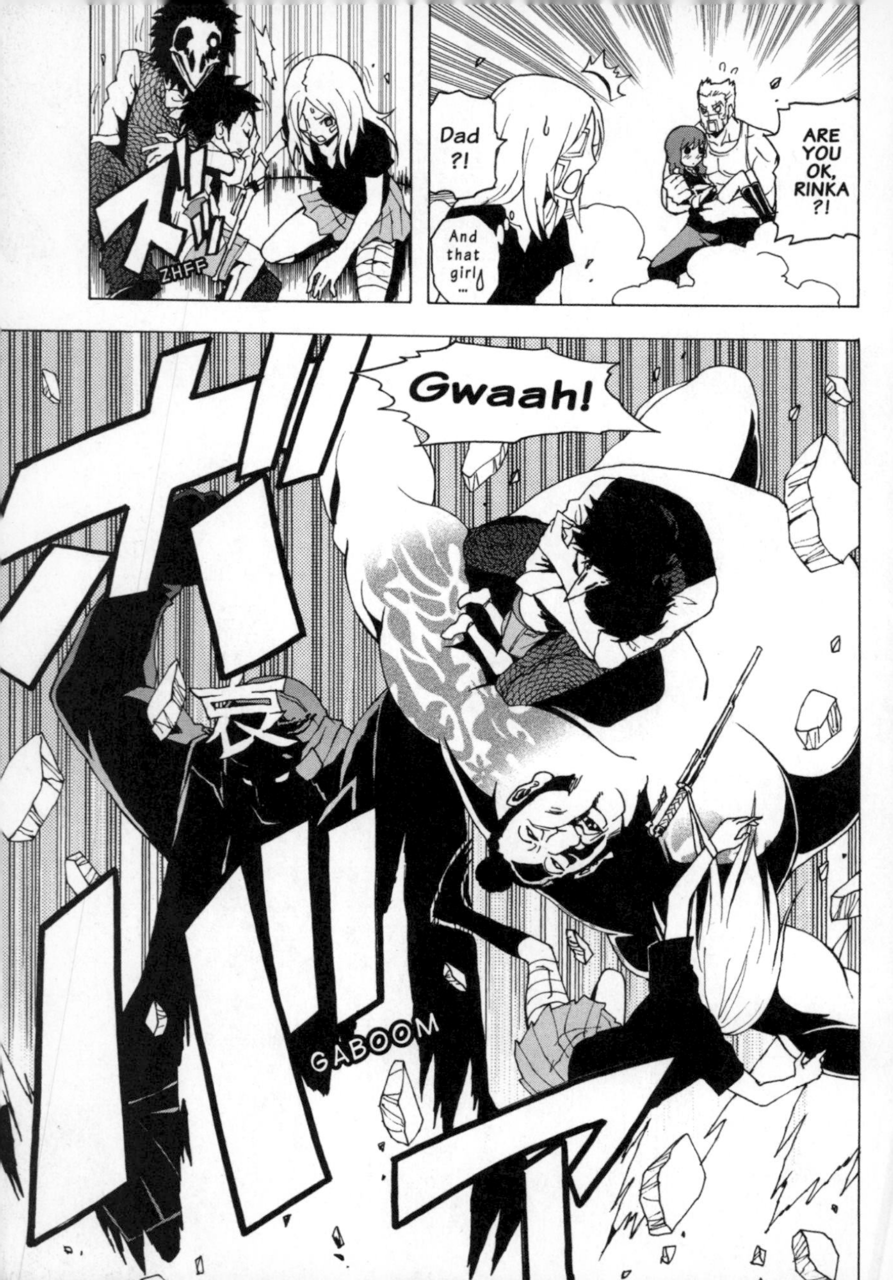
ARE YOU OK, RINKA ?!
Dad ?!
And that girl ...
ZHFF
Gwaah!
GABOOM

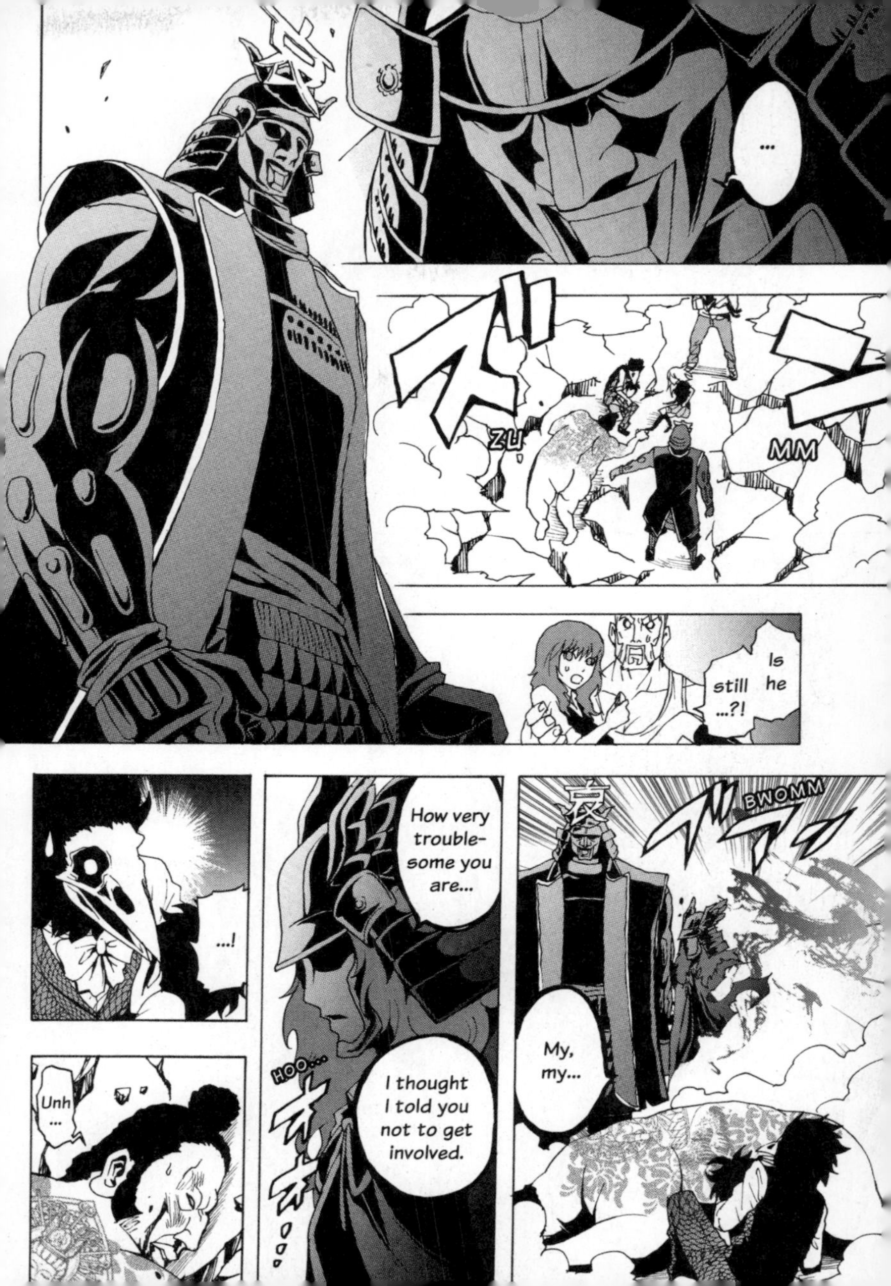
...
ZU
MM
Is he still ...?!
BWOMM
My, my...
How very trouble-some you are...
HOO...
I thought I told you not to get involved.
...!
Unh ...

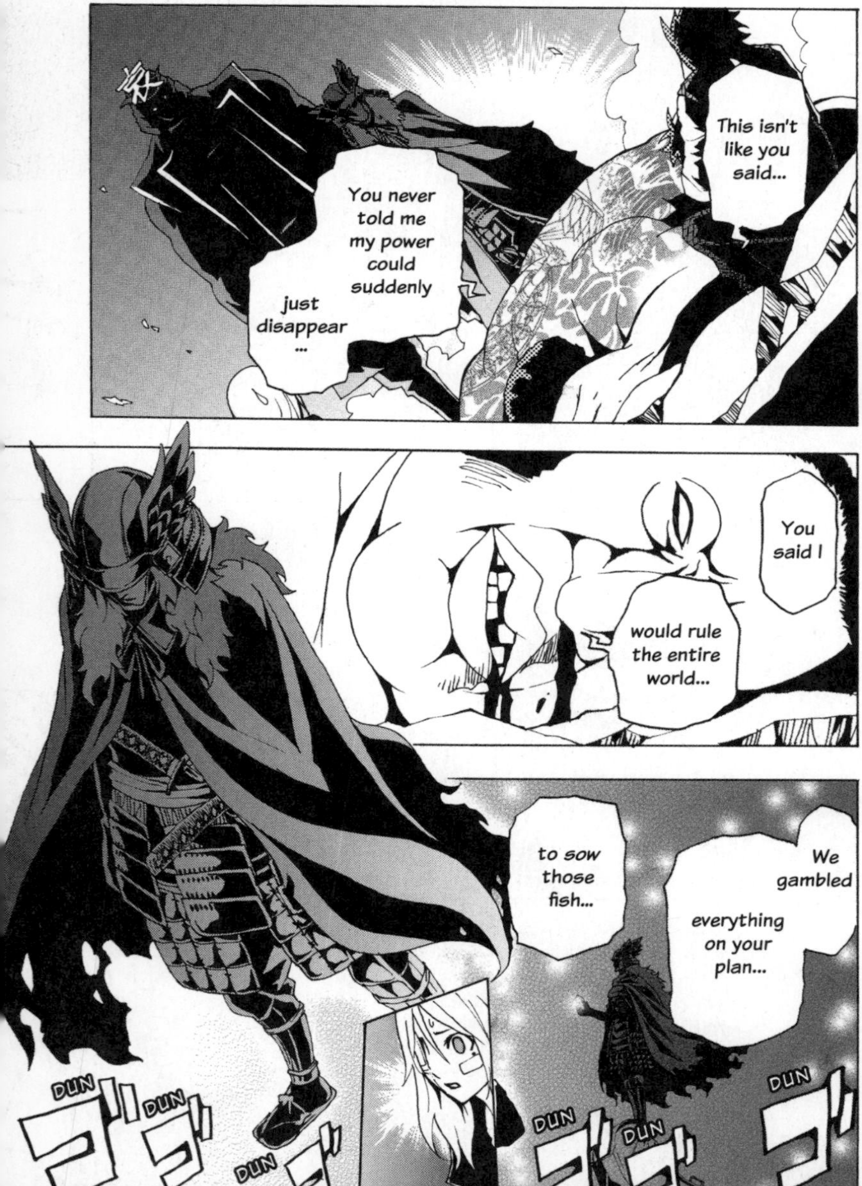
This isn't like you said...
You never told me my power could suddenly just disappear...
You said I
would rule the entire world...
We gambled everything on your plan...
to sow those fish...
DUN
DUN
DUN
DUN
DUN
DUN

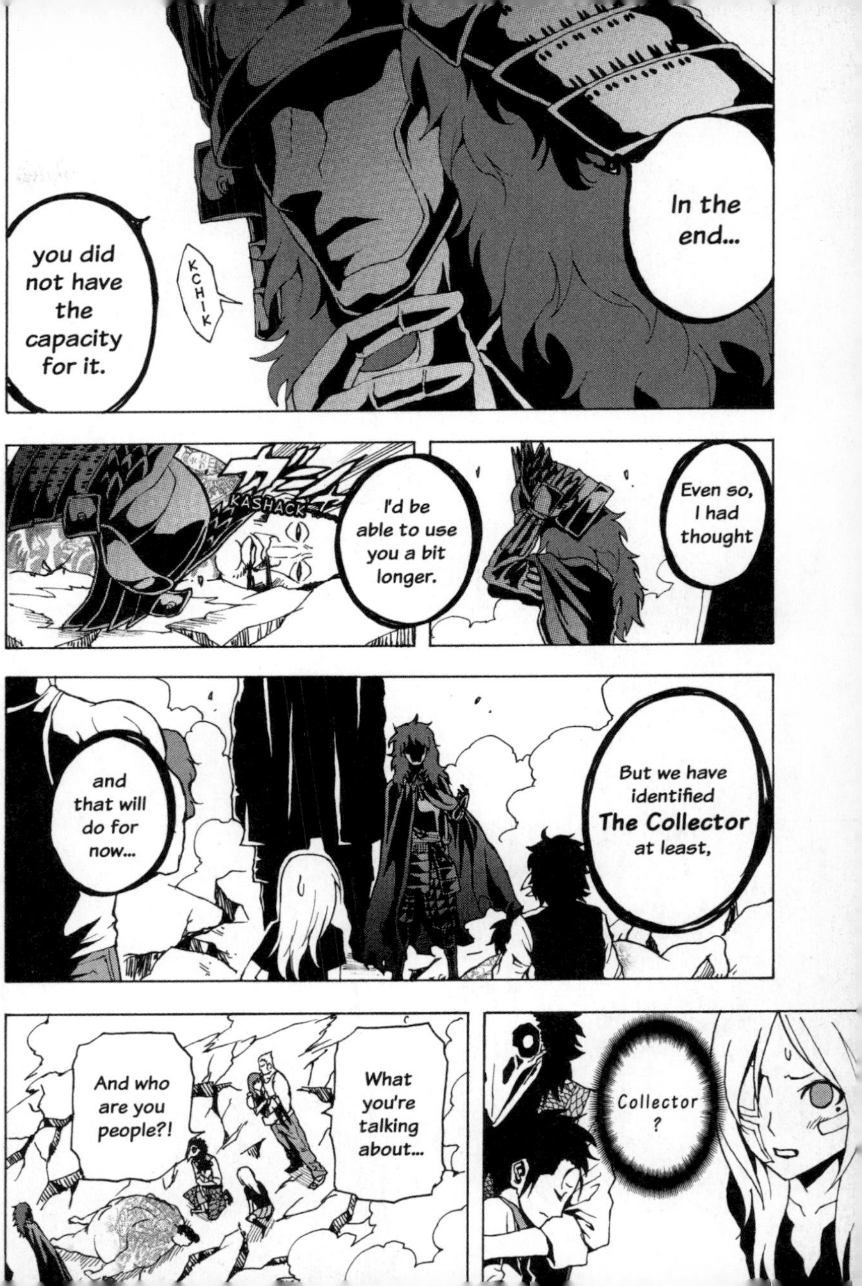
In the end...
KCHIK
you did not have the capacity for it.
Even so, I had thought
KASHACK
I'd be able to use you a bit longer.
But we have identified The Collector at least,
and that will do for now...
Collector ?
What you're talking about...
And who are you people?!

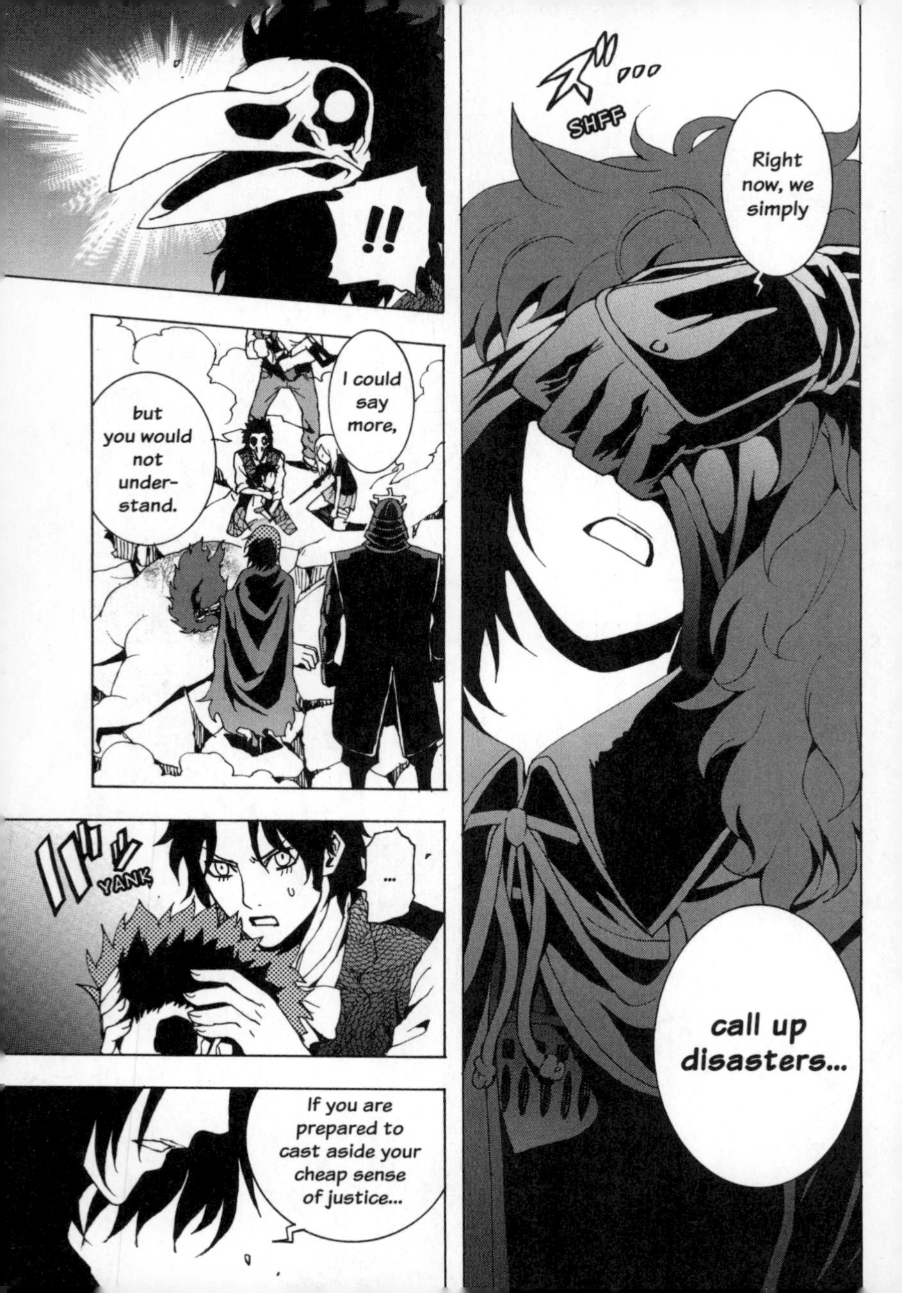
SHFF
Right now, we simply
call up disasters...
!!
I could say more,
but you would not understand.
YANK
...
If you are prepared to cast aside your cheap sense of justice...

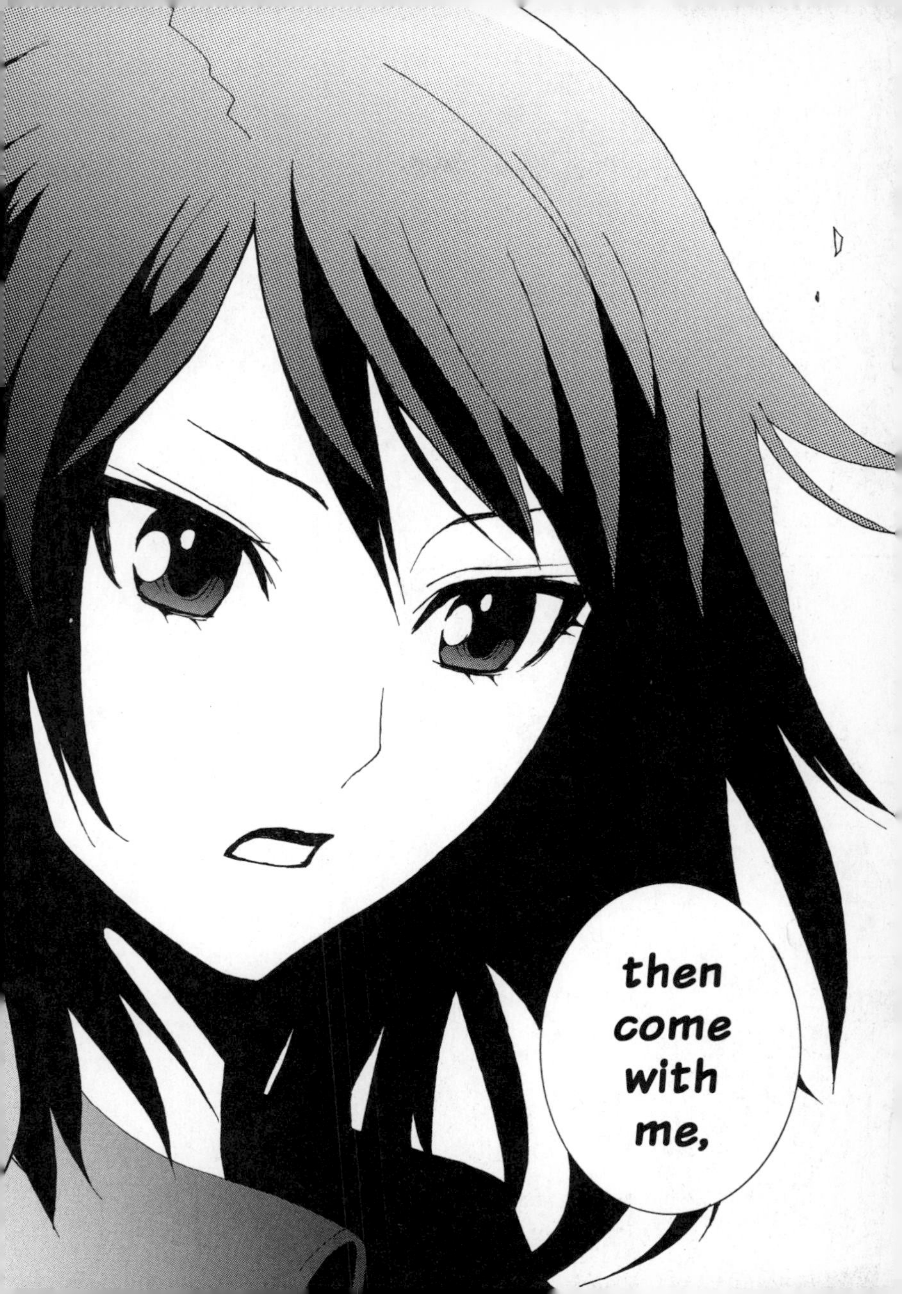
then come with me,

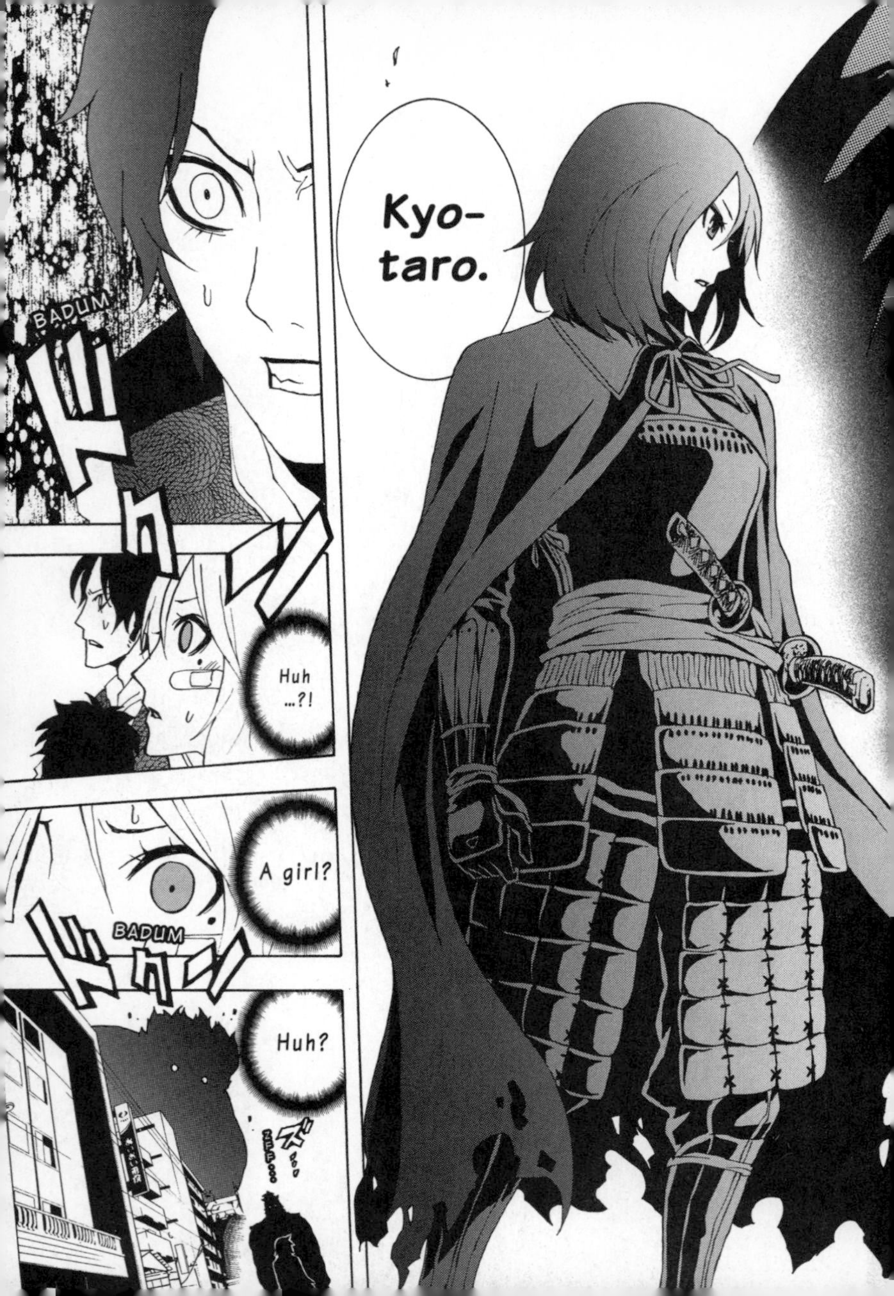
Kyo-
taro.
BADUM
Huh
...?!
A girl?
BADUM
Huh?
ZFF...

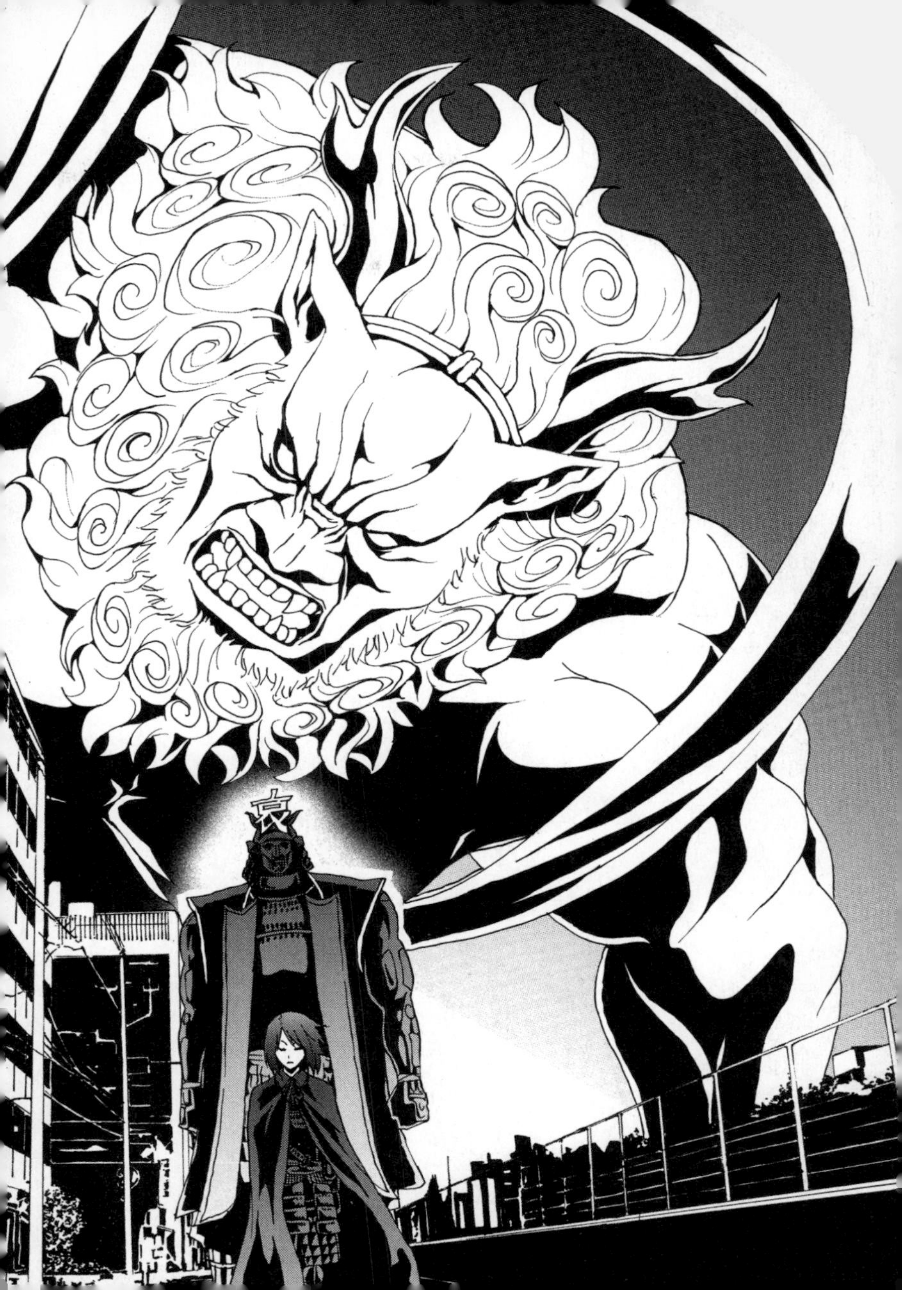
哀

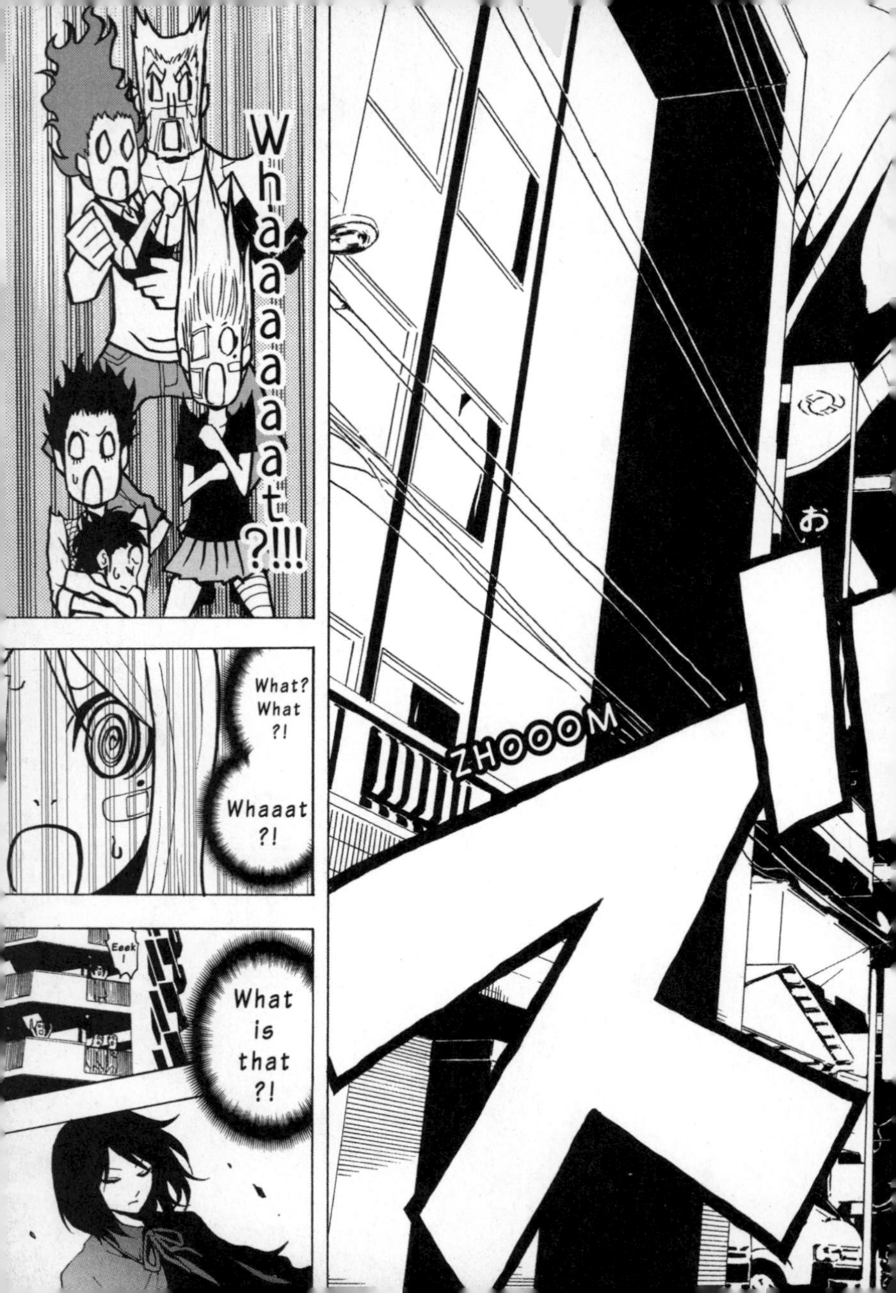
お
ZHOOOM
Whaaaaaat?!!!
What? What ?!
Whaaat ?!
Eeek !
What is that ?!

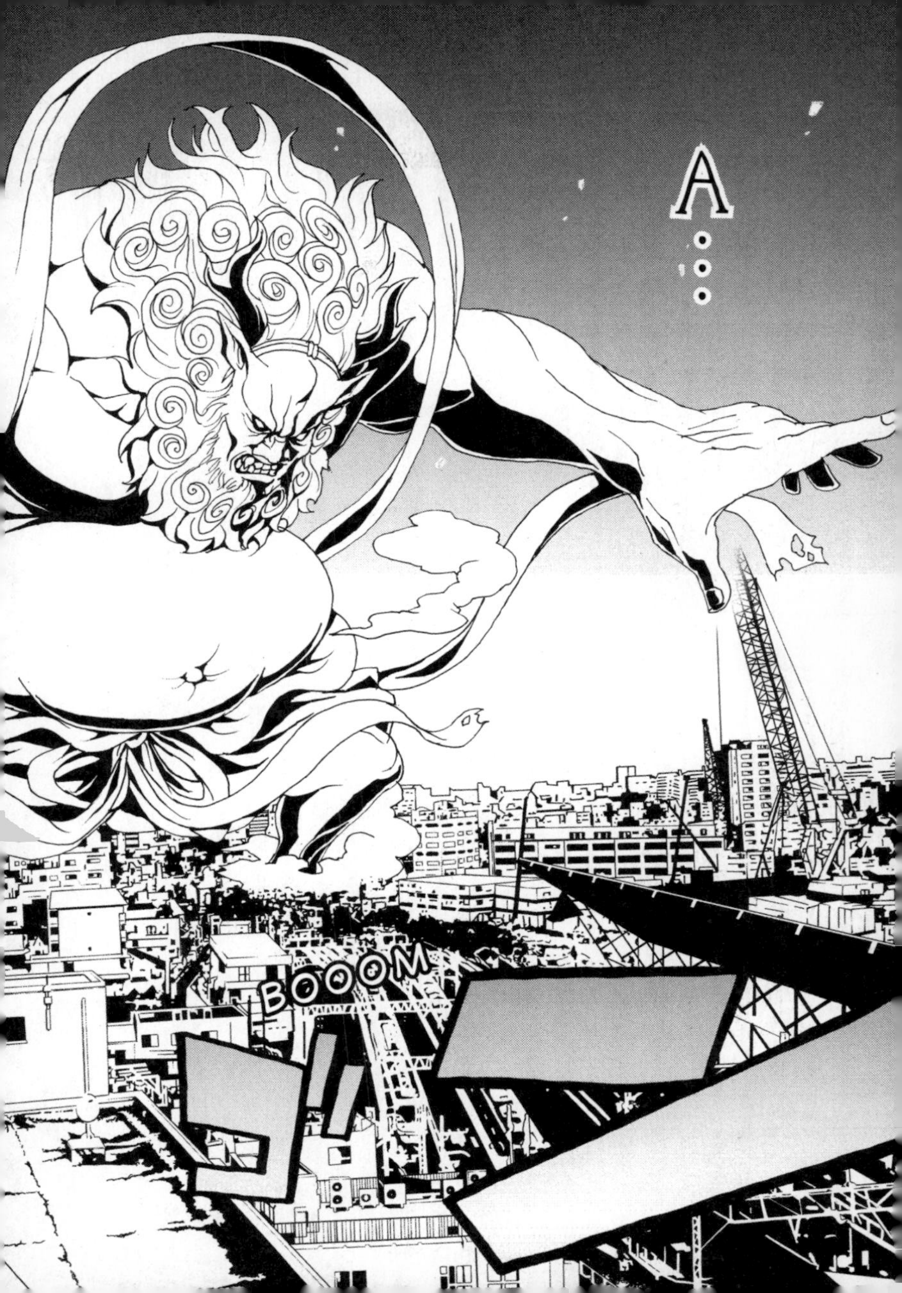
A...
BOOOM

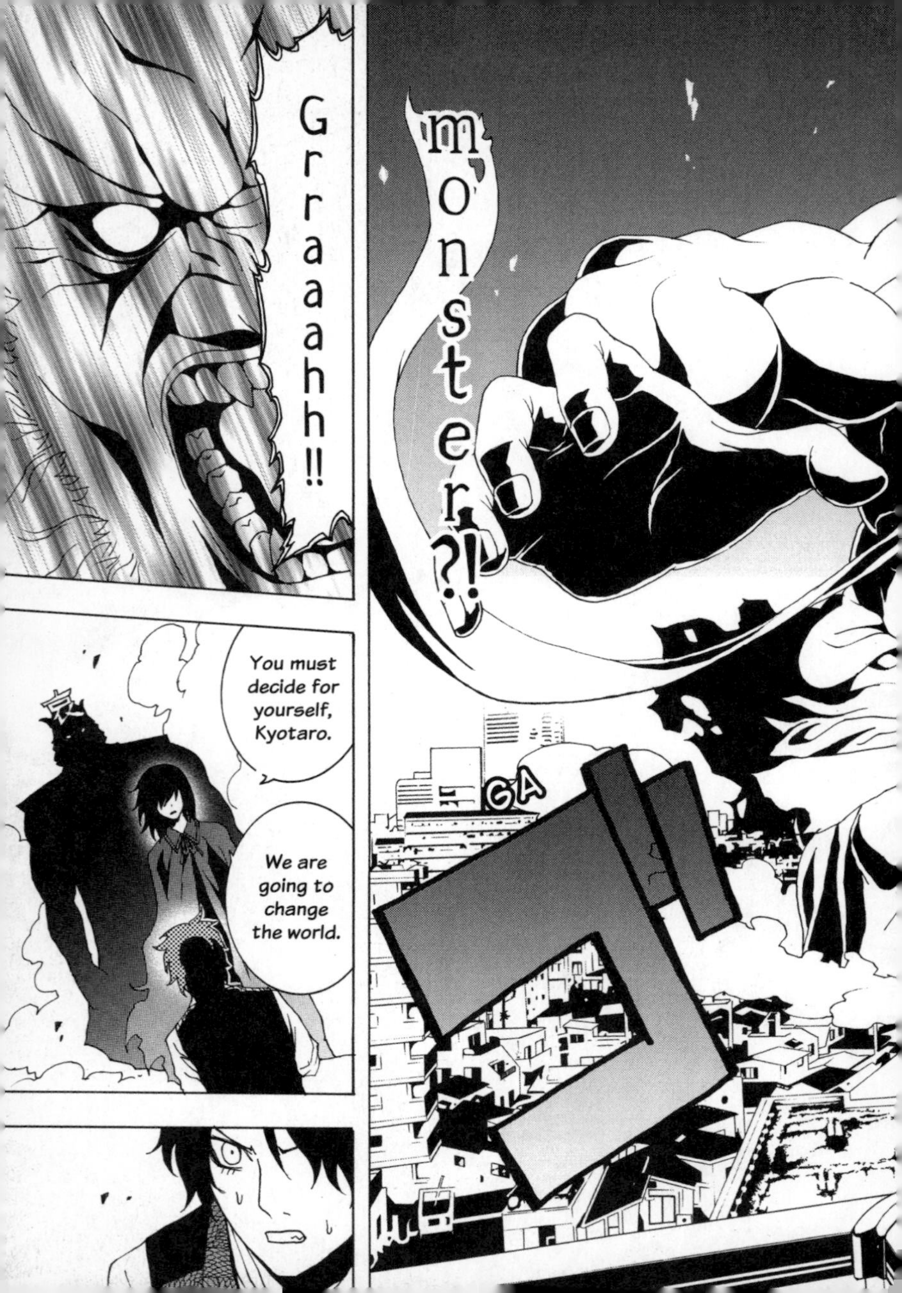
monster?!
GA
Grraaahh!!
You must decide for yourself, Kyotaro.
We are going to change the world.

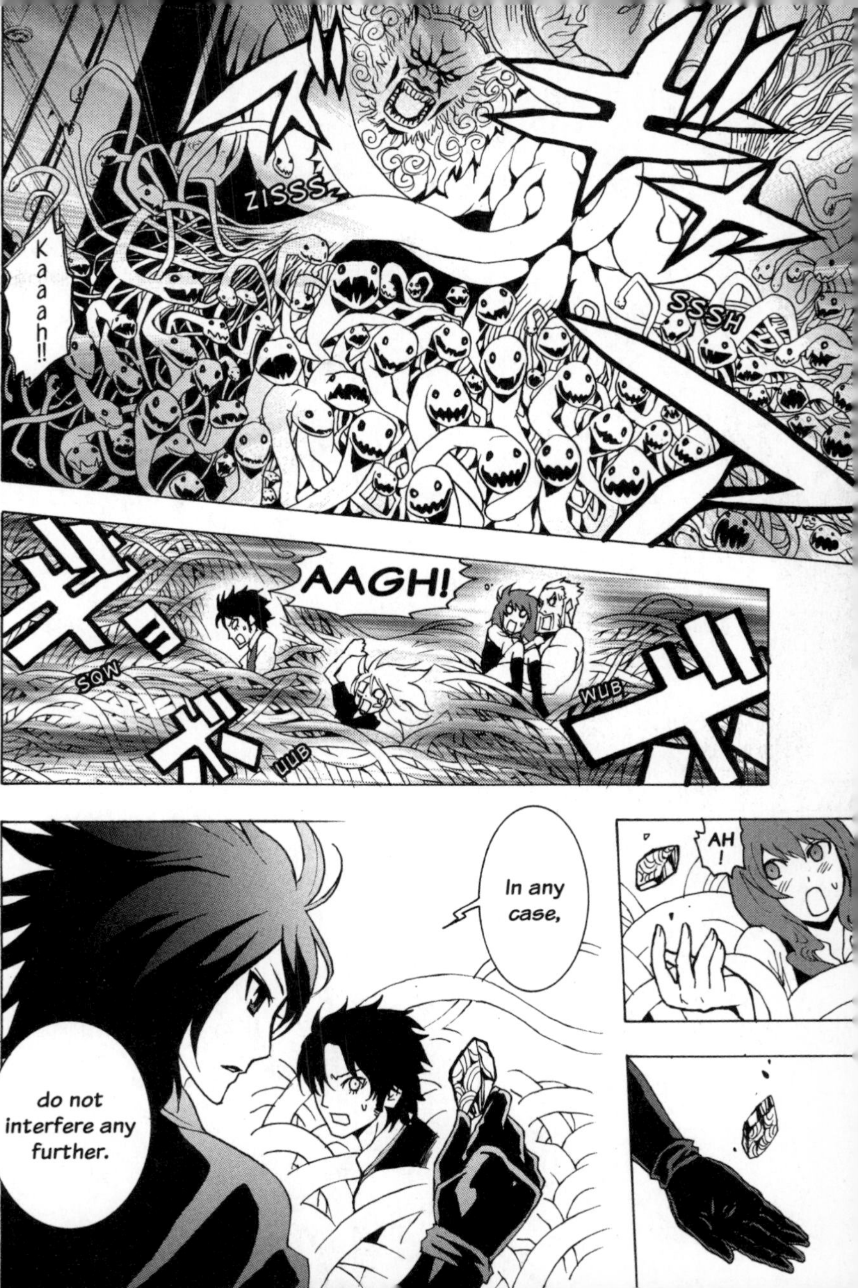
ZISSS
Kaaah!!
SSSH
AAGH!
WUB
SQW
UUB
AH!
In any case,
do not interfere any further.

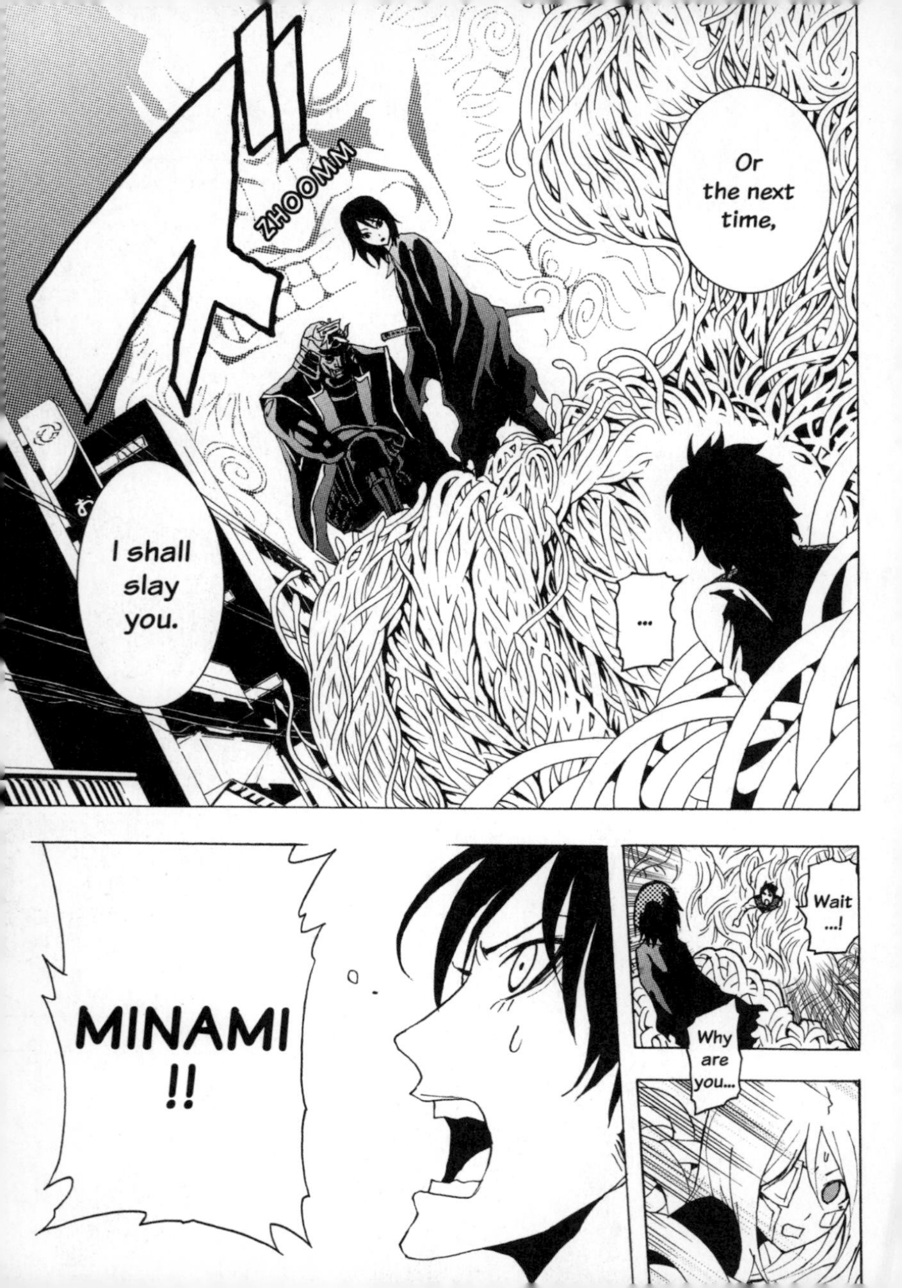
Or the next time,
ZHOOMM
...
I shall slay you.
Wait ...!
Why are you...
MINAMI !!

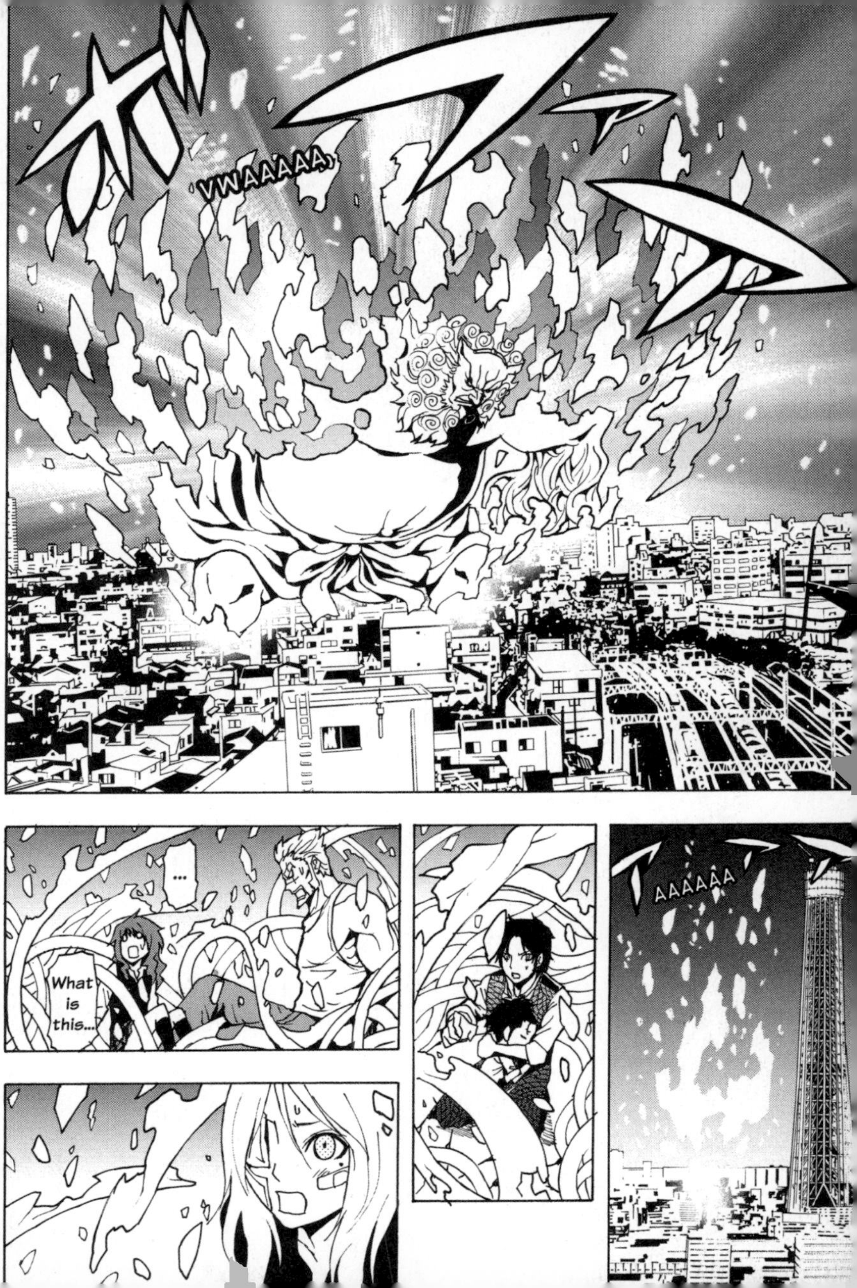
VWAAAAA
AAAAAA
...
What is this...

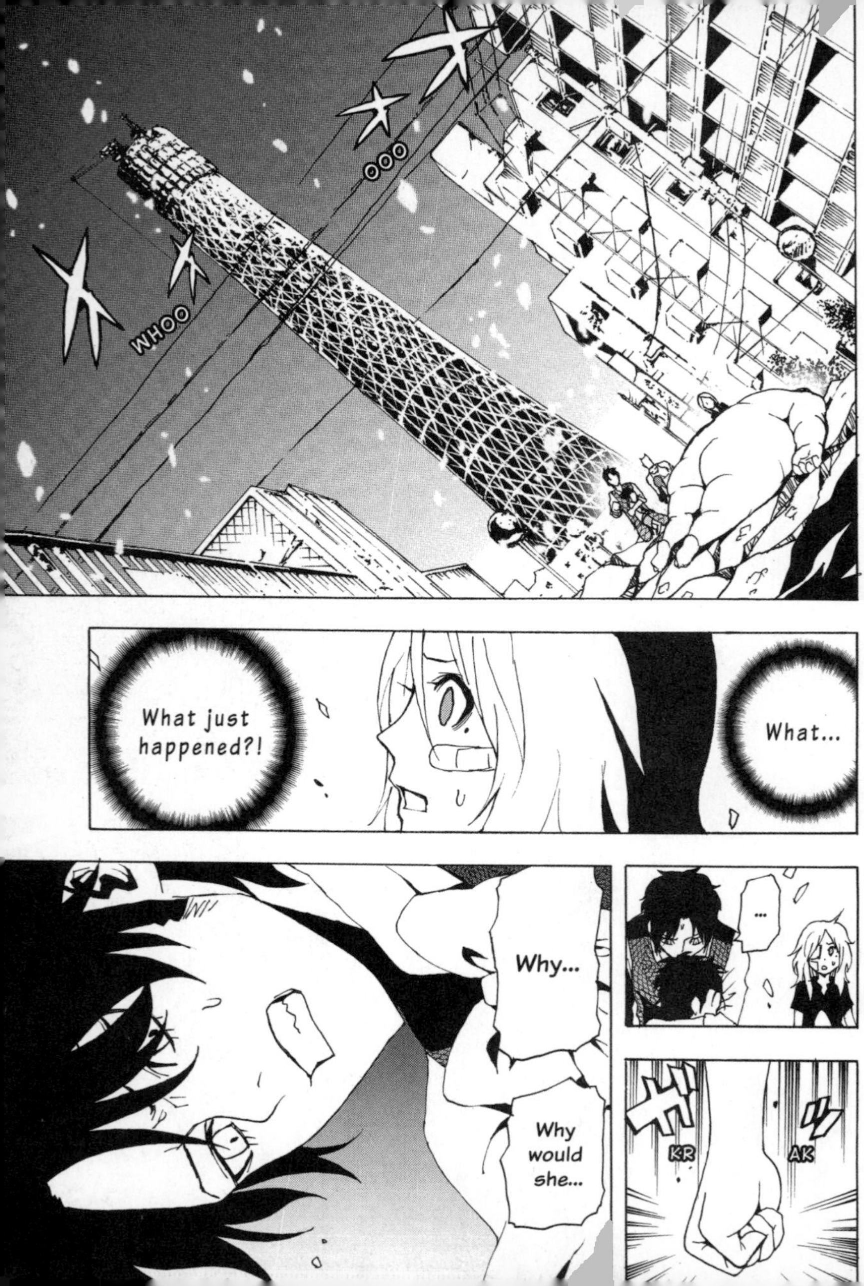
WHOO
OOO
What...
What just happened?!
...
KR
AK
Why...
Why would she...

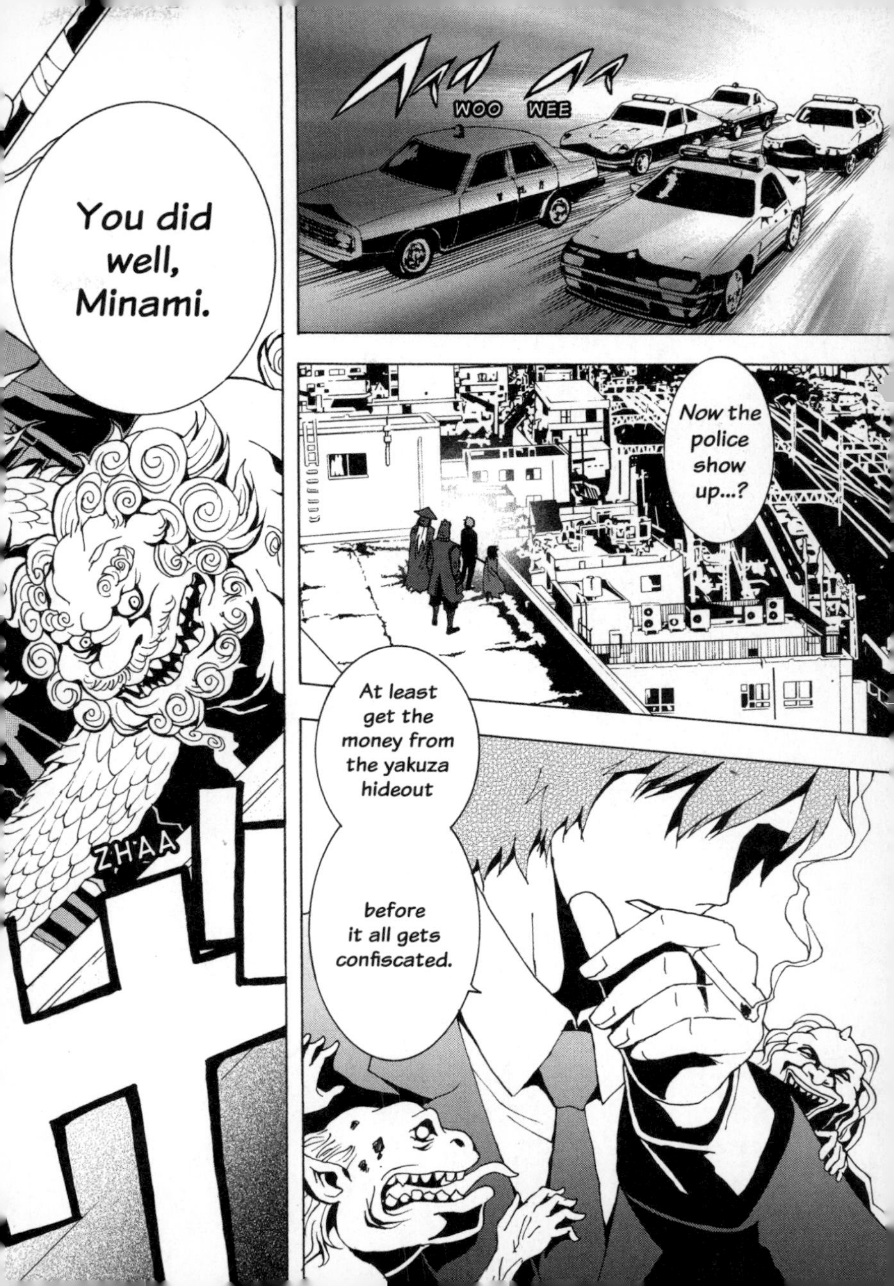
WOO WEE
Now the police show up...?
At least get the money from the yakuza hideout
before it all gets confiscated.
You did well, Minami.
ZHAA

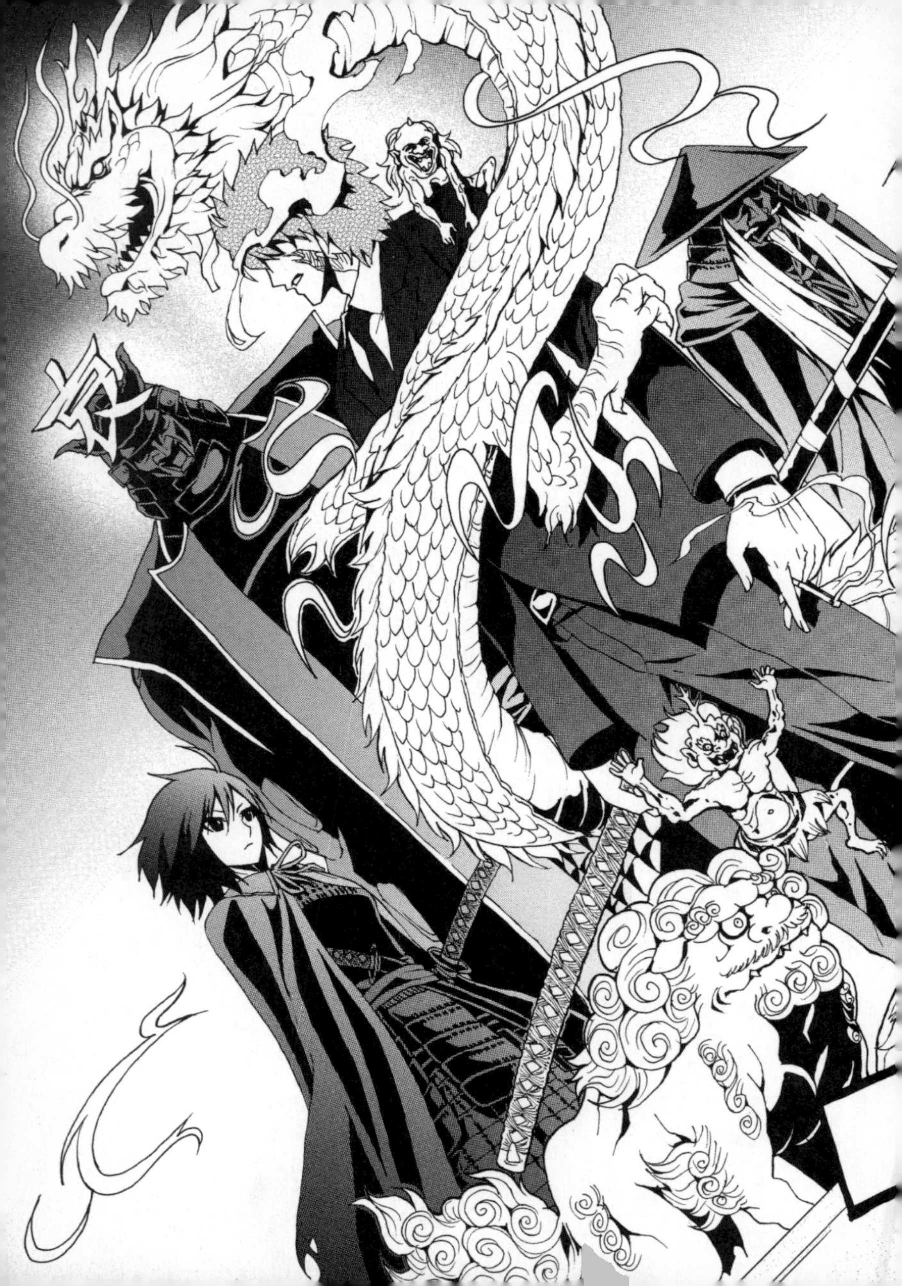

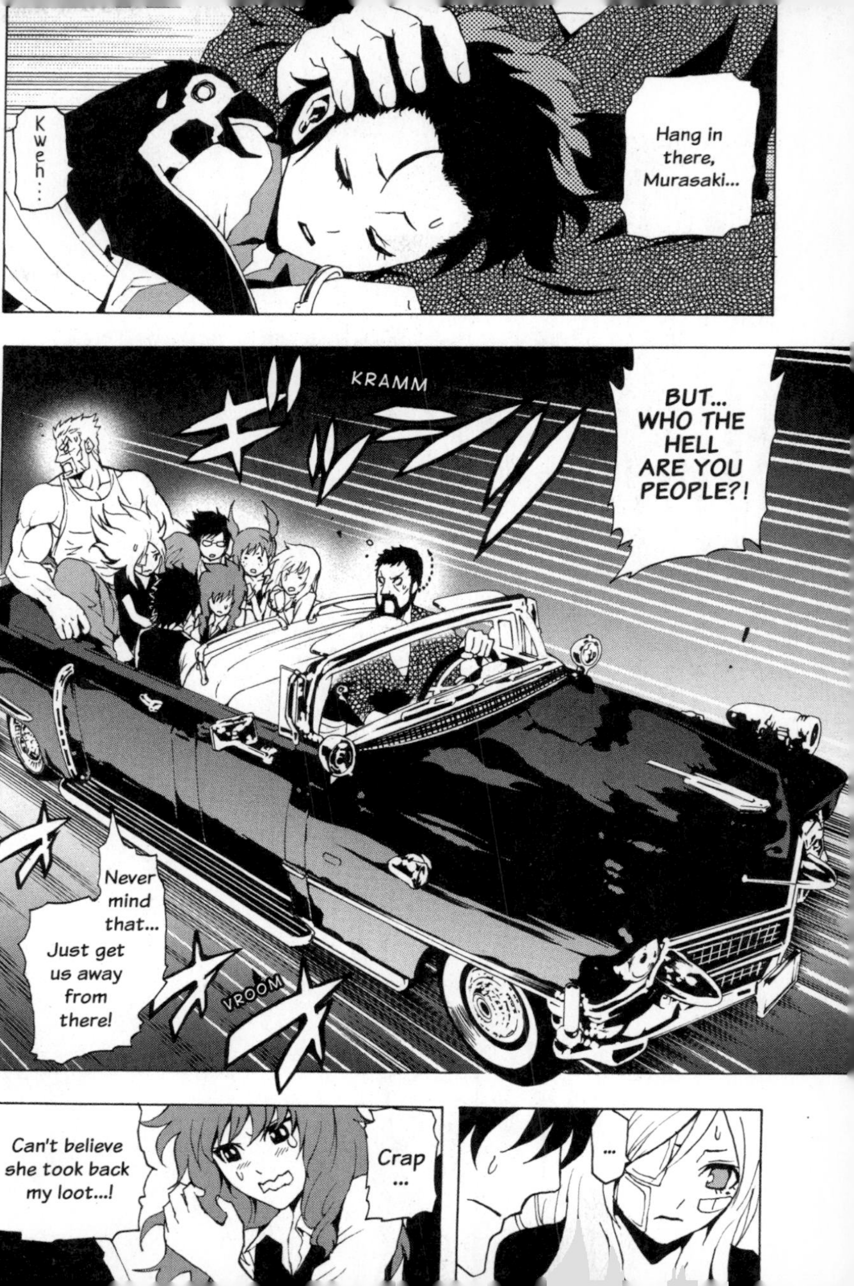
Hang in there, Murasaki...
Kweh...
BUT... WHO THE HELL ARE YOU PEOPLE?!
KRAMM
Never mind that... Just get us away from there!
VROOM
...
Crap ...
Can't believe she took back my loot...!

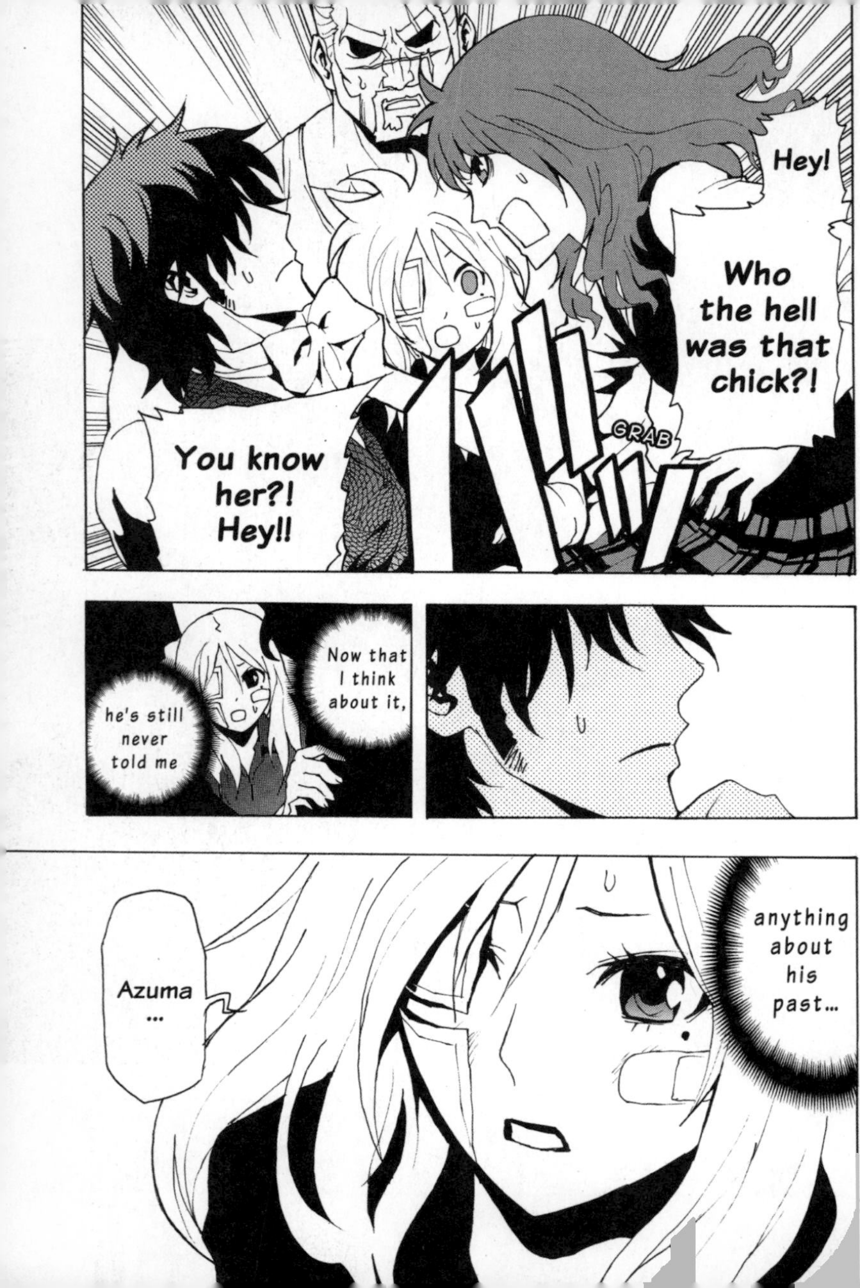
Hey!
Who the hell was that chick?!
GRAB
You know her?! Hey!!
Now that I think about it,
he's still never told me
anything about his past...
Azuma ...

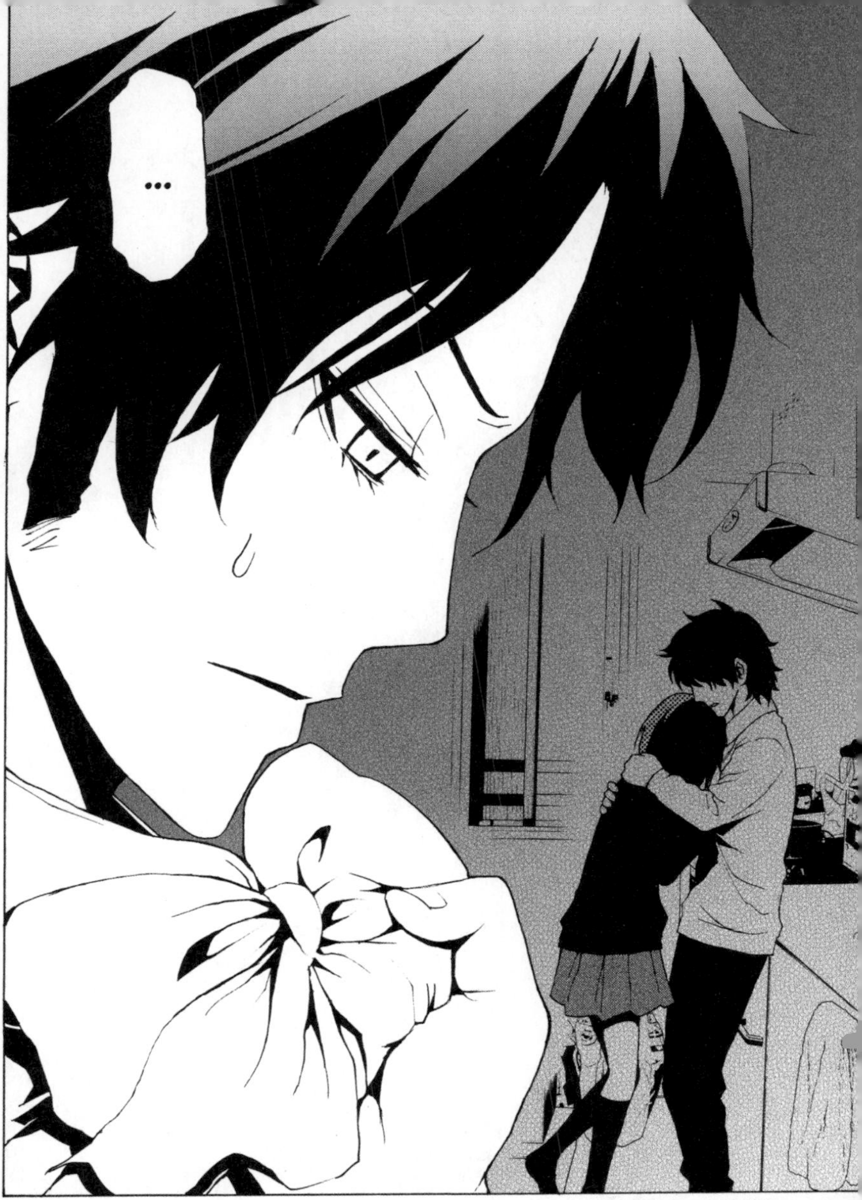
...

SCENE 8 /// END

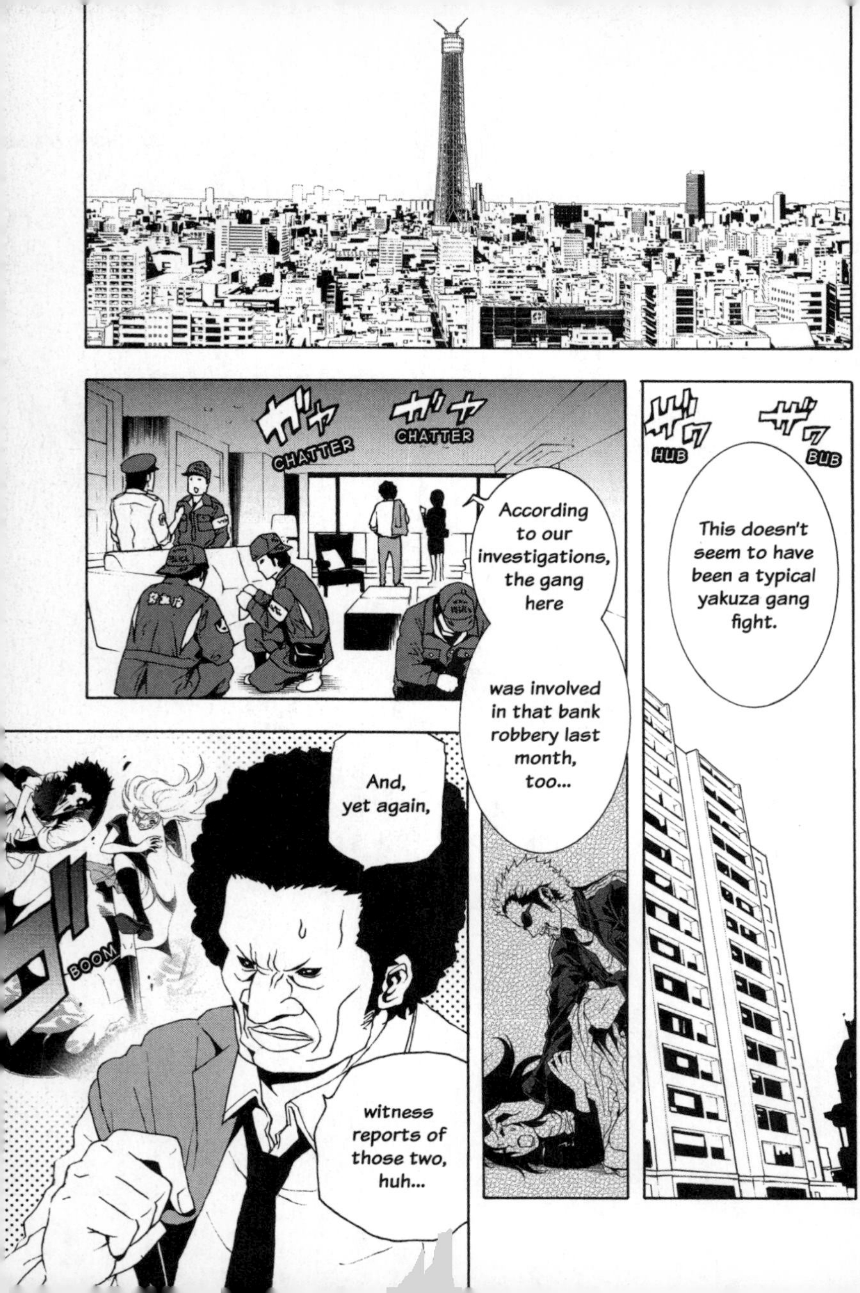
HUB
BUB
This doesn't seem to have been a typical yakuza gang fight.
CHATTER
CHATTER
According to our investigations, the gang here
was involved in that bank robbery last month, too...
BOOM
And, yet again,
witness reports of those two, huh...

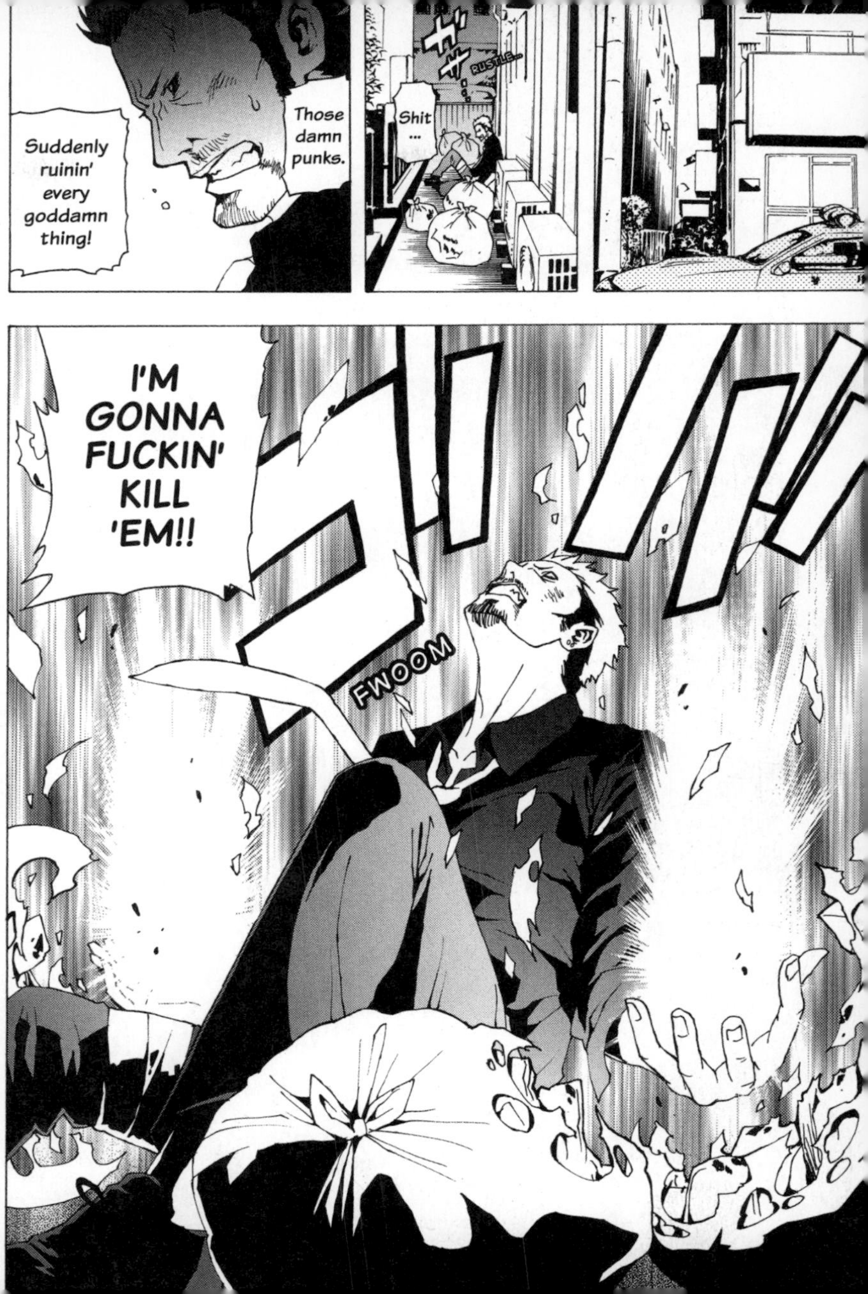
RUSTLE...
Shit ...
Those damn punks.
Suddenly ruinin' every goddamn thing!
I'M GONNA FUCKIN' KILL 'EM!!
FWOOM

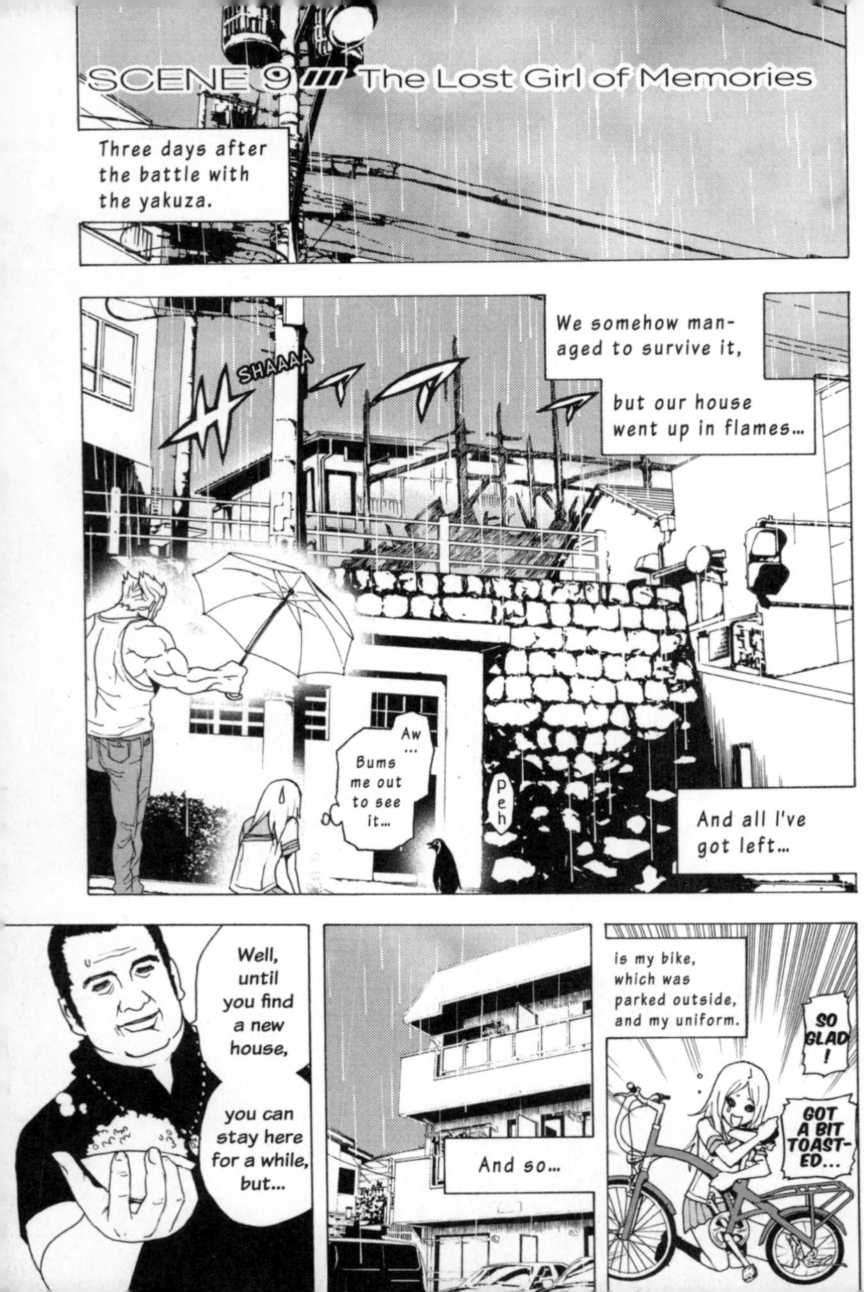
SCENE 9 /// The Lost Girl of Memories
Three days after the battle with the yakuza.
We somehow man-aged to survive it,
but our house went up in flames...
SHAAAA
Aw... Bums me out to see it...
peh
And all I've got left...
is my bike, which was parked outside, and my uniform.
SO GLAD!
GOT A BIT TOAST-ED...
And so...
Well, until you find a new house,
you can stay here for a while, but...

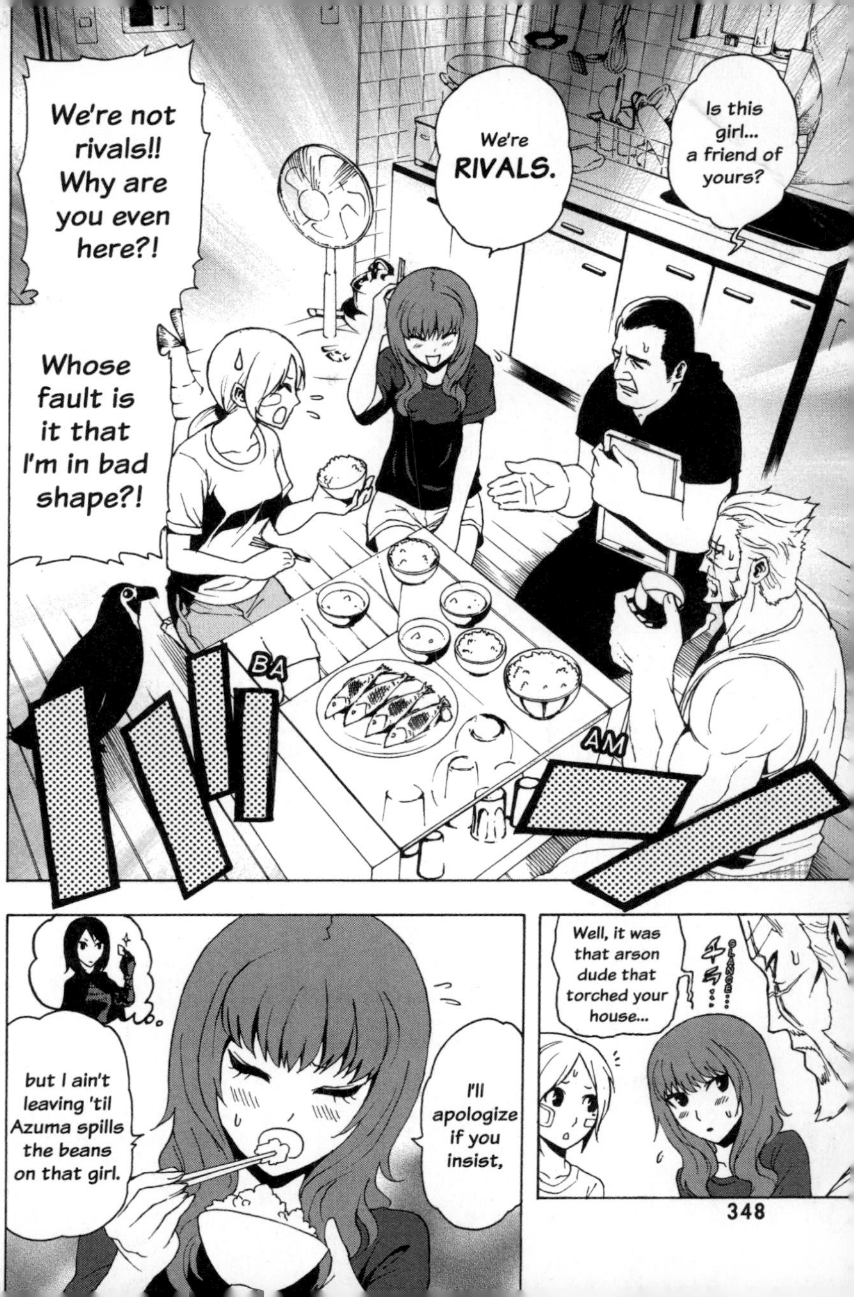

Is this girl... a friend of yours?
We're RIVALS.
We're not rivals!! Why are you even here?!
Whose fault is it that I'm in bad shape?!
BA
AM
Well, it was that arson dude that torched your house...
GLANCE...
I'll apologize if you insist,
but I ain't leaving 'til Azuma spills the beans on that girl.

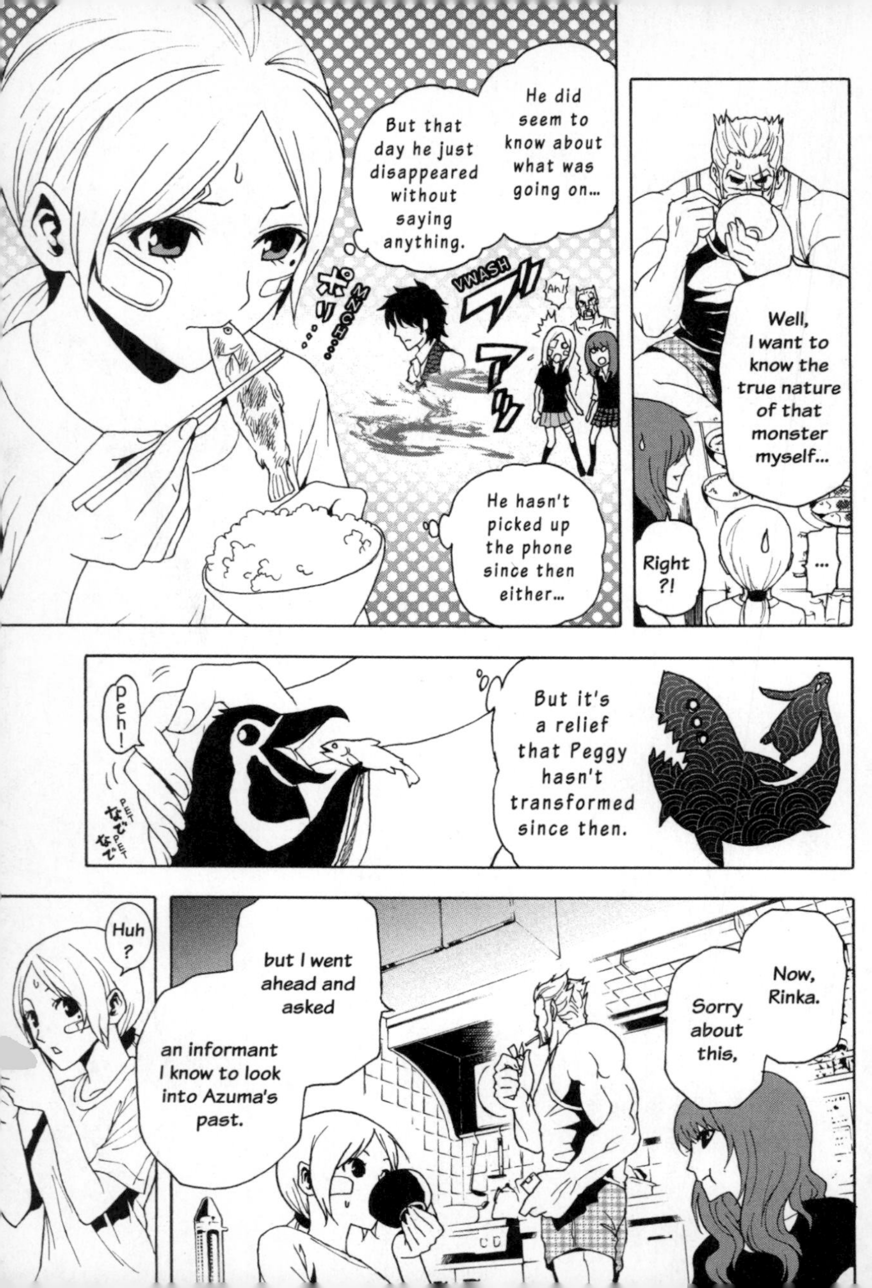
Well, I want to know the true nature of that monster myself...
...
Right?!
He did seem to know about what was going on...
But that day he just disappeared without saying anything.
VWASH
Ah!
MNCH...
He hasn't picked up the phone since then either...
But it's a relief that Peggy hasn't transformed since then.
Peh!
なで PET なで PET
Now, Rinka.
Sorry about this,
but I went ahead and asked
an informant I know to look into Azuma's past.
Huh?

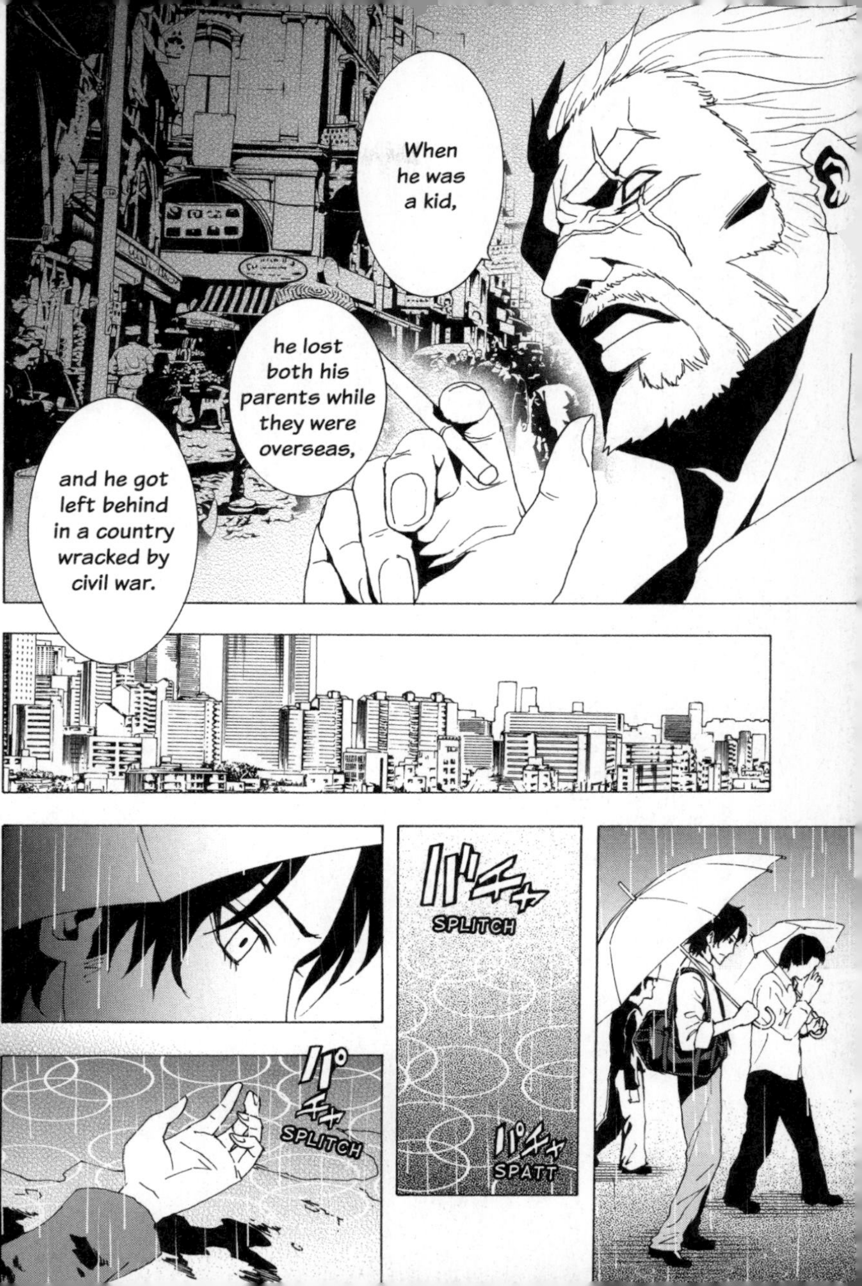
When he was a kid,
he lost both his parents while they were overseas,
and he got left behind in a country wracked by civil war.
SPLITCH
SPATT
SPLITCH

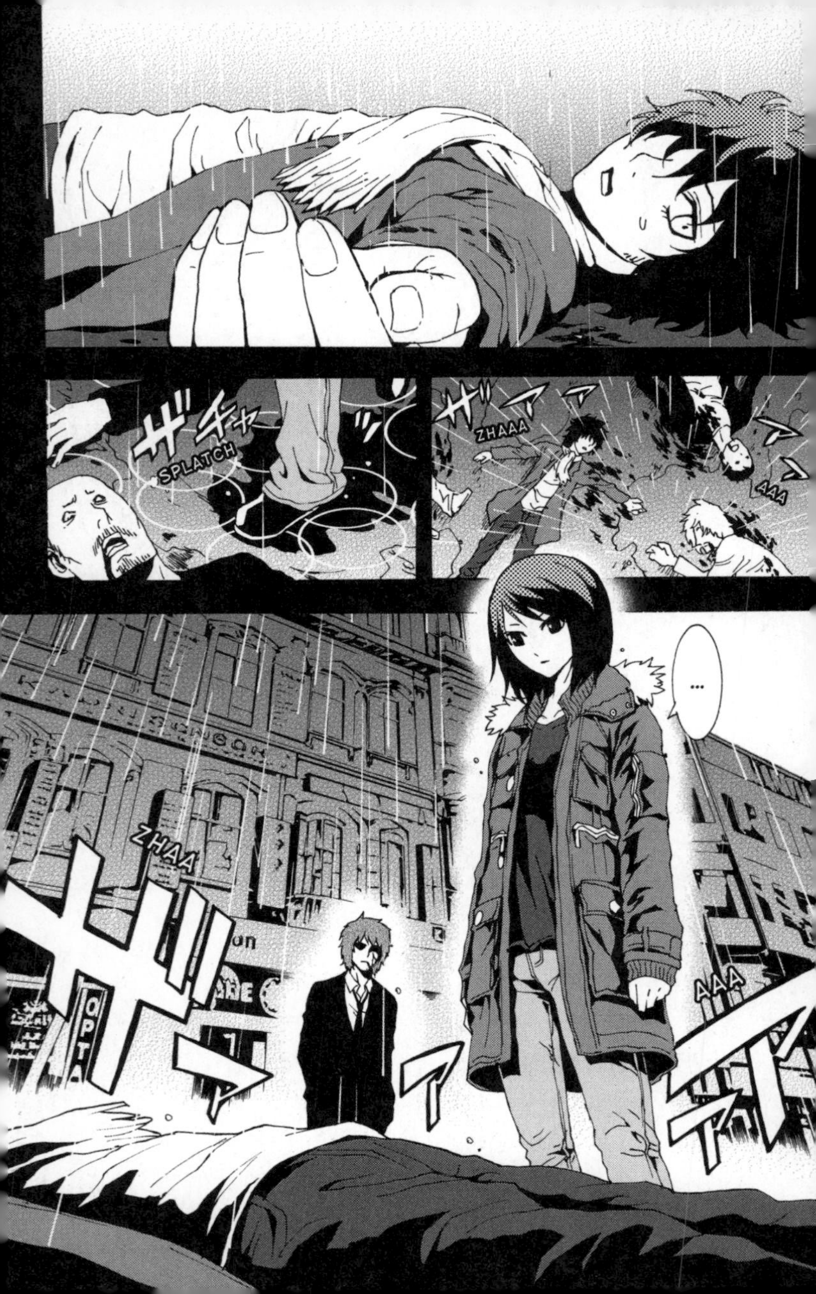
ZHAAA
AAA
SPLATCH
...
ZHAAA
AAA

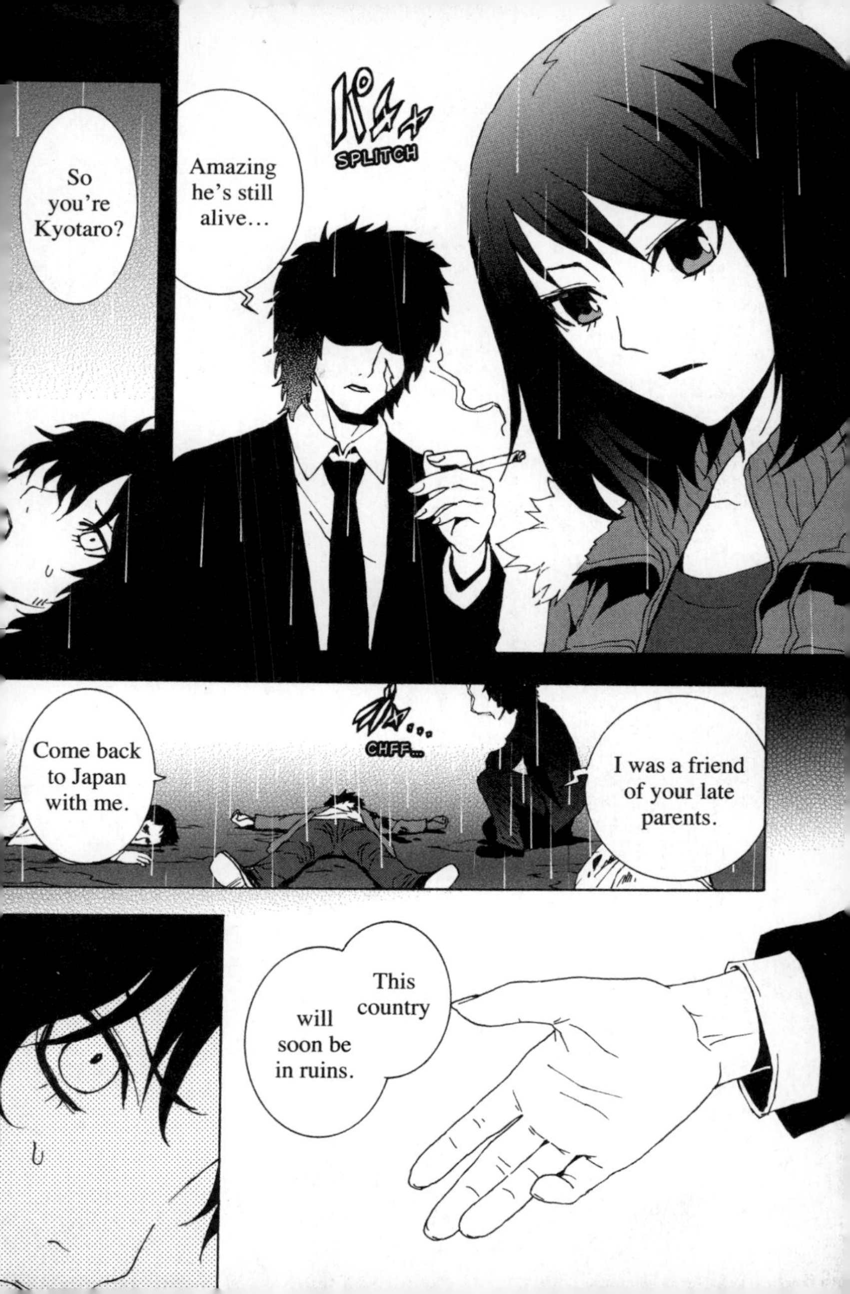
SPLITCH
Amazing he's still alive…
So you're Kyotaro?
I was a friend of your late parents.
CHFF...
Come back to Japan with me.
This country will soon be in ruins.

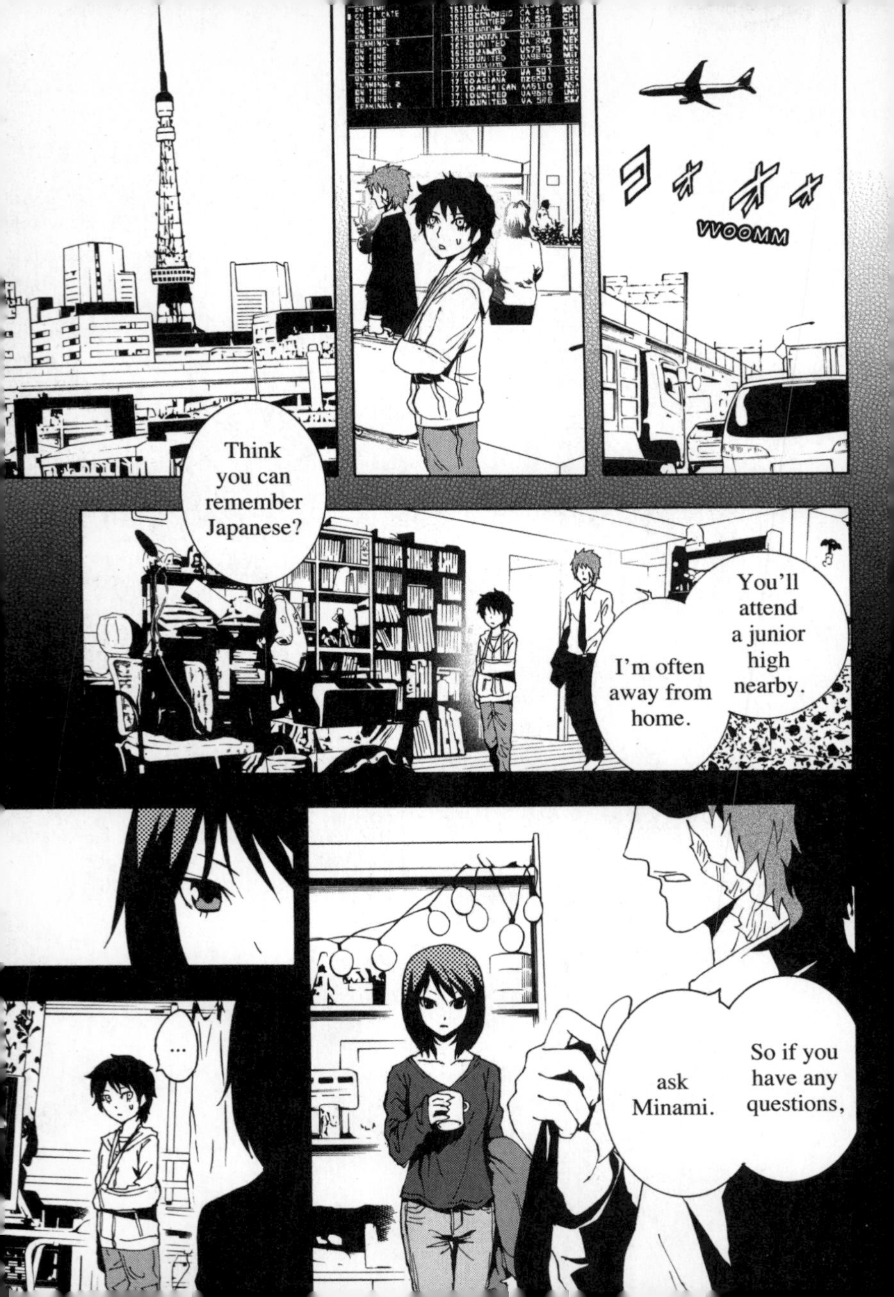
コォオォ
VVOOMM
Think you can remember Japanese?
You'll attend a junior high nearby.
I'm often away from home.
So if you have any questions,
ask Minami.
...

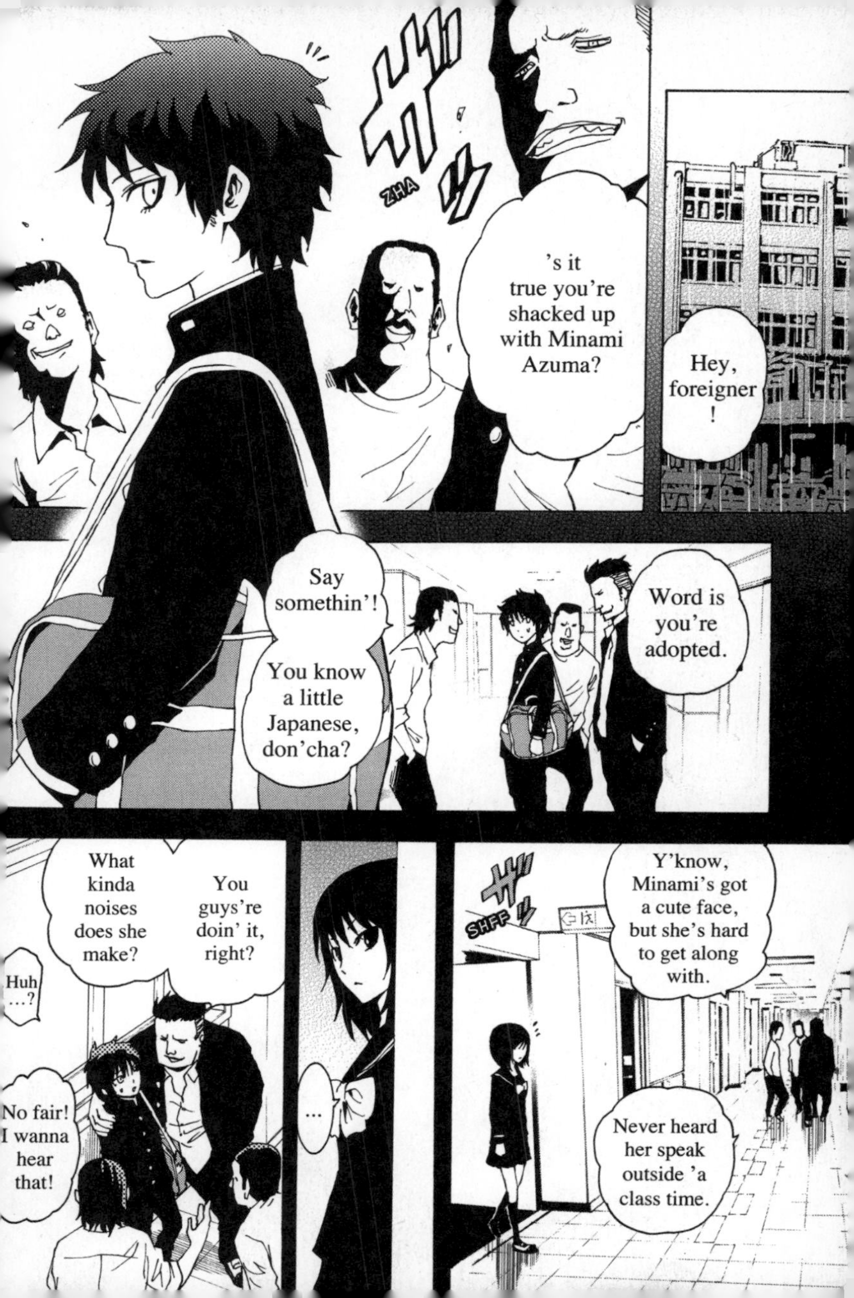
Hey, foreigner!
's it true you're shacked up with Minami Azuma?
ZHA
Word is you're adopted.
Say somethin'!
You know a little Japanese, don'cha?
Y'know, Minami's got a cute face, but she's hard to get along with.
SHFF
Never heard her speak outside 'a class time.
...
You guys're doin' it, right?
What kinda noises does she make?
Huh ...?
No fair! I wanna hear that!

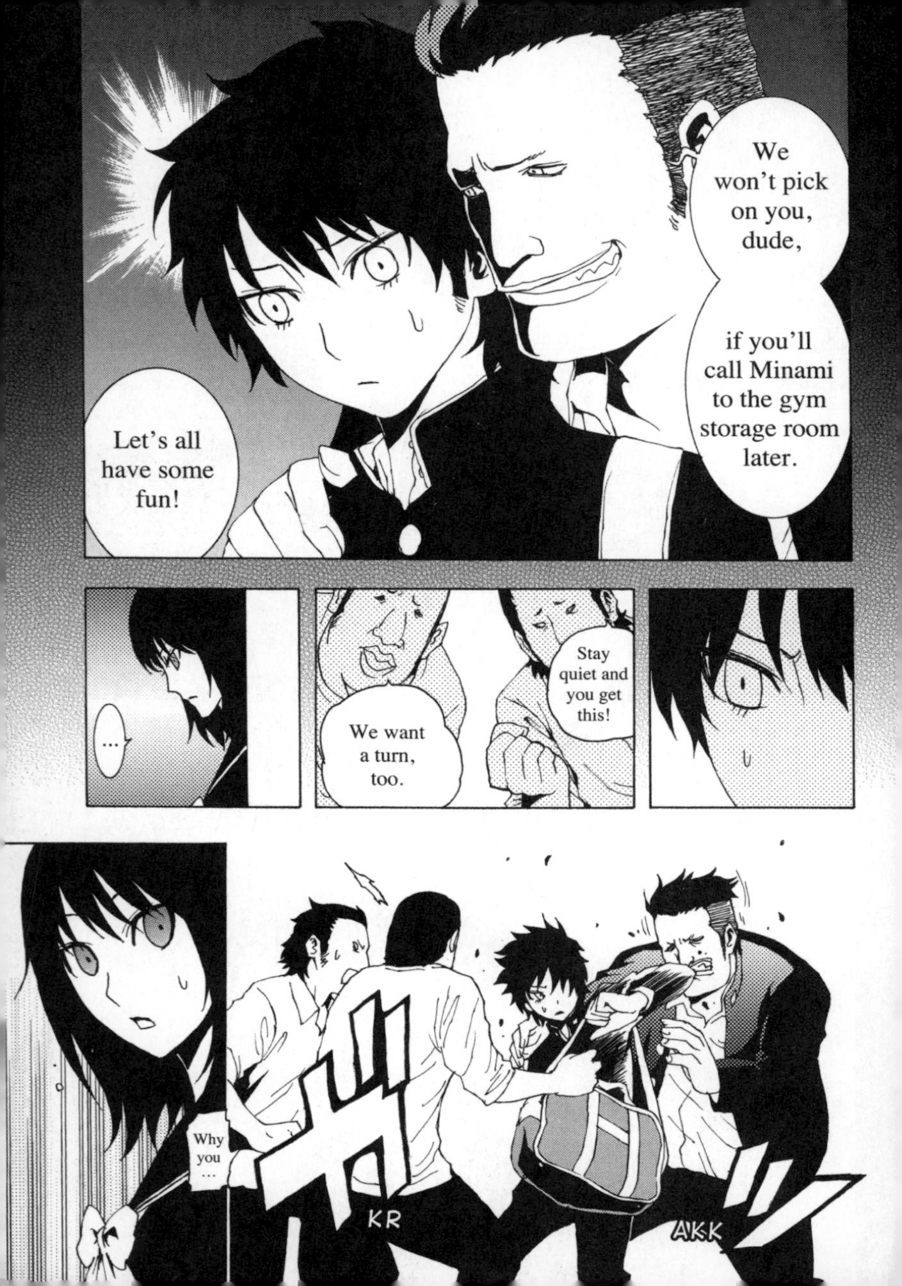
We won't pick on you, dude,
if you'll call Minami to the gym storage room later.
Let's all have some fun!
Stay quiet and you get this!
We want a turn, too.
...
Why you ...
KR
AKK

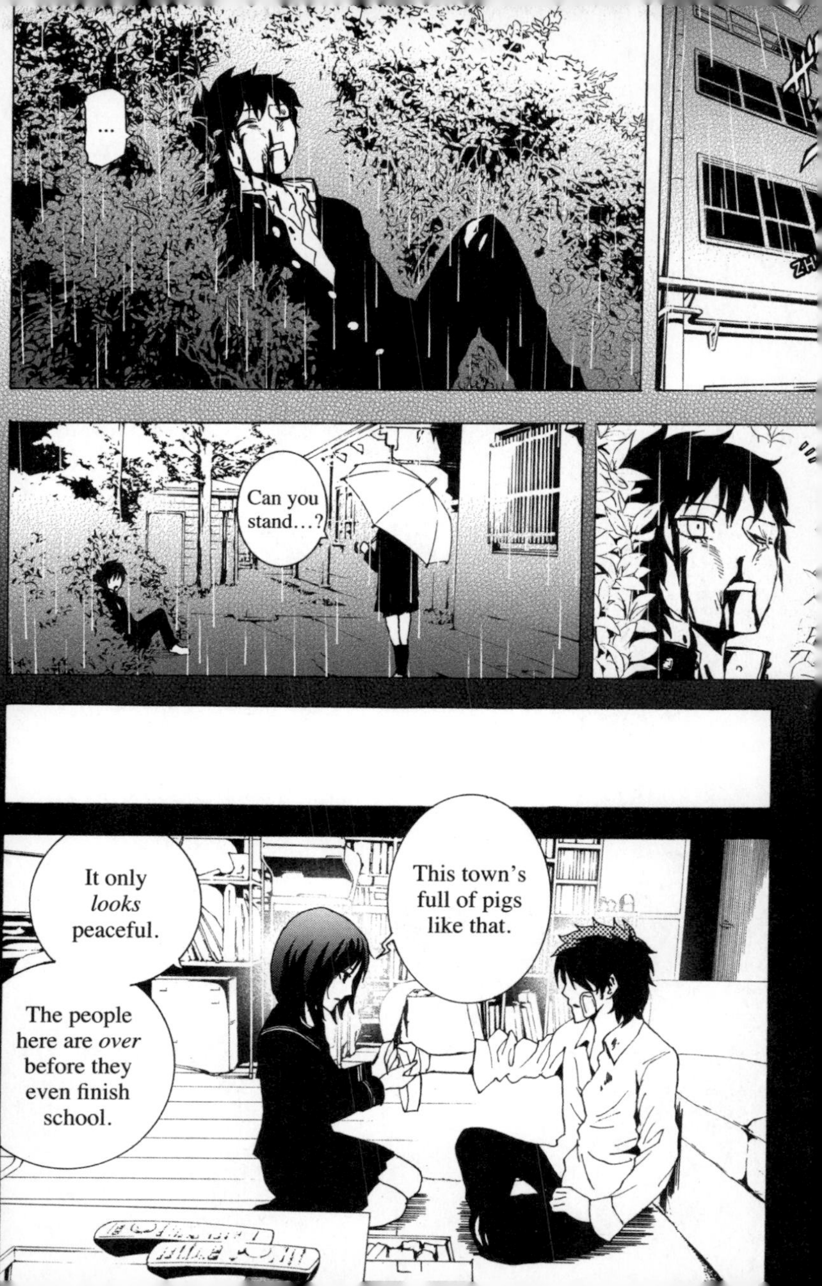
...
ZH
Can you stand…?
This town's full of pigs like that.
It only *looks* peaceful.
The people here are *over* before they even finish school.

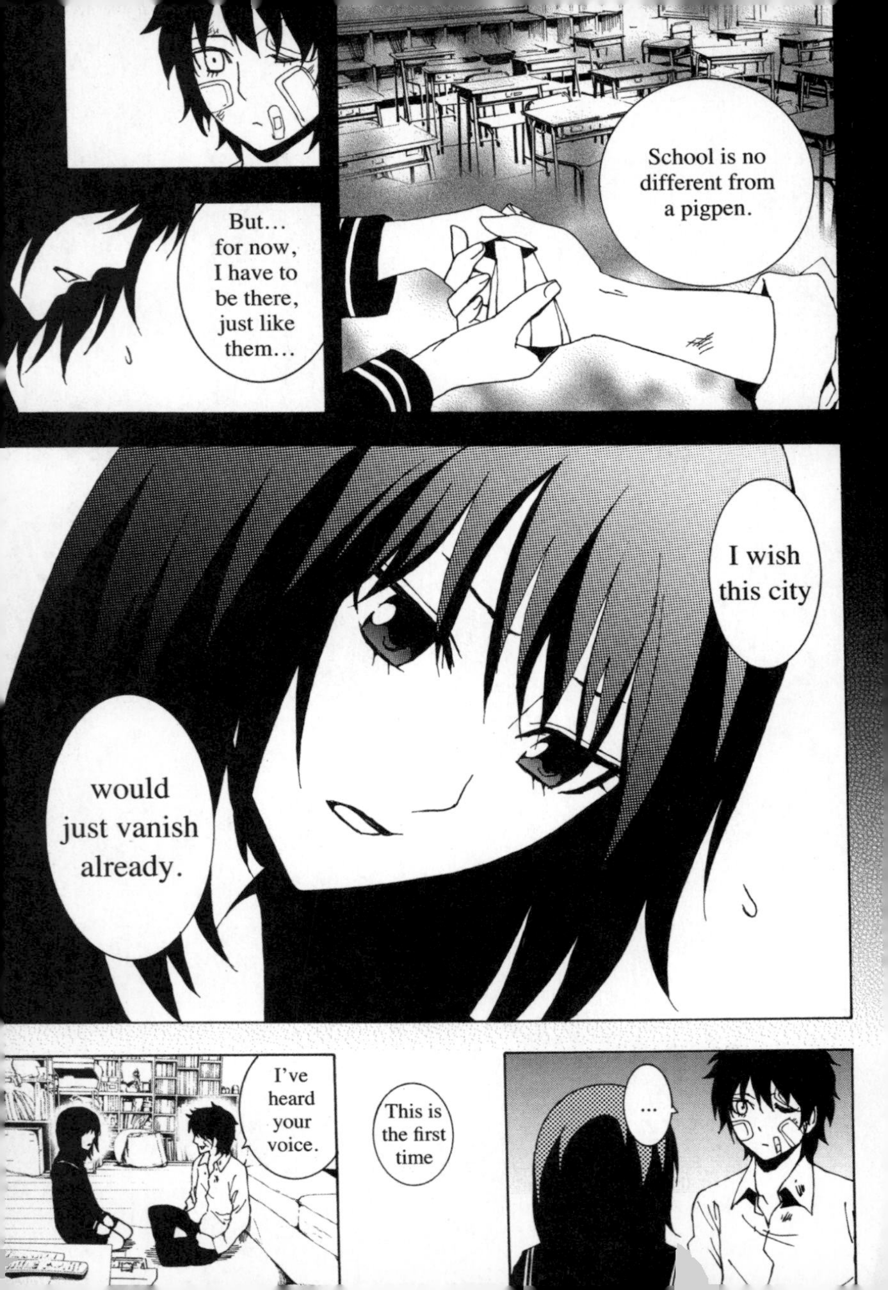
School is no different from a pigpen.
But… for now, I have to be there, just like them…
I wish this city
would just vanish already.
…
This is the first time
I've heard your voice.

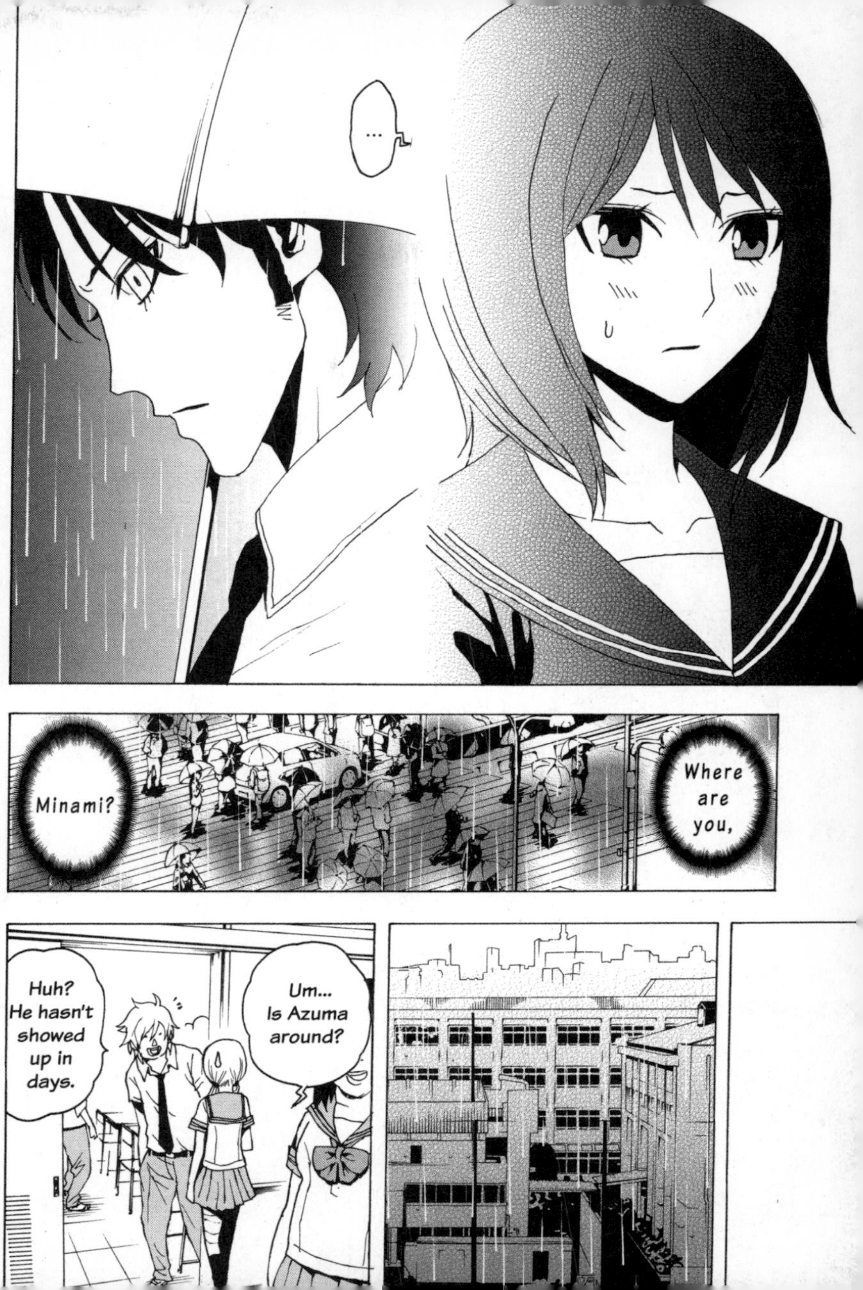
...
Where are you,
Minami?
Um... Is Azuma around?
Huh? He hasn't showed up in days.

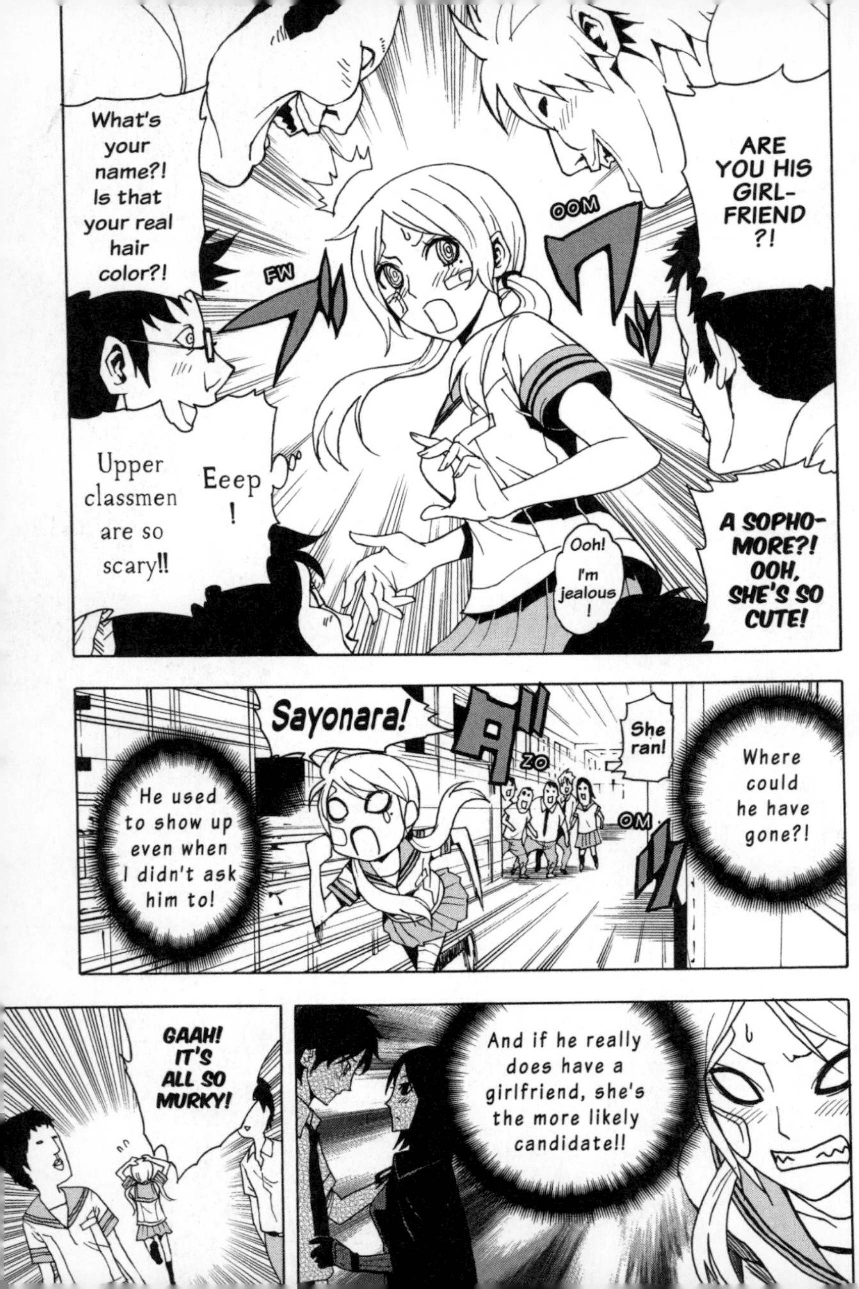
ARE YOU HIS GIRL-FRIEND ?!
OOM
What's your name?! Is that your real hair color?!
FW
A SOPHO-MORE?! OOH, SHE'S SO CUTE!
Ooh! I'm jealous !
Eeep !
Upper classmen are so scary!!
Where could he have gone?!
She ran!
OM
ZO
Sayonara!
He used to show up even when I didn't ask him to!
And if he really does have a girlfriend, she's the more likely candidate!!
GAAH! IT'S ALL SO MURKY!

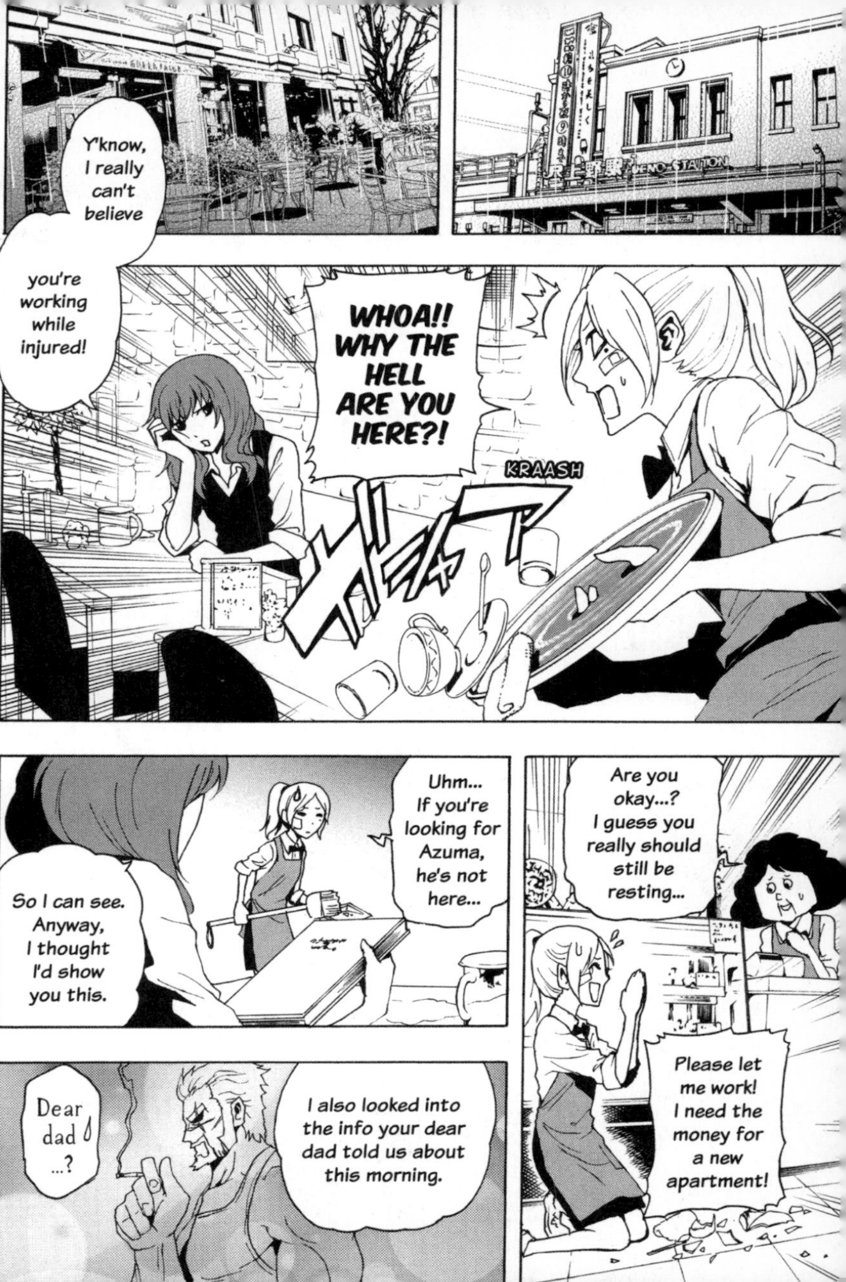
UENO STATION
Y'know, I really can't believe
you're working while injured!
WHOA!! WHY THE HELL ARE YOU HERE?!
KRAASH
Are you okay...? I guess you really should still be resting...
Please let me work! I need the money for a new apartment!
Uhm... If you're looking for Azuma, he's not here...
So I can see. Anyway, I thought I'd show you this.
I also looked into the info your dear dad told us about this morning.
Dear dad ...?

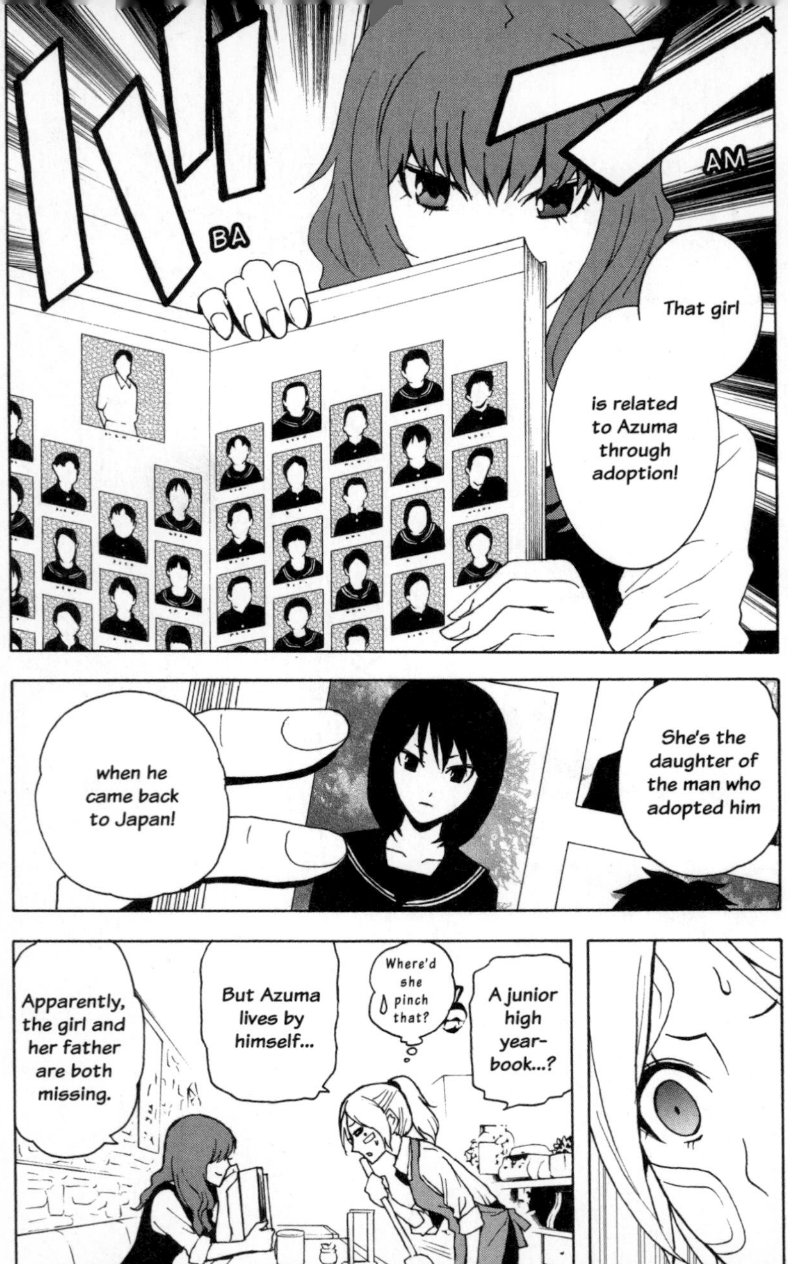
AM
BA
That girl
is related to Azuma through adoption!
She's the daughter of the man who adopted him
when he came back to Japan!
A junior high year-book...?
Where'd she pinch that?
But Azuma lives by himself...
Apparently, the girl and her father are both missing.

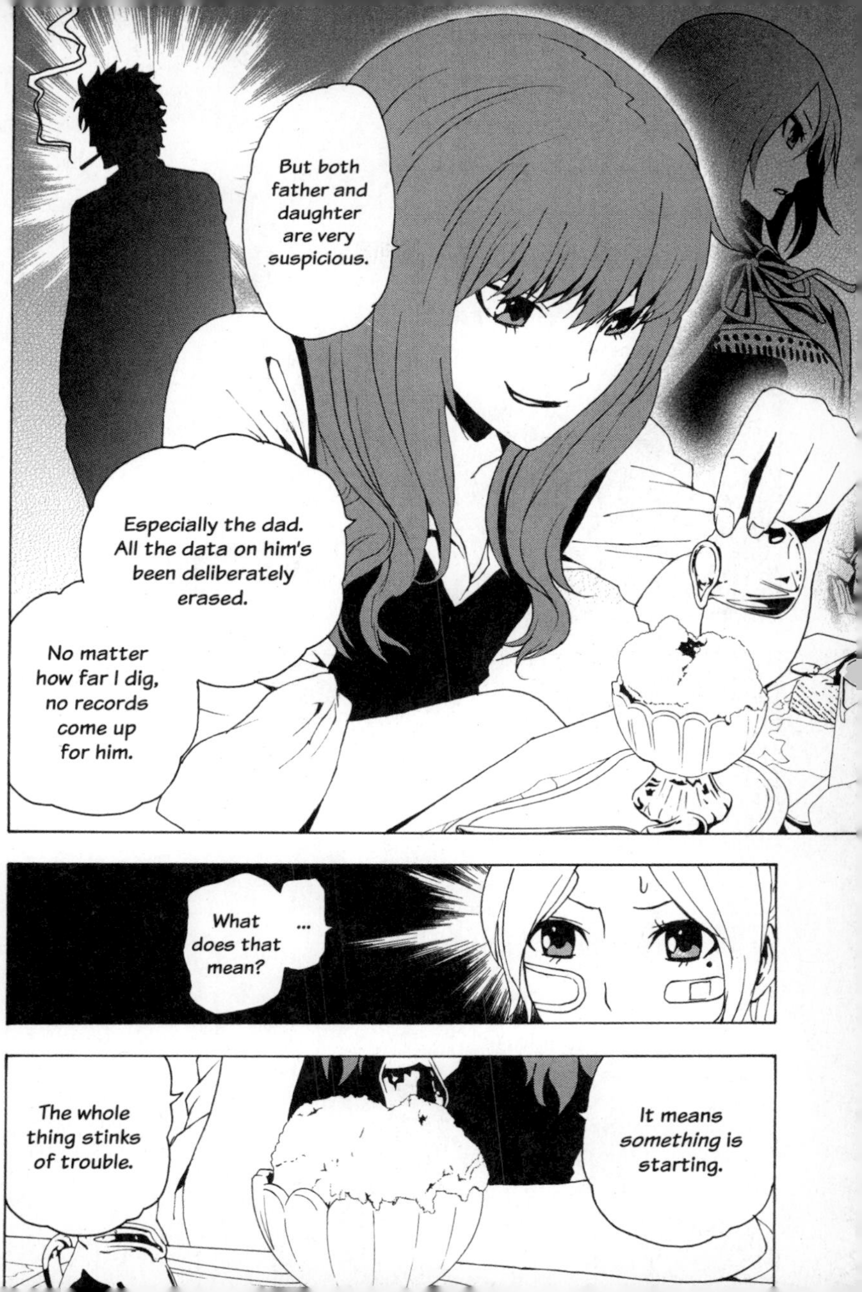
But both father and daughter are very suspicious.
Especially the dad. All the data on him's been deliberately erased.
No matter how far I dig, no records come up for him.
...
What does that mean?
It means *something* is starting.
The whole thing stinks of trouble.

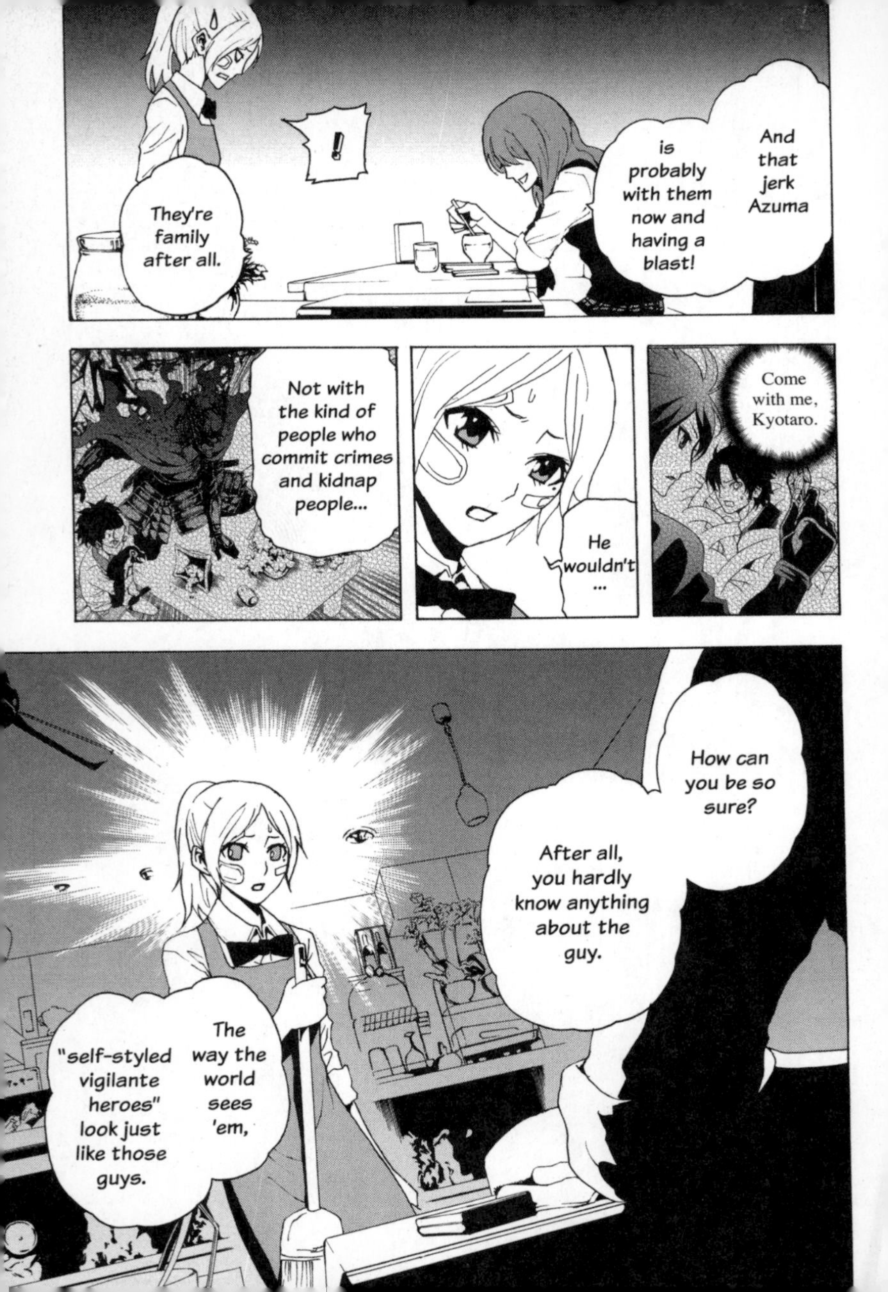
And that jerk Azuma
is probably with them now and having a blast!
!
They're family after all.
Come with me, Kyotaro.
He wouldn't ...
Not with the kind of people who commit crimes and kidnap people...
How can you be so sure?
After all, you hardly know anything about the guy.
The way the world sees 'em,
"self-styled vigilante heroes" look just like those guys.

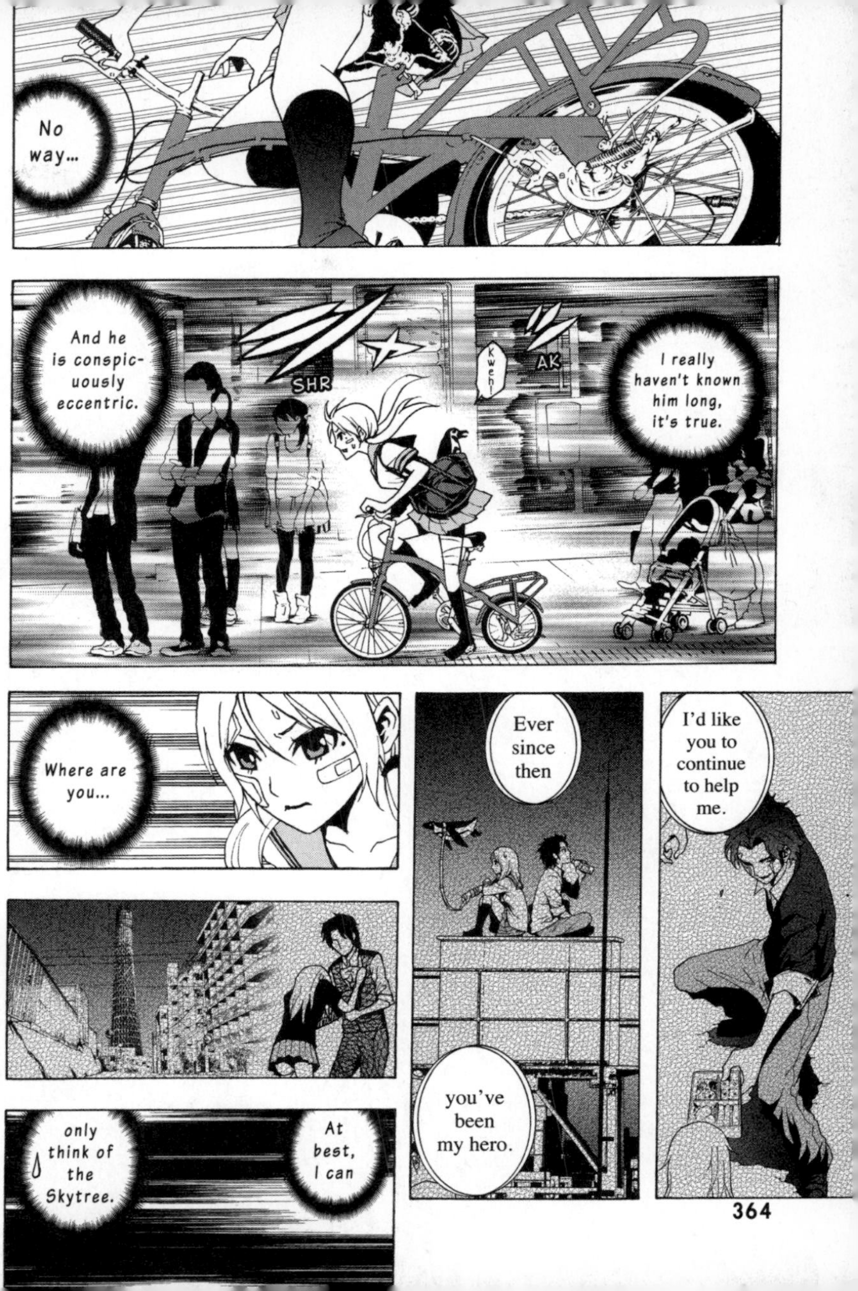
No way...
I really haven't known him long, it's true.
AK
Kweh!
SHR
And he is conspicuously eccentric.
I'd like you to continue to help me.
Ever since then
you've been my hero.
Where are you...
At best, I can
only think of the Skytree.

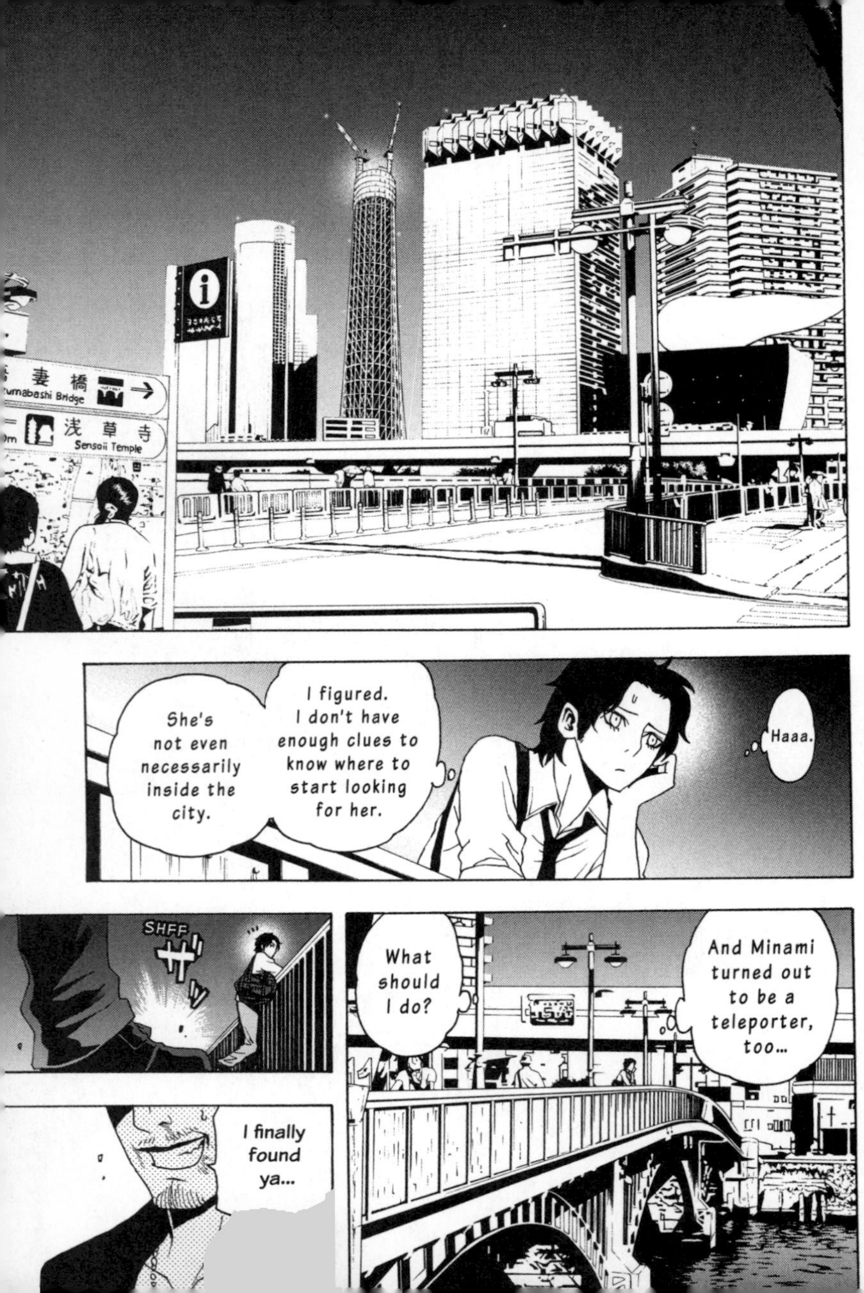
妻橋
umabashi Bridge
浅草寺
Sensoji Temple
Haaa.
I figured. I don't have enough clues to know where to start looking for her.
She's not even necessarily inside the city.
And Minami turned out to be a teleporter, too...
What should I do?
SHFF
I finally found ya...

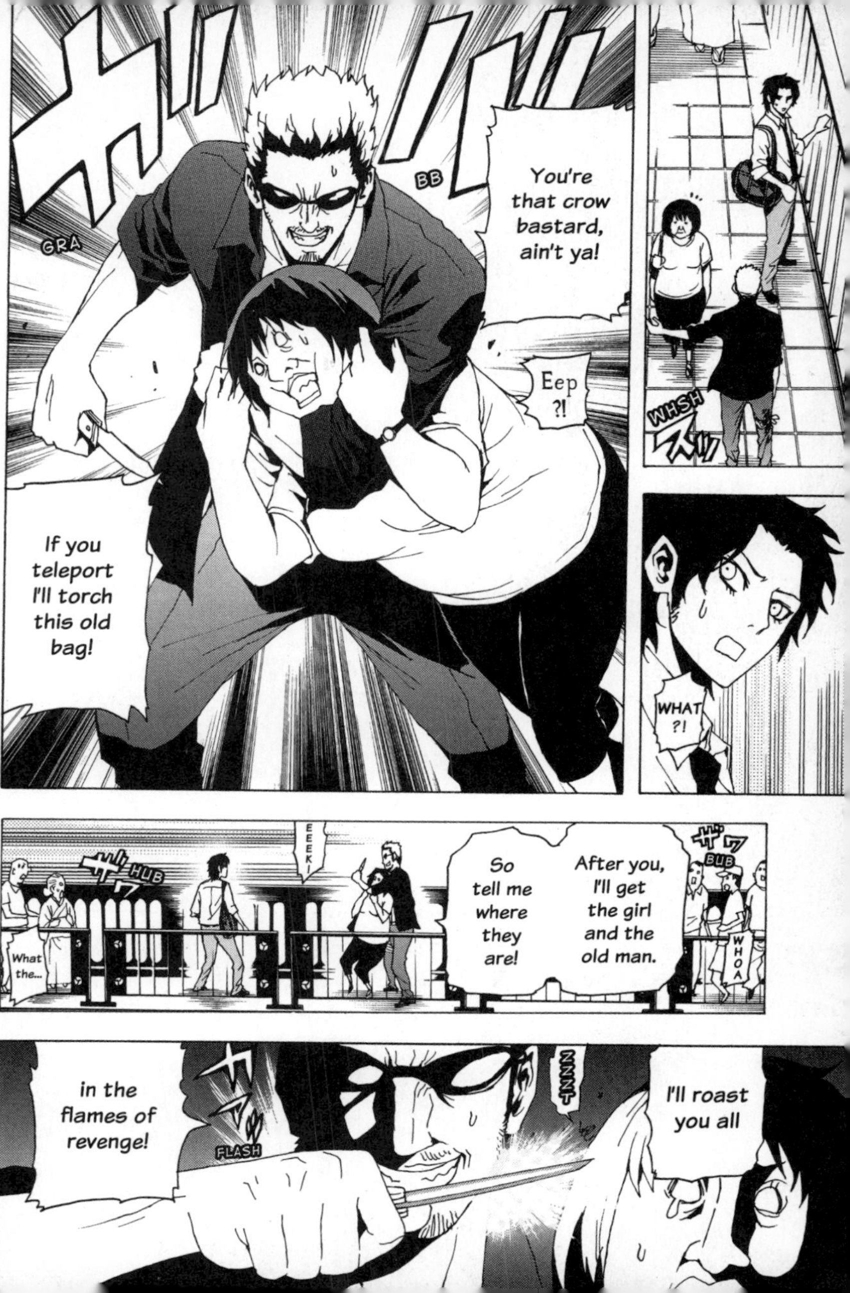
WHSH
WHAT ?!
You're that crow bastard, ain't ya!
BB
Eep ?!
GRA
If you teleport I'll torch this old bag!
BUB
WHOA
After you, I'll get the girl and the old man.
So tell me where they are!
EEEK!
HUB
What the...
I'll roast you all
ZZZT
in the flames of revenge!
FLASH

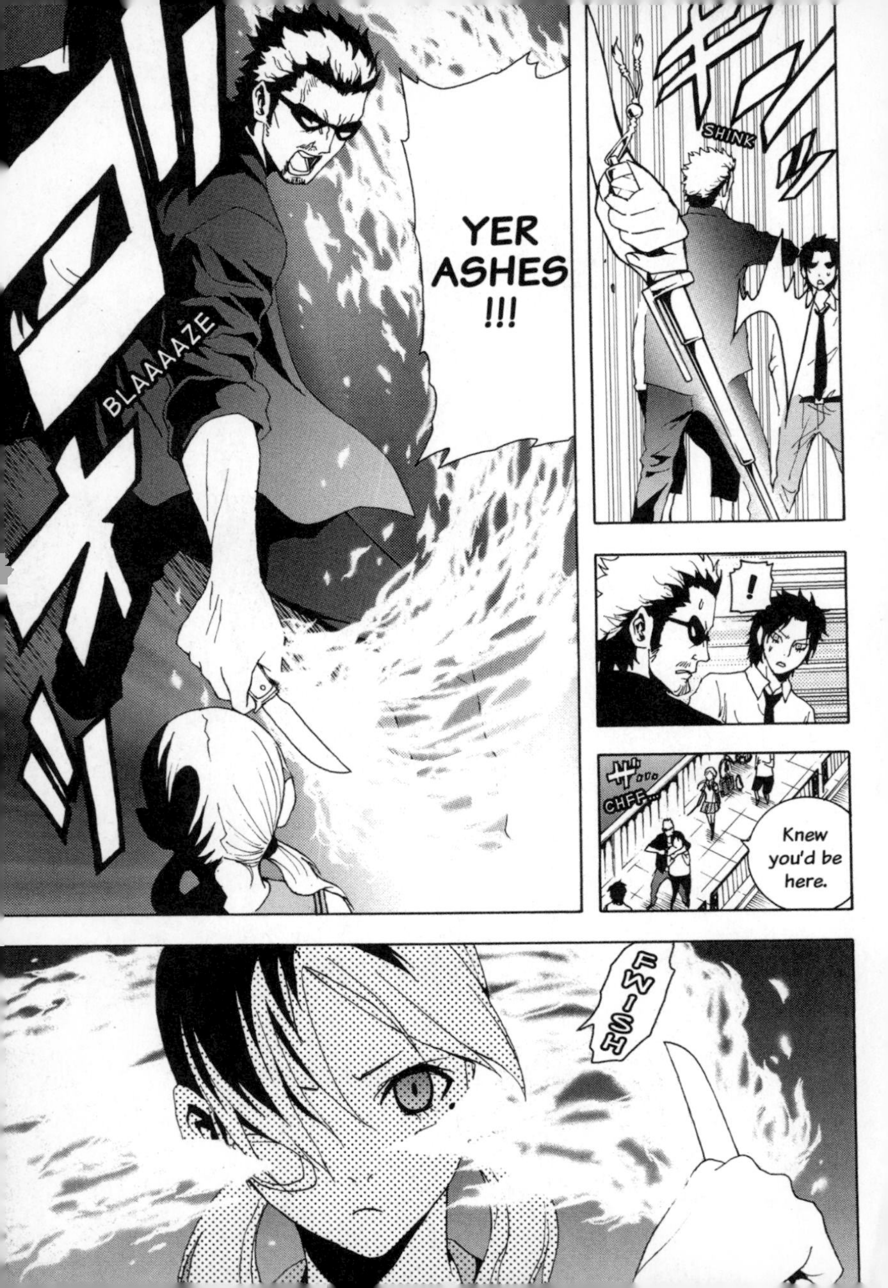
SHINK
!
CHFF...
Knew you'd be here.
BLAAAAZE
YER ASHES !!!
FWISH

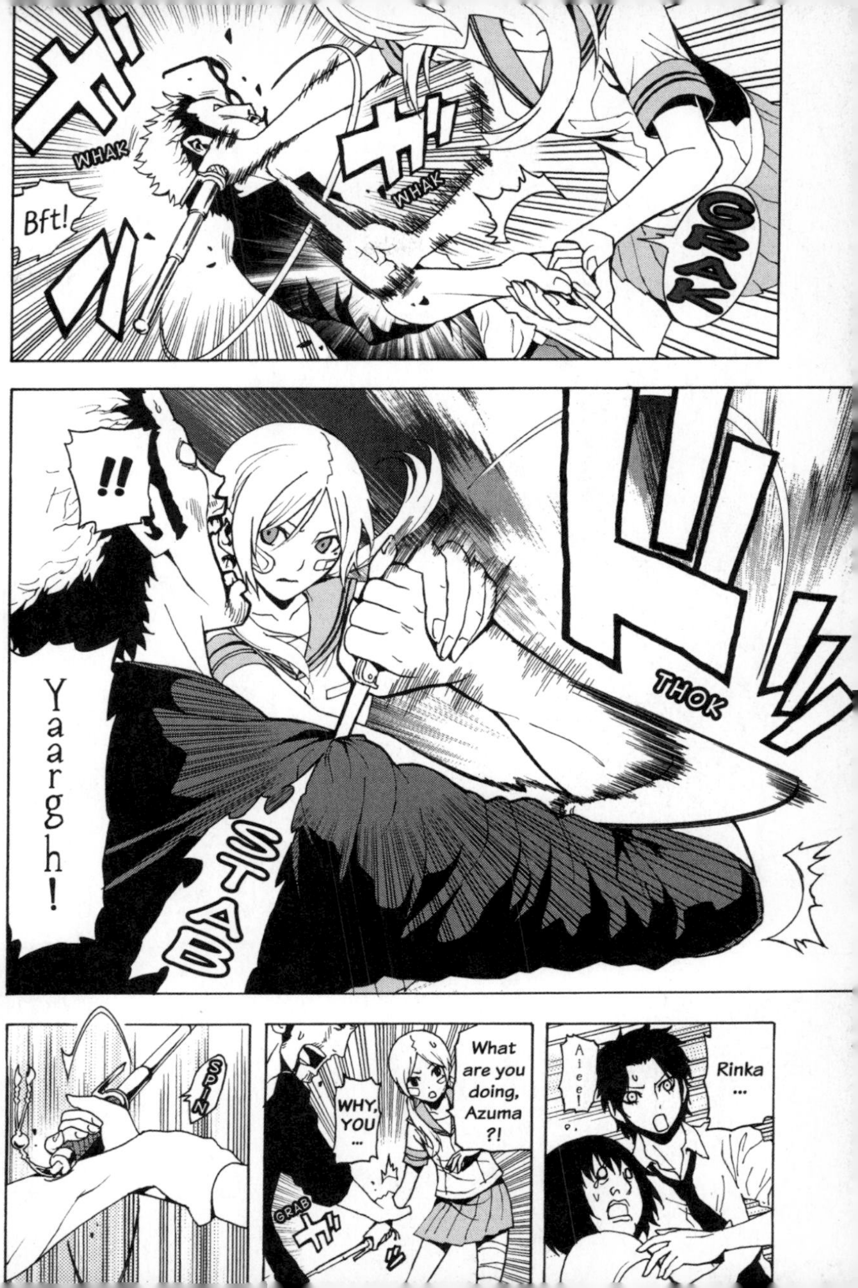
GRAK
WHAK
WHAK
Bft!
THOK
!!
STAB
Yaaargh!
Rinka ...
Aieee!
What are you doing, Azuma ?!
WHY, YOU ...
GRAB
SPIN

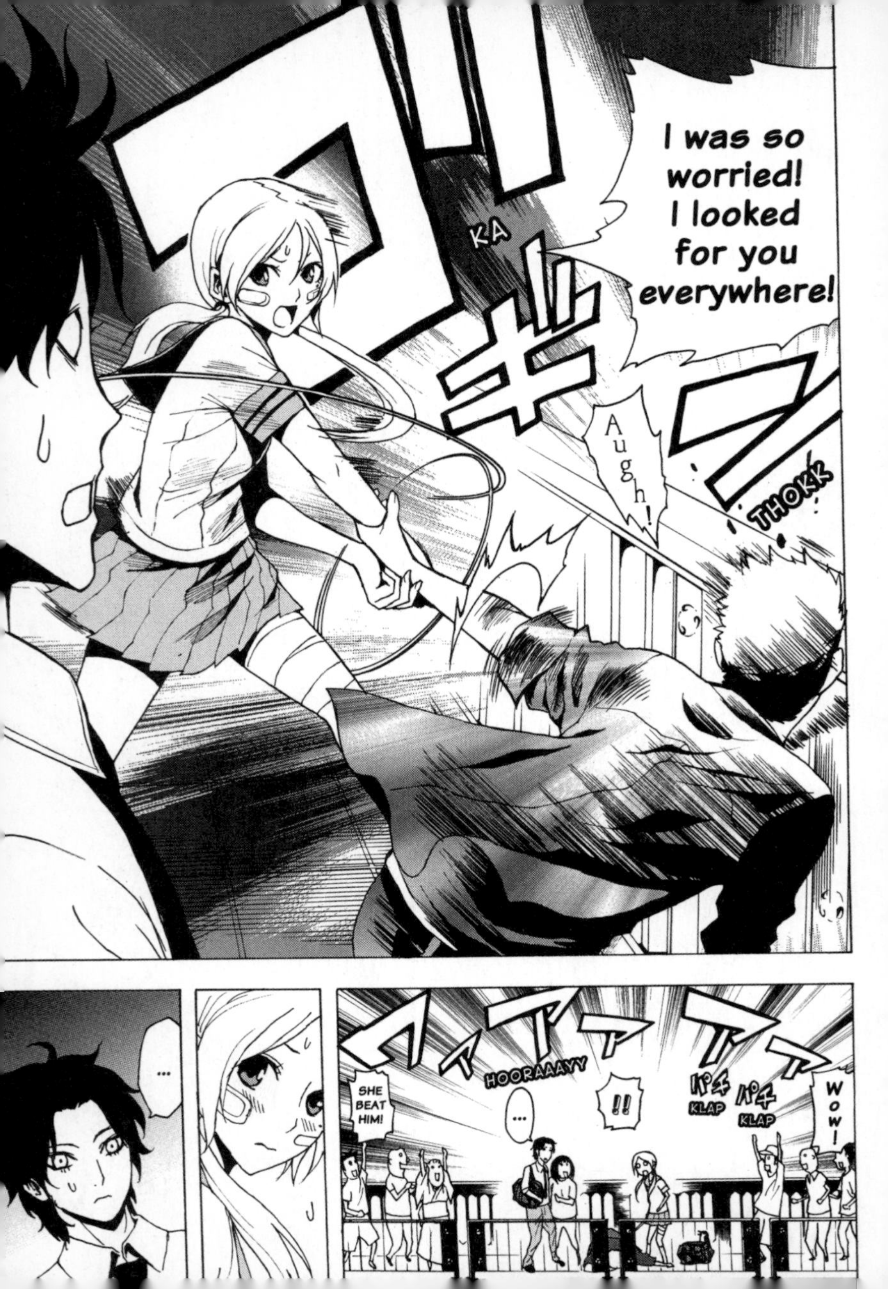
I was so worried! I looked for you everywhere!
KA
Augh!
THOKK
Wow!
KLAP
KLAP
HOORAAAYY
!!
...
SHE BEAT HIM!
...

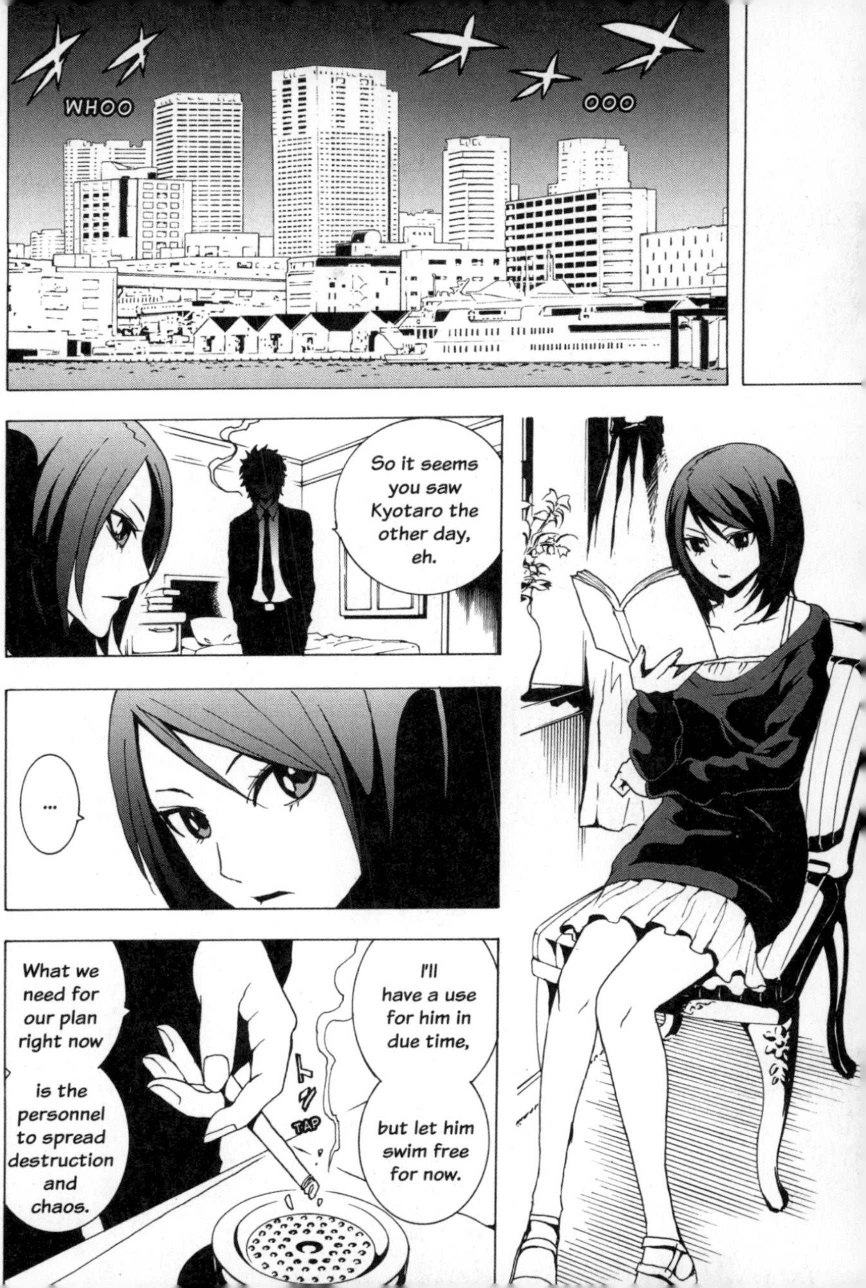
WHOO
OOO
So it seems you saw Kyotaro the other day, eh.
...
I'll have a use for him in due time,
but let him swim free for now.
TAP
What we need for our plan right now
is the personnel to spread destruction and chaos.

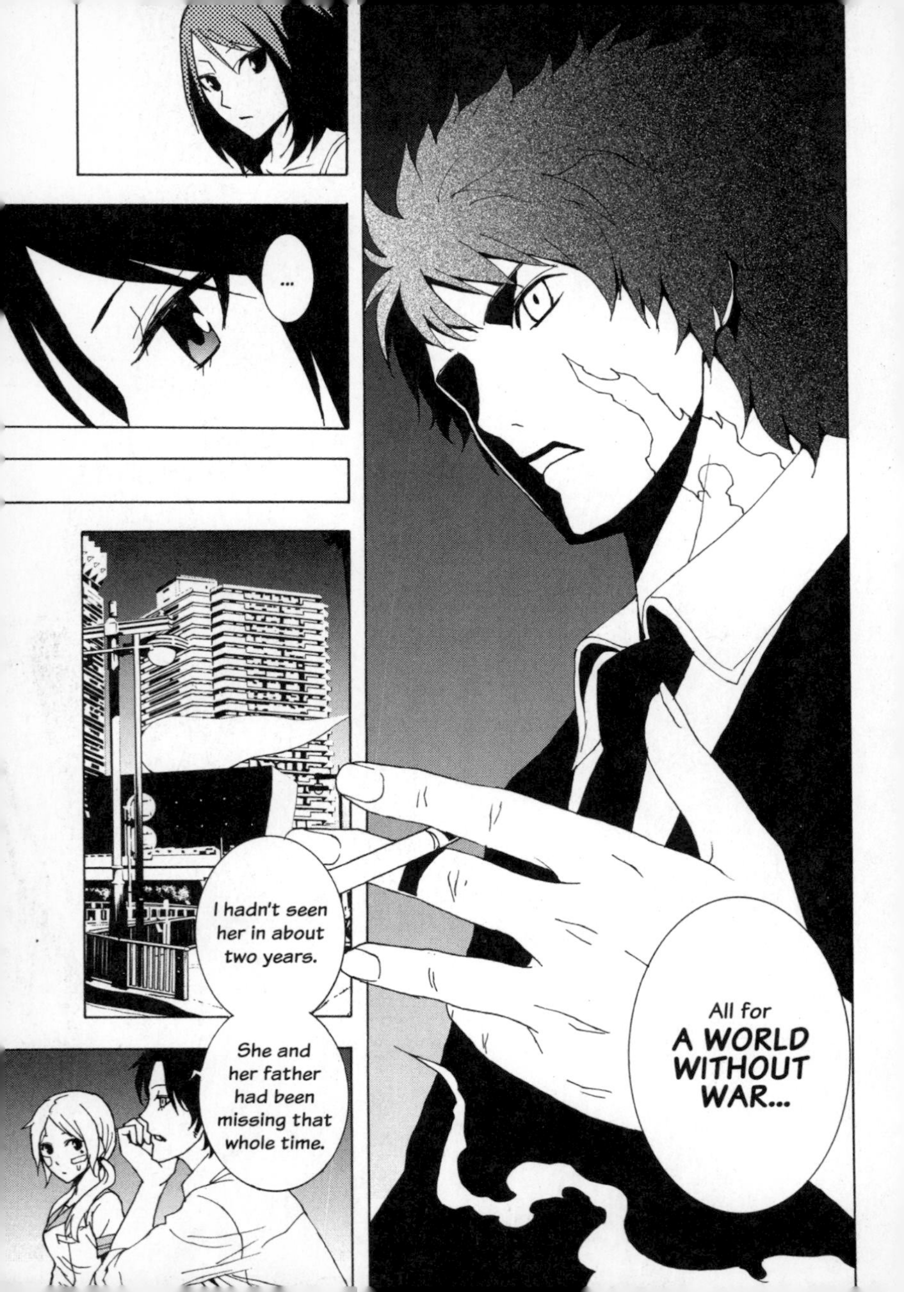
All for A WORLD WITHOUT WAR...
...
I hadn't seen her in about two years.
She and her father had been missing that whole time.

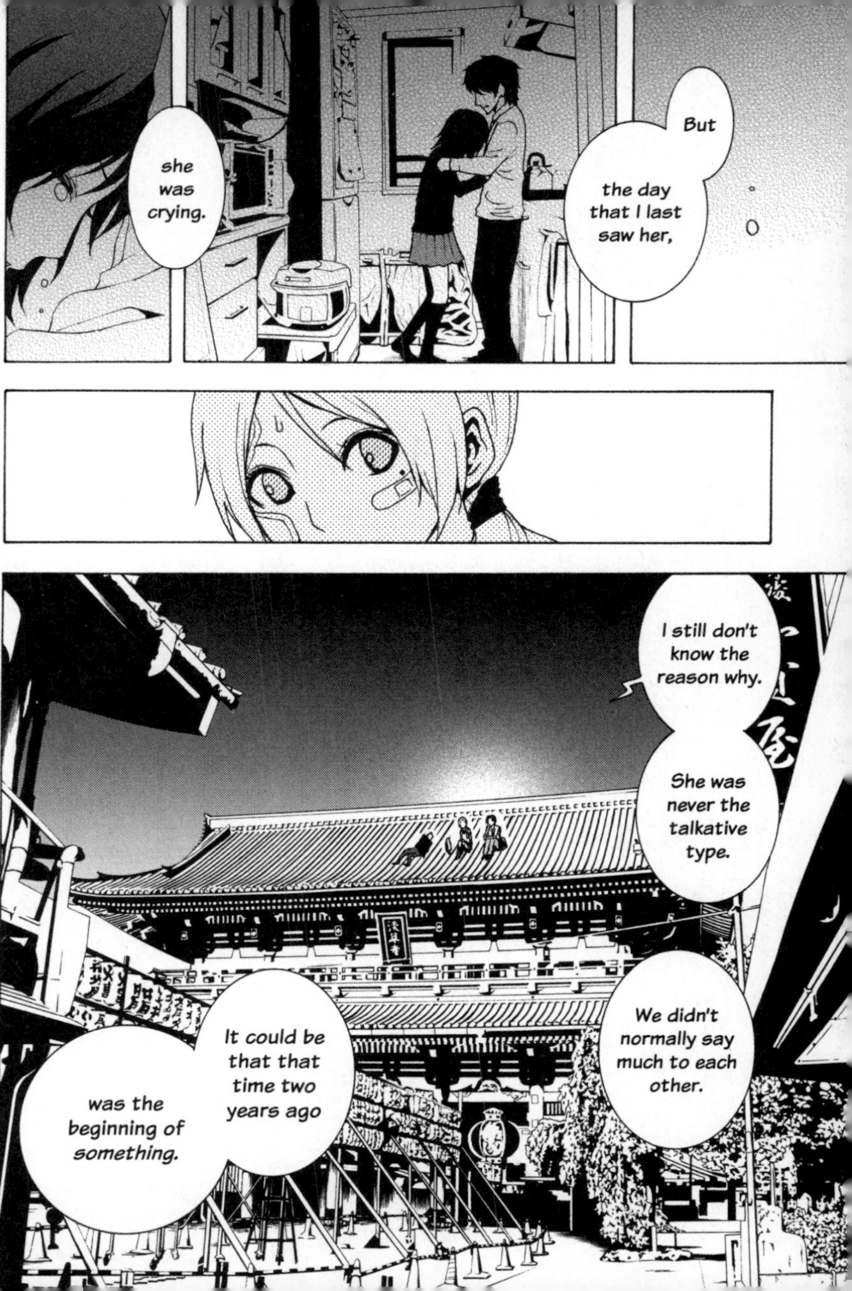
But
the day that I last saw her,
she was crying.
I still don't know the reason why.
She was never the talkative type.
We didn't normally say much to each other.
It could be that that time two years ago
was the beginning of something.

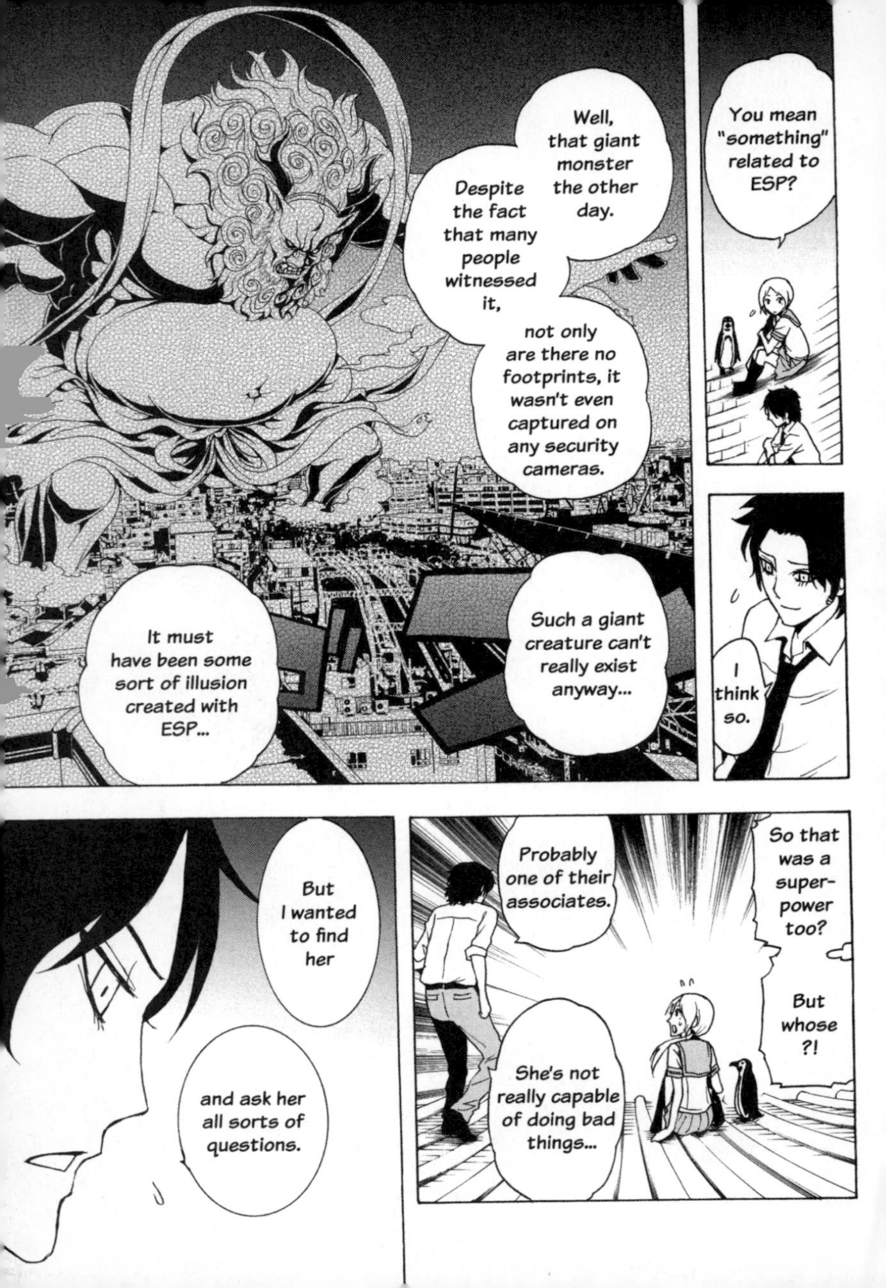
You mean "something" related to ESP?
I think so.
Well, that giant monster the other day.
Despite the fact that many people witnessed it,
not only are there no footprints, it wasn't even captured on any security cameras.
Such a giant creature can't really exist anyway...
It must have been some sort of illusion created with ESP...
So that was a super-power too?
But whose ?!
Probably one of their associates.
She's not really capable of doing bad things...
But I wanted to find her
and ask her all sorts of questions.

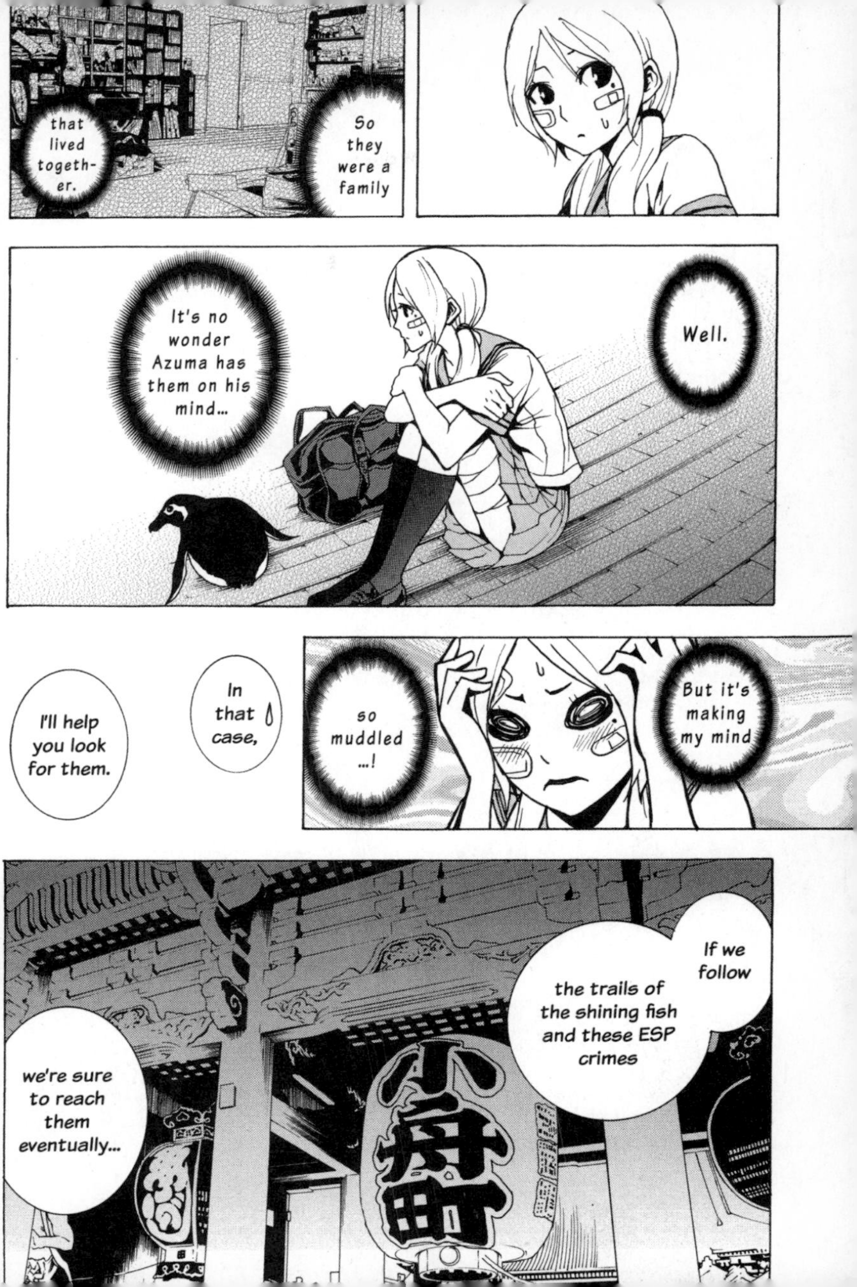
So they were a family
that lived togeth-er.
Well.
It's no wonder Azuma has them on his mind...
But it's making my mind
so muddled ...!
In that case,
I'll help you look for them.
If we follow
the trails of the shining fish and these ESP crimes
we're sure to reach them eventually...

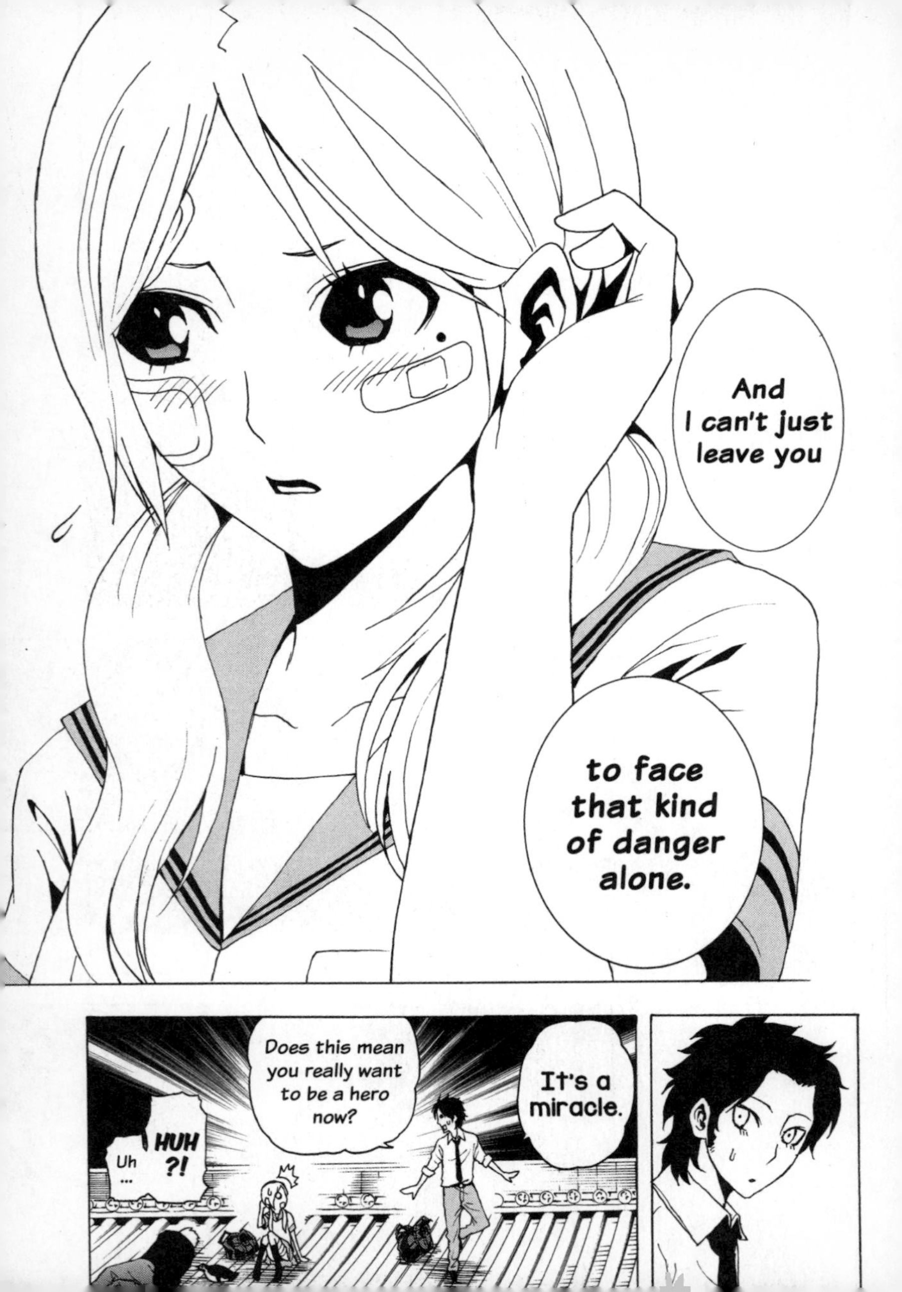
And I can't just leave you
to face that kind of danger alone.
It's a miracle.
Does this mean you really want to be a hero now?
HUH ?!
Uh ...

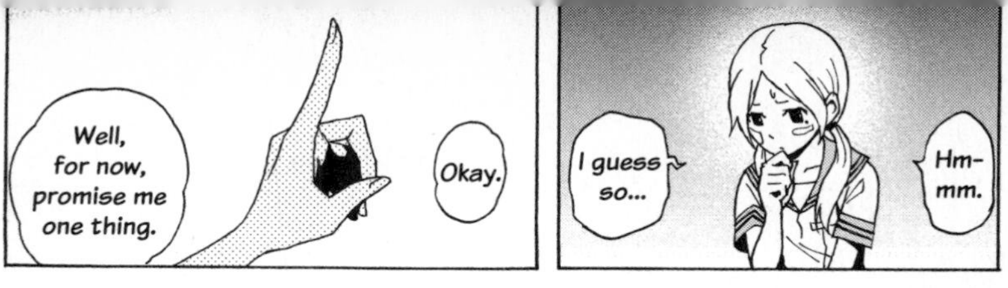
Hm-mm.
I guess so...
Okay.
Well, for now, promise me one thing.

As usual, I don't really understand him or what a hero of justice really is...

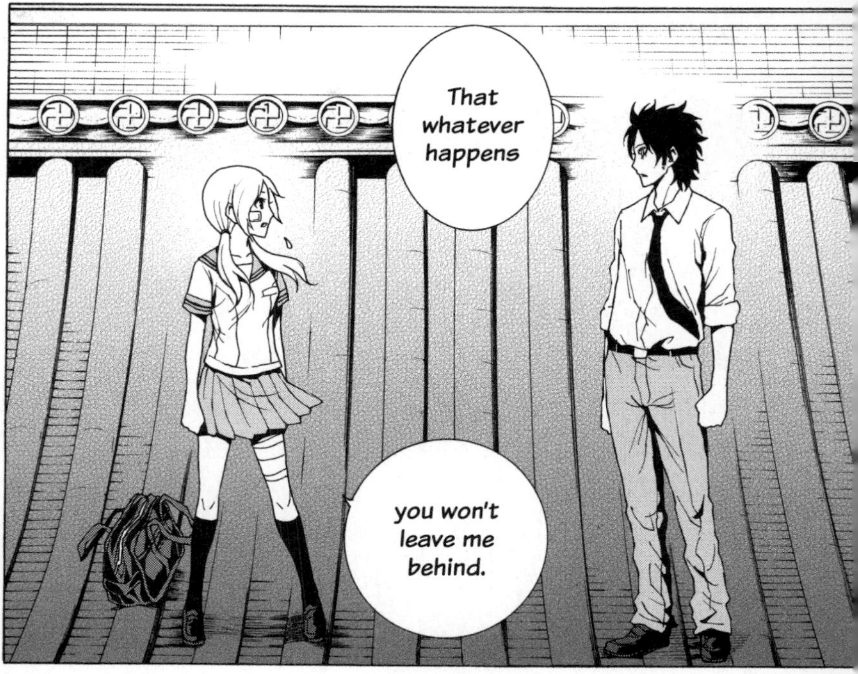
That whatever happens
you won't leave me behind.

And if something is going to happen, I have to admit I'm nervous.

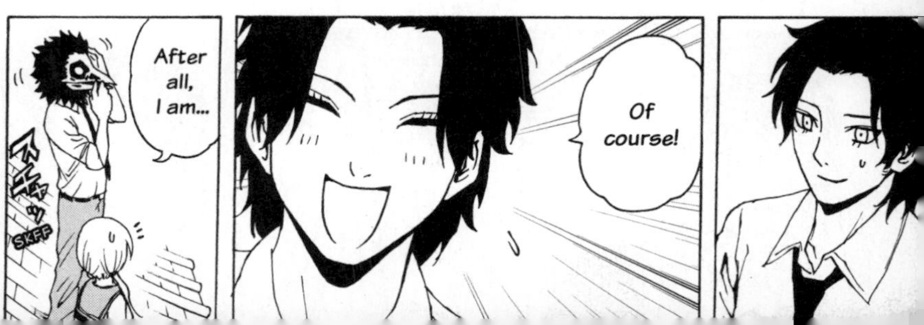
Of course!
After all, I am...
SKFF

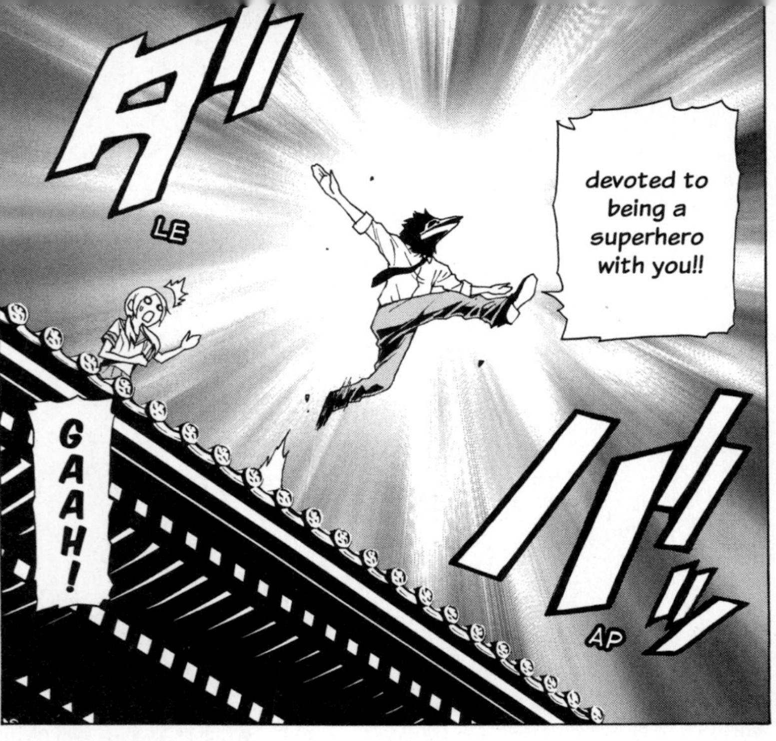
devoted to being a superhero with you!!
LE
GAAH!
AP

And I'm nervous about leaving this guy to his own devices.

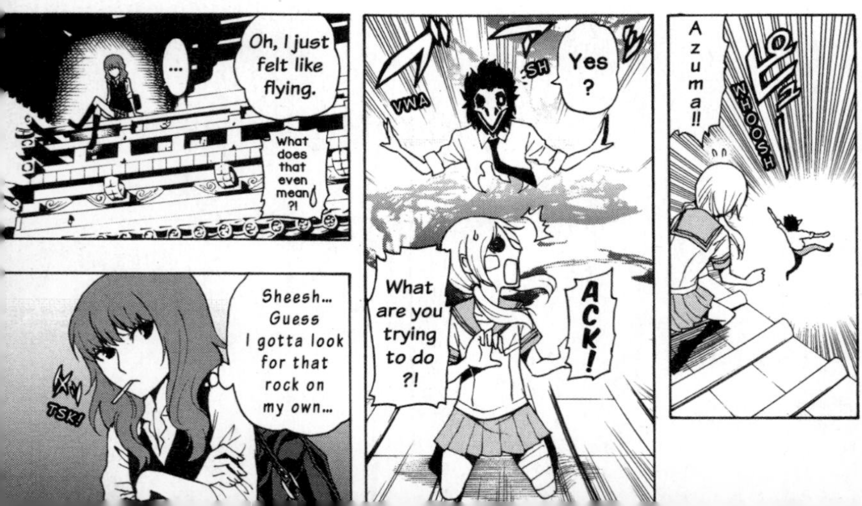
Azuma!!
WHOOSH
SH
Yes?
VWA
ACK!
What are you trying to do?!
Oh, I just felt like flying.
...
What does that even mean?!
Sheesh... Guess I gotta look for that rock on my own...
TSK!

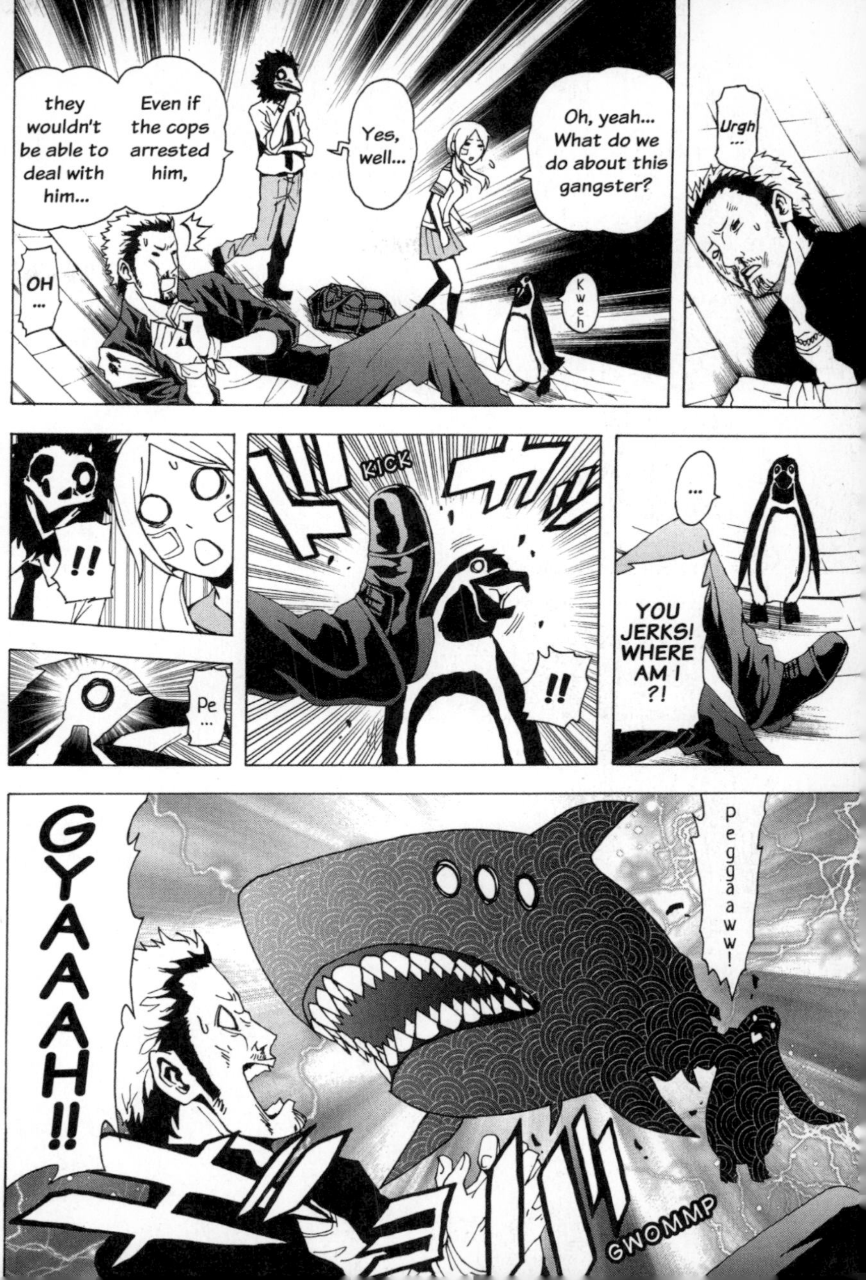
Urgh...
Oh, yeah... What do we do about this gangster?
Kweh
Yes, well...
Even if the cops arrested him,
they wouldn't be able to deal with him...
OH...
...
YOU JERKS! WHERE AM I?!
KICK
!!
!!
Pe...
Peggaaww!
GWOMMP
GYAAAH!!

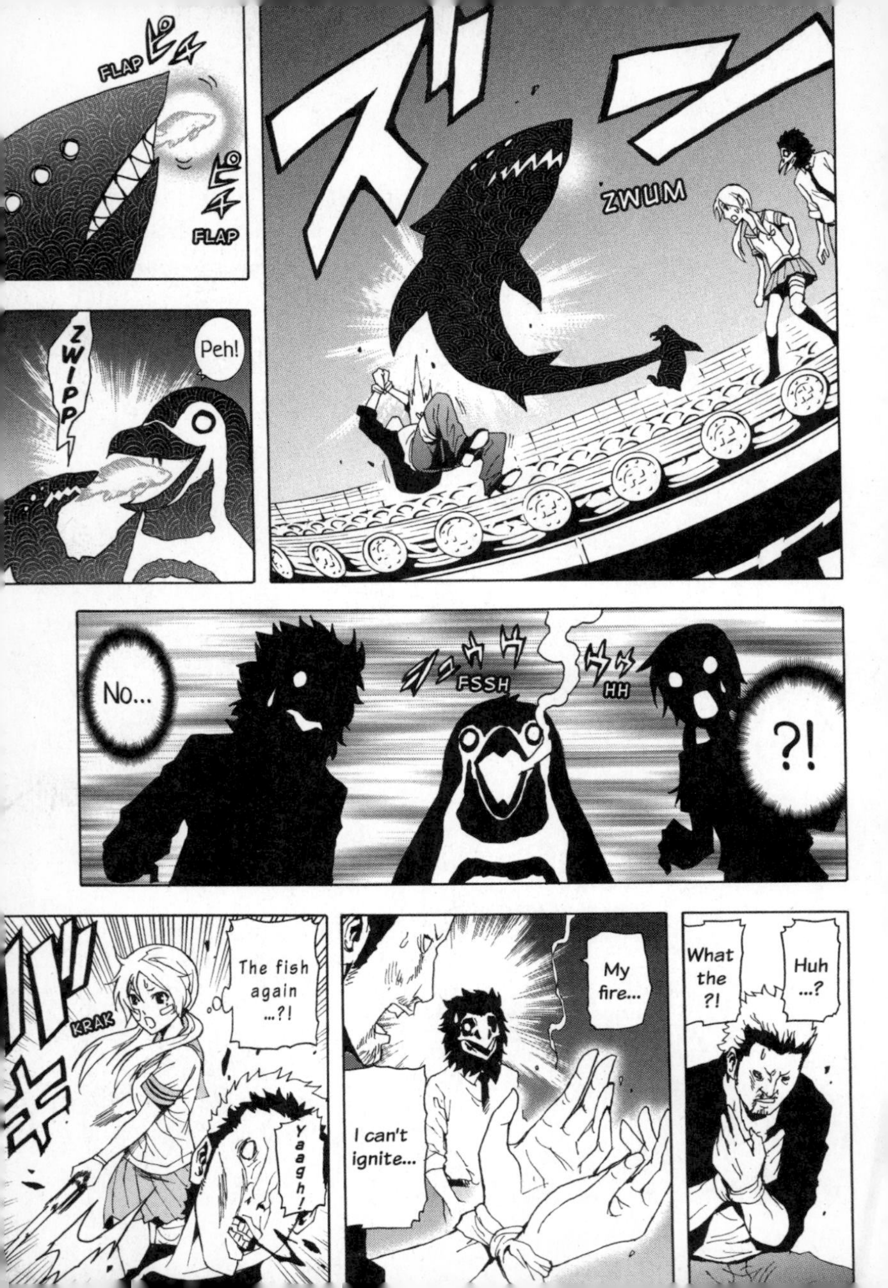
ZWUM
FLAP
FLAP
ZWIPP
Peh!
?!
HH
FSSH
No...
Huh ...?
What the ?!
My fire...
I can't ignite...
The fish again ...?!
KRAK
Yaagh!

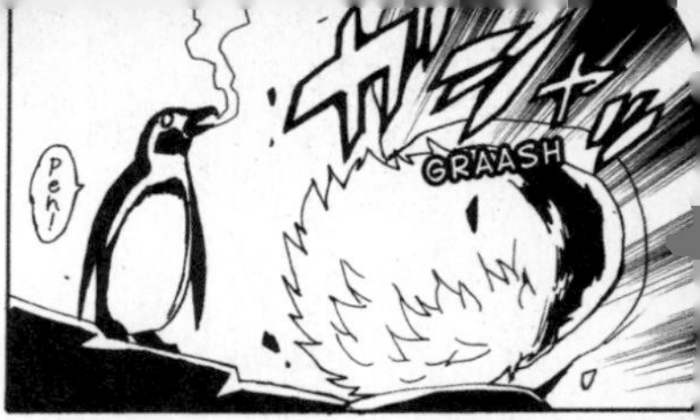
Pen!
GRAASH

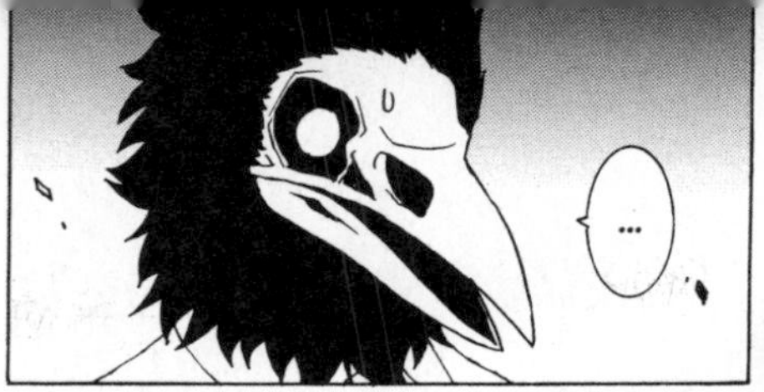
...

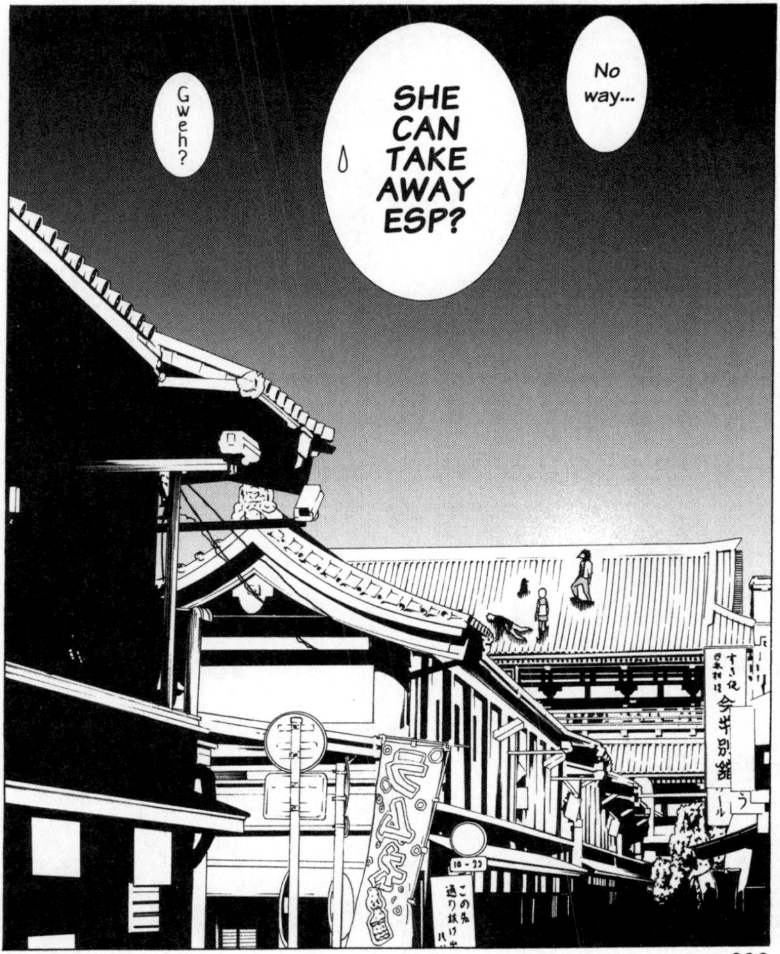
No way...
SHE CAN TAKE AWAY ESP?
Gweh?

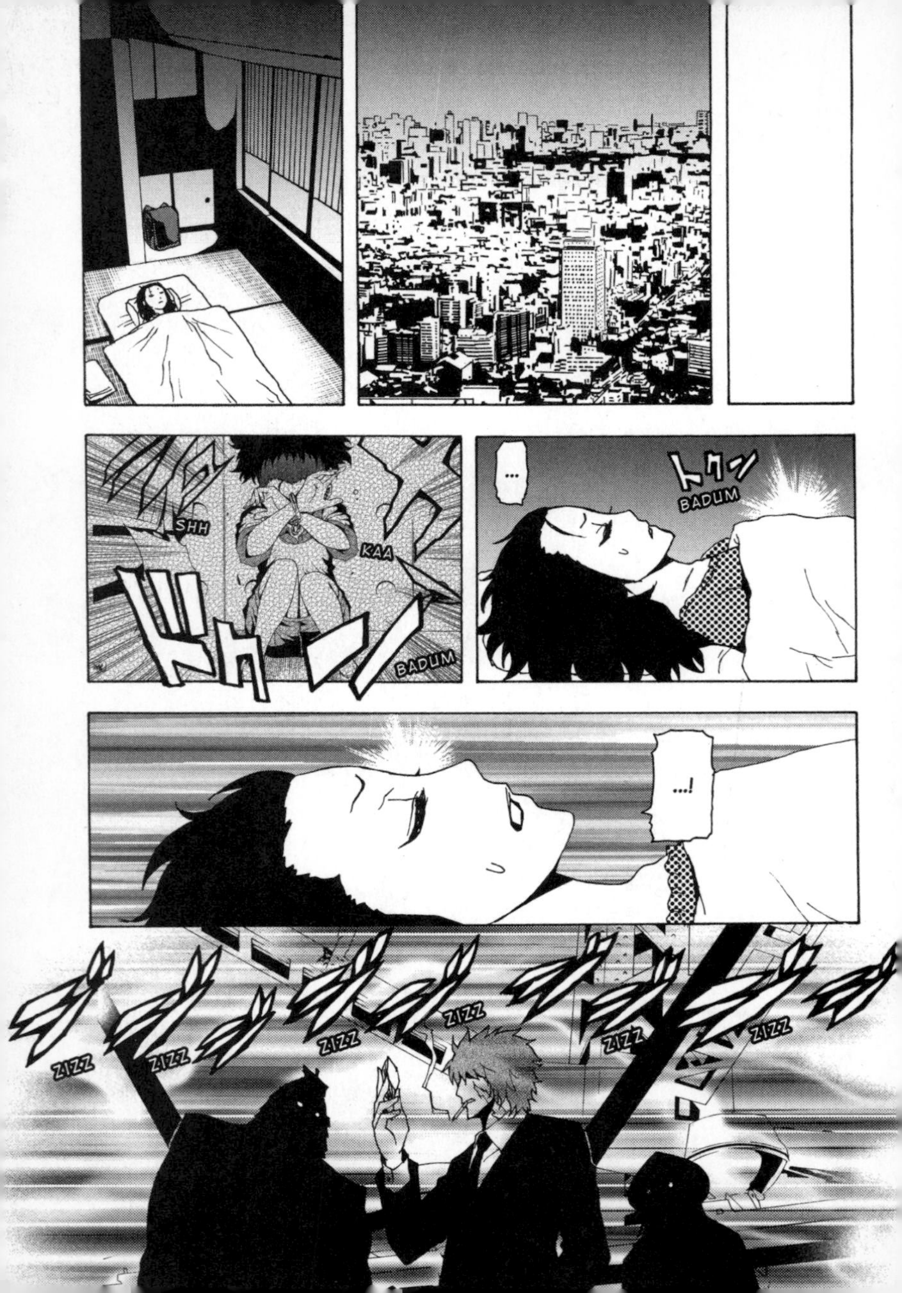
...
トクン
BADUM
SHH
KAA
BADUM
...!
ZIZZ
ZIZZ
ZIZZ
ZIZZ
ZIZZ
ZIZZ

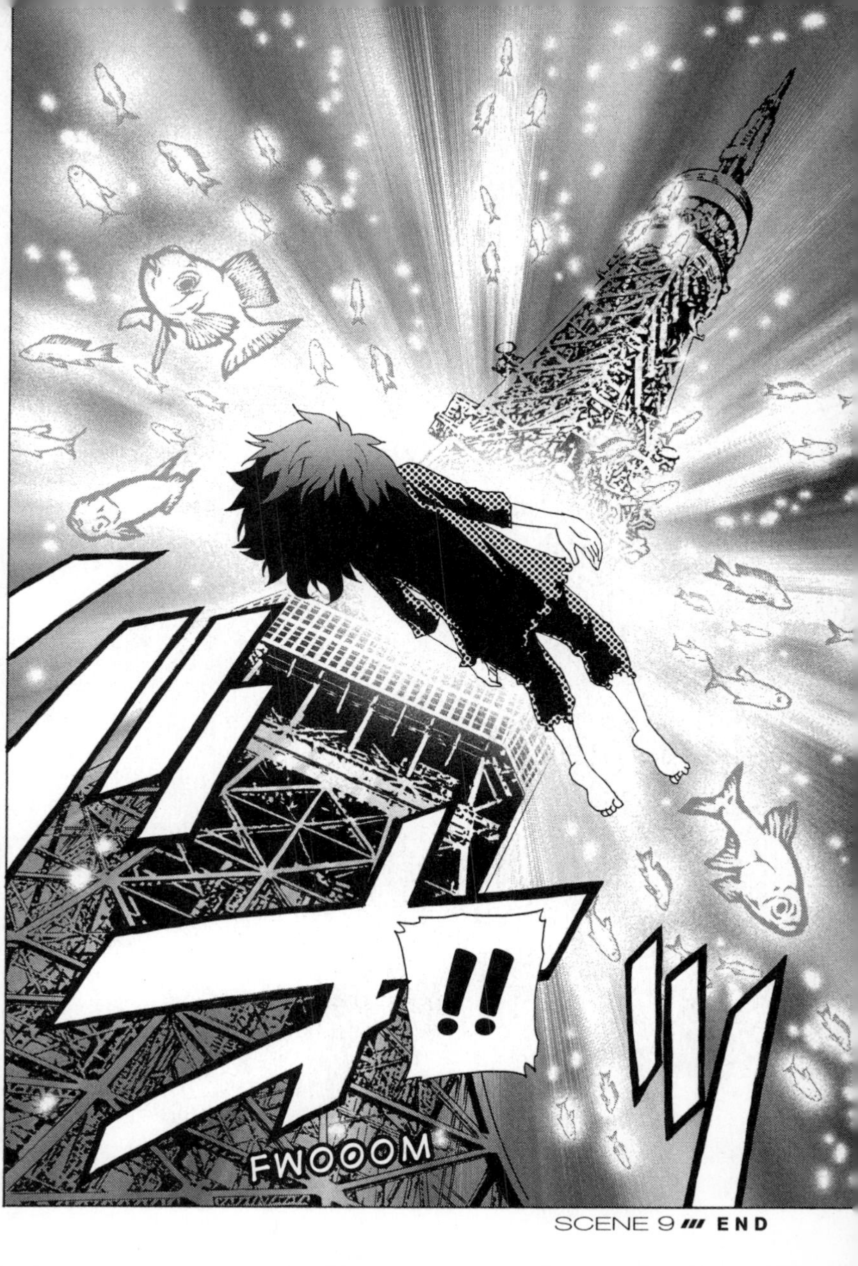
!!
FWOOOM

SCENE 9 /// END

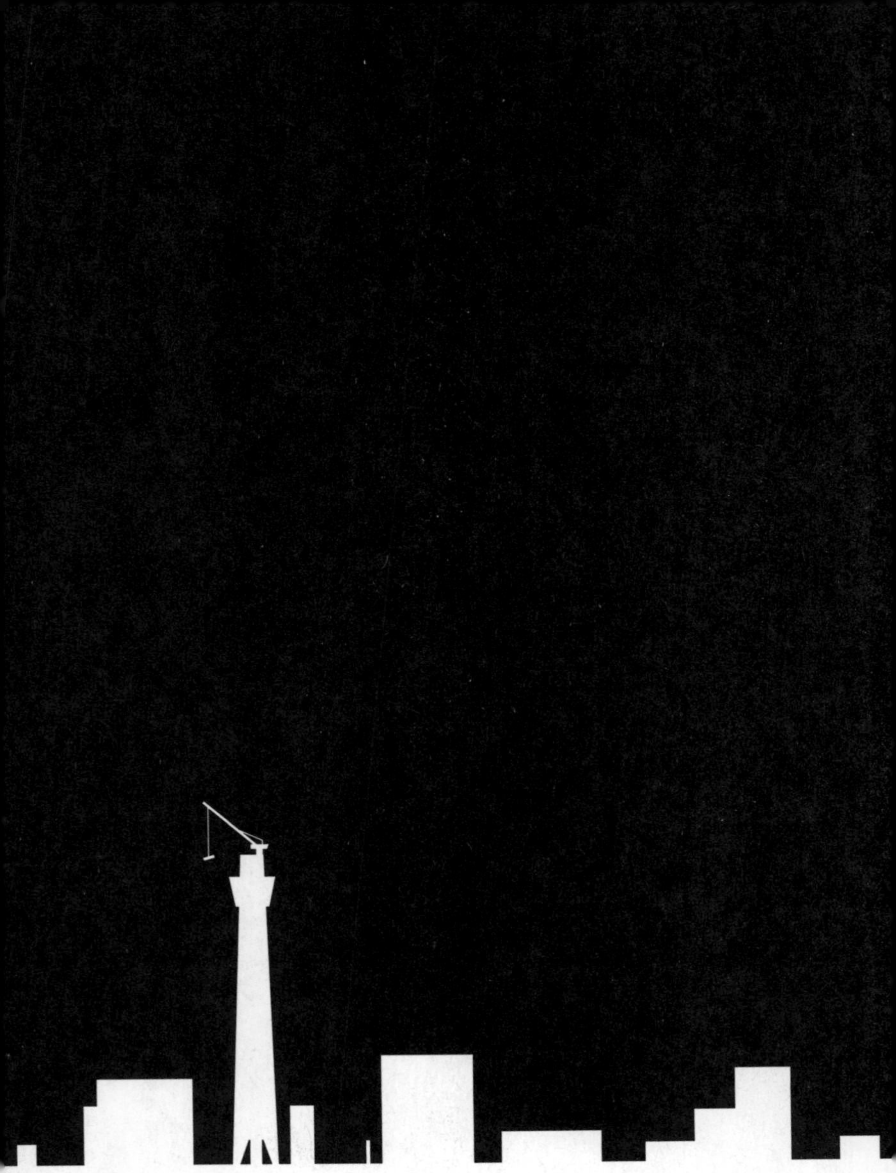

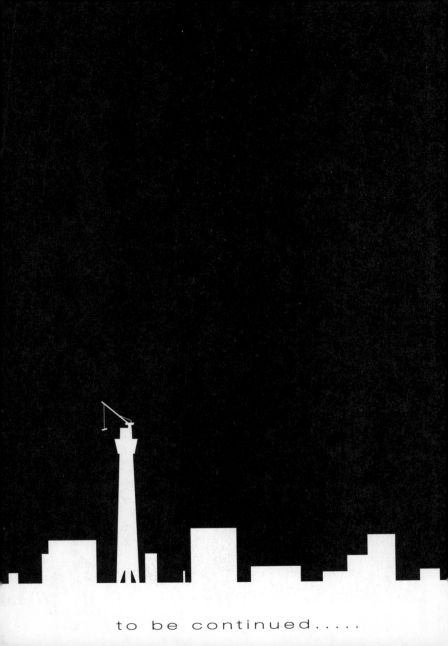

to be continued.....

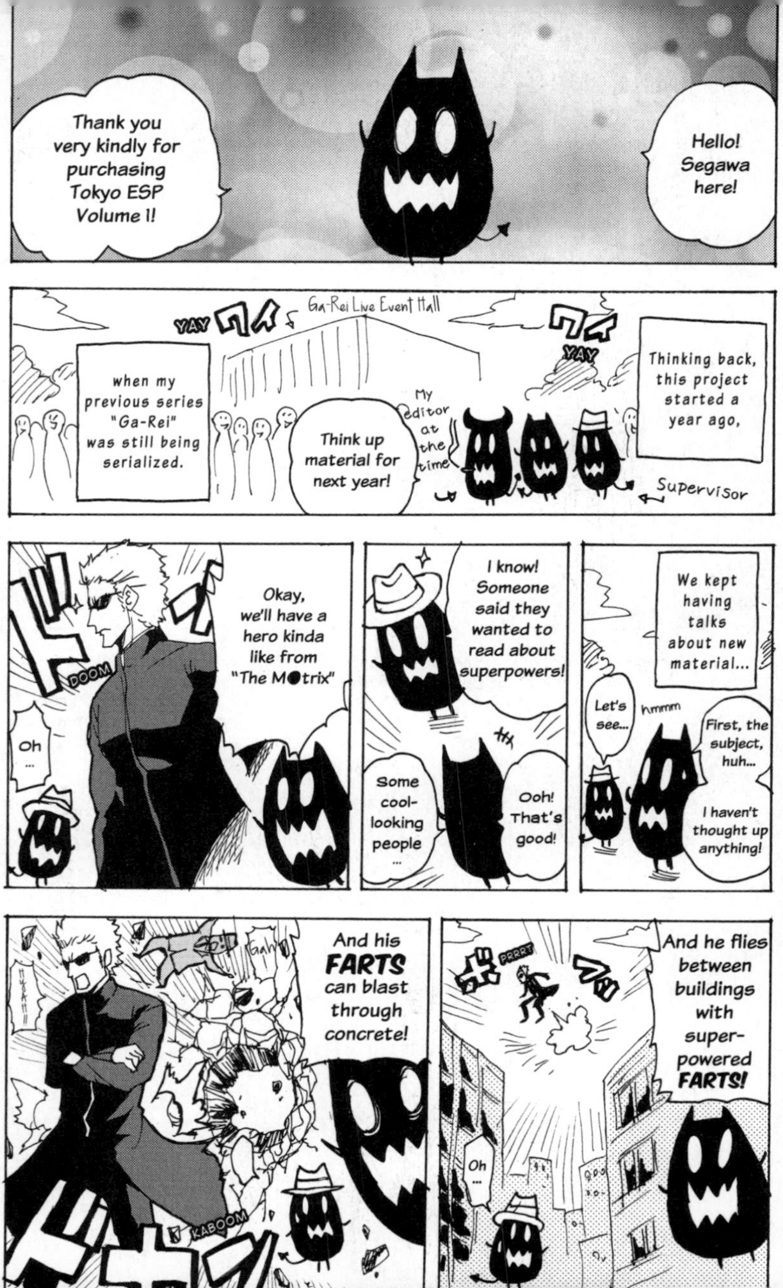

Hello! Segawa here!
Thank you very kindly for purchasing Tokyo ESP Volume 1!
Thinking back, this project started a year ago,
YAY
Supervisor
My editor at the time
Think up material for next year!
Ga-Rei Live Event Hall
YAY
when my previous series "Ga-Rei" was still being serialized.
We kept having talks about new material...
hmmm
First, the subject, huh...
Let's see...
I haven't thought up anything!
I know! Someone said they wanted to read about superpowers!
Ooh! That's good!
Some cool-looking people ...
Okay, we'll have a hero kinda like from "The M●trix"
DOOM
Oh ...
And he flies between buildings with super-powered FARTS!
PRRRT
Oh ...
And his FARTS can blast through concrete!
KABOOM

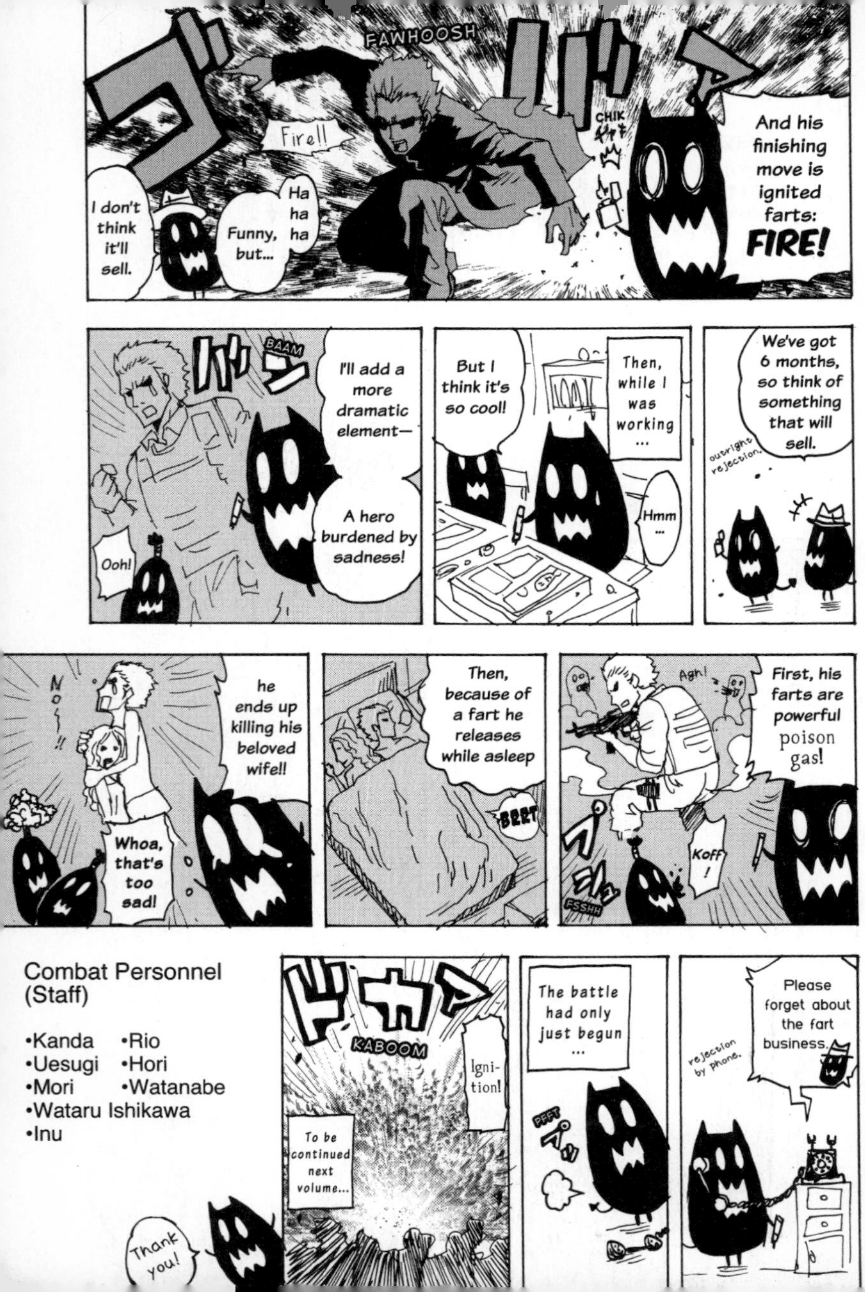
FAWHOOSH
CHIK
And his finishing move is ignited farts: FIRE!
Fire!!
Ha ha ha
Funny, but...
I don't think it'll sell.
We've got 6 months, so think of something that will sell.
outright rejection.
Then, while I was working...
But I think it's so cool!
Hmm...
BAAM
I'll add a more dramatic element—
A hero burdened by sadness!
Ooh!
First, his farts are powerful poison gas!
Agh!
Koff!
FSSHH
Then, because of a fart he releases while asleep
BRRT
he ends up killing his beloved wife!!
Whoa, that's too sad!
Please forget about the fart business.
rejection by phone.
The battle had only just begun...
PFFT
KABOOM
Igni-tion!
To be continued next volume...
Thank you!

Combat Personnel (Staff)

- Kanda
- Rio
- Uesugi
- Hori
- Mori
- Watanabe
- Wataru Ishikawa
- Inu

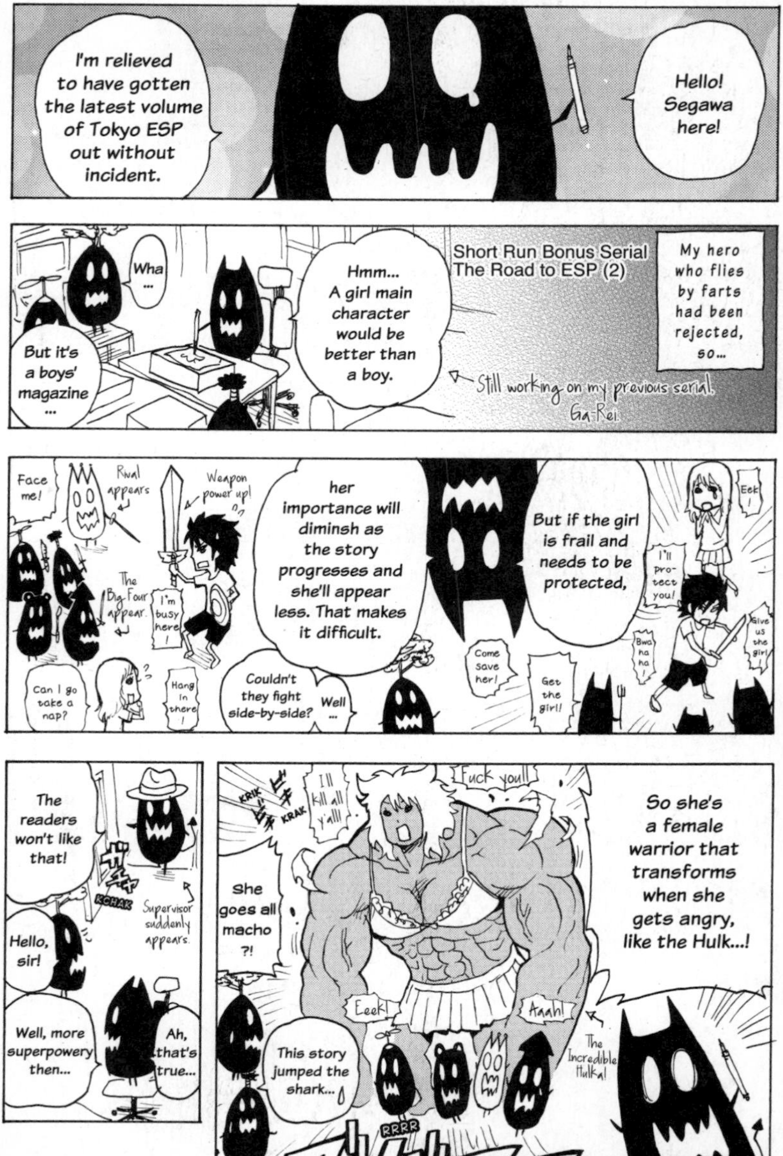
Hello! Segawa here!
I'm relieved to have gotten the latest volume of Tokyo ESP out without incident.
My hero who flies by farts had been rejected, so...
Short Run Bonus Serial The Road to ESP (2)
Hmm... A girl main character would be better than a boy.
Still working on my previous serial, Ga-Rei
Wha...
But it's a boys' magazine...
Eek!
But if the girl is frail and needs to be protected,
I'll protect you!
Give us the girl!
Bwa ha ha!
Come save her!
Get the girl!
her importance will diminsh as the story progresses and she'll appear less. That makes it difficult.
Well...
Couldn't they fight side-by-side?
Weapon power up!
Rival appears
Face me!
I'm busy here!
The Big Four appear.
Hang in there!
Can I go take a nap?
So she's a female warrior that transforms when she gets angry, like the Hulk...!
Fuck you!!
I'll kill all y'all!
KRIK
KRAK
She goes all macho?!
Aaah!
Eeek!
The Incredible Hulka!
This story jumped the shark...
RRRR
The readers won't like that!
KCHAK
Supervisor suddenly appears.
Hello, sir!
Ah, that's true...
Well, more superpowery then...

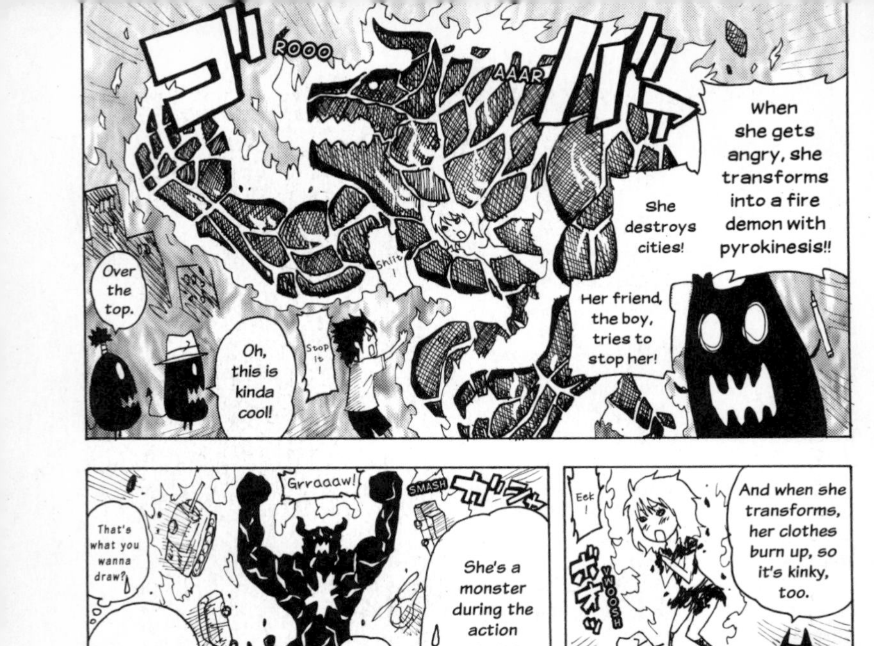
ROOO
AAAR
When she gets angry, she transforms into a fire demon with pyrokinesis!!
She destroys cities!
Her friend, the boy, tries to stop her!
Shit!
Stop it!
Oh, this is kinda cool!
Over the top.
Eek!
And when she transforms, her clothes burn up, so it's kinky, too.
VWOOSH
Ooh! But...
SMASH
Grraaaw!
She's a monster during the action scenes.
Of course!
She smashes tanks and stuff!
That's what you wanna draw?
So we won't get to see much of the girl then?
!!
Work on it a bit more please!
See ya!
And so, after this and that...
gentle rejection.
BTAM
VWOOSH
death by pyro-kinesis
GAH!
KABOOM
GYAAH!
The road to ESP stretched on and on...

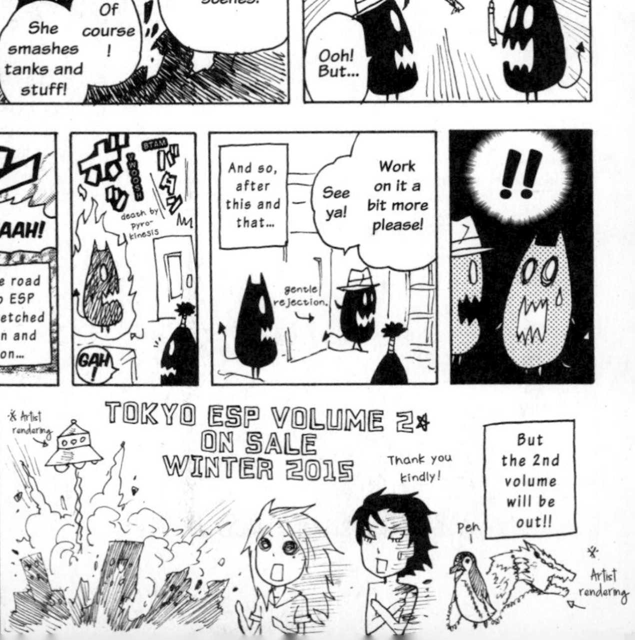
But the 2nd volume will be out!!
TOKYO ESP VOLUME 2 ON SALE WINTER 2015
Thank you kindly!
※ Artist rendering
Peh!
※ Artist rendering

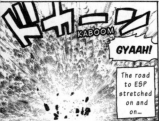

Combat Personnel (Staff)

- Kanda
- Uesugi
- Mori
- Rio
- Hori
- Watanabe
- Reference Material: Edo-Tokyo Open Air Architectural Museum

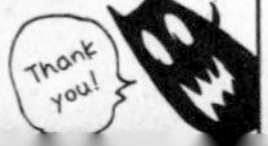
Thank you!

P9-DGZ-908

Tokyo ESP, volume 1

A Vertical Comics Edition

Translation: Kumar Sivasubramanian
Production: Risa Cho
          Tomoe Tsutsumi

© Hajime SEGAWA 2010
Edited by KADOKAWA SHOTEN
First published in Japan in 2010 by KADOKAWA CORPORATION, Tokyo.
English translation rights arranged with KADOKAWA CORPORATION, Tokyo
through TUTTLE-MORI AGENCY, INC., Tokyo.

Translation provided by Vertical Comics, 2015
Published by Vertical, Inc., New York

Originally published in Japanese as *Toukyou ESP 1 & 2* by Kadokawa Corporation, 2010
Tokyo ESP first serialized in *Gekkan Shounen Eisu*, Kadokawa Corporation, 2010-

This is a work of fiction.

ISBN: 978-1-941220-60-3

Manufactured in the United States of America

First Edition

Vertical, Inc.
451 Park Avenue South
7th Floor
New York, NY 10016
www.vertical-comics.com

Vertical books are distributed through Penguin-Random House Publisher Services.